W9-DHG-236

THE FIRST FREEDOM TODAY

THE FIRST FREEDOM TODAY

CRITICAL ISSUES RELATING TO

CENSORSHIP AND TO INTELLECTUAL FREEDOM

EDITED BY

ROBERT B. DOWNS AND RALPH E. McCOY

AMERICAN LIBRARY ASSOCIATION

CHICAGO 1984

Designed by Raymond Machura

Composed by Modern Typographers, Inc.
  in Linotron Times Roman

Printed on 50-pound Glatfelter,
  a pH-neutral stock, and bound in
  B-grade Holliston cloth by
  Malloy Lithographing, Inc.

**Library of Congress Cataloging in
Publication Data**
Main entry under title:

The First freedom today.

  1. Censorship—United States—Addresses,
essays, lectures. 2. Freedom of
information—United States—Addresses,
essays, lectures. 3. Freedom of
speech—United States—Addresses, essays,
lectures. I. Downs, Robert Bingham,
1903–   . II. McCoy, Ralph E. (Ralph
Edward), 1915–
Z658.U5F57 1984   323.44′5   84-461
ISBN 0-8389-0412-2

CONTENTS

ACKNOWLEDGMENTS

Numerous authors and publishers provided valuable assistance by granting permission to reprint copyrighted material from books, periodicals, and other publications. Their contributions are noted throughout the present anthology.

As in so many other publishing undertakings in which the senior editor has been involved, preparation of the manuscript for the present work was substantially aided by Deloris Holiman of the University of Illinois Library staff. Her assistance is gratefully acknowledged.

ROBERT B. DOWNS

INTRODUCTION

Notable historical precedents inspired the title THE FIRST FREEDOM TODAY for the present work, the first edition of which was published in 1960. When the Bill of Rights was added to the U.S. Constitution in December 1791, after being ratified by the required three-fourths of the states, the First Amendment specifically stated, in part, "Congress shall make no law . . . abridging the freedom of speech or of the press."

One hundred fifty years later, when America was on the verge of war with the Axis powers, Franklin D. Roosevelt addressed the U.S. Congress, enunciating the Four Freedoms: "In the future days, which we wish to make secure," he said, "we look forward to a world founded upon four essential human freedoms. The first is freedom of speech and expression everywhere in the world."

Reaffirmation from another distinguished source came on December 14, 1946, when the United Nations General Assembly resolved, "Freedom of information is a fundamental human right, and the touchstone of all the freedoms to which the United Nations is consecrated."

Few, if any, principles have inspired as eloquent statements of faith as the belief in free expression.

In an address before the Fund for the Republic, February 21, 1957, a leading American historian, Bruce Catton, restated this basic truth:

> The greatest of all American traditions is the simple tradition of freedom. From our earliest days as a people, this tradition has provided us with a faith to live by. It has shaped what Americans have done and what they have dreamed. If any one word tells what America really is, it is the one word—freedom. . . . The secret of the American tradition is freedom— freedom unabridged and unadulterated, freedom that applies to everybody in the land at all times and places, freedom for those with whom we disagree as well as for those with whom we do agree.

The Modern Language Association recently observed that "Censorship is everywhere—left, right, and center" and that it is worldwide. A professor of English at San Diego State University, who specializes in Iranian literature, compiled the names of all contemporary Iranian writers whose work he knew. They fell into three groups: those who are in prison, those who are in hiding, and those who have been executed. The situation in South Africa, North Korea, Cuba, and Eastern Europe is little better. At a 1982 meeting of MLA, John Leonard, former editor of the *New York Times Book Review*, noted the pervasive nature of censorship in the United States:

> Blacks—having entirely missed the moral point of Mark Twain—would ban *Huckleberry Finn*. . . . Gays disrupt the filming and obstruct the screening of a film, 'Cruising,' that they don't like, whether they have seen it or not. . . . Liberated women campaign against pornography as if such toads in the erotic garden as Larry Flynt weren't good enough for a genteel Bill of Rights.

Leonard went on to point out that the U.S. government is the biggest censor of all, "hiding behind national security and executive privilege."

The editors concede that THE FIRST FREEDOM TODAY has a bias, reflecting the liberal view as opposed to advocates of censorship. In any case, from the standpoint of the literature of the field, the writings of the leading American and British authors during the present century have shown unyielding opposition to the idea and practice of censorship in all its forms. With rare exceptions, the banners and burners of books have not been highly literate folk.

The general plan of organization of THE FIRST FREEDOM TODAY follows what the editors believe are logical sequences. At the outset, an attempt has been made to provide a broad background in order to place matters of censorship and intellectual freedom in their proper historical setting. The second step is briefly to examine some of the key issues in the field, especially those that have developed during the past two decades. A chapter is then devoted to the most important, most basic, and perhaps most misunderstood document on which nearly everything depends: the First Amendment to the Constitution of the United States.

With the perspective coming from this general approach, the editors have gone on to explore in greater depth some of the most troublesome problems of censorship and intellectual freedom now confronting American society. One of the seriously threatened areas, dealt with in the third chapter, is public schools where censorship of textbooks and the contents of school libraries is rampant.

No profession is more directly affected by censorship than librarianship. Chapter five demonstrates convincingly that librarians are meeting the challenge and are strongly resisting misguided efforts to restrict freedom in the exercise of their profession.

Two of the most controversial issues to emerge in recent times are the concern of the fifth and sixth chapters. Darwin's theory of evolution has been the focus of bitter debate for more than a century. The 1925 Scopes trial was once thought to have been the last great battle over the truth or falsity of the doctrine, but a new war has erupted between advocates of "creationism" and evolution, with legislation on the subject being tested in courts of law. Equally controversial is a favorite scapegoat of educational and religious conservatives, "secular humanism."

The fight over obscenity and pornography has raged off and on in the United States since the time of Anthony Comstock in the 1870s. Chapter seven, relating to this perennial subject, devotes considerable attention to a key document, the report of the U.S. Commission on Obscenity and Pornography released in 1970. This subject is undoubtedly one on which full agreement among contending parties will never be reached.

More vital during the past decade or two have been questions relating to freedom of the press, broadly conceived. Included here are such aspects as increasing secrecy concerning government operations, the conflict between a free press and fair trial for defendants in court cases, libel and invasion of privacy, and new problems emerging with censorship of radio and television.

These, then, in the editors' view, are the liveliest and most aggravating issues confronting librarians, authors, editors, publishers, educators, students, general readers, television watchers, and the citizenry as a whole in the last quarter of the twentieth century. Emphases change, but the basic questions differ little from those posed in the 1960 edition of *The First Freedom*.

CHAPTER ONE

HISTORICAL BACKGROUND

The roads to the formulation of the First Amendment and from the First Amendment to its legal interpretation today have been both long and difficult, with not only uphill stretches but also detours, switchbacks, and barriers. The applications of freedom of the press and freedom of speech have consistently grown. However, two areas in particular—politics and religion—have frequently required reexamination of the First Amendment as they gain or lose importance. Whenever such a shift occurs, new questions of applications are raised. If the times of change are noteworthy, so are the times of no change. Before independence from England, the colonial legislatures had done little or nothing to facilitate exercise of the freedoms later protected by the First Amendment; in fact, the colonial legislators often censored more scrupulously than the crown.

That a change in the role of a government raises questions of censorship is most clearly seen during times when the reciprocal roles of religion and government are changing. For example, a very great movement toward censorship happened when, under the English Tudors the aims of church and state became unified in the establishment of a national church. In the opposite situation with the same message, the First Amendment protects the freedoms of the press and of speech only by forbidding the establishment of religion by Congress.

A shift in the relationship between government and religion has reappeared in the 1970s and 1980s in the political resurgence of religious fundamentalism. Again, an attempt politically to enforce cultural behavior that is called Christian by its proponents has resulted in restrictions on publication and dissemination of information with contrary viewpoints. The conflict occurs with regard not only to the religious doctrine, as in the evolution-creationism battle, but even more to the ethics of the culture as a whole—in forms of patriotism and sexual morality.

Although the most striking examples have to do with religion, it seems that almost any broad change in the range of activities to which a government applies itself, or any new exercise of its claimed powers, may result in new questions on freedom of information. The first tests of the First Amendment occurred when the new government faced its first challenges, during preparations in 1798 for a war with France (a war that never, in fact, began) and during the early abolition movement, which ultimately tested the Constitution in the Civil War. In this century, we have seen a similar test, as the new worldwide role of the United States has periodically raised concerns about the security of the government to exercise the responsibilities presumed by that role. Frequently this test results in attempts to censor—the McCarthy hearings, the Pentagon Papers controversy, and, in the 1980s, the restrictions on publications of works by former CIA employees.

The three articles in this chapter trace this development, mostly in the histories of England, the American colonies, and the United States. The first, "Freedom of Speech and Press: Development of a Concept," provides the background of the First Amendment and its history to roughly 1970. The second, "Freedom of the Press and Unbelief," considers freedom of the press in relation to religious dissent and unbelief. The third, "Issues of the Past Decade," considers more recent history, the issues raised in the 1970s.

Robert B. Downs

FREEDOM OF SPEECH AND PRESS: DEVELOPMENT OF A CONCEPT

The Founding Fathers acted with premeditation and forethought when in adopting the Bill of Rights they placed the freedom of information at the top of the first ten amendments to the Constitution. Burned into our consciences and consciousness for nearly two hundred years—though not infrequently violated in practice—are the admonitions in the First Amendment: "Congress shall make no law . . . abridging the freedom of speech, or of the press."

To understand the motivations and strong emotional involvement of the framers of the Constitution, with its appended Bill of Rights, one must retrace a series of events in English and colonial American history. The First Amendment's prohibition against interference with free speech and free press was a direct consequence of centuries of bitter experience living under extremely repressive English laws controlling speech and

Reprinted with permission from *Library Trends* 19:(1) 8–18. © 1970 The Board of Trustees of The University of Illinois. Footnotes have been omitted.

press. The authority of government was long regarded as supreme, irresistible, and absolute. Prior to the English Revolution of 1688, unqualified sovereignty had been exercised by the Crown; subsequently, the same power was vested in parliamentary authority. Any criticism of the government was considered not only objectionable but dangerous heresy which must be ruthlessly suppressed. That entire concept was rejected by the First Amendment.

For five hundred years before adoption of the American Constitution, a struggle between tyranny and freedom had been under way in England. The Anglo-Saxon precedents in the field may be dated from the English treason statute of 1351, during the reign of Edward III. Parliament persuaded or compelled Edward III to narrow the crime of treason by limiting it to making war on the King or compassing or imagining his death. But in subsequent centuries the statute was broken down by judicial interpretation and expanded by new acts of Parliament. Officials in power used the charge of treason to send their adversaries to the scaffold—and then lost their own heads when they fell out of favor with the King. Parliament added new treasons to the statutory list, with no requirement that an overt act be proved. The omission, noted Sir Matthew Hale in his *Pleas of the Crown*, "subjected men to the great punishment of treason for their very thought." The body of repressive laws continued to build up until the death of Henry VIII, when legislation was enacted wiping out all forms of treason except those contained in the statute of Edward III.

Nevertheless, with or without the sanction of law, the slaughter of dissidents persisted. Catholic Queen Mary killed off the Protestants and Protestant Elizabeth similarly dispatched the Catholics—along with sundry rivals and ex-lovers. The orgy of persecution continued without diminution during the eighty-five year Stuart epoch and Cromwell's Puritan Revolution.

The significance of the written and printed word was fully recognized by Elizabeth, Cromwell, and the Stuarts. From the time William Caxton set up the first printing press in England, in 1476, a new force was released in the world, but until Henry VIII's split with the Catholic Church, printed books were predominantly concerned with orthodox religion or were non-controversial in subject matter. Thereafter the country was flooded with Anabaptist, Presbyterian, Quaker, and Papist tracts. As soon as products of the printing press started to reach the masses, restraints began to be set up. Treason, felony, and heresy statutes directed against authors and publishers were enacted in Elizabeth's time and strengthened by a licensing system to control the printers and their presses. Only the government was free to express opinion through the spoken or written word.

A blow against censorship and prior restraint was struck by John Milton in 1644 in his classic polemic, *Areopagitica*, contending against parliamentary censorship and for unlicensed printing. Milton's stirring defense for liberty of the press went unheeded, and governmental censorship continued for another fifty years. The Licensing Act of 1662, made law after the Restoration, prohibited seditious and heretical books and pamphlets; forbade printing any material unlicensed by the Stationers' Company, a governmental monopoly; made illegal the importation or selling of a book without a license, and required that all printing presses be registered with the Stationers' Company. The system did not come to an end until 1694, six years after the "Glorious Revolution" threw out the last of the Stuarts.

Meanwhile, on the other side of the Atlantic, the English colonies in America, forced to operate under the laws of the motherland, were experiencing similar travails. One myth that should be dispelled is the popular belief that freedom of expression was cherished in the colonial American society. As Leonard W. Levy points out in his *Freedom of Speech and Press in Early American History*:

The evidence provides little comfort for the notion that the colonies hospitably received advocates of obnoxious or detestable ideas on matters that counted. Nor is there reason to believe that rambunctious unorthodoxies suffered only from Puritan bigots and tyrannous royal judges. The American people simply did not understand that freedom of thought and expression means equal freedom for the other fellow, especially the one with hated ideas.

Colonial America was marked by great diversity of opinion on religion, politics, and other matters, but violent conflicts were avoided for the most part by the separation of groups with varying points of view. John P. Roche sums up the prevailing situation quite accurately: "Colonial America was an open society dotted with closed enclaves, and one could generally settle in with his cobelievers in safety and comfort and exercise the right of oppression." Thus, Unitarians avoided Anglican or Puritan communities; Puritans stayed away from the Anglican colonies; Quakers and Anabaptists confined their activities principally to Pennsylvania and Rhode Island; and Catholics were concentrated in Maryland. The atheist met with toleration nowhere.

Strangely, again contrary to tradition, the most severe suppression of freedom of expression came not from royal judges or governors appointed by the Crown, but from the popularly elected assemblies. During the eighteenth century especially, the law of seditious libel was enforced in America chiefly by the provincial legislatures. The assemblies, considering themselves immune from criticism, issued warrants of arrest for, interrogated, fined, and imprisoned anyone accused of libeling its members, or the body as a whole, by written, printed, or spoken words. One historian concludes, "Literally scores of persons, probably hundreds, throughout the colonies were tracked down by the various messengers and sergeants and brought into the house to make inglorious submission for words spoken in the heat of anger or for writings which intentionally or otherwise had given offense."

None of the colonies was an exception. The first assembly to meet on American soil, the Virginia House of Burgesses, decided that a Captain Henry Spellman was guilty of "treasonable words" and stripped him of his rank. The prevailing attitude in the Old Dominion was expressed in Governor William Berkeley's famous remark, "I thank God, *there are no free schools* nor *printing*, and I hope we shall not have these hundred years; for *learning* has brought disobedience, and heresy, and sects into the world, and *printing* has divulged them, and libels against the best government. God keep us from both!"

Even in Pennsylvania, reputedly the most tolerant of the colonies, printing was stringently regulated. William Penn himself presided over a council meeting in 1683 when it was ordered that the laws of the colony should not be printed. In what is believed to be the first criminal trial in American involving freedom of the press, Pennsylvania's first printer, William Bradford, had his press seized by the government, was charged with seditious libel, and spent more than a year in prison for printing a pamphlet entitled the *Frame of Government* which was a copy of the colony's charter.

The ruling powers were especially suspicious of newspapers. The first newspaper to be published in the American colonies, entitled *Publick Occurrences*, expired after its first issue. Issued by Benjamin Harris in 1690 in Boston, the paper was immediately suppressed because it mentioned the Indian Wars and commented on local affairs.

A more celebrated event was the trial of John Peter Zenger, a case which contributed greatly to establishing the principle of a free press in British North America. Zenger's newspaper, *The New York Weekly Journal*, had printed satirical ballads reflecting on William Cosby, the highly unpopular governor, and his council. The issues condemned were described "as having in them many things tending to raise seditions and tumults among the people of this province, and to fill their minds with a contempt for his majesty's government." The grand jury failed to indict Zenger and the General Assembly refused to take action, but acting under the Governor's orders, the attorney general filed an information. At the trial of the prisoner, in 1735, the defense was conducted by Andrew Hamilton, a Quaker lawyer from Philadelphia who was Speaker of the Pennsylvania Assembly. Despite a packed court, the defendant was acquitted with a verdict based on the principle that in cases of libel the jury should judge both the law and the facts.

The concept of freedom of speech and press, so strikingly absent in America before the Zenger case of 1735, remained inconspicuous for a considerable period afterward. Leonard Levy's assertion that "it is difficult to find a libertarian theory in America before the American Revolution—or even before the First Amendment" is doubtless accurate. Benjamin Franklin's celebrated "Apology for Printers," though influential, could hardly be characterized as profound. The first colonial writer to develop a true philosophy of freedom of speech and press was James Alexander, founder of the American Philosophical Society, a prominent public figure and man of versatile talents, who masterminded the Zenger defense. Alexander's *A Brief Narrative of the Case and Tryal of John Peter Zenger* (1736) was a widely known source of libertarian thought in America and England during the eighteenth century. Less familiar, but of outstanding quality, was his four-part essay on the history and theory of freedom of speech, published in Franklin's *Pennsylvania Gazette* in 1737. A primary principle stated by Alexander is that "Freedom of speech is a principal pillar in a free government: when this support is taken away, the constitution is dissolved and tyranny is erected on its ruins."

The framers of the U.S. Constitution of 1787 were educated, highly literate, and widely-read men intimately acquainted with the centuries of struggle between tyranny and freedom that had been going on in England and more recently in America. The long record of oppression and suppression formed a backdrop as the leaders proceeded to build the government of the United States on the sovereignty of the people and their rights as citizens of a republic.

Originally, however, the Constitution did not contain a bill of rights, because the convention delegates at Philadelphia felt that individual rights were in no danger and would be protected by the states. Nonetheless, the absence of a bill of rights became the strongest objection to the ratification of the Constitution. Under the influence of his friend Thomas Jefferson, and yielding to the general demand for a bill of rights, James Madison became the principal draftsman of the first ten amendments.

A basically new approach to the crime of seditious libel was made by the authors of the First Amendment. Even after the victory over censorship in England in 1695, the people continued to view their rulers as their superiors who must not be censured directly in newspapers and pamphlets, but only through petitions to elected parliamentary representatives. Now came Madison and his associates who regarded governmental authorities as servants of the people. As stated by Madison, "If we advert to the nature of Republican Government, we shall find that the censorial power is in the people over the Government, and not in the Government over the people." In effect, sedition ceased to be a crime under the broad prohibitions of the First Amendment, though breaches of the peace which destroyed or endangered life, limb, or property, were still punishable by law.

The Bill of Rights had been in effect less than a decade when it met with its first serious challenge. In 1798, war with France seemed imminent. Thousands of French refugees were in the United States, espionage activities were prevalent, and radicals supported the French cause. President John Adams even objected to the visit of a group of French scientists, arguing that "learned societies" had "disorganized the world" and were "incompatible with social order." The popular hysteria led to Congress' enactment of a series of alien and sedition laws. One such law made it a crime, for example, to publish any "false, scandalous and malicious" writing against the government, the Congress, or the President "with intent to defame" them or to bring them "into contempt or disrepute" or "to stir up sedition." The crime carried a penalty of $2,000 fine and two years in jail.

An immediate uproar ensued. One side contended that "a conspiracy against the Constitution, the government, the peace and safety of this country is formed and is in full operation. It embraces members of all classes; the Representatives of the people on this floor, the wild and visionary theorist in the bloody philosophy of the day, the learned and the ignorant." Such arguments were met with impassioned pleas for freedom of speech and the press, led by Thomas Jefferson and James Madison. The alien and sedition laws became a prime issue in the presidential campaign of 1800. When Jefferson was elected he promptly pardoned all those who had been convicted under the 1798 laws. Congress passed laws remitting fines, and the Sedition Act expired with the Fifth Congress in 1801.

The next major attack on the First Amendment's proscriptions against any law abridging freedom of speech and of the press occurred in 1835, when President Andrew Jackson proposed to Congress the passage of a law which would prohibit the use of the mails for "incendiary publications intended to instigate the slaves to insurrection." A special committee, under the chairmanship of John C. Calhoun of South Carolina, reported adversely on the proposal on the ground that it was in conflict with the First Amendment, though a majority of the committee was in sympathy with the bill's intent. Calhoun, in turn, introduced a bill to make it unlawful "for any deputy postmaster, in any State, Territory, or District of the United States, knowingly to deliver to any person whatever, any pamphlet, newspaper, handbill, or other printed matter or pictorial representation touching the subject of slavery, where, by the laws of the said State, Territory, or District, their circulation is prohibited; and any deputy postmaster who shall be guilty thereof, shall be forthwith removed from office." The Calhoun bill was likewise defeated.

Counterattacking, the opponents of Calhoun's proposal introduced and succeeded in passing an act that in principle prohibited the post office department from censoring the mail. More than a century later, Judge Thurman W. Arnold in his opinion in the *Esquire* case stated: "We believe that the Post Office officials should experience a feeling of relief if they are limited to the more prosaic function of seeing to it that 'neither snow nor rain nor heat nor gloom of night stays these couriers from the swift completion of their appointed rounds.'"

Three so-called "Civil War amendments," destined to have a profound impact on civil liberties and intellectual freedom, were adopted from 1865 to 1870. The Thirteenth Amendment abolished slavery and the Fifteenth provided that "The rights of citizens of the United States to vote shall not be abridged . . . on account of race, color, or previous condition of servitude." It is the Fourteenth Amendment, however, which is most frequently linked with the First as a protection against censorship and as a guarantee of free expression. Pertinent sections state: "No State shall make or enforce any law which shall abridge the privileges or immunities of citizens of the United States; nor shall any State deprive any person of life, liberty, or property, without due process of law; nor deny to any person within its jurisdiction the equal protection of the law."

The significance of the Fourteenth

Amendment from the point of view of civil liberties lies in the growth of national power as opposed to state power. As John P. Roche points out so cogently:

Specifically, the growth of federal power has led to the implementation of a principle of national protection of individual liberty against the actions of states or municipalities by the judiciary and to judicial decisions excluding the states from areas of jurisdiction of vital significance in civil liberty. Moreover, with a full recognition of the dangerous potentialities of unchecked national power, it is contended that the national institutions have provided a far higher level of juridical defense and have shown a far greater sensitivity to the rights of the individual than have the states.

Every generation since 1790—in fact, virtually every decade—has redefined and reinterpreted the First Amendment. Though the language is clear and explicit, "Congress shall make no law . . . abridging the freedom of speech, or of the press," Congress, the courts, and executive powers have repeatedly done, or at least attempted to do, exactly that. One theory used to circumscribe or circumvent the Amendment was use—abuse or liberty versus license. Under this notion, a distinction was made between right and wrong use of speech and press, i.e., liberty as against license. Superseding that doctrine to some extent was Justice Holmes' "clear and present danger" test, according to which liberty of press and speech would remain unrestricted as long as public safety was not imperiled. A classic example is Justice Holmes' "fire in a crowded theatre" statement. A new theory that has come into vogue in more recent judicial decisions is "balancing of interests," as between public and private rights and welfare. All of these theories, it should be noted, infringe on the unqualified guarantees of the First Amendment.

The most blatant attacks on the principles contained in the First Amendment occurred after the two world wars. A notorious case was the raids carried on under the direction of A. Mitchell Palmer, Woodrow Wilson's Attorney General. On January 2, 1920, one minute after midnight, about 500 FBI agents and police swooped down on 3,000 Russian, Finnish, Polish, German, Italian, and other alien workmen, looking for Communists to deport. The victims were hustled off to jail and arrested without warrants, homes were ransacked without legal authorization, and all literature and letters were seized. Irving Brant suggests that the actual substance of the supposed crime of these hapless victims of Palmer's "Red Raids" was nothing more nor less than the ancient crime of "compassing or imagining the death of the King," in this instance "compassing or imagining the death of the Republic."

An even more virulent epidemic, from which the nation has not yet fully recovered, is "McCarthyism," a phenomenon of the early nineteen fifties. The Senate Permanent Subcommittee on Investigations of the Committee on Government Operations was used as a platform by its chairman, Senator Joseph R. McCarthy of Wisconsin, to air his unsubstantiated, irresponsible charges that the federal government was thoroughly infiltrated by Communist agents. McCarthy's attacks on the U.S. information libraries abroad led to the burning of some books accused of being Communist propaganda, the resignations of numerous librarians, and the closing of a considerable number of libraries because of reduced congressional support.

In past eras religious heresy was a common basis for thought suppression. There is rarely a case of censorship for religious heresy in present-day society. A more persistent ground for attacks on intellectual freedom is unorthodox political opinions, as has been shown in the foregoing discussion. Political questions remain lively and controversial issues in the modern world. A third area for censorial attacks is the problem of obscenity and pornography.

For almost a century after the American Revolution, the United States managed to get along without any censorship laws in the field of obscenity. The full flower of repression bloomed with the Comstock era in 1868, under the inspiration of a young man by the name of Anthony Comstock, who had emerged from the backwoods of Connecticut to lead a crusade against what he considered indecent literature. Under a special act of the New York State Legislature, Comstock organized the New York Society for the Suppression of Vice. The law gave the Society a monopoly in its field and its agents the rights of search, seizure, and arrest—rights which had previously belonged exclusively to the police authorities. The crowning touch came in 1873, when the moral forces obtained the passage of the federal statute entitled the "Comstock Law," which provided penalties for mailing allegedly obscene publications. Hundreds of thousands of books were confiscated and thousands of defendants arrested. Eventually, this kind of censorship was discredited by ridicule, by the growth of liberal thought, by changing literary taste, and by certain landmark court decisions.

In its 1957 decision in the *Roth* case, the Supreme Court made solid progress in striking the shackles of censorship from literature. The Court ruled that a work could not be considered obscene unless it met all of three separate and distinct tests: it had to go substantially beyond customary limits of candor in the description or representation of matters pertaining to sex or nudity; the work must appeal to the prurient interest of the average adult; and the work must be utterly without redeeming social importance. Under the Court's liberalizing influence of the past decade, literature has become increasingly free and candid, though a step backward was taken in the *Ginzburg* case in 1965, when the Court ruled that the publisher's method of advertising and promoting a book must be taken into account in judging questions of obscenity.

A new dimension was added in 1968 when an eighteen-member Commission on Obscenity and Pornography was appointed by President Lyndon B. Johnson. It is anticipated that under President Nixon's urging, the commission will recommend some type of strict federal legislation, possibly aimed at counteracting the liberal opinions of the Supreme Court.

The fundamental freedom of the press is constantly under attack and "eternal vigilance," as Thomas Jefferson warned, is required to preserve it. The First Amendment is presumably in no danger of repeal, but it is always imperiled by erosion and qualification. As the federal bureaucracy grows steadily larger and more complex, official interference with the public's right to know is common practice. In his Pulitzer Prize-winning editorial of many years ago, William Allen White had a highly relevant statement applicable to current conditions:

You say that freedom of utterance is not for time of stress, and I reply with the sad truth that only in time of stress is freedom of utterance in danger. No one questions it in calm days, because it is not needed. And the reverse is true also; only when free utterance is suppressed is it needed, and when it is most needed, it is most vital to justice. . . . This state . . . is in more danger from suppression than from violence, because, in the end, suppression leads to violence. Violence indeed, is the child of suppression.

Also memorable is a defense of freedom of expression stated by Supreme Court Justice Brandeis, concurred in by his colleague Justice Holmes:

[Those who won our independence] believed that freedom to think as you will and to speak as you think are means indispensable to the discovery and spread of political truth; that without free speech and assembly, discussion would be futile; that with them, discussion affords ordinarily adequate protection against the dissemination of noxious doctrine; that the greatest menace to freedom is an inert people; that public discussion is a political duty; and that this should be a fundamental principle of the American government.

Perhaps psychologists and psychiatrists may be able to offer explanations for the state of mind which produces censorship pressures. In the United States, since the end of World War II, many Americans have been uneasy about revolutions around the world, the growth in power of the Soviet Union and Red China, and the tensions of the Cold War. At home, the people find themselves trapped in a collective nightmare of choking cities, polluted land, water, and air, casual murders of tens of thousands along the highways, mammoth problems of racial integration, student unrest, and large-scale juvenile delinquency. In a period of tension, frustration, and worry, therefore, the people are prone to attack what they consider a visible enemy, e.g., threatening ideas in published form. Removing subversive books from circulation, they reason, will undermine the Communist controversy, and taking obscure books off the shelves will end juvenile delinquency and stop the crime wave.

But despite the psychological and other handicaps under which the literary world labors, reading materials of all kinds are available to Americans in greater quantities than ever before. Viewed objectively, we remain a free people in the field of reading. It is a freedom, however, that cannot be taken for granted, casually and indifferently.

Ralph E. McCoy

FREEDOM OF THE PRESS AND UNBELIEF

ENGLISH EXPERIENCE

The invention of printing in the middle of the fifteenth century was welcomed by the two great powers of Western Europe—the church and the state. But within a generation it was clear that the same instrument that was capable of propagating the faith and bringing prestige to secular rulers could also spread heresy and sedition. Printing was being put to use with dangerous effectiveness in the growing movement to reform the medieval church. In 1520 Pope Leo X issued a bull against unlicensed printing, employing the Inquisition to identify and prosecute authors and printers of heretical works, and relying on temporal rulers to exact punishment. The Council of Trent (1545–63) established rules for an index of forbidden books that continued in one form or another until

Reprinted by permission of the publisher, Prometheus Books, Buffalo, N.Y., from its forthcoming publication, *Encyclopedia of Unbelief*, edited by Gordon Stein.

repealed by the Second Vatican Council (1962–65).

In England Henry VIII issued his first list of prohibited books in 1526, a total of eighteen theological titles, five of which were written by Reformation leader Martin Luther. The Tudors, from Henry VIII to Elizabeth, acted upon the premise that published dissent of any kind, civil or religious, was a threat to the peace of the realm and required suppression. The spread of the Protestant Reformation in Europe in the sixteenth century, while weakening the power of the papacy to control printing, brought its own hostility to religious dissent. In place of the authority of the Pope, the Reformation substituted the authority of the Bible as interpreted by Protestant clergy.

When Henry VIII broke with the Pope in 1534 and became spiritual as well as temporal ruler of England, religious publishing came under state control and violators were subjected to severe punishment, including torture and death. Press censorship under the Tudors was accomplished first by granting monopolies and privileges to compliant printers and then, beginning in 1538, by a system of licensing that continued until 1694. The Star Chamber, until abolished during the Puritan Revolution, was the focal point for press control, establishing its first decree on printing in 1586 and relying on church officials, ecclesiastical courts, and the Stationers' Company (a trade organization) for enforcement.

Elizabethan Puritans were among the first religious groups to defy the Star Chamber's edict against unlicensed printing. The Marprelate Tracts, issued in 1588–89 from a secret unlicensed press, attacked with witty and satirical language the episcopacy of the Church of England and lead to the deaths of the suspected authors, John Penry and John Udall. The early Stuart monarchs continued the severe Tudor restrictions on the publication of both political and religious dissent, efforts that reached a climax with the zeal of Archbishop of Canterbury William Laud, who served both as prosecutor and judge before the Star Chamber. Laud was re-sponsible for the persecution of three leading Puritan writers—William Prynne, a lawyer; John Bastwick, a physician; and Henry Burton, a minister. For their published criticisms of "papist" practices by church prelates, the three were fined, pilloried, shorn of their ears, and given life imprisonment. They were released, along with other political prisoners, when the Puritans came into power.

During the Puritan Revolution, ushered in by the Long Parliament in 1640, the persecuted Puritans became the persecutors, suppressing both Roman Catholic and Church of England doctrines and beheading their archenemy, William Laud. Parliament replaced the Star Chamber as censors during the Commonwealth (1649–60), and ecclesiastical courts that had been a major factor in enforcing offenses against religion were shorn of their coercive powers, leaving them with only spiritual sanctions. Licensing the press begun by the Puritans was reaffirmed by a 1643 ordinance.

Principal among the dissenters in Puritan England was a group of civil libertarians known as the Levellers. Unlike either the Puritans or the prelates of the established church, who favored press freedom only to protect their own doctrines, Leveller pamphleteers championed freedom of conscience and of the press as rights of every freeborn English subject. They opposed the monopoly in religion granted the clergy and the monopoly in printing granted the Stationers' Company. Their crusade for religious toleration and for the separation of church and state introduced revolutionary concepts that were unacceptable to the Puritan theocracy. Those who preached tolerance as well as those who espoused dissenting theological views were dealt with harshly. In 1644 William Walwyn, one of the first Englishmen to write forcefully on behalf of the liberty of conscience, called for the relaxation of Commonwealth press controls on religious dissent and criticized the impracticality of licensing. At the same time Richard Overton's tracts, combining passion with humor, espoused religious freedom as the natural right of man and Henry C. Robinson pled for press freedom as a logical extension of a laissez-faire economic doctrine. "No man can have a natural monopoly of truth," Robinson wrote. Religious opinions should be "fought out upon eaven ground, on equall termes, neither side must expect to have greater liberty of speech, writing, Printing . . . than the other." All three Leveller pamphleteers, along with their leader John Lilbourne, were imprisoned for their unlicensed tracts.

Also in 1644 Puritan John Milton wrote *Aereopagitica*, an eloquent plea for freedom of the press which was published without a license in defiance of authorities. Directing his remarks against the 1643 printing ordinance, Milton argued for abolishing state censorship before publication and for freedom from punishment after publication, except for legally proved libel or blasphemy. Only "papist" views and ephemeral journalism would be exempt from protection under the law. "Give me the liberty to know, to utter, and to argue freely according to conscience, above all liberties," Milton wrote. Neither the persistent agitations of the Levellers nor the eloquence of John Milton, one of their own, convinced Puritan authorities to relax press controls, and prior censorship in England continued for another fifty years.

With the fall of the Commonwealth in 1660 and the restoration of the Stuart monarchy, Puritan morality and religious dogma were rejected and the Anglican church once again became supreme. Parliament continued to exercise control over printing under an Act of 1662, supplemented by various royal proclamations. In 1694, after years of debate over press controls and agitation from Deist pamphleteers, including Charles Blount, Parliament allowed the Licensing Act to expire. The decision was made not by accepting the principle of press freedom but on the basis of expediency. Licensing had proved difficult to administer and ineffective in suppressing dissent.

Unorthodox or contemptuous commentary on religion continued to be a recognized offense at common law. Chief Justice Sir Matthew Hale, in the 1676 blasphemy case against John Taylor, wrote, "Christianity is a parcel of the Laws of England; and therefore to reproach the Christian religion is to speak in subversion of the law." Authors, printers, publishers, and vendors of printed works considered blasphemous or seditious could be brought to trial before either house of Parliament or before the courts. Beginning with the Taylor case, blasphemy, especially when expressed with ridicule and contempt, replaced doctrinal heresy as the more serious offense at common law. In addition to the suppression of antireligious publications under common law, a statute of 1698 specifically forbade publications denying the Holy Trinity, the divine authority of the Bible, or the truth of the Christian religion. However, it was an apostasy law, applying only to persons brought up as Christians or who had at one time professed the Christian faith.

Fear of attacks on church dogma and the church hierarchy that had prompted censorship in the past was largely replaced during the eighteenth century by fear of the spread of rationalism that challenged Christianity itself. The fear was fed by the rising tide of Deist literature that came with the end of licensing. Typical of Deist attacks on revealed Christianity were the tracts of Matthew Tindal who wrote in his *Christianity as Old as the Creation* (1730), "It's an odd jumble to prove the truth of a book by the truth of doctrines it contains, and at the same time conclude those doctrines to be true because contained in that book." During the years 1727–30 Thomas Woolston, a Cambridge scholar, published six essays arguing that the biblical miracles were absurd and intended only as allegories. Tindal's tracts were burned by the common hangman, a frequent fate of unorthodox religious works, and Woolston died in prison, where he had been committed for blasphemous libel.

A new approach to control of the English press was introduced in 1712 with the passage of the first Stamp Act, which was designed not so much as a means of revenue as it was a means to curtail and eradicate the growing number of radical newspapers and pamphlets intended for distribution among the lower classes. Government subsidization of supportive newspapers was also employed by the political party in power, whether Tory or Whig; Daniel Defoe and Jonathan Swift both used their talents as paid propagandists. The eighteenth century witnessed a lively pamphleteering war, reflecting controversies in both politics and religion. Parliament continued to exercise authority over both seditious and blasphemous libel, issuing warrants, conducting trials, and prescribing punishment. One of the most celebrated cases was that of John Wilkes who in 1764–68 was charged with seditious libel for criticizing the king in his paper, *North Briton*. Wilkes was expelled from Parliament and eventually spent almost two years in prison, but he became the idol of the common people for championing freedom to criticize an unpopular government. Obscenity appeared for the first time as a major issue in one of the Wilkes trials.

Government suppression of press criticism reached a climax in the hysteria that engulfed England during the period of the French Revolution. Many Englishmen feared the spread of French rationalism as well as the political radicalism of the Jacobins. The most censored author of the period, for his radicalism in both politics (*Rights of Man*) and religion (*Age of Reason*), was Thomas Paine. The eminent lawyer Thomas Erskine defended Paine unsuccessfully in his sedition trial following publication of *Rights of Man*, but acted successfully for the prosecution in the trial of Thomas Williams for publishing *Age of Reason*, a defense of Deism. Erskine declared that he could not grant the same freedom to attack the Christian religion as he granted to attack the political system.

Fear of Jacobin influence led to the formation in London in 1792 of the Association for Preserving Liberty and Property against Republicans and Levellers, a vigilante group with branches throughout England. Members served as informers and assisted in prosecuting persons believed to be subversive. To counteract the tactics of this association and to support press freedom, Thomas Erskine and a group of associates formed Friends to the Liberty of the Press. An aggressive government campaign against Jacobin propaganda in Scotland resulted in imprisonment or transporation of Thomas Muir and other supporters of the French Revolution and British constitutional reform. Treason trials were also held in London for Thomas Hardy and eight others, including John Horne Tooke, who had opposed the war with America, but a vigorous defense by Thomas Erskine and public revulsion against the harshness of the Scottish treason trials led to their acquittal.

One of the most eloquent, if unlikely, defenders of press freedom and an opponent of both the sedition trials that had taken place during the late eighteenth century and the blasphemy prosecutions of the 1820s was Robert Hall, a Baptist minister. In his *Apology for the Freedom of the Press* (1793) Hall wrote, "The law hath amply provided against overt acts of sedition and disorder, and to suppress mere opinion by any other method than reason and argument, is the height of tyranny." All men, he argued, should have absolute liberty to discuss "every subject which can fall within the compass of the human mind." His radical views on press freedom were widely denounced by fellow clergymen.

Increased refusal of juries to convict in sedition and treason trials, despite instructions to do so by strict judges, led to the passage of the Fox Libel Act of 1792. Chief Justice William Mansfield, in the 1770 libel case against newspaper publisher Henry S. Woodfall, had ruled that the jury in a libel trial was limited to establishing the fact of publication only (often admitted by the accused); the judge must decide whether or not the work constituted seditious or blasphemous libel. Mansfield's ruling was widely followed in libel cases until the Fox Libel Act removed these restrictions on the power of juries.

The French Revolution had led to the

separation of church and state in that nation, but no such change took place in England. Once the fear of French revolutionary ideas spreading to England had subsided, however, there appeared to be greater tolerance for political dissent. But the government continued to assume responsibility for the protection of the Christian religion, and conflict over religious heterodoxy continued throughout the nineteenth century. In 1802 the Society for the Suppression of Vice was formed, with the blessing of George III, "to encourage religion and virtue among the humbler ranks of society and to suppress blasphemous, licentious and obscene books and prints." Like the vigilante association of an earlier decade that had moved against sedition, the vice society was chief informer and prosecutor against blasphemy and obscenity for two decades, obtaining more than seven hundred convictions by the end of its second year. Between 1817 and 1825 the Society dealt with fourteen important blasphemy cases and twenty important obscenity cases, the latter with greater success.

The newspaper stamp duty was increased in 1815. During the next twenty years almost a thousand publishers and news vendors were brought to trial for circulating unstamped papers that, it was feared, would spread Deism and republicanism among the "lower orders." Civil authorities seemed more concerned than church leaders in protecting disaffection with established religion, fearing that radicalism in religion might lead to political radicalism. In 1819 Parliament passed two press acts which supplemented the common law of libel: the Blasphemous and Seditious Libels Act and the Publications Act. The latter was directed against the cheap weeklies (and pamphlets) that tended "to excite hatred and contempt of the Government and the Constitution . . . and also vilifying our holy religion. . . ."

England in the 1820s witnessed a spirited campaign for greater press freedom in the realm of both politics and religion. So-called scientific radicals, such as James Mill, Francis Place, and Jeremy Bentham, pled their case for press freedom through reasoned pamphlets and journal articles, and a number of prominent Whigs attempted Parliamentary reform. The greatest challenge to press restrictions, however, came from Richard Carlile, a radical freethinker and republican, considered by historian Trevelyan to have done more for the liberty of the press than any other Englishman of the nineteenth century. Carlile spent a large part of his adult life either in jail or under indictment for publication of such works as Paine's *Age of Reason*, Elihu Palmer's *Principles of Nature*, and his own paper, the *Republican*, in which he reviled Christian doctrine. Carlile, his wife, sister, and a series of shopmen joined in a relentless campaign against the press law and, particularly, against the activities of the vice society, collectively serving more than two hundred years in prison. Carlile and the Bridge Street Gang, as his associates were known, invited arrest to challenge the common law of blasphemy and other press restraints.

William Hone, a less fanatical publisher, was three times brought to trial for publishing political satires and cartoons that took the form of parodies on the Lord's Prayer, the Apostle's Creed, the Book of Common Prayer, and the Ten Commandments. Hone's parodies, illustrated by Cruikshank, ridiculed the Prince Regent, the constitution, Parliament, the vice society, and press law. Unable to get a conviction for sedition, authorities brought Hone to trial for blasphemous libel. The jury disregarded the judge's instructions to convict, finding Hone "not guilty" and defending the right of political criticism, even when it employed religious symbols. It was said that more than 100,000 copies of Hone's parodies were sold, largely stimulated by the trials.

A national campaign to remove the tax on newspapers took place in the 1830s, with hundreds of papers and tracts being published without payment of the tax. Several hundred vendors and a smaller number of printers and publishers were imprisoned. A leader in the "war of the unstamped" was Henry Hetherington whose *Poor Man's Guardian*, published in defiance of the tax law, resulted in his imprisonment and the arrest of some five hundred persons for its sale. One of the most notable blasphemy cases of the nineteenth century was that of George Jacob Holyoake, Chartist and "apostle of secularism," who, along with Charles Southwell, founded the *Oracle of Reason*, the first English journal devoted wholly to atheist thought. During the three years of its existence (1841–43) four successive editors were imprisoned for blasphemy. In 1841 Edward Moxon was convicted of malicious libel on the Christian religion for publishing Shelley's *Queen Mab*, but he was never called up for sentencing. The judge suggested that it was more appropriate to refute objectionable views on religion by other publication than to prosecute the author or publisher.

Despite the combined efforts of reformers, pamphleteers, and courageous publishers and news vendors and the support of a number of liberal Whigs in Parliament, the tax on newspapers was not removed until 1855 and the tax on paper continued until 1869. During the latter years of the paper tax, Holyoake was brought to trial for non-payment of the tax on his paper, the *Reasoner*, but the case was dismissed with the repeal of the tax in 1869. Charles Bradlaugh published his weekly *National Reformer*, a paper devoted to atheism, republicanism, and neo-Malthusianism, "in Defiance of His Majesty's Government," under an almost forgotten ordinance of 1819 that required the posting of a surety bond in the publication of a newspaper. Bradlaugh was brought to trial but his case was also dismissed with the repeal of that law in 1869. Thus ended 157 years of struggle to abolish the "taxes on knowledge." It has been estimated that within a year of the repeal of the last stamp tax more than 150 new papers, mostly small weeklies, appeared in England.

Blasphemy continued to be a serious crime in England during the remainder of the nineteenth century, with eighty-eight prosecutions and sixty-one convictions under common law, mostly involving atheist thought and vilification of Judeo-Christian

beliefs and personages rather than dissent over doctrinal issues. George W. Foote and W. J. Ramsey, editors of the *Freethinker*, an atheist journal that mixed satire and comic cartoons with more serious attacks on Judeo-Christian thought and the Bible, were brought to trial in 1883 under the common law of blasphemous libel. The indictment charged the editors with "disregarding the laws and religion of the realm, and wickedly and profanely devising and intending to asperse and villify Almighty God, and to bring the Holy Scriptures and the Christian religion into disbelief and Contempt among the people of this kingdom and against the peace of our lady the Queen, her crown and dignity." Foote and Ramsey were found guilty and given jail sentences of one year, but Chief Justice Coleridge, in summarizing for the jury, modified the existing common law of blasphemy by declaring that Christianity was no longer part of the law of the land and that "if the decencies of controversy are observed, even the fundamentals of religion may be attacked without the person being guilty of blasphemy." This dictum was reaffirmed in the John W. Gott blasphemy trials in 1911–12.

Following the Gott conviction, the Committee for the Repeal of the Blasphemy Laws was formed, including representatives from Unitarians, ethical societies, the Rationalist Press Association, and the Freethought Socialist League. The committee sought to abolish all laws against heresy and blasphemy, noting that even under the Coleridge rule the court could decide what expressions were "decent" and that, while immunity was given to "the scholar and gentleman," it was denied to the poor and unlearned. The committee noted further that during the past year (1912) there had been more prosecutions for blasphemy in England than during the previous fifty years and that there were at least seven laws still in effect for punishment of "offenses against religion." Furthermore, the blasphemy laws did not protect all religion but only the Church of England and that even without blasphemy laws indecent language would be subject to laws against disturbing the peace. Despite many efforts in Parliament, spearheaded by this committee and later the Society for the Abolition of the Blasphemy Laws, the laws remained in force. But fewer cases were brought to trial, probably the last conviction being that of John W. Gott, imprisoned in 1922 for the fourth time for a ribald antireligious pamphlet.

Opposition to English blasphemy laws over the years came not only from nonconformists and athesists but also from prominent churchmen who felt that using the force of law to protect the Christian faith was morally wrong and counterproductive; that Christianity could and should stand on its own merits. During the prosecutions of Richard Carlile in 1819 one minister wrote, "If Deists will listen to you, persuade them; if they will reason, argue with them; if they write and publish, reply to them; if they misrepresent, expose them; but in the name of Christ, do not persecute them, do not abet or sanction persecution." During the trial of the editors of the *Freethinker* in 1883, Charles Gill wrote that there should be a recognition that "as there is a fanaticism of faith, so also there may be a fanaticism of unbelief." He condemned blasphemy prosecutions as a survival of a legal heritage that conscientiously burnt heretics and was associated with the trials and condemnation of Socrates and Jesus. Writing in 1875, Sir James F. Stephen, a legal scholar, observed that blasphemy prosecutions had not checked the open growth of scepticism. "They helped to complete the alliance between religious and political dissaffection and they forced serious and quiet unbelievers to take up a line of covert hostility to Christianity which was injurious to their own honesty and directness of purpose on the one hand and doubly injurious to Christianity itself in the long run."

In 1929 a bill to abolish the crimes of blasphemy and blasphemous libel by repealing five statutory laws was withdrawn after considerable debate in Parliament indicated that there was no clear consensus for passage. It is interesting to note that the 1929 bill excluded Northern Ireland, the assumption being that protection of the church was still needed in those counties or that passage would have been impossible without the exception. Several subsequent repeal attempts also failed. Those opposing repeal expressed concern over the scurrilous and obscene attacks on religion and the effect of such attacks on the sensibilities of Christians, particularly children. But underlying the difficulties of repeal, as it had for generations, was the political establishment of the Church of England. Despite retention of both statutory and common law against blasphemy in England, there has been no major threat to freedom of publication for more than a half century, so that the issue now seems moot.

AMERICAN EXPERIENCE

The English who settled the North American colonies in the seventeenth century brought with them the restrictive views on press freedom that prevailed in the mother country. While they protected zealously the rights of their own creeds—Church of England, Puritan, Quaker, or Roman Catholic, they did not recognize a legal right of free discussion. They believed that to preserve public order and morality they must suppress heresy in the church and sedition in the state. Most of the colonies established licensing systems, and royal governors and assemblies quarreled over who should control the press. Legislative assemblies were, on the whole, more restrictive than royal governors, and presses were only as free as the legislatures permitted.

The first challenge to the Puritan theocracy in America came from Roger Williams, whose advocacy of religious toleration resulted in his banishment from the Massachusetts colony in 1635. In the colony of Rhode Island that he and associates founded, complete religious freedom was guaranteed, with tolerance extended "to Jews, pagans and Turks." Williams's treatise on toleration, *The Bloudy Tenent of Persecution*, appeared in 1644, the year in which Milton issued his *Areopagitica*. Rhode Island was an exception among the colonies in guaranteeing freedom of expression.

The first book to be burnt by the common executioner, following the English custom, was William Pynchon's *The Meritorious Price of Our Redemption* (1650), which expressed "erronyous and hereticale" views on Christ's suffering. Pynchon fled to England to avoid trial by the Massachusetts legislature. Pennsylvania's first printer, William Bradford, was arrested three times by the Quaker government for his printing. In 1693 he fled to New York, where he became official government printer. Following the Bradford affair, Pennsylvania established a formal licensing system which prevailed for a generation. A quarrel among Pennsylvania Quakers led to the arrest of Thomas Maule for disturbing the peace by importing copies of his tract *Truth Held Forth & Maintained*. During his 1695 trial Maule shocked the court by maintaining that the Bible was as fallible as his own work. He was acquitted by the jury, which reacted to the excesses of the Salem witchcraft trials.

In New York two Presbyterian ministers, Francis Makemie and John Hampton, were brought to trial in 1707 for preaching without a license and for publishing sermons critical of the Church of England. The jury found them "not guilty" on grounds that the Church of England was not officially established in the province. The most famous freedom of the press case in colonial America was the New York trial in 1734–35 of John Peter Zenger, whose paper the *New-York Weekly Journal* had incurred the wrath of the royal governor. Zenger's acquittal by a jury, despite an unfriendly judge, was attributed to the eloquent logic of his legal counsel, James Alexander. The Zenger decision was a landmark because it introduced four principles of press freedom: (1) the royal governor had no right to challenge freedom of the press; (2) the people had a right to information about their government; (3) "truth" could be considered a mitigating factor in a libel case; and (4) the

jury could consider the law as well as the fact of publication. The last issue was not settled in England until the Fox Libel Act of 1792. Although the Zenger decision made a great impression in England where several editions of the trial were published, it failed to establish a basis for press freedom either in New York or in other American colonies.

Censorship of the press in the colonies was conducted under both common law against seditious and blasphemous libel and under specific statutes governing speech and press which criticized government or religion. Action against the press was also taken under ordinances governing the preservation of the public peace. During the American Revolution and the decade of agitation against English oppression before the Revolution, the colonial press devoted its energies to criticism, often vitriolic, of the British government in England and its representatives in America, exercising a broad and unbridled freedom for political dissent.

By the time the federal Constitution was adopted in 1787, most state constitutions included some guarantees of freedom for speech and press, although often expressed in general terms. The most compelling guarantee was the Virginia Statute of Religious Freedom, adopted in 1785. For political expediency the federal Constitution was adopted without a free-press clause. But in the Bill of Rights, adopted in 1791 with strong support from Jefferson and Madison, the First Amendment forbade Congress from enacting any law "respecting an establishment of religion, or prohibiting the free exercise thereof; or abridging the freedom of speech, or of the press. . . ." While this statement would seem to settle the matter of freedom of expression, the issue continued to be the subject of Federalist and Anti-Federalist tracts and, intermittently over the years, came before the courts for interpretation. There is considerable evidence to indicate that the drafters of the First Amendment had in mind only the contemporary English common law concept of press freedom as stated by Jurist William Blackstone:

"The liberty of the Press is, indeed, essential to the nature of the free state, but this consists in laying no previous restraints upon publication, and not in freedom from censure for criminal matters, when published." And, of course, the First Amendment applied only to federal legislation and placed no constraint on the states until passage of the Fourteenth Amendment in 1868. (This interpretation of the Fourteenth Amendment was not established by the Supreme Court until the *Near v. Minnesota* case in 1931.)

A challenge to the speech and press clause in the First Amendment came within seven years of its adoption with the passage of the Sedition Act of 1798. The press that had attacked the British during the Revolution now turned its venom on the policies and officials of the new government, often with such scurrility that many, including President John Adams, feared for the survival of the republic. The Sedition Act virtually abolished press freedom for political dissent. Some twenty-five Republican editors and printers were prosecuted for criticizing Federalist officials and their policies before the Jefferson administration allowed the act to expire in 1800. Despite guarantees of a free press in both federal and state constitutions, blasphemy statutes remained in force in a number of states and offenses against religion were still actionable under common law. Over the years, however, with the gradual secularization of society and the wide diversity of sect, blasphemy trials became fewer in number and convictions rare unless the offense was coupled with elements of sedition or obscenity.

The most notable American blasphemy case in the nineteenth century was that of Abner Kneeland, freethinking editor of the *Boston Investigator*, who was brought to trial in 1834 for irreverently ridiculing the doctrine of prayer and the miracles and for denying the divinity of Christ. The case dragged through the courts for four years, resulting in Kneeland's conviction and sentencing to sixty days in jail and in a ruling by the Supreme Judicial Court of Mas-

sachusetts that the commonwealth's blasphemy law was constitutional. One of the issues in the case was the association of blasphemy and obscenity in a compound crime. In an earlier New York blasphemy case (1811) Chief Justice Kent had upheld that state's blasphemy law as not violating the guarantee of separation of church and state, noting that since public morality was grounded in the Christian faith, protection of that faith contributed to the peace and safety of the state.

In 1887 Charles B. Reynolds, a freethinker, was arrested in New Jersey for blasphemy and convicted, despite an able defense by Robert G. Ingersoll. In 1894 the editor of a Lexington, Kentucky freethought paper, *Blue Grass Blade*, who had previously spent time in jail for blasphemy, was brought to trial for a blasphemous account of the birth of Christ. The judge dismissed the case, accepting the argument of the defense that under the First Amendment there was no place for the common law crime of blasphemy and that for a publication to be prohibited from the mails it must be obscene as well as blasphemous.

One of the last blasphemy cases in the United States took place over a period of years, beginning in 1916, against a Lithuanian free-thought lecturer, Francis X. Mockus, charged with blasphemy in three states—Illinois, Connecticut, and Maine. The Illinois judge quashed the indictment, ruling that "no legislative inhibition against blasphemy exists in this state." Theodore Schroeder of the Free Speech League, who devoted a lifetime to opposing blasphemy laws, defended Mockus in several trials, attempting to establish the unconstitutionality of blasphemy laws. Despite Schroeder's efforts to bring the issue to a head, the case in Connecticut was dropped when the defendant disappeared. In 1926 a Lithuanian socialist, Anthony Bimba, was cleared of blasphemy in a Massachusetts court but was found guilty of seditious libel for which he had not been charged.

For the past half century, blasphemy and other offenses against religion in print or in public speech have been largely ignored, public attention having turned to issues of greater concern—sexual immorality and political radicalism, the latter reaching peaks in the "red scare" following World War I and during the McCarthy era. Although direct censorship of the press for religious dissent is a remnant of the past, Americans have been faced with a number of related issues involving freedom of religious or antireligious expression: the Jehovah's Witnesses' use of electronic devices in attacking other religions, radio response time for atheists, censorship of motion pictures deemed offensive to certain religious groups, the dissemination of birth control information, and evolution versus creationism in public school textbooks.

In *Cantwell v. Connecticut* (1940), one of several Jehovah's Witnesses cases involving free speech for religious dissent, the U.S. Supreme Court ruled that speech is protected by the First Amendment regardless of its offensiveness, unless it is deliberately abusive and obscene and is likely to incite a breach of the peace. In response to a petition, the Federal Communications Commission ruled in 1946 that atheists were entitled to response time on radio to reply to religious broadcasts. However, a House of Representatives Select Committee objected to the ruling, asserting that "the broadcast of a regular public worship . . . did not present a public controversy which in the public interest requires that time be granted to those who would destroy the church in America." Under pressure from Roman Catholics, the New York Film Censorship Board in 1952 refused a license to the film *The Miracle* considered to be blasphemous, but the U.S. Supreme Court (*Burstyn v. Wilson*) ruled that "under the Constitution and Amendments thereto a state may not ban a film on the basis of a censor's conclusion that it is sacrilegious."

Religious objections to the dissemination of birth control information, particularly from Roman Catholics, resulted in both federal and state prohibitions, but in 1965 the U.S. Supreme Court struck down a Connecticut statute (*Griswold v. Connecticut*), invalidating as well an anti-birth control law in Massachusetts. In areas where fundamentalist religious sects are influential there have been efforts to censor school textbooks that present the theory of evolution and to demand equal treatment for the Genesis version of creation. The challenge to the teaching of evolution in the classroom, which seemed to have ended with the celebrated Tennessee "monkey trial" in 1925, has recently been revived, with anti-evolution or creationism statutes enacted in a number of states. Arkansas and Mississippi statutes have been declared unconstitutional and similar laws in other states are being challenged in the courts. It is too soon to determine what effect, if any, the current Moral Majority movement will have on freedom of religious or antireligious expression.

Robert B. Downs

ISSUES OF THE PAST DECADE

The old aphorism that the more things change the more they remain the same applies to a considerable extent in the field of censorship and intellectual freedom. Nevertheless, old issues take new directions, legal aspects receive new interpretations, opposing forces re-group and fluctuate, while the objects of attack vary from perennial favorites to nine day's wonders. The overall impression is described by the French phrase *déjà vu*.

Dr. Ralph McCoy's monumental bibliography on *Freedom of the Press* is predominantly concerned with the American scene, but it contains a representative selection of British, Canadian, Australian, and other entries from English-speaking areas of the world to demonstrate the international nature of the struggle to maintain the freedom of the mind everywhere. The picture would be far grimmer, of course, in the re-

Based on the Foreword to Ralph E. McCoy's *Freedom of the Press: Ten Year Supplement, 1967–1977*, published by the Southern Illinois University Press in 1979. Reprinted by permission of the Press.

pressive dictatorial regimes behind the Iron Curtain and among many nations of Africa, Asia, and Latin America, whose people remain helpless under the heels of ruthless tyrants.

It is refreshing and heartening to note the continued interest in the historical aspects of speech and press freedom. One who refuses to learn from the lessons of history is doomed to repeat its mistakes. We should never forget that the First Amendment's prohibition against interference with free speech and free press was a direct consequence of centuries of bitter experience living under extremely repressive English laws controlling speech and press. The authority of government was long regarded as supreme, irresistible, and absolute. Any criticism of the government was viewed as dangerous heresy which must be ruthlessly put down. That entire concept was rejected by the First Amendment. Thomas Jefferson's warning that the price of liberty is eternal vigilance is borne out by the unremitting efforts in the Supreme Court, the U.S. Congress, state legislatures, and other agencies to modify, soften, weaken, or redefine the simple principle that "Congress shall make no law . . . abridging the freedom of speech, or of the press."

Scattered throughout the McCoy record are numerous references to past events, such as the trial of Peter Zenger, the martyrdom of Elijah Lovejoy, and the fanaticism of Comstockery, as well as more recent happenings, such as the A. Mitchell Palmer "Red Raids" of the nineteen twenties and Senator Joseph McCarthy's witchhunts of the nineteen fifties. But recent writings on these historical matters have not been simply threshing over old straw. Through sound research and proper historical perspective, they have brought new interpretations and new insights to bear on familiar subjects.

Though we have continued to be preoccupied with the same or similar problems year after year, new issues have risen during the past decade, in response to new pressures, new legislation, and recent legal decisions, especially at the Supreme Court level. It will be the purpose of the present discussion to review and analyse a number of the most vital issues as they have developed during the ten-year period, 1967–77.

PENTAGON PAPERS

Complex issues relating to freedom of the press were raised in 1971 by publication of the Pentagon Papers, a collection of documents, totaling forty-seven volumes, on the "History of U.S. Decision-Making Process on Vietnam Policy." The principal questions at stake were the constitutional ban on prior restraint in publication, national security, and government censorship policies, especially excessive use of "classification" by the federal government to conceal information. The Pentagon Papers had been secretly taken from Defense Department files by a staff member, Daniel Ellsberg, and turned over to the *New York Times*, *Washington Post*, *Boston Globe*, and *St. Louis Post-Dispatch*. The study, which had been commissioned by DOD Secretary Robert McNamara, was a critique of U.S. Indochina policy up to 1968, plus texts of relevant documents. The papers showed that four successive administrations (Truman, Eisenhower, Kennedy, and Johnson) had made major military and political decisions without the knowledge of the Congress and of the American people.

The celebrated Pentagon Papers case opened in June 1971 after publication by the *New York Times* of three installments of the material. The Justice Department filed a civil suit in District Court seeking a permanent injunction against further publication. Judge Murray I. Gurfein issued a temporary restraining order against the newspaper, but four days later denied a permanent injunction, stating that "A cantankerous press, an obstinate press, an ubiquitous press must be suffered by those in authority in order to preserve the even greater values of freedom of expression and the right of the people to know."

The Justice Department refused to accept defeat, basing its arguments on violation of a statute by the *Times* against "unauthorized possession" of government documents, publication of which would cause irreparable injury to defense interests of the United States. The Espionage Act adopted by Congress in 1951, on which the Department rested its case, it was noted by one judge, "provides for criminal penalties, but not prior restraint." The New York Appellate Court ruled that the *Times* could resume publication, though it could not use any material deemed dangerous to national security. On the same day, the Washington Circuit Court ruled seven to two in favor of the *Washington Post*, holding that publication of the documents would not endanger national security.

The next act of the drama occurred at the Supreme Court level, to which both the *Times* and the Justice Department appealed. Newspaper executives in general took the view that the Pentagon Papers dealt with events long past and thus constituted a historical treatise that the public was entitled to read. The information in the documents was not damaging to national security, they held, though it was probably embarrassing to high officials responsible for making Vietnamese policy. In any event, on June 30, 1971, in a split decision (Justices Burger, Blackmun, and Harlan dissenting), the Supreme Court found in favor of the *Times* and the *Post*, holding that any government attempt to block a news article prior to publication bears "a heavy burdon of presumption against its constitutionality." In the Court's opinion, "the government had not met that burden," and so this first attempt to suppress publication of material held dangerous to national security was denied.

Despite the victory achieved in the Supreme Court's Pentagon Papers ruling, civil libertarians were inclined to view it as a flawed decision. They noted that all nine justices filed separate opinions on widely varying grounds. Furthermore, though the press had ultimately been permitted to publish, it had been silenced for fifteen days by the government, during which time the First Amendment guarantees of freedom from government control had been suspended.

CLASSIFIED INFORMATION

The tremendous effort by Federal Government officials to halt publication of the Pentagon Papers for political reasons made clear a fundamental democratic dilemma: how to reconcile demands for suppression of information in the name of national security with democratic beliefs in an open society and the people's right to know, or in other words to determine where to draw the line between the fullest flow of information and publication of material deemed contrary to national security. The legal arguments advanced by the Justice Department in the Pentagon Papers case grew out of an assertion that the President has "inherent" power to decide what information can be released, both military and political. In recent decades, the concept of "executive privilege," which has no constitutional or legal basis, has been frequently invoked by the President in refusing to release information requested by Congress, the press, or other agencies. As the power of the Chief Executive has expanded, steadily and relentlessly, mountains of "Top-Secret Sensitive," "Top-Secret," and "Secret" documents have piled up, remaining concealed even from the eyes of historians, long after any possible justification for their "classified" status has ceased.

Controversy over the Pentagon Papers affair brought charges of excessive secrecy and improperly concealed information on the part of the executive branch of the government. The Department of Defense conceded that ninety-five percent of the material in the papers had already been published or declassified when the furor began. Nevertheless, administration spokemen claimed that for the President or his representatives to withhold information was a right intrinsic in the doctrine of separation of powers.

Adhering to that principle, efforts by Congress to obtain information on the Laotian campaign were blocked, together with data on the deployment of nuclear weapons abroad and the gross budget of the Central Intelligence Agency. President Nixon also denied a request of Congress to inspect the Defense Department's foreign military assistance plan.

Spearheaded by then Vice-President Spiro Agnew, attacks by the Nixon administration on news media became virulent. Evidence seemed convincing that the executive branch was attempting to intimidate the media, especially television, in order to stifle criticisms of administrative policies. A study by the American Civil Liberties Union characterized the situation as follows: "attacks on the press by officers of government have become so widespread and all pervasive that they constitute a massive federal-level attempt to subvert the letter and the intent of the First Amendment." Among the tactics used was the government's increased use of its subpoena power to force newsmen to turn over news notes and film footage from their files and to name sources of information. A natural consequence was self-censorship by the media, particularly radio and television stations operating under licenses, causing them to avoid discussion of controversial issues.

Somewhat analogous to the Pentagon Papers affair was a subsequent much-publicized case which brought on a confrontation with the House Ethics Committee. CBS television reporter Daniel Schorr had procured a copy of a House Intelligence Committee report and passed it on to a newspaper, the *Village Voice*, for publication. Schorr refused to turn over his copy of the report to the Ethics Committee or to name the person who gave it to him. In a statement to the House Committee, Schorr said: "For a journalist the most crucial kind of confidence is the identity of a source of information. To betray a confidential source would mean to dry up many future sources for many future reporters. The reporter and the news organization would be the immedi-

ate loser. I would submit to you that the ultimate losers would be the American people and their free institutions." The House Committee refused to cite Schorr for contempt of Congress, but the incident led to the loss of Schorr's position with CBS.

PRIOR RESTRAINT

The question of prior restraint, a key issue in the Pentagon Papers case, has cropped up in other connections during the past decade.

In 1974, a unique case of censorship arose when a book by Victor Marchetti and John A. Marks, *The CIA and the Cult of Intelligence* was published with deletions demanded by the Central Intelligence Agency and approved by a federal district court judge. There had been several years of litigation preceding publication. Such prior restraint by government had never been imposed previously in the United States. Marchetti had been an agent of the CIA at one time, and it was claimed that as a condition of employment years before, he had signed an agreement not to reveal any information without the consent of CIA officials. In accordance with the court order, the manuscript was submitted to the agency, which deleted 339 passages. The publisher, Alfred Knopf, and the author prepared to sue for restoration, after which the number of deletions was reduced to 168. In a later court action, it was found that publication would affect national security in only 27 passages. Further legal appeals by the CIA, however, resulted in the book being issued with the full 168 deletions.

The Supreme Court refused to intervene in the Marchetti case, letting stand the lower court's ruling permitting extensive censorship by the CIA. Another dimension was added in 1975 by a second book about the CIA, *Inside the Company*, published in England. This work is subject to seizure on entering the United States.

At about the same time, a proposed revision of the federal criminal code was submitted to Congress containing a provision for press censorship that would have imposed heavy fines and long prison sentences on reporters, editors, and authors who released information considered damaging to national security or to the nation's foreign relations. Fortunately, because of wide protests, it appears that the legislation will not be approved by Congress.

The United States was not alone in practicing prior restraint. Britain's attorney general temporarily blocked publication of a deceased government official's diary, by asserting that its revelations would damage future confidential exchanges between officers of the government. The order was set aside later by a high court. National security was the claimed basis in Israel for banning publication of a book *Confrontation and Disengagement*; the author's manuscript and notes were seized.

PRESS GAG ORDERS

Another type of prior restraint, press gag orders by trial court judges, became an increasingly common practice during the decade. Judges sought to limit information by orders of silence to defense lawyers, prosecutors, and police officials and by restricting access of reporters to the proceedings. Artists for two television networks were forbidden to sketch courtroom scenes either in the courtroom or from memory outside it. Such orders have generally been held unconstituional on appeal. In one instance, a New Orleans court restricted reporting of a murder trial until after the jury was seated and all editorial comment until the trial was concluded. The order was stayed by Justice Powell of the Supreme Court, who declared that it "imposes significant prior restraint on media publication," and therefore carried "a heavy presumption against its constitutional validity." In several instances, violators of secrecy orders were found guilty of contempt by judges. A leading writer on censorship, Paul Fisher, Director of the University of Missouri's Freedom of Information Center, commented that "the strict enforcement of these restrictions raised judicial censoring power to heights not known in the last half century." The laudable motive behind the orders, the guarantee of a fair

trial, came into direct conflict with guarantees of free speech and free press.

An important victory was won by the press in 1976 when the Supreme Court found a Nebraska court's order suppressing facts concerning a sensational murder case unconstitutional on grounds of prior restraint. The ruling described the order as "the most serious and least tolerable infringement on First Amendment rights," especially "as applied to reporting of criminal proceedings." A five-judge majority of the Court envisioned no situation in which the danger of prejudicial pretrial publicity would justify prior restraint or an injunction against publication of information obtained by the press concerning crimes of accused defendants, even if it was claimed that the facts might threaten the right to trial by an impartial jury. The court went on to hold that in balancing competing constitutional rights, a vague fear that publication of information may be harmful to a defendant's Sixth Amendment rights could not support violation of equally significant First Amendment principles.

FAIR TRIAL *VS.* FREE PRESS

Nevertheless, controversy continued over the rights of individuals as against the rights of the press in dealing with courtroom trials. A prime question is the apparent difference between the First and Sixth Amendments to the U.S. Constitution. The First Amendment states clearly that "Congress shall make no law . . . abridging the freedom of speech, or of the press," while the Sixth Amendment offers various kinds of protection to accused persons in court and to suspects in police custody. The best solution to this complex issue, it is generally agreed, is a strong sense of responsibility on the part of the media. However, as Paul M. Chalfin points out, "If we are to expect the press to exercise proper self-restraint, we also have a right to demand that the law enforcement officers, district attorneys and defense lawyers refrain from trying their cases in the newspapers. This is dictated not only by wise law enforcement and courtroom procedure but also by an adherence to the canons of professional ethics."

PRIVACY

Not necessarily involving criminal charges but somewhat related to the fair trial question is the privacy issue. A growing concern for an individual's right to privacy is shown by references in the McCoy bibliography—a right which sometimes seems to be in conflict with the public's right to know. Enactment of "sunshine laws" has resulted in revelations about public business. Noteworthy are the federal Freedom of Information Act and numerous similar laws in the states involving public records and public meetings. A far more touchy issue, however, is publicity relating to individual citizens.

In a 1967 decision involving *Life* magazine the Supreme Court ruled that a person seeking to collect damages for invasion of privacy must prove that the publicity was false and that it was published with knowledge of its falsity or with a reckless disregard of whether it was false or not. A 1975 decision had broad implications for publishers of newspapers, magazines, and books. In an eight to one decision (Justice Douglas dissenting), the Court ruled that the *Cleveland Plain Dealer* must pay $60,000 to a West Virginia family for invading its privacy because one of its reporters published two articles containing knowingly false statements. In March 1976, in a decision that narrowed the First Amendment shield protecting the news media against libel suits, the Court declared that a prominent Florida socialite could not be considered a "public figure" for the purpose of deciding libel claims against *Time* magazine, the charge being the alleged misquoting of a 1968 divorce decree. Justice Brennan dissented from the opinion in these words: "At stake in the present case is the ability of the press to report to the citizenry the events transpiring in the nation's judicial systems. There is no meaningful or constitutionally adequate way to report such events without reference to those persons and transactions that form the subject matter in controversy."

There is considerable evidence to the effect that the concept of privacy is being used inceasingly to deny the public information that traditionally was fully available. Individual's past records and convictions cannot be revealed without peril. The trend of recent Supreme Court decisions is effectively to narrow the definition of a "public figure," leaving publishers vulnerable to libel suits. The key issue is to find a proper balance between the privacy rights of individuals and the necessity for society to inform and govern itself.

A new agency, the Federal Privacy Protection Study Commission, was established in 1975, chiefly for the purpose of protecting the privacy of U.S. citizens by restricting access to personal information. The Commission has announced plans to recommend legislation dealing with personal data contained in medical records, federal income tax forms, and insurance company files, for example, and every person would be guaranteed the right to see, copy, and correct any files that any organization has concerning him or her.

The most flagrant and unjustifiable invasions of personal privacy, recent investigations reveal, have been the work of two federal agencies, the Central Intelligence Agency and the Federal Bureau of Investigation. Among illegal acts were the opening and photographing of mail, including the correspondence of many prominent Americans, spying on every black student union or group on U.S. college campuses, and efforts to break up so-called hate groups.

Such activities on the part of the CIA and FBI had been sanctioned and encouraged by the White House. The Nixon administration asserted its power to engage in wiretapping and eavesdropping, without prior judicial approval, of persons whom the Attorney General thought were a threat to the nation's domestic security. When the matter reached the Supreme Court, it was ruled that eavesdropping without a warrant is unconstitutional. Justice Powell noted that "The price of lawful public dissent must not be a dread of subjection to an unchecked surveillance power. Nor must the fear of unauthorized official eavesdropping deter vigorous citizen dissent and discussion of government action in private conversation. For private dissent, no less than open public discourse, is essential to our society."

RIGHTS OF SPECIAL GROUPS

Increasing concern has been shown during the past decade in the rights of special groups in society: prisoners, military personnel, mental patients, children, students, and teachers. It has been remarked that four public institutions in the United States have traditionally ignored the Bill of Rights—the military, the schools, mental "hospitals," and prisons. First Amendment rights are severely restricted and often prohibited in all four. They deny the right of free trial to persons accused of misconduct, and consider authority more important than freedom, order more precious than liberty, and discipline more valuable than individual expression. Military commanders, school principals, chief psychiatrists, and prison wardens, it is suggested, have similar characteristics in the governance of their respective organizations.

An estimated 1,500,000 Americans are presently confined in penal institutions. During the past few years, four principal issues concerning their rights have emerged in legal actions: (1) the right of a prisoner to have access to materials without prior screening or censorship, including receipt of personal correspondence and reading published literature; (2) the right of a prisoner to publish his own writings without restraint or interference with royalties; (3) the right of a prisoner to correspond with or to be interviewed by the public press; and (4) the right of a prisoner to have access to legal research materials.

A growing number of court decisions have been made clarifying these points. For example, U.S. District Court Judge Walter T. McGovern ruled that prisoners had the right to subscribe to newspapers, periodicals, and books, and specified that reading materials "can be denied an inmate only if such cen-

sorship furthers one or more of the substantial governmental interests of security against escape or unauthorized entry, or if the publication is obscene." Another District Court Judge, Wilbur D. Owens, Jr., joined other federal judges in California, Alabama, Florida, and Georgia in upholding the right of prisoners to law library service. If other suitable legal assistance is unavailable, Judge Owens declared, prison officials must make an adequate law library available as an aid in the preparation of prisoner's habeas corpus and civil rights petitions.

Writing in the *New Republic*, Peter Barnes declares that "for three-and-a-half million Americans in uniform, justice is what the brass says it is, damn the Constitution and full speed ahead." The author was commenting on the arrest and sentencing to four years hard labor and dishonorable discharge of two army privates for producing and distributing a mimeographed protest against the Vietnamese war to soldiers at Fort Ord, California.

Underground newspapers have proliferated at army bases during the past several years, especially before the end of the war in Vietnam. Invariably, they were suppressed. Dissent against the war was stamped out by military commanders. GI protesters were punished for leafleting, for distributing underground newspapers, for demonstrating, and for voicing unpopular opinions. According to the Uniform Code of Military Justice, words that are "unbecoming," "provocative," "defamatory," or "reproachful" are crimes. Actually, as a practical matter, the words mean anything the commanding officer wants them to mean. A commentator on one famous case, that of Captain Howard Levy, noted that during the trial the captain's "words were invested with meanings so terrible that the existence of the nation as well as the army seemed to be at stake."

A case before the Supreme Court in 1976 involved an attempt by Benjamin Spock and others to campaign at Fort Dix, New Jersey. In a six-to-two decision, the Court declared that the business of military bases is "to train soldiers, not to provide a public forum" for political debate. The decision cited the American tradition of "a politically neutral military" and drew a sharp distinction between the rights of civilians and those of military personnel, holding that base commanders have broad powers to bar political campaigning on United States installations. Later in the same year, U.S. District Court Judge Barrington D. Parker overturned as unconstitutional a Marine Corps regulation prohibiting the distribution of "political literature" on Marine bases without the approval of commanders, and remarked that "Perhaps encouragement of more freedom of thought would have sparked recognition of unlawful orders in the Vietnam War and prevented atrocities such as the massacre of civilians at My-lai."

Teachers' and students' rights also received judicial review at various levels. A series of articles in the *New Yorker* brought national notice to the case of Charles James, an eleventh-grade English teacher at Addison High School near Elmira, New York. James had been fired by his school board for wearing a black armband symbolizing his opposition to the Vietnam war. A lower court approved the right of a teacher to express political views in the classroom so long as there was no threat of disruption. Because the school board failed to show that his action disrupted classroom activities or interfered with his teaching, the court concluded that the board dismissed James simply because it disagreed with his political views, and ordered his reinstatement. The board appealed to the Supreme Court, which let stand the lower court ruling.

A prominent library educator, Martha Boaz, maintains that "the student has a right to read; he has a right to free access to books. He has a right to a wide variety and an extensive selection of materials. He has a right to examine all ideas, to explore all forms of learning, to investigate all cultures. He has a right to investigate every medium of art and every mode of expression of it. He has a right to search for truth wherever it may be found." Interference with student freedom has most frequently taken the form of cen-

sorship of student newspapers. The College Press Service has reported numerous instances of "overt acts of censorship" against campus newspapers, often involving the disciplining of editors and reporters and sometimes suppression of the papers. The principal issues, generally, were the extent to which student editors and reporters can legitimately express controversial views, whether they may use allegedly indecent words, and whether university and college administrators can censor or suppress student publications unacceptable to them. A University of California Special Commission on the Student Press, apparently reflecting the opinion of the American Society of Newspaper Editors, concluded: "It is the Commission's first and basic recommendation that it be accepted and made repeatedly clear to all concerned—regents, administrators, and campus newspaper staffs—that these newspapers are not 'official' organs of the University." Cases that have reached the courts have for the most part ended in rejection of attempts by campus administrators to censor the student press.

OBSCENITY AND PORNOGRAPHY

On June 21, 1973, the Supreme Court issued new obscenity guidelines. Henceforth, it was ruled, "community standards," as opposed to "national standards," would become the measure for determining whether a work is "prurient." The basic criteria, the Court ruled, must be (1) whether "the average person applying contemporary community standards" would find that the work, taken as a whole, appeals to the prurient interest; (2) whether the work depicts or describes, in a patently offensive way, sexual conduct specifically defined by the applicable state law; and (3) whether the work, taken as a whole, lacks serious literary, artistic, political, or scientific value.

In the wake of the Court's decision, the question immediately arose: what is the "local" community? The state or the city, or county, or neighborhood? The question was not directly answered by the Court. Authors, publishers, and motion picture producers were concerned that "contemporary community standards" would become defined as "local community standards," reducing the range of ideas and expression to the least tolerant segment of the "community." Thus a single county might have the power to censor books for the entire country, since, from an economic point of view, publishers would be inclined to produce only titles acceptable everywhere.

In effect, the Court's new ruling substantively altered previous Supreme Court definitions of what constitutes the obscene and the nature of criminal proceedings against its purveyors. Most significant was the denial of any nationwide standard. "It is neither realistic nor constitutionally sound," declared Chief Justice Burger, "to read the First Amendment as requiring that the people of Maine or Mississippi accept public depiction of conduct found tolerable in Las Vegas or New York City." (Counting states, territories, counties, townships, etc., there are some 20,000 local jurisdictions in the United States.) Justice Burger stated further that in the prosecution of allegedly obscene works the testimony of expert witnesses need not be introduced; the defense may introduce such witness, but their testimony may be disregarded.

Justice Rehnquist, who delivered the opinion of the Court in *Miller v. California*, the case establishing the concept of community standards, commenting on the meaning of "local community standards," held that the Court did not refer to any "precise geographical area." It was the Court's view, he stated, that the First and Fourteenth Amendments do not require uniform national standards and "A juror is entitled to draw on his own knowledge of the view of the average person in the community or vicinage from which he comes for making the required determination for obscenity."

A flood of new state laws and local ordinances followed the Supreme Court's *Miller v. California* decision. Now that local rather than national standards may determine whether a publication is obscene or not, publishers were discovering how widely standards vary. Thus the movie *Deep Throat*, often a target for censors, plays without interference in some cities while it is banned in others. A notorious case arose in Memphis, Tennessee, where Larry Parrish, an assistant U.S. attorney, won convictions against sixteen defendants and four corporations on charges of conspiring to distribute *Deep Throat*, and sixteen persons (few, if any of whom had ever been in Memphis) were indicted for conspiring to distribute a movie called *School Girl*. Actors and producers of *The Devil in Miss Jones* were next on the schedule. Serious constitutional questions are raised by the Memphis convictions. It appears that any person who contributes in any way to the production or distribution of a motion picture can be indicted and prosecuted, based on standards in some Bible Belt town. Such prosecutors as Parrish and other officials around the nation would impose on the entire country the standards of their own districts. Richard A. Blake, in an article entitled "Will Fig Leaves Blossom Again?" concluded that "Good state laws and sound judicial procedures might make it [the community standards decision] work; a new wave of suppression and neo-Victorian censorship will bring the debate back to zero."

COMMISSION REPORT

During the Johnson administration, a commission to investigate obscenity and pornography was appointed. The commission's report was not submitted until 1970, during President Richard Nixon's first term. The commission recommended the abolition of obscenity laws that prohibit the distribution of materials to adults who choose to receive them—a proposal in accord with Supreme Court decisions ruling that the First Amendment protects an adult's right to read and see whatever he chooses. The COP report found against all laws banning pornography, citing evidence gathered in the United States and Denmark to the effect that pornography did no discernible harm to man's character; it discovered no proof to the contrary.

President Nixon promptly disavowed the report's "morally bankrupt conclusions and major recommendations . . . American morality is not to be trifled with. The Commission on Pornography and Obscenity has performed a disservice and I totally reject its report." In response, the commission's chairman, William B. Lockhart, Dean of the University of Minnesota School of Law, suggested that President Nixon was unhappy with the report because its "scientific studies do not support the assumptions congenial to his viewpoint." Lockhart pointed out that the commission had been directed by Congress to test assumptions about the harmful effects of sexual materials, and "this we did through extensive scientific studies of many kinds." Since the commission's findings were politically unpopular, the long-range influence of its report has remained uncertain.

TEXTBOOKS

Another highly sensitive area in the field of free expression was textbooks for public schools. Pressures continued to be exerted on textbook publishers, school boards, and school librarians. A much publicized case in 1974 occurred in Kanawha County, West Virginia, where fundamentalists raised loud and demonstrative protests against the school board's adoption of "un-Godly and un-American" textbooks, deemed unfit for their children. At issue was a series of textbooks primarily for high school English literature and language skills—books which included selections from works by Eldridge Cleaver, Malcolm X, Allen Ginsberg, and Gwendolyn Brooks. Dissident parents kept their children out of school for over nine weeks, led boycotts, inspired coal mine strikes, and led a march on the state capital. The protests were marked by bombings and other violence. At the height of the controversy, the Heath textbooks, prime targets of the parents, were removed from classrooms and relegated to libraries, where only children with permission slips from home were allowed to use them. A series of alternative texts was adopted by the Kanawha County Board of Education in July 1975. The antitextbook forces were success-

ful in forcing the removal of more than three hundred books from the schools and the development of new guidelines for the purchase of textbooks. By mid-1975, however, many of the books were returned to the schools, though some principals refused to accept them or placed them in storage.

Fifty years after the famous Scopes anti-evolution trial in Dayton, Tennessee, a new anti-evolution law was enacted by the Tennessee legislature. At about the same time, California and Texas passed laws requiring that equal time be given to the Book of Genesis when the theory of evolution was taught in the public schools. On the same day, in August 1975, a federal judge and the Tennessee Supreme Court declared unconstitutional the Tennessee law requiring textbooks to provide equal space to biblical and scientific theories on the creation of the universe. In finding the law unreasonable, U.S. District Court Judge Frank Gray, Jr. noted, "Every religious sect, from the worshipers of Apollo to the followers of Zoroaster, has its belief or theory. It is beyond the comprehension of this court how the legislature, if indeed it did, expected that all such theories should be included in any textbook of reasonable size." In California, when the State Board of Education adopted new science and social science textbooks in 1975, none of the works contained any reference to the biblical theory of the creation of the world.

A major decision affecting school libraries was rendered by the U.S. Court of Appeals for the Sixth Circuit (Kentucky, Michigan, and Ohio, and Tennessee) in 1976. The Court ruled that school officials cannot go through a school library and arbitrarily remove and ban books they dislike. The decision elaborated on four principal points concerning what sort of books should be (1) selected as high school textbooks, (2) purchased for a high school library, (3) removed from a high school library, and (4) forbidden to be taught or assigned in a high school classroom. In a stirring conclusion, the judges declared, "A library is a mighty resource in the free marketplace of ideas. It is specially dedicated to broad dissemination of ideas. It is a forum for silent speech. . . . Here we are concerned with the right of students to receive information which they and their teachers desire them to have."

The evidence is overwhelming that censorship and governmental repression is on the increase throughout the world. As President, Jimmy Carter spoke out strongly for universal human rights. How much influence his outspoken sentiments have had outside the United States remains to be seen. Indeed, there are indications that President Carter's stand led to increased oppression of dissidents in the Soviet Union and other Iron Curtain nations.

The colossal nature of the problem of human freedom and human rights is revealed by reports issued by the Anti-Slavery Society for the Protection of Human Rights, founded in 1834, in Britain. As recently as 1955, the Society estimated that there were 62 million people classifiable as slaves. The United Nations failed to adopt a convention against the practice of slavery until 1956, after years of lobbying by the Anti-Slavery Society. Only 85 of the 147 UN members have ratified the convention. The United Nations Human Rights Committee reported in 1982 that millions were in bondage in India and other countries.

CHAPTER TWO

NEW VIEWS OF THE FIRST AMENDMENT

The most basic law protecting freedom of speech and the press in America was the first amendment to be added to the U.S. Constitution—a recognition of its profound importance.

There are three guarantees of personal liberties in the First Amendment: Congress shall make no law (1) respecting an establishment of religion or prohibiting the free exercise thereof; (2) abridging the freedom of speech or of the press; or (3) abridging the right of the people peaceably to assemble and to petition the government for a redress of grievances. The language is simple and implicit. Nevertheless, a sizable segment of a library could be filled with judicial and other attempts to interpret the fundamental law, and often to pervert its meaning. Controversy continues to swirl around the amendment as each age brings new points of view to bear upon it. In his study, "The Evolution of the First Amendment," Ralph McCoy examines some of the changing concepts as the public and the courts have confronted new issues in politics, religion, sex, and personal libel. He also discusses the First Amendment as it has been applied to new forms of mass communication—motion pictures, radio, and television.

Ralph E. McCoy

THE EVOLUTION OF THE FIRST AMENDMENT

Freedom of expression, as guaranteed by our federal Constitution, is both an end in itself, insofar as the right of an individual is concerned and a process or a method for arriving at other goals in our society. In fact,

Howard Rusk Long Honor Lecture, School of Journalism, Southern Illinois University at Carbondale, June 22, 1982.

a democratic society would soon fail if its citizens were not sufficiently informed to pass judgment on matters affecting their lives.

The basic guarantee of freedom of expression is contained in the First Amendment to our Constitution, adopted in 1791:

Congress shall make no law respecting an establishment of religion, or prohibiting the free exercise thereof; or abridging the freedom of speech, or of the press; or the right of the people peaceably to assemble, and to petition the Government for a redress of grievances.

There are other constitutional provisions which relate to freedom of expression or support it: there is the prohibition against unreasonable searches and seizures, contained in the Fourth Amendment; the privilege against self-incrimination, contained in the Fifth Amendment; and the right of due process, contained in the Sixth Amendment. Also, the Fourteenth Amendment prohibits the individual states from enacting laws abridging freedom of speech and of the press.

The wording of the First Amendment—"Congress shall make no law . . . abridging the freedom of speech, or of the press"—would seem to be clear and unequivocal; but for almost two centuries the meaning of these words has been the subject of widespread debate in American society and deliberation in the courts. Our present understanding of freedom of the press is the result of an evolutionary process which, in fact, is still taking place.

SEDITION ACT

The first challenge to freedom of the press from Congress came within seven years of the adoption of the First Amendment—with the passage of the Sedition Act. Under this act numerous editors were brought to trial, convicted, and sent to prison for criticizing the administration of President John Adams. It was argued by the Federalists who supported the Sedition Act that the First Amendment was intended only to forbid prior restraint on the press through licensing, not to be a guarantee against prosecution for abuse of that freedom after the fact. This was the prevailing British doctrine espoused by Sir William Blackstone, whose views were so influential in early American jurisprudence. Criticism of the President or his administration was considered a form of seditious libel and punishable as an abuse of press freedom. The sedition law was allowed to expire under Thomas Jefferson's administration without its constitutionality having been tested by the courts. It was not until World War I that a significant First Amend-

ment case came before the United States Supreme Court.

During the nineteenth century, American jurisprudence developed the "bad tendency" test, derived from the English law of seditious libel, by which utterances were punishable whenever they had a reasonable tendency to undermine government stability. The test was broadly applied so that Congress, the courts, or the state legislatures could take action against an oral or printed expression if it tended to lead to an evil consequence—corrupting public morals, inciting the commission of a crime, disturbing the peace, fostering disrespect for the law, or endangering national security.

The endangering of national security has frequently been an area in which First Amendment freedoms have been set aside. In time of war or grave national emergency the courts and the general public have accepted limited abridgment of press freedom. During World War I, when freedom for dissent in this country was at an all-time low, the government, often with court approval, took action against pacifists who opposed the draft and against socialists, anarchists, and labor unionists. Such dissenters were prosecuted under the guise of extinguishing any spark that might endanger the war effort. These actions were taken under the Espionage Act of 1917, which has never been repealed. Government has so often cried "wolf," claiming national security when, in fact, no real threat existed (as in the case of the Pentagon Papers), that the courts have been skeptical.

OBSCENITY

In the area of obscenity a bad tendency test (also known as the "Hicklin rule" from an 1868 British case) was in general use in the United States until the 1930s. The Hicklin rule stated that any work was actionable if it tended "to deprave or corrupt those whose minds were open to such immoral influences and into whose hands a publication of this sort might fall." Obscenity, of course, was not an issue faced by the framers of the Bill of Rights; it was not considered a threat to the survival of the republic. As in Britain at the time, obscenity was an issue to be addressed by ecclesiastical rather than civil authorities; the latter were chiefly concerned with protecting freedom of expression in the realm of politics and religion. Obscenity did not become a civil offense in the United States until the 1870s. In 1957 the United States Supreme Court in the *Roth* case ruled that obscenity was outside the protection of the First Amendment. This judgment still stands.

It is significant that in the same sentence of the First Amendment that protects press freedom, Congress is also prohibited from making any law either establishing religion or prohibiting its exercise. This separation of church and state, so important in our democracy, was a reaction to the British experience in which civil authorities had power to control religious expression and often considered religious heterodoxy a more serious crime than political dissent. In 1792 the British barrister Thomas Erskine successfully defended Thomas Paine against charges of sedition for his political tract, *Rights of Man*, but Erskine also successfully prosecuted the publisher of Paine's Deist tract, *Age of Reason*. Erskine expressed the prevailing British view when he declared that he could not grant the same freedom to attack religion that he granted to attack the political system. In America the separation of church and state and the guarantee of freedom of religious expression has been firmly established under the First Amendment and, over the years, has been upheld by the courts.

Despite some efforts by the courts to liberalize the establishment of press freedom and to guard against undue prosecution after publication, many controversial issues were unsafe for discussion under the bad tendency test, and this test was superseded eventually by what has become known as the "clear-and-present-danger" test. This doctrine was first suggested by Justice Oliver Wendell Holmes in a World War I espionage case, *Schenck v. United States*, and was expanded and applied in a number of subsequent decisions and dissenting opinions. It is not sufficient justification, according to Justice

Holmes, to suppress an expression because it has bad tendencies; the expression must pose an obvious and immediate danger to individuals and society. And Holmes gave the now familiar example of an incident that was both clear and dangerous, the false cry of "fire" in a crowded theater. The clear-and-present-danger test was generally welcomed by supporters of freedom of expression, but while it widened the area of protection under the First Amendment, it did not invariably take into consideration either the nature or the gravity of the evil that might follow. It also seemed to place a penalty on the effectiveness of expression—the more convincing the rhetoric, the greater the crime. And it left freedom of expression subject to the temper of the times and the philosophical disposition of judges.

BALANCING OF INTERESTS

Almost every First Amendment case that has come before the nation's higher courts down through the years has involved the examination of the principle of freedom of speech and press against some other basic American right also guaranteed by the Constitution or established under common law: the right of the accused to a fair trial, the right of privacy for every citizen, the state's responsibility to protect the welfare of the child, the security of the nation against foreign aggression, and the preservation of public health and safety. In attempting to weigh the right of freedom of expression with these other constitutional guarantees, the court in recent years has evolved the doctrine of "balancing of interests." This technique has been generally applied on an ad hoc basis, weighing in each case the loss or danger to the individual or to society if one or the other right prevailed. In discussion of "balancing" it has been suggested that First Amendment rights occupy a preferred or superior position with respect to other constitutional rights. Freedom of thought and speech, wrote Mr. Justice Cardozo in 1937, "is the matrix, the indispensable condition, of nearly every other form of freedom."

Another view of press freedom which has

been vigorously, if not widely, espoused by certain members of the Supreme Court is the so-called absolutist theory. Justice Hugo Black, a strict constructionist, along with liberal Justice William O. Douglas, developed this interpretation of the Constitution during long and distinguished careers on the court. What does the First Amendment mean? It means just what it says, according to Justice Black: "Congress shall make *no law* abridging the freedom of speech or of the press," and, by the Fourteenth Amendment, this absolute prohibition is extended to legislative acts of the states. What about balancing press freedom with other constitutional rights? The framers of the Bill of Rights, according to Justice Black, already balanced these rights in the course of their deliberations, arriving at the absolute prohibition against laws restricting speech and press. What about expressions that lead directly to criminal acts? The acts themselves are subject to punishment under the criminal code, but speech that might have prompted the act is protected. Justice Black made it clear, however, that the First Amendment, while it guaranteed absolute freedom of speech and press, did not guarantee freedom of speech and press *plus*. He would not, for example, use the First Amendment to protect the occupying of private property, an action that might accompany free speech.

Another advocate of the absolutist theory of press freedom was Professor Alexander Meiklejohn, one of the great thinkers and writers on the First Amendment. Professor Meiklejohn would give absolute protection to speech and press, but *only* in the realm of *political* belief and discussion, which he believed was the original intention of the framers of the document. The First Amendment, according to Meiklejohn, "declares that with respect to political belief, political discussion, political advocacy, and political planning, our citizens are sovereign, and the Congress is their subordinate agent."

Even under an absolutist interpretation of the First Amendment, however, there could be no guarantee that, in the absence of any law of Congress, the nation's press would carry out its role of informing the people about political affairs, would serve as an adequate forum for political debate, and would open its facilities to broad sectors of public opinion. In fact, there was considerable evidence to the contrary. Many newspapers, while defending their privilege to be free from external control, were not carrying out their responsibility to society. Indifference, overriding business interests, and political bias could be as threatening to a free press as government interference.

Great concern has been expressed in recent years over the growing monopoly of press ownership, as one after another city is served by only one newspaper and that paper is often part of a national chain, which might also include radio and television stations. There was a time when almost every county seat in Illinois had at least one newspaper and often two, a Republican paper and a Democratic paper; today many such towns have no papers at all. The Congress and the courts have been faced with the problem of curbing monopolistic practices in the communications industry that might seriously reduce the diversity of opinion, without doing violence to free enterprise and the First Amendment. Newspaper owners have often cited the First Amendment as an argument against applying to newspapers the controls that are normally, under the antitrust laws, applied to other trade monopolies. Balancing interests in the area of press monopoly has resulted, on the one hand, in placing restrictions on cross-media ownership and, on the other hand, in relaxing the antitrust laws to the extent that newspapers in danger of financial collapse might combine certain business and operational functions, provided they retain separate editorial controls.

FREEDOM WITH RESPONSIBILITY

The rising demand for positive government action to assure a *responsible* as well as a *free* press was brought into focus in 1947 by the report of the prestigious Commission on Freedom of the Press. The commission endorsed a concept that would extend the First Amendment's negative prohibition against abridging the press to embrace a positive freedom that would promote public enlightenment. For the most part the nation's press resented this implied criticism of its performance and the suggestion of possible social controls, but the seed for change had been planted and continued to grow. More recently Professor Thomas I. Emerson, in a scholarly study of First Amendment freedom, concluded that modern society requires a deliberate, affirmative, and aggressive effort to support a system of freedom of expression, a theory which, he noted, the Supreme Court has failed to produce in its ad hoc balancing of issues. Other legal scholars have called for judicial activism by the Supreme Court on behalf of press freedom that would match its landmark decisions on civil rights and apportionment voting. With the present court such activism is unlikely.

RADIO AND TELEVISION

In one segment of the press, radio and television (media never envisioned by the framers of the First Amendment two centuries ago), the concept of social responsibility has been generally recognized. Almost from the beginning, Congress found it necessary to pass laws which seemingly abridged the freedom of the so-called electronic press, arguing that with a limited number of channels available government must assign and regulate their use in the interest of the public. While control of content has not been regulated directly—in fact, the Federal Communications Commission is expressly prohibited from exercising such controls—there is indirect control of content through periodic review of station performance at the time of license renewal.

The most controversial involvement of government in the regulation of the electronic press has been the requirement of fairness in programming. Under the so-called fairness doctrine a radio or television station that airs controversial issues must present opposing views or give the opposition opportunity to reply. And another regulation requires stations to provide equal time to candidates in a presidential election.

In 1969 the Supreme Court ruled in the case of *Red Lion Broadcasting Co. v. Federal Communications Commission* that the "fairness doctrine" was indeed constitutional. Five years later, however, the court ruled in the case of *Miami Herald Publishing Co. v. Tornillo* that the same principle could not be applied to a newspaper, requiring it to give balanced treatment to public issues. The different treatment of the print and the electronic media has generated considerable controversy, and there is growing sentiment both within FCC and Congress for repeal of the fairness doctrine.

At the same time that leaders in radio and television want to abolish federal controls over public access to their facilities, there has been an opposing opinion, first voiced by Professor Jerome Barron of George Washington University Law School, to extend the fairness doctrine to newspapers. The mounting pressures for government enforcement of broader access to the press— both printed and electronic—reflects the doctrine of social responsibility enunciated by the 1947 commission. The social upheaval of the 1960s and 1970s added fuel to the movement for forced access and posed a challenge to the traditional interpretation of the Bill of Rights.

MOTION PICTURES

Motion pictures are another form of mass communication for which exceptions have been made to the First Amendment mandate. Up until *The Miracle* case of 1952, the Supreme Court's attitude toward films was that they were "a business, pure and simple, originated and conducted for profit" and that they were outside the protection of the First Amendment. This decision in the 1915 Mutual Film Corporation case supported a system of prior licensing by cities and states. In 1952, however, in the case of *Burstyn v. Wilson* involving the motion picture *The Miracle* which had been denied a license in New York state on grounds that it was "sacrilegious," the court held that a sacrilegious test was not grounds for denying a license, citing the First Amendment's protection of religious dissent. Subsequent decisions went further, virtually invalidating the entire system of motion picture licensing by cities and states, so that the film today enjoys much the same protection from prior restraint as the printed word. The rigid controls over film content, particularly in the area of sex, once exercised by the film industry itself through the so-called Hays Office code has given way to a voluntary rating system that leaves the decision of attendance up to the individual and, in the case of X-rated movies, policing to the theater management. Thus, motion pictures enjoy a greater freedom than radio and television.

LIBEL AND INVASION OF PRIVACY

One of the restrictions placed upon freedom of speech and of the press from the very earliest time has been an attack on the character and reputation of an individual—either verbal attacks known as slander or printed attacks, the more serious, known as libel. Because of their pervasive nature radio and television are considered by the courts as coming under the law of libel rather than slander. The balancing of the right of the press to criticize versus the right of an individual to protect reputation and privacy has been a frequent issue before the Congress and the courts. Even Justice Black found himself unwilling to deny this exception in pressing his absolutist views. The pendulum has been swinging from one side to the other in determining whether the press or the individual needed greater protection from government. In 1964 the Supreme Court in *New York Times v. Sullivan* gave increased protection to the press in its criticism of public officials, adding proof of malicious intent to the well-established tests of falsity and harm that the plaintiff must establish. Common law has generally allowed the press greater freedom to criticize public officials and public figures than persons in private life. Recent jury trials, however, have tended to support the plaintiff, a reflection of public disapproval of press excesses and an aggressive legal profession that stands to benefit financially from large damages awarded.

The Supreme Court has also moved away from the level of protection offered the press under *New York Times v. Sullivan* guidelines, so that the press—printed and electronic—is in greater danger under present interpretation of the libel laws. The recent judgment against the *Alton* (Ill.) *Telegraph* is a case in point.

In recent years there has been growing public concern for what was the original rationale for the First Amendment, to ensure an informed electorate. The right to discuss public policy, which Professor Meiklejohn saw as the paramount purpose of press freedom, would have little meaning if the press, and ultimtely the people, did not have access to information about the operation of their government and the behavior of public officials. Citizens, it is argued, should not be dependent upon what information reluctant public officials are willing to release or upon what an aggressive press is able to ferret out. The events of Watergate and the systematic attack on the press during the Nixon administration led to the passage of a strengthened Freedom of Information Act, intended to prevent the federal government from conducting public business in private, from hiding inefficiency and devious behavior of public officials under false claims of national security or the need for executive secrecy. A number of states have passed similar open records and open meeting laws. Efforts of the Reagan administration to weaken the federal Freedom of Information Act and to return to the secrecy of the past have thus far been repulsed by the Congress. The concept that the people have the "right to know" is probably the most significant recent development in First Amendment doctrine.

OTHER EMERGING CONCEPTS

There are a number of other emerging concepts, largely limited to discussion within the academic community, which either extend or limit the First Amendment, depending upon one's point of view.

Does the freedom to speak and to print imply a converse right—the freedom *not* to speak and *not* to print? The Fifth Amendment clearly protects the right of an accused to remain silent, to refuse to be a witness against oneself. But during the McCarthy hearings of the 1950s, men went to jail for using the First Amendment to protect the right not to express their political views. In a Jehovah's Witnesses case the Supreme Court upheld the right of the Witnesses not to be required to salute the flag or pledge allegiance, based largely on the right of religious freedom under the First Amendment. In another area involving the right not to speak, newspaper reporters have gone to jail rather than reveal their news sources, claiming a reporter's privilege not to speak, even when ordered to do so by a court, a privilege comparable to that historically enjoyed by lawyers, doctors, and clergymen. The Supreme Court has not sustained such absolute immunity, and the press has turned to state legislatures for protective laws. The freedom not to speak is related to the common law concept of privacy. Greater concern with protecting an individual's right to privacy in recent years has been prompted not only by press invasion of personal lives but also by the growing probes of government agencies, and by the insidious threat of the computer.

In the concept of press freedom which encourages an informed electorate, is there also an implied freedom of an individual *not* to read, *not* to listen, and *not* to see? This concept also reflects concern over invasion of privacy by the media. Many years ago G. K. Chesterton, in arguing for greater British control of stage productions than of books, noted that it was easier for a reader to snap shut an offending book than to climb over the laps of a half-dozen theatergoers when a play was offensive. While it is always a viewer's prerogative to switch to another television channel, some critics of the media have argued that television, more than books and newspapers, invades the privacy of the home and that greater government controls of broadcasting content are needed. In some instances the right of privacy from media invasion has been supported by the courts. Municipalities are free to enact ordi-

nances against noise from loudspeakers in public conveyances and on public streets, provided that they are even-handed in applying the rules. While the Postal Service is enjoined from interfering with the distribution of obscene materials through the mails (the Supreme Court having ruled in the 1946 *Esquire* case that it was the business of the post office to deliver the mail not to read it), individuals may request in writing that unsolicited sexually oriented matter be excluded from delivery to their mailboxes. In most states explicit sexual matter, even if permitted to be sold, must not be publicly displayed because it would be an unwarranted intrusion on individual privacy.

MARXIAN VIEWS

A discussion of the various interpretations of the First Amendment should at least mention the point of view of the "New Left," a view perhaps best expressed by Professor Herbert Marcuse. To him freedom of the press is freedom to express the truth. And the truth is what Professor Marcuse and other Marxists say it is. Intolerance to the untruthful ideas of others, Marcuse asserts, is a virtue, and the libertarian doctrine of press freedom is an opiate of the people and fails to provide a genuine access to social change. This Marxist view prevented several international freedom of the press conferences, held under the auspices of the United Nations, from reaching any mutually acceptable agreement.

After almost two centuries of experimentation with one of the most radical of social doctrines—the right of free expression—where do we as a nation stand? What concepts and understandings seem to be well established in common law and practice? What concepts are undergoing change and revision? What concepts are under attack and in danger? It is difficult to make categorical judgments. But we know that prior censorship or licensing of the press, which was abolished in England as early as 1694, has never been acceptable in the United States. Attempts at prior censorship have arisen from time to time but have been consistently knocked down by the Supreme Court, most notably in the 1931 case of *Near v. Minnesota*, in which there had been attempts to prohibit publication of an offensive radical paper, and in the 1976 case *Nebraska Press Association v. Stuart*, in which a lower court judge had attempted to gag the press in the coverage of a trial. And, in the first attempt in American history of the federal government to invoke prior censorship, the case of the Pentagon Papers, the Supreme Court ruled against the Nixon administration. But even in this relatively safe area, vigilance is needed to prevent municipalities, state legislatures, and the lower courts from taking unconstitutional action in response to local passions and pressures.

Freedom of the press from prosecution after the fact also has been well established in the realm of politics and religion. The Supreme Court's commitment to free expression is perhaps best expressed by that oft-quoted dictum from the *New York Times v. Sullivan* decision: "Debate on public issues should be uninhibited, robust, and wide open." Also, despite a lack of constitutional support, no serious challenges are posed today in the area of sex expression. The courts have protected works of serious literature since the 1930s and works of any "redeeming social value" are likely to be safe if the case reaches the higher federal courts. The extent to which First Amendment guarantees are withheld or extended to radio and television is a major unresolved controversy, with impressive arguments offered on both sides. Ultimately the issue will have to be decided by a balancing of interests—not what is best for the industry but what is best for society.

In no other nation do the people have greater access to information about the operation of their government than in the United States. In Britain, for example, the press still operates under the restriction of the Official Secrets Act, which limits both access to government information and the freedom to publish it, restrictions that we in the United States would find intolerable.

But again, a vigilant press and an aware public are necessary to preserve this open society as a new generation of public officials attempts to alter the rules. Unfortunately, the public itself has not always identified the newspaper's right of free expression with its own right as citizens.

Two other areas where press freedom could be in danger in this country have already been mentioned—the increase in libel judgments against the press and the monopoly of press ownership. Excessive awards of actual and punitive damages (often running into millions of dollars) and the high cost of legal services that must be paid even though the paper is vindicated have threatened the life of newspapers and magazines. And fear of such litigation is bound to have a chilling effect on the freedom to report and to comment editorially.

Monopoly of ownership of the nation's press, both print and electronic, has been the subject of a number of congressional investigations and court decisions. Such a monopoly in the agencies of mass communication could be as damaging to diversity in public information as action by a government agency.

PRESSURE GROUPS

Finally, there is the threat of pressure groups, ethnic, religious, and ideological, whose freedom to speak and write is guaranteed by the First Amendment but who are not always willing to grant such freedom to those who hold opposing views. Many actions of pressure groups in both minority and majority groups are extralegal, in the form of boycotts and threats of boycotts. Their challenges, therefore, may not reach the courts, but such actions nonetheless result in restrictions on free expression. Pressure groups are an essential ingredient in a democracy and contribute to the formation of public policy, but history has shown that they can also be a negative and restrictive force, and we must be aware of that danger.

The fact that the American people today enjoy greater freedom of expression than any other peoples of the world is a tribute to the Bill of Rights, to the fidelity of our courts in upholding these rights, and to the performance of a substantial body of the nation's press that has been responsible as well as free. It is remarkable that each generation has been able to adapt the First Amendment's broad and enduring principles to the changing needs of the times.

A Yale University professor of law discusses the scope and limitations of the First Amendment as it has been interpreted by the courts, including the concept of "full protection," the conflict with other societal interests, the right of access, and the right to know, in a Public Affairs Committee pamphlet entitled *The Bill of Rights Today*.

Thomas I. Emerson

FREEDOM OF EXPRESSION

The First Amendment provides that "Congress shall make no law . . . abridging the freedom of speech, or of the press; or the right of the people peaceably to assemble, and to petition the Government for a redress of grievances." (Although this provision mentions only Congress, it is recognized as applying to all branches of government—legislative, executive, and judicial.).

The ultimate purpose of the First Amendment is to protect and maintain an effective system of freedom of expression. Such a system protects the individual's right to self-fulfillment—to express ideas, communicate with others, live according to one's own style. It provides a rational method for discovering the truth and making judgments, by obtaining all the facts and listening to all opposing views. It is essential to the democratic process, in which the people make the decisions and instruct their government. And it facilitates social change without resort to violence. In short, freedom of expression is the heart of an open society.

The protection of the First Amendment extends to all forms of expression. "Expression" includes communication of information or ideas by speech, writing, art, or in any other way. It may be conveyed through a speech, book, newspaper, motion picture, television, play, or by any other medium. It may deal with politics, religion, culture, or any other sphere of interest. It includes the holding of a meeting, marching in a parade, participating in a demonstration. Expression may be "symbolic speech," such as wearing an armband or conducting a silent vigil. First Amendment protection also embraces the right to associate with other persons in order to facilitate expression or increase its effect.

The major current questions concerning the First Amendment fall into three categories: (1) to what degree, if any, may the government interfere with the content or the manner of expression; (2) what rights of access do individuals have to the means of communication; and (3) what "right to know" does a person have who wishes to communicate or to receive a communication.

Two propositions concerning governmental interference are well established. First, the nature of the interference—whether by imposing a criminal penalty, denying a privilege, compelling a person to appear before a legislative committee, or otherwise—is immaterial. If the government's action has a "chilling effect" upon expression, it is subject to the limitations of the First Amendment. Second, while the government may regulate the *time, place,* and *manner* of expression where necessary to accommodate different interests, the government may not as a general rule control, restrain, or otherwise interfere with the *content* of expression. It does not matter whether the expression is friendly or hostile to government policies, whether it voices an accepted or an unpopular opinion, whether it is couched in moderate or intemperate language, whether it is racist, totalitarian, sexist, or otherwise obnoxious, whether it is true, false, or some-

Reprinted from *The Bill of Rights Today*, by Thomas I. Emerson, Public Affairs Pamphlet No. 489A. Copyright 1973, 1980 by the Public Affairs Committee, Inc. Used with permission. The pamphlet is available from the Public Affairs Committee, 381 Park Avenue South, New York, N.Y. 10016 for 50 cents.

where in between. The basic starting point is that all expression, as long as it is expression and not action, is protected.

Justices Hugo L. Black and William O. Douglas argued that there should be no exception or qualification to either of these basic propositions. The Supreme Court as a whole, however, has never accepted this "full protection" view. Broadly speaking, the Court has recognized three exceptions and two qualifications.

The exceptions are for obscenity, libel, and "fighting words," all of which the Court has held are not protected by the First Amendment. But those terms have been narrowly construed.

The first qualification concerns expression that advocates violation of law, particularly the use of force or violence. Here the Supreme Court originally employed the "clear and present danger" test, holding that expression could be prohibited only if uttered under circumstances that created a clear and present danger of a substantial violation of law. The Court has ruled, too, that the expression must also incite to action. The present test, sometimes called the Brandenburg test, is that limitations on freedom of expression can be imposed only where "advocacy is directed to inciting or producing imminent lawless action and is likely to incite or produce such action." Either formulation allows expression to be cut off at any point where the Court believes the expression comes too close to causing a violation of law.

The other qualification applies more broadly to cases in which the right to freedom of expression comes into conflict with other individual or social interests, such as a right to a fair trial, safeguarding national security, or avoiding corruption in the electoral process. In such situations the Supreme Court has come to apply a balancing test, weighing the values of freedom of expression against the advantages sought to be gained by the restriction imposed. The balancing test has been vigorously criticized as failing to recognize the preferred position accorded to freedom of expression in our society and as being so vague that it allows the court to decide a case either way.

In general, the courts have afforded a substantial degree of protection against interference by the government with freedom of expression. But significant weaknesses remain. The Supreme Court's rules concerning speech that may lead to violation of law leave the door open to suppression of a range of groups that engage in, or some of whose members engage in, militant rhetoric. The balancing test gives the courts leeway to curtail speech in the name of other interests, rather than requiring the government to achieve its objectives through measures that do not restrict expression. Moreover, the rules laid down by the Supreme Court are not necessarily the rules enforced by local mayors, prosecutors, police, or other officials.

The law concerning the right of access to the means of communication has developed very slowly. The system of freedom of expression operates largely on a laissez-faire basis, and must continue to do so. Complete government control of all access to communication would hardly be a free or independent system. Nevertheless, the system is now subject to serious distortion. Most of our means of communication, particularly the mass media, lean toward a single economic, political, and social viewpoint. Indeed, failure to provide access for more varied interests is the most glaring weakness of the system of free expression today.

The law has always recognized some rights of access. As far back as 1937 the Supreme Court ruled that streets, parks, and similar open places "have immemorially been held in trust for use of the public and, time out of mind, have been used for purposes of assembly, communicating thoughts between citizens, and discussing public questions." And the Federal Communications Act makes provision for equal time for political candidates and imposes upon broadcasting stations a requirement of general fairness in airing controversial issues.

Under the Warren Court the right of access made some progress. The rule allowing use of the streets and parks was extended to their modern equivalent—malls and shopping centers—even where the property was privately owned. And the Federal Communications Commission (FCC) regulations were upheld in a broad ruling that laid down the principle: "It is the right of the viewers and listeners, not the right of the broadcasters, which is paramount."

Under the Burger Court, however, progress came to a halt. The shopping center cases were reversed and the authority of broadcasting stations to refuse political advertisements, while accepting commercial advertisements, was sustained. Moreover, cable television, which would provide much greater access to the electronic media, has received little encouragement from Congress or the FCC. Thus, a serious problem for the system of freedom of expression continues unsolved.

The right to know is a crucial aspect of a system of freedom of expression. Unless every person has a right to hear what is being said, and unless a person desiring to communicate can obtain information, the system cannot operate effectively.

Although the First Amendment does not expressly mention the right to know, the Supreme Court has consistently ruled that the rights guaranteed by the First Amendment include "the right to receive information and ideas." On the whole, the Court has protected the right to hear against direct interference by the government. But it has done little or nothing to promote the right of journalists and others to obtain information. It has refused to allow reporters to protect their sources of information against disclosure in court proceedings and has ruled that there is no constitutional right to compel the government to disclose information it desires to withhold, even on a subject such as conditions within a prison. The 1967 Freedom of Information Act, amended in 1974, and similar state legislation have forced the government to produce substantial quantities of information, but such laws contain broad exceptions. Government secrecy is still the rule.

Professor Emerson attempts to formulate a general theory on freedom of the press in which "a fundamental distinction must be drawn between conduct which consists of expression and conduct which consists of action." He applies this theory to the publication of classified government information in testimony before a United States Senate Judiciary Committee subcommittee looking into questions on freedom of the press. A more elaborate development of the theory is given in Emerson's book *The System of Freedom of Expression* (Random House, 1970)

Thomas I. Emerson

STATEMENT ON THE FIRST AMENDMENT

My testimony . . . is an attempt to formulate in terms of legal principle, and to apply to modern conditions, the absolutist theory that Madison and Jefferson had of the First Amendment.

One of the most remarkable features of the First Amendment is that, in the 180 years of its history, the courts have never developed a coherent theory of just what constitutional protection it affords. The Supreme Court did not, of course, have much occasion to interpret or apply the First Amendment until the suppression of free speech which grew out of World War I began to be challenged in the courts. The first major decision of the Supreme Court, *Schenck v. United States* (249 U.S. 47), did not come until 1919. Since that time, however, the Supreme Court has decided hundreds of First Amendment cases and the lower courts many thousands.

In the course of these decisions various legal doctrines have from time to time prevailed, or been advanced in concurring and dissenting opinions. These formulations include the bad tendency test, the clear and

Reprinted from U.S. Judiciary Committee, Subcommittee on Constitutional Rights, *Hearings*, October 13, 1971, pp. 199–205. Footnotes have been omitted.

present danger test, ad hoc balancing of interests, an incitement test, a test of grave and irreparable danger to national security, and the so-called absolute position. But the shifting majorities and minorities have never been able to settle on any single theory by which to determine how far the First Amendment protects freedom of expression. The extent of disagreement is dramatically reflected in the last Supreme Court decision, the *New York Times* and *Washington Post* cases, where nine separate opinions were rendered. A lawyer arguing a First Amendment case before the Supreme Court today literally does not know where to begin or where the Court will come out.

This unfortunate state of affairs seriously jeopardizes the system of freedom of expression in this country. If the courts cannot make up their minds there is no way for the citizen to know what his rights are. This is particularly damaging to freedom of the press. In the absence of a clearcut theory of First Amendment protection the press must either take daily risks or curtail its expression. Moreover, a system of freedom of expression can only exist if the community as a whole understands that system and supports it. But little understanding or support is possible when there is no agreement upon the basic constitutional doctrines which should govern.

It is true that no one simple formula can be devised which could apply to all the varied situations in which First Amendment issues are presented. Nevertheless, I think it is possible to construct a comprehensive theory which takes into account the underlying purposes of the First Amendment and formulates the basic legal doctrines necessary to achieve those goals. I have attempted such a formulation in my book, *The System of Freedom of Expression*, and will try briefly to summarize my conclusions for the committee.

I. A GENERAL THEORY

The central idea of a system of freedom of expression is that a fundamental distinction must be drawn between conduct which consists of expression and conduct which consists of action. Expression must be freely allowed and encouraged. Action can be controlled, subject to other constitutional requirements, but not by controlling expression. A system of freedom of expression cannot exist effectively on any other foundation, and a decision to maintain such a system necessarily implies acceptance of this proposition.

The line between expression and action is often entirely clear. At other times, however, the line may be obscure and the distinction more difficult to formulate. All expression has some physical element. Moreover, a communication may take place in a contest of action, as in the familiar example of the false cry of "fire" in a crowded theater. Or, a communication may be closely linked to action, as in the gang leader's command to his triggerman. In these cases it is necessary to decide, however fine the distinction may appear to be, whether the conduct is to be classified as one or the other. This judgment must be guided by consideration of whether the conduct partakes of the essential qualities of expression or action, that is, whether expression or action is the dominant element. And the concept of expression must be related to the fundamental purposes of the system of freedom of expression and the dynamics of its operation.

Freedom of expression can flourish and the goals of the system can be realized, only if expression receives full protection under the First Amendment. This principle of full protection means that the First Amendment must be interpreted as embodying the following rules of law.

1. The Government may not prohibit, curtail, or restrict expression in any way for the purpose of achieving other social objectives or advancing its own interests. In such a context the expression must be given full protection regardless of its tendency, its likelihood to create a clear and present danger, or any balancing of interests. Government controls must be confined to regulation of action. Where the Government regulation is directed toward conduct consisting of

action and conduct consisting of expression it must be drawn in such a way as to restrict only the action, leaving the expression uncurtailed.

2. It follows, *a fortiori*, that no controls can be exercised over expression by a system of prior restraint.

3. The Government may regulate the internal operations of the system of freedom of expression in order to resolve conflicts between participants in the system, such as by requiring a permit for a parade or allocating use of facilities in short supply. Such regulation must relate only to the time, place, and manner of the expression, not to its content, and must conform to the principle of fair accommodation between participants.

4. Where exercise of the right of expression involves the use of physical facilities also utilized for other purposes, such as an assembly on the streets or in a park, the Government may allocate the use of the facilities between the competing interests. Such regulations must likewise conform to the principle of fair accommodation and, so far as it relates to expression, control only time, place and manner, not content.

5. The status of an individual in a limited-purpose organization, such as a Government agency or a labor union, imposes upon him certain obligations different from those of the ordinary citizen to the general community. Hence the freedom of expression of such person, vis-à-vis the organization, may be subjected to the minimum regulation necessary to secure the specific purposes the organization is designed to achieve.

6. The Government may exercise its power to eliminate obstructions to, or to affirmatively promote, the effective functioning of the system of freedom of expression. Regulation of this type is valid under the First Amendment provided it advances, rather than retards, the operation of the system in terms of its basic nature and functions.

Other legal doctrines are necessary to solve particular problems. These pertain to the place where First Amendment rights may be exercised, the relationship of the system of freedom of expression to the system of privacy, and similar matters. Such issues likewise must be resolved on a functional basis, taking into account the objectives and operation of the system.

The foregoing principles are applicable to the basic "system of freedom of expression" which exists in this country. They do not necessarily apply, or apply in the same way, to certain sectors of social conduct in which the rules for protecting freedom of expression must be framed in a different context. Such areas include commercial activities, the activities of children, certain aspects of the military, and some aspects of communication with foreign countries. This does not mean that the First Amendment has no application in these sectors. It simply recognizes that the functions of expression and the principles needed to protect expression in such areas are different from those in the main system, and that different legal rules may therefore be required.

II. APPLICATION OF THE THEORY TO THE PUBLICATION OF CLASSIFIED INFORMATION

We may test the general theory by applying it to the problems involved in the publication of the Pentagon Papers. To what extent, if any, may the Government attempt to prevent or punish the publication of classified information without violating the First Amendment?

The issues must be considered in a realistic context. We must take into account both how the classification process works and the role of the press in reporting on national affairs. It is well known that there are millions of Government documents classified and that over-classification is endemic to the process. Moreover, the technique of classification is an easy way for the Government to cover up its mistakes or take dubious action behind a cloak of secrecy, and is frequently used for these purposes. In addition, large quantities of classified information are constantly being disclosed and published. Some of this is released by high Government officials to promote administration policies;

some is leaked by Government officials who disagree with administration policies in order to apply pressure for their viewpoint; some is revealed to a favorite reporter or disclosed in an off-the-record briefing session in order to put a reporter under obligation to the official; some appears in memoirs. The fact is that the Government and its officials allow a continuous flow of classified information to become public in order to advance their own interests. Disclosure is part of the government process.

The other half of the picture is equally significant. The function of the press is not limited to the mere reporting of official handouts. Its great role is to probe behind the scenes and inform the public of what is going on back of closed official doors. The press must be skeptical, critical, and above all informative. There is no other way by which the American people can obtain the information necessary to understand public issues and control its public servants. This is particularly important in an era of mounting Government secrecy and massive credibility gaps. In performing this vital function the press has the duty to dig out all the information it can, classified or unclassified. Disclosure is part of the democratic process.

Under these circumstances, the imposition of sanctions for the publication of classified materials would simply operate to give the Government a one-way opportunity to use the classification system to conceal its mistakes and to promote its own interests, while throttling the press as a major countervailing source of information. The only way in which our system of freedom of expression can operate effectively is to treat all so-called classified material which escapes from Government possession as part of the pool of information available to the whole community in the conduct of its public affairs.

Against this background we can proceed to a more detailed analysis of the constitutional issues. The first step is to determine what conduct connected with the publication of classified material involves "action" and what involves "expression." It would seem that stealing classified information from Government files or obtaining it through fraud or deception of the Government would constitute "action."

In securing physical possession in this way the "action" element of the conduct appears predominant. Similarly, obtaining or divulging classified information as part of an espionage operation would also appear to be "action," not "expression." Surreptitious conveyance of information to the agent of a foreign country, in the context of an espionage apparatus, is not part of the system of communicating ideas protected by the First Amendment. But publication of the material, after the "action" had terminated, would plainly constitute "expression." This would certainly hold as to publication by the press or by any third party who obtained information from the person who originally took possession. I think it would also apply to publication of the material by the very person who obtained illegal possession. At that point the "action" is completed and the "expression" commences.

Under this analysis the Government could apply sanctions to the theft of classified information, or other illegal procurement, as well as to espionage. But subsequent publication of the material, after it had escaped the Government's possession and thereby became part of the general pool of information, could not be prevented or punished. As "expression," the conduct would be fully protected.

Two other aspects of First Amendment theory are also relevant. First, what about the conduct of an employee in a Government agency who, having authorized possession of classified material, conveys this information to a third party in violation of a lawful regulation? One might consider this conduct as engaging in "expression." Even so, obligations necessary to the effective achievement of the agency function could be imposed upon members of that organization. Hence, assuming the regulation was in fact necessary, the Government could apply sanctions to the Government employee. Second, the legal doctrines applicable to classified information relating to military operations in an actual theater of war might be different. A reporter in a battle zone is not governed by the same principles as pertain to the civilian world. Hence, without attempting to formulate the rules applicable to military operations, it is sufficient to say that ordinary First Amendment principles would not necessarily control.

The question may be raised at this point whether it would not be possible to prevent or punish the publication of only that part of classified materials which might do serious damage to our national security. The issue is a crucial one in First Amendment theory. The basis of the full protection theory and, I believe, of an effective system of free expression is that partial suppression of expression is wrong in principle and destructive of the system in practice. In the case of classified materials, with which we are here concerned, I think it can be demonstrated that anything short of full protection would lead to a degree of press repression that would far outweigh any gains to national security.

One way for the Government to proceed would be, as in the *New York Times* and *Washington Post* cases, by attempting to enjoin or otherwise prevent in advance the publication of classified material. This mode of procedure calls into play the most repressive of all methods of control—advance censorship or prior restraint. I have elsewhere attempted to summarize the impact of prior restraint upon freedom of expression.

A system of prior restraint is in many ways more inhibiting than a system of subsequent punishment: It is likely to bring under Government scrutiny a far wider range of expression; it shuts off communication before it takes place; suppression by a stroke of the pen is more likely to be applied than suppression through a criminal process; the system allows less opportunity for public appraisal and criticism; the dynamics of the system drive toward excesses, as the history of all censorship shows.

If a free press is to survive, all forms of prior restraint without qualification or exception, must be rejected.

Indeed, it is not possible as a practical matter to introduce qualifications or exceptions to the rule against prior restraint without undermining the rule altogether. In the *Times-Post* case, for example, the Government argued that a prior restraint should be permissible where the publication of classified material might "gravely and irreparably" damage national security. Should the courts accept such a doctrine all the government would need do in any case would be to allege "grave and irreparable damage" and ask the court for a restraining order. In order to consider the Government's contention the court would be constrained to issue such an order, hold a hearing (probably in secret), and ultimately decide whether or not the newspaper could publish the material. The very process of determining whether the exception to the prior restraint rule should apply would itself constitute a prior restraint. This is exactly what happened in the *Times-Post* case. In short, no rule other than the rule of full protection is feasible when the Government attempts to cut off expression before it has occurred.

The other method of control—sanctions applied after publication has taken place—presents similar difficulties. None of the legal tests proposed, other than full protection, affords any real safeguard to the press. The "grave and irreparable damage" test is wide open and impossible to reduce to specific terms. The same is true of the clear and present danger test, the balancing test, or any other that can be devised. There is no way to define precisely in advance where the cutoff point is to be. The best those legal doctrines can do is to determine after trial that the point has been passed.

As a result, the press can never know beforehand what is criminal and what is not. Nor can it ever be sure when the Government may claim the publication is criminal and start a prosecution. Hence the press is put under intolerable pressure. Its function is to criticize and expose. In doing this it often causes embarrassment, arouses hostility, or provokes vengeance. It is not possible to perform such a function if the Government is able to institute a criminal proceeding whenever in its judgment the publication might create a danger to "national security." In the end the press would be put under a form of control very similar to prior restraint. In order to be certain there would be no retaliation it would have to make sure that the Government did not oppose publication.

We conclude, therefore, that there is no way to preserve a free and vigorous press except by a rule which extends to publication of classified material that has entered the public domain the full protection of the First Amendment. It has been argued that such a doctrine will jeopardize our national security. The history of this country, however, affords no support for such fear. On the contrary an independent press, encouraged to perform its traditional role, is a far better instrument than repression for preserving our national security.

I have confined myself here to application of the full protection theory of the First Amendment to the single instance of the publication of classified material. I believe that a similar analysis made in other areas would lead to similar conclusions. The major task in First Amendment cases should be to determine what is expression, as distinct from action, and to give expression complete protection. Legal doctrines which attempt to afford expression only partial protection are inconsistent with the purposes of the First Amendment and in practice defeat its objectives. It is true that the First Amendment as thus applied may entail some risks. But there is no way to eliminate all risks. And the attempt to do so leads only to a closed society. On the other hand I know of no society that has been overturned because of overprotection of freedom of expression.

A New York lawyer who has specialized in First Amendment cases considers categories that make up the constituent parts of an extended freedom of the press: freedom to speak, to listen, not to speak, not to listen, to speak anonymously, to know, and to have access to the media.

Harriet F. Pilpel

FREEDOM OF THE PRESS— AMERICAN STYLE

All of us reading this magazine are apt to agree that the First Amendment guaranteeing freedom of the press should be "first in the hearts of our countrymen" and that from a variety of sources that freedom is in danger today. The trouble is we talk about freedom of the press as if it were one and indissoluble whereas, in fact, like other generalities, it is composed of a large number of specifics.

Perhaps what we have and what we try to keep would be clearer if we bore those specifics in mind. Indeed, there is a school of thought which believes that the first order of business in the solution of any problem is the application of the technique of fragmentation—the ability to talk and think in terms of the component parts that together make up our large lump concepts—love, peace, war, truth, goodness, and, of course, freedom of speech and the press which the First Amendment forbids the government to abridge. (I shall refer throughout to "freedom of speech" as including all forms of expression, including, of course, freedom of the press.)

It is necessary to define "abridgment" as well as "freedom." Clearly, it can take many forms which break down under two main headings: "Prior restraint," which usually means an injunction against speech, or subsequent punishment, which can be a fine, a jail sentence or even in extreme cases a loss

Reprinted by permission from the March 12, 1973, issue of *Publishers Weekly*, published by R. R. Bowker Company, a Xerox company. Copyright © 1973 by Xerox Corporation.

of life (e.g., as in treason—cf. Ethel and Julius Rosenberg). Often, however, the abridgment takes much more subtle forms. A "prior restraint" can inhere in a requirement that in order to receive certain types of mail from abroad you must put your name on a list. A "subsequent punishment" need not be criminal—it may "merely" mean you lose your job for something you have said (e.g., the "Hollywood 10").

Now, let us look at the constituent parts of the freedom itself. It breaks down into at least eight categories:

1. First, there is freedom to speak, the right to communicate freely and without restraint.

2. Second is the right to listen, the freedom to read, to watch and to hear.

3. Third is the right *not* to speak or write, to refuse to communicate.

4. Fourth, there is the right not to be forced to listen or see, which has been said to be part of another basic constitutional right, the "right of privacy." In this context, "privacy" means the right of the individual not to be subjected to sight, sound or smell which he wishes to avoid but has no way of avoiding.

5. Fifth is the right of anonymity, the right to communicate and receive communications anonymously.

6. Sixth is the right to know, the right not to have government keep secrets from us, except those absolutely necessary to the security of government itself.

7. Seventh, and in a way part of the first, is the "right of access." It is not enough to have freedom to speak if all the effective media of communication are unavailable either as the result of government action or non-action on the part of "private interests" which control the media.

8. And, finally, we come to the question: Against whom does this constitutional guarantee apply? Is only government forbidden to abridge freedom of expression? Can the Constitution be read to guarantee that freedom against nongovernmental forces as well?

1. FREEDOM TO SPEAK

Freedom to speak, in the sense of the right to communicate, was no doubt paramount in the minds of those who first promulgated the First Amendment. Yet this freedom has perhaps the most exceptions grafted upon it today. We are all familiar with and accept the fact that one's speech may be prohibited because it threatens what the courts call a "clear and present danger." As Mr. Justice Holmes, himself a true apostle of freedom of speech, put it, no one has the right to cry "Fire" in a crowded theatre. Recently, however, the government has tried to suppress freedom to communicate in situations where no "clear and present danger," no matter how defined, was present. There are, for example, the "Pentagon Papers" actions, both the original attempts to prevent the New York *Times* and the Washington *Post* from printing the Pentagon material and the later controversies such as the one involving Senator Mike Gravel and the Beacon Press. Even more recently, there have been the efforts of the CIA to prevent former employees from writing about it at all.

Less generally recognized as limitations on freedom to speak are such civil actions as those for libel and violation of the right of privacy. With reference to libel, the rule of *New York Times v. Sullivan* and its offspring has been in the direction of permitting greater freedom of speech in the libel area. Today there is greater freedom of speech about public officials, candidates for public office, public personages and persons in the context of public issues as far as libel is concerned than ever before. As to these categories of persons, there is actionable libel only if they can prove that what was said about them was knowingly or recklessly false. However, the mere existence of this exception, so deplored by Justices Black and Douglas, has resulted in many cases being brought by such persons, and while it seems that they lose more often than they win, the continued danger of exposure to a libel suit—which is expensive and time-consuming—remains something of a throttle on free discussion about public issues. Since public officials themselves are absolutely immune from libel liability for any statements they make in their capacity as public officials, a rule of absolute immunity for those who libel them in that capacity may well be called for.

Today, oddly enough, the threat of freedom of expression on the civil side—that is, in the form of private suits—comes much more from actions alleging violation of the right of privacy than from suits claiming libel. Since the United States Supreme Court has held that the test is substantially the same with reference to the same categories of people, there is far more risk of violating someone's right of privacy than there is of libel. Almost anything said about a person, even a public person, and even though not libelous, can be made the basis of a successful privacy suit if the plaintiff alleges and proves that there was a "substantial" deliberate falsification or a reckless disregard of the truth. And again, even if the plaintiff loses a privacy suit, he can, by bringing it, subject a publisher or broadcaster or producer or distributor to such enormous expense in defending the suit that they may be seriously damaged even if they win. Perhaps in libel and privacy cases the law ought to allow the courts to award costs against the plaintiff if he loses, as is the situation in unsuccessful copyright infringement suits today.

Then there are the obscenity laws. Almost no attention is being paid to the Report of the Commission on Obscenity and Pornography which, based on extensive study, recommended that there be no law proscribing obscenity for adults and a very limited one as to children. A few groups, such as the Committee on Civil Rights of the Association of the Bar of the City of New York, have called for the enactment of these recommendations into law in New York State: the probability of this being done anywhere in the present climate of public opinion is remote. On the contrary, much of the pending legislation would tighten the present Supreme Court definitions of obscenity by, for example, eliminating "redeeming social importance" as part of the test and/or by declaring that the "community standards," by which a work attacked as obscene is to be judged, are to be solely the standards of the particular local community where the case is brought. An effort along such lines was defeated in November 1972 by popular referendum in California, but nonetheless Congress and many state legislatures are contemplating tightening controls on obscenity and thus further restricting the freedom to speak.

Especially disquieting are recent attempts of the Federal and state governments to "get" underground newspapers for publishing, for example, abortion referral ads. By and large, these efforts have been defeated in the lower courts but such suits against publications with dissident points of view have caused considerable concern.

There are many more restrictions on the freedom to speak which, by and large, are not recognized as such. In addition to the Post Office laws and regulations, there are the civil laws against fraud, the Federal Trade Commission, the SEC, the increasingly frequent bans on "abusive language," epithets and "insulting words," the imposition of license requirements for news vendors and theaters, and many others. Finally, there are entire groups of people whose freedom of expression, at least until recently, has been totally abridged and whch even today have very little: persons in the military service, persons in mental institutions, and to considerable extent minors. Yet these are "persons" too, entitled, within limits that must surely be definable, to the First Amendment's guarantee of the right to speak.

2. FREEDOM TO LISTEN

We come now to the second aspect of the basic constitutional guarantee of freedom of expression, the right correlative to the right to speak, namely, the right to listen. This is a freedom the contours of which are only now beginning to be drawn, primarily with respect to radio and television. The United States Supreme Court, in the *Red Lion* case, specifically held that the constitutional guarantee exists not only for those who wish to speak but also for those who wish to listen. In sustaining the Fairness Doctrine for broadcasters, the Court said:

> . . .It is the right of the viewers and listeners, not the right of the broadcasters, which is paramount. . . .It is the right of the public to receive suitable access to social, political, esthetic, moral, and other ideas and experiences which is crucial.

It has been suggested that this freedom of the receiver as well as the transmitter of speech should also be recognized with respect to the print media, but no such recognition has yet been accorded or even seriously considered as law.

3. THE RIGHT NOT TO SPEAK

The right not to speak has been very much in the news because of the *Caldwell* and like cases, involving the right of newsmen to refuse to disclose their sources or to reveal material which they choose not to publish. Because of the United States Supreme Court decisions in the recent newsmen subpoena cases, this right at the moment appears to be on somewhat shaky ground. However, many states have already passed shield laws to protect the confidentiality of news sources and material, and proposals for such laws are presently pending in many state legislatures and before Congress.

To some extent the right not to speak is closely related to the right to listen since, as the United States Supreme Court pointed out in the *Red Lion* case, the real point of the First Amendment guarantee is not only the protection of the reporter and his source but the public itself, which will inevitably be deprived of important information if the sources of that information dry up because of forced disclosure.

4. THE RIGHT NOT TO LISTEN

This right is also not clearly delineated. It is part of the rapidly evolving doctrine of the "right of privacy." This doctrine is still so amorphous that, as Justice Stewart said with respect to hardcore pornography: "I can't define it but I know it when I see it." The "right of privacy" today already stretches all the way from contraception and abortion to protection against electric eyes, computerized personal dossiers, and knowingly false statements (see 1 above). In the context of the affirmative constitutional guarantee of free expression, the right means that no one should be exposed to having "thrust" upon him material he doesn't want to see. This concept figured largely in one of the recent key United States Supreme Court obscenity cases, the *Redrup* case. Under the view expressed in that case, the criterion of obscenity seemed to be not the content of any material which people, in the exercise of a free choice, choose to see, but whether it is distributed in such a manner that it is *forced* upon those who choose not to see it. Examples are outdoor signs, window displays and sounds in public places or facilities from which there is no escape. Obviously, one man's right not to listen may conflict with another man's freedom to speak, but the *Redrup* limitation on public display and "thrusting" may be moving toward the necessary balance.

5. THE RIGHT TO SPEAK ANONYMOUSLY

The right of anonymity is claimed infrequently in the context of oral speech, although even here it can be in issue if a speaker chooses not to be seen or identified. However, when it comes to printed matter in the mails or otherwise, it is argued that the constitutional guarantee to be meaningful must embrace the right to be anonymous. Exponents of unpopular points of view may well be "chilled" into silence if they are not permitted to circulate their views without having to attach their names to it. Similarly, it has been held by the United States Supreme Court that those who wish to receive certain types of mail from abroad must have a right to receive it without having to notify the Post Office in order to have it delivered to them. Except for this decision, there would have been in Post Office hands a rapidly lengthening list of those seeking material which in the eyes of the Post Office or some other government agency might be considered "subversive."

6. THE RIGHT TO KNOW

This aspect of freedom of the press is also today very much in the news. It is what the Freedom of Information Act is all about. In a sense, it, too, was involved in the Pentagon Papers case. It poses the distinct and separate question: how much can the government keep to itself and what are guiding criteria? It looks as if the recent decision of the Supreme Court upholding government secrecy classifications may have struck a serious blow at this concept of the right to know, but, clearly, the last word has not yet been spoken.

7. THE RIGHT OF ACCESS

In the past few years, it has been suggested that perhaps there are situations where, if the government does not intervene to assure access to the press, the failure may be a violation of the First Amendment. The argument is that *no action* by government can infringe a basic freedom. What good does it do for a person to have the right to speak, it asked, if private individuals control the arteries of speech and block access to them? A partial right of access to the electronic media is assured by the Fairness Doctrine promulgated and enforced by the FCC. Under that doctrine, a person attacked on the airwaves has a right to reply. In addition, the doctrine reposes on all broadcast licensees the obligation to air a variety of different viewpoints on controversial public issues. The Communications Act itself requires all licensees which permit any candidate to use their facilities to accord equal time to all other candidates for the same office. It also calls for every licensee to devote some of its broadcast time to issues of public importance. It is the duty of the Federal Communications Commission thus affirmatively to make possible the exercise of free speech on the air at least to this

extent. The Fairness Doctrine is grounded on the First Amendment and the fact that the airwaves constitute public property as to which the government has the right and the obligation to insure access for persons attacked and for different points of view on controversial issues.

As mentioned above, it has recently been suggested that a similar obligation should be imposed to implement the First Amendment with regard to the print media. Here there is, theoretically, no scarcity element as there is in the case of the still limited number of available air channels, a scarcity, incidentally, which is apt to disappear as cable TV comes into its own. On the other hand, theoretically, anyone can publish a newspaper or a magazine or a book.

Actually, however, there is realistically in the case of the print media even a greater scarcity of channels, dictated not by technology but by economic realities. Thus, while in New York City there are only three general daily newspapers, there are more than 35 radio and television stations. It is true that anyone can distribute handbills expressing their opinions and many people may be able to hire halls in which speeches can be made. In these days of mass media covering our "global village," however, it is hardly realistic to say that such limited right of access to the print media creates any real right of access on the part of most of us. The proponents and opponents of establishing "right of access" to the print media are equally ardent and civil libertarians are lined up on both sides. The ultimate resolution even with respect to the airways, now that we have virtually unlimited cable potential with a requirement of public access channels, is far from clear.

8. AGAINST WHOM THE
   GUARANTEE APPLIES

So much for a brief indication of the major components of the constitutional guarantee of freedom of expression here and now. Equally important is the question against whom, in all its various meanings, it applies. Primarily, it applies against the government itself in all its branches—the prohibition of abridgment of freedom of speech and the press extends to the legislative, executive and judicial departments of government, to federal, state and local officials, down to the town dog catcher and the ski instructor in a national park. In addition, there are other so-called private groups which in effect exercise governmental power which should be, and in some respects have been, held also to be bound by the guarantees of the First Amendment. Thus, the United States Supreme Court has held that where a private company "owns" a town, lock, stock and barrel—its streets, its parks, its playgrounds and public buildings—then, for purposes of the First Amendment, that company *is* the government and subject to the same inhibitions against abridgment of free speech. Similarly, when a shopping center prohibits picketing relating to a labor controversy involving one of its stores, the United States Supreme Court has applied the First Amendment guarantee to the shopping center. More recently, the present Court has stepped back a little from this position and has held, for example, that anti-Vietnam forces did not, under the First Amendment, have the right to protest inside a shopping plaza.

On occasion, the freedom of expression guaranteed by the First Amendment can be asserted even against private individuals although they are not exercising the prerogatives of government, as did the company in the company-town case and the shopping center in the labor dispute. The Federal Civil Rights Act prohibits private persons from conspiring to deprive others of their civil rights, one of which, of course, is freedom of expression. Generally, however, the guarantees of free speech and free press do not apply against private individuals. If, however, a "right of access" to all the media is recognized, the government might have an affirmative obligation to insure freedom of expression against the private interests which control the media, and in that sense the scope of the First Amendment may come

to apply to those who own and control the mass media.

THE BATTLEGROUND TODAY

Many commentators and students of the First Amendment today discern what may be a many-pronged attack by the government on freedom of expression in many of its aspects. They point to an apparent government effort to fragment each medium of the press. Looked at from one point of view, this might not be such a bad idea. The three major networks have dominated and continue to dominate the airwaves and, like such newspapers as the New York *Times* and the Washington *Post*, have enormous influence on millions of Americans. Theoretically and ideally, the more diverse and numerous the sources of the press, the greater the freedom of each one of us to arrive at our own conclusions. In fact, however, this hypothesis may not hold up in the face of a big government getting bigger, with more power concentrated in the Chief Executive.

In an article published in the *Harvard Law Review* some years ago, the writer reluctantly concluded that, bad as big networks may be in terms of their competitive effect on individual station licensees, it may well be that they are the only effective defense against big government in the area of freedom of speech. By its attacks on the major news media, electronic and print, the stand of the present Administration that the networks are too powerful has had an appeal for those who would like to see more newspapers, more radio and TV stations, and more mass magazines. However, it may well be that only giants can fight giants. The result of a diminution of the power of the giants in the media is all too likely to be an increase in the power of the government. The government's present efforts to break up the public broadcasting service is another example of its apparent effort to divide the media into small ineffective fragments, which individually could not possibly represent a counter-force to government pressures.

There is no question, as Mayor Lindsay pointed out as recently as January 26, 1973, that

. . . the press has an obligation to examine its own biases and to review constantly 'its own efforts to separate fact and opinion.' In this area of self-criticism, the media could do a great deal more to gain public confidence.

But the most serious threat to the goal of an informed public comes from government itself.

It has been said that the power to tax is the power to destroy. In a much more fundamental and important sense, the power to control the media is the power to destroy a democratic society. As was pointed out recently in a Civil Liberties publication, in banner headlines, "CONTROL THE MEDIA AND YOU CONTROL THE MINDS." Now must be the time for all good men to come to the aid of the media and demonstrate, as the good citizens of California did by rejecting Proposition 14 (the anti-obscenity provision), that freedom of the press continues to be our "first freedom" and that here, as elsewhere, eternal vigilance is indeed the price of liberty.

The Free Speech Movement that swept college campuses in the late 1960s showed signs of repudiating its original commitment in the following decade. Dissident students on campuses across the country (including Princeton and Amherst) often harassed or otherwise denied freedom to speak to speakers with unpopular views. Recognizing the need "to examine the condition of free expression, peaceful dissent, mutual respect and tolerance at Yale," President Kingman Brewster, Jr., appointed a committee headed by historian C. Vann Woodward "to draft recommendations for any measures it may deem necessary for the maintainance of these principles. . . ." The following statement of values and priorities introduced the committee's report, submitted December 23, 1974.

Committee on Freedom of Expression at Yale University

FREEDOM OF EXPRESSION AT YALE

THE REPORT OF THE COMMITTEE

The primary function of a university is to discover and disseminate knowledge by means of research and teaching. To fulfill this function a free interchange of ideas is necessary not only within its walls but with the world beyond as well. It follows that the university must do everything possible to ensure within it the fullest degree of intellectual freedom. The history of intellectual growth and discovery clearly demonstrates the need for unfettered freedom, the right to think the unthinkable, discuss the unmentionable, and challenge the unchallengeable. To curtail free expression strikes twice at intellectual freedom, for whoever deprives another of the right to state unpopular views necessarily also deprives others of the right to listen to those views.

We take a chance, as the First Amendment takes a chance, when we commit ourselves to the idea that the results of free expression are to the general benefit in the long run, however unpleasant they may appear at the time. The validity of such a belief cannot be demonstrated conclusively. It is a belief of recent historical development, even within universities, one embodied in American constitutional doctrine but not widely shared outside the academic world, and denied in theory and in practice by much of the world most of the time.

Because few other institutions in our society have the same central function, few assign such high priority to freedom of expression. Few are expected to. Because no other kind of institution combines the discovery and dissemination of basic knowledge with teaching, none confronts quite the same problems as a university.

Reprinted with permission from *AAUP Bulletin*, 61: 29–30, 38–40 (Spring 1976).

For if a university is a place for knowledge, it is also a special kind of small society. Yet it is not primarily a fellowship, a club, a circle of friends, a replica of the civil society outside it. Without sacrificing its central purpose, it cannot make its primary and dominant value the fostering of friendship, solidarity, harmony, civility, or mutual respect. To be sure, these are important values; other institutions may properly assign them the highest, and not merely a subordinate priority; and a good university will seek and may in some significant measure attain these ends. But it will never let these values, important as they are, override its central purpose. We value freedom of expression precisely because it provides a forum for the new, the provocative, the disturbing, and the unorthodox. Free speech is a barrier to the tyranny of authoritarian or even majority opinion as to the rightness or wrongness of particular doctrines or thoughts.

If the priority assigned to free expression by the nature of a university is to be maintained in practice, clearly the reponsibility for maintaining that priority rests with its members. By voluntarily taking up membership in a university and thereby asserting a claim to its rights and privileges, members also acknowledge the existence of certain obligations upon themselves and their fellows. Above all, every member of the university has an obligation to permit free expression in the university. No member has a right to prevent such expression. Every official of the university, moreover, has a special obligation to foster free expression and to ensure that it is not obstructed.

The strength of these obligations, and the willingness to respect and comply with them, probably depend less on the expectation of punishment for violation than they do on the presence of a widely shared belief in the primacy of free expression. Nonetheless, we believe that the positive obligation to protect and respect free expression shared by all members of the university should be enforced by appropriate formal sanctions, because obstruction of such expression threatens the central function of the university. We further believe that such

sanctions should be made explicit, so that potential violators will be aware of the consequences of their intended acts.

In addition to the university's primary obligation to protect free expression there are also ethical responsibilities assumed by each member of the university community, along with the right to enjoy free expression. Though these are much more difficult to state clearly, they are of great importance. If freedom of expression is to serve its purpose, and thus the purpose of the university, it should seek to enhance understanding. Shock, hurt, and anger are not consequences to be weighed lightly. No member of the community with a decent respect for others should use, or encourage others to use, slurs and epithets intended to discredit another's race, ethnic groups, religion, or sex. It may sometimes be necessary in a university for civility and mutual respect to be superseded by the need to guarantee free expression. The values superseded are nevertheless important, and every member of the university community should consider them in exercising the fundamental right to free expression.

We have considered the opposing argument that behavior which violates these social and ethical considerations should be made subject to formal sanctions, and the argument that such behavior entitles others to prevent speech they might regard as offensive. Our conviction that the central purpose of the university is to foster the free access of knowledge compels us to reject both of these arguments. They assert a right to prevent free expression. They rest upon the assumption that speech can be suppressed by anyone who deems it false or offensive. They deny what Justice Holmes termed "freedom for the thought that we hate." They make the majority, or any willful minority, the arbiters of truth for all. If expression may be prevented, censored, or punished, because of its content or because of the motives attributed to those who promote it, then it is no longer free. It will be subordinated to other values that we believe to be of lower priority in a university.

The conclusions we draw, then, are these: even when some members of the university community fail to meet their social and ethical responsibilities, the paramount obligation of the university is to protect their right to free expression. This obligation can and should be enforced by appropriate formal sanctions. If the university's overriding commitment to free expression is to be sustained, secondary social and ethical responsibilities must be left to the informal processes of suasion, example, and argument. . . .

[In a minority report, law student Kenneth J. Barnes takes issue with the view that free expression should always supersede any other values which might conflict with it. He challenges this theory on several fronts. The following statements are excerpted from Mr. Barnes' report.]

A MINORITY REPORT

Because of the degree to which free speech is undermined by power relationships and ideological coloring, we should recognize that holding up a *pure model* of "free speech" to dissident oppressed groups (as the Majority does) often serves the cause of oppression more than that of free speech.

Even if "truth" were not colored by ideology and power relations, it is not clear that a "free marketplace of ideas" would discover this "truth" at all, much less discover it efficiently. . . .

Even if a free exchange of ideas were the best means of discovering truth, a university has other important purposes and values besides the discovery and dissemination of academic knowledge, and other functions besides merely research and discussion of academic theory. . . . In addition to free expression, other moral questions must be dealt with. . . . I believe that the university *should* take a stand for its ideals on erupting national issues, and not merely cloister itself within the walls of knowledge-seeking. And I believe that the university's commitment to minority groups, and to equal opportunity is at least as laudable a value as free expression.

The First Amendment, let us recall, only protects against government interference with expression; it does *not* create an obligation to provide a forum nor to guarantee a polite reception to all ideas. . . . Nor should a university feel obligated to go beyond the canons of academic freedom—i.e., noninterference with faculty research and teaching—by providing a forum for unscholarly or socially harmful ideas. . . .

I agree that free expression is an important value, which we must cherish and protect. But it is not the *only* value which we uphold, either in society or in our universities. Under certain circumstances, free expression is outweighed by more pressing issues, including liberation of all oppressed people and equal opportunities for minority groups.

Perhaps the foremost advocate of the point of view expressed in the minority report of the Committee on Freedom of Expression at Yale is Marxian philosopher Herbert Marcuse. In his essay *Critique of Pure Tolerance* Marcuse argues that tolerance, as it is practiced today, serves the cause of oppression by supporting prevailing social and political attitudes and opinions. Marcuse calls for the liberalizing of tolerance which would mean "intolerance against movements from the Right, and toleration of movements from the Left." Such tolerance and intolerance "would extend to the stage of action as well as of discussion and propaganda, of deed as well as of word. The traditional criterion of clear and present danger seems no longer adequate to a stage where the whole society is in the situation of the theater audience when somebody cries: 'fire.' " He acknowledges that such a point of view would incorporate censorship, even precensorship, but it would be "openly directed against the more or less hidden censorship that permeates the free media."

CHAPTER 3

SCHOOLS UNDER SIEGE

Reminiscent of Nazi Germany's book-burning orgies are recent incidents in the United States. Book burning in Warsaw, Indiana, and Drake, North Dakota, was nationally publicized. In Warsaw all forty school copies of a textbook, *Values Classification*, were burned. In Drake the school board ordered confiscated and burned all copies of three books assigned in English classes, Kurt Vonnegut's *Slaughterhouse Five*, James Dickey's *Deliverance*, and an anthology of short stories by Hemingway, Conrad, Steinbeck, Faulkner, and others.

Less violent but harsh responses have been reported in innumerable communities nationwide as censorship pressures on public schools have mounted in recent years. Across the country parents and school board members, outraged by books they consider immoral, un-American, or "just plain filthy," have mounted campaigns to remove materials that they find offensive off the school library shelves and out of classrooms. Not infrequently, teachers using the books are fired.

The present chapter aims to deal with both the philosophical and practical aspects of the situation. A number of specific cases involving school censorship are reviewed, all of which have received national attention: selection of textbooks in Kanawha County, West Virginia; the removal by the school board of the Island Trees Free School District in Long Island, New York, of certain books from school library shelves; the banning of a book, *365 Days*, relating to the war in Vietnam, by a school library committee in Baileyville, Maine; and attacks on individual books throughout the country. Also considered at some length is the report on a nationwide survey of censorship in public schools, sponsored by the American Library Association and other organizations. Finally, the rampant campaign to ban textbooks, led by the Gablers in Texas, is reviewed and its present status discussed.

The issues at stake are complex and by no means clear cut. America is a pluralistic society, including elements often working at cross purposes, from extreme conservatism to total permissiveness. Key roles are played by parents, teachers, librarians, administrators, and school boards. Textbook publishers have frequently submitted to censorship for financial reasons. Efforts to resolve the problems have reached all the way to the U.S. Supreme Court. The only certain factor is that controversies will continue to erupt. The main objective here is to try to define and clarify the basic issues.

A short article by Stanley N. Wellborn, in *U.S. News & World Report* summarizes recent developments.

Stanley N. Wellborn

DRIVE TO BAN BOOKS SPREADS IN U.S.

Black parents in Davenport, Iowa, and Houston are pressing schools to drop *Huckleberry Finn* because the word "nigger" is used in the book.

In Bangor, Me., a school committee banned the book *365 Days*, which often uses profanity to describe the effects of the Vietnam War on 17 young soldiers who were wounded in battle. In January, a federal judge struck down the ban.

These episodes are part of a new wave of ban-the-book drives across the country, with both conservative and liberal activists taking aim at school materials they find objectionable.

The list of banned items includes textbooks, dictionaries, novels, plays and musical productions. In some cases, bonfires have been built with books and magazines purged from schoolroom shelves, and some libraries have used scissors and ink to delete certain passages of other volumes.

The controversy was expected to be fueled even further by a U.S. Supreme Court hearing March 2 on a New York censorship case—the first time the court has ever heard oral arguments on the issue of book banning in schools.

TAKING SIDES

School and library officials say attempts to curb access to books is the most divisive issue to hit many communities in years.

"No book is being spared scrutiny," says

Judith Krug, director of the American Library Association's intellectual-freedom office. "Every school system in the country faces potential challenges on literary works or periodicals that somebody finds offensive."

A recent report by the Association of American Publishers, the American Library Association and the Association for Supervision and Curriculum Development concludes: "Censorship pressures on books and other learning materials in the public schools are real, nationwide and growing."

The report, "Limiting What Students Shall Read," surveyed 7,500 school administrators and found that 25 percent reported stepped-up efforts to ban books in their districts in the previous year.

Several schools banished *The Diary of Anne Frank*, an account of a Jewish family in hiding from the Nazis, because the book describes a young girl's physical development too explicitly and because it discusses Anne's conflicts with her mother.

The Supreme Court case involves the Board of Education of the Island Trees Union Free School District on Long Island, which in 1976 voted to remove nine books from the high-school library. Titles included *Slaughterhouse Five* by Kurt Vonnegut, Jr., *The Naked Ape* by Desmond Morris and *Soul on Ice* by Eldridge Cleaver.

The board ruled that the books contain "indecent matter, vulgarities, profanities, explicit descriptions of sexual relations . . . or disparaging remarks about blacks, Jews or Christ." Schoolboard members said that such writings were "inconsistent with the basic values of the community."

Opponents of the decision contend that the school board's action prevented all students in the district from access to certain books, and thus was unconstitutional under First Amendment guarantees of freedom of speech.

Many disputes arise because of the far greater range of what is read and discussed in today's classrooms compared with 25 years ago. Contemporary literature deals frankly with such topics as sexuality, death, justice, social inequity and family life—often in graphic vocabulary and style.

A parent group in Girard, Pa., recently objected to including on school reading lists the book *Working*, a 1974 best seller, which contains a series of interviews with working persons. Author Studs Terkel became so concerned about the issue that he defended his book at a town meeting in Girard.

"The trouble with censorship is that once it starts it is hard to stop," says Terkel. "Do you ban the Bible, or 'Hamlet'? Just about every book contains something that someone objects to."

SUPPORT FOR SCREENING

Now a growing number of educational authorities, including U.S. Education Secretary Terrel H. Bell, believe that parents and elected officials have the right to screen materials required by schools. Asserts Scott D. Thomson, executive director of the National Association of Secondary School Principals: "If society willingly accepts R ratings for films—thus restricting their viewing by youth—then how can we immediately scream 'censorship' when similar criteria are applied to schoolbooks?"

Critics of that view say it permits a small group of individuals to force removal of books that other students and parents find commendable. They point to a recent Associated Press poll finding that 62 percent of Americans believe that librarians and teachers, rather than school boards, should have the final say in banning controversial books from the school curriculum.

Some educators also contend that because nearly one third of all books sold are purchased by educational systems, the ripple effect of a book-banning decision can spread widely. Says Sherry Keith, author of "Politics of Textbook Selection," a new study by the Institute for Research on Educational Finance and Governance at Stanford University:

"Schoolchildren are one of the largest captive reading audiences in the world today. Because of the high cost of textbook publishing, relatively small interest groups can influence the content of textbooks throughout the U.S. It has become a very politicized process."

Few educators expect book bans to disappear unless the Supreme Court specifically orders such action. What they are hoping for is clearer guidelines from the Court on how schools can resolve future book controversies without tearing their communities apart.

A special report issued by the Washington, D.C., organization People for the American Way describes the situation in even stronger terms.

People for the American Way

MIND CONTROL IN THE SCHOOLS: THE CENSORSHIP BATTLE

The Radical Religious Right has launched a systematic, national "battle for the mind" of tomorrow's leaders. Its latest inspirational book, titled *The Battle for the Mind*, thunders that "the godless religion of secular humanism" controls public education. Thus, moral majoritarians intend to "purge" all books and classroom discussions that question the existence of absolute truth, imply that there may be more than one answer to a question or introduce "alien" ideas. They are attacking the very purpose of education: to teach children how to think.

This battle is being waged by a number of national Radical Religious Right groups in public school classrooms and libraries all over the country, and it exemplifies the moral majoritarians' broader goal: to impose their view of the world on all Americans. They not only want to prevent people from learning about ideas; they view the

Reprinted by permission of People for the American Way, 1015 18th St., N.W., Washington, D.C. 20036.

discussion of ideas as a threat. In short, the Radical Religious Right's goal is mind control.

It is not a hidden agenda. One moral majoritarian leader boasts that "After the Christian majority takes control, pluralism will be seen as immoral and evil, and the state will not permit anybody the right to practice evil."

CENSORSHIP NATIONWIDE:
A 500% LEAP

Attempts by moral majoritarians to impose their "standards" on the nation's school children are succeeding in communities all over the country. Dorothy Massie of the National Education Association recently wrote of textbook censorship, "Probably at no time have the pressures been more severe than they are just now." According to a comprehensive national survey, one quarter of the school administrators and librarians surveyed reported that books, films and magazines were challenged during the 1979–1980 study period, and that half of these challenges resulted in some form of censorship. Reported censorship cases skyrocketed 500% after last November, according to another survey by Judith Krug of the American Library Association.

Among the material reported restricted, altered, removed or destroyed: Hemingway's *A Farewell to Arms*, Steinbeck's *The Grapes of Wrath* and *Of Mice and Men*, Orwell's *1984*, Huxley's *Brave New World*, "Bill Cosby on Prejudice" (film), Weekly Reader's *Our Freedom*, Laura Ingalls Wilder's *Little House in the Big Woods* and the story books *Mr. & Mrs. Pig's Evening Out* and *The Twelve Days of Christmas*. One school banned *Making It with Mademoiselle* until it was pointed out that the book, published by *Mademoiselle* magazine, was a how-to dressmaking book for teen-agers.

THE MIND-CONTROL AGENDA:
BOOK BURNING AND
INDOCTRINATION

The Radical Religious Right insists that young people must not be exposed to any book, film, idea or discussion that conflicts with their orthodoxy. A Warsaw, Indiana, school board member recently declared that the real issue is *who* will control young people's minds. Moral majoritarians claim they are engaged in a battle to determine *who* will use the schools to indoctrinate young people. They aren't content to decide what their own children should read; they want to dictate what *everyone's* children shall read and learn and discuss in school. (Carrying this mission to the extreme, the Maryland Family Protection Lobby is trying to ban textbooks used in *optional* sex education courses in one county school system. The head of the group admits he has not read the books he wants banned.)

This goal is not just a pipe dream. Actual book burnings have occurred across the nation, the bonfires fueled by volumes from literary masterpieces to *National Geographic*. Illinois Moral Majority chairman Rev. George Zarris says that "some stuff is so far out, you have to ban it. . . . I would think that moral [sic] minded people might object to books that are philosophically alien to what they believe. If they have the books and feel like burning them, fine."

In one Wisconsin community, nine parents checked out 33 books from two school libraries and refused to return them. Included in the seizure was *The Diary of Anne Frank*, under national attack because it "perpetrates the hoax" that the Holocaust actually occurred.

The two most ironic targets of the moral majoritarian assault are *1984* and *Brave New World*. Because these two classics warn of the dangers of a mind-controlled society, the present-day mind controllers are understandably threatened by them. *Brave New World* recently withstood an attack in Sumner, Iowa, despite charges that it "promotes the seeds of secular humanist propaganda." The moral majoritarians, claiming the book is anti-christian and anti-motherhood, were not satisfied with a school policy that allowed them to select alternative reading material for their own children. They insisted on preventing *other* people's children from learning of the dangers of a *Brave New World*.

COMBATTING AN IMAGINARY ENEMY: "SECULAR HUMANISM"

At the national level, the mind control campaign is coordinated and directed by three major groups: Jerry Falwell's Moral Majority, Inc., Mel and Norma Gabler's Educational Research Analysts, and Phyllis Schlafly's "Stop Textbook Censorship Committee." (Schlafly reasons that "secular humanists" now censor all textbooks and must be stopped, and Falwell condemns most textbooks as nothing more than "Soviet propaganda.")

The Gablers warn parents in numerous national mailings that textbook content "appears so natural, reasonable and convincing" that they should not risk reading the texts themselves. Instead, they provide thousands of "detailed reviews [that] can save countless hours of painstaking work." The Gablers demand that schools "teach absolutes." Why? "Textbooks mold nations because textbooks largely determine how a nation votes, what it becomes and where it goes!"

In their *Handbook No. 1*, the Gablers preach: "The teaching of Humanism in public schools not only defies Christian values and authority of parents, but borders on treason and violates the U.S. Constitution by teaching a religion." The manual continues:

As long as the schools continue to teach ABNORMAL ATTITUDES and ALIEN THOUGHTS, we caution parents NOT to urge their children to pursue high grades and class discussion, because the harder students work, the greater their chances of brainwashing.

The Gabler's "reviews" urge readers to "purge" schools of all material that encourages thinking and discussion or is inconsistent with moral majoritarian orthodoxy. A few samples:

Textbook material: a discussion of the civil rights movement and the slogan, "Freedom!" Objection: everyone in this country has always been free unless they were in jail.

Textbook material: suggested discussion of whether computers are capable of creative thinking. Objection: "Infers [sic] that there can be more than one answer."

Textbook material: description of America as a nation of immigrants from other countries. Objection: presents a derogatory view of America that does not foster patriotism.

Textbook material: all discussions of "women's contribution to history." Objection: undermines women's traditional role.

MIND CONTROL BATTLES: WITCH HUNTS AND HATE MAIL

North Carolina Moral Majority distributed to families across the state a 28-page "review" of textbooks and novels it found objectionable. A social studies text was condemned by this "local" group because it asked, "Do we really need fifty state governments plus one national government?" The objection: "the importance of federalism should be clearly taught, not questioned." Another social studies text was attacked because students are not "emotionally or intellectually capable" of discussing food shortages, overpopulation and ecology.

North Carolina Moral Majority spawned a group, called Parents Actively Concerned, which is circulating throughout the state a list of "26 Don'ts" to help parents purge certain teaching methods from local schools. The "Don'ts" include "Don't discuss the future," "Don't exchange 'opinions' on political or social issues" and "Don't participate in any classroom discussion which begins with such phrases as 'What is your opinion of' . . . or 'Do you think' . . .?"

The Wyoming Family Rights Forum has sued a school board to suppress a history text because it is "anti-family" (not all women described were mothers and homemakers) and "anti-free enterprise" (it accurately stated that the 19th century populist movement favored a graduated income tax).

A moral majoritarian minister in Abington, Virginia, demanded to know the names of those who had checked certain materials out of the public library. The Washington Moral Majority chapter sued the state's library board to obtain a list of everyone who has borrowed sex education materials. And the Camas, Washington, school system adopted a policy that allows individual parents and school administrators to ban books from school libraries without a formal hearing.

The Baileyville, Maine, school board voted to remove from the library a book of interviews with wounded soldiers titled *365 Days*. High-school senior Michael Sheck led the fight to restore the book. Sheck received anonymous phone calls and hate letters. One read: "Dear Michael; I hope you burn in hell, you heathen bastard." Signed, "a Concerned Christian."

UP IN SMOKE: BOOKS OR THE CONSTITUTION?

While most states allow schools to select texts locally a substantial number (including Alabama, California and Texas) have state-level textbook selection procedures. Thus, if the mind controllers can censor an idea from texts in one of these states, publishers will be pressured to revise those texts for every other community in America, since it is not economically feasible to produce different versions for different states.

The national censorship survey reveals that the majority of state-level textbook challenges focus on "secular humanism" and "agnostic views," and that most state censorship groups use materials prepared by out-of-state organizations. In fact, *half* of the state-level respondents reported that the Gablers had influenced their state's textbook selection process.

A recent *Miami Herald* editorial warned:

. . . the Far Right's book burners may set their sights next on gaining control of local school boards. If they succeed, Americans might as well get ready to gather 'round the bonfires. They'll start by incinerating the works most often found on the hit lists of the Far Right. . . . What will really be going up in smoke, however, is the U.S. Constitution and its guarantees of freedom of thought, expression and belief.

In the next article Mark G. Yudof, a law professor at the University of Texas at Austin, considers recent court decisions in the light of the role of public schools in the process of socialization. The aim of public education must be distinguished from indoctrination. The achievement of that aim requires a complex structure for making decisions, which would ensure First Amendment rights, academic freedom, and the pursuit of legitimate educational goals, including preparation for professional and civic life. The explicitness of the decision-making structure allows light easily to be shed on attempts to restrict legitimate freedoms for doctrinaire motives.

Mark G. Yudof

THE STATE AS EDITOR OR CENSOR: BOOK SELECTION AND THE PUBLIC SCHOOLS

Over the last ten years there have probably been more constitutional challenges to public school library and textbook decisions than in the previous one hundred years. I suspect that there are many reasons for this increase. Resolution of disputes in the public schools is increasingly dominated by rules and formal procedures and legislation and lawsuits, and it is natural that the legalization apparent with regard to collective bargaining, student records, desegregation, treatment of the handicapped, and the like, should spill over into the textbook area. Public opinion polls also show a declining confidence in professionals and public officials, and many are perhaps less accepting of decisions made by experts or elected school representatives. This is particularly true if one is a member of a minority group which feels that the majority's curriculum, textbook, and other school decisions do not

Reprinted by permission of Mark G. Yudof from *Censorship Litigation and the Schools* (Chicago: American Library Assn., 1983), pp. 49–67. Footnotes have been omitted.

reflect its preferences. And with the decline in the view that public schools are above politics, the dissension in values that pervades so many areas—for example, in the role of women—may result in an increased willingness of the losers in the political process to do battle in the courts. This is particularly evident in the movement to dismantle whatever barriers have "separated government from personal morality and religion." As the Public Agenda Foundation put it in a recent study,

This mode of thinking can be seen . . . in increasing demands for "reviews" of school textbooks. Many Americans have come to feel that the state cannot be neutral to questions of lifestyle; they believe that the forces of government should be harnessed to bring the country back to a particular moral and religious standard.

Textbook controversies arise in many settings. School officials assert their wisdom in educating the young. Elected officials often perceive of themselves as the conduits for transporting the community's values into the schools. Writers, editors, and publishers are gravely concerned with their freedom of expression and they fear government efforts to eliminate particular ideas and perspectives from school classrooms. Parents have an interest in directing the upbringing of their children and in inculcating particular secular and nonsecular values. Teachers and librarians assert rights to academic freedom, particularly the right to be reasonably autonomous in carrying out their professional responsibilities. Students may assert a right to know, to read, to learn, or to acquire information, or a right not to be subjected to materials they find fundamentally objectionable. And some, including myself, fear government expression itself; for government may take advantage of the captive and immature audience in public schools to indoctrinate children to values that enhance the *status quo*, to undermine their ability in the future to act as "self-controlled" citizens expressing preferences about political, economic, and social questions. The government's capacity to shape beliefs and attitudes may be as destructive of democratic values as direct censorship. And government may accomplish this by picking and choosing among private communicators, by subsidizing the voices of the uncritical, and by denying subsidies to strong and critical voices. Book selection for public school students is an excellent example of a policy arena in which such dangers lurk. But for all its importance, judicial decisions remind one of the ancient Latin motto "Crescit occulto velut arbor aevo" (which loosely translated means "Nothing great has great beginnings"). Courts have reacted tentatively, inconsistently, and sometimes incoherently, notwithstanding (or perhaps because of) the delicate and important nature of the problem. I am reminded of the nineteenth-century reactionary Joseph De Maistre, who admonished that the pure of heart and righteous do not need books; precepts are "imprinted by grace in our hearts." It is only because of our sinful ways that "books and laws became necessary."

Perhaps it is best to begin with the notion that indoctrination is much of what schools are about. But it is not all that schools are about. If government is to educate children, to operate public schools, and to select teachers, books, and courses, a basic decision has been made about the communication of skills, attitudes, values, and beliefs, between generations. Education and indoctrination, information and values, cannot be neatly disentangled. Education, after all, is often a process of persuasion. As Elliot Aronson has remarked, one man's propaganda is another's truth. More importantly, socialization and education are not only inextricably linked, but the failure of the adult generation, through the policy, to bring the young into the larger political, economic, and social culture would have disastrous consequences. We have no reason to think that children are inherently good or democratic or tolerant or peaceful. We have even less reason to believe that they are capable of inventing, on their own and without the benefit of the community's experiences, gasoline engines, theories of relativity, and neurosurgical techniques. The dominant languages, modes of computation, and the specific customs and history of the people will and should be taught. And this learning is not value neutral.

The problem, however, lies in devising educational systems that prepare children for adult life without simultaneously sacrificing their ability to reflect upon the ends for which they are being prepared, without indoctrinating them to unbridled allegiance to the *status quo* or to the rightness of current institutional arrangements. Basic knowledge should be communicated while attempting, as best we can, to give the young "ample opportunity of making the decisions upon which these principles are based, and by which they are modified, improved, adapted to changed circumstances or even abandoned if they become entirely unsuited to the new environment." Education can expand the mind and imagination or contract them. The child who is taught nothing of his or her country's cultural, political, and intellectual heritage must be pitied as much as the child who is compelled to conform in all respects to the conventional wisdom. As Ruth Benedict put it, "No civilization has in it any element which in the last analysis is not the contribution of an individual." Yet, individuality does not exist in a vacuum; it is defined by the background of the community.

The inevitable question then is, Who determines what is to be taught in public schools, who does the necessary balancing? The answer, by and large, is that elected representatives, school board members, and school administrators make the choices and are, at least in theory, accountable to the citizenry for their performance. There is no necessary reason why affairs have to be arranged this way; many have proposed alternatives which would enhance, for example, the power of families to make educational choices. But these are our existing legal and institutional arrangements. As the Seventh Circuit recently stated in *Zykan v. Warsaw Community School Corporation*,

[Public schools have a] broad formative role . . . [which encompasses] the encouragement and nurturing of those fundamental social, political, and moral values that will permit a student to take his place in the community. . . . As a result, the community has a legitimate, even a vital and compelling interest in "the choice [of] and adherence to a suitable curriculum for the benefit of our young citizens. . . .

Educational decisions necessarily involve choices regarding what students should read and hear, and particularly in light of the formative purpose of secondary school education, local discretion thus means the freedom to form an opinion regarding the instructional content that will best transmit the basic values of the community.

This necessarily puts the state in the business of editing the curriculum, including making selections of books for inclusion in the school library and for optional or required reading in designated courses. If no such authority existed, if disgruntled parents and others had a "right" to equal time to reply to the state's program, if public schools were public forums in the fullest sense of the phrase (like parks, for example), the educational mission of the schools, including acculturation, would become impossible. As a general matter, despite some wishful thinking to the contrary, schools are not subject to the various balancing of the message doctrines including fairness, a right to reply, equal time, and the like. As Professor (now Judge) Canby has stated,

"[E]diting is what editors are for; and editing is selection and choice of material." To forbid the managers of . . . [public communication] enterprises to select material for inclusion and, necessarily, exclusion would for all practical purposes destroy these endeavors.

If we pause a moment to reflect on these matters, it becomes clear why curricular and book purchasing decisions generally should be left to the state under current institutional arrangements. It simply cannot be the case that because government owns and operates an enterprise devoted to communication it cannot, in good faith, carry out its editorial functions. Where time and resources are scarce, selectivity is inherent in communication. A person does not have a constitutional right to publish his or her article in the law review of a state university, for that undermines the mission of publishing high quality, scholarly articles. Nor should prison rehabilitation programs, state-sponsored psychiatric programs for the mentally infirm, or, for that matter, the President's State of the Union Address be subject to dilution by requirements of fairness, balance, or rights of reply as a matter of constitutional law. Of course such standards sometimes have been voluntarily adopted by statute or regulation or practice for government communications. But if one concedes that public schooling, prison rehabilitation programs, military training, and other government communication efforts are legitimate and, indeed, essential for well-being, then government cannot be denied the editorial power which is the wherewithal to accomplish its objectives. And this logic is bolstered by the fact that school children are a captive audience, an audience captured for the purpose of accomplishing particular educational objectives. They are in school because, through democratic processes, the people have decided they should be there, and hence the duly elected representatives of the people should make the basic editorial decisions. The loss of liberty to parents and children is difficult to justify if the students are a captive audience to private communicators with their own educational or indoctrinational agenda. As Professor Shiffrin succinctly writes,

To make education compulsory was itself to challenge liberal ideology.

The essence of compulsory education is that the state and not parents will ultimately decide what is best for children.

This is not to say that there are not situations in which the editorial functions of the state may not be limited. There are constitutional doctrines of limitation, and I will soon elaborate on them. Nor is it to say that persons should not have access to schools for communication purposes, or that students do not have First Amendment rights of communication which they take with them to public schools. But the standard is one of nondisruption or compatibility of the educational process, the mission of the schools,

and private expression. My point is that the loss of the power to choose and select textbooks and courses is inherently incompatible with the schooling enterprise. For this reason, and many of you may disagree, I do not know how the various derivative First Amendment rights entitled rights to know, to learn, or to acquire information can be given much credence in the public school setting. In my view the "right to know," as articulated by the Supreme Court, is no more than artistic camouflage to protect the interest of a willing speaker who seeks to communicate with a willing listener. If students have a right to know, then they should have a constitutional right to demand courses in public schools that are not offered for financial or other reasons. Any question in a class, as a constitutional matter, would require an answer—no matter that the question relates to the French Revolution and is asked in an algebra class or that every other student in the class has no desire to acquire such information at that time and place. Students, presumably, would be entitled to choose their own books at government expense. And no librarian could refuse to purchase a book sought by a student. In other spheres, public libraries devoted to particular subjects, say the social sciences, would fall under the constitutional axe if nineteenth-century Russian novels were requested. Museum collections would quickly follow. There simply is no limiting principle, apart from the question of the uncertain constitutional pedigree of such a right. This is a far cry from situations where a lawyer or pharmacist wishes to communicate information about his or her services and products to the public, where many consumers of the services and products wish to acquire the information, and where government forbids the willing parties from communicating with each other by particular means.

If students and parents cannot edit the curriculum and choose books for themselves in the guise of a right to know, surely authors, editors, and publishers have no constitutional right to have their books purchased by the state for dissemination in public schools. To my knowledge, no court has arrived at such a holding. This would effectively place the power to edit the curriculum in the hands of private, disinterested parties—neither parents nor the state—and they would have an audience captured for them by governmental coercion. Further, it is one thing for government to censor books and limit their distribution, and quite another to require the state to purchase books in the name of the First Amendment rights of its producers. Surely such absolutists as Justices Black and Douglas, who did not believe that federal and state governments had any authority to ban books on obscenity, national security, or other grounds would blanch at requiring governments to purchase *Fanny Hill*, *Ulysses*, or the *Pentagon Papers*. By analogy, state officials may not ban a magazine with offensive language or refuse to allow a sexually explicit artwork to be shown, but this does not necessarily mean that they are required to fund the magazine or to provide a state-owned exhibit place for the artwork. Even if this is debatable, qualitative judgments are an inherent part of the funding process—unless one's position is that the state must support all magazine publishers and struggling artists who seek state subsidies, if it supports any.

IRREVOCABLE DELEGATIONS: DUE PROCESS AND THE FIRST AMENDMENT

If the state has wide reign to select books and determine the curriculum, what mechanisms are there to limit the state's ability to indoctrinate without sacrificing its editorial powers? One answer is to strengthen private centers of communication, including the rights of students, teachers, and others to engage in speech on school premises so long as there is no undue disturbance of the state's own expression. Both Professor Shiffrin and I have advocated this approach. It is one thing to forbid a person wishing to speak on drug abuse to take over a gym class, and it is quite another to forbid him from distributing pamphlets on the problem in the school hall-

ways between classes. But another way to think about the problem is to focus on what we mean by such fudge words as government, state, public officials, and the like. Governments are made up of people, and these people have different perspectives and different places in the hierarchy. The reality is that government communication powers and activities are so extensive that inevitably editorial responsibility is delegated to "professional" editors, those "street-level bureaucrats" responsible for the actual delivery of services. In the education context, the state legislature could vote on each book to be used in every school in the state, applying its editorial judgments. But in the nature of things authority is delegated to state departments of education, state textbook commissions, local school boards, principals, and even the teachers and school librarians themselves. This delegation of editorial authority, which often parallels the balkanization of governments responsible for education (the thousands of school districts and hundreds of thousands of schools, librarians, and teachers) is a bulwark against the centralized orchestration of a publicly established orthodoxy that Justice Jackson warned us about nearly forty years ago. Safety lies in keeping politicians too busy to intervene in daily decisions about book acquisitions or student newspaper articles, in the sense that professionals should make the judgments in custom and practice. What is to be feared is dilettante politicians and special interest groups with political muscle.

The concept of delegated editorial responsibility is a powerful one. Consider, for example, the doctrine of academic freedom for teachers. These cases seem difficult to justify, and the Supreme Court has never embraced the right explicitly and distinguished it from traditional First Amendment doctrine. Should the fortuity of speaking and teaching for a living entitle an instructor to some special autonomy that other government employees do not share? Is it because they deal in words? And what of a librarian's asserted right to academic freedom? Why should a government employee who purchases books have any greater latitude than a government supply officer responsible for ordering paper and office equipment? Part of the answer, surely, is that books and words have a peculiarly important position in democracy. But this could equally as well argue for greater supervision of teachers and librarians in public schools. What students learn is more important than which copying machine is purchased by a state highway department. And if the government is truly an editor, then why should not the government have the same rights of control and hiring and firing as private schools, newspapers, and broadcast stations?

The answer lies in the place which teachers and librarians occupy in the system of government expression, not *per se* in their own constitutional entitlements. The greater the ability of higher echelon officials to control what goes on in each school, school library, and classroom, the greater the danger of the promulgation of a uniform message to its captive listeners. If teachers were automatons, required to adhere rigidly to lesson plans, book selections, and the like, ideological indoctrination could become a reality. If librarians were responsible only for processing book orders, with no discretion over what was ordered, the same risks could be incurred. In practice, varying discretion is given to teachers and librarians and the system works reasonably well. But what if editorial authority is not delegated to them? Is there a constitutional rule, derived from the First Amendment concern for government-established orthodoxy, that would require such delegations? In my own work, I have answered this question negatively. If, for example, a school board establishes objective rules in advance that allow it to make judgments about textbook and library acquisitions, and if the school board in fact makes such decisions over time, then their decisionmaking apparatus is not subject to constitutional attack on the grounds that delegation and the division of authority over textbooks and library books is required. But you should be aware of the fact that the student-newspaper cases implicitly reach a

contrary result. The conventional wisdom is that once a public school establishes a newspaper, although it need not have done so, it generally may not interfere with the editorial judgments of the student editors. And the cases do not appear to turn on how much editorial discretion was given the students or whether faculty supervision was established in advance by objective rules.

How then does one explain cases like *Parducci v. Rutland* in which Judge Johnson upheld the teacher's right to select a book for her students over the protestations of school authorities? *Cary v. Board of Education*, a recent Tenth Circuit case, begins to unravel the answer. Judge Logan, in referring to *Parducci* and similar academic freedom cases, noted that

the cases which held for the teachers and placed emphasis upon teachers' right to exercise discretion in the classroom, seemed to be situations where school authorities acted in the absence of a general policy, after the fact, and had little to charge against the teacher other than the assignment with which they were unhappy.

Thus, if higher authorities have no policy on book assignment or selection and thereby *de facto* delegate such authority to teachers and librarians, they cannot later intervene on an *ad hoc* basis to limit the dissemination of the books or their acquisition. Similarly, where school authorities have promulgated in advance a set of rules delegating authority to teachers, librarians, special textbook committees, and so forth, they should not be able to undo that delegation on a selective basis merely because they are dissatisfied with the results of that delegation in a particular instance. In other words, the First Amendment should be construed to embody a doctrine of irrevocable delegations of authority in book selection policies, at least where the revocation operates retroactively or on an *ad hoc* basis.

The irrevocable delegation doctrine is rooted in Supreme Court opinions that require federal agencies to follow their own procedures, even if those procedures would not be constitutionally required in the first instance under the due process clause. If one wishes to be technical about it, the argument might well be that established procedures for book selection and removal create a sort of property interest, settled and relied upon expectations as to how the state will behave, which are embodied in positive law. A student may not have a "right to know" and a publisher may have no right to government largesse, but they should have a right to compel a government entity to honor the procedures that have been established for determining what is taught and what books will be used. Less technically, an analogy may be drawn to the obscenity area where, as Professor Monaghan has noted, "the Court has placed little reliance upon the due process requirements of the Fifth and Fourteenth Amendments, but instead has turned directly to the First Amendment as the source of rules." If the problem is that government communication in schools may overwhelm students, that in the process of learning they may lose their ability to think critically and independently, then the irrevocable delegation doctrine makes good sense. Courts are not put in the position of deciding what is propaganda or indoctrination and what is education. The state remains free to alter prospectively its decisional structure. But having created a structure which is conducive to decentralized, balkanized, and professional decision-making about schoolbooks (whether intended or not), school authorities should be required to abide by that structure. If they wish to take on the job of editing the school curriculum and selecting books, it should be a full-time job. There should be no room for "Lone Rangers" who react to isolated book selection decisions, while ignoring the need to cultivate both community and individuality in the mass of curricular, library, and book assignment decisions.

The irrevocability doctrine has not always been clearly applied by the courts. In the *Cary* case itself, from which I just quoted, the school board had established a high school Language Arts Text Evaluation Committee to review materials for language arts courses. The committee consisted of teachers, administrators, parents, and students, and apparently it was charged with reporting its book recommendations to the school board. The books were not to be purchased by the district but by individual students. Only one book was rejected by a majority of the committee, but nine more were rejected in a minority. The school board approved 1275 books for the language art classes, but rejected ten others—only six of which were listed in the minority report. The excluded books included *A Clockwork Orange* by Anthony Burgess, *The Exorcist* by William P. Blatty, *Coney Island of the Mind* by Lawrence Ferlinghetti, and *Kaddish and Other Poems* by Allen Ginsberg. The court upheld the expulsion, reasoning that if the board could decide not to offer contemporary poetry and if it could select the major textbook for the course, why could it not prevent the assignment of other books? But with all due respect, that was not the question for review as the court had articulated it. The board established a review procedure, and it is not at all clear that the board abided by it. The case should have been remanded for such a determination. For example, was the board required to select books on the basis of the information provided by the majority and minority reports? If it was free to disregard all recommendations, then what was the point of the procedure? Was the board, like the committee members, required to follow objective standards and to give reasons for rejecting particular books? References to the general statutory powers of school boards do not answer these questions.

Perhaps the most plausible explanation of the case is that the parties stipulated that the books were not obscene, that no systematic attempt had been made to exclude any particular philosophy, and that a "constitutionally proper decisionmaker" might well determine that the books were proper for high school language art classes. These stipulations may well have given away the game. The presumption of censorship of ideas that an *ad hoc* revocation of the committee's book selection authority normally entails, assuming that this was the case, was rebutted by plaintiff's own concessions. The only plausible reason for nonselection was a judgment about the educational appropriateness of the books. Defendants conceded that students were not prohibited from reading the books and teachers were free to comment upon them and recommend them. Only protracted discussion, which would in effect reinstate the forbidden books, was prohibited. But even so, the *Cary* court should have held the board to its own rules, thereby retaining a structure preservative of Fifth Amendment values and satisfying the expectations of the participants.

In contrast to *Cary*, the court in *Salvail* v. *Nashua Board of Education* relied heavily on the failure of the board of education to follow its own procedures in a decision to remove all and then parts of *Ms.* magazine from the school library. In that case the board approved guidelines for the selection of instructional materials, delegating its editorial function to the "professionally trained personnel employed by the school district." The guidelines contained criteria for selection, including quality of presentation, appropriateness for age, subject, and ability levels, and literary quality. The guidelines also provided that the chosen books should help students be aware of the contributions of both sexes and of various religious, ethnic, and subcultural groups, and that on controversial issues, the collection should be balanced and insure the representation of various religious, ethnic, and subcultural groups; and that on controversial issues, the collection should be balanced and insure the representation of various points of view. In the event of a citizen complaint or question about book selection, the guidelines provided for appeals to an Instructional Materials Reconsideration Committee, with subsequent appeals to the superintendent and school board. Bypassing these procedures a board member presented a formal resolution to remove *Ms.* magazine from the school library, and this was

approved by the board despite the protestations of the superintendent that the established procedures should be followed. The court held that the board "was required to follow [the guidelines] in its attempt at removal of *Ms.* magazine from the shelves of the high school library." This conclusion of law was sufficient to support the court injunction against banning the magazine from the school library. It was unnecessary for the court to address broader censorship issues, relating to whether the alleged "sexual overtones" of the magazine were simply a pretext for banning an objectional point of view.

This last point is worthy of elaboration. The remedy for violating preestablished book selection and removal policies should be the acquisition or reshelving of the books in question. There are other possibilities. The board might decide or be ordered to submit the book for review through the existing procedures. But this is time consuming and the passage of time alone might well sustain the board's original unlawful action. Further, the knowledge of the board's previous decision might well taint the decision-making process of the selection committee. Many members of the selection committee are likely to be school employees. And even the promulgation of new policies empowering the board to make such decisions, and applying these policies prospectively, invites disingenuous behavior with respect to the specific books that have been at the center of controversy. In other words, an effective deterrent needs to be created, and a requirement of further proceedings would not create such a deterrent.

BOOK SELECTION AND PROCEDURAL DUE PROCESS

Apart from bolstering the delegation of authority, one may think about applying more traditional due process techniques to the book selection process. I have found only one case adopting this position, *Loewen* v. *Turnipseed*, a district court case arising in the Northern District of Mississippi. In that case the "rating committee" appointed by the governor and state superintendent of education of Mississippi approved a book entitled *Your Mississippi* for purchase by the State Textbook Purchasing Board and disapproved a book entitled *Mississippi: Conflict and Change*. The books were considered for use in ninth-grade classes in Mississippi history, and apparently the state would purchase approved books for both public and parochial schools. The controversy arose because *Mississippi: Conflict and Change* allegedly emphasized the mistreatment of blacks in Mississippi, while the alternative selection did not. The "rating committee" split on the issue, with the white majority outvoting the black minority. The court ultimately held that the selection was motivated by racial discrimination, intended to perpetuate segregation, and was therefore unconstitutional.

But along the way the court held that the rating committee procedure for selecting textbooks was also unconstitutional. Mississippi law did not provide for review of the rating committee's decision, "without giving those adversely affected by it a voice in the matter." Since the publishers of the books were given an opportunity to present their positions to the committee, presumably the court had in mind the authors, and students, faculty, and school districts across the state. And indeed they were the plaintiffs. At first blush the holding appears difficult to sustain. In the jargon, the decision appears to be a legislative and not an adjudicative matter. A governmental body is not constitutionally required to hold an adversary hearing in deciding to award a construction contract for a public building. But perhaps, as in the case of the irrevocable delegation doctrine, guidance should be sought more in First Amendment interests than in the due process clause. A loose parallel may be found in the obscenity cases where adversary hearings are required, notwithstanding the fact that the publisher's property interest alone would not justify such stringent procedural safeguards.

The stigma or non-stigma plus cases decided under the due process clause may also provide a rough parallel. Where governmental communications may stigmatize a person and where he is simultaneously deprived of some entitlement, the government may be required to hold a hearing to determine the facts of the matter. The notion is that a liberty interest has been violated. A classic case would be the dismissal of a public employee, accompanied by publicized charges that he had engaged in some reprehensible behavior.

I have argued elsewhere that these cases are best understood from the perspective of government expression that may do untold damage to an individual's life chances. In a modern industrial society, widely publicized government accusations may do as much harm to a person as the loss of liberty through incarceration or the taking of his physical property. A hearing requirement does not mean that the government may not speak badly about individuals, but only that, under some circumstances, it must abide by procedures designed to insure the accuracy of the government's remarks. In *Loewen*, government is expressing itself through its textbook selections. The potential harm to authors, students, and others is great, and perhaps a due process hearing makes sense despite the lack of fit between these facts and prior due process decisions.

While I am dubious about this aspect of *Loewen* surviving appellate review, it is clear that even affirmance would require the adoption of some limiting principle. Surely, governments are not required to hold a due process hearing every time they wish to make a decision about funding research, purchasing a book, subsidizing the arts, or publishing a manuscript at the Government Printing Office. One tentative suggestion is that a distinction might be drawn between books that may be marketed only in schools and those that have a more general market. That is, in the case of textbooks an adverse decision is financially devastating and the book is unlikely to be read widely. For novels by Graham Greene or Howard Fast, the impact is far less grave. Thus, a hearing might be required for textbook selections, whereas it would not be required for the general run of books acquired by school libraries.

Finally, I cannot resist making one last point about the *Loewen* case. The court did not order the rating committee to alter its procedures to conform to its opinion. Rather, as in *Cary*, the court enjoined the defendants to approve *Mississippi: Conflict and Change*. The practical result of the case was that both books under consideration were approved and local Mississippi school districts and dioceses were free to choose the one they preferred. This is indeed a Solomonic remedy. But more importantly, the decision effectively placed the power to make textbook selections in the hands of local communities and local school officials. Not only is this consistent with the irrevocable delegation doctrine, but it also has overtones of structural due process. Perhaps, as in the Supreme Court's pornography, school financing, and zoning cases the district court intended to emphasize the need for community and not statewide decisionmaking. If schools are to reflect the values of the communities in which they are located, then each community should be able to determine its own standards for schoolbooks. Parents and publishers do not decide, but neither should distant state officials. While I admit that the constitutional underpinnings of the argument are subject to question, community decisionmaking is consistent both with the mission of schools and with the First Amendment interest in avoiding wholesale indoctrination through a centralized decisionmaking process.

ILLICIT MOTIVATION

In a number of fascinating recent decisions, circuit courts have gone a full step further than the irrevocable delegation doctrine. They have sought to distinguish good faith pedagogic judgments about books from an effort to indoctrinate to a particular school of thought or political point of view. This is a task of immense difficulty, largely dependent on a motivational analysis. In my own writing, I have been skeptical about such efforts except in situations where the state cannot even plausibly argue that it is pursuing the goal of education. Professor Shiffrin, on the other hand, sees more possibilities in this approach, and the weight of authority appears, at the moment, to be more consistent with this approach. Perhaps the best exposition of the principle occurred in the *Zykan* case:

[T]he Constitution [does not] permit the courts to interfere with local educational discretion until local authorities begin to substitute rigid and exclusive indoctrination for the mere exercise of their prerogative to make pedagogic choices regarding matters of legitimate dispute.

Noticeably absent from the amended complaint is any hint that the decisions of these administrators flow from . . . some systematic effort to exclude a particular type of thought, or even from some identifiable ideological preference.

Not surprisingly, the court remanded the case to allow amendment of the pleadings and presentation of evidence on the motivation issue.

The *Warsaw* case is rather complex. Essentially, the student plaintiffs filed suit under Section 1983 alleging that their First and Fourteenth Amendment rights had been violated by a series of related school board decisions. A textbook was removed from the school premises (*Values Classification*) and given to a senior citizens' group for public burning. Four books ordered for a Women in Literature course (*Growing Up Female in America*, *Go Ask Alice*, *The Bell Jar*, and *The Stepford Wives*) were not permitted to be used. The school board, under a new policy prohibiting reading materials that might be objectionable, also excised portions of *Student Critic* and permanently removed *Go Ask Alice* from the school library. Adding icing to the cake, the established school procedures for book selection decisions were not followed, seven courses were eliminated from the curriculum, and the English teacher who planned to offer the

Women in Literature course was not re-hired. The plaintiffs alleged that these actions were largely taken because particular words in the books offended the school board's social, political, and moral tastes. The court found this insufficient, however, because school boards are supposed to act on such tastes and beliefs in making book selection, curricular, and other decisions. In the court's words,

The amended complaint nowhere suggests that in taking these actions defendants have been guided by an interest in imposing some religious or scientific orthodoxy to eliminate a particular kind of inquiry generally.

Apparently, if one is to credit the court's account of the case, plaintiffs erred in not specifically alleging that the board was attempting to eliminate feminist thought from the public schools.

With all my reservations about the workability of the motivation test, the court's treatment of the facts and pleadings in *Zykan* is bizarre. The court might have held that all public education casts a pall of orthodoxy and eliminates some kinds of inquiries. That is its purpose. If anthropology books and courses are not available in the schools, a sort of orthodoxy and limit on inquiry is evident. But the court had a case in which a series of books relating to feminism were banished, the school board shortcircuited normal procedures for book selection and retention, and the teacher who proposed to discuss the banned books lost her job. If there is a distinction between imposed orthodoxy and education, the Warsaw community board clearly was on the wrong side of the distinction.

From any reasonable perspective, *Zykan* illustrates the type of facts that shed light on a school board's motivation to censor or edit. First, there was a series of related, but nonetheless *ad hoc* determinations, all of which pointed in the direction of eliminating feminist thought from the schools. Second, the book decisions clearly did not rest on considerations of economy or scarce resources. Third, the school board was not selecting among disciplines or subjects so much as it was addressing itself to a current political issue that cut across many disciplines. Fourth, the reasonable evidentiary presumption that the failure of the board to abide by its own procedures is a sign that it is engaging in a censorship was not rebutted by the extrinsic evidence. Fifth, the removal of a book from a library and the nonrenewal of a teacher lends itself better to motivational analysis. In a sense, it is easier to figure out why someone was fired or why a book was removed than it is to determine why someone was hired among hundreds of applicants or why a book was not purchased from the thousands available. This is consistent with the *Minarcini* decision, distinguishing book acquisition and book removal policies.

In this multifactored motivational analysis, *Zykan* indicates that courts should not decide school book controversies without detailed examination of the facts. As a general matter, judges should not be dismissing complaints with prejudice or rendering summary decisions if they are to take seriously their extremely difficult task. And certainly plaintiffs should not move for summary judgment and should resist all of defendants' efforts to short-cut the fact-finding process. Beyond this, however, *Zykan* reveals precious little about what the lower court should do with those facts. With some hesitancy, let me propose a legal text. Borrowing from the racial discrimination context, the standard should be whether the defendants would have taken the action they in fact took, but for the illegitimate desire to suppress objectionable and controversial ideas. While perhaps orthodoxy and education cannot be easily distinguished, the point may well be that the effort to censor, rather than to edit, is a corruption of the political processes by which schooling decisions are made. In any given case, the impact of censorship and editing may be the same (for example, Russian history books are not read in schools), but the polity has a strong interest in insuring that the intergenerational communication of knowledge and values is not guided by principles inconsistent with democratic and First Amendments precepts relating to the creation of self-controlled citizens.

In my view, the leading case on removal of books from public school libraries, *Pico* v. *Board of Education, Island Trees Union Free School District*, is consistent with the standard that I have articulated. *Pico* involves such outlandish and bizarre official behavior that it would be difficult (but not impossible) for any court to resist some form of intervention. The case involved the removal of ten books from school libraries, including *The Fixer, Slaughterhouse-Five, The Naked Ape, Soul on Ice*, and others. As Judge Sifton noted with amusing understatement, this was accomplished through "unusual and irregular intervention in school libraries' operations by persons not routinely concerned with their contents." Three school board members had attended a conference sponsored by a conservative organization and had obtained a copy of a list of objectionable books. The list was annotated with remarks that particular books were seditious, disloyal, anti-white women, anti-Christian, and pro-feminist. Sensing an emergency, two of the board members gained entry to a school library at night and found ten of the most objectionable books in the card catalog. Over the objections of the superintendent, the board then bypassed normal selection and removal procedures and banned the books. The removal became a *cause célèbre*, and the incumbent board members were reelected, in part at least because of their stance on the book removal issue. After the suit was filed, defendants emphasized that their decision was premised on "the repellent and vulgar language present in the books." Not surprisingly, Judge Sifton did not believe them. Judge Newman was not sure, and he and Judge Sifton ordered the case remanded for full trial (the case arose as an appeal from the granting of summary judgment for defendants). Judge Mansfield dissented.

Judge Sifton's opinion could not be more to the point. He did not for a moment deny the socialization function of public schools. And socialization inevitably involves the suppression of some facts and ideas. But his view was that the facts gave rise to "an inference . . . that political views and personal taste are being asserted not in the interests of the children's well-being, but rather for the purpose of establishing those views as the correct and orthodox ones for all purposes in the particular community." Thus, it was clear that the defendants would not have removed the books but for the desire to impose an orthodoxy and to suppress inconsistent ideas. The decisionmaking process of the school system had been corrupted by an effort "to express an official policy with regard to God and country. . . ." If the school board had been interested in an editing process designed to ferret out educationally inappropriate reading matter, many of the same books might well have been removed. But the similarity of impact of censorship and editing would not obviate a motive so patently inconsistent with First Amendment values. Judge Newman said much the same thing, opining that education may sometimes involve the suppression of ideas. But he could not accept such suppression "when exclusion of particular views is motivated by the authorities' opinion about the proper way to organize and run society in general." But given the defendants' formally expressed reasons for removing the books, he courteously insisted that a full trial was necessary "to determine precisely what happened."

Bicknel v. *Vergennes Union High School Board* was decided by the same panel on the same day as *Pico*, and it also involved the removal of books from the school library. This time, however, Judge Newman changed his vote and affirmed the lower court's dismissal of the complaint for failure to state a claim upon which relief could be granted. Judge Mansfield concurred, and Judge Sifton dissented. My impression is that Judge Newman wished to illuminate the law by contrasting the results in *Pico* and *Bicknell*, and to create one of those "but see" or "compare" footnotes that would gain immortality in the pages of law reviews and law reports. In any event, the defendant board had created a "School Library Bill of Rights for School Library Media Center Program"; and this document gave the professional staff the "right" "to freely select, in accordance with Board policy, organize and administer the media collection to best serve teachers and students." If a complaint were received about a staff book selection, the librarian was to attempt to resolve the matter. Any unresolved matters were for the board. Without following the procedure, the board, upon complaint, removed *Dog Day Afternoon* and *The Wanderers* from the school library, asserting that they employed "vulgar and indecent language." The board also voted to prohibit the librarian from purchasing any additional major works of fiction, and required that library purchases in other areas be reviewed by both the school administration and the board. Subsequent to these actions, a number of students, parents, and library employees and the Right to Read Defense Fund brought suit.

To begin with the obvious, the facts of *Bicknell* are much less compelling from the plaintiff's standpoint than those in *Pico*. The board's actions appear to be much less of an ideological witch-hunt, and there is nothing about the decision to review books jointly in the future that violates First Amendment doctrine. But the most straightforward explanation of *Bicknell* is that it is a pleading case. While plaintiffs claimed that the board's action was motivated "by personal tastes and values," they did not assert (according to Judge Newman) that the removal of the books was motivated by political concerns. They admitted "that the books were removed because of vulgarity and obscenity." The plaintiffs also claimed that the failure of the school board to follow its own procedures was a violation of due process of law. Judge Newman, while not commenting on the district court's finding to the contrary, held as a matter of law that the claim was without merit. Judge Sifton

agreed in his dissenting opinion, but argued that these procedural irregularities should be explored at trial in the context of determining the motivation of the board.

In my view, *Bicknell* is wrongly decided under applicable constitutional doctrines. As in *Cary*, if the plaintiffs did not use the magic words about motivation to achieve political orthodoxy, they should have had an opportunity to amend their complaint or refile the suit with the appropriate pleadings. Again, if the Second Circuit is going into the motivation business with regard to book selection and removal policies (I tried to warn them), summary procedures are entirely inappropriate. If the motives were mixed, and according to Judge Newman the plaintiffs unwisely conceded on the obscenity issue, there still is the question of whether the removal would have occurred but for a political motivation to suppress ideas. Further, both Judges Sifton and Newman did not clearly articulate or understand the irrevocable delegation doctrine. Judge Newman opines that the sort of right recognized in *Pico*, presumably a right to avoid ideologically motivated official efforts to suppress ideas through book selections, is not the sort of interest in liberty or property that typically gives rise to a requirement for a due process hearing. Judge Sifton agreed. Even if *Loewen* were the law of the land, which it is not, I agree. But the entitlement is not a property or liberty interest in avoiding orthodoxy; it is the property and liberty interest, combined with First Amendment values, in assuring that a school board follows its own procedures for removing library books. The emphasis on procedural due process in its usual sense and not in the sense of reinforcing the board's delegation of selection and removal functions is a fundamental error in the decision. And this causes the judges to ignore the value of decentralized, balkanized, and professional decisionmaking in advancing First Amendment values.

RESERVATIONS AND REFLECTIONS
Having examined the recent case law on

book selection and removal policies, permit me to make a number of observations and to express a certain uneasiness. The irrevocable delegation doctrine strikes me as the wisest compromise in terms of avoiding the quagmire of motivation theory and in terms of playing to the demonstrated competencies of courts. On the other hand, it is not as protecting of First Amendment values as other approaches, and it invites school boards to take on limited review functions that may meet the letter, if not the spirit, of the doctrine. And the constitutional status of the doctrine is not assured, with some recent Supreme Court *dicta* pointing in the opposite direction. With regard to traditional due process guarantees, recent Supreme Court decisions do not bode well for their extension even to a limited class of book selection cases. The Court also has shown an inclination to dilute the remedies for the failure to follow due process procedures, and reinstatement of rejected books may be much too much for it to swallow. Interestingly enough, the structural due process approach, requiring that local communities make book decisions, is highly consistent with the prevailing philosophy of many of the Justices. But the precedents are few, they are easily distinguishable, and it is far from certain the Court will be impressed by the structural due process writings of such distinguished scholars as Laurence Tribe and Professor (now Judge) Hans Linde.

But for all of these doubts, I believe it remains an open question as to whether the sort of lines which the Second and Seventh Circuits have sought to draw are workable or desirable. How does one know an "orthodoxy" when one sees one? Is not all education centered on establishing certain orthodoxies and editing out of the curriculum ideas and facts which are deemed wrong or unimportant by the community? To raise a specific example, the *Pico, Bicknell, Zykan*, and *Salvail* decisions all assume that the ex-clusion of sexually oriented books or books with dirty words is constitutionally permissible. But why is this not as much of an imposition of values as is implicit in the exclusion of a feminist or a civil rights point of view? Is not the inculcation of standards of morality and sexual behavior one of the purposes of public schooling? Or is it, as the court in *Right to Read Defense Committee* v. *School Committee of the City of Chelsea*, that school boards should have no constitutional power to remove an allegedly offensive library book unless the book meets constitutional standards of obscenity? But is this not inconsistent with the accepted notion that school authorities may pass on the educational appropriateness of books for youngsters in the schools, with the notion that the vast majority of people in a particular community may not wish their sons and daughters subjected to such materials?

There is also the danger that courts will intrude too far into the curriculum of public schools, and that there will be a loss of accountability for book selection and removal decisions. At the moment this danger appears remote. Whatever the articulated standard, plaintiffs have gained few victories. And a few well publicized victories may well do more to influence school officials than a multitude of losses. But this suggests to me what everyone should realize. The primary restraints on excessive government communication activities are political and attitudinal. Restraint depends on the independence of private publishers and their willingness to do political battle over their First Amendment beliefs. It depends on persuading public officials and the public itself that censorship is not the way. It depends on revitalizing our traditions of local control of education and on keeping state and federal governments as far removed as possible from school book decisions. In the last analysis, people will have the kind of schools that they want and deserve.

SCHOOL CENSORSHIP CASES

Kanawha County

The first case to receive major national attention originated in Kanawha County, West Virginia, in 1974. The long-drawn-out battle there was precipitated by a number of school board members, egged on frequently by outside agencies. As the controversy went on, groups of citizens were drawn in, leaving the community deeply divided. At the outset, the basic issue was selection of textbooks and supplementary reading for English courses. The texts approved by the State of West Virginia were tentatively accepted, pending further investigation. A member of the school board then consulted Mel and Norma Gabler, founders of Educational Research Analysts in Texas, and was informed that most of the books in the list of 325 titles for the language arts were disrespectful of authority and religion, destructive of social and cultural values, obscene, pornographic, unpatriotic, or in violation of individual and familial rights of privacy. A thousand citizens attended a special meeting of the school board, which voted to drop some books and to retain others. The ministers of the community were divided in their views, pro and con. When the school term began in the fall of 1974, 8,000 students stayed home and 4,000 miners struck to show their displeasure with the books. The board of education building in Charleston was forcibly closed and some of its windows blown out by shotgun blasts. The Gablers were invited up from Texas and added to the ferment by a whirlwind tour of lectures in the Charleston area.

In 1974 the Kanawha County Board of Education adopted the following guidelines for textbook selection, as summarized by Edward B. Jenkinson in his *Censors in the Classroom*:

    I. Textbooks for use in the classrooms of Kanawha County shall recognize the sanctity of the home and emphasize its importance as the basic unit of American society.

        Textbooks must not intrude into the privacy of student's homes by asking personal questions about inner feelings or behavior of themselves or their parents, or encourage them to criticize their parents by direct questions, statements or inferences.

    II. Textbooks must not contain profanity.

    III. Textbooks must respect the right of ethnic, religious or racial groups to their values and practices and not ridicule those values or practices.

    IV. Textbooks must not encourage or promote racial hatred.

    V. Textbooks must encourage loyalty to the United States and the several states and emphasize the responsibilities of citizenship and the obligation to redress grievances through legal processes.

VI. Textbooks shall teach the true history and heritage of the United States and of any other countries studied in the curriculum. Textbooks must not defame our nation's founders or misrepresent the ideals and causes for which they struggled and sacrificed.

VII. Textbooks used in the study of the English language shall teach that traditional rules of grammar are a worthwhile subject for academic pursuit and are essential for effective communication among English speaking people.

Jenkinson points out that if the guidelines were interpreted as the protesters viewed them, "enforcement would impose upon the public schools the task of indoctrinating students to one system of cultural and religious values, inflexible and unexamined."

Eventually, all the disputed textbooks were returned to the schools. Two series, however, could be used as supplemental reading only with parental approval.

The battle of the books in Kanawha County was a complex affair, extensively commented upon by educators, religious leaders, reporters, and others. Superintendent of Schools Underwood stated, "It might take a decade before we can understand what happened."

Island Trees

A second school library censorship case eventually ended up in the U.S. Supreme Court. Pitted against each other at Levittown, New York were the school board of the Island Trees Free School District and a group of opposing students, led by Steven Pico. The case began on the night of November 7, 1975, when two members of the school board slipped out of a school sports festival and persuaded the night janitor to admit them to the high school library. Using a list of "objectionable books," prepared by a conservative organization called Parents of New York— United, they searched the card catalog for books later described by them as "mentally dangerous." They found nine, a majority dealing with the experiences of Jews, blacks, and Hispanics. Some time later the school board voted to remove eleven books from the library and to ban their use in the school's curriculum. They were: Anonymous, *Go Ask Alice*; Jerome W. Archer, editor, *A Reader for Writers*; Alice Childress, *A Hero Ain't Nothin' but a Sandwich*; Eldridge Cleaver, *Soul on Ice*; Langston Hughes, editor, *Best Short Stories by Negro Writers*; Oliver La Farge, *Laughing Boy*; Bernard Malamud, *The Fixer*; Desmond Morris, *The Naked Ape*; Piri Thomas, *Down These Mean Streets*; Kurt Vonnegut, *Slaughterhouse Five*; and Richard Wright, *Black Boy*.

As the superintendent of schools had predicted, this suburb of New York City, described by one observer as "usually placid, middle class, and predominantly white," was thrown into turmoil by the board's action. In January 1977 Steven Pico and four other students filed suit against removal of the books. Four years of legal action followed. The students maintained that their First Amendment rights to be free of "the pall of orthodoxy" had been infringed, while the board held that it had unlimited power to indoctrinate students in community values and to protect traditional morality. As the school board president stated the matter, the question was "whether parents have the right to exercise power over what is taught in public schools they pay for." The books banned, it was argued, were anti-American, anti-Christian, anti-Semitic, and just plain dirty. The American Civil Liberties Union, acting on behalf of the students, claimed that the board's decision was politically based, was not founded on educational criteria, and violated the First Amendment.

A district court supported the school board and denied a trial. In March 1981, however, a U.S. Circuit Court of Appeals disagreed and ordered that the case be brought to trial. The school board then appealed to the U.S. Supreme Court, and the high court agreed to hear the case. The ACLU was joined by the Association of American Publishers, American Booksellers Association, the American Library Association, and five other groups in filing friends of the court briefs. Among those directly interested in the outcome were librarians, literary agents, book publishers and distributors, writers, and book stores.

It was assumed that whatever the justices decided would have an impact on the entire issue of school board censorship and, furthermore, could have an impact beyond schools. A clear-cut decision was hoped for. The Supreme Court heard arguments on March 2, 1982. In the process, the justices expressed concern over the failure of either side to suggest guidelines that school boards might follow in deciding to censor books.

On June 25, 1982, a deeply divided Supreme Court rendered its decision. It ruled that the Island Trees school board may have erred in removing nine books from its public school libraries, but the justices failed to come up with a new rule that would guide the nation's school boards on the limits of their power to remove controversial books from schools. A bare majority of five justices agreed only that the dispute had to be sent back to a federal court to see if the school board members had "constitutionally valid concerns that justified their removal of the books"; only three justices agreed with Justice William J. Brennan's opinion that would sharply limit the power of officials to remove such books. Four justices would give broad discretion to officials to ban books they find offensive: Chief Justice Warren Burger wrote that subjecting a school board's actions to federal review would bring the Supreme Court perilously close to becoming a "super-censor" of school board library decisions. The court's decision contained no binding precedent for future cases.

Following is a summary of the U.S. Supreme Court decision in the Island Trees case.

R. Bruce Rich

THE SUPREME COURT'S DECISION IN ISLAND TREES

On June 25, 1982, the United States Supreme Court announced its long-awaited decision in the celebrated school book censorship case involving the removal of nine well-known works from the school library shelves of the Island Trees Union Free School District in Long Island, New York. The case posed for the Court the issue of whether and, if so, in what circumstances, such book removals in the school setting can deprive students of their First Amendment rights. Not surprisingly, the Court divided sharply on the issue, with the decision reflected in seven separate opinions, none of which commanded a majority of the Justices. Nevertheless, a majority of the Court voted to return the case for further trial proceedings to determine the underlying motivations of the local school board in removing the books, thereby preserving the First Amendment claims of the students and rejecting the notion that there are not potential constitutional constraints on school board actions in this area. Viewed in this light, the decision, for all of its uncertainties, must be regarded as a significant victory for the proponents of a vigorous First Amendment and of the freedom to read.

THE COURT'S DECISION

Justice Brennan, writing for four of the Justices, stated the issue presented by the *Island Trees* case in extremely narrow terms: whether the First Amendment limits the discretion of a local school board to remove library books from junior and senior high school library shelves. The case, Justice Brennan emphasized, did not involve the school board's discretion to prescribe the curricula of the schools; neither did it deal

Reprinted from *Newsletter on Intellectual Freedom* 31 (5): 149, 173–81 (September 1982).

with the *acquisition* of the books for a school library.

As to the narrow issue presented, Justice Brennan, with Justices Marshall, Stevens and Blackmun, determined that there are indeed constitutional limitations on the school board's authority: "We think that the First Amendment rights of students may be directly and sharply implicated by the removal of books from the shelves of a school library." In what circumstances? Here the four Justices found the school board's motivations essential:

Our Constitution does not permit the official suppression of *ideas*. . . . If [the school board] *intended* by their removal decision to deny [the students] access to ideas with which [the school board] disagreed, and if this intent was a decisive factor in [the school board's] decision, then [the school board] *intended* by their removal decision to deny [the students] access to ideas with which [the school board] disagreed, and if this intent was a decisive factor in [the school board's] decision, then [the school board] have exercised their discretion in violation of the Constitution. . . . [emphasis in original]
[W]e hold that local school boards may not remove books from school library shelves simply because they dislike the ideas contained in those books and seek by their removal to "pre-scribe what shall be orthodox in politics, nationalism, religion, or other matters of opinion". . . . Such purposes stand inescapably condemned by our precedents.

In reaching its conclusion, the Brennan opinion relies heavily on the concept that the "right to receive ideas" is "a necessary predicate" to the meaningful exercise of speech, press and political freedom. Such access to ideas "prepares students for active and effective participation in the pluralistic, often contentious society in which they will soon be adult members." In this connection, the opinion reasons further, the school library plays an especially important role. Noting that "students must always remain free to inquire, to study and to evaluate," the Brennan opinion concludes that "the school library is the principal locus of such freedom." Since the students' selection of books from the school library "is entirely a matter of free choice," the school board's claim of a duty to inculcate community values was misplaced in the school library, "where the regime of voluntary inquiry holds sway."

Finally noteworthy in the Brennan opinion is the concern over the procedures followed by the school board in reviewing the challenged books. Indicating that "[t]his would be a very different case if the record demonstrated that [the school board] had employed established, regular, and facially unbiased procedures for the review of controversial materials," the opinion expresses concern over the possibility that, instead, the school board had resorted to "highly irregular and ad hoc" removal procedures— "the antithesis of those procedures that might tend to allay suspicions regarding petitioners' motivations."

For four of the Justices, then, whether or not the removals were constitutionally permissible was dependent upon whether or not it was the school board's intent to suppress ideas, to create a "pall of orthodoxy" in the school setting. Short of such intent, these Justices, along with the rest of the Court, appeared willingly to defer to the school board's discretion in removing books that were determined to be, for instance, "educationally unsuitable" or "pervasively vulgar."

The fifth Justice voting to explore the school board's motivations—Justice White—preferred to await the outcome of the trial before expressing an opinion as to the circumstances that would amount to unconstitutional action by the school board. (Justice White's ducking of the constitutional issue presented was roundly criticized by other Justices who expressed the view that, since the Court had agreed to decide the case, it was inappropriate for a member of the Court to refrain from addressing the issue squarely before it.) In spite of Justice White's noncommittal posture, one must conclude from his willingness to explore the school board's motivations further that some set of facts could present themselves which would cause Justice White to conclude that the school board had exceeded their constitutional authority.

Scathing dissents were registered by the remaining four justices—Burger, Powell, Rehnquist and O'Connor. The gist of these dissents was that no substantial restraints had been placed by the school board upon the students (the books could be freely discussed and are available in the public library and bookstores); that there is no constitutional "right of access" to particular books in a school library ("schools in particular ought not to be made a slavish courier of the material of third parties"); and that an analysis of the school board's motivations amounts to an impermissible effort to undermine local school boards' judgments as to the educational suitability of particular materials.

Justice Burger, having cast the issue as involving "whether local schools are to be administered by an elected school board, or by federal judges and teenage pupils," rejected "categorically" the "notion that the Constitution dictates that judges, rather than parents, teachers, and local school boards, must determine how the standards of morality and vulgarity are to be treated in the classroom." Justice Powell, a former school board president, lamented the decision as a "debilitating encroachment upon the institutions of a free people."

The dissenters, with some considerable force, also took Justice Brennan to task for erecting what they perceived to be an unprincipled analytical distinction between library acquisition, on the one hand, and library removals, on the other, as well as between curricular decisions and library removal decisions. As Justice Burger asked rhetorically: "[I]f the First Amendment commands that certain books cannot be *removed*, does it not equally require that the same books be *acquired*? . . . Similarly, a decision to eliminate certain materials from the curriculum, history for example, would carry an equal—probably greater—prospect of 'official suppression'. Would the decision be subject to our review?"

THE SIGNIFICANCE OF THE DECISION

If nothing else, the *Island Trees* decision sends an important message to school officials who may be intent on cleansing school library shelves of works which they view as personally offensive. That message is that such actions will be subject to searching scrutiny—in the federal courts if necessary—to assure that they are properly motivated. More generally, by preserving the students' constitutional claims, the Court placed school library book removals within the class of official conduct in the school setting which is subject to First Amendment limitations.

At the same time, it is important to recognize that the decision contains a number of self-stated limitations, as well as ambiguities. It is thus unclear what, if any, constitutional limitations attend a school system's textbook acquisition decisions, or its library acquisition policies. In this connection, one must wonder how absolutely Justice Brennan intended his statement that "[Local school boards] might well defend their claim of absolute discretion in matters of curriculum by reliance upon their duty to inculcate community values."

Equally unclear is the meaning of such concepts as "pervasive vulgarity" and "educational suitability" as rationales for book removals. Could such terms not be used by a school board intent on developing a "proper" record to justify a vast range of questionable book removals?

Similarly left unclear by the decision is the extent to which procedures must be adopted and adhered to in connection with book removals. Are such procedures a constitutional requirement or is a failure to utilize procedures merely a factor which the courts will examine in evaluating the motivation underlying particular removals?

These and other unresolved issues may or may not be clarified by subsequent court decisions (including a possible further Supreme Court decision in *Island Trees* should the trial proceed and further appeals be taken). In the meanwhile, librarians, publishers and others committed to the First Amendment principles at stake in this area can be pleased that the Supreme Court— even if in less than compelling fashion—has recognized and preserved those principles.

EXCERPTS FROM THE OPINIONS

Justice Brennan

The principal question presented is whether the First Amendment imposes limitations upon the exercise by a local school board of its discretion to remove library books from high school and junior high school libraries. . . .

We emphasize at the outset the limited nature of the substantive question presented by the case before us. . . .

For as this case is presented to us, it does not involve textbooks, or indeed any books that Island Trees students would be required to read. Respondents do not seek in this Court to impose limitations upon their school board's discretion to prescribe the curricula of the Island Trees schools. On the contrary, the only books at issue in this case are *library* books, books that by their nature are optional rather than required reading. Our adjudication of the present case thus does not intrude into the classroom, or into the compulsory courses taught there. Furthermore, even as to library books, the action before us does not involve the *acquisition* of books. Respondents have not sought to compel their school board to add to the school library shelves any books that students desire to read. Rather, the only action challenged in this case is the *removal* from school libraries of books originally placed there by the school authorities, or without objection from them. . . .

The Court has long recognized that local school boards have broad discretion in the management of school affairs. . . .

At the same time, however, we have necessarily recognized that the discretion of the States and local school boards in matters of education must be exercised in a manner that comports with the transcendent imperatives of the First Amendment. . . .

Of course, courts should not "intervene in the resolution of conflicts which arise in the daily operations of school systems" unless "basic constitutional values" are "directly and sharply implicate[d]" in those conflicts. But we think that the First Amendment rights of students may be directly and sharply implicated by the removal of books from the shelves of a school library. Our precedents have focused "not only on the role of the First Amendment in fostering individual self-expression, but also on its role in affording the public access to discussion, debate, and the dissemination of information and ideas." And we have recognized that "the State may not, consistently with the spirit of the First Amendment, contract the spectrum of available knowledge." In keeping with this principle, we have held that in a variety of contexts "the Constitution protects the right to receive information and ideas." This right is an inherent corollary of the rights of free speech and press that are explicitly guaranteed by the Constitution, in two senses. First, the right to receive ideas follows ineluctably from the *sender's* First Amendment right to send them: "The right of freedom of speech and press . . . embraces the right to distribute literature, . . . and necessarily protects the right to receive and consider them. It would be a barren marketplace of ideas that had only sellers and no buyers."

More importantly, the right to receive ideas is a necessary predicate to the *recipient's* meaningful exercise of his own rights of speech, press, and political freedom. Madison admonished us that "A popular Government, without popular information, or the means of acquiring it, is but a Prologue to a Farce or a Tragedy; or, perhaps both. Knowledge will forever govern ignorance: And a people who mean to be their own Governors, must arm themselves with the power which knowledge gives."

. . . In sum, just as access to ideas makes it possible for citizens generally to exercise their rights of free speech and press in a meaningful manner, such access prepares students for active and effective participation in the pluralistic, often contentious society in which they will soon be adult members. Of course all First Amendment rights accorded to students must be construed "in light of the special characteristics of the school environment." But the special characteristics of the school *library* make that environment especially appropriate for the recognition of the First Amendment rights of students.

A school library, no less than any other public library, is "a place dedicated to quiet, to knowledge, and to beauty." *Keyishian* v. *Board of Regents* observed that "students must always remain free to inquire, to study and to evaluate, to gain new maturity and understanding." The school library is the principal locus of such freedom. . . .

Petitioners emphasize the inculcative function of secondary education, and argue that they must be allowed *unfettered* discretion to "transmit community values" through the Island Trees schools. But that sweeping claim overlooks the unique role of the school library. It appears from the record that use of the Island Trees school libraries is completely voluntary on the part of students.

Their selection of books from these libraries is entirely a matter of free choice; the libraries afford them an opportunity at self-education and individual enrichment that is wholly optional. Petitioners might well defend their claim of absolute discretion in matters of *curriculum* by reliance upon their duty to inculcate community values. But we think that petitioners' reliance upon that duty is misplaced where, as here, they attempt to extend their claim of absolute discretion beyond the compulsory environment of the classroom, into the school library and the regime of voluntary inquiry that there holds sway.

In rejecting petitioners' claim of absolute discretion to remove books from their school libraries, we do not deny that local school boards have a substantial legitimate role to play in the determination of school library content. We thus must turn to the question of the extent to which the First Amendment places limitations upon the discretion of petitioners to remove books from their libraries. In this inquiry we enjoy the guidance of several precedents. . . .

As noted earlier, nothing in our decision today affects in any way the discretion of a local school board to choose books to *add* to the libraries of their schools. Because we are concerned in this case with the suppression of ideas, our holding today affects only the discretion to *remove* books. In brief, we hold that local school boards may not remove books from school library shelves simply because they dislike the ideas contained in those books and seek by their removal to "prescribe what shall be orthodox in politics, nationalism, religion, or other matters of opinion." Such purposes stand inescapably condemned by our precedents.

. . . This would be a very different case if the record demonstrated that petitioners had employed established, regular, and facially unbiased procedures for the review of controversial materials. But the actual record in the case before us suggests the exact opposite. Petitioners' removal procedures were vigorously challenged below by respondents, and the evidence on this issue sheds further light on the issue of petitioners' motivations. Respondents alleged that in making their removal decision petitioners ignored "the advice of literary experts," the view of "librarians and teachers within the Island Trees Schools system," the advice of the superintendent of schools, and the guidance of "publications that rate books for junior and senior high school students." Respondents also claimed that petitioners' decision was based solely on the fact that the books were named on the PONYU list received by petitioners Ahrens, Martin, and Hughes, and that petitioners "did not undertake an independent review of other books in the [school] libraries." Evidence before the District Court lends support to these claims. The record shows that immediately after petitioners first ordered the books removed from the library shelves, the superintendent of schools reminded them that "we already have a policy . . . designed expressly to handle such problems," and recommended that the removal decision be approached through this established channel. But the Board disregarded the superintendent's advice, and instead resorted to the extraordinary procedure of appointing a Book Review Committee—the advice of which was later rejected without explanation. In sum, respondents' allegations and some of the evidentiary materials presented below do not rule out the possibility that petitioners' removal procedures were highly irregular and ad hoc—the antithesis of those procedures that might tend to allay suspicions regarding petitioners' motivations.

Justice Blackmun

In combination . . . with more generally applicable First Amendment rules . . . the cases outlined above yield a general principle: the State may not suppress exposure to ideas—for the sole *purpose* of suppressing exposure to those ideas— absent sufficiently compelling reasons. Because the school board must perform all its functions "within the limits of the Bill of Rights," this principle necessarily applies in at least a limited way to public education. Surely this is true in an extreme case: as the plurality notes, it is difficult to see how a school board, consistent with the First Amendment, could refuse for political reasons to buy books written by Democrats or by Negroes, or books that are "anti-American" in the broadest sense of that term. Indeed Justice Rehnquist appears "cheerfully [to] concede" this point.

In my view, then, the principle involved here is both narrower and more basic than the "right to receive information" identified by the plurality. I do not suggest that the State has any affirmative obligation to provide students with information or ideas, something that may well be associated with a "right to receive." And I do not believe, as the plurality suggests, that the right at issue here is somehow associated with the peculiar nature of the school library; if schools may be used to inculcate ideas, surely libraries may play a role in that

process. Instead, I suggest that certain forms of state discrimination *between* ideas are improper. In particular, our precedents command the conclusion that the state may not act to deny access to an idea simply because state officials disapprove of that idea for partisan or political reasons.

Certainly, the unique environment of the school places substantial limits on the extent to which official decisions may be restrained by First Amendment values. But that environment also makes it particularly important that *some* limits be imposed. The school is designed to, and inevitably will, inculcate ways of thought and outlooks; if educators intentionally may eliminate all diversity of thought, the school will "strangle the free mind at its source and teach youth to discount important principles of our government as mere platitudes." As I see it, then, the question in this case is how to make the delicate accommodation between the limited constitutional restriction that I think is imposed by the First Amendment, and the necessarily broad state authority to regulate education. In starker terms, we must reconcile the schools' "inculcative" function with the First Amendment's bar on "prescriptions of orthodoxy."

In my view, we strike a proper balance here by holding that school officials may not remove books for the *purpose* of restricting access to the political ideas or social perspectives discussed in them, when that action is motivated simply by the officials' disapproval of the ideas involved. It does not seem radical to suggest that state action calculated to suppress novel ideas or concepts is fundamentally antithetical to the values of the First Amendment. At a minimum, allowing a school board to engage in such conduct hardly teaches children to respect the diversity of ideas that is fundamental to the American system. In this context, then, the school board must "be able to show that its action was caused by something more than a mere desire to avoid the discomfort and unpleasantness that always accompany an unpopular viewpoint," and that the board had something in mind in addition to the suppression of partisan or political views it did not share.

As I view it, this is a narrow principle. School officials must be able to choose one book over another, without outside interference, when the first book is deemed more relevant to the curriculum, or better written, or when one of a host of other politically neutral reasons is present. These decisions obviously will not implicate First Amendment values. And even absent space or financial limitations, First Amendment principles would allow a school board to refuse to make a book available to students because it contains offensive language, or because it is psychologically or intellectually inappropriate for the age group, or even, perhaps, because the ideas it advances are "manifestly inimical to the public welfare." And, of course, school officials may choose one book over another because they believe that one subject is more important, or is more deserving of emphasis. . . .

Concededly, a tension exists between the properly inculcative purposes of public education and any limitation on the school board's absolute discretion to choose academic materials. but that tension demonstrates only that the problem here is a difficult one, not that the problem should be resolved by choosing one principle over another. As the Court has recognized, school officials must have the authority to make educationally appropriate choices in designing a curriculum: "the State may 'require teaching by instruction and study of all in our history and in the structure and organization of our government, including the guaranties of civil liberty, which tend to inspire patriotism and love of country.' " Thus school officials may seek to instill certain values "by persuasion and example," or by choice of emphasis. That sort of positive educational action, however, is the converse of an intentional attempt to shield students from certain ideas that officials find politically distasteful.

Chief Justice Burger

The First Amendment, as with other parts of the Constitution, must deal with new problems in a changing world. In an attempt to deal with a problem in an area traditionally left to the states, a plurality of the Court, in a lavish expansion going beyond any prior holding under the First Amendment, expresses its view that a school board's decision concerning what books are to be in the school library is subject to federal court review. Were this to become the law, this Court would come perilously close to becoming a "super censor" of the school board library decisions. Stripped to its essentials, the issue comes down to two important propositions: *first*, whether local schools are to be administered by elected school boards, or by federal judges and teenage pupils; and *second*, whether the values of morality, good taste, and relevance to education are valid reasons for school board decisions concerning the contents of a school library. In an attempt to place this case within the protection of the First Amend-

ment, the plurality suggests a new "right" that, when shorn of the plurality's rhetoric, allows this Court to impose its own views about what books must be made available to students.

I agree with the fundamental proposition that "students do not 'shed their rights to freedom of speech or expression at the schoolhouse gate.' " For example, the Court has held that a school board cannot compel a student to participate in a flag salute ceremony, or *prohibit* a student from expressing certain views, so long as that expression does not disrupt the educational process. Here, however, no restraints of any kind are placed on the students. They are free to read the books in question, which are available at public libraries and bookstores; they are free to discuss them in the classroom or elsewhere. Despite this absence of any direct external control on the students' ability to express themselves, the plurality suggest that there is a new First Amendment "entitlement" to have access to particular books in a school library.

. . . The apparent underlying basis of the plurality's view seems to be that students have an enforceable "right" to receive the information and ideas that are contained in junior and senior high school library books. This "right" purportedly follows "ineluctably" from the sender's First Amendment right to freedom of speech and as a "necessary predicate" to the recipient's meaningful exercise of his own rights of speech, press, and political freedom. No such right, however, has previously been recognized.

. . . In short, even assuming the desirability of the policy expressed by the plurality, there is not a hint in the First Amendment, or in any holding of this Court, of a "right" to have the government provide continuing access to certain books.

Whatever role the government might play as a conduit of information, schools in particular ought not be made a slavish courier of the material of third parties. The plurality pays homage to the ancient verity that in the administration of the public schools "there is a legitimate and substantial community interest in promoting respect for authority and traditional values be they social, moral, or political." If, as we have held, schools may legitimately be used as vehicles for "inculcating fundamental values necessary to the maintenance of a democratic political system," school authorities must have broad discretion to fulfill that obligation. Presumably all activity within a primary or secondary school involves the conveyance of information and at least an implied approval of the worth of that information. How are "fundamental values" to be inculcated except by having school boards make content-based decisions about the appropriateness of retaining materials in the school library and curriculum. In order to fulfill its function, an elected school board *must* express its views on the subjects which are taught to its students. In doing so those elected officials express the views of their community; they may err, of course, and the voters may remove them. It is a startling erosion of the very idea of democratic government to have this Court arrogate to itself the power the plurality asserts today.

The plurality concludes that under the Constitution school boards cannot choose to retain or dispense with books if their discretion is exercised in a "narrowly partisan or political manner." The plurality concedes that permissible factors are whether the books are "pervasively vulgar," or educationally unsuitable. "Educational suitability," however, is a standardless phrase. This conclusion will undoubtedly be drawn in many—if not most—instances because the decision-maker's content-based judgment that the ideas contained in the book or the idea expressed from the author's method of communication are inappropriate for teenage pupils.

The plurality also tells us that a book may be removed from a school library if it is "pervasively vulgar." But why must the vulgarity be "pervasive" to be offensive? Vulgarity might be concentrated in a single poem or a single chapter or a single page, yet still be inappropriate. Or a school board might reasonably conclude that even "random" vulgarity is inappropriate for teenage school students. A school board might also reasonably conclude that the school board's retention of such books gives those volumes an implicit endorsement.

Further, there is no guidance whatsoever as to what constitutes "political" factors. This Court has previously recognized that public education involves an area of broad public policy and "go[es] to the heart of representative government." As such, virtually all educational decisions necessarily involve "political" determinations.

What the plurality views as valid reasons for removing a book at their core involve partisan judgments. Ultimately the federal courts will be the judge of whether the motivation for book removal was "valid" or "reasonable." Undoubtedly the validity of many book removals will ultimately turn on a judge's evaluation of the books. Discretion must be used, and the appropri-

ate body to exercise that discretion is the local elected school board, not judges.

We can all agree that as a matter of *educational policy* students should have wide access to information and ideas. But the people elect school boards, who in turn select administrators, who select the teachers, and these are the individuals best able to determine the substance of that policy. The plurality fails to recognize the fact that local control of education involves democracy in a microcosm. In most public schools in the United States the *parents* have a large voice in running the school. Through participation in the election of school board members, the parents influence, if not control, the direction of their childrens' education. A school board is not a giant bureaucracy far removed from accountability for its actions; it is truly "of the people and by the people." A school board reflects its constituency in a very real sense and thus could not long exercise unchecked discretion in its choice to acquire or remove books. If the parents disagree with the educational decisions of the school board, they can take steps to remove the board members from office. Finally, even if parents and students cannot convince the school board that book removal is inappropriate, they have alternative sources to the same end. Books may be acquired from book stores, public libraries, or other alternative sources unconnected with the unique environment of the local public schools.

Through use of bits and pieces of prior opinions unrelated to the issue of this case, the plurality demeans our function of constitutional adjudication. Today the plurality suggests that the *Constitution* distinguishes between school libraries and school classrooms, between *removing* unwanted books and *acquiring* books. Even more extreme, the plurality concludes that the Constitution *requires* school boards to justify to its teenage pupils the decision to remove a particular book from a school library. I categorically reject this notion that the Constitution dictates that judges, rather than parents, teachers, and local school boards, must determine how the standards of morality and vulgarity are to be treated in the classroom.

Justice Powell

The plurality opinion today rejects a basic concept of public school education in our country: that the States and locally elected school boards should have the responsibility for determining the educational policy of the public schools. After today's decision any junior high school student, by instituting a suit against a school board or teacher, may invite a judge to overrule an educational decision by the official body designated by the people to operate the schools.

School boards are uniquely local and democratic institutions. Unlike the governing bodies of cities and counties, school boards have only one responsibility: the education of the youth of our country during their most formative and impressionable years. Apart from health, no subject is closer to the hearts of parents than their children's education during those years. For these reasons, the governance of elementary and secondary education traditionally has been placed in the hands of a local board, responsible locally to the parents and citizens of school districts. Through parent-teacher associations (PTAs), and even less formal arrangements that vary with schools, parents are informed and often may influence decisions of the board. Frequently, parents know the teachers and visit classes. It is fair to say that no single agency of government at any level is closer to the people whom it serves than the typical school board.

I therefore view today's decision with genuine dismay. Whatever the final outcome of this suit and suits like it, the resolution of educational policy decisions through litigation, and the exposure of school board members to liability for such decisions, can be expected to corrode the school board's authority and effectiveness. . . .

The plurality's reasoning is marked by contradiction. It purports to acknowledge the traditional role of school boards and parents in deciding what should be taught in the schools. It states the truism that the schools are "vitally important 'in the preparation of individuals for participation as citizens,' and as vehicles for 'inculcating fundamental values necessary to the maintenance of a democratic political system.' " Yet when a school board, as in this case, takes its responsibilities seriously and seeks to decide what the fundamental values are that should be imparted, the plurality finds a constitutional violation.

. . . A school board's attempt to instill in its students the ideas and values on which a democratic system depends is viewed as an impermissible suppression of other ideas and values on which other systems of government and other societies thrive. Books may not be removed because they are indecent; extoll violence, intolerance and racism; or degrade the dignity of the individual. Human history, not the least of the twentieth century, records the power and political life of these very ideas. But they are not our ideas or values.

Although I would leave this educational decision to the duly constituted board, I certainly would not require a school board to promote ideas and values repugnant to a democratic society or to teach such values to *children*.

In different contexts and in different times, the destruction of written materials has been the symbol of despotism and intolerance. But the removal of nine vulgar or racist books from a high school library by a concerned local school board does not raise this specter. For me, today's decision symbolizes a debilitating encroachment upon the institutions of a free people.

Justice Rehnquist

Considerable light is shed on the correct resolution of the constitutional question in this case by examining the role played by petitioners. Had petitioners been the members of a town council, I suppose all would agree that, absent a good deal more than is present in this record, they could not have prohibited the sale of these books by private booksellers within the municipality. But we have also recognized that the government may act in other capacities than as sovereign, and when it does the First Amendment may speak with a different voice. . . .

With these differentiated roles of government in mind, it is helpful to assess the role of government as educator, as compared with the role of government as sovereign. When it acts as an educator, at least at the elementary and secondary school level, the government is engaged in inculcating social values and knowledge in relatively impressionable young people. Obviously there are innumerable decisions to be made as to what courses should be taught, what books should be purchased, or what teachers should be employed. In every one of these areas the members of a school board will act on the basis of their own personal or moral values, will attempt to mirror those of the community, or will abdicate the making of such decisions to so-called "experts." In this connection I find myself entirely in agreement with the observation of the Court of Appeals for the Seventh Circuit in *Zykan* v. *Warsaw Community School Corp.*, that it is "permissible and appropriate for local boards to make educational decisions based upon their personal social, political and moral views." In the very course of administering the many-faceted operations of a school district, the mere decision to purchase some books will necessarily preclude the possibility of purchasing others. The decision to teach a particular subject may preclude the possibility of teaching another subject. A decision to replace a teacher because of ineffectiveness may by implication be seen as a disparagement of the subject matter taught. In each of these instances, however, the book or the exposure to the subject matter may be acquired elsewhere. The managers of the school district are not proscribing it as to the citizenry in general, but are simply determining that it will not be included in the curriculum or school library. In short, actions by the government as educator do not raise the same First Amendment concerns as actions by the government as sovereign.

Justice Brennan would hold that the First Amendment gives high school and junior high school students a "right to receive ideas" in the school. This right is a curious entitlement. It exists only in the library of the school, and only if the idea previously has been acquired by the school in book form. It provides no protection against a school board's decision not to acquire a particular book, even though that decision denies access to ideas as fully as removal of the book from the library, and it prohibits removal of previously acquired books only if the remover "dislike[s] the ideas contained in those books," even though removal for any other reason also denies the students access to the books. . . .

Education consists of the selective presentation and explanation of ideas. The effective acquisition of knowledge depends upon an orderly exposure to relevant information. Nowhere is this more true than in elementary and secondary schools, where, unlike the broad-ranging inquiry available to university students, the courses taught are those thought most relevant to the young students' individual development. Of necessity, elementary and secondary educators must separate the relevant from the irrelevant, the appropriate from the inappropriate. Determining what information *not* to present to the students is often as important as identifying relevant material. This winnowing process necessarily leaves much information to be discovered by students at another time or in another place, and is fundamentally inconsistent with any constitutionally required eclecticism in public education.

Justice Brennan rejects this idea, claiming that it "overlooks the unique role of library." But the unique role referred to appears to be one of Justice Brennan's own creation. . . .

As already mentioned, elementary and secondary schools are inculcative in nature. The libraries of such schools serve as supplements to this inculcative role. Unlike university or public librar-

ies, elementary and secondary school libraries are not designed for free-wheeling inquiry; they are tailored, as the public school curriculum is tailored, to the teaching of basic skills and ideas. Thus, Justice Brennan cannot rely upon the nature of school libraries to escape the fact that the First Amendment right to receive information simply has no application to the one public institution which, by its very nature, is a place for the selective conveyance of ideas. After all else is said, however, the most obvious reason that petitioners' removal of the books did not violate respondents' right to receive information is the ready availability of the books elsewhere. Students are not denied books by their removal from a school library. The books may be borrowed from a public library, read at a university library, purchased at a bookstore, or loaned by a friend. The government as educator does not seek to reach beyond the confines of the school. Indeed, following the removal from the school library of the books at issue in this case, the local public library put all nine books on display for public inspection. Their contents were fully accessible to any inquisitive student.

Intertwined as a basis for Justice Brennan's opinion, along with the "right to receive information," is the statement that "our Constitution does not permit the official suppression of *ideas*." There would be few champions, I suppose, of the idea that our Constitution *does* permit the official suppression of ideas; my difficulty is not with the admittedly appealing catchiness of the phrase, but with my doubt that it is really a useful analytical tool in solving difficult First Amendment problems. Since the phrase appears in the opinion "out of the blue," without any reference to previous First Amendment decisions of this Court, it would appear that the Court for years has managed to decide First Amendment cases without it.

I would think that prior cases decided under established First Amendment doctrine afford adequate guides in this area without resorting to a phrase which seeks to express "a complicated process of constitutional adjudication by a deceptive formula." A school board which publicly adopts a policy forbidding the criticism of United States foreign policy by any student, any teacher, or any book on the library shelves is indulging in one kind of "suppression of ideas." A school board which adopts a policy that there shall be no discussion of current events in a class for high school sophmores devoted to second-year Latin "suppresses ideas" in quite a different context. A teacher who had a lesson plan consisting of 14 weeks of study of

United States history from 1607 to the present time, but who because of a week's illness is forced to forego the most recent 20 years of American history, may "suppress ideas" in still another way.

In the case before us the petitioners may in one sense be said to have "suppressed" the "ideas" of vulgarity and profanity, but that is hardly an apt description of what was done. They ordered the removal of books containing vulgarity and profanity, but they did not attempt to preclude discussion about the themes of the books or the books themselves. Such a decision, on respondents' version of the facts in this case, is sufficiently related to "educational suitability" to pass muster under the First Amendment.

Justice O'Connor

If the school board can set the curriculum, select teachers, and determine initially what books to purchase for the school library, it surely can decide which books to discontinue or remove from the school library so long as it does not also interfere with the right of students to read the material and to discuss it. . . .

I do not personally agree with the board's action with respect to some of the books in question here, but it is not the function of the courts to make the decisions that have been properly relegated to the elected members of school boards. It is the school board that must determine educational suitability, and it has done so in this case.

On August 14, 1982, it was reported that after six years of banishment, *Slaughterhouse Five, The Naked Ape, Soul on Ice* and six other books were back on the Island Trees school library shelves. The school board voted six to one to return the books to the schools, two months after the Supreme Court decision. School librarians are required, however, to inform parents of children who check out any of the nine books.

Despite the fragmented Supreme Court ruling, librarians, civil liberties advocates, and book publishers generally interpreted the decision as a victory. As stated by the attorney for the ACLU, "It sends a very important message to school boards: act carefully."

Commenting on the Island Trees case and the Supreme Court action, a well-known columnist Jeffrey M. Shaman wrote in the *Chicago Tribune* (July 29, 1982):

A school library is an integral part of the marketplace of ideas. It has been eloquently described as a place where a student can explore the unknown and discover thoughts and information not covered by the prescribed curriculum. The student learns that a library is a place for testing ideas, expanding upon them, a place for self-education and enrichment.

Baileyville

A third school library censorship controversy that received wide publicity arose in a small northeastern Maine community, Baileyville, and centered on a single book. Acting on the complaint of parents of a high school student, the school committee of Baileyville voted to remove *365 Days*, Dr. Ronald Glasser's graphic account of a year spent treating wounded soldiers in Vietnam. At first the book was placed on a reserved shelf in the high school library, to be read only with parents' permission, and later it was completely banned.

According to the chairman of the Baileyville school committee, the book was taken off the library's shelves not because it dealt with the Vietnam War or because of its anti-war theme but because of the "offensive and abusive language" soldiers are quoted as using. The book's publisher, George Braziller, wrote to the chairman:

I would ask you to reconsider your decision for the sake of your students, the ideals of education and knowledge, and also the freedom of speech and thought. We shall not be protecting our youth if we swathe them in ignorance, nor shall we earn or deserve their respect, if we cannot place enough trust and faith in them to reason and respond on their own behalves.

Another communication to the chairman came from Harrison E. Salisbury, president of the Authors League, who wrote:

Each book banning by a school board increases the tide of suppression that threatens the freedom of the First Amendment. Today your board restrains a book a few parents disapprove. Tomorrow, other parents may urge you to ban books they dislike. Ultimately, if the Amendment continues to be eroded by such restraints, others may deny your board's members the right to read books they choose.

Salisbury added,

Offensive language in books does not hurt high school students, but a restriction of their freedom to read will injure them. It stunts their intellectual development; it offends their dignity; and it feeds the process of censorship that threatens their most precious heritage as citizens in a democratic society—the full freedom to exercise their rights under the First Amendment.

With help from a Maine Civil Liberties Union attorney, three parents and a former student filed a class action suit against the Baileyville school committee, seeking a permanent injunction to order the committee to restore *365 Days* to the high school library. The class in the complaint filed in federal district court represented "adult community residents, present students and future students within School Union No. 107 who have access to and use of the library located at Woodland High School." The plaintiffs argued that the school committee violated their civil rights of "freedom of access and freedom of expression under the First Amendment and procedural due process under the Fourteenth Amendment."

The complaint also charged that "the school committee and individual defendants categorized certain words taken out of context from *365 Days* as being 'offensive and abusive' " Furthermore, "that prior and up to April 28, 1981, individual defendants had not read *365 Days* in its entirety; that upon information and belief up to the filing of this complaint, said individual defendants still have not read *365 Days* in its entirety."

Early in 1982, a federal district judge granted the temporary injunction requested, ordering the Baileyville school committee to return *365 Days* to the shelves of the Woodland High School library. Judge Conrad K. Cyr found that the school committee's actions had violated the plaintiff's First and Fourteenth Amendment rights. His opinion stated, "As long as words convey ideas, federal courts must remain on First Amendment alert in book banning cases, even those ostensibly based strictly on vocabulary considerations. The less vigilant rule would leave the care of the flock to the fox that is only after their feathers." The decision came after two days of hearings held in the district court at Bangor. Among those testifying for the plaintiffs were the author, Dr. Glasser; Ward Just, writer for the *Atlantic*; and Frances Fitzgerald, author of *Fire in the Lake*, a history of the Vietnam War. Amicus briefs were submitted by the Authors League, George Braziller, the publisher, the Maine Teachers Association, and the Maine Library Association.

In his fourteen-page decision, Judge Cyr made clear that the First Amendment included high school students. As he wrote, "Public schools are major marketplaces for ideas, and First Amendment rights must be accorded all 'persons' in the market for ideas, including secondary school students." The judge added:

It stands to reason that the state may have a greater responsibility to protect youth from obscenity than from materials merely deemed objectionable on vocabulary grounds. Yet the state may not impede individual expression even on obscenity grounds except in accordance with judicially supervised standards requiring a showing that the challenged expression, taken as a whole lacks "serious literary, artistic, political, or scientific value" and "appeals to prurient interest in sex."

The judge did not accept defense arguments that the committee's action was not intended to limit free speech. He wrote, "How anomalous and dangerous then to *presume* that state action banning an entire book, where the social value of the content is roundly praised and stands unchallenged by the state, does not directly and sharply implicate First Amendment rights because the ban was not *intended* to suppress ideas." The judge also found serious fault with the procedures followed by the school committee, which did not set up a policy for challenged material until after it had voted to ban *365 Days*, and then decided to exclude *365 Days* from the newly enacted policy. The judge questioned the committee's judgment, noting:

The Committee's rationale was neither articulated nor memorialized. The record discloses no finding that harm might result to students exposed to the coarse language in *365 Days*. It may be considered implicit in the Committee vote that three of its members found the language "objectionable," but it does not appear that the ban was predicated on a *Committee* determination that exposure might be harmful to students. Two committee members testified that certain words in *365 Days* were considered *inappropriate* for use by or to students, but no evidence has been presented that even three committee members believed that harm might result to all students exposed to such language.

In conclusion, the judge suggested that the book ban might also be unconstitutionally overturned:

The entire book has been banned, not only its "objectionable" language. The ban applies to adults as well as students and to mature as well as immature students, regardless of their age or sophistication. The ban prohibits peaceable possession of private copies of the book anywhere on school property, including buses.

The foregoing account of the Baileyville case is based in part on John Mutter's report in the *Publishers Weekly*, February 2, 1982. A lively, detailed, and often entertaining story, "Banned in Baileyville," was written by Scott Campbell.

Scott Campbell

BANNED IN BAILEYVILLE

Out past Brewer, out past Beddington, out past Wesley, Crawford and Alexander, 100 miles from Bangor, at the edge of the eastern time zone, lies the town of Baileyville. Thirty-three sqaure miles stretched out along the banks of the St. Croix River, the border separating Maine from New Brunswick, Canada, it is home to 2,167 people, 2,166 of whom are white. Its primary settlement, Woodland, was established in 1905 when the St. Croix paper mill was built. In 1963, the Georgia-Pacific Corporation bought the St. Croix Paper Company and now runs the pulp and paper mill there, plus a stud sawmill and a plywood plant. Except for a few months of tourism, it is the only industry in the entire county. As anyone in Woodland will tell you: "If it weren't for Georgia-Pacific, none of us would be here at all."

It is a simple, friendly town, not at all as isolated or fearful as one might expect from its remoteness. It is, after all, on Route 1, so the townsfolk are accustomed to having passers-by around; and they get eight TV channels, including Toronto and Atlanta, on cable. They are in touch with the world.

The central core of the village consists of maybe a dozen blocks of frame houses across the tracks from the mill. On the fringes of that settlement and scattered around the countryside, people live largely in housetrailers set up on cinder blocks. Some of the people are poor enough that when their young start growing too fast, instead of buying new shoes for them, cut toe-holes in the old ones. In a place like this, where

winter comes early and stays well past its welcome, the comforts of church can come in handy. That may be why, in a town which tends to have just one of everything—one beauty shop, one library, one liquor store, one high school—there are no fewer than five churches (Baptist, Catholic, Methodist, Episcopal and Pentecostal) and radio programs which play "contemporary Christian music." According to the radio preachers, in between rock 'n' roll songs about Jesus, you do not have to get educated, or obey the Ten Commandments, or even go to church every day or follow a bunch of church rules. All you have to do is to believe in Jesus Christ, and invoke His name when you pray. "People who pray and omit the name of Christ," pronounces Pastor Roy Blevins of the Woodland Baptist Church, "their prayer will not be heard. Never gets above the ceiling."

Carol Davenport was born and raised in this environment. An agreeable, soft-spoken woman, she has had, so far in her life, five husbands and three 18-wheel logging trucks—trucks which she sometimes drives herself (her handle is "Diamond Girl") and sometimes hires others to drive. A year ago last March, she joined the Woodland Baptist Church. One month later, her daughter Betsy—15 years old and a ninth-grader—signed a book out of the school library, grew bored with it, and passed it along to a friend on the school bus. That night, Carol Davenport got a call from the mother of Betsy's friend, Sandy Turner. She wanted to know if Mrs. Davenport knew what her daughter was reading. There were lots of dirty words in it. "I was quite shocked," Mrs. Davenport told me later, "when I saw what they were reading. That they got it in the school library."

It is tempting to speculate that what happened next happened because Carol Davenport was embarrassed in front of her friend, that she felt somehow responsible for the fact that Mrs. Turner's daughter had gotten this book from Betsy, and therefore felt a responsibility to do something about it— something more than simply asking Betsy not to read it. It is also tempting to speculate that Mrs. Davenport was especially embarrassed because she had just become a member of the Baptist Church. But she does not see it that way. From her point of view, her motivation was as simple as she said it. She stated her feelings simply, and with an air of innocence. "It was just so repetitious," she said. "It would be just as good a story without using all that language. I don't think any writing needs to include four-letter words."

Taking the book from her daughter and engaging the help of her husband, she started talking to people. She talked to the high school principal. She talked to the librarian. She talked to her pastor, Roy Blevins, who promptly talked to four other people in the community. She talked to Thomas Golden, Chairman of the School Committee, and finally talked to Raymond Freve, the Superintendent of Schools, urging that the book be removed. She says she never intended to try to shackle the minds of the children of Woodland, or to impose her political or social views on anyone. She was simply reacting to a personal sense of propriety.

At the School Committee meeting on April 28, the Superintendent presented photocopies of parts of Chapter Eight, and read some reviews of the book aloud. The committee discussed it briefly, then voted 5-to-0 for removal. Neither Carol Davenport, nor her husband, nor the Pastor Roy Blevins, nor the Superintendent of Schools, nor the School Committee members had read the book before it was banned.

The book was *365 Days*. It was written by Ronald Glasser, a pediatrician assigned to one of several Army hospitals in Japan during the Vietnam War, to treat the children of the military dependents there. He wasn't there long before he realized that the soldiers who were being lifted in from combat—on the average of 6,000–8,000 a month—were little more than children themselves: teenagers struggling to survive their 365-day tour of duty and often not succeeding. Trained in school to ask his patients how they felt and what had happened to them, Glasser listened in horror to the boys' combat experiences. *365 Days* is a collection of some of the stories they told him, often in their own words.

When it was released in 1971, the book was praised by all its reviewers and nominated for a National Book Award. *The Library Journal* called it "a moving, well-written book for all libraries." But for all its critical praise, it was not always well received. When it was performed as a play that year at the Kennedy Center, some members of the audience, upset by the four-letter words and by the gruesome descriptions of injuries, got up and started to leave the theater. Others blocked their way, insisting they stay and pay attention, and it finally broke into a scuffle.

More fighting was never what Glasser intended. He wrote the book, he says in its foreword, "to give something to these kids that was all theirs, without doctrine, something they could use to explain themselves." What the book succeeds in explaining, and the reason a lot of people object, is the experience of being involved in relentless and random murder. Part of the book's success in putting the reader inside that chaos is its fastidiousness of detail: it is so dense with medical and military lingo that its glossary does not begin to be sufficient. The swearing, which is not included in the glossary, might have been: it is every bit as much a part of medical and military lingo as "chopper," "cobra," "nephrectomy" and "bouncing betty."

Just so we know what we're talking about, there are a total of 452 words in the book which might be considered objectionable by one person or another. About 40 per cent of them are "dirty," having mostly to do with body parts and functions. The other 60 per cent or so are to do with the loss of those body parts and functions, often by a violent and unspeakably painful death. Many of the "dirty" words were spoken by 18- and 19-year-olds who had just awakened, for instance, to find that both their legs were missing. Or who had just returned from a night in the jungle, covered with Viet Cong blood, to find there were no cornflakes left. For high schoolers who some day might be called upon to fight another war like this, it could be an important book. If it hadn't been for Michael Sheck, its banning on April 28 could have been the end of it in Baileyville.

At a time in life when most people are preoccupied with fitting in, Michael Sheck wears his individuality like a badge. When he transferred to Woodland High School that winter from a high school outside Baltimore—his father was retiring to the village where Michael's mother grew up: Grand Lake Stream, just down the road—on his first day of school in Woodland, he wore what he always wore in Baltimore: flannel pants, saddle shoes, a sweater, a tweed jacket and a pair of tortoise-shell horn-rimmed glasses. He had his sights on getting a Ph.D. in theoretical mathematics and physics. Until one of his cousins said hello, most of the other students thought he was a substitute teacher. It did not surprise him in the least. He has always looked older than he is, and has always made friends with older people.

When one of the teachers told him that *365 Days* had been banned, Michael took his friend Heather Beebe and headed straight for the school library. He had been involved in these things before. In Maryland, he had served on a committee which reviewed materials for a sex education program; when the committee chose a book and a film which came into controversy, a suit was ultimately filed and Sheck appeared as a witness. So when the high school librarian told him he couldn't have the book, he knew he had his first piece of admissible evidence, in case it ever came to court, witness carefully arranged.

At the School Committee meeting May 5, Michael and Heather asked the committee members to reconsider their decision. They would not. On the morning of May 18, the day of the next Committee meeting, Michael brought a copy of *365 Days* to school—for which he had had to drive 100 miles, to the Bangor Library—as a way of protesting the ban. At lunchtime, he purposely walked past the principal's office, just to see what would happen. The principal, John Morrison, rose beautifully to the bait. If Sheck did not leave the book in the office, or put it in his car, he said, it would be confiscated just as if it were *Hustler* or *Penthouse*. Since he was leaving at the end of that period anyway, Michael put the book in his car. Along with the second piece of evidence for a possible lawsuit.

That night, the Committee meeting was packed. There were more than 50 people there, students and parents alike, alerted by a front-page article in *The Bangor Daily News*. The student council announced it had voted unanimously to ask the Committee to put the book back on the shelf. Ten of 15 people stood up to add their support to the request. A Methodist minister read a passage from the Song of Solomon and said that that was dirty too, by the standards that were being used, and that they might as well ban the Bible. Three of the Committee members by now had read the book, and two of them had changed their minds about it, agreeing with the townspeople that the book should be put back on the shelves. But when one of them, Susan White, suggested the book be returned to the library on a restricted basis, so students could check it unless their parents filed written objection, her motion was defeated. Only one person at that meeting spoke in favor of the ban. Pastor Roy Blevins, of the Woodland Baptist Church: "I don't see it as banning," he said, "but as selectivity of education." The ban stood.

Michael Sheck was furious. At the next committee meeting, in June, he proffered a formal procedure for reviewing the challenged materials. When the committee decided it needed time to think the proposal over, again he asked that the book be put on a restricted shelf. When the committee again refused, he announced he would sue by August first. At that point, Superintendent Freve stepped in. Sheck's proposal, he reasoned, would put the book on the shelf only over the summer, and no one was likely to check it out over the summer anyway. Persuaded by that logic, Thomas Golden changed his vote and the issue was tabled until August. But by now bad feelings had festered. Sheck had received anonymous phone calls and a few hate letters. One of the letters was reprinted in *The Maine Times*. It read:

Dear Michael,
I hope you burn in hell,
you heathen bastard.
     Signed,
     A Concerned Christian

"Bastard" appeared in the book five times. "Hell" appeared nineteen. "Burn" as in "burned alive" appeared a total of fifty-five times. . . .

By the end of the summer, the Baileyville case had begun to attract some attention in the national media. The TV networks had picked it up, *The Washington Post* and *The New York Times*, and the attention was arousing the nation's awareness and interest. Betsy Davenport got a letter from a boy in Worcester, Mass., who enclosed a button for her to wear. *I read all banned books*, it said. Michael Sheck, by now, was receiving letters from around the country in support of his cause, including one from a former soldier who had served in Vietnam: "Don't let them stop us from telling our story just because of the words we had to use to tell it."

But for all the support he was receiving, Sheck was not all that sure. At times, he became obsessed with the issue: eating, sleeping, drinking the bookban. At times, his parents had to insist that he go out and spend the day fishing, or drive to Canada to fill the car with gas at the lower rates. It wasn't that he was wavering on the principle; it was that he was unsure of how far he really wanted to go. He was leaving for college soon—he didn't have to worry about it—but his family was settled there now and he had a 12-year-old sister who still had to go through the school system. What might a lawsuit bring upon them? In spite of the fact that his mother's family had been in Maine for six generations and his aunt was even the postmistress, his father was from New York City and Michael grew up in Baltimore: in a way, he was an outsider. But he finally decided to

take the case as far as it needed to go. "The chance," he said, "there might be one person who wanted to read that book and didn't get the chance to is what frightened me."

When the school committee convened in August, it was a very different scene from the mobbed Committee meeting in May. Except for Michael and a friend, the only people at the meeting besides the committee members were three newspaper reporters. At the outset, the people had thought it "neat" that Michael was "taking on" the committee, but after an entire summer, their interest had cooled somewhat, as indeed it appears the school committee was hoping Michael's would. At the August meeting, as promised, the Committee adopted a formal review procedure for challenged materials. But when Susan White submitted a motion to put *365 Days* through the newly-adopted process, the motion was voted down. The decision had been made. As stated by Thomas Golden, the School Committee chairman, "It's just that *365 Days* had too much gross language. I think there's a lot better books on war. Books like *The Red Badge of Courage* or *All Quiet on the Western Front*. Maybe I've heard some of these offensive words, but I sure don't use them as part of my vocabulary and I don't like to be around people who use them. I guess that most of John Steinbeck's books also have such words in them, but not that many, and we haven't removed his books."

When Ronald Coles heard Michael's story, he was fascinated with it, and more than a little impressed with Michael. "The kid is brilliant," he told me later. "He is your perfect plaintiff." If Sheck was the perfect plaintiff, however, Ronald Coles may very well have been the perfect prosecutor. An energetic 42, he speaks dramatically, underlining his words with inflection, charging them with enthusiasm. He had had a good practice in New York City until, in the fall of 1976, he decided, at last, to get away from it all and moved to Machias, 35 miles to the south of Baileyville. He set up a new practice and listed himself with the Maine Civil Liberties Union as available for volunteer work. *Sheck* v. *Baileyville* was the first opportunity of his career to argue for the freedom of speech. He worked four weeks, full-time, without pay.

In September, when the class action suit was filed on behalf of the students and parents of students in Baileyville, it named Thomas Golden, Raymond Freve and the other two dissenting members of the School Committee, Clifford McPhee and Stephen Neale, both of whom were also members of the Woodland Baptist Church. It charged them with violation of the plaintiff's civil rights and of the first and fourteenth amendments to the U.S. Constitution—the freedom of speech and due process. It also said that the Committee's action was "unusual, irregular, capricious and arbitrary" and sought a preliminary injunction to place the book back on the shelf for the duration of the suit. When Baileyville's town attorney received his notice of the suit, he passed it along to another lawyer in his Calais office who was familiar with the precedents. At 25, Daniel Lacasse was the youngest and newest member of the firm. He had just graduated from law school.

In a town as small as Baileyville, people can't afford to get too divided over things— all they've got is each other—so the people did not gossip and argue a lot about this case. Once in a while, Carol Davenport might hear some people talking about it when she went to the grocery, but as soon as she rounded the corner they would quickly quiet down. In the Wagon Wheel, the men stood around sipping Bud and waiting their turns to play pool, and the talk was as likely to center on who could identify all fifty states as it was to be about bookbanning. But if anybody had missed the fact there was something going on in town, they could not miss it for long. As the hearing approached, the streets of Woodland were inundated with journalists, photographers and filmmakers, sometimes trying to sneak in the school to get a couple of pictures, sometimes flying overhead in hired helicopters. The press had been alerted.

And they were out in force. On the first day of the hearing in Bangor, a brilliant, biting cold Monday morning before Christmas, the steps to the courthouse were crowded with TV cameras and journalists surrounding a small contingent of veterans dressed in camouflage fatigues. One of the soldiers carried a flag. The others carried hand-lettered signs:

> Censor War, Not History
> The Moral Majority Sent Us There,
>   Now Let Them Listen To What Happened
> War Is Obscene, Not History

On his way into the courthouse, Ron Glasser stopped to chat with the men. Inside, in a third-floor courtroom panelled with acoustic tile, ten rows of spectators collected, the first four rows of whom were the press.

The judge in charge of the hearing was Conrad Cyr, who had been on the federal bench for just two months when *Sheck* vs. *Bailey* came into his courtroom. He began with a curious irony: the four-letter word for intercourse, which was the focus of the hearing, was not to be used in court. It would instead be referred to as The Word. In a situation already ripe with religious overtones, it was an odd choice of euphemisms. Other words were also banned: excrement would be the "s-word," female dogs and illigitmate children would be the "b-words," and so on, until the whole assembly began to sound like Mr. Rogers. In a case where the issue at stake was the banning of those very words, it seemed an inauspicious beginning.

With the rules of play understood, Ronald Coles began by calling Carol Davenport to the stand. He asked her what she thought of the book, and when she answered her voice was quiet, not at all the voice of a crusader: "They didn't need to use that language."

"Mrs. Davenport," Coles went on, "do you know what the purpose of the book is?"

"To teach the children about the war."

Coles asked if she used these words in her conversation. "No," she said. In the last five years? "No," she said. "Or ten."

Coles read her an erotic passage from an unidentified book and asked if that would also offend her to the point of wanting it removed from the library. She replied it would. The passage, Coles revealed, was from James Joyce's *Ulysses*. Would she also want to remove a book for using phrases like "Jewish Devil?" Mrs. Davenport said she would, and Coles introduced *The Merchant of Venice*. Coles then showed Mrs. Davenport certain words in a book which was wrapped in brown paper and asked if she thought the words offensive. She did. He then revealed the book was *Love Story*, and that her daughter had checked the book out of the Woodland High School library the previous spring.

Next Coles called to the stand John Boyce, Mrs. Davenport's fourth husband, who testified that she used the banned words frequently during their marriage, especially during the last six months, and in front of the children. "She had a general vocabulary of four-letter words," he said, and he added he did not think her vocabulary had changed very much. Then John Morrison, the high school principal, testified that he was only joking when he told a teachers' meeting that teachers objecting to the Committee's ruling shouldn't forget who pays them.

Then the writers took the stand: Ron Glasser, Ward Just, Frances Fitzgerald and Gloria Emerson, all of whom had been in Vietnam and written about it. (Fitzgerald won the Pulitzer Prize for *Fire in the Lake* and Emerson won the National Book Award for *Winners and Losers*.) All of them testified that the language used was indigenous and necessary to the story. "They couldn't say 'golly gee,' " said Glasser. "War is not a world of Jane Austen people," said Emerson. "Language lost its conventional meaning over there," said Just. And Frances Fitzgerald testified that some of the soldiers she met swore "sometimes almost exclusively."

When the court adjourned at the end of the day, Carol Davenport and her husband headed quickly for the door. "I was quite upset," she told me later. "I mean, I didn't know why he went about everything the way he did. Taking my ex-husband in and all that. But I guess that's the way he works," she mused. "From what I understand now."

As she pressed her way through the crowd a reporter asked her for an interview, and when she refused, tried to follow her out. At that point, her pastor, Roy Blevins, braced himself in the doorway to block the exit until she could get away. And what happened next depends upon whom you talk to. The reporter claims that Blevins kneed him firmly in the crotch. Blevins admits he brought his knee up, "but nowhere near that high." How high exactly he meant, of course, he was not at liberty to say. That would have been a "b-word."

The next day, Blevins was called to the stand. He testified that he did not try to start a campaign against the book after talking to Mrs. Davenport. "I visited four influential members of the community," he said, "to try to get a pulse of how the community felt about it. I didn't start a campaign, but I was interested in what was going on." He admitted he did advise the Davenports to take their complaint to the School Committee.

Next, two Vietnam veterans were called to testify that the book was accurate in all respects, including the language used. Clifford McPhee took the stand to say he believed that students should be protected from a book that used The Word even once and that he did not believe they should have freedom of choice in a library. "I think the school committee should have the right to set the standards for that school and what they're going to allow in that school."

Michael Sheck testified that he heard The Word used by students "at least once a day", and Heather Beebe reported the book gave her "an outlook on the war I had never had before. I knew next to nothing about Vietnam when I read the book. Vietnam is not a topic of teaching in high schools." With the end of her testimony, Coles rested his case. He had called, all told, thirteen witnesses.

Lacasse did not call any. He simply argued to the judge that the plaintiffs did not demonstrate "irreparable injury," that both Beebe and Sheck had been able to get the book in other places, that Sheck, in fact, had read the book four times. He also cited court decisions indicating a judge should stay out of local school matters unless a "sharp" constitutional violation could be demonstrated. Which, he maintained, was not the case here.

Judge Cyr, in the end, did not agree. When his 34-page decision came out just two days before the Super Bowl, it was far more extensive than anything anyone had anticipated. "As long as words convey ideas," he wrote, "federal courts must remain on first amendment alert in bookbanning cases, even those ostensibly based strictly on vocabulary considerations. A less vigilant rule would leave the care of the flock to the fox that is only after their feathers." On a somewhat less metaphorical note, he went on: "The information and ideas in books placed in a school library by proper authority is protected speech. And the first amendment right of students to receive that information and those ideas is entitled to constitutional protection. A book may not be banned," he continued, "from a public school library in disregard of the requirements of the fourteenth amendment." He went on to say that the Committee action appeared to be seriously deficient because of "procedural irregularity, arbitrariness, vagueness and overbreadth," and in ordering that the book be put back on the school library shelf, he became the first federal judge in history to make such a ruling about a book which had ostensibly been banned only for dirty words.

Coles was ecstatic. "It's the best-written decision on book-banning I've ever seen." he told me. "It's going to make school boards extremely reluctant to ban a book not only on first amendment grounds but on fourteenth amendment due process grounds." Francis Brown, the Baileyville town attorney, was not surprised by the decision. "We told them the most they could expect realistically was a restricted shelf ruling." He said he only wanted to find out whether or not there might be some sort of restriction possible, and what a school board does when faced with pressure to ban a book—a question, according to Lacasse, that really has not been answered yet.

So while the book is back on the shelf, the story is not yet over. Lacasse wants the case to go to trial, admitting to feeling that, in presenting all those witnesses in a preliminary hearing, Coles' approach was akin to going all the way on a first date. As far as Coles is concerned, however, one date was all he needed. But when he submitted a movement to make the injunction permanent, his motion was denied. Both sides instead have been instructed to submit proposals for a challenged book review policy, and to review each other's proposals. What will then be done with these proposals remains to be seen, but the chances are very likely that any book review policies will be significantly affected by the Supreme Court ruling on the Pico case this summer.

Meanwhile, the town of Baileyville has returned to normal. Michael Sheck has gone on to college, Carol Davenport has returned to the village where she grew up, and Pastor Roy Blevins has returned to the radio, plying his preacherly promises at bargain-basement rates: People who pray and omit the name of Christ, their prayer will not be heard. To be heard, you just have to say The Word.

There exists in this world great faith in The Word. The power is believed to be contained in The Word itself. It is a totem, a talisman, a touchstone for the powerless to unending power. In a world where we send our children into the jungle to be maimed and killed, then affect shock at how those children express their terror and rage, the need for words of such power is clear. That is why soldiers sometimes swear "almost exclusively." But in this case, the need for powerful words had an unspoken corollary: if you can save yourself by simply uttering one word, then you can save your children by simply banishing another. You do not have to draw the distinction between the use and abuse of language, do not have to try to explain about pain and rage and powerlessness, do not even have to try to understand those things yourself. All you have to do is invoke one word and ban the other. It is seductively simple.

Of course, not everyone buys that magic, even in Baileyville. But then, as Pastor Roy Blevins says: "A lot of people are confused today about the word of God. . . ."

The denouement of the Baileyville case came on August 27, 1982, when a consent agreement was reached between the opposing forces. The agreement had been sent to U.S. District Judge Conrad Cyr for final approval. The four-page agreement prohibited the school committee from ordering books placed on a "restricted shelf" and empowered a monitor to assure that the agreement was being followed. Under the agreement the school committee would not be allowed to ban, or to use other means than an outright ban, a book from the library, though librarians would still be allowed to use the normal weeding process to remove old, deteriorated or out-of-date books.

Huckleberry Finn

One of the most extraordinary instances of school censorship is aimed at Mark Twain's *The Adventures of Huckleberry Finn*, considered by many critics to be the great American novel. Ironically, a bitter attack on the book originated in the Mark Twain Intermediate School in Fairfax, Virginia. On the recommendation of a committee of faculty, administrators, and parents, the book was restricted to use in the school's library. The charge was racism, and the work was also described as anti-American, hostile to the melting pot theory, the Declaration of Independence, and even the Fourteenth Amendment. Black parents have considered the frequent use of the word *nigger* as demeaning or even traumatic for their children. In defense of the book, the well-known columnist Edwin M. Yoder, Jr., wrote:

In fact, Huck is a "bad" boy—a vagrant, a liar, a pipe-puffing fugitive from respectability and bathtubs. His virtue is that he speaks for the heart against the legalistic morality of his time, when it is regarded as an act of "conscience" to report or help track down a fugitive slave. As Twain himself put it, Huck Finn is "a book of mine where a sound heart and a deformed conscience come into collision and conscience suffers defeat."

Another case arose in Springfield, Illinois, where a high school business teacher filed a complaint against the use of *Huck Finn* in classroom instruction. Robert Doyle of the American Library Association's Office of Intellectual Freedom informed the press that schools in Illinois, Texas, Virginia, and Pennsylvania had received challenges about the book with increasing frequency since 1980. In most cases, according to Doyle, the book had been retained in school libraries but several schools had dropped it from required reading lists.

BANNING TEXTBOOKS

The *National Law Journal* in its May 25, 1981, issue reports that numerous censorship groups concentrating solely on books have sprung up. Mentioned specifically is an organization called Educational Research Analysts of Longview, Texas, operated by Mel and Norma Gabler, who, according to the *Journal*, "have turned reviewing textbooks into a cottage industry, with reviews of thousands of 'objection-able' or 'acceptable' textbooks sent to a mailing list of more than 12,000 parents, teachers or school board members in all 50 states and 25 foreign countries."

The Gablers started with history texts, which were critically examined for feminist bias, negative attitudes toward free enterprise, and preoccupation with ecology. The scope of the enterprise was soon expanded to everything from geology (making certain that the creation theory received as much attention as the theory of evolution) to the New Math. One of the Gabler's primary concerns is economic texts. They charge that textbooks in that field are either Keynesian or socialistic, ignoring or expressing a bias against free enterprise and a free market.

As described by Stephen Arons in "The Crusade to Ban Books" (*Saturday Review*, June 1981, p. 19), the Gablers "provide book 'reviews' that, by quotation and page reference, make it unnecessary for local citizens to read a book in order to condemn it." The Association of American Publishers, in an April 1981 survey report, found that more than half the state-level school officials responding noted the involvement of the Gablers in textbook selection.

A special report issued by the Washington-based organization People for the American Way lays down a broadside against the textbook censorship campaign and proposes to take countermeasures. The text of the report, in part, follows.

People for the American Way

THE TEXAS CONNECTION: COUNTERING THE TEXTBOOK CENSORSHIP CRUSADE

As Texas goes, so goes the nation.
—Professor Edward Jenkinson
Indiana University

Professor Jenkinson isn't referring to pace-setting football teams, trends in oil exploration or the origins of new fashions in western wear. He's talking about the effect that successful textbook censorship campaigns in Texas have on books available to students in schools all over the country.

Texas shapes textbook content through-out the nation for one simple reason: eco-nomics. Texas approves texts at the state level for every school in the state's 1,152 school districts, and it is the second largest textbook purchaser in the nation. A national censorship study explains that "Textbook publishers . . . can rarely afford to turn away potential sales in a major adoption state" like Texas. "Nor can they, in most cases, afford the luxury of maintaining two separate editions. Thus, an edition prepared for Texas or California often becomes the sole edition available nationwide."

In response, some publishers have begun to precensor their new textbooks to ensure they'll meet Texas "standards." For example, publishers dropped the classic short story, "The Lottery" from the national editions of four literature anthologies because the Texas State Textbook Committee re-fused to purchase any books that included the story for Texas schools. Last year, hop-ing to make *The American Heritage Dictionary* acceptable for Texas classrooms, Houghton Mifflin publishing representatives agreed to delete "offensive words" from the dictionary's latest edition.

Anticipating pressure from Radical Right creationism advocates, a number of publishers of biology texts have recently slashed

Reprinted by permission of People for the American Way, 1015 18th St., N.W. Washington, D.C. 20036 their coverage of evolution. Holt, Rinehart & Winston, which publishes a biology book used by almost half the nation's high school biology students, has cut the text's discussion of evolution by 25% in the last four years. Laidlaw Bros. (a division of Doubleday) publishing executive Eugene Frank admits, "You're not going to find the word 'evolution' " in the new textbook, *Experiences in Biology*. Why not? "The reason for self-censorship is to avoid the publicity that would be involved in a controversy over a textbook. We'd like to sell thousands of copies."

The process by which Texas selects textbooks for its schools encourages censorship by vocal minorities. Only those who *object* to books can file formal complaints and testify before the textbook committee each year. Texas citizens who want to *defend* a book or its ideas are excluded from the formal process and have no forum in which to be heard.

HIT LISTS IGNITE TEXTBOOK BATTLES

For almost a decade, the leading objectors to textbook content have been Mel and Norma Gabler of Longview, Texas. Their Educational Research Analysts' full-time staff helps them write textbook "reviews" which are then distributed as hit lists to thousands of censorship activists in communities all over the country.

Reported textbook censorship cases have sky-rocketed 300% since November 1980, according to the American Library Association. The Gablers' "reviews" have ignited textbook controversies in all 50 states; half of all state-level respondents to a national censorship survey reported that the Gablers' censorship campaigns had affected their state's textbook adoption proceedings.

The Gablers warn readers in their numerous national mailings that textbook content "appears so natural, reasonable and convincing" that would-be censors should not risk reading the texts themselves. Instead, the Gablers provide thousands of "detailed reviews [that] can save countless hours of painstaking work."

In their *Handbook No. 1*, the Gablers warn:

As long as the schools continue to teach ABNORMAL ATTITUDES and ALIEN THOUGHTS, we caution parents NOT to urge their children to pursue high grades and class discussion because the harder students work, the greater their chances of brainwashing.

"A concept will never do anyone as much good as a fact," is the credo that guides the Gablers. "Too many discussions and textbooks leave students to make up their minds about things," complains Norma Gabler, adding, "Now that's just not fair to our children." Schools must teach "absolutes," say the Gablers. Why? "Textbooks mold nations because textbooks largely determine how a nation votes, what it becomes and where it goes." Mel Gabler adds, "When a student reads in a math book that there are no absolutes, suddenly every value he's been taught is destroyed. And the next thing you know, the student turns to crime and drugs."

The Gablers also oppose role-playing, polling students on issues discussed in class and posing open-ended questions to encourage students to understand that not all problems have black-and-white solutions. The Gablers object even to *discussions* of segregation, women's rights, trade unions, the civil rights movement, slavery in America, world hunger and poverty.

A COORDINATED ASSAULT ON PUBLIC EDUCATION

The Gablers provide thousands of textbook "reviews" to three other organizations that direct the national censorship movement: Rev. Jerry Falwell's Moral Majority, Phyllis Schlafly's Eagle Forum, and the Texas-based Pro-Family Forum. These groups can produce thousands of local foot soldiers to launch censorship battles in communities all over the country. The Gablers' censorship crusade is applauded by powerful New Right political strategists Howard Phillips, Paul Weyrich and Richard Viguerie. Mel and Norma Gabler are popular speakers at major Radical Right conventions and rallies.

By working to censor all books and classroom discussions that question the existence of absolute truth, imply that there may be more than one answer to a question or introduce "alien" ideas, the Gablers and other national censorship leaders are attacking the very purpose of education: to teach children how to think. They are determined to prevent all young people from being exposed to any book, idea or discussion that escapes the boundaries of their narrow view of the world.

The Gablers celebrated their first major censorship success in 1974. After filing 163 objections to a 10-volume reading series up for adoption in Texas, the state rejected seven of the books and ordered extensive changes in the eighth. The Gablers objected, for example, to one story character's anguished question, "How could they sing of the land of the free, when there was still racial discrimination?" Their objection? "Majority of people are free. Only people in jail are not free."

Two years after their first victory, the Gablers helped prevent school systems throughout the state from acquiring five dictionaries which they claimed contained "vulgar language and unreasonable definitions." In 1978, the Gablers claimed credit for banning from all Texas schools 18 of the 28 textbooks they targeted. Last year, 10 of the 21 texts the Gablers attacked were rejected by the state.

This year, the Texas State Textbook Committee received more than 900 pages of objections; almost 600 pages of attacks were filed by the Gablers. They included:

Textbook material: (Teacher's Guide) "Organize a brain-storming session for students to give examples of activities that encourage independence in children."
Gabler's objection: "This activity . . . could lead to permissive childrearing, which is now acknowledged to be a probable cause of our increased crime rate."

Determined to rewrite history to reflect their own dogmatic beliefs, the Gablers criticize one textbook's discussion of the Equal Rights Amendment for "misleading students to believe that women are not guaranteed equal rights already. This is totally untrue." The Gablers complain that other texts fail to tell students that child labor laws, federal unemployment compensation and urban renewal programs may be unconstitutional.

PEOPLE FOR'S TEXAS TEXTBOOK PROJECT

In past years, the Gablers and their allies have been virtually unopposed in their crusade against Texas textbooks. Because their victories are defeats for school children around the country, People For the American Way is launching a major project to protect students' access to information and ideas in our nation's public schools. Our Texas Textbook Project is monitoring the state's textbook adoption hearings, educating the public about the nature and extent of the censorship threat, and helping Texas citizens who want to increase public participation in the textbook adoption process to ensure students' intellectual freedom. . . .

A proclamation by the Texas State Board of Education in 1982 reads as follows: "Textbook content shall promote citizenship and the understanding of the free-enterprise system, emphasize patriotism and respect for recognized authority. Textbook content shall not encourage life-styles deviating from generally accepted standards of society."

At hearings held by the Texas State Textbook Committee in August 1982, People for the American Way, (PFAW), an organization based in Washington, D.C., went on the attack against the Gablers' Educational Research Analysts. Representatives of PFAW were not permitted to defend textbooks blacklisted by the Gablers, since only negative testimony was allowed, but the Board agreed to accept written statements defending criticized texts.

Among admirers of the Gablers and their methods are such New Right leaders as the Reverend Jerry Falwell and Phyllis Schlafly. A member of the Texas board is quoted as saying, "I feel the Gablers are doing a great service. They're ferreting out slang, vulgarities, and also things that are unpatriotic."

Many classroom teachers in Texas and elsewhere, however, object to the Gablers' narrow viewpoints. The Texas State Teach-

ers Association aided People for the American Way by providing copies of the Gablers' textbook criticisms in advance of the hearings. Publishers are also deeply concerned because Texas is the nation's second largest purchaser of textbooks and is in a key position to influence the content of texts coming from publishers.

PFAW has petitioned the Texas Commissioner of Education to admit positive as well as critical testimony in future hearings. The organization plans to continue on the offensive.

BOOK AND MATERIALS SELECTION FOR SCHOOL LIBRARIES AND CLASSROOMS

A landmark report on a nationwide survey of censorship in U.S. public schools, sponsored by the Association of American Publishers, American Library Association, and Association for Supervision and Curriculum Development, was released in July 1981. The report surveys 1,891 public elementary and secondary school administrators and librarians. It is the most extensive study undertaken to date on the selection practices and censorship pressures affecting books and other materials in the classrooms and libraries of the nation's public schools. The following introduction to this report outlines the reasons for initiating and the objectives of the study.

Association of American Publishers, American Library Association, and Association for Supervision and Curriculum Development

LIMITING WHAT STUDENTS MAY READ

Censorship in America's public schools has become an issue of rising national concern. In recent years, reports from educators, librarians, and the press, from all sections of

the country, have told increasingly of attempts to challenge or restrict the books and teaching materials available to students in the classroom and the school library. According to these reports, the pressures come from both the right and the left of the political spectrum, from individual parents as well as from organized special-interest groups, and sometimes from educators within the schools themselves.

The issue of censorship in our schools—its extent, the origin and nature of the challenges to books and materials, the resolution of those challenges, their perceived impact on the educational environment, and their relationship to the overall process by which instructional and library materials are selected—is too important to be evaluated solely on the basis of scattered reports, occasional headlines about book-burning, celebrated cases of high-court litigation, or unsupported claims by contestants in the educational or political arena. At the heart of the issue lie the difficult questions of what and how students shall learn—questions crucial to all who vie for influence over the future direction of our pluralistic society.

While previous surveys have dealt with either the selection of school books and learning materials or the censorship pressures on them, until now no broad survey has been undertaken to provide comprehensive data on the relationship between the censorship problem and the larger selection process. To obtain fuller, more up-to-date information on both aspects, and to examine their interaction, three national organizations closely involved with the question—the Association of American Publishers (AAP), the American Library Association (ALA), and the Association for Supervision and Curriculum Development (ASCD)—undertook, in 1980, a nationwide survey.

The survey, "Book and Materials Selection for School Libraries and Classrooms: Procedures, Challenges, and Responses," was conducted in two parts during the spring and summer of 1980. In April 1980, a detailed (52-item) questionnaire was mailed to a randomly selected stratified sample of 7,572 public elementary and secondary school librarians, library-supervisors, principals, and district superintendents in the 50 states and the District of Columbia; a total of 1,891 respondents participated. . . . From May to August 1980, a mail-and-telephone survey was conducted of the state-level administrators who oversee the evaluation and adoption of textbooks in the 22 states that have statewide adoption procedures for school books. (Each of the 22 "adoption" states compiles and publishes its own lists of books mandated or recommended for use in its public schools; the 28 "open" states leave school book selection entirely to their local education agencies.) All but one of the adoption states returned a completed ques-

tionnaire; and officials in 20 of the 22 adoption states participated in the phone interviews.

This report summarizes and interprets the major findings of the AAP-ALA-ASCD survey—particularly those findings which shed light on the censorship problem—and makes certain recommendations. The full report of the survey results can be obtained from the sponsoring organizations or through the facilities of ERIC (the Educational Resources Information Center).

Neither the report itself nor the survey data should be taken as precise indicators of the rate or impact of censorship pressures nationwide. Nonetheless, the experiences reported here by a meaningful number of school administrators and librarians warrant concern in themselves, and may well reflect a more general situation extending beyond the sample. (It is important to note that, since the survey requested information on the two school years preceding June 1980, the data do not reflect any intensification of pressures that may have resulted from changes in the political climate after that time.)

What the experiences reported here do indicate is that censorship pressures on books and other learning materials in the public schools are real, nationwide, and growing.

SUMMARY

In summary, the survey findings analyzed in this report point to the following conclusions:

challenges to classroom—and, more frequently, library—materials occur in schools in all regions and in all types of communities across the nation;

such challenges arise from within as well as from without the educational establishment;

the challenges often result in limiting students' access to materials, information, and ideas;

many schools not only lack, or fail to follow, written policies and procedures for selecting materials but also lack, or fail to follow, written procedures for reconsidering materials when challenges arise; and

schools that do have written selection policies and reconsideration procedures appear to resolve conflicts with fewer restrictions on the instructional and library materials available to students, and therefore with less negative impact on the educational environment.

The survey findings also indicate that

many schools fail to communicate their educational objectives and methods to the local community;

the public relations efforts of many schools are more often crisis-oriented than ongoing; and

finally, responses to the state-level survey in particular have suggested that local and national pressure groups, especially those of the political right-of-center, increasingly attempt to exploit the controversial arena of school book selection for political ends.

In our pluralistic society, choosing what students shall read and learn can never be an easy process. Nor can it be free of controversy. In that difficult process, challenges to instructional and library materials in our public schools have a legitimate function. As a check both on unavoidable human error and on the occasionally arbitrary exercise of authority, such challenges may be viewed as an essential element in the overall selection process.

While administrators and librarians should not expect the school arena to be free of such challenges, they can take steps to ensure that the entire selection process, including the procedures for challenge and review, will be carried on both professionally and equitably; and that the range of materials thereby made available to students will not only reflect established professional criteria but also reflect the values, and address the needs, of the entire school community. To that end, the following recommendations are offered:

RECOMMENDATIONS

Before challenges arise, school districts should:

1. *Establish in writing, a materials selection policy.* The policy statement should specify the local criteria and procedures for selecting curricular and library materials. School personnel, including administrators at all levels, should strictly adhere to the established policy and procedures in the selection of all materials.

2. *Establish, in writing, a clearly defined method for dealing with complaints.* Formal procedures for the review of challenged materials should be an integral part of the selection policy statement. Survey data strongly suggest that review procedures include the following provisions:

a. That a "request-for-review" form be used to identify, in writing, the complainant's specific concerns and objections, for evaluation during the review process;

b. That a broad-based committee including parents and other community residents, as well as school personnel, be established to review challenged materials; and

c. That no restrictions be placed on the use of challenged materials until the entire review process has been completed.

3. *Establish continuing communication with the public served by the schools.* School personnel should keep the local community informed, on a regular basis, about educational objectives, curricula, and classroom and library programs, and should be accessible to all concerned local residents to hear their views. It is especially important that the community be informed about the policies and procedures for selecting and reviewing books and other instructional and library materials, since these materials form the basis for the school's educational program.

If a challenge arises, school districts should:

1. *Attempt to resolve the challenge informally.* When the complaint is first received,

appropriate personnel should meet informally with the complainant to hear the specific objections being raised and to explain how and why the challenged material was selected. If, at the end of this informal discussion, the complainant still wishes to challenge the material in question, the request-for-review form should be provided.

2. *Take no action to review challenged materials until a written request for review is filed.* When the formal request has been filed, established review procedures should be implemented immediately. At this time, the school board or other governing body should be fully informed of the details of the complaint. If there is no standing review committee, the necessary committee should now be established.

3. *Strictly adhere to established procedures throughout the review process.* All school personnel should be reminded that no restrictions are to be placed on the use of the challenged materials until the entire review process has been completed.

4. *Inform the general public.* Any review of challenged materials should be conducted openly, and the community the district serves should be kept informed through the media and/or local organizational channels, such as the parents' association or school newsletters.

5. *Seek support.* Many local and national groups can offer advice and support. It is best to alert such groups when a complaint is first received. They can often help schools resolve challenges equitably; at the very least, they can provide moral support. Publishers in particular, through the Association of American Publishers, may be able to provide assistance in resolving challenges.

A 1982 study of censorship in 860 high school libraries across the nation made by Lee and David Burress revealed a steady increase in censorship pressures on books, periodicals, and films. Of those librarians surveyed 34 percent reported challenges to books, frequently by a parent or group lodging a complaint with school officials. This number compared with 20 percent in a similar survey made in 1966. The most frequently censored title reported was *Go Ask Alice*, a diary of an anonymous teenage girl who fell into drug use and committed suicide. It replaced J. D. Salinger's *Catcher in the Rye*, which had headed the list in earlier surveys but moved into second place. *Our Bodies, Ourselves* was third.

A disturbing result of the 1982 survey was the increased number of locally active pressure groups, from less than 1 percent in previous surveys to 17 percent in the current survey. The project was co-sponsored by the Committee Against Censorship of the National Council of Teachers of English.

CHAPTER FOUR

LIBRARIANS FIGHT BACK

Librarians have long been in the forefront, nationwide, in resisting censorship and attacks on intellectual freedom. Particularly effective has been the Office for Intellectual Freedom of the American Library Association, which serves as a national clearinghouse for information and advice to libraries and librarians under attack and cooperates with other like-minded organizations. Not infrequently its activities have involved it in legal testimony and in friends-of-the-court statements.

The association as a whole has taken official positions on a number of key issues involving intellectual freedom, the basic one being the *Library Bill of Rights*, first adopted in 1939.

Library Bill of Rights
The American Library Association affirms that all libraries are forums for information and ideas, and that the following basic policies should guide their services.

1. Books and other library resources should be provided for the interest, information, and enlightenment of all people of the community the library serves. Materials should not be excluded because of the origin, background, or views of those contributing to their creation.
2. Libraries should provide materials and information presenting all points of view on current and historical issues. Materials should not be proscribed or removed because of partisan or doctrinal disapproval.
3. Libraries should challenge censorship in the fulfillment of their responsibility to provide information and enlightenment.
4. Libraries should cooperate with all persons and groups concerned with resisting abridgment of free expression and free access to ideas.
5. A person's right to use a library should not be denied or abridged because of origin, age, background, or views.
6. Libraries which make exhibit spaces and meeting rooms available to the public they serve should make such facilities available on an equitable basis, regardless of the beliefs or affiliations of individuals or groups requesting their use.

The present statement was adopted by the ALA Council June 18, 1948 and amended February 2, 1961, June 27, 1967, and January 23, 1980.

By way of interpreting the *Library Bill of Rights*, the association in 1971 adopted these seven propositions:

1. We will make available to everyone who needs or desires them the widest possible diversity of views and modes of expression, including those which are strange, unorthodox, or unpopular.

2. We need not endorse every idea contained in the materials we produce and make available.

3. We regard as irrelevant to the acceptance and distribution of any creative work the personal history or political affiliations of the author or others responsible for it or its publication.

4. With every available legal means, we will challenge laws or governmental action restricting or prohibiting the publication of certain materials or limiting free access to such materials.

5. We oppose labeling any work of literature or art, or any persons responsible for its creation, as subversive, dangerous, or otherwise undesirable.

6. We, as guardians of intellectual freedom, oppose and will resist every encroachment upon that freedom by individuals or groups, private or official.

7. Both as citizens and professionals, we will strive by all legitimate means open to us to be relieved of the threat of personal, economic, and legal reprisals resulting from our support and defense of the principles of intellectual freedom.

Additional statements have expressed the association's objections to practices that would restrict access to certain materials held by libraries or would expurgate portions of library materials. The full rights of minors to use library facilities also has been affirmed. A policy statement recognizing the confidentiality of library circulation records which would identify names of library users with specific materials borrowed was adopted by the association in 1971.

LeRoy C. Merritt, long-time editor of the ALA *Newsletter on Intellectual Freedom* and dean of the School of Librarianship at the University of Oregon, was an articulate and highly literate opponent of censorship. Here he examines problems of book selection in relation to intellectual freedom.

LeRoy C. Merritt
BOOK SELECTION AND INTELLECTUAL FREEDOM

In very general terms, it may be said that there are two theories of public library book selection which are almost as diametrically opposed to each other as the two poles. Too simply, perhaps, they may be designated as the value theory and the demand theory. The value theory posits the public library as an educational institution containing books that provide inspiration, information, and recreation, with insistence that even the last-mentioned should embody some measure of creative imagination. The collection should include only those books which one way or another tend toward the development and enrichment of life. In short, "give them what they should have."

The demand theory, on the other hand, sees the public library as a democratic institution, supported by taxes paid by the whole community, each member of which has an equal right to find what he wishes to read in the library collection. In short, "give them what they want." Just as no man can live well or for long at either pole, so no librarian can espouse either the value theory or the demand theory to the exclusion of the other. Nor is life on the equator especially salutary or easily possible. So it is that each librarian works out some sort of "temperate" compromise, and if all goes well, his library acquires and holds a clientele which is comfortable with the collection it finds.

The relative weight of the two theories

Reprinted by permission of the H. W. Wilson Company from *Book Selection and Intellectual Freedom*, by LeRoy Charles Merritt. Copyright © 1970 by Mary L. Merritt, executor. Footnotes have been omitted.

varies from field to field within a given library, varies somewhat between libraries of the same type, and may vary greatly between different types of libraries. In the context of intellectual freedom, the librarian needs to be in the position of being able to argue for the value of his collection to his community and, by corollary, for the place of every book in that collection as being of value to some group of readers in the community.

Acting in good conscience and without fear of intimidation, the librarian must select each book as being in fact a positive contribution to the collection and of potential benefit or usefulness to some portion of the library's clientele. He must select each book not because it will do no harm but because it may do some good. There is an important corollary to this. A book is selected because of its usefulness to a group of readers, even though it may not be useful to others, or may even be distasteful, repugnant, or objectionable to them. It is selected for its positive value to a certain group of patrons, despite the possibility of another patron's objecting or the likelihood of controversy.

It is important also that the librarian harbor no fear that he is engaging in censorship himself when a title is rejected as not belonging in the library according to established policy. The distinction made by Asheim between selection and censorship on the librarian's part is a valid one and must be completely understood, felt, and believed if the librarian is to be in a proper frame of mind to withstand an onslaught from people with tendencies toward censorship. The librarian who feels, believes, or suspects that he himself engages in a measure of censorship in the process of selection is in a poor psychological position when the real thing comes, either as a request to remove a book or to add one the librarian considers unacceptable.

That some librarians consciously or unconsciously do engage in censorship in the selection process is an unfortunate irrelevancy. The Fiske report, with its evidence of conscious and subconscious censorship by librarians engaged in book selection, stands on its own merits. The *Newsletter on Intellec-*

tual Freedom gives almost issue-by-issue testimony that Fiske's findings are as valid now as they were a decade ago, and not only in California but in all parts of the country. The purpose of this chapter is to assist the librarian in moving toward a firm and sound position on intellectual freedom in the selection process. The remainder of the volume is devoted to precepts, techniques, and practices which it is hoped will assist the librarian to withstand tendencies toward censorship from outside the library. This chapter is primarily concerned with those sensitive areas of book selection where librarians are divided in theory and in practice, where they find a conflict between selection theory and legal requirements, and where their selection policies and practices have been challenged.

OBSCENITY AND PORNOGRAPHY

Let us begin by attempting to define the indefinable. Etymologically, *pornography*, which is derived from the Greek, means writing about prostitutes or prostitution. In common usage it is defined as meaning "a depiction (as in writing or painting) of licentiousness or lewdness: a portrayal of erotic behavior designed to cause sexual excitement." The definition is clear, but it reveals that the application of the term to any work is bound to be subjective. Only the author himself can say what effect a particular work or passage in a work is "designed" to produce. What the reader concludes about the author's intentions can only be an inference.

Obscene, from the Latin, applies to whatever is indecent, disgusting, or grossly offensive, including, although not limited to, things sexual or scatological. What is considered obscene varies greatly from culture to culture, from time to time, from place to place, from art form to art form. Hardly any instrumental music could be considered obscene. Much that would be regarded as obscene if performed on stage is portrayed in books, the reading of which is essentially a private activity. This is still broadly true, even though there is now much more freedom in regard to nudity and erotic behavior

on stage and screen than would have seemed possible a generation ago.

In law, the word *obscene* may be described as indefinable. The best legal minds, including those on the Supreme Court, have labored mightily, and failed. They will continue to fail, for like beauty, obscenity is in the eye of the beholder (as noted above, *pornography* is an equally subjective term). In literature the effort at definition is just as impossible, and as pointless. Books fall above or below the level of critical acceptability according to contemporary theories and standards of literary criticism, of which obscenity is not one. A book achieves critical acceptance on criteria other than the amount or the frankness of its sexual content. A book with little or no other content fails to achieve acceptance on those same literary criteria.

So it is also with library book selection. An actual or theoretical obscenity quotient is not a criterion of selection. Neither Haines, nor Carter and Bonk, nor Ranganathan mention it. The librarian who rejects *Valley of the Dolls* or *The Arrangement* as trash is on firm literary ground; the librarian who rejects either because of its sexual content must in consistency withdraw a host of much better books from his collections. The librarian willing to work at selecting fiction and other creative writing by good literary standards will be in a sound position to defend any of his selections against charges of their alleged obscenity.

SEX EDUCATION

Broderick reported that three quarters of the public libraries buying books on sex consider it necessary to keep them in protective custody. Libraries not buying such books gave as a reason that "This type material disappears from shelves." Conversely, libraries keeping the books on open shelves reported little or no theft or mutilation. Some librarians expressed annoyance that such books wear out and need to be replaced. These differences in practice can possibly be explained by differences in clientele in various parts of the country and in communities of various sizes. The more probable explanation, however, is the difference in attitude on the part of the librarians concerned. The importance of having such books in the library was disputed by none of Broderick's respondents. Considering the known reluctance on the part of many library patrons to ask for books on sex education, there is a correspondingly strong argument for keeping them on the open shelves. Providing for a certain amount of loss by theft must be considered part of the cost of purveying authoritative information in this sensitive area in our society.

RELIGION

The paragraph on religion in the composite selection policy in Chapter 3 sets forth a standard library position on the selection of religious books in the public library. The field is usually not touched on in school library selection policies, but no school library can be considered complete without the Bible and some histories of religion, both ancient and modern. Religion is a major part of our culture and can be dealt with as such without being presented as doctrine.

Not covered in public library selection policies, probably because their occurrence is rare, are the occasional books critical of a particular religion. Paul Blanshard's critical works on Roman Catholicism will serve as cases in point of books which should be in public libraries in communities where there is public interest in them. Members of a faith are not all of a piece in their attitude toward such works. Even a devout Catholic may want to know what a sincere critic has to say about his faith. The librarian need only follow the normal selection criteria for nonfiction in this sensitive area; and having thus selected such titles, he will be in a strong position to defend their presence in the collection.

The obverse problem may be more difficult—that of the citizen who protests the absence of books which have not been selected. Such protests almost invariably come not from people who wish to read the books but from those who want them in the library for other people to read. They want the library to serve their propagandistic purposes. Suggested here is possibly a new principle of book selection. All public librarians consider very carefully every request from a patron for the addition of a particular title when it is clear that the patron wants to read the book. When it seems unlikely that anyone else in the community will want to read the title in question, the book is borrowed from another library. There is no reason, however, either to buy the book or borrow it because an interested citizen wants it to be available for others to read. The principle applies not only to books in the field of religion but to all other areas in which the patron may have an ulterior motive, be it politics, his views on the fluoridation of water, or parental interest in his own deathless prose or poetry. It applies equally to books offered as gifts. The librarian who would not buy a volume presented with the author's compliments should feel under no compulsion to add it to his library's collection.

POLITICS

"The Myth of Library Impartiality," first so described by Berelson, is here generally recognized as such. Libraries cannot supply an equal number of titles on both or all sides of every political issue. They must follow the pattern of book publication and cannot wait for a title to appear on the "other" side before making a purchase. It is necessary, however, that the authentic and important books on every political issue which meets the normal selection criteria be acquired as they are published. And certain landmark books need to be added regardless of those criteria. *The Communist Manifesto*, *Mein Kampf*, and the *Blue Book* of the John Birch Society are classic examples.

The ulterior motive principle is relevant here also, particularly during presidential campaign years. *A Texan Looks at Lyndon*, by J. Evetts Haley, is only one example of books which many public libraries were urged to add to their collections for the propagandistic purposes of the donors. Some libraries added them; some did not; some placed them in pamphlet files as being "ephemeral" material—not a bad hiding place. One librarian added them with a flourish of local newspaper publicity as to why he did so. This may have been good public relations but seems clearly inconsistent with the ALA Statement on Labeling.

BOOKS AS NEWS

It happens occasionally that a book which does not meet the normal selection criteria of a public library is added later when, for one reason or another, it becomes news. *Peyton Place* will serve as an example. Literary trash by almost anyone's standards, this book was rejected by many public libraries following the normal selection process. "But," as one librarian has said, "when a book sells seven million copies, it becomes news as a literary phenomenon, and should be added so that readers in general can discover what the fuss is all about."

In another area, *Race and Reason*, by Carleton Putnam, was not bought by the Arlington (Virginia) County Public Library because it gave biased, inaccurate information on the alleged basic inferiority of Negroes. The book's supporters protested vehemently to the library, then placed a bill before the Virginia General Assembly requiring mandatory inclusion of the book on the Board of Education's approved list for public schools. Thus the title acquired news value, and it became important for libraries to have it so that interested citizens could form their own opinions about the controversy. The director of the Arlington County Public Library then added *Race and Reason* to the book collection. Neither *Peyton Place* nor *Race and Reason* acquired intrinsic value because of their topical interest. One remains trash and the other remains inaccurate, and now that they are no longer in the limelight, no librarian should feel any compulsion to add them in violation of normal selection criteria.

CLOSED SHELVES AND LOCKED CASES

A substantial number of librarians whose book selection policies are relatively unre-strictive limit the practice of intellectual freedom by restricting the circulation of certain titles and certain classes of books. To say the books are shown in the card catalog and are available at the desk on request still places a barrier between book and patron. Nearly 80 per cent of public library patrons do not come to the library to obtain a specific book; hence the book which cannot be found by browsing through the open shelves is lost to the overwhelming majority of library patrons.

Many of the titles which are not freely available on the open shelves are precisely the ones which ought to be there to be found and read by the patron who has no one to ask or consult for the needed information and who is too timid to allow a librarian to become aware of his need. Once the selection decision has been made to add a title to a library collection, that title should find its rightful place on the open shelves of the library.

Such closed shelf collections are justified in the minds of many librarians by a real or alleged need for the library to protect the books from theft or mutilation. The need may well be real for some books, including those which must be segregated for reasons other than their possible controversiality.

Segregation to protect the book, however, is probably overemphasized. To have several copies of a ten-dollar book stolen in a single year is a painful experience for library personnel and involves both budgetary and processing costs; a librarian's natural response is to find a way of putting a stop to it—such as placing all such books on closed shelves. The fact of the matter is that we have no evidence that titles with an alleged high theft potential are stolen at a greater rate than the average volume in the collection. It just seems that way. Some loss by theft is part of the cost of doing business on an open shelf basis and should be budgeted for in the same manner as losses by depreciation and obsolescence. Good unrestrictive selection policies developed in the cause of intellectual freedom should not be vitiated by restrictive administrative practices.

AGE OF READER

Closed shelves are sometimes considered necessary as a means of keeping children and young people from finding books considered suitable only for adults. Other administrative practices are used to the same end under the presumption that some books are harmful to the young or in an effort to avoid controversy with parents who might think so. Indeed, the protest of only one patron about a book on the open shelves has served as a jail sentence for many books in many libraries. Librarians generally resist the withdrawal or destruction of a book, but too many do not hesitate to place it under lock and key.

Beginning on June 27, 1967, when the American Library Association Council unanimously approved a revised Library Bill of Rights as "basic policies which should govern the services of all libraries," any restriction on the use of the library by reason of the reader's age clearly became contrary to ALA policy. Paragraph 5 of the Library Bill of Rights now [1970] reads: "The rights of an individual to the use of a library should not be denied or abridged because of his age, race, religion, national origins or social or political views."

The insertion of the word "age" was a direct result of the 1967 Preconference Institute on Intellectual Freedom and the Teenager, sponsored by the Intellectual Freedom Committee, the American Association of School Librarians, and the Young Adult Services Division. Beginning with a brilliant address by Edgar Z. Friedenberg, then Professor of Sociology on the Davis campus of the University of California, speaker after speaker brought authority to bear on the fact that no evidence exists of a correlation between the reading of allegedly obscene materials and juvenile delinquency, and that, in fact, the typical juvenile delinquent reads hardly anything at all. A summary by Intellectual Freedom Committee chairman Ervin J. Gaines of the conference papers, which have not yet been published, may be found in the September 1967 issue of the *Newsletter on Intellectual Freedom*. In brief, the young person who is ready for the con-

tent of a book is also ready to handle that content; if he is not ready he will either not be interested in the book or will not understand and will pass over the portions his elders are concerned about on his behalf.

The librarian who would restrict the availability of books to young people because of actual or suspected parental objection to certain books being freely available to young people on the open shelves needs to bear in mind that he is not *in loco parentis* in his position as librarian. The job of the public and school librarian is to select books for a particular clientele in accordance with established policy. Not all books can be suitable for all members of a clientele, but all must be there for the use of those who can and want to read them. The parent who would rather his child did not read certain books or certain categories of books should advise the child, not the librarian.

HEALTH AND MEDICINE

Librarians are from time to time charged with censorship for not adding to their collections in the field of health, nutrition, and medicine books not regarded by the medical profession as authentic and reliable. *Dianetics*, by L. Ronald Hubbard, for example, was not added to the collections of the Brooklyn Public Library on the basis of a negative review in the *Journal of the American Medical Association*. More recently the Madison (Wisconsin) Public Library came under criticism for not stocking the books on nutrition written by Adele Davis. In a letter dated October 4, 1966, Assistant Director Orrilla Blackshear responded as follows:

When a person comes to the public library to obtain books on nutrition or on health, he has a right to expect that the books he receives will fall within the broad area of accepted nutritional and medical practice. Anyone using the library to obtain technical information has the right to assume that the library will furnish such information from authoritative sources. In technical matters, we must depend upon authorities in the field for evaluation.

This problem was also touched on by Broderick, who noted that some librarians responding to her questionnaire about problem nonfiction were caught in a dilemma in connection with books in the field of nutrition. One librarian who considered Taller's *Calories Don't Count* to be dangerous said the reserve list was too heavy for the library to withdraw the book. On the other hand, six libraries holding the book withdrew it from circulation when the United States Government instituted action against it. Both situations point up a failure to think through the principles involved and reveal a lack of confidence in the librarian's own book selection judgment. Certainly a book which is dangerous should not be circulated by a library no matter how long the reserve list. Nor, when a library has decided a book is a desirable addition to the collection, should it be withdrawn just because a legal action has been instituted against it. Let librarians not be guilty of equating accusation with a formal determination of guilt by a court of competent jurisdiction.

IN GENERAL

Other subject areas which librarians consider sensitive could be adduced, but enough examples have been presented to work toward some generalizations in behalf of complete intellectual freedom in the book selection process by the wholly intellectually honest librarian. A few words more need to be said in criticism of efforts by school administrators and public librarians to rationalize a restrictive attitude or position.

The pressure toward censorship in school libraries has sometimes been alleviated or eliminated by a compromise: the reading of the book in question is permitted rather than required. This serves to remove the impasse between the parent who objects to a particular book and his child who feels he must read it because it is in his school assignment. Thus a strong parental protest against one of four books on a required reading list in a Philadelphia high school was resolved amicably by the addition of three to the list and the requirement that any four of the seven be read. In Oceanside, California, when parents representing nine families requested that their children be kept out of the school

library because of the presence of the *Dictionary of American Slang*, the request was denied; but school authorities agreed that the *Dictionary* would not be made available to these children, in accordance with general district policy to deny children access to books their own parents deemed objectionable. This practice seems to remove or to alleviate pressure, but it does not solve the problem concerning those materials which librarians or teachers believe every student should have access to or should be required to read. Were the principle to be generally extended to permit adjustment of curriculum and library resources for each individual child according to the predilections of his parents, public education soon would be a mockery and the school library an administrative shambles. School authorities and librarians must realize that there is no easy way to escape around the pressures toward censorship. Inevitably, sooner or later, they must be met head-on with a forthright defense of the principle of the freedom to read along with a very sincere and dedicated effort to educate the public concerned in the importance of the principle and the value of the books to which a vocal minority objects.

The public librarian frequently states that his reason for not buying a particular book is "lack of funds." The reason is used almost indiscriminately for books the librarian considers of dubious worth, those potentially a subject of controversy, and those so obviously superior as to be very expensive. Art books are a usual example. While most readers allow themselves to be put off by this specious answer, the reader who chooses to argue can almost invariably place the librarian in an untenable position. If the book in question is of dubious value the reader can find a host of volumes already on the shelves equally if not more dubious. It is the same with the potentially controversial book. Any good collection already contains many books which have been involved in controversy and a good many more which may be.

Even in the case of the expensive art book, the librarian who says he cannot afford it because there are other needs that take precedence at a particular time is saying only that he considers those other needs to be more important to his community than the art book. There can hardly be a library so poor that it could not purchase a one-hundred-dollar art book if the selector considered that book to be more important to the community than the twenty or thirty other books the same one hundred dollars could buy. The plea of poverty is one which librarians must learn to avoid as being too easy an answer to an important question and one which only the casual inquirer will accept and which the intelligent reader considers either evasive or dishonest.

Another frequently stated reason for not purchasing a book is that there is no demand for it. The joker in the sentence is the absent modifier *known*. Some books are so obviously important or potentially of such great value that they must be purchased even if there is no known demand. Furthermore, since most books borrowed from the public library are found on the shelf by borrowers who did not know of their existence upon entering the library, the librarian has the obligation to provide the good and important books of our time so that his clientele may have the opportunity of finding them while browsing. Thus the argument of demand, or lack of demand, is equally specious. It causes the librarian to say or imply that no one in his community has the wit or the will to read the book in question—a stand no librarian can afford to take.

The librarian who understands Asheim's distinction between selection and censorship, who is wholly serious and conscientious in the process of selection need have no fear of a censor's success in a legal determination of an issue by a competent court. This position was admirably set forth by Edward de Grazia at the Washington Conference on Intellectual Freedom:

It is my opinion that under present law no book selected by a librarian for his shelves can constitutionally be found obscene. Why? Because any such book must have at least some slight redeeming social importance. The very act of library

selection testifies to and engrafts such importance upon it.

This is why, for example, the Kinsey Institute was able to vindicate in court its constitutional right to import even so-called hard-core pornography. The process of selection, the institutional interest, can lend even otherwise "worthless" material the kind of importance necessary to activate the constitutional guarantees of free expression. Therefore, I believe that libraries must have something like total immunity from prosecution or external coercion in the exercise of their vital functions. The basic principle for librarians might best be described thus: Any material selected by a librarian, in the exercise of his function as a librarian, is protected. The protection extends both to his acquisition and retention of the material, and also precludes any valid prosecution of the librarian for acquiring or retaining it.

Richard L. Darling, dean of the School of Library Service, Columbia University, surveys the field from the point of view of the library profession.

Richard L. Darling

CENSORSHIP—AN OLD STORY

No one will question that censorship is an old story. It must be as old as recorded literature, perhaps older. Certainly it was well underway the first time two men disagreed, and one felt strong enough to suppress the ideas of the other. History is filled with censorship tales. Horror stories to those who believe that ideas have a right to be heard and weighed in the balance. Stories of evil suppressed by those who believe that ideas not held by the majority are necessarily evil.

Socrates, Galileo, Bruno, Milton—these are only a few of the names of famous men whose ideas and writings have been suppressed as dangerous and heretical. An equally illustrious group of men have defended the right to be heard. John Locke, Thomas Jefferson, John Stuart Mill, and again, John Milton, are on that list. Through

Reprinted by permission of the National Council of Teachers of English from *Elementary English* 51: 691–96 (May 1974). Footnotes have been omitted.

the centuries conflicting forces have battled on this issue, freedom of expression and of publication, and underlying both, freedom of thought. Skirmishes have been won, on either side, occasionally even a battle, but neither has ever succeeded in making its frontiers secure. Those who defend intellectual freedom succeed sometimes, in defending the reading and distribution of a work, only to find themselves embattled again over the same work or still a new one.

Censorship is an old story, but it seems always to be a new one too. The objects of censorship change, even the general subjects held suspect, but in generation after generation, the attempts to suppress publications with which someone disagrees continue. Censorship is peculiarly a new story as it relates to children's books.

It is all but impossible to find a record of censorship of children's books until recent times. No doubt the late development of a unique literature for children explains this absence. The earliest literature that children enjoyed was adult literature, and an oral literature. Whether it was a vulgar age, fine sensibilities attuned to protecting children not yet developed, or whether the children were already asleep when the minstrel began his songs, we have no record. By the time printing had evolved, and the first needs for religious books, school books, and other practical books had been satisfied, those who turned to the production of children's books had specific purposes in mind, and highly moral ones, specifically to indoctrinate the children in a particular creed or dogma, religious or secular.

Those early books for children, describing the exemplary lives of saintly children who earned early, though pious deaths, dreadful as they were, appear not to have aroused a censor asking for life-affirming books, though they surely might have if they had continued into our own time. But perhaps few children actually read them. There is evidence that the nursery set preferred the broadsides and chapbooks, bearing exciting tales of heroes and adventure, delivered by roving peddlers to the books that pious printers prepared for their betterment.

We do know that the Puritans objected to the "ungodly ballad" and foolish story, but there is no evidence that they succeeded in suppressing them. Their influence must have taken its toll, though, for even when the great Newbery began to issue his books for the young, every one had its moral.

Despite the brief flurry of imaginative tales in 17th-century France, the 18th century presents an almost unrelieved parade of didactic books for the young. Whatever resistance school books, thinly disguised as story books, may have aroused in the young, they did not elicit the ire of a censor. Even the objections of the Puritans were not aimed at the young alone, for they believed all light reading inherently bad.

We reach the 19th century before we find well documented attempts to suppress books in order to protect children. The most notorious censor in 19th-century America, Anthony Comstock, certainly believed that he was protecting the young, along with society in general, when he persuaded the Federal Government to pass the Comstock Act and to begin using the mails to suppress books. But in the tons of books and magazines he succeeded in confiscating, we do not find children's books. His target was the *Police Gazette*, not Peter Parley. Attention to children's books came from another source, and one that professed to select books for children rather than censor them.

Early in the century the American Sunday School Union was founded. Rather, the idea was imported from England and quickly took root and spread in America. Well before the Civil War every Christian denomination had its Sunday Schools and each Sunday School had its library and a host of publishers, both denominational and secular, issuing new books and whole series to meet its needs.

In 1830 the American Sunday School Union set up standards for juvenile literature. Their emphasis was on the moral and religious character of the books, although other criteria, including style and appropriateness for the growing mind of the child were also included.

In the next several decades specific denominations took up the evaluation of children's books and, in the process, developed their own standards. No doubt the most influential effort of this sort was that of the Ladies' Commission on Sunday-School Books. On October 12, 1865, at a meeting of ladies called at the Rooms of the American Unitarian Association in Boston, the Rev. Charles Lowe proposed that the ladies form a group to prepare a list of books for Sunday-School libraries to be "selected with scrupulous care" and recommended to the churches. The ladies responded and soon had fifty members cooperating in their reviewing. They prepared a three part list, divided as follows:

1. Books for Unitarian Sunday-Schools.
2. Books highly recommended for their religious tone, but not in accord with Unitarian tenets.
3. Books "valuable and profitable, though not so fully adapted to the purpose of a Sunday-School library."

Publisher's Weekly, for Nov. 22, 1873, gave a summary of the work of the Unitarian Ladies Commission from its first catalog in 1867 through the 1873 supplement.

The supplement published in May reports the work of this year—182 books examined, 38 accepted. The three reading committees into which the commission is divided report as follows:
One committee has rejected 40 books, accepted 12; another rejected 50 books, accepted 10; a third rejected 54 books, accepted 16. It may be interesting to compare the percentage of accepted books, as it stands in our different catalogues and supplements:

The Catalogue of 1867 gives . . . . . 30 per cent
The Supplement of 1868 gives. . . . 24 per cent
The Supplement of 1869 gives. . . . 30 per cent
The Supplement of 1870 gives. . . . 18 per cent
The revised catalogue of
  1871 gives . . . . 28 per cent
The Supplement of 1872 gives. . . . 22 per cent
The Supplement of 1873 gives. . . . 21 per cent

The whole number of books accepted in the six years is 1087. The number of books read is 4042.

The *Unitarian Review* for June, 1874, contained an article, "Literature for the Young" signed "Ladies Commission on Sunday-School Books." In an introduction to this article, the editor praised these ladies "of the highest literary and religious culture," for their "wise judgment and taste and fairness," and added, "If once public sentiment shall fairly be aroused to the importance of the right sort of reading for the young—and to the poisoning nature of much that is now most circulated—the makers of books will be compelled to conform to a higher moral and religious and literary standard."

The article submitted by the Ladies Commission described their work from Oct., 1873 to May, 1874. They had examined 343 books, and had approved 82. They listed the most common reasons for rejection. Most of the reasons were literary, relating to style, structure, characterization, motivation, and stereotyped character and action, but many were condemned for their sensationalism, exaggeration of incident, lack of proper connection between cause and effect, a "startling and even horrible character of events," for "vulgar words" and "vulgar thoughts." They suggested that writers for children take the advice of St. Paul, with one word changed. "Whatsoever things are true, whatsoever things are honest, whatsoever things are just, whatsoever things are lovely, whatsoever things are of good report, '*write*' on those things."

Attacks on sensational books, usually sensational boys books, were by no means uncommon throughout the seventies. No less a writer than Louisa May Alcott attacked them in her *Eight Cousins*, particularly the works of William T. Adams, who wrote under the pen name, Oliver Optic. Miss Alcott referred to his books as *optical* delusions, and earned a stinging reply from Mr. Adams in return.

No doubt there were a great many second-rate children's books, deserving to be rejected by Miss Alcott and the Unitarian

Ladies Commission. What makes the work of the Commission Ladies, who were not censors certainly, since they never forced their opinions on others, most interesting in our context is that they did use non-literary criteria, and they had great influence on the growing public library movement.

The Boston conference of the American Library Association devoted its attention in 1879 to a series of papers on Fiction and the Reading of School Children. On that occasion "sensational" books had both their attackers and defenders. In the opening paper Kate Gannett Wells called for closer supervision of children's reading, saying that some parents are either lazy or have "a mistaken notion of a child's right to freedom . . ." and called for "stricter rules" to protect children from indiscriminate reading. A second paper by Martha H. Brooks, of the (Unitarian) Commission on Sunday-School Books described that organization's work, and set forth their criteria for judgment. Miss M. A. Bean attacked the reading of fiction by the young, indiscriminately, as the cause of "inattention, want of application, distaste for study, and unretentive memory. . . ."

Mr. S. S. Green headed the opposition, defending the right of children to read story books, including the sensational books of Oliver Optic and Horatio Alger. He praised the work of the Ladies Commission, saying he had used their lists in the Worcester, Mass., Public Library. However, he added a caution.

In using the Catalogues of the Ladies' Commission it is important to remember that this organization seeks to provide books especially for children brought up under refining influences, and that were the ladies who compose it aiming to provide for the needs of public libraries they would use a little more latitude in the selection of books. Perhaps, also, the fact that gentlemen do not aid in making out the lists, limits somewhat their value.

James Freeman Clarke, and especially, Thomas Wentworth Higginson gave their support to Green. Higginson said, "If, as Mr. Green has said, nothing takes hold of a neglected Irish boy for instance, like Oliver Optic's stories, then I would give him Oliver Optic in copious draughts, and give it at the public expense. . . ."

They did not have the last word. William P. Atkinson felt that the Optics of the day had a "mischievous influence." In the final paper Mellen Chamberlain cautioned against prohibitions and urged the librarians present to inspire boys and girls to better literature.

Dorothy Broderick, with quite another purpose, reported a symposium held at the 1895 ALA Conference. The subject was "Improper Books: Methods Employed to Discover and Exclude Them." Miss Broderick chose her quotations to indicate that the librarians of 1895 were open minded on factual matters and opinion, which though unpopular now, might be "accepted belief" later, but not on questions of morals, which were, apparently, immutable.

She continues quoting articles with titles such as "What Shall Libraries Do About Bad Books?" "What Makes a Book Immoral?" and "Questionable Books in Public Libraries." She makes a fairly convincing argument that American librarians did censor books, some of them proudly, until at least the middle of this century. Her thesis is that there is historical precedent for library censorship which, she reasons, justifys it. But we shall return to Miss Broderick again, on all sides of the argument, and also to the American Library Association and its stand on censorship today.

I said earlier that censorship is peculiarly new as it relates to children's books. I might almost have said that it is a 20th-century phenomenon. It is also peculiar, too, in that there has never yet been a children's book declared illegal by a court of competent jurisdiction. The story of censorship of children's books and other reading materials is a tale of pressure groups, illegal actions, of timidity, even cowardice among librarians and other educators, and of almost unbelievable prejudice and stupidity.

Textbooks and comic books have been subject to more pressure even than trade books. With textbooks, the most common charge has been that they are un-American or subversive, or both. Powerful right-wing groups have been able to prevent the use of certain titles in the schools of an entire state. Magruder's *American Government* has served as a favorite target, but many other books have also suffered. More recently, textbooks used in sex education have become an increasingly favored target for both right-wing political organizations and for fundamentalist religious groups.

Comic books have been attacked for their use of crime, violence, and, sometimes, obscenity. A national group, the National Organization for Decent Literature made the comic a prime target and used pressure tactics and attempted economic boycotts to force news dealers to stop selling them. The major claim against the comics is that they contribute to juvenile delinquency, though there is no research evidence to show that they do.

More recently trade books have become the censor's target. Each issue of the *Intellectual Freedom Newsletter* reports new cases of banning or attempts to ban children's books. Everyone knows of the banishment of *Huckleberry Finn* from the curriculum of New York City's public schools, and we have all read of the banning of Helen Bannerman's *Little Black Sambo* from a growing number of public and school libraries. The history of attacks on children's books in the last several years is so voluminous, in fact, that all I can do in the brief time remaining is talk about a few celebrated cases.

The day when children's books are excluded because of "vulgar words" would appear to be near an end. The attack by Mrs. A. Randall, Head, Children's Services, Memphis Public Library, on Dorothy Broderick's review of *Comeback Guy* in 1962, because Miss Broderick failed to warn her readers that the book contained a "damn" seems quaint today. But the amazing defacement of Sendak's *In the Night Kitchen* in a Louisiana library shows that morbid Puritanism is by no means dead. Fortunately, most of the world of children's

books was shocked that a grundyish librarian would paint tempera diapers on a naked boy. Writers, illustrators, publishers, and librarians have joined forces to combat this kind of censorship, and the American Library Association has adopted a policy statement opposing such defacement of books.

The ALA also took a strong stand when the International Conference of Police Associations and its affiliates attempted to bring strong pressure against libraries to remove William Steig's *Sylvester and the Magic Pebble* from their collections. The ALA Intellectual Freedom Committee was embarrassed, however, when a police officer asked, "Why is it that some librarians were quick to comply with requests to remove another children's book, *Little Black Sambo*, from their collections when blacks complained that its illustrations were degrading? Yet now, when police officers find William Steig's pigs dressed as law enforcement officers to be degrading, librarians object vociferously to taking books out of their collections?"

Many librarians have argued that *Little Black Sambo* is a different thing. Somehow, removing it is not censorship, but removing Sylvester is. Librarians and others find themselves on the horns of a dilemma, their social views on racial justice in conflict with their devotion to intellectual freedom and their opposition to censorship. Dorothy Broderick is honest. She simply would abandon intellectual freedom. She says, "Some things are right and some things are wrong and it is that simple." While we can all sympathize with her opposition to racism and other ills, her solution—censorship—is too simplistic. And her notion that the librarian is an infallible judge of the good and true is dangerous. It was not many years ago that certain libraries, in some Southern states, banned Garth Williams' *The Rabbits' Wedding* because a white rabbit married a black one. Banning books, if we accept the principle, can go both ways.

Robert W. Haney, in his book, *Comstockery in America; Patterns of Censorship and Control* deplores the tendency of many otherwise liberal groups to attempt to impose censorship on books of which they disapprove using the tactics of their enemies. He then says:

There is a threat to our society, but it does not come from literature. It arises from a warped set of values which renders human life sterile. It comes from an intolerable amalgamation of political, social and economic problems, all of which have made a shambles of our lives simply because we shirked them when they first confronted us. Now we are terrified at the prospect of having to solve them full grown.

He continues:

Crime, lust, bloodshed, hate, greed, cruelty, and selfishness are threads of life. The child had better have a little knowledge of them lest he be so startled when he comes of age that he will be unable to deal with them.

The banning of literature will not cure the real ills of our world. In fact, book banning can only hide them. The ALA Intellectual Freedom Committee has taken a stand in favor of children's freedom and against the banning of any books. When librarians, or teachers, begin to censor books because those books reflect the social climate and conscience of the era in which they were produced, it sounds ominously as though they have adopted the philosophy of *1984*. We must oppose that kind of philosophy, and oppose censorship of whatever kind. When we waste our energies on banning books which reflect the world, we neglect the world's real problems.

Ralph E. McCoy

SOCIAL RESPONSIBILITY VS. THE LIBRARY BILL OF RIGHTS

The Library Bill of Rights, initially adopted by the American Library Association in 1939, had declared the responsibility of libraries to maintain a fair and equitable representation of materials representing the full spectrum of political and social points of view. Over the years intellectual freedom has been a frequent topic of discussion in various forums of the association, and the concept has been expanded and interpreted by action of subsequent assemblies of the ALA Council, the governing body of the association.

During the late 1960s and early 1970s the historic meaning of intellectual freedom was challenged by an aggressive sector of the association that supported an advocacy concept under which libraries would play an active role in providing materials that would promote certain social goals. Predominant among these goals was assuring equitable treatment of racial minorities and women. A heated controversy developed within the profession between those who supported the traditional interpretation of the Library Bill of Rights and those who placed a higher value on effecting social change.

"If American librarians were to accept this substitution of a 'social responsibility' concept of the role of libraries in society for the concept described in the Library Bill of Rights and other ALA policies," wrote David Berninghausen, Director of the University of Minnesota Library School, in *Library Journal*, November 15, 1972, "then freedom of access to all points of view in libraries could not exist. . . . In the American society, which, by its Constitution forbids a state religion or a monolithic political organization, a *publicly-supported* library cannot legally limit its information services to media expressing any party-line orthodoxy, whether it is that of librarians, the government, or any one segment of society."

Ervin J. Gaines, then Director of the Minneapolis Public Library, also saw the advocacy movement as an erosion of the traditional role of libraries in providing a diversification of information and ideas in a pluralistic society. In the winter 1976 issue of *Minnesota English Journal*, Gaines wrote:

There is at the present time in the United States a powerful move to imbue libraries and schools with a sense of mission to uproot social injustice. The duty is pressed upon us to modify behavior by manipulation—by what you teach in the classroom and what we have available for reading in the library. In the teaching profession and in the profession of librarianship there are eloquent spokesmen who are passionate advocates of social control through manipulation and censorship. They would have us suppress evil books, and would also have us rewrite our history to conform to the current scale of values. . . . The fallacy of this attempt at advocacy should be apparent to intelligent and thoughtful people—but I am somewhat saddened that my expectations about the free mind are not realized. Free thought and full information are seen by many as expendable if they do not immediately and directly lead to increased social justice.

Other librarians saw no conflict between the concepts of intellectual freedom and social responsibility. William DeJohn, then at the Missouri State Library, wrote in *Library Journal* for January 1, 1973:

Librarians can actively focus attention on the various ideas and information contained in their libraries that relate to the problems facing society without being accused of "advocating partisan causes." . . . The concept of social responsibility does not mean that librarians should use their libraries to further their partisan, nonlibrary causes. It does mean that librarians and ALA "should endeavor to devise means whereby libraries can become more effective instruments of social change."

In the same issue of *Library Journal* Katherine Laich, then President of ALA, wrote: "There is no reason to believe that because librarians, acting as members of ALA, take a stand on a social issue, they will jettison their commitment to the continuing obligation to supply opposing views in their library collections."

In no area has there been greater controversy over the meaning of intellectual freedom than in children's librarianship where some librarians proposed "re-evaluation" of children's collections as a means of achieving social change.

In an article on re-evaluation of books for children appearing in *Children's Book Council, New York Calendar* for January-April 1972, Sara I. Fenwick, of the University of Chicago Graduate Library School, suggested that, in addition to the continuous

process of deciding whether to retain or replace materials that are less acceptable in quality or usefulness, recognition be given to "a revised set of criteria directed toward specific problems in our society. . . . Thus, one set of criteria is being evolved to identify those books that are effective in their presentation of the equality of the sexes, and, at the other end of the scale, those that present girls and women in roles less than equal in opportunities and expectations than boys and men." A similar re-assessment, Fenwick noted, had been employed in examining the presentation and treatment of minorities in writing for children. "The re-evaluation involved in both cases is a retrospective look at titles in book collections and on bibliographies while testing old and new criteria in response to current social concerns."

Dorothy M. Broderick, then columnist for the *School Library Journal*, in an article entitled "Censorship—Reevaluated" (*Library Journal*, November 15, 1971) charged that in the name of intellectual freedom "we defend materials that perpetuate attitudes that hinder the growth of individuals who are intellectually free." Librarians are faced with two alternatives, she stated: "The first is to go right on doing what we've been doing, namely, reflecting attitudes rather than affecting them. The second is to fight to make the library an instrument of social change." Before we can take the second course, according to Broderick, the traditional role of the library must be redefined through public debate. Also, the concept of intellectual freedom must be "redefined to mean that we will do all in our power to offer individuals experiences through materials that will broaden, not limit, their possibilities for growth. That means making value judgments. . . . The whole concept of social responsibility implies value judgments— some things are right and some things are wrong and it is that simple."

In the February 15, 1973, issue of *Library Journal*, James A. Harvey, then Executive Secretary of the Illinois Library Association, rejected the advocacy concept in selecting library books for children in the following statement excerpted from his article, "Acting for the Children?"

These contemporary efforts to rid libraries of objectionable children's materials, under the guise of reevaluation, are not much different in substance from traditional efforts. In some instances, the identity of the censors and the means they use have changed, but the motivation remains the same. The *superficial* motivation involved in such efforts has always been one of moral values, whether the subject matter was sex, politics, religion, race, or drugs. As Ms. Broderick so succinctly illustrates, rare is the censor who does not believe he is acting in a socially responsible manner, and "some things are right and some things are wrong and it is that simple" has been the credo of all censors since before the invention of the eraser.

The roots of contemporary and traditional censorship efforts, however, go deeper than the surface issues of moral values and value judgments. At the core of the problem in schools and libraries is a confused and potentially dangerous definition of education. Rather than viewing education as the development of the ability to think critically about social issues, some consider education to be the learning of a prescribed body of knowledge, and the learning of nothing which conflicts with that prescribed body of knowledge. This brand of education is a thinly disguised, refined form of propaganda. . . . The possibilities for the content of the prescribed body of knowledge seem as endless as the hangups of the individuals doing the prescribing . . . and proscribing. Invariably, in this view of education, censorship and propaganda are mutual essentials. That which is "right" becomes the subject of propaganda; that which is "wrong" becomes the subject of censorship. It is as simple as that, and to hell with critical thinking.

Addressing the issue of evaluating library collections, the ALA Council in 1973 issued a statement (revised in 1981) that recognized the continuous review of library materials as a necessary "means of maintaining an active library collection of current interest to users. In the process, materials may be added and physically deteriorated or obsolete materials may be replaced or removed in accordance with the collection maintenance policy of a given library and the needs of the community it serves." However, the statement pointed out, it is an abuse of the evaluation function and violates the principles of intellectual freedom to use the procedure as "a convenient means to remove materials presumed to be controversial or disapproved of by segments of the community."

On the broader issue of diversity in collection development, the ALA Council in 1982 approved a statement which affirmed its historic position calling for libraries to provide a broad-based selection of political and social points of view. The statement said in part:

Throughout history, the focus of censorship has vacillated from generation to generation. Books and other materials have not been selected or have been removed from library collections for many reasons, among which are prejudicial language and ideas, political content, economic theory, social philosophies, religious beliefs, and/or sexual forms of expression.

Some examples of this may include removing or not selecting materials because they are considered by some as racist or sexist; not purchasing conservative religious materials; not selecting materials about or by minorities because it is thought these groups or interests are not represented in a community; or not providing information on or materials from nonmainstream political entitities.

. . . Librarians have a professional responsibility to be inclusive, not exclusive, in collection development and in the provision of interlibrary loan. . . .

Intellectual freedom, the essence of equitable library services promotes no causes, furthers no movements, and favors no viewpoints. It only provides for free access to all expressions of ideas through which any and all sides of a question, cause, or movement may be explored. Toleration is meaningless without tolerance for what some may consider detestable. Librarians cannot justly permit their own preferences to limit their degree of tolerance in collection development, because freedom is indivisible.

Divergent points of view on preselection censorship by librarians are expressed in point-counterpoint format in a program at the 1982 American Library Association conference. The speakers were: Cal Thomas, vice-president of the Moral Majority and former reporter for NBC News, whose book *Book Burning* expands his point of view, and Nat Hentoff, columnist for the *Village Voice*, whose novel *The Day They Came to Arrest the Book* involves censorship of *The Adventures of Huckleberry Finn*. Excerpts from their remarks follow.

ARE LIBRARIANS FAIR? PRESELECTION CENSORSHIP IN A TIME OF RESURGENT CONSERVATISM

Cal Thomas

Item: The federal government is currently supplying hundreds of thousands of dollars through something called the Women's Educational Equity Act to groups who are rewriting the textbooks used by children in public schools to reflect the feminist world view.

Item: George Gilder, the author of the best-selling *Wealth and Poverty*, has complained that some feminists have kept several publishing companies from reissuing his book *Sexual Suicide* and that Harper and Row, Basic Books, Simon and Schuster, and Times Books have bowed to pressure from their own women employees in choosing not to publish a new paperback edition. Hugh Van Dusen, head of Harper and Row's paperback division, says of *Sexual Suicide*, "It's a red flag. Out of loyalty to those people [meaning the feminists on his staff] and to the integrity of our list, I decided not to bid for the rights. But that doesn't constitute censorship."

Item: The Virginia Board of Education withdrew three Virginia history textbooks from its list of approved texts, primarily because of criticism concerning the treatment

Reprinted from *Newsletter on Intellectual Freedom* 31 (5): 151, 181–88 (September 1982).

of racial issues. Since that time, 1973, no replacements have been available.

Item: A Fairfax County, Virginia, public school official attempted to ban Mark Twain's *The Adventures of Huckleberry Finn* because he thinks it is "racist trash." Says John Wallace, an administrator at the Mark Twain Intermediate School, of all things, "anybody who teaches this book is racist."

Item: Something called the Council on Interracial Books for Children has this passage in an introduction to its publication, *Guidelines for Selecting Bias-Free Textbooks and Storybooks*: "Implicit in all textbooks surveyed is the assumption that the U.S. society is a true democracy. . . . The distortion which results is serious, for by calling government and economic systems "democratic" the textbooks deny the realities of capitalism and all that goes with it—classes, conflicting class interests, and the ongoing struggle between those few who control wealth and those many who are trying to share wealth." The Council wants to "reeducate" children by producing new textbooks that would reflect these views. Here's another quote from the same publication designed to rewrite American school textbooks: "Let's make it clear that we have no desire to see children's books that would solely help the dominated get a bigger piece of the pie. We don't like the pie, period. . . . We are not interested in seeing different people win a place in the status quo, the present social structure. We are challenging the structure itself because it promotes anti-human values."

Writing last December 28 in the "My Turn" column of *Newsweek* magazine, Margarita Levin, who is working on her Ph.D. in the philosophy of mathematics, attacks the censorship from the left that portrays women as "Jackies of all trades." After mentioning a number of children's books that show women as auto mechanics, traffic cops, doctors, and telephone repair persons (and there is nothing wrong with that), she says that Mr. Fireman and Mr. Grocer were there, too, but almost none of the women in the books were doing anything that could be considered "traditional." In other words, wives and mothers weren't treated as history, much less as contemporary role models.

Says Levin: "By now every bookstore and library stocks tales that feature one version or another of a brave heroine and a timid, sensitive boy." She notes that until recently changes in roles came about naturally but now they are being forced upon us by activist groups determined to shape society according to their own perceptions of it.

Levin continues: "We approved of having a few female doctors and fathers shown playing with their children since such examples would be true to life. But the portrayal of women in these latest books is completely distorted . . . lots of bricklayers and lawyers, but few, if any, mothers with their children.

"Complaining about this imbalance is apt to provoke the response, 'We must counter centuries of oppression against women.' At the risk of being called a spoilsport, I have to point out that a three year old girl today has not experienced centuries, or even five year's worth, of oppression. Libland is not real and never will be so long as boys are boys and girls are girls.

"The media have helped blind us to those home truths by the tendency to label feminist doctrine as progressive and 'liberating,' and attempts to tell the truth as right-wing brainwashing. Let a conservative try feminist-style pressure tactics to get religion into books and up go the howls. Let him remove violence or scatology from a classic and he's a Savonarola."

I take the time to share some of these examples and some of this philosophy with you because I believe there is far more danger in contemporary America from the censorship of the left than the censorship of the right.

There will always be people on the right and the left who believe they should force everyone else to believe as they believe and read only what they read . . . if, indeed, they read at all. To paraphrase a Bible verse with which I am familiar, "The jerks you will

always have with you!" As a journalist for twenty-one years before coming to the Moral Majority, I am aware of the danger of allowing that attitude to prevail.

It is not the presence of Kurt Vonnegut or *Soul on Ice* or any number of other books that are available in libraries and classrooms that disturbs me. It is the context in which they are so often taught . . . a context of moral laxity and situational ethics, a lack of absolutes or personal accountability or responsibility, of a do-your-own-thing philosophy, because there is no right or wrong, no truth or falsehood. It is wonderful to expose children and adults to ideas and philosophies, new and old, but children, especially, must be given a framework in which they can make reasonable choices based on at least some certainties or we expose them to a stormy sea without a compass or a rudder. That, I believe, is at the heart of what we are seeing develop today.

Let me say right here that the Moral Majority, Incorporated, is not now involved, has not been involved, and will not be involved in libraries in any way except that some of our members carry library cards and occasionally borrow books from them and pay fines when they are overdue. That is the extent of our involvement in libraries and I can promise you that will be the extent of our involvement in the future. . . .

There are, of course, more subtle forms of censorship than somebody running into a library and trying to ban a book. There is a form of censorship practiced by reviewers, who refuse to take notice of or review most books that uphold the Judeo-Christian ethic. A case in point: Dr. Francis Schaeffer is a world-renowned philosopher and theologian. He counts among his friends and those who have been influenced by his writings— presidents, cabinet members, and members of Congress. His influence is worldwide. His books are never reviewed by the major newspapers or magazines. They never show up on best-seller lists, despite the fact that they outsell every book on the *New York Times* and other prestigious lists. As a result of this subtle censorship, libraries often do not select them. They are placed in a category that says what we the "elite" regard as important, *is* important. Therefore, you are not important because you have a perspective that we consider conservative-religious and so you won't find room for consideration here. So much for academic freedom, openness, tolerance, and pluralism.

The practical effect of this attitude is to ban books from libraries more completely than a legislative act or court order could ever do.

The most blatant example of book banning by libraries is the way that so many of them have bought dozens, even scores or even hundreds of books that promote the now dead Equal Rights Amendment, thereby directly or indirectly promoting the so-called women's liberation movement. These same libraries have refused to buy any book which opposed the ERA.

Since the anti-ERA folks won that battle, there must be millions of people interested in reading the arguments against it. Yet this book banning by many libraries means that the American reading public of this and future generations will never be able to learn why ERA lost unless they spend a small fortune to buy the books. There is no excuse for every public, college, and school library not to have the anti-ERA book written by the leader of the STOP-ERA movement (*The Power of the Positive Woman* by Phyllis Schlafly) and the biography of the leader of the STOP-ERA movement (*The Sweetheart of the Silent Majority*). . . .

All conservatives are asking for . . . with the exception of the kooks . . . is fairness and balance. Why is it that some people fight so long and hard to defend the right of young children to read dirty words in certain books and at the same time fight just as hard to prevent them from voluntarily praying or studying the Bible on school property during nonschool hours? Which poses the greater danger to young people? Exposure to the possibility of the existence of God or exposure to scatalogical words and atheism? Our courts have allowed community standards to determine what is obscene and porno-

graphic. They have allowed local option liquor by the drink. Does anyone seriously suggest that young people, particularly, can be hurt more by exposure to traditional values and morals than they can be hurt by getting drunk or overdosing on *Hustler* and *Penthouse*?

Censorship is really the current cliché slogan of the liberals who today are trying to intimidate profamily activists who object to obscenity, profanity, blasphemy, immorality, and violence in textbooks, other school materials, and television to the exclusion of proper counter-balance. The pressure groups against traditional moral standards are really the most ruthless censors of all. . . .

An unlikely ally in explaining what has upset so many Americans is liberal theologian Harvey Cox of Harvard University Divinity School. . . . Said Professor Cox, "One of the major problems in this country is that people don't give a damn what is being taught to their children. If I were to discover that my children were being taught things I thought were completely against my beliefs or family beliefs, I would complain, too."

Now I'm not here today to label you or to accuse you or to attack you. I just want to explain that conservatives are people, too. Educators and politicians don't own children. If anybody "owns them," or, more precisely, is ultimately responsible for them, it is the parents. School teachers, administrators, and librarians have been placed in positions of trust to teach young people not only how to make a living but also how to live. It is not enough to say the kids will get those values from home. The school has far more influence than the parents in the growing-up years and at a minimum should be expected not to go against what is being taught at home.

But how can we start to communicate better with one another and avoid name calling and political posturing for our mutual benefit and the nation's benefit?

First, open up the book selection process to the public. Seminars, information brochures that might be available to citizens at public places throughout the community, an invitation to attend a meeting at which books are selected and rejected so that the people can see for themselves what goes into the process, the adoption of an attitude that librarians are public servants, not dictators. That means that libraries and librarians are to serve the needs and interests of conservatives as well as liberals. Most conservatives I know want only balance in the reading material their tax dollars pay for. If Gloria Steinham and Betty Friedan are to be bought, then Phyllis Schlafly and George Gilder should be as well.

Second, most libraries have "youth" sections, but as I understand it, no child or young teenager may be prohibited from checking out any book he or she wishes to read. I wonder if that is a wise policy. There are restrictions on movie admissions (ostensible ones at least) by which children under 17 are not admitted without an adult to accompany them at R-rated pictures and under 17 are supposedly not admitted at all to X-rated films. Laws in most states ostensibly prevent minors from purchasing cigarettes and beer, wine, or liquor. All states have minimum ages for driver's licenses. There are many other such restrictions. Couldn't some minimal standards be established and publicized that certain books (and you know, I think, the kind I'm talking about) should not necessarily be banned, but that access to them should be restricted or require a note from home or an accompanying parent before they are borrowed? Is this unreasonable? I don't think so.

We are what we read as much as we are what we eat. The activism of the left has put them in the hypocritical position of criticizing the right when we raise certain questions concerning the values that are being taught in our literature and in our public schools. The press and others who report on the activities of the left find no fault at all in what they are doing because they very often share the same goals. . . .

All I can say is that conservatives are people, too; people who have seen the cherished traditions and values we believe built America challenged as they have never been challenged before. Our views and values and even religion (and we are made up not only of Christians of many denominations, but conservative Jews, Mormons, and even a few atheists and agnostics) are said not to matter anymore. The left wants us to sit on the sidelines while they run the country. We will be allowed to participate so long as we adopt a pluralistic attitude. To the liberal, pluralism means that if you disagree with him, then you give in to his position and you are pluralistic and tolerant—a supporter of the First Amendment rights and worthy of involvement in the American Way. But should you hold to your views as matters of principle and refuse to compromise them, then you are an intolerant, racist, bigoted book banner and book burner, seeking to undermine our precious First Amendment freedoms, a shover of values down other people's throats, a religious fanatic, a fundamentalist, who even believes the Bible is true and not a collection of myths and fables.

The most responsible conservatives (and I admit, as I said earlier, there are some irresponsible ones on the right as well as on the left) don't want to ban books and establish a precedent that could result in the banning of something they would like to read or write in the future. But they . . . we . . . do seek balance.

Could we possibly begin again at the beginning and could we move away from this establishment of armed camps of the left and the right from which we lob our artillery shells at each other and never get together to talk peace? This is America, not the Soviet Union. We should be able to talk out our differences and see the merit of each other's positions, protecting the right of each to be heard and read and leaving it up to educated minds to then make informed decisions based on the availability of all the facts and not based on a limited set of choices or a limited selection of books. We at the Moral Majority are ready to talk and "reason together." We'd like to hear the same from you.

Nat Hentoff

I was much intrigued with the first part of Cal Thomas's talk. As he was pillorying censorship from the left, with which I thoroughly agree (which is why, by the way, I am so beloved of the Council for Interracial Books for Children, which would be delighted to ban me, not just my books, but me permanently—they are the paradigmatic example of people who claim they're not censors and are indeed pervasive, or try to be pervasive, censors), I thought, my God—if I may use that term—we might have here an historic occasion on which there would be a pact between the Moral Majority and this representative of that ancient tradition of Jewish free-thinking atheism, in which we would both agree on the banning of all banning. And that might even make a lead paragraph somewhere!

But as I heard the rest of the speech, I realized that the talk about balance was based upon what seemed to me a kind of plebiscite notion, namely, that because everybody pays taxes, then everybody ought to be consulted as to what goes into a library. Therefore, there ought to be kind of a vote for almost every book that gets into a library. At least that seems to me to be the concept. And that reminded me of what James Madison said shortly after the Revolution was successfully concluded, and here I paraphrase somewhat idiomatically. He said, "You know, George III was the enemy until now. We got rid of him, and now the enemy is us, the enemy is majoritarianism." (James Madison sort of foresaw Walt Kelly and "Pogo.") That's why the Supreme Court, in its better moments, has pointed out from time to time that there are certain things that are not up for popular vote, certainly those things in the Bill of Rights. And I think the notion of the popular election of school books is so appalling that conservatives themselves—particularly if they happen to be in the minority, let's say, where I live in Manhattan County—would find it very, very disturbing. . . .

[In comments on the *Island Trees* decision of the U.S. Supreme Court, Hentoff expressed concern over "two dangerous holes": The decision protects books from being rejected from the school library but excludes curricular materials from First Amendment protection. It makes a distinction between a library's initial selection of a book (not a First Amendment matter) and removing it after it has been acquired (a protected right).]

School boards with any amount of intelligence (and some do have some—you remember the Mark Twain comment about that: first God made idiots and that was for practice, and then he made school boards) can still censor because they will simply make sure the books don't get into the library. And in this they have complete control. According to [Justice] Brennan, who is our champion, they have complete control over the acquisition of library materials and they have complete control over curriculum. . . .

Preselection censorship is really a free ballgame, not only for the school board people but for librarians and administrators, as well. I know a librarian in a medium-sized town in Illinois who is a Catholic and who is honestly convinced that it is bad for the soul of any child to read any book that encourages abortion. There are no books that encourage abortion in her library. That's preselection censorship of the rawest kind.

Of course, it can happen the other way just as easily. In fact, I know another librarian in Massachusetts who thought that it is wrong to give a child a book that indicates that life begins at conception and that abortion is murder. In fact, any book that says that would have trouble getting into some YA collections. So it works both ways.

This kind of preselection censorship, whether it's self-censorship or the kind of censorship I characterize as Council-for-Interracial-Books kind—which is censorship for the good of everybody, whether they like it or not—that kind of censorship will increase unless you people begin to examine what you're doing.

Another thing that struck me, particularly

in relationship to what is now left for censorship after the *Island Trees* decision, is the study that came out last summer. To me, it is the most useful, intriguing, dismaying, and sometimes encouraging study on censorship I've ever read. It's titled *Limiting What Students Shall Read*, and was sponsored by the American Library Association, the Association of American Publishers, and the Association for Supervision and Curriculum Development. According to this survey, library materials were challenged more often than classroom materials and were more often changed as a result of challenges. (By the way, I trust I don't have to make the obvious jump, but I'm doing it anyway: public libraries or school libraries, what's the difference? It's all indivisible. The First Amendment is entirely indivisible. It's the same for Nazis in Skokie as it is for the Communist Workers Party in Greensboro. It's the same for school libraries and public libraries. And if you think there's an assault that's not going to reach you, you ain't been reading much lately.) Perhaps one of the most startling findings of the survey was that librarians named school personnel—teachers, administrators, and librarians—as initiating over thirty percent of the challenges cited.

The enemy is us, right?

To give you an example, suppose a certain book comes your way. Let's say it's a YA novel that tells about a school censorship case, a library censorship case. And the particular book described in the novel, which everybody—or just about everybody—wants to censor, repeatedly uses racial epithets—very, very vile racial epithets. Naturally, the black students and the black parents don't want it in the library. Feminists object to it because the women described in the book are foolish, and they're all subservient to their husbands. They read Phyllis Schlafly religiously. The leading character in the book is a male adolescent who is a thief and a liar. He's contemptuous of his father and of church-going people, and for long stretches of time he cavorts stark naked. You know, I hope, what the name of the book is.

I think that book is going to have trouble. Of course, I'm talking about *my* book, which I referred to earlier—*The Day They Came to Arrest the Book*. I think because it is about *Huckleberry Finn*, there are some YA librarians who are not going to want it, who are not going to pick it. It's going to be too much trouble.

I'll tell you what some people might want to buy, though. John Wallace, an administrator at the Mark Twain Intermediate School in Fairfax, Virginia, who tried to ban *Huckleberry Finn* and failed, has almost completed a revision of *Huckleberry Finn*, in which all the insulting words have been taken out. Last week, he said to a reporter for the local Fairfax daily, I think my book is going to be adopted eventually in more schools and taken by more libraries than the original.

You think about whether he's right or not.

By the way, I don't mean to suggest that, the *Island Trees* case notwithstanding, you're still not going to have a lot of trouble with head-on conflicts like the one between Kathy Russell and the Rev. Tom Williams. There's still going to be more of that. But I think that the essential danger to come is more and more in self-censorship or in the kind of censorship that comes from people inside the system, like administrators, principals, etc.

Let me tell you a brief story. I was in Mobile, Alabama, not too long ago, talking before the Alabama Library Association, and various librarians were telling their tales of hardship and exultant victory when they fought to keep books from being censored. One said, "You know, nonetheless, I select books very carefully now. And that way I don't have any trouble at all." Which is, of course, what you do in Korea or Chile or Russia or wherever. Another one said, "No, I don't do that, but I keep a rein on those books that might cause me some trouble—like your books." She pointed at me. She was talking about *This School Is Driving Me Crazy*. And she said, "What I do with your book, because I've had some complaints, is require the kid to get a note from his parents before he can take out the book." Which is great motivation! You know, "What's this dirty book you need my permission for?" Then the kid has to sign a contract with the librarian that he or she will read the book only at home. That way, the kid won't get busted for spreading the dirty word among the other kids.

I could not figure it out. I'm both Jewish and from Boston originally, and there's nothing more prudish than that combination. I don't even write about *im*plicit sex. And I couldn't figure out what words were causing this trouble, not only in Alabama, but in several places around the country. I finally ran into a librarian in a small town in southern Illinois who said the objectionable words were "damn" and "hell." She said, "In this town, and I think it could probably explain some of your problems elsewhere, there are some very religious people who are very careful about what their kids watch on television and what they see in the movies. Sure, the kids hear other kinds of words they're not supposed to hear from their peers, but they know that they're not supposed to use them. And when they see those words in a book, words like 'damn' and 'hell,' which are blasphemous to those parents, they blanch. So what I tell those parents, obviously, is, your kids don't have to read that book. I'll give them another book. But you can't decide what all the other kids in the library are going to read." Which, of course, is the basic, common-sense position which is not too prevalent.

In a way, it's a lot easier, paradoxically, to engage in a real shootout, in which everyone's outfront, and the press is in and the television is in, and the other side is afraid of looking like yahoos (and they probably are yahoos), and Judy Krug is as close as your nearest phone, and reporters are coming again, and you could lose your job. But the adrenalin's up and you're a public figure, and you're a brave one. And goddamnit, the issues are clear. I mean, really clear. Once you've gotten into that kind of fight, that's it.

Preselection censorship works very differently. None of the above is going on—no cannon fire, no press, no public tumult. You're going over a list of books you might or might not buy. It's quiet. It's nice and quiet. Who needs trouble next year? You see some names—Blume, Vonnegut. If you're at the bottom of the list, Hentoff. Nothing but trouble, every one of them. You look around. You don't want to call Judy Krug about this decision—she'll never let you forget it! And Lord knows, there are more books than you have the budget for anyway. So here's an author who never gets anyone into trouble—Peaceable Shronsky, or whatever his name is. Some nice book, some appreciative book—about cats, cats with anthropomorphic features and humor. No time bombs in there. If you're going down that road—it's like the river of Lethe—it takes more courage to stop and turn around and decide, oh, the hell with it, we'll take the Blume and the Vonnegut and the Hentoff, and we'll fight it out—but why don't those writers go into some other line of work!

I saw something this morning that I hope you all get before you leave. It's put out by the Young Adult Services Division Intellectual Freedom Committee and is titled, "Does Your Library Violate the Library Bill of Rights and Not Know It? A Library Pre-Censorship Quiz." Read it yourselves, and bring it around to your colleagues. Challenge yourselves with questions like, "Have you not purchased a popular young adult title such as *Forever* because it might be unpopular with parents?" Or, "Have you not purchased teenage sex books from a conservative religious point of view, such as *How to Be Happy Though Young*, because a staff member found them personally repugnant?" Very good stuff in here.

I started with a couple of librarians in Minnesota and I think in all fairness I ought to end with another kind. Also on that trip, I ran into a librarian who said, "I wish professionals would become more courageous. I realize that there are jobs on the line, but it is the most important role we can play because if we don't, who will?"

There is a "fundamental First Amendment corollary of the right to read. And that is the right of a student to not be forced to read a book that goes against his conscience." In the *Village Voice* (May 3 and 10, 1983) Nat Hentoff discusses the controversy over the reading of Studs Terkel's *Working* in the Girard, Pennsylvania, high school. While the school board affirmed the rightful place of *Working* in the high school, a victory for the right of students to read a book that some people in town thought blasphemous and vulgar, it refused to provide an alternative

book for any student who objected to being forced to read *Working* against his or her moral or religious principles. Two boys from fundamentalist Christian homes were denied diplomas for refusing on grounds of conscience to read the Terkel book. Hentoff cites as precedent for the right *not* to read a book Supreme Court Justice Robert Jackson's opinion (*West Virginia State Board of Education v. Barnette*, 1943) vigorously supporting the right of children of Jehovah's Witnesses not to salute the flag in the public schools.

The president of the University of Wisconsin, former vice-president for Academic Affairs at Harvard University, and legal scholar Robert M. O'Neil in the following article defines the status of libraries and librarians in relation to the First Amendment.

Robert M. O'Neil

LIBRARIES, LIBRARIANS, AND FIRST AMENDMENT FREEDOMS

Few professions more clearly deserve the protection of the first amendment than librarians. Yet few groups—perhaps none engaged in sensitive intellectual activity—have gained fewer constitutional safeguards. Decisions comparable to those defining the free expression of professors, teachers, reporters, theatrical performers, authors and others simply do not exist in the library field. As a consequence, professional librarians understandably fear censorship and repression—not only in "book burning" communities but in more tranquil and civilized parts of the country as well. There are several reasons for this paucity of constitutional protection, which we shall review shortly. There are also some persuasive, if untested, legal

Reprinted by permission from *Human Rights Review* 4: 295–312 (Summer 1975). Copyright 1975 by the British Institute of Human Rights. Footnotes in the orginal article have been omitted, but key cases have been identified in the text.

bases for a new and much needed first amendment freedom. The major concern of this article will be to explore these intriguing constitutional issues.

The neglect of libraries and librarians as an object of constitutional concern can be readily demonstrated. In his seminal treatise on first amendment law, Professor Thomas I. Emerson does not mention libraries, though he develops at length the arguments for a broad definition of free expression and inquiry. The relatively few court cases dealing with libraries have concerned such collateral matters as racial segregation or employment policies, and not the vital and sensitive central function for which libraries exist. In the one instance where a federal appellate court has discussed library circulation policies and access to controversial materials, the presence of a substantial first amendment issue was all but overlooked. In the one pertinent state case, now pending in the California courts, the profoundly important and delicate constitutional issue has been avoided through artful statutory construction.* Thus the constitutional rights and liberties of libraries and librarians remain a virtually uncharted area of law—bad-

*Moore v. Younger, L.A. Sup. Ct. C85493. On January 13, 1975, Los Angeles County Superior Court Judge Robert P. Schifferman ruled that "it was the intention of the Legislature to provide librarians with exemption from application of the Harmful Matter Statute when acting in the discharge of their duties." California's Attorney General informed the State Librarian that the State of California would be bound by the decision.

ly in need of attention, but curiously neglected.

I. NEGLECT OF LIBRARIES IN THE LAW—SPECULATIONS AND CONJECTURES

There are two possible explanations for the paucity of library safeguards. One theory, of course, is that such protection does not exist because it is not needed. This hypothesis deserves relatively little attention, in light of the very major and persistent threats to the freedom of libraries—threats reported bimonthly in the American Library Association's *Newsletter on Intellectual Freedom* and recounted in larger perspective at the Association's annual meeting. Few attacks on public school curricula or teaching materials fail to include or at least invite attacks upon the school libraries as well. Often the library is the first, rather than the last, object of repression in a community determined to stamp out a particular book or magazine, or all the works of a controversial author. There should be no need of elaborate refutation before we set the first hypothesis to rest. We turn instead to a subtler and more complex, but ultimately more satisfying explanation for the law's neglect of libraries and librarians.

Librarians are perhaps in the worst possible position to press their interests and assert their rights through the courts. On one hand, they lack the massive economic stake that has generated most first amendment test litigation; unlike movie distributors and exhibitors, magazine and newspaper publishers, theatrical producers, book publishers and others that have successfully asserted free press or speech claims, librarians simply cannot finance test cases as part of a commercial operation. Nor are they likely to be the beneficiaries of wealthy patrons, as in the case of the Oregon student editor whose criminal appeal (for refusing to disclose a source) was financed by the late Senator (and publisher) William Knowland. Book publishers may support test litigation by distributors or authors, but are far less likely to come to the aid of beleaguered librarians.

On the other hand, librarians are remote from the legal services programs that have enabled low income groups to assert their constitutional rights through test suits. Most librarians, if underpaid, are not indigent, and are thus well above the income levels for public or private legal services. Even the national civil rights and civil liberties groups have been relatively slow to respond to the plight of the librarian. Thus, the librarian is too poor to afford costly counsel or prolonged test litigation, yet not poor enough to have the costs borne by others.

A second factor explaining the lack of precedent may be the nature of the library profession. Unlike school teachers and other groups that are increasingly well organized for economic and other matters, librarians have been historically reluctant to press for redress of grievances. When the American Library Association filed an amicus curiae brief in the United States Supreme Court, seeking a rehearing of the 1973 obscenity decision [*Miller v. California*, 413 U.S. 15 (1973)], the New York Times remarked editorially:

Professional librarians as a group are hardly known as flaming radicals. As civil servants they find themselves in the delicate position of being the guardians of much that is necessarily controversial, while their place on the totem pole of Authority gives them very little power to defend their professional opinions and their personal security.

The editorial concludes, with obvious approval, that ALA's plea for a rehearing "represents an expert judgment based on experience at the firing line." Since that time the Association has filed at least one other amicus brief in a major intellectual freedom case [*Jenkins v. Georgia*, 418 U.S. 153 (1974)] and has mounted a major test suit of its own [*Moore v. Younger*]. But these are quite recent developments, and are in some ways out of character for librarians.

There are two other possible explanations for the paucity of library litigation. One is the lack of clarity about the nature of the librarian's constitutional claim. When a publisher is enjoined from releasing (or a dealer from selling) a book, or a producer is barred from presenting a play to a community, or a movie is seized from the hands of a distributor, the issues are starkly clear. But when a librarian is deterred from circulating a controversial volume, the source of the pressure may be much harder to pin down. Moreover, there appears to be a substantial amount of self-censorship by librarians fearful of reprimands or reprisals; however reprehensible may be the pressures that cause such behavior, they are beyond challenge in the wake of voluntary compliance or even anticipation.

Such complexities as these led the Court of Appeals for the Second Circuit several years ago to dismiss rather callously a librarian's first amendment claim:

The administration of any library, whether it be a university or particularly a public junior high school, involves a constant process of selection and winnowing based not only on educational needs but financial and architectural realities. To suggest that the shelving or unshelving of books presents a constitutional issue, particularly where there is no showing of a curtailment of freedom of speech or thought, is a proposition we cannot accept.

The very issue, of course, is whether a "curtailment of freedom of speech" may be shown where external pressures distort or thwart professional judgment about circulation. But the fact that the pressures are sometimes internal, even self-generated, and that many other factors may impinge on that process, may deprive the librarian's constitutional claim of the clarity that marks comparable claims in other sectors.

It may also be less than clear how various laws affect the librarian and his functions. In the current test suit brought by the American Library Association against the California "harmful to minors" statute, the state attorney general has argued that librarians need not fear prosecution because they neither "distribute" nor "exhibit" anything that could be deemed harmful matter [*Moore v. Younger*]. This is curious reasoning in two respects. For one, it is hard to see what professional librarians do if it is not

distribution or exhibition of materials. Moreover, the attorney general himself had specifically brought librarians within the ambit of the "harmful matter" law, thus generating a quite reasonable apprehension of liability. Yet the later attempt to confuse the issue by taking the librarian's function out of the statute simply illustrates the difficulty of framing viable test cases.

Finally, one suspects that librarians are understandably reluctant to identify themselves publicly in the way that a test case plaintiff must do. Since most controversial volumes are suspect in the public mind—whatever may be their literary merits—their advocacy may entail certain risks. No one likes to be identified as a purveyor of pornography, although if one makes his living by peddling dirty books to susceptible customers at inflated prices, the risk is at least a calculated one. Such a public posture for a librarian is even less comfortable in the growing numbers of cases in which books are attacked for allegedly biased treatment of issues of sex and race. It is one thing to risk attack by the John Birch Society; it is quite another to run afoul of the NAACP, CORE, NOW or WEAL. The complexity of the pressures underlying book censorship, and the risks of a strong public stand against those pressures, may have deterred many potential plaintiffs from library test cases.

Whatever the cause of the current condition, the clear result has been the underdevelopment of a major branch of the law of free thought and expression. But is such a situation harmful, either to librarians or to those with whom they deal? One might rely simply upon the rapidly evolving first amendment law affecting other professional groups, and hope to reason by analogy in the case of librarians. Yet the needs and problems of librarians are quite different from those of booksellers, publishers, newsdealers, theatrical producers, professors and reporters. The whole process of deciding whether to acquire and how to catalog and circulate a controversial work—not to mention the complex challenge of new nonprint formats—is simply different from the judgments required of professionals in other fields.

These differences alone would call for development of a discrete body of library law. The need to do so is underscored by the increasing specialization of other branches of first amendment law. Fifteen or twenty years ago there were simply free speech and free press cases. Today we have relatively discrete bodies of law protecting the expression of students, teachers, reporters, publishers, broadcasters, prisoners, and even rock musical producers. If the librarian fails to seek comparably specialized redress from the courts, the protection accorded other professionals may be progressively less helpful as it becomes more specialized. Thus it is no longer simply a matter of librarians seeking generalized first amendment protection; the critical need now is to develop a body of law that meets the particular needs of a distinctive group.

Against this background, it is now time to consider the prospects for the development of such a branch of first amendment law. We begin with analogies simply because we have no holdings precisely in point. The necessary starting point is the relationship between the librarian and the patron, for if the prospective reader has a constitutional right to read, it would appear that the librarian has a constitutional right (if not responsibility) to serve that interest. Apart from this derivative interest, it may be that the librarian's own professional activity—selection, classification, shelving and circulation of literary materials—warrants first amendment protection independent of the reader's interests. We will examine both branches of the law.

II. THE RIGHT TO READ AS A SOURCE OF LIBRARIANS' LIBERTIES

One would naturally expect a clear judicial declaration of any human interest as widely accepted as the right to read. Yet no such declaration exists. From time to time the Supreme Court has observed, always in dictum, that the first amendment "embraces the right to distribute literature . . . and necessarily protects the right to receive it" [*Martin v. City of Struthers*, 319 U.S. 141 (1943); *Kleindienst v. Mandel*, 408 U.S. 753 (1972); *Stanley v. Georgia*, 394 U.S. 557 (1969)]. Yet the Court has always stopped short of a clear holding that the right to read (or to hear) controversial messages enjoys the same constitutional protection as the right to disseminate. The best we can do is to reason by analogy from a number of cases in which the receipt of information is at least implicated, though never expressly protected.

First, there is a group of decisions involving the right to receive publications. The case most closely in point is *Lamont v. Postmaster General* [381 U.S. 301 (1965)]. In holding that Congress could not require postal patrons to return address cards in order to receive mail from Communist countries, the Court strongly implied that the first amendment encompassed the receipt of controversial publications. Justices Brennan and Goldberg made the implication explicit in their separate opinion:

> [T]he protection of the Bill of Rights goes beyond the specific guarantees to protect from constitutional abridgments those equally fundamental personal rights necessary to make the express guarantees fully meaningful. . . . [T]he right to receive publications is such a fundamental right. The dissemination of ideas can accomplish nothing if otherwise willing addressees are not free to receive and consider them. It would be a barren marketplace of ideas that had only sellers and no buyers.

Before reading this passage too broadly, several qualifications are in order. This is only the view of two Justices, one of whom has since left the Court. The Communist publications involved in the *Lamont* case—unlike most objects of library controversy—would have been unavailable anywhere else if the addressee could not get them through the mails. Moreover, the detained publications bore the name of the individual addressees, and might be thought (in contrast to library materials or bookstore displays) the property of that addressee. Finally,

Lamont does not say (even in the concurring opinions) that there is a right to receive *particular* materials in the mail, but only that Congress cannot require the postal patron to sign his name and reveal his identity as a condition of receiving *any* mail from particular countries. The case would be precisely on point if, for example, a public library required all patrons wishing books about homosexuality, or Communism, or explosives, to sign a special card which would then be circulated throughout the system where anyone might see it. Such a practice would almost certainly be struck down without deciding whether the patron had a right of access to particular materials; a disclosure requirement of this type would be an unconstitutional condition even if there were no clear right to read.

A second group of cases deals with the right to hear a controversial speaker. Several years ago the Supreme Court stopped short of deciding the broad issue in the case involving Belgian Marxist Ernest Mandel, who had been denied a visa and thus could not accept speaking invitations in the United States. The Court dismissed Mandel's claim on the grounds that Congress had plenary power to exclude aliens for virtually any reason, even though citizens might wish to hear him speak [*Kleindienst v. Mandel*, 408 U.S. 753 (1972)]. In the course of the opinion, however, the Court strongly implied a constitutional interest on the part of potential citizen audiences. The majority rejected the government's claim that persons who wished to receive Mandel's message could buy his books, read his articles, or even listen to recordings of his speeches outside the United States. "This argument," replied Mr. Justice Blackmun, "overlooks what may be particular qualities inherent in sustained, face-to-face debate, discussion and questioning." Justice Marshall, in dissent, insisted that "the right to speak and hear—including the right to inform others and to be informed about public issues—are inextricably part of that process."

Earlier cases involving college and university speaker bans also imply a right to

hear. In most cases of the late 1960's and early '70's, the speaker was among the plaintiffs, so the rights of the audience never came into issue. In one case, however, the speaker had dropped out of the suit. The court nonetheless went on to strike down the speaker ban at the behest of the prospective listeners: "[T]here is respectable authority indicating that the audience, which is, after all, a principal beneficiary of the First Amendment, also has standing to seek relief against illegal censorship. . . . There is a First Amendment right to peacefully assemble to listen to the speaker of one's choice, which may not be impaired by state legislation any more than the right of the speaker may be impaired" [*Snyder v. Board of Trustees of the University of Illinois*, 286 F. Supp. 927 (N.D. Ill. 1968)].

In the speaker ban cases, as with *Lamont*, several cautions are appropriate. The constitutional barrier has usually been only one of standing, with the disposition of the merits fairly clear if the court could reach them. Moreover, there are obvious differences between the speaker-audience relationship and the reader-author or reader-publisher relationship. Without an audience, there literally is no speech and no way in which the speaker can exercise his undoubted first amendment right. Also, the close concurrence between listener's and speaker's interests suggest a particular urgency here that may not be present in the reader-publisher or reader-writer context, where distinctive interests exist and can be independently recognized by the courts. Thus the analogical value of the speaker cases, though substantial, must be qualified.

Some additional support may come from recent decisions involving broadcast licensing and the "public interest." In sustaining the "personal attack" rules promulgated by the Federal Communications Commission, the Supreme Court identified a strong listener-viewer first amendment interest in the receipt of balanced material: "It is the right of the viewers and listeners, not the right of the broadcasters," observed the unanimous Court, "which is paramount" [*Red Lion*

Broadcasting Co. v. FCC, 395 U.S. (1969)]. The Court spoke also of the "right of the public to receive suitable access to social, political, esthetic, moral, and other ideas and experiences" as an interest of a high constitutional order. Several years later, while holding that a particular group had no constitutional right to present its message on the air, the Supreme Court reaffirmed the primacy of the listener-viewer interest in receiving information over the air [*Columbia Broadcasting System, Inc. v. Democratic National Committee* 412 U.S. 94 (1973)]. Perhaps even closer to the mark, a court of appeals has held that the format of a radio station may not be altered (*e.g.*, from classical or education to "top forty") if such alteration would seriously deprive the community of an important medium. In such cases the courts' emphasis has rested most specifically and clearly upon the listener interest, even when contrary to the broadcaster's desires.

The informational access claims of two groups have received specific attention by the courts. Nearly thirty years ago the Supreme Court recognized the interests of residents of company towns to receive material from outside sources without broad censorship by the town's owners. Later the Court upheld similar claims of access to shopping centers—again stressing as much the interests of persons inside who wished to receive information as of persons outside the center wishing to impart information. While the most recent shopping center case somewhat limits the right of access defined in the earlier decisions, the basic principle—a right to receive information unaffected by the private status of the enclave—remains unimpaired.

The courts have also begun to deal with access rights of prisoners to receive even controversial materials from outside prison walls. Although the issue has not yet reached the Supreme Court, lower courts have insisted that prison restrictions on reading material be narrowly drawn and may only serve the vital needs of institutional security. Such decisions, even more clearly than those

involving company town residents or shopping center patrons, imply a right to receive information which can be curtailed only by specific and substantial governmental needs.

Also closely related is the Supreme Court's holding that a person may constitutionally possess obscene material in the privacy of his own home. In *Stanley v. Georgia* [394 U.S. 557 (1969)] the majority found it "now well established that the Constitution protects the right to receive information and ideas"—a right which was "fundamental to our free society." Of course the case dealt only with possession and not with acquisition; four years later, the Court refused to extend the implications of *Stanley* to cover the dissemination of obscene materials, thus placing the doctrine more on grounds of the privacy of the home than of freedom of expression.

We have saved until last the one decision that comes closest to recognizing a first amendment right to read. In 1962 the California Supreme Court struck down a ban on Henry Miller's *Tropic of Cancer* [*Zeitlin v. Arnebergh*, 59 Cal. 2d 901, 383 P. 2d 152, 31 Cal. Rptr. 800 (1963)]. The case had two plaintiffs—one, a bookseller who wished to sell the book, and the other a reader who wished to buy it. Had the bookseller been in court alone, the decision would doubtless have come out the same way, so there may be a superfluous quality to the reader's role. Yet the government did move to dismiss the reader's complaint, alleging a lack of standing to raise the constitutional issues. The Supreme Court responded:

Unless [the reader] is able to find a bookseller willing to face the possibility of criminal prosecution and the attendant . . . risks, he will be deprived of his basic constitutional right to read. Thus declaratory relief may offer the only method for vindication of this constitutional right.

It is true that the reader was unnecessary to the decision. It is also true that the case came up on a demurrer, though there is no indication the court felt its judgment limited by the procedural posture. At least in California, the right to read seems fairly well entrenched in the freedoms of expression and communication.

If analogies do not provide a complete answer to the constitutional question with which we began, logical analysis may give added support. The argument for recognition of a freedom to read seems at least as compelling in the case of a publicly-supported institution like a library as in the case of a company town, a shopping center, a college campus, etc. Clearly the constitutional range of access to information, any more than of expression, cannot be narrower in a public place or facility than in a comparable private entity. The Supreme Court has quite recently stressed, in holding that municipal auditoriums could not bar the controversial musical "Hair," the importance of public function and responsibility in this regard [*Southeastern Promotions, Ltd. v. Conrad*, 420 U.S. 546 (1975)]. It would be anomalous if courts were to hold that the reader has less right to receive controversial material from a public library than from a private bookstore or lending library or from a privately-owned radio or television station. Indeed, the first amendment responsibility of a tax supported library system to its patrons would seem at least as broad as the responsibility of a company town to its residents or a broadcast licensee to its listeners. The public library is as integral a part of the public forum as the municipal park or auditorium, and access to its intellectual resources should be unfettered for similar reasons.

Before bringing this discussion to a close, one possibly troublesome question must be considered: Does not the existence of alternative channels in most communities ensure that readers will have access to controversial materials even if the library refuses to carry them or make them available? There are two quite dispositive answers.

The first is that only the *public* library is free, and thus constitutes the only channel within reach of many people. Few can afford to buy all the books they want to read, or rent them from a lending library—even if the range of selection were as broad in the private sector. For many people of limited means, the public library is the *only* source even for daily newspapers and weekly magazines, and even more clearly for such costly items as hardcover books. Thus the availability of private sector alternatives is constitutionally defective because, for many citizens, it is illusory.

There is a second and better answer. The public library has certain responsbilities simply because it is public. In the recent "Hair" case, the City of Chattanooga argued that it should not be required to open its auditorium to an abhorrent musical because there were plenty of other facilities in the community. Even if private theaters would welcome a chance to present "Hair" in Chattanooga, that would be constitutionally irrelevant: " '[O]ne is not to have the exercise of his liberty of expression in appropriate places abridged on the plea that it may be exercised in some other place.' " What goes for rock musicals must apply with even greater force to libraries: the existence of private outlets (quite apart from the cost factor) seems constitutionally immaterial to the right of access to information.

To this point we have talked only of the right to receive materials. The librarian's rights, of course, are derivative or corollary. The author, printer, and publisher need not invoke the reader's rights because they have personal first amendment rights of dissemination. But the librarian is not directly in the channel of distribution and thus cannot invoke the same kind of interest. Instead, the argument must be that the reader cannot read if there is no material available, and that the librarian is a principal source of such material.

The argument needs to be developed a bit more fully. First, it seems clear that a librarian cannot be required to violate the constitutional rights of readers by withholding materials to which the first amendment ensures them access. The California Supreme Court has held that a social worker may not be compelled to violate the privacy rights of his clients by conducting unannounced pre-dawn raids. In other settings it seems clear that the public employee may not be forced to choose between losing his job and violating the rights of others. The same principle should apply no less to the librarian faced with a threat or demand to abridge a patron's right to read. Quite apart from the broad constitutional principle, there is a practical risk of civil liability for depriving the patron of his rights. Surely, then, the desire to respect the first amendment interests of persons whom he serves should protect the librarian against reprisal. If the right to read enjoys the constitutional status we have suggested it should, the librarian is surely a most appropriate, if indirect, beneficiary.

This constitutional claim is, however, a derivative one. The question remains whether the librarian enjoys *personal* first amendment rights. Although no court has so held, it would be surprising if the sensitive intellectual work of the librarian could not claim constitutional protection. Yet here again we must reason by analogy.

The most obvious and apposite analogy is to academic freedom. A substantial body of case law now protects freedom of expression and association of professors and researchers. Clearly this freedom encompasses more than simply classroom instruction. Also included are political activity and association off campus, participation in labor organizations, writing letters to the local press, and of course academic relationships with students and colleagues. Over the last twenty years or so, the courts have struck down a broad range of invasions of academic freedom that chill free thought and inquiry even though they do not directly stifle discussion in the classroom.

The relevance of libraries and librarians to academic freedom should be obvious. Professors cannot pursue controversial issues or invite student research on the frontiers of human knowledge unless the university library is free to order and circulate all relevant materials. Indeed, a free and unfettered university library may well be the cornerstone of academic freedom. Thus the college or university librarian is engaged in a pursuit which seems no less deserving of direct first

amendment protection, within the academic community, than the teaching and research of the professor.

The relevance of academic freedom to the public school or community library is less obvious. Yet the public library shares with the university a responsibility for the gathering and transmission of knowledge from one generation to another. Effective participation in the political process requires ready access to the shelves of the library. Censorship of the acquisition and circulation of controversial materials by the public library cannot help but constrict the total intellectual and political environment of the community. If librarians are not free to gather and disseminate a broad range of materials, then the civic life of the community and the vigor of political debate are bound to suffer. Thus the function of the public library—and the need for constitutional protection of that function—relate closely to the mission of the college or university from which academic freedom springs.

There is still a missing step, however, by which to bring the librarians' professional activity under the purview of the first amendment. What is needed is a new concept of free expression which would encompass the librarian's intellectual and creative processes. Such a concept should not be difficult to fashion. In fact, some of the librarian's functions are "speech" in the narrowest and most traditional sense. Yet it would hardly do to stop there—that is, to tell the librarian that he may order any book he wishes (because that involves "speech" in the technical sense) but that he may not catalog, shelve, or circulate the work since these functions are not traditionally within the first amendment. Rather than parsing the librarian's work in this arcane fashion, we need a much broader concept which will include all the elements vital to the exercise of a librarian's professional judgment and responsiblity.

Such an extension of the traditional concept of free expression hardly seems radical or novel. The Supreme Court has already recognized the concept of "symbolic speech"—notably in the case of a student wearing a black armband in protest against the Vietnam war. A lawyer's freedom of expression necessarily involves the solicitation of clients. An architect's "speech" must include drawing blueprints and the designing of buildings, as well as verbal descriptions of these works. For the sculptor and painter, the only meaningful concept of expression includes the tangible artistic work which results from the creative process, even though the only traditional "speech" involved may be the title or the catalog. Most recently the Supreme Court has brought within the protection of the first amendment the performance of a rock musical, whatever might be the Justices' views of the literary merits of the particular work.

In this setting the professional activity of the librarian seems to merit comparable constitutional protection. When the librarian speaks or writes words of his own, the first amendment unmistakably applies, but simply does not go far enough. Most of what the librarian does is to review, select and disseminate the words of others. Yet the preparation of acquisition lists, cataloging and shelving and circulating books all require a measure of judgment and intellectual evaluation comparable to that required of other protected professions. Moreover, the courts have never had difficulty bringing under the first amendment the bookseller, the newsdealer or the movie exhibitor, all of whom disseminate the words and works of others rather than their own. Surely the librarian, who performs a similar function in a noncommercial context, should not enjoy a lower level of constitutional protection.

III. ASSERTING THE LIBRARIANS' RIGHTS

The current state of affairs is anomalous. We have a plausible basis for a new constitutional right, but no court decisions recognizing it. Librarians ought to be protected, but in fact they are not. The next critical step is to take measures which will bridge the gap between constitutional theory and practical application. What measures might be appropriate?

The first and most obvious step is test litigation. Already underway in the California courts the suit challenging the "harmful minors" law [*Moore v. Younger*]. The result in the first round was favorable to the librarian-plaintiff's interests but on so narrow and nonconstitutional a ground that they, along with the state, have appealed. The California appellate courts may well render the first clear constitutional decision on the rights and liberties of librarians. Should this case fail to produce a constitutional judgment, then undoubtedly other suits will be brought under the auspices of the American Library Association. Once librarians have begun to assert their legal interests, they are not likely to back away simply because the first suit stops short of the constitutional issue—especially when, as in the California case, the narrow decision is favorable to their position.

Litigation should not be the only approach, however. Much can be done through legislation. Recently representatives of state library associations have become much more active in opposing obscenity and other censorship legislation, and in pressing for protection for librarians. (A number of states have adopted exemptions which either expressly or by implication spare librarians from liability for good faith circulation of obscene materials.) If properly organized, and working together with publishers, authors and distributors groups, librarians could become a far more effective political force for intellectual freedom than they have been to date.

The third approach lies through education. Most citizens know far too little either about the incidence or the risks of censorship especially as it affects libraries. It is raids on pornographic book stores and seizure of X-rated movies that capture the headlines—not the slow undermining or erosion of a librarian's will or confidence. Ways must be found to dramatize the plight of the beleaguered librarian in a repressive community. The ALA's superb *Newsletter on Intellectual Freedom* has begun to do this in a most effective way, but to a circulation list of 3000 (less than 10% of the total ALA membership). The newspapers pay far too little attention to developments affecting libraries. Throughout the Kanawha County, West Virginia school textbook crisis in the Fall and Winter of 1974, little was written about the potential and actual threats to school libraries; all the attention in the press was given to school classrooms, school board meetings, bombings and the like. (Happily the Director of the ALA Office of Intellectual Freedom was asked by the National Education Association to serve, and did serve, as a member of the panel investigating the West Virginia situation.) Much more needs to be done simply to make the public aware both of the dangers of library censorship, and of steps that can be taken to combat such repression.

Finally, there is a need for more and better *professional* education on the subject of library freedom and librarians' rights. The simple fact is that professionals in the field often do not fight back because they are not fully cognizant of their legal rights. Every university that has both a law school and a library school should offer at least one course on the legal rights of librarians (as well as the more frequently taught legal liabilities and obligations). There should be casebooks and other teaching materials dealing with librarians' rights, and a host of paper topics for students who wish to pursue the subject in depth. Collaboration between lawyers and library specialists offers a most promising prospect both for teaching and for research. The wonder is that such collaboration has been so limited to date.

IV. CONCLUSION
The constitutional rights and liberties of professional librarians seem to be a constitutional concept in search of a decision. If the California suit does not provide the vehiele for judicial recognition of this vital set of first amendment interests, another case will do so before long. Meanwhile, the risks of repression and censorship—the stifling of a major artery of free inquiry and public debate—cannot be minimized simply because adequate precedent is lacking. If the problem exists, and surely it does, the courts will get to it soon enough.

CHAPTER FIVE

HOW DID IT ALL BEGIN?

The basic principles of Charles Darwin's theory of evolution, as set forth in *The Origin of Species*, are today almost universally accepted in the scientific world, though controversies have raged around them for more than a century.

The most important event in Darwin's life, determining his whole career, was his five-year voyage as naturalist on HMS *Beagle*, 1831–36. During this period the *Beagle* touched on nearly every continent and major island as she circled the world. Darwin was called upon to serve as geologist, botanist, zoologist, and general man of science—superb preparation for his subsequent life of research and writing.

Everywhere Darwin went, he made extensive collections of plants and animals, fossil and living, earth-dwelling and marine forms. He investigated, with the eye of a naturalist, the pampas of Argentina, the dry slopes of the Andes, the salt lakes and deserts of Chile and Argentina, the dense forests of Brazil, Tierra del Fuego, and Tahiti, the deforested Cape de Verde Islands, geological formations of the South American coast and mountains, active and dead volcanoes on islands and mainland, coral reefs, fossil mammals of Patagonia, extinct races of man in Peru, and the aborigines of Tierra del Fuego and Patagonia.

Of all the regions visited none impressed Darwin so forcibly as the Galapagos Islands, five hundred miles off the west coast of South America. There he saw giant tortoises, elsewhere found only as fossils, huge lizards long since extinct in other parts of the world, enormous crabs, and sea lions. The birds on the islands were similar to those on the neighboring continent but not identical. The strange phenomena of the Galapagos Islands, added to certain facts previously noted in South America, reinforced the ideas on evolution beginning to take shape in Darwin's mind.

Immediately upon his return to England, Darwin began keeping a notebook on evolution and collecting facts on the variation of species, thus taking the first steps toward his *Origin of Species*. In the beginning the great riddle was how to explain the appearance and disappearance of species. Why did species originate, become modified with the passage of time, diverge into numerous branches, and often vanish from the scene completely?

The key to the mystery for Darwin came through a chance reading of Malthus' *Essay on Population*. Malthus had shown that mankind's rate of increase was retarded by such checks as disease, accidents, wars, and famine. It occurred to Darwin that similar factors might keep down the populations of animals and plants. Thus was born the famous Darwinian doctrine of natural selection, struggle for existence, or survival of the fittest—the foundation stone for *The Origin of Species*.

For twenty years Darwin's notebooks expanded to substantiate his theories. He read a vast range of literature, talked with expert breeders of animals and plants, studied skeletons of wild and domesticated birds, made crossing experiments with pigeons, and investigated seed transport.

Strong support for the principle of natural selection, Darwin thought, came from a study of "artificial selection." In the case of domestic animals and plants, humans have selected and bred the varieties most advantageous to their own needs, causing radical modifications. If evolution could be brought about by artificial selection, Darwin reasoned, nature might function in the same manner, except that natural selection would result from the struggle for existence. Among all forms of life, he observed, an enormous number of individuals must perish; only a fraction of those born can survive. Some species furnish food for other species. The battle goes on ceaselessly, and the fierce competition eliminates animals and plants unfitted to survive. Variations in species take place to meet the conditions necessary for survival.

The first announcement of the theory of evolution by natural selection came in 1858, shortly after Darwin learned that a fellow scientist, Alfred Russel Wallace, carrying on natural history observations in the Malay Archipelago, had reached the same conclusions. *The Origin of Species* was published the following year.

At the outset Darwin describes the changes that have occurred in domesticated animals and plants as a result of human control, and these are compared with variations resulting from natural selection. Wherever there is life, it is concluded, change is constant. To variation there is added the struggle for existence, and Darwin offers dramatic illustrations of how far the ability of living organisms to reproduce outstrips their capacity to survive.

The Origin of Species demonstrates the operation of the principle of natural selection in checking population increases. Some individuals in a species are stronger, can run faster, are more intelligent, more immune to disease, sexually more aggressive, or better able to endure the rigors of climate than their fellows. These will survive and reproduce as the weaker members perish. In the course of many millenniums, variations lead to the creation of essentially new species.

As expressed by Darwin: "Natural selection is daily and hourly scrutinizing, throughout the world, the slightest variations; rejecting those that are bad, preserving and adding up all that are good." In this fashion is the theory of unending evolution presented in *The Origin of Species*.

The contemporary reception of Darwin's celebrated book has been compared to "a conflagration like lightning in a full barn." If the revolutionary new theory were valid, the biblical story of creation could no longer be accepted. Church authorities immediately viewed the Darwinian thesis as dangerous to religion and roused a storm of opposition. In *The Origin of Species* Darwin intentionally avoided any discussion of man's beginning, because he thought that any emphasis on this phase of evolution would cause his entire theory to be rejected. In a later work, *The Descent of Man*, however, a massive amount of evidence is advanced to demonstrate that the human race is also a product of evolution from lower forms.

Viewed in retrospect, Darwin's impression on nearly all major fields of learning was, and continues to be, profound. The doctrine of organic evolution has been accepted by biologists, geologists, chemists, and physicists, by anthropologists, psychologists, educators, philosophers, and sociologists, and even by historians, political scientists, and philologists.

Because Darwin was an extraordinarily acute observer and experimenter, his findings for the most part have stood up well against the test of time. Even though his theories have been modified by the discoveries of modern science, Darwin succeeded in foreshadowing in a remarkable fashion the ideas prevailing today in genetics, paleontology, and a variety of other fields.

Nevertheless, violent controversy continues to rage around the evolutionary theory, especially in the United States. Even a U.S. President has expressed doubts as to its validity, and fundamentalist religious groups, known as creationists, continue to bring pressure on state legislatures to require the biblical account of creation to be taught on an equal basis, or as an alternative, to the theory of evolution. Many years after the famous 1925 "Monkey Trial" of John Scopes for teaching evolution in Dayton, Tennessee, stormy debates go on in educational, religious, and legislative circles.

The most recent phase of a conflict now exceeding the Hundred Years' War in duration is the rise of "creation science" to challenge the theory of evolution. According to a well-known paleontologist, Stephen Jay Gould, the basic text for creationism was written by John Whitcomb and Henry Morris, *The Genesis Flood*, published in 1961. The authors were convinced that they had found a scientific alternative to Darwin, based on Genesis 1:6–7.

Responding to pressure from religious groups, the California legislature enacted a law requiring teachers of evolutionary biology to describe God and the six days of creation. A suit to force compliance was filed in 1979 by Kelly Seagraves, director of the San Diego–based Creation Science Research Center. By mutual consent the scope of the ensuing trial was limited. Eminent scientists waiting to testify were not called as witnesses. The only substantive judicial finding was that the California Board of Education was not communicating clearly enough to teachers the "undogmatic" intent of the guidelines for teaching evolution. The creationists saw the guidelines as opening new inroads for teaching the biblical view of creation.

The court decided, however, that the guidelines did not violate the rights of the creationists.

The California case was simply a prelude to epic courtroom battles to follow.

Among the arguments advanced by creationists to support their case is that the evolutionary theory does not have the characteristics of a normal scientific theory. For example, evolutionists are unable to make significant predictions about future events. From a legal standpoint creationists maintain that teaching of evolution constitutes a religion in the form of secular humanism, thus violating two provisions of the U.S. Constitution: one forbidding the state from establishing a religion and the other protecting an individual's right to practice religion.

The stage was set for the nationally publicized trial held in Little Rock, Arkansas, early in 1982. In March 1981 the governor of Arkansas had signed into law, without reading it, a statute entitled "Balanced Treatment for Creation Science and Evolution Science Act." It mandated that "public schools within this state shall give balanced treatment to creation science and to evolution science." Shortly thereafter the act was challenged on constitutional grounds.

Some background for the conflict is supplied by two articles; "The Science-Textbook Controversies," by Dorothy Nelkin in the April 1976 issue of the *Scientific American* and "Repealing the Enlightenment" by Gene Lyons, a resident of Little Rock, in *Harper's* magazine for April 1982.

Dorothy Nelkin

THE SCIENCE-TEXTBOOK CONTROVERSIES

In 1969 the California Board of Education issued new guidelines for the biology curriculum of the state's public schools. The guidelines included a statement that the Book of Genesis presents a reasonable explanation of the origin of life and that the concept of special creation should be taught as an alternative to the concept of organic evolution. It was only fair, it asserted, that "equal time" should be given to the two concepts and that students should be allowed to choose between them.

Why is it that objection to the concept of evolution, dormant as a public issue since the Scopes trial of 1925, has gathered new impetus? How have comparatively small groups of people who believe in special cre-

ation been able to insist that their belief have a place in public education and even in the deliberations of science policy at the Federal level? What are the issues that have forced public recognition of concerns long ignored as being merely the private views of religious fundamentalists?

The California guidelines dramatically manifested the wide public interest in the values conveyed to students through the teaching of biology and the social sciences. The evolutionary concepts of modern biology are attacked by publications distributed in the millions by Jehovah's Witnesses and other missionary sects. The issue even reached the courts in 1972, when the religion editor of the *Washington Star*, who maintained that he was acting in the interest of 40 million evangelical Christians in the U.S., sued the National Science Foundation for using public funds to support education that violated religious beliefs. School boards and curriculum committees in many communities have been effectively prevented from recommending textbooks that discuss evolution.

The controversy over the science curriculum, which threatens to end a 20-year effort to modernize the precollege science curriculum in the public schools, has been bitter and filled with paradoxes. Although the evolutionary concepts of biology are among the most firmly established generalizations of modern science, public demands for the teaching of alternative explanations have exerted remarkable political influence. Although public education in science has fostered the widespread belief that natural phenomena can be rationally explained, there are vigorous efforts to reintroduce traditional religious explanations. Although the complexities of modern technology call for specialized knowledge, there is an increasing demand for participation by lay groups in the teaching of science on the grounds that education should reflect the values of the community. Perhaps the greatest paradox of all is that the critics of science textbooks do not represent the poorly educated or deprived sectors of the population only. Most textbook controversies issue not from rural folk in Appalachia but from middle-class citizens, many of whom are technically trained.

After the Scopes trial antievolutionary sentiment had a quiet but pervasive influence on the teaching of biology in the public schools. Textbooks for the most part avoided the topic: the word "evolution" or the name of Darwin can scarcely be found in books published in the 1930's. A national survey made in 1942 indicated that fewer than half of all high school biology teachers even mentioned evolution in their courses. As late as 1959, the centennial of the publication of Darwin's *Origin of Species*, the geneticist Hermann J. Muller could state that the teaching of biology in public schools was dominated by "antiquated religious traditions" and that it barely referred to modern research in population genetics and related areas that increasingly refined and supported the concept of evolution.

To help remedy the situation the National Science Foundation set up a program called the Biological Sciences Curriculum Study (BSCS) and gave it $7 million to create modern biology courses for the public schools. Three textbooks were developed, each emphasizing a different aspect of current biological research: molecular biology, cell biology and ecology. All three reflected the fact that modern biological research is based on evolutionary assumptions, which were described as "the warp and woof of modern biology."

The BSCS series was actually part of a larger National Science Foundation program that had been inaugurated in the late 1950's after the U.S.S.R. had launched its first Sputnik. The program was intended to build up the scientific and engineering manpower of the U.S. by bringing modern scientific concepts, methods and knowledge to the nation's public schools. The program as a whole had a considerable impact on precollege science education. A new curriculum in physics was devised by the Physical Science Study Committee (PSSC). It was soon followed by new curricula in mathematics, chemistry, biology (BSCS) and finally the social sciences. In all, the National Science Foundation financed 53 such projects.

Initially there was little problem with public acceptance of the new curricula in physics, chemistry and mathematics. A shadow of future problems appeared, however, when the BSCS biology series was introduced in 1964. That immediately touched off several intense, although short-lived, disputes. For example, in Texas critics of the curriculum declared that the teaching of such "atheistic" material was associated with the kind of "godless behavior" that had led to the assassination of President Kennedy the year before. The fact that the assassin fired from the Texas School Book Depository Building was not neglected by those who fought the adoption of the BSCS textbooks. All three books were finally approved in Texas, however, and the series was soon in service throughout the country.

The development of the social-science curriculum, titled *Man: A Course of Study* (MACOS), was launched in 1963 wnen a group of scholars from the Education Development Center, Inc. (then Educational Services, Inc.), of Cambridge, Mass., received a grant from the National Science Foundation to develop an integrated program of precollege social-science courses. Until MACOS was introduced the teaching of social science in the public schools had consisted mostly of descriptive presentations of American history. MACOS, designed for children in the fifth and sixth grades, asks three questions: What is human about human beings? How did they get that way? How can they become more so?

The MACOS curriculum relies on studies of animal behavior and of the culture of the Netsilik Eskimos to explore questions about the nature of human beings, patterns of social interaction and child rearing, and the development of a culture's total view of the world. To the social scientists who worked on the MACOS curriculum the study of animal behavior provided a provocative metaphor to illuminate features of human behavior. The study of a traditional tribal culture showed how human beings as well as animals adapt to a particular environment; in order for the Netsilik to survive in an environment with limited food resources they practice infanticide and senilicide as means of controlling the population. MACOS suggested that in some societies such practices, disturbing as they would be in our own culture, were functional, and that neither behavior nor beliefs have an absolute value apart from their social and physical context.

It was difficult to find a publisher for a curriculum that was innovative and costly and required special training for teachers. Accordingly the National Science Foundation provided credit to back the publication of MACOS, and it set up workshops for training the teachers who would be adopting the program. In all, the National Science Foundation granted $4.8 million to develop MACOS and $2.16 million to implement it. By 1974 the MACOS curriculum, widely praised as an imaginative contribution to education, had found its place in some 1,700 schools in 47 states.

Elementary education in the public schools has always been one of the more volatile areas of public policy. Any effort at innovation can count on provoking conflict for two reasons: first, parents are persistently anxious about what influences their offspring, and second, parents and teachers alike are ambivalent about the proper role of public education in disseminating values as well as knowledge. An army of "textbook-watchers" has long been on guard for changes in textbooks that threaten various concepts of basic education, public morality or patriotism. More recently textbook-watchers have also been concerned with eliminating ethnic and sex bias. With the notable exception of the Scopes trial, however, there had been relatively few disputes over the teaching of science. Science was generally perceived as being morally neutral and associated with material progress. Thus it was dissociated from the questions of values that concerned the textbook-watchers.

By the late 1960's attitudes appeared to shift. The change became evident in the growing criticism of scientific rationality and in the proliferation of cults and sects based on Eastern mysticism. Less visible, but perhaps more important in the light of subsequent events, was a remarkable growth in the membership of fundamentalist churches, particularly in urban Texas and southern California—the very centers of industry based on high technology.

In those areas some citizens were disillusioned with what they called the "decadence of scientism" and with political authority that seemed to remove their sense of local power. They expressed their resentment by attacking science courses in the local schools. In fact, they formed the financial, social and political base for a nationwide movement to challenge science textbooks. Their answer to the uncertainties of a technological society was not to reject technology but to return to fundamentalist religion and traditional beliefs. It was in this atmosphere that the National Science Foundation precollege curricula in biology and the social sciences became the focus of extended and bitter controversy.

The activists at the core of the antievolution movement are the "scientific creationists," people with degrees in science who work out of "creation research centers." They maintain that they are scientists who are engaged not in a controversy between religion and science but in a debate about the validity of two scientific theories. Their organizations and activities are patterned on those of organized science. Titles and credentials are offered as proof of their legitimacy. Research projects are designed to examine their hypotheses. Journals and textbooks disseminate their findings. They believe "all basic types of living things, including man, were made by direct creative acts of God during the creation week" and they seek to reinterpret the evolution of organisms according to biblical authority.

It was creationists of this kind who in 1969 convinced the California Board of Education that creation and evolution should be taught as alternative theories. Bills with similar provisions were introduced in state legislatures throughout the country. In Tennessee legislation requiring equal time for the concept of special creation was passed in 1973. The California creationists eventually failed, however, to implement the teaching of the creation concept in the public schools, and even in Tennessee the law requiring equal time for the creation concept was declared unconstitutional and was repealed in 1975. The creationist movement has nonetheless retained a strong base of support among people who think that their traditional values are in some way threatened by the rational explanation of natural phenomena.

The strength of that fear became apparent in the reaction against MACOS. The controversy involved many of the same people who had earlier fought the BSCS series of biology textbooks. Initially the MACOS materials sold well and were enthusiastically received in many communities. The only early resistance was a protest in Florida in 1970 and another a year later in Phoenix, Ariz., where the superintendent of schools banned the materials throughout the state.

In 1973, however, a rash of disputes broke out across the nation. MACOS suddenly became a symbol for local frustrations. The specific nature of the protests varied from one region to another. In university communities strains in the "town-gown" relationship became apparent when groups of local citizens leveled protests at "those experts on the campus who try to determine our values." In the South religious issues were predominant. In small towns there was criticism of the message of cultural relativism in MACOS suggesting that beliefs and values unacceptable in our culture might be acceptable in others. In urban centers a major concern was that such "irreligious teaching" would cause "immoral behavior."

These seemingly isolated disputes were linked by a network of communications. The same activists showed up in many different communities disputing MACOS, and they repeatedly issued identical documentation of the problems the course allegedly presented. Several organizations based in Washington provided legal assistance and circulated reports and out-of-context inflammatory material from the course to arouse parental concern. By 1975 the sales of MACOS had declined by 70 percent.

The moral content of MACOS caused some to question the propriety of Federal financing of a controversial curriculum. Soon the controversy became a national issue. Representative John B. Conlan of Arizona carried the issue to the House Committee on Science and Technology. He found little support for his suggestion that Congress censor the curriculum, but he did find that his colleagues sought some control over "unaccountable executive bureaucracies" such as the National Science Foundation. Congressional attitudes had been primed in part by Senator William Proxmire's criticism of "those damn fool projects in the behavioral sciences," by the perennial concern over the spending of public funds and by the post-Watergate mistrust of executive agencies.

Last April, Conlan proposed to the entire House of Representatives that the bill authorizing the National Science Foundation to finance the development of science curricula for public schools be amended to require Congressional approval for specific science-curriculum projects. The amendment was defeated by a vote of only 215 to 196. A different amendment was passed, requiring that all material pioneered by the foundation (including the guidelines for training the teachers) be open to parental inspection. Funds for MACOS, however, were terminated, and further support of science-curriculum projects was suspended pending a review of the entire National Science Foundation educational program.

Several review committees were formed, including a group within the foundation and the Science Curriculum Implementation Review Group, under the chairmanship of J. M. Moudy, chancellor of Texas Christian University. The Moudy group was appointed by Representative Olin E. Teague of Texas, chairman of the House Committee on Science and Technology. The committee of the National Science Foundation recommended that the system for reviewing specific science-curriculum projects before they are implemented in the public schools be tightened and that the review system include laymen such as parents and community leaders. It further recommended that the National Science Foundation itself remain "at arm's length" from the implementation process.

The Moudy study group represented a spectrum of opinion on the issue and agreed on only a few recommendations. Nevertheless, it recommended that the National Science Foundation continue to fund the implementation of MACOS, provided that initiative for implementation projects came from local institutions. Such separation would help to shield local communities against being unduly influenced by the Federal Government. The Moudy study group also agreed that laymen should be included in the review system. Specifically it suggested that representative parents who are "innocent of professional and scholarly bias" be involved in decisions regarding curricula that impinge on widely observed customs and long-held religious beliefs.

As the Moudy study group was considering whether or not the National Science Foundation's system of reviewing educational materials was adequate, Representative Conlan extended his criticism of the review system to include the foundation's other policies. His criticism helped to stimulate a Congressional examination of the foundation's peer-review system of evaluating proposals for grants for scientific research, and also a call for more public accountability for funds expended on such research.

The National Science Foundation is faced with the task of how to evaluate and monitor its educational projects, a task that presents many dilemmas. If the foundation finds it cannot approve a course of study for dissemination to the public, it is open to accusations of censorship. If it does approve a course for dissemination and parents and community leaders object to it, then it is even more open to accusations of trying to impose Federal standards on education.

It is easy to label those who question the validity and limits of modern science as ignorant, irrational or crackpot. Those labels throw no light on the social and political tensions that sustain objections to the teachings of science in the public schools. Three themes pervade the science-textbook controversies. First, the protests reflect the fact that a non-negligible fraction of the population is disillusioned with science and is concerned that it threatens traditional religious and moral values. Second, the protests reflect the fact that many people clearly resent the authority represented by scientific dogmatism, particularly when that authority is expressed in an increased professionalism of the school science curriculum. Third, the protests reflect the fact that many people are afraid that the structured, meritocratic processes operating within science threaten more egalitarian, pluralistic values.

Let us examine those three themes in more detail. First, for many fundamentalists the social disruptions of the 1960's are evidence that the quality of American values is declining. These people associate what they perceive as an expanding immorality with the dominance of "liberal" secular and scientific values, and they blame the decline of religion on the rise of a technological society. They do not react by opposing technology, however. They focus instead on the uncertainties and disruptions that they feel characterize modern life as a result of secularism and scientific rationality. They seek to alleviate these uncertainties and disruptions by turning toward a traditional and fundamentalist religious outlook. The creationist who wrote the California guidelines proposing equal time for the theory of the creation in biology textbooks associates the concept of evolution with "a campaign of secularization in a scientific-materialistic society—a campaign to totally neutralize religious convictions, to destroy any concept of absolute moral values, to deny any racial difference, to mix all ethnic groups in cookbook proportions, and finally [to destroy] the differences between male and female."

Fundamentalist textbook critics are particularly distressed by the teaching of modern biology and social science because of the emphasis on the similarities between man and other animals, because of the implication that moral values are relative and because of the denial that an omnipotent and omniscient force determines human development and behavior. They argue that emphasizing the genetic similarities between human beings and other animals may encourage "animal-like," socially dangerous behavior. One creationist stated: "If man is an evolved animal, then the morals of the barnyard or jungle are more natural . . . than the artificially imposed restrictions of premarital chastity and marital fidelity. Instead of monogamy, why not promiscuity and polygamy? . . . Self-preservation is the first law of nature; only the fittest will survive. Be the cock-of-the-walk and the king-of-the-mountain. Eat, drink and be merry, for life is short and that's the end. So says evolution." One woman even blamed the "streaking" fad of 1974 on the concept of evolution. "If young people are taught they are animals long enough, they'll soon begin to act like them."

Many of the disturbing values that are implicit in the concept of evolution became explicit in MACOS. Some critics asked: Why should a discussion of man concentrate in such detail on animals? Others argued that the curriculum was a pernicious attempt to spread the religion of secular humanism, an anthropocentric view of the world that emphasizes man's capacity to achieve self-realization through reason and denies the importance of God and a spiritual order. Critics were particularly disturbed by the MACOS material on the adaptation of the Netsilik Eskimos to their harsh environment. MACOS suggested that values and behavior were based not on God's law but on specific environmental pressures. To some critics this point of view implied that scientists were expounding a philosophy of relativism that denies absolute standards. Such relativistic assumptions, it was thought, were morally destructive and harmful to family life. One critic remarked: "Already we condone feticide and abortion and devalue human life, all in the name of biological principles." To stengthen their case some textbook-watchers cite examples in which science has been misused, thus associating themselves with widely held concerns about the social impact of modern science and technology.

The second theme in the textbook controversies is the resentment of the role played by scientists and other professionals in the development of science curricula for the public schools. Representative Conlan declared: "An elite corps of unelected professional academics and their government friends run things in the schools." Creationists spoke of arrogance and the absence of humility among scientists. One sympathetic journalist wrote of his joy in "seeing science humbled" and of witnessing a break in the "monopoly of truth." A creationist observed: "After all, scientists put on their trousers in the morning one leg at a time, just like the rest of the world." And a Jehovah's Witness wrote about the "arrogant authoritarianism required by evolutionists to sustain what they cannot prove." Such concerns are not, of course, unique to textbook-watchers; resentment against professional authority is expressed at nearly every public confrontation between experts and laymen.

In California the attack on scientific authority resulted in a number of changes in textbooks that were intended to remove dogmatic statements and to indicate the limits of scientific explanation. The creationists also attacked the National Science Foundation for its support of the BSCS materials. The theme of "a Federal takeover of education" emerged in full force during the MACOS disputes and during the 1975 Congressional hearings on the annual appropriation for the National Science Foundation. At that time Representative Conlan found that one way to arouse interest in MACOS among his Congressional colleagues was to describe the curriculum as an "insidious attempt to impose particular school courses . . . on local school districts, using the power and financial resources of the Federal Government to set up a network of educator lobbyists to control education throughout America."

Textbook disputes are organized around demands for the increased participation of laymen in decisions about the school curriculum. The demands for local control have been stimulated by the decade-old ruling of the U.S. Supreme Court to the effect that decisions on obscenity and pornography were to be made locally. Textbook-watchers, who had been concerned with "smut in the schools," had watched the obscenity case with interest. They have used the Supreme Court ruling to back their argument that any issue impinging on local values, including how science is to be taught, should be judged within the community. One organizer in Texas who is active in anti-MACOS and pro-creationist protests throughout the country summarized the prevailing philosophy of the movement: "Unless people take an active voice in assisting the authorized units of government in a process of selecting textbooks, the selection will continue to deteriorate."

The public education system has been one of the last grass-roots institutions in Amer-

ica. School systems were traditionally decentralized, run by local school boards composed of elected nonprofessional citizens. Local control has gradually been eroded, however, through court decisions, through the reliance of schools on nonlocal funds, through the merging of school districts and through the trend toward professionalism. The curriculum in a public school today is guided more by national testing standards and college entrance requirements than by local values. The influence of individuals who expect to retain local control over educational policy is threatened by the growing power of statewide curriculum committees and by the increasingly professional departments of education. Federally funded programs devised by professionals are an additional threat.

The decline of local control has been a major source of tension in the controversies over ethnic balance and the busing of students as well as in the controversies over curricula and textbooks. Hence when textbook-watchers reject professional control of the curricula that influence their children, they can count on support from diverse groups ranging from the "radical right" to the "new left," all concerned with Government infringement on local powers and all sympathetic to any movement that seeks to increase individual political activity.

Demands for increased nonprofessional participation in curriculum decisions raise difficult practical questions. Does the state have a responsibility to require that certain textbooks be used in all classes? What kinds of constraints or standards can be imposed to balance academic interests with local and individual religious concerns? What happens if local values deny students access to widely accepted knowledge and wisdom?

From the professional perspective designing a school curriculum is a technical enterprise that is best organized by experts, so that the curricula will provide the student with the best available information. From a local perspective, however, public education also transmits values and beliefs. Since such values and beliefs are very much family matters, parents must be involved. Clearly science education is no longer exempt from that perspective.

The third theme in the textbook controversies is a defensiveness toward the egalitarian, pluralistic processes that operate outside science, processes that lean heavily on the notion that there are two sides to every question and that each side should be treated fairly and given equal time.

In January, 1973, Henry M. Morris, Jr., the director of the Institute for Creation Research, wrote to the director of the BSCS project and challenged him to a public debate. The debate would take up the statement: "Resolved, that the special-creation model of the history of the earth and its inhabitants is more effective in the correlation and prediction of scientific data than is the evolution model." Morris proposed that the winner of the debate would be determined by the applause from the audience. According to Morris, the issue was one of free public choice, of equality and of fairness. Creationists argue that since the biblical account of the origin of man and other living things is scientifically valid, it deserves equal time with the concept of evolution. Whenever there are two equally valid hypotheses, it is only fair that students be exposed to both of them and be allowed to choose for themselves.

The modern concept of equal time originated with the Fairness Doctrine of the Federal Communications Commission, which states that broadcasters are responsible for affording a "reasonable opportunity for the presentation of contrasting viewpoints on controversial issues of public importance." The Fairness Doctrine was based on the rationale that television, as a costly and monopolistic medium, did not sufficiently allow dissenting viewpoints to be expressed. In practice the doctrine has been extraordinarily difficult to define and to implement on television. In principle, however, it has had an enormous appeal in American society because it is equated with fairness and justice and is rooted in the democratic attitude.

The concept of equal time has been particularly influential in American education. Over the past decade textbooks have been challenged by minority groups and by women who see the presentation of history as ethnically and sexually biased and who seek to have their interests more fairly represented in the educational process. The concept of equal time, of pluralism, implies that all groups have a right to maintain their cultural and religious traditions in the face of pressures for conformity. The textbook-watchers have extended the concept to the teaching of science; they believe the struggle against cultural conformity is paralleled by their struggle against scientific conformity.

The theme of equal time appeared in the disputes over MACOS in the form of demands that diverse values be represented in social-science courses. MACOS, it was argued, presented a one-sided view. The attorney for groups protesting against MACOS in Kanawha County, W. Va., in 1975 commented: "Under the banner of science, value systems are being marched into the schoolroom with a shameless disregard of the will of the polity. . . . The truth dawning on parents—be they creekers and rednecks from West Virginia or Gold Coasters from Connecticut—is that education is a sectarian occupation."

One report on MACOS from a conservative organization in Washington that provides legal counsel for textbook controversies specifically asserted that science education should either avoid all questions of values or provide equal time for the presentation of alternative values. The Moudy study group said that MACOS implicitly promotes "an evolutionary and relative humanism" because it does not allow any "hints of patriotism, theism, creationism or other explicit values." An aide to Representative Conlan added: "Diverse facts should be taught fairly and the student allowed to make up his own mind."

The suggestion that questions of scientific fact and scientific education should be settled by public debate has left most scientists amazed. Would the lay community really want to give quack doctors equal time with licensed doctors? To include the doctrines of Christian Science in books on health? To include astrological lore in books on astronomy? For that matter, would the community entertain putting a paragraph in the Book of Genesis to indicate that the scientific method rejects supernatural explanations of the universe?

Concepts of pluralism, of equity and of participatory democracy, as they are defined in the political context, are incongruous in science. Scientific concepts are taught when they are generally accepted by the scientific community. In fact, it is precisely that acceptance by the scientific community that acts to validate one concept and reject another; acceptance by those outside the scientific community is irrelevant. Moreover, although science is an open system in terms of social class, the reputation of a scientist depends on his achievements and their rigorous evaluation by his peers. Indeed, the internal standards of science may run counter to egalitarian principles. Hence scientists are particularly distressed by the proposal that laymen participate in defining the nature of an appropriate education in science.

The suggestion that egalitarian principles be extended to science indicates that the character and the content of science, as they are understood by scientists, are perceived quite differently by many laymen. Conversely, when scientists dismiss the critics of science as simply being "irrational," they fail to grasp the differences between the structured, meritocratic processes that operate within science and the more egalitarian, pluralistic processes that operate outside it.

The differences between the attitudes of scientists and those of nonscientists naturally hinder efforts to communicate scientific information to the public effectively. Indeed, the way in which such information is communicated may partly explain why public resistance to the authority of science is so persistent. Where scientists themselves understand that their work is approximate, conditional and open to critical examination, many nonscientists believe science is authoritative, exact and definitive. The

organized skepticism toward scientific findings that is tacitly understood by those who practice science contrasts sharply with the external view of science.

Perhaps the most difficult concept for scientists to convey to those who are not scientists is the delicate balance between certainty and doubt that is so essential to the scientific spirit. Textbooks in particular tend to convey a message of certainty to the nonspecialist. In the process of simplifying concepts, findings may become explanations, explanations may become axioms and tentative judgments may become definitive conclusions. Few textbooks are careful to stress the distinction between fact and interpretation or to suggest that intuition and speculation actually guide the development of scientific concepts.

Authoritarian public representations of science are reinforced by scientists who deeply desire to avoid challenge and criticism from people outside their own profession. They tend to respond to criticism with a kind of scientific fundamentalism: by citing the value-free character of their work or the weight of the factual evidence that supports their conclusions. To those whose religious faith is challenged, however, the scientific merits of a concept that defines man's place in the universe may be less to the point than the concept's social and moral implications. The concept of evolution, after all, has had a remarkable social impact. It was described as "a secure basis for ethics" by C. H. Waddington. It was called a naturalistic religion by Julian Huxley. It was a justification of laissez faire economics for the 19th-century entrepreneurs who called the growth of large companies "the survival of the fittest." The moral implications that can be drawn from the concept of evolution and the threat it presents to absolute ethical values are clearly far more important to many laymen than the details of the concept's scientific verification.

Those details can, in fact, easily be ignored or rationalized by such laymen. The persistence of creationism and the controversy over MACOS are reminders that many people are reluctant to surrender their deepest convictions to the authority of science, and that intuitive expectations and beliefs can easily take precedence over scientific explanations. Furthermore, simply increasing the amount of available technical information is unlikely to change well-rooted beliefs. Selection operates within the mind of the individual to determine the way in which such information is interpreted, particularly when the information is not fully understood.

Nevertheless, it is not accurate to dismiss the critics of science textbooks as being merely an antiscience fringe group. Creationism is an unlikely combination of religion and science in which theological beliefs are conveyed in a context of research monographs and scientific societies. And most of the people who have been working against MACOS do not deny that science is a useful activity. They object primarily to an impersonal educational bureaucracy that fails to represent their interests and that insults their personal beliefs. They are not reacting against science so much as resisting its image as an infallible source of truth that denies their sense of place in the universe.

In these respects the textbook critics are part of the romantic resistance to science that is reflected in the popularity of astrology, mystical cults and the imaginary cosmologies of Immanual Velikovsky and Erich Von Daniken. They are also part of a political resistance to science that is reflected in increased social action against innovation and in the demands for lay participation in scientific and technical decisions. As questions that are normally resolved by professional consensus are brought into the political arena, and as democratic values such as freedom of choice, equality and fairness enter into science policy, the consequences of such resistance to science may be painful.

Gene Lyons

REPEALING THE ENLIGHTENMENT

The subspecies *Homo nesciens arkansas* comprises two distinct varieties: Country, and Country-Come-to-Town. It was ever thus. Back in the bad old days before the invention of polyester suits and communications satellites, however, genuine yokels held all the power in the state we call "the Land of Opportunity." In fact the first Arkansas antievolution law was not a product of the legislature. Passed on November 6, 1928, the day of Herbert Hoover's ascension to the presidency, the statute forbidding mention of godless, atheistic Darwinism in public schools was enacted by popular referendum.

A couple of days before the election, advertisements appeared in newspapers across the state. THE BIBLE OR ATHEISM, WHICH? read the headline on one favoring the passage of Act No. 1. But more than a hundred prominent citizens, including two former governors and the editor of the *Arkansas Gazette*—most of them from the sinful metropolis of Little Rock—signed another advertisement, urging common sense. Only three years earlier, after all, in 1925, Arkansas's neighbor to the east had convicted John Scopes for uttering heresies within the hearing of school children, and in the process had made the word "Tennessee" a synonym for "benighted." The people at large, the second advertisement maintained, were not qualified to pass on the veracity of a theory taught "in every first-class university and college in America, Europe, Asia, Africa and Australia." It was not the credibility of science that was at stake, but the state's reputation.

Voter turnout was heavy, for not only were science and religion contending on the ballot but Arkansas faced an excruciating presidential choice. Al Smith, the Democrat, represented both Demon Rum and the Pope of Rome. Hoover, though, was a Republican, the party of Lincoln. Hayseeds emerged from every God-intoxicated hollow in the Ozarks; automobile and mule jams clogged the flat dirt roads of the Delta. Al Smith won the Wonder State, but evolution lost. The vote for banning biological science was 108,991 to 63,406. Only Pulaski County (Little Rock) dissented.

Having made a ritual gesture in favor of the Lord, fundamentalists returned to the sleep of ages. Darwin made little headway in the boondocks, but then neither did any other sort of civilized learning. Most persons capable of reason in those districts found out about evolutionary theory anyway. In Little Rock and the other larger towns the law was ignored, albeit with caution. Acquaintances of mine who grew up in country towns tell stories of science teachers' voices dropping into conspiratorial whispers, of books being slipped to them on the sly as if they were racy French novels. A cruder version of the Moral Majority has been regnant in the Arkansas outback for at least 150 years, after all, without having effected a diminution of freelance sin. Alcohol in drinkable form is still forbidden the rustics across vast swatches of the state. While a federal court in Little Rock wrestled recently with creationism, the school board in Paragould voted not to allow a school prom on the grounds that dancin' leads to drinkin' and drinkin' to lust. Even so, Arkansas leads the nation in teenage pregnancies and ranks high in the incidence of venereal disease. By setting up coherent thought as temptation, Arkansas's antievolution law has probably lured as many young Arkansans to science over the years as it has prevented from hearing about it.

Initiated Act No. 1, in any event, remained on the books for forty years with nary a prosecution. It was removed in 1968 by the United States Supreme Court after a Little Rock Central High biology teacher made an issue of it. *Epperson* v. *Arkansas* was the second Supreme Court case involving Central High in little more than a decade. The first, of course, concerned racial segregation.

KNOW-NOTHINGISM IN A LAB COAT

Act 590, or the "Balanced Treatment of Creation-Science and Evolution-Science Act," as adepts call it, has a more socially acceptable pedigree than the 1928 monkey law. Reporters who came to Little Rock to cover the recent trial about this one's constitutionality found no snake handlers or fulminating barefoot hillbillies. Yessir, folks, with Act 590, country has done come to town. Dress up an ambitious fraud in a suit made of synthetic fiber, style his hair like a health-spa instructor's, give him a pocketful of credit cards, a push-button phone with a "hold" button, electric windows in his late model car, stick a Bible in his pocket, provide a neatly coiffed wife who knows how to make goo-goo eyes at the back of his head for TV cameras, and that man can play the media like a church organ. The statute's very concept of "balanced treatment" derives from, and therefore appeals to, the idea of journalistic fairness taught in the nation's "Schools of Communication." Are there not, after all, "two sides to every question"? Unfortunately that concept, which is shallow enough when dealing with persons holding a post-Enlightenment world view, ill equips a reporter to get at the truth when confronted with persons who do not. Creationists, you see, do not believe that there is or can be a distinction between the sacred and the secular. All ideas to them are religious ideas. Hence they do not hold themselves to the arbitration of facts, evidence, and logic; they reject the metaphysics of science even while claiming its cultural authority.

Neither do creationists believe, accordingly, in the separation of church and state, although they will prevaricate and squirm like sixteenth-century Jesuits when the question is put to them directly. So if the story of the 1981 Monkey Trial strikes you as ludicrous, which I hope it will, do not therefore be deceived into taking creationism lightly. Theirs is a coherent and internally consistent world view. The "scientists" in the movement do science as one does literary criticism, picking among facts and theories for ones that support a preexisting point of view—which in their case is a literal reading of Genesis—and either twisting whatever does not fit, or simply discarding it. Creationism is no more science than is astrology or palm-reading; it is William Jennings Bryan's know-nothingism in a lab coat. Creationists claim the designation "scientific" partly as propaganda, but, as with most propaganda, they are their own first victims. Oddly, while not believing in real science, which strikes them as pessimistic, European, and anti-Christian—perhaps even "Jewish"—they believe quite heartily, most of them, in technology and progress. Up to the day of Armageddon, that is. Most would also be shocked to hear themselves described as Social Darwinists, but are all free-enterprise zealots whose views are perfectly congruent with that turn-of-the-century philosophy. And there are a whole lot more of them in California, to come to the point, than there are in Arkansas.

But the Arkansas experience with creationism is instructive. The sponsor of the "Balanced Treatment" Act was one Sen. James L. Holsted of North Little Rock, a tall, handsome graduate of Vanderbilt University who was at the time president of the Providential Life Insurance Company, a family concern. Creationism zipped through the senate on the last day of the 1981 session, with no hearings and only a few comments from the floor. The house of representatives held no hearings either, having scheduled the bill for a period reserved for "noncontroversial" legislation. Debate consumed all of fifteen minutes, some of which was spent refusing to hear Arkansas's Methodist bishop Kenneth Hicks, who had rushed in vain to the capitol when a member of his flock warned him what was up. The tally there was 69–18.

BETTER THAN THE CIRCUS
Arkansans in general are probably no more ignorant than the American public at large, but all the ignoramuses do agree. Political tradition here pardons a legislator who votes on symbolic issues to soothe the prejudices of the mouth-breathing element in the dirt-road churches. Arkansas is more than 90 percent Protestant, the hard-shell sects predominate, and ambitious youths yearn to be television evangelists as others wish to emulate Reggie Jackson or Donny Osmond. No sense, runs the usual logic, in stirring people up; the federal courts can take care of it. Then everybody can whoop it up in the next campaign about meddlin' judges thwarting the will of the people, can get reelected, and can continue to work on the truly important business of democracy, like exempting farm equipment from the sales tax or allowing the poultry industry to load as many chickens as can be jammed into a semi-trailer regardless of highway weight limits.

Indeed, it appears that many of the legislators mistook the creationist bill for yet another in the series of harmless resolutions in praise of Christianity that they customarily endorse. Others were simply gulled. Had scientists uncovered evidence proving Genesis to be biologically and historically accurate? Who could doubt it? Were atheists and "secular humanists" laboring to suppress the truth? It sounded logical. The legislature was besieged by a well-organized phalanx not of backwoods fulminators but of live-wire "Christian" bidnessmen and doctors' wives from the newer suburbs of Little Rock. The creationists have laid their traps where the money is: among the semieducated who, by their prosperity, deem themselves members of contemporary Puritanism's visible elect, but who cling to the childish theology of their fathers because contemporary life has flooded them with a confusion of moral values that will not compute unless the Bible is accepted as a rule book. At the time of the "debate," only the Moral Majority and a local organization called FLAG (Family, Life, America, and God) seemed to know that Act 590 had been introduced at all, much less made it to the floor.

In fact, Act 590 was not written in Arkansas, and there is reason to doubt that anybody here read it all the way through until after it was already law. Senator Holsted got it from an employee of his, who in turn took it from a group of fundamentalist ministers who received it by mail from its author, a respiration therapist named Paul Ellwanger of Anderson, South Carolina. Ellwanger, founder and proprietor of an organization he calls Citizens for Fairness in Education, wrote it with the help of an outfit called the Institute for Creation Research in (where else?) San Diego. The "scientific" godfathers of creationism are Henry Morris and one Dr. Duane Gish, a preposterous buncombe artist about whom more later. The principal legal consultant was Wendell Bird, also of the ICR and author, for those readers who may be tempted to dismiss creationism as mere regional delusion, of a very long article in the *Yale Law Journal* three years ago that not only posited creationism as a science but proposed its inclusion in public school curricula to "balance" and thereby "neutralize" the teaching of evolution, which it equated with atheism.

Governor Frank White certainly did not read the creationism bill. A Little Rock bank executive and a graduate of the U.S. Naval Academy, White ran for office as God's own candidate. The Lord, he said repeatedly during his campaign against incumbent Democrat Bill Clinton, had told him to declare his candidacy. On winning a narrow victory in the Reagan landslide, he declared the deity well pleased. White's equally pious second wife told the press that God had not only introduced her to her second husband but He had even done a turn as celestial realtor, divinely inspiring their choice of a home. After he signed the bill, White boasted to reporters that Arkansas had assumed the scientific leadership of the known world. White asserted that the new law was undoubtedly constitutional. But when asked specifically about the clause forbidding the "establishment of Theologically Liberal, Humanist, Nontheist, or Atheistic religions," the governor confessed that he was ignorant of the text. His office issued a clarification saying he had been thoroughly briefed, but the aide responsible for keeping track of legislation told the *Arkansas Gazette* that to her knowledge nothing of the sort had transpired. Sponsor Holsted told the same newspaper that "of course" his motives were religious, but, he added, "If I'd known people were going to be asking me about the specifics of creation science, I might have gotten scared off because I don't know anything about that stuff." Democratic Attorney General Steve Clark, in a remark that would come back to haunt him, said he had his doubts the law could be defended.

When the educated portion of the citizenry heard about the law, reaction was strong. There was a near unanimous outcry from the universities, teacher organizations, and the Arkansas Academy of Sciences. Editorial scorn was heaped on the perpetrators by virtually every newspaper in the state. So far have we come since 1928 that editorialists in places like Warren, McGehee, Stuttgart, Searcy, and Lonoke felt free to denounce Act 590 without having to fear for burning crosses. The prevailing theme was that the thoughtless bozos of the legislature had again made Arkansas a national joke, just when its image had begun to improve after the damage done by Orval Faubus in the 1957 Central High integration crisis. A Little Rock man had lapel pins made with a banana logo and sold them to benefit the monkey house at a zoo; he raised hundreds of dollars. A series of derisively funny editorial cartoons has appeared in the *Arkansas Gazette* in which Governor White always appears holding a half-eaten banana. Only the *Arkansas Democrat*, the capital's second-string newspaper, involved in a circulation war with the *Gazette* and seeking the lowest common denominator, has defended the law.

Senator Holsted was prevented from reaping what glory there was to be had from creationism by an untimely indictment for embezzling $105,000 from the family business, but Frank White has got himself an issue. The governor's genius consists of a total inability to be embarrassed. His 1980 campaign was a masterpiece of fraudulent innuendo. Besides the usual denunciations of taxes, Big Government, and welfare cheats—Arkansas has the lowest taxes of any of the fifty states, and thus of the industrial world—White spent most of his money on a series of television commercials showing a minor riot by Cuban refugees housed on a former Army base near Fort Smith. Most of the Cubans were black. Had Governor Bill Clinton "stood up" to Jimmy Carter, he asserted, this threat to Arkansas's peace and security could have been prevented.

Whether or not White is the crassest religious hypocrite seen in these parts since Billy Sunday seems to me a question not worth pausing over. Americans overrate sincerity. Morally speaking, it matters little whether a person can't think, won't think, or merely feigns the credulity of a child. In any case, creationism has become so volatile an issue that the governor is welcome to it, should he decide to flog it in the 1982 campaign. Creationism cuts unpredictably across party and ideological lines. As always, the imponderable mystery is how the monkey law plays in the country; White couldn't be elected county assessor in Little Rock. But there are no polls to tell us how many Arkansans favor the law, much less whether its proponents care deeply enough to vote on that basis alone. Many legislators got nervous when they began hearing from their educated constituents, particularly from ministers and churchgoers from nonfundamentalist sects, which have long since given up militant opposition to the visible world, and who believe correctly that antics like those of last year degrade religion rather than advance it. Chambers of commerce anxious to lure new industries, especially of the clean, high-tech variety, found themselves facing embarrassing questions. Some even wondered whether creationism might not hamper the Arkansas Razorback football and basketball coaches in their quest for out-of-state talent. If *that* could be proved, only Jehovah himself could save White from popular wrath. Many legislators said they thought they had made a mistake; there was talk of repeal. But that required the cooperation of the governor, and White stood petulantly firm. If anybody was going to save Arkansas's public school students from necromancy, it would have to be a federal judge. Again.

GOD TAKES THE STAND

If one wished to understand why the adult forms of Christianity in America seem afflicted with polite senility while the kindergarten churches bulge with sinners, Little Rock's creationism trial offered many clues. When the American Civil Liberties Union first announced that it would challenge the law and presented its twenty-three plaintiffs to the public, creationism looked to be set up for a quick knockout. Of the twenty-three, twelve were clerics. Their number included not only the Methodist, Roman Catholic, Episcopal, and African Methodist Episcopal bishops of Arkansas but also representatives of the Presbyterians, Southern Baptists, and Reform Jews as well. Here was a perfect opportunity to seize the high rhetorical ground from the electronic fundamentalists. In aligning themselves with an easily exposed religious hoax, the Moral Majority and company would seem finally to have gone too far. To require that a sectarian dogma inimical to most churches be taught *as science* in public schools violates virtually everything six graders are taught about Americanism.

But the churchmen blew it, locally at least. They allowed themselves to be muzzled by a platoon of lawyers. Perhaps "muzzled" is a bit strong. Although the trial was political in its essence, the ACLU conducted it as if it were a corporate merger. In their own pulpits and newsletters, the clergy expressed themselves forcefully and with some eloquence. Bishop Hicks of the Arkansas Methodist Church delivered himself early on of a well-written letter to the *Gazette* on the vast presumption underlying fundamentalist bibliolatry: that puny man sets himself up to limit God's power to the dimensions of his own mind. But only a small fraction of readers see the editorial page; Hicks was preaching to the converted. If the churchmen had appeared on the evening news bearing such messages, if they had held regular news conferences and distributed press releases at regular intervals commenting on the trial, if they had put together a paid religious telecast on the subject using some of the very erudite and committed scientists and theologians who came to Little Rock on their own time to testify, they might have dealt creationism a crippling blow. They did not conduct such a campaign. But the Moral Majority and the Institute for Creation Research did. So the fundamentalist line that the trial was a contest between atheism and the Lord went unchallenged, at least in volume and stridency.

But that is a cavil next to the brilliant show the ACLU's witnesses made during the trial last December. Arkansans can thank their governor and legislature for provoking a first-rate seminar on science and theology, featuring an array of erudite men and women whose like we would not otherwise have seen in five years of visiting lecturers. University of Chicago theologian Langdon Gilkey made such a forceful witness that he had the fundamentalist preachers who crowded the back of the courtroom nodding and buzzing in agreement when he dissected the language of Act 590 to reveal at every turn the unacknowledged authority of Genesis, the very phrase "sudden creation of the universe, energy, and life from nothing" implying not only God, but the God of the Old Testament alone.

Of course most of those preachers are simple souls, not up to the rapid donning and doffing of hats required to maintain that creationism is "scientific" and Act 590's purpose is secular. Unlike many of the state's witnesses, they have never wandered in the wood of materialism and doubt. Evolution is to them an unholy fairy tale whose premises they have never credited for one moment. As for the U.S. Constitution, why, if the Founding Fathers had meant for us to separate God's word from our government, the word "Creator" would not appear in the Declaration of Independence. Only communists think otherwise. When Cornell sociologist Dorothy Nelkin said in cross-examination that she was an atheist, there was a muted gasp in the back of the courtroom. Several heads bowed in prayer.

As the plaintiff's witnesses went on, the courtroom took on most of the aspects not of a religious, but an academic, camp meeting. Except for Moral Majoritarians and creationists taking notes, most of the militant godly among the spectators disappeared, to be replaced by honors biology classes from the local high schools and professors from the Little Rock campuses of the University of Arkansas. Even had I not recognized many of the latter, style would have told: in our corner of the world, as the British reporters on hand rapidly established, creationists go in for synthetic fabrics, styled hair, or toupees, while evolutionists sport khaki, wool, and facial hair.

As an academic camp meeting, the first week of the trial was most inspiring to this apostate English professor. Having years ago wearied of the posturings of most academic literary types, I suppose I had grown more than half dubious that useful thinking was going on anywhere in the academic world. But to hear philosopher of science Michael Ruse of the University of Guelph explain how science both limits and lays claim to knowledge, and to be able to listen to such literate practitioners as geneticist Francisco Ayala of the University of California, biophysicist Harold Morowitz of Yale, Harvard's versatile paleontologist Stephen Jay Gould, and Brent Dalrymple of the U.S. Geological Survey was a rare privilege. There may be something more to our species after all than the lust for power and things. Thank you, Governor White.

It was hard not to pity Attorney General Steve Clark and his outgunned staff, attempting to show that the creationism law had no religious origins. The record contained letters from the law's author. "I view this whole battle as one between God and anti-God forces," Paul Ellwanger had written. He advised his supporters to conceal their sacred motives, lest the courts catch on; if they could not forbear witnessing for the Lord when petitioning their representatives, they should reserve the apologetics for a separate sheet of paper.

The text of the law itself betrayed its intent at every turn. Here, for example, is the definition of the law of creationism:

"Creation-science" means the scientific evidences for creation and inferences from those scientific evidences. Creation-science includes the scientific evidences and related inferences that indicate: (1) Sudden creation of the universe, energy, and life from nothing; (2) The insufficiency of mutation and natural selection in bringing about development of all living kinds from a single organism; (3) Changes only within fixed limits of originally created kinds of plants and animals; (4) Separate ancestry for man and apes; (5) Explanation of the earth's geology by catastrophism, including the occurrence of a worldwide flood; and (6) A relatively recent inception of the earth and living kinds.

In nearly two weeks of testimony, no scientist, whether "creation" or otherwise, could enlighten the court as to the exact meaning of "kind." Creationist Wayne A. Farir of King's College, Briarcliff Manor, N.Y., said it could mean "species," "genus," "family," or even "order," in which case number four above stands contradicted, since Adam and Eve, Governor White, and Bonzo the Chimp all belong to the order of primates. Farir, who labors at refuting Darwin by comparing the blood-cell sizes of various turtles, said he was still working on the problem of whether or not the shelled beasts constitute a kind. Neither turtles nor tortoises, of course, are specifically mentioned in Genesis 1:11–12 and 21–25, where the concept of "kinds" originates; some, indeed, are "swimming creatures, with which the waters abound," others "animals that crawl on the earth." It is a difficult problem.

Perhaps no more difficult, though, than the attorney general faced in seeking expert witnesses for creationism. Everybody, both in the movement and outside it, cites Henry Morris and Duane Gish of the Institute for Creation Research as not simply *the* authorities on the subject, but in fact its originators. Both, unfortunately, are prolific authors. Putting them on the stand to prove creationism to be science would be like calling Richard Nixon to testify that politicians never lie. In his treatise *Scientific Creationism*, for example, Morris says:

A. Creation cannot be proved
   1. Creation . . . is inaccessible to the scientific method.
   2. It is impossible to devise a scientific experiment to describe the creation process, or even to ascertain whether such a process *can* take place. The creator does not create at the whim of a scientist.

The learned Dr. Gish—he has a Ph.D. in biochemistry from Berkeley—is similarly honest, at least part of the time. In *Evolution? The Fossils Say No!*, he puts it this way:

We do not know how the Creator created, what processes He used, for *He used processes which are not now operating anywhere in the natural universe* [his emphasis]. This is why we refer to creation as special creation. We cannot discover by scientific investigations anything about the creative processes used by the Creator.

As an article of faith, of course, Gish's is a perfectly sound position and places creationism exactly where it belongs: outside science's claim to know. In a recent letter to *Discover* magazine, though, Gish went further. He was responding to an article attacking creationism's pretensions:

Stephen Jay Gould states that creationists claim creation is a scientific theory. *This is a false accusation.* Creationists have repeatedly stated that neither creation nor evolution is a scientific theory (and each is equally religious).

Yet this same eminence was everywhere in Little Rock during the trial, sitting two rows behind the state's lawyers, passing them notes, indulging in heated colloquies during the recesses, and making pronouncements about the indubitable scientific merits of creationism for the television reporters. Indeed, the man's creator seems to have blessed him with a tropism for bright lights and camera lenses.

Despite a definitely simian aspect, which made him the butt of many cruel jokes in the press row, Gish is in fact a masterful artist of the televised debate, that bastard form of showmanship first visited on us by presidential politics. During the trial, good old Jerry

Falwell, of Moral Majority and "Old Time Gospel Hour" fame, staged just such a confrontation between Gish and Prof. Russell Doolittle, a chemist from the University of California, who was naïve enough to think that the winners and losers of such events are determined by evidence and logic. Perhaps in graduate seminars and laboratories they are, but for all of his earnest learning, Doolittle might as well have been trading insults with Johnny Carson. Gish's presentation was timed to the minute and consisted of a premium assortment of half-truths, semifacts, quasi-logic, outright falsehoods, and simple balderdash. All replete, of course, with scriptural authority. In front of the audience in Falwell's Lynchburg church, cheering and whistling to see the infidel routed, Gish was triumphant.

Gish argued, for example, that the Second Law of Thermodynamics renders evolution impossible. How childish of "evolution scientists" to imagine, he implied, that they could push this ludicrous hoax past such a learned and reverent authority as himself. What the cheering faithful do not know, however, is that the Second Law of Thermodynamics states almost the opposite of what Gish says it does. In a closed system, it is true, greater organization of heat energy cannot occur. A closed system is one that energy is not entering from the outside. In an open system, into which energy does flow, increased organization of energy can and does occur. Until very recently, when scientists simply ignored the creationists, Gish and his followers did not trouble to make the distinction, although if the Second Law meant what they said it did, not only evolution but life itself would be impossible. On the "Old Time Gospel Hour" debate Gish even slipped for a brief moment into the Old Time Second Law of Thermodynamics, telling the audience that "on the hypothetical primordial earth, you did not have an energy conversion machine." This is heresy.

With creationism's chief apologists eliminated as potential witnesses by reason of their own past words, Attorney General Clark had no recourse but to call creationists who had published little or nothing. What began in the first week as a fine seminar degenerated into a boring farce with overtones of pathos. That the state's case was incoherent was no fault of the lawyers: it was Act 590 that bequeathed to them the "two-model approach," in turn taken from creationist authors, who in turn plagiarized the notion, as I have suggested earlier, from the "equal time" doctrine that allots television coverage to political candidates in our imperfect world of Republicans and Democrats. Briefly stated, the argument runs like this: "evolution science" posits atheism. "Creation science," while not religious, of course, posits theism. There are no other possibilities. Either there is a God, in which case "evolution science" is falsified, or there is not, in which case . . . But let us not get into that thicket. Suffice it to say, though, that the theory of evolution does not posit atheism. Science agrees to exclude the supernatural, yes. But so do accounting, law, and the rules of baseball. Are we now to have Bowie Kuhn denounced as a godless purveyor of materialistic satanism? Perhaps a creation baseball league will be next.

The "two-model approach" allowed Clark to pretend what creationists pretend: that all evidence against any aspect of any scientific theory tending to support evolution constitutes proof of creationism. Logically, of course, this is like saying that evidence I was not in Little Rock last Wednesday establishes that I was in fact golfing on Mars. Hence scientists were easily convicted of doing science. Does Stephen Jay Gould's theory of "punctuated equilibrium"—i.e., of evolutionary change in relatively rapid bursts, with cataclysms altering the environment—disagree with those of more orthodox theorists who think the process has been more gradual? Very well. Both are refuted and creationism proved. One of the funnier moments in the trial's first week came when one young barrister tried to ensnare the wickedly articulate Francisco Ayala, a former priest with scientific training *and* the equivalent of a doctorate in theology, into admitting the validity of the two-model approach. "Your name," the scientist told the expectant young lawyer, "is Mr. Williams. But my name isn't not-Mr. Williams. The courtroom is full of people whose name isn't not-Mr. Williams." The real Mr. Williams changed his line of questioning. At another point, a state's attorney asked Professor Morowitz of Yale: "Can you tell me the name of one Ivy League university that has a creation scientist on its staff?" Morowitz could not. Neither could he name any other prestigious graduate school or journal that employed creationists. Morowitz added, "I can't give you the name of an Ivy League school, graduate school or journal which houses a flat earth theorist either."

The state's most coherent witness by far was Dr. Norman Geisler of the Dallas Theological Seminary. It was Geisler who admitted, under cross-examination, that besides the two-model theory, he also believed that UFOs were "a satanic manifestation in the world for the purpose of deception." As nearly as I can work it out, Geisler believes that any abstract idea held strongly by any number of people constitutes what he calls "transcendence," and answers his definition of religion. He quoted, as all good fundamentalists do, from something called *The Humanist Manifesto*, and intimated that because there is such an organization, and because a footnote in a Supreme Court decision once classified that organization as a religious one, that all persons who are "humanists" are acolytes of that faith. I shall refrain from insulting *Harper's* readers by letting them work out the syllogism themselves. It is by such arguments that fundamentalist "intellectuals" propose to render the First Amendment tautological and thus useless: if all intellectual positions are equally "religious" in nature, then why bother?

The most profound part of Geisler's testimony was his attempt to prove that the "Creator" of the universe and life mentioned in Act 590 was not an inherently religious concept. After citing Aristotle, Plato, and one or two other classical philosophers who supposedly believed in a God or gods without worshipping them—albeit not as

creators of the world "from nothing"—Geisler offered his most thundering proof: the Epistle of James. He cited a line of Scripture to the effect that Satan acknowledges God, but chooses not to worship Him. "The Devil," he said, "believes that there is a God." Whee! If Geisler has not yet squared the circle in his meditations, he has at least, well, circled it. Who would have thought one could prove the Creator a nonreligious idea by means of hearsay evidence from Beelzebub? After unloading that bombshell, Geisler, too, hastened to face the cameras in the courtroom hallway. "We don't rule out stones from a geology class just because some people have worshiped stones, and we don't rule God out of science class because some believe in him." As I listened to Geisler I could not help but recall the words of the Rev. C. O. Magee, a Presbyterian minister who is a member of the Little Rock School Board. "Any time religion gets involved in science," Magee told the *Gazette*, "religion comes off looking like a bunch of nerds. . . . The Book of Genesis told who created the world and why it was created and science tells how it was done." Amen.

After Geisler, the state's case went straight downhill. These witnesses were supposedly learned men, possessing advanced degrees, most of them resident in institutions that purported to be colleges and universities. Some of my own prejudices against academia would have revived, except that this collection of sad sacks, flub-a-dubs, and third-rate hobbyists had been gleaned mostly from the kinds of schools where the faculty must sign pledges certifying their literal belief in the factual inerrancy of the Bible, and were not, in the post-Enlightenment sense, really academic institutions at all. (The Institute for Creation Research requires such a pledge.) Most were like Donald Chittick, a physical chemist from George Fox College in Newberg, Oregon. Chittick spent hours telling the court how fuel could actually be made very rapidly from "biomass" materials. (In the Ozarks, of course, a good deal of biomass fuel has been distilled and drunk over the years.) To Chittick's mind, this proves that the world does not have to be 4.5 billion years old at all. Chittick's most telling point was that the amount of helium present in the earth's atmosphere indicates that radioactive decay has been taking place on earth for about 10,000 years only. That is just about how old creationists say the earth is. Either Chittick did not mention, or does not know, that helium is too light to be held by the earth's gravity and disperses constantly into space.

The trial's only poignant moment came during cross-examination of Harold Coffin, a dreadfully earnest Seventh Day Adventist who spends his time floating horsetail ferns in tanks of water to demonstrate that their fossilized ancestors found standing upright in coal seams hundreds of feet thick could have floated to that position during Noah's flood. Coffin was asked to say how old the earth would seem to a person unaided by Scripture, and considering only the available scientific evidence. Coffin paused for what seemed five minutes before answering, so it must have been at least fifteen seconds. As old as evolutionists claim, he said, about 4.5 billion years.

To his credit, Judge Overton kept his patience throughout, although he did seem to be losing it once with a pompous faculty lounge-lizard type from Wofford College in South Carolina, one W. Scott Morrow, a chemist who claimed to be an "evolutionist," but took it upon himself to testify to the closed-mindedness of "my fellow evolutionists." After more than an hour's worth of plausible generalities about how scientists are slow to accept new ideas, Overton asked Morrow if scientific papers were ever rightly rejected. He said he couldn't answer, as he'd never been an editor. Pressed by Overton for one specific example of a scientifically valid creationist's paper's ever having been rejected, Morrow could not provide one. (Indeed, in the course of the trial the state could not produce a single creationist paper that had been published in a refereed scientific journal anywhere in the world, nor even one that had been submitted.) "Are you saying," the judge challenged, "that the entire national and international scientific community is engaged in a conspiracy?"

Morrow replied that he knew a lot of his colleagues in science and "I know a closed mind when I see one." Afterward, Morrow, too, hustled in the direction of the cameras, and told the press that the judge wasn't paying attention and was obviously biased. Then he beat it back to South Carolina, which is welcome to him. Have I mentioned that there was only one Arkansan among the creationist witnesses?

The pro-creationist witness who traveled farthest for the trial, however, was one Dr. Chandra Wickramasinghe, a native of Sri Lanka who teaches mathematics in Wales. Having allied himself several years ago with Sir Fred Hoyle, the notable English astronomer, who seems to have slipped into scientific dotage, Wickramasinghe has collaborated with his mentor on two books that have done very well on best-seller lists in England, *Life Cloud* and *Diseases from Space*. The first book is an elaboration of a science-fiction novel by Hoyle which I read about twenty-five years ago. It posits that life originated in swirling clouds of intergalactic dust and was brought to earth by a comet. So far the hypothesis has not been falsified, but at the moment it cannot be seriously tested either.

Diseases from Space elaborates on the idea that viral epidemics are in fact visited on us from the great beyond and asserts that viruses cannot be transmitted horizontally from one human being to another. This hypothesis provoked the best joke of the trial. If viruses cannot be transmitted from one person to another, some unknown wag on the ACLU side wondered, then how about the following scenario: a man comes home and tells his wife, "Honey, I've got good news and bad news. The bad news is I've caught herpes. The good news is it came from outer space." As for the creationist notion that the universe is just 10,000 years old, Dr. Wickramasinghe said, "one would have to be crazy to believe that."

A BLOW FOR THEOCRACIES

We are all the poorer for Attorney General Clark's decision not to appeal Judge Overton's ruling that the creationism law is unconstitutional. No rationally consequent adult who sat through Little Rock's creationism trial can have expected another outcome. Even the Moral Majority's fulminations were clearly a reaction to the dismal showing the creationist witnesses made. Examined in the light of reason, with evidence honestly given and logically assessed, creationism cannot prevail. Unlike a televised debate or a local school-board committee meeting, the trial was a fair fight. But nothing said that Overton's opinion—and I hope readers will have patience with my pointing out that he was educated at Malvern (Ark.) High School and the University of Arkansas—would be as cogent and well written as it was. Many of the creationist faithful were privately contacting the attorney general's office here to advise against appeal. They would like to believe they have a better chance in Louisiana, where the local authorities have deputized the Institute for Creation Research's Wendell Bird. Overton dismissed Bird's argument as having no legal merit:

If creation science is, in fact, science and not religion, as the defendants claim, it is difficult to see how the teaching of such a science could "neutralize" the religious nature of evolution.

Assuming for the purposes of argument, however, that evolution is a religion or religious tenet, the remedy is to stop the teaching of evolution, not establish another religion in opposition to it. Yet it is clearly established in the case law, and perhaps also in common sense, that evolution is not a religion and that teaching evolution does not violate the establishment clause.

It is equally clear that the state has a "compelling interest" in the teaching not only of biological science, of which the theory of evolution is the fundamental organizing principle, but also of chemistry, physics, geology, and even history, all subjects that would have required "balancing" with creationist gibberish if Act 590 had stood. Where that is the case, the Supreme Court has ruled many times, aggrieved fundamentalists who do not wish to have their children hear what offends them, and wish the shelter of the "free exercise" clause of the First Amendment, are permitted to withdraw their children from science classes or from public school.

Ultimately, the creationists cannot prevail in the courts. Now that the scientific community and the educated public are aroused by the Little Rock spectacle, I doubt that a bill in the U.S. Congress of Rep. William Dannemeyer's (Rep.-Calif.), which would limit funding for the Smithsonian Institution if it refuses to put up creationist exhibits, will get anywhere either. So long as current attempts to limit the power of the federal judiciary are fought back—Arkansas's Act 590 controversy being a textbook example of the political cowardice that has led to courts currently having more power than most of us are comfortable with—we will not have a theocracy in this country, fundamentalist or otherwise. Leave it up to the Arkansas legislature, and in five years we would have an Inquisition.

Creationism was mortally damaged by the Little Rock spectacle. That is why the slippery Dr. Duane Gish now says he thinks state laws mandating its teaching are a mistake; he wants to go back to strong-arming local school boards, as in the past. In fact, the Moral Majority and its politico-religious allies, I believe, will soon be muttering only to each other again. One could not observe the Arkansas Moral Majority head, Rev. Roy McLaughlin, in action in his modernistic pulpit in Vilonia without speculating that his boyish charm—he looks like a sort of cross between Pat Boone and Howdy Doody—might just be wearing a mite thin. Arkansans may be hotter than most citizens for that old-time fundamental religion, but are they really ready to credit McLaughlin when he says, with unmistakable reference to the clergymen on the opposite side of the creationism case, that "a preacher who does not believe the word of God to be the inspired, inerrant, infallible word of God . . . is a crook and he ought to resign his pulpit . . . and quit robbing money from God's people"? Even out on the dirt roads, they know McLaughlin is talking about their friends and neighbors. In the long run, Arkansas folks aren't *mean* enough for that.

On January 5, 1982, Judge William R. Overton, U.S. District Court, Eastern District of Arkansas, Western Division, permanently enjoined the Arkansas Board of Education from implementing the "Balanced Treatment for Creation-Science and Evolution-Science Act" of that state legislature. The act had been challenged by a group of Arkansas religious leaders of various faiths, the Arkansas Education Association, parents of children attending Arkansas public schools, and others. Defendants included the Arkansas Board of Education, the Department of Education, and the State Textbooks and Instructional Materials Selecting Committee.

The suit challenged the validity of the statute (Act 590 of 1981) on three grounds: first, that the act constituted an establishment of religion prohibited by the establishment clause of the First Amendment to the Constitution; second, that the act violated a right to academic freedom guaranteed to students and teachers by the free speech clause of the First Amendment; and third, that the act was impermissibly vague in violation of the due process clause of the Fourteenth Amendment.

The legal standards under which the establishment of religion clause of the First Amendment must be judged are clear, according to Judge Overton. He cited the 1971 Supreme Court decision *Lemon v. Kurtzman* (403 U.S. 607), which formulated a three-part test on which this case must be judged:

First, the statute must have a secular legislative purpose: second, its principal or primary effect must be one that neither advances nor inhibits religion . . . ; finally, the statute must not foster "an excessive government entanglement with religion." [*Stone v. Graham.* 449 U.S. at 40]

Judge Overton's opinion traced the development of the religious movement known as fundamentalism and the emergence of the term "scientific creationism."

William R. Overton

CREATIONISM IN SCHOOLS: THE DECISION IN McLEAN V. THE ARKANSAS BOARD OF EDUCATION

Fundamentalism began in nineteenth century America as part of evangelical Protestantism's response to social changes, new religious thought and Darwinism. Fundamentalists viewed these developments as attacks on the Bible and as responsible for a decline in traditional values.

The various manifestations of Fundamentalism have had a number of common characteristics, but a central premise has always been a literal interpretation of the Bible and a belief in the inerrancy of the Scriptures. Following World War I, there was again a perceived decline in traditional morality, and Fundamentalism focused on evolution as responsible for the decline. One aspect of their efforts, particularly in the South, was the promotion of statutes prohibiting the teaching of evolution in public schools. In Arkansas, this resulted in the adoption of Initiated Act 1 of 1929.

Between the 1920's and early 1960's, anti-evolutionary sentiment had a subtle but pervasive influence on the teaching of biology in public schools. Generally, textbooks avoided the topic of evolution and did not mention the name of Darwin. Following the launch of the Sputnik satellite by the Soviet Union in 1957, the National Science Foundation funded several programs designed to modernize the teaching of science in the nation's schools. The Biological Sciences Curriculum Study (BSCS), a nonprofit organization, was among those receiving grants for curriculum study and revision. Working with scientists and teachers, BSCS developed a series of biology texts which, although emphasizing different aspects of biology, incorporated the theory of evolution as a major theme. The success of the BSCS effort is shown by the fact that fifty percent of Amer-

The complete text of the decision (*McLean* v. *The Arkansas Board of Education*), including footnotes that have been omitted from these excerpts, may be found in the *Federal Supplement* (529 F. Supp. 1255).

ican school children currently use BSCS books directly and the curriculum is incorporated indirectly in virtually all biology texts.

In the early 1960's, there was again a resurgence of concern among Fundamentalists about the loss of traditional values and a fear of growing secularism in society. The Fundamentalist movement became more active and has steadily grown in numbers and political influence. There is an emphasis among current Fundamentalists on the literal interpretation of the Bible and the Book of Genesis as the sole source of knowledge about origins.

The term "scientific creationism" first gained currency around 1965 following publication of *The Genesis Flood* in 1961 by Whitcomb and Morris. There is undoubtedly some connection between the appearance of the BSCS texts emphasizing evolutionary thought and efforts by Fundamentalists to attack the theory.

In the 1960's and early 1970's, several Fundamentalist organizations were formed to promote the idea that the Book of Genesis was supported by scientific data. The terms "creation science" and "scientific creationism" have been adopted by these Fundamentalists as descriptive of their study of creation and the origins of man. Perhaps the leading creationist organization is the Institute for Creation Research (ICR), which is affiliated with the Christian Heritage College and supported by the Scott Memorial Baptist Church in San Diego, California. The ICR, through the Creation-Life Publishing Company, is the leading publisher of creation science material. . . .

Creationists have adopted the view of Fundamentalists generally that there are only two positions with respect to the origins of the earth and life: belief in the inerrancy of the Genesis story of creation and of a worldwide flood as fact, or belief in what they call evolution. . . .

The creationist organizations consider the introduction of creation science into the public schools part of their ministry. The ICR has published at least two pamphlets containing suggested methods for convincing school boards, administrators and teachers that creationism should be taught in public schools. The ICR has urged its proponents to encourage school officials to voluntarily add creationism to the curriculum.

Citizens For Fairness in Education is an organization based in Anderson, South Carolina, formed by Paul Ellwanger, a respiratory therapist who is trained in neither law nor science. Mr. Ellwanger is of the opinion that evolution is the forerunner of many social ills, including Nazism, racism and abortion. About 1977, Ellwanger collected several proposed legislative acts with the idea of preparing a model state act requiring the teaching of creationism as science in opposition to evolution. . . . From these various proposals, Ellwanger prepared a "model act" which calls for "balanced treatment" of "scientific creationism" and "evolution" in public schools. He circulated the proposed act to various people and organizations around the country. . . .

[The Greater Little Rock Evangelical Fellowship unanimously adopted a resolution to seek introduction of Ellwanger's Act in the Arkansas Legislature. Senator James L.] Holsted, a self-described "born again" Christian Fundamentalist, introduced the act in the Arkansas Senate. He did not consult the State Department of Education, scientists, science educators or the Arkansas Attorney General. The Act was not referred to any Senate committee for hearing and was passed after only a few minutes' discussion on the Senate floor. In the House of Representatives, the bill was referred to the Education Committee which conducted a perfunctory fifteen minute hearing. No scientist testified at the hearing, nor was any representative from the State Deparment of Education called to testify.

Ellwanger's model act was enacted into law in Arkansas as Act 590 without amendment or modification other than minor typographical changes. The legislative "findings of fact" in Ellwanger's act and Act 590 are identical, although no meaningful fact-finding process was employed by the General Assembly

Ellwanger's efforts in preparation of the model act and campaign for its adoption in the states were motivated by his opposition to the theory of evolution and his desire to see the Biblical version of creation taught in the public schools. . . . Senator Holsted's sponsorship and lobbying efforts in behalf of the Act were motivated solely by his religious beliefs and desire to see the Biblical version of creation taught in the public schools.

The State of Arkansas, like a number of states whose citizens have relatively homogeneous religious beliefs, has a long history of official opposition to evolution which is motivated by adherence to Fundamentalist beliefs in the inerrancy of the Book of Genesis. This history is documented in Justice Fortas' opinion in *Epperson* v. *Arkansas*, 393 U.S. 97 (1968), which struck down Initiated Act 1 of 1929, prohibiting the teaching of the theory of evolution. . . .

The unusual circumstances surrounding the passage of Act 590, as well as the substantive law of the First Amendment, warrant an inquiry into the stated legislative purposes. The author of the Act had publicly proclaimed the sectarian purpose of the proposal. The Arkansas residents who sought legislative sponsorship of the bill did so for a purely sectarian purpose. These circumstances alone may not be particularly persuasive, but when considered with the publicly announced motives of the legislative sponsor made contemporaneously with the legislative process; the lack of any legislative investigation, debate or consultation with any educators or scientists; the unprecedented intrusion in school curriculum; and official history of the State of Arkansas on the subject, it is obvious that the statement of purposes has little, if any, support in fact. The State failed to produce any evidence which would warrant an inference or conclusion that at any point in the process anyone considered the legitimate educational value of the Act. It was simply and purely an effort to introduce the Biblical version of creation into the public school curricula. The only inference which can be drawn from these circumstances is that the Act was passed with the specific purpose by the General Assembly of advancing religion. The Act therefore fails the first prong of the three-pronged test, that of secular legislative purpose, as articulated in *Lemon* v. *Kurtzman*, *supra*, and *Stone* v. *Graham*, *supra*.

III

If the defendants are correct and the Court is limited to an examination of the language of the Act, the evidence is overwhelming that both the purpose and effect of Act 590 is the advancement of religion in the public schools.

Section 4 of the Act provides:

Definitions as used in this Act:

(a) "Creation-science" means the scientific evidences for creation and inferences from those scientific evidences. Creation-science includes the scientific evidences and related inferences that indicate (1) Sudden creation of the universe, energy, and life from nothing; (2) The insufficiency of mutation and natural selection in bringing about development of all living kinds from a single organism; (3) Changes only within fixed limits of originally created kinds of plants and animals; (4) Separate ancestry for man and apes; (5) Explanation of the earth's geology by catastrophism, including the occurrence of a worldwide flood; and (6) A relatively recent inception of the earth and living kinds.

(b) "Evolution-science" means the scientific evidences for evolution and inferences from those scientific evidences. Evolution-science includes the scientific evidences and related inferences that indicate (1) Emergence by naturalistic processes of the universe from disordered matter and emergence of life from nonlife; (2) The sufficiency of mutation and natural selection in bringing about development of present living kinds from simple earlier kinds; (3) Emergence by mutation and natural selection of present living kinds from simpler earlier kinds; (4) Emergence of man from a common ancestor with apes; (5) Explanation of the earth's geology and the evolutionary sequence by uniformitarianism; and (6) An inception several billion years ago of the earth and somewhat later of life.

(c) "Public schools" mean public secondary and elementary schools.

The evidence establishes that the definition of "creation science" contained in 4(a) has as its unmentioned reference the first 11 chapters of the Book of Genesis. Among the many creation epics in human history, the account of sudden creation from nothing, or *creatio ex nihilo*, and subsequent destruction of the world by flood is unique to Genesis. The concepts of 4(a) are the literal Fundamentalists' view of Genesis. Section 4(a) is unquestionably a statement of religion, with the exception of 4(a)(2) which is a negative thrust aimed at what the creationists understand to be the theory of evolution.

Both the concepts and wording of Section 4(a) convey an inescapable religiosity. Section 4(a)(1) describes "sudden creation of the universe, energy and life from nothing." Every theologian who testified, including defense witnesses, expressed the opinion that the statement referred to a supernatural creation which was performed by God.

Defendants argue that: (1) the fact that 4(a) conveys ideas similar to the literal interpretation of Genesis does not make it conclusively a statement of religion; (2) that reference to a creation from nothing is not necessarily a religious concept since the Act only suggests a creator who has power, intelligence and a sense of design and not necessarily the attributes of love, compassion and justice; and (3) that simply teaching about the concept of a creator is not a religious exercise unless the student is required to make a commitment to the concept of a creator.

The evidence fully answers these arguments. The ideas of 4(a)(1) are not merely similar to the literal interpretation of Genesis; they are identical and parallel to no other story of creation.

The argument that creation from nothing in 4(a)(1) does not involve a supernatural deity has no evidentiary or rational support. To the contrary, "creation out of nothing" is a concept unique to Western religions. In traditional Western religious thought, the conception of a creator of the world is a conception of God. Indeed, creation of the world "out of nothing" is the ultimate religious statement because God is the only actor. . . .

The facts that creation science is inspired by the Book of Genesis and that Section 4(a) is consistent with a literal interpretation of Genesis leave no doubt that a major effect of the Act is the advancement of particular religious beliefs. . . .

IV(A)

The approach to teaching "creation science" and "evolution science" found in Act 590 is identical to the two-model approach espoused by the Institute for Creation Research and is taken almost verbatim from ICR writings. It is an extension of Fundamentalists' view that one must either accept the literal interpretation of Genesis or else believe in the godless system of evolution.

The two model approach of the creationists is simply a contrived dualism which has no scientific factual basis or legitimate educational purpose. It assumes only two explanations for the origins of life and existence of man, plants and animals: It was either the work of a creator or it was not. Application of these two models, according to creationists, and the defendants, dictates that all scientific evidence which fails to support the theory of evolution is necessarily scientific evidence in support of creationism and is, therefore, creation science "evidence" in support of Section 4(a).

IV(B)

The emphasis on origins as an aspect of the theory of evolution is peculiar to creationist literature. Although the subject of origins of life is within the province of biology, the scientific community does not consider origins of life a part of evolutionary theory. The theory of evolution assumes the existence of life and is directed to an explanation of *how* life evolved. Evolution does not presuppose the absence of a creator or God and the plain inference conveyed by Section 4 is erroneous.

As a statement of the theory of evolution, Section 4(b) is simply a hodgepodge of limited assertions, many of which are factually inaccurate. . . .

IV(C)

In addition to the fallacious pedagogy of the two model approach, Section 4(a) lacks legitimate educational value because "creation science" as defined in that section is simply not science. Several witnesses suggested definitions of science. A descriptive definition was said to be that science is what is "accepted by the scientific community" and is "what scientists do." The obvious implication of this description is that, in a free society, knowledge does not require the imprimatur of legislation in order to become science.

More precisely, the essential characteristics of science are:

(1) It is guided by natural law;
(2) It has to be explanatory by reference to natural law;
(3) It is testable against the empirical world;
(4) Its conclusions are tentative, i.e., are not necessarily the final word; and
(5) It is falsifiable. (Ruse and other science witnesses).

Creation science as described in Section 4(a) fails to meet these essential characteristics. . . .

Creation science, as defined in Section 4(a), not only fails to follow the canons defining scientific theory, it also fails to fit the more general descriptions of "what scientists think" and "what scientists do." The scientific community consists of individuals and groups, nationally and internationally, who work independently in such varied fields as biology, paleontology, geology and astronomy. Their work is published and subject to review and testing by their peers. The journals for publication are both numerous and varied. There is, however, not one recognized scientific journal which has published an article espousing the creation science theory described in Section 4(a). Some of the State's witnesses suggested that the scientific community was "close-minded" on the subject of creationism and that explained the lack of acceptance of the creation science arguments. Yet no witness produced a scientific article for whch publication had been refused. Perhaps some members of the scientific community are resistant to new ideas. It is, however, inconceivable that such a loose knit group of independent thinkers in all the varied fields of science could, or would, so effectively censor new scientific thought. . . .

The methodology employed by creationists is another factor which is indicative that

their work is not science. A scientific theory must be tentative and always subject to revision or abandonment in light of facts that are inconsistent with, or falsify, the theory. A theory that is by its own terms dogmatic, absolutist and never subject to revision is not a scientific theory.

The creationists' methods do not take data, weigh it against the opposing scientific data, and thereafter reach the conclusions stated in Section 4(a). Instead, they take the literal wording of the Book of Genesis and attempt to find scientific support for it. . . . The Creation Research Society employs the same unscientific approach to the issue of creationism. Its applicants for membership must subscribe to the belief that the Book of Genesis is "historically and scientifically true in all of the original autographs." The Court would never criticize or discredit any person's testimony based on his or her religious beliefs. While anybody is free to approach a scientific inquiry in any fashion they choose, they cannot properly describe the methodology used as scientific, if they start with a conclusion and refuse to change it regardless of the evidence developed during the course of the investigation.

IV(D)

In efforts to establish "evidence" in support of creation science, the defendants relied upon the same false premise as the two model approach contained in Section 4, i.e., all evidence which criticized evolutionary theory was proof in support of creation science. For example, the defendants established that the mathematical probability of a chance chemical combination resulting in life from non-life is so remote that such an occurrence is almost beyond imagination. Those mathematical facts, the defendants argue, are scientific evidences that life was the product of a creator. While the statistical figures may be impressive evidence against the theory of chance chemical combinations as an explanation of origins, it requires a leap of faith to interpret those figures so as to support a complex doctrine which includes a sudden creation from nothing, a worldwide flood, separate ancestry of man and apes, and a young earth.

The defendants' argument would be more persuasive if, in fact, there were only two theories or ideas about the origins of life and the world. That there are a number of theories was acknowledged by the State's witnesses, Dr. Wickramasinghe and Dr. Geisler. Dr. Wickramasinghe testified at length in support of a theory that life on earth was "seeded" by comets which delivered genetic material and perhaps organisms to the earth's surface from interstellar dust far outside the solar system. The "seeding" theory further hypothesizes that the earth remains under the continuing influence of genetic material from space which continues to affect life. While Wickramasinghe's theory about the origins of life on earth has not received general acceptance within the scientific community, he has, at least, used scientific methodology to produce a theory of origins which meets the essential characteristics of science. . . .

The proof in support of creation science consisted almost entirely of efforts to discredit the theory of evolution through a rehash of data and theories which have been before the scientific community for decades. The arguments asserted by creationists are not based upon new scientific evidence or laboratory data which has been ignored by the scientific community. . . .

[Judge Overton referred to the findings of Robert Gentry used as an argument against evolution by the creationists. Gentry had raised some questions about radiometric-dating methods. "The discoveries have not, however, led to the formulation of any scientific hypothesis or theory which would explain a relatively recent inception of the earth or a worldwide flood." The testimony of Marianne Wilson, in charge of the science curriculum for Pulaski County Special School District, "was persuasive evidence that creation science is not science." Ms. Wilson and a committee of science teachers who were assigned the job of providing a creation-science curriculum guide, "reached the unanimous conclusion that creationism is not science; it is religion. They so reported to the Board. The Board ignored the recommendation and insisted that a curriculum guide be prepared." Ms. Wilson found all available creationists' materials unacceptable because they were permeated with religious references and reliance upon religious beliefs.]

Without using creationist literature, Ms. Wilson was unable to locate one genuinely scientific article or work which supported Section 4(a). . . . The curriculum guide which she prepared cannot be taught and has no educational value as science. . . .

The conclusion that creation science has no scientific merit or educational value as science has legal significance in light of the Court's previous conclusion that creation science has, as one major effect, the advancement of religion. The second part of the three-pronged test for establishment reaches only those statutes having as their *primary* effect the advancement of religion. Secondary effects which advance religion are not constitutionally fatal. Since creation science is not science, the conclusion is inescapable that the *only* real effect of Act 590 is the advancement of religion. The Act therefore fails both the first and second portions of the test in *Lemon v. Kurtzman*, 403 U.S. 602 (1971).

IV(E)

Act 590 mandates "balanced treatment" for creation science and evolution science. The Act prohibits instruction in any religious doctrine or references to religious writings. The Act is self-contradictory and compliance is impossible unless the public schools elect to forego significant portions of subjects such as biology, world history, geology, zoology, botany, psychology, anthropology, sociology, philosophy, physics and chemistry. Presently, the concepts of evolutionary theory as described in 4(b) permeate the public school textbooks. There is no way teachers can teach the Genesis account of creation in a secular manner.

The State Department of Education, through its textbook selection committee, school boards and school administrators will be required to constantly monitor materials to avoid using religious references. The school boards, administrators and teachers face an impossible task. How is the teacher to respond to questions about a creation suddenly and out of nothing? How will a teacher explain the occurrence of a worldwide flood? How will a teacher explain the concept of a relatively recent age of the earth? The answer is obvious because the only source of this information is ultimately contained in the Book of Genesis.

References to the pervasive nature of religious concepts in creation science texts amply demonstrate why State entanglement with religion is inevitable under Act 590. Involvement of the State in screening texts for impermissible religious references will require State officials to make delicate religious judgments. The need to monitor classroom discussion in order to uphold the Act's prohibition against religious instruction will necessarily involve administrators in questions concerning religion. These continuing involvements of State officials in questions and issues of religion create an excessive and prohibited entanglement with religion.

[The court rejected plaintiffs' charges that the term "balanced treatment" was too vague and therefore in violation of due process, finding to the contrary that the meaning for the purpose of the establishment clause of the First Amendment was "all too clear."]

V(B)

The plaintiffs other argument revolves around the alleged infringement by the defendants upon the academic freedom of teachers and students. It is contended this unprecedented intrusion in the curriculum by the State prohibits teachers from teaching what they believe should be taught or requires them to teach that which they do not believe is proper. The evidence reflects that traditionally the State Department of Education, local school boards and administration officials exercise little, if any, influence upon the subject matter taught by classroom teachers. Teachers have been given freedom to teach and emphasize those portions of subjects the individual teacher considered important. The limits to this discretion have generally been derived from the approval of textbooks by the State Depart-

ment and preparation of curriculum guides by the school districts.

[The court did not accept the testimony of some witnesses that academic freedom means that the teacher should be permitted unlimited discretion, subject only to the bounds of professional ethics.]

In any event, if Act 590 is implemented, many teachers will be required to teach material in support of creation science which they do not consider academically sound. Many teachers will simply forego teaching subjects which might trigger the "balanced treatment" aspects of Act 590 even though they think the subjects are important to a proper presentation of a course.

Implementation of Act 590 will have serious and untoward consequences for students, particularly those planning to attend college. Evolution is the cornerstone of modern biology, and many courses in public schools contain subject matter relating to such varied topics as the age of the earth, geology and relationships among living things. Any student who is deprived of instruction as to the prevailing scientific thought on these topics will be denied a significant part of science education. Such a deprivation through the high school level would undoubtedly have an impact upon the quality of education in the State's colleges and universities, especially including the pre-professional and professional programs in the health sciences. . . .

[The court denied the charge made by the defendants that evolution is a religion. "It is clearly established in the case law, and perhaps also in common sense, that evolution is not a religion and that teaching evolution does not violate the Establishment Clause." Finally, the court responded to a defense witness's statement that polls indicated a significant majority of the American public thought that creation science should be taught if evolution was taught.]

The application and content of First Amendment principles are not determined by public opinion polls or by a majority vote. Whether the proponents of Act 590 constitute the majority or the minority is quite irrelevant under a constitutional system of government. No group, no matter how large or small, may use the organs of government, of which the public schools are the most conspicuous and influential, to foist its religious beliefs on others. . . .

Judge Overton's decision did not, of course, end the creation versus evolution controversy. The Louisiana and Mississippi legislatures enacted laws similar to the one in Arkansas invalidated by Judge Overton.

Virtually the entire contents of the March-April 1982 issue of *Academe*, official journal of the American Association of University Professors, is devoted to the subject of creationism. Previously, at its 1981 Annual Meeting, the AAUP had adopted the following resolution:

The Sixty-seventh Annual Meeting of the American Association of University Professors declares its firm opposition to legislation, recently adopted by the State of Arkansas and pending before other state legislatures, that requires "balanced treatment" of "creation science" and evolution in public schools. This legislation, by requiring that a religious doctrine (sometimes disguised) be taught as a condition for the teaching of science, serves to impair the soundness of scientific education preparatory for college study and to violate the academic freedom of public school teachers.

The potential consequences of this legislation for higher education science curricula are of particular concern to this Meeting. Faculty members who educate public school teachers would presumably have to be trained in "creation science" so that they can educate their students accordingly. Members of college and university faculties in Arkansas and elsewhere should be able to teach and criticize freely in accord with professional standards. "Creation-science" legislation would impose an unacceptable limitation upon the faculty member's ability to carry out these obligations.

The Sixty-seventh Annual Meeting of the American Association of University Professors calls on state governments to reject "creation-science" legislation as utterly inconsistent with the principles of academic freedom.

Louisiana's "creation science" statute, which required schools to teach the Bible's version of the origin of the species along with Darwin's, is plagued with state-constitutional infirmity, the U.S. District Court for the Eastern District of Louisiana decided, in November 1982. Examining the state supreme court's interpretation of state law, the district court enjoined enforcement of the statute, reasoning that it violated the commandment of the Louisiana constitution that the State Board of Elementary and Secondary Education, and not the state legislature, have the ultimate policy-making power over public elementary and secondary curricula. By disposing of the case on state-law grounds, the court avoided the First Amendment claims of the numerous individuals and organizations challenging the statute.

An article by a geologist who specializes in paleontology, Stephen Jay Gould, in the *Atlantic* sheds further light on the on-going discussion.

Stephen Jay Gould

CREATIONISM: GENESIS VS. GEOLOGY

G. K. Chesterton once mused over Noah's dinnertime conversations during those long nights on a vast and tempestuous sea:

> And Noah he often said to his wife
>   when he sat down to dine,
> "I don't care where the water goes if
>   it doesn't get into the wine."

Noah's insouciance has not been matched by defenders of his famous flood. For centuries, fundamentalists have tried very hard to find a place for the subsiding torrents. They have struggled even more valiantly to devise a source for all that water. Our modern oceans, extensive as they are, will not override Mt. Everest. One seventeenth-century searcher said: "I can as soon believe that a man would be drowned in his own spittle as that the world should be deluged by the water in it."

With the advent of creationism, a solution to this old dilemma has been put forward. In *The Genesis Flood* (1961), the founding document of the creationist movement, John Whitcomb and Henry Morris seek guidance from Genesis 1:6–7, which states that God created the firmament and then slid it into place amidst the waters, thus dividing "the waters which were under the firmament from the waters which were above the firmament: and it was so." The waters under the firmament include seas and interior fluid that may rise in volcanic eruptions. But what are the waters above the firmament? Whitcomb and Morris reason that Moses cannot refer here to transient rain clouds, because he also tells us (Genesis 2:5) that "the Lord God had not caused it to rain upon the earth." The authors therefore imagine that the earth, in those palmy days, was surrounded by a gigantic canopy of water vapor (which, being invisible, did not obscure the light of Genesis 1:3). "These upper waters," Whitcomb and Morris write, "were therefore placed in that position by divine creativity, not by the normal processes of the hydrological cycle of the present day." Upwelling from the depths together with the liquefaction, puncturing, and descent of the celestial canopy produced more than enough water for Noah's worldwide flood.

Fanciful solutions often generate a cascade of additional difficulties. In this case, Morris, a hydraulic engineer by training, and Whitcomb invoke a divine assist to gather the waters into their canopy, but then can't find a natural way to get them down. So they invoke a miracle: God put the water there in the first place; let him then release it.

The simple fact of the matter is that one cannot have *any* kind of a Genesis Flood without acknowledging the presence of supernatural elements. . . . It is obvious that the opening of the "windows of heaven" in order to allow "the waters which were above the firmament" to fall upon the earth, and the breaking up of "all the fountains of the great deep" were supernatural acts of God.

Since we usually define science, at least in part, as a system of explanation that relies upon invariant natural laws, this charmingly

direct invocation of miracles (suspensions of natural law) would seem to negate the central claims of the modern creationist movement—that creationism is not religion but a scientific alternative to evolution; that creationism has been disregarded by scientists because they are a fanatical and dogmatic lot who cannot appreciate new advances; and that creationists must therefore seek legislative redress in their attempts to force a "balanced treatment" for both creationism and evolution in the science classrooms of our public schools.

Legislative history has driven creationists to this strategy of claiming scientific status for their religious view. The older laws, which banned the teaching of evolution outright and led to John Scopes's conviction in 1925, were overturned by the Supreme Court in 1968, but not before they had exerted a chilling effect upon teaching for forty years. (Evolution is the indispensable organizing principle of the life sciences, but I did not hear the word in my 1956 high school biology class. New York City, to be sure, suffered no restrictive ordinances, but publishers, following the principle of the "least common denominator" as a sales strategy, tailored the national editions of their textbooks to the few states that considered it criminal to place an ape on the family escutcheon.) A second attempt to mandate equal time for frankly religious views of life's history passed the Tennessee state legislature in the 1970s but failed a constitutional challenge in the court. This judicial blocking left only one legislative path open—the claim that creationism is a science.

The third strategy had some initial success, and "balanced treatment" acts to equate "evolution science" and "creation science" in classrooms passed the Arkansas and Louisiana legislatures in 1981. The ACLU has sued for a federal court ruling on the Louisiana law's constitutionality, and a trial is likely this year. The Arkansas law was challenged by the ACLU in 1981, on behalf of local plaintiffs (including twelve practicing theologians who felt more threatened by the bill than many scientists did). Federal Judge William R. Overton heard the Arkansas case in Little Rock last December. I spent the better part of a day on the stand, a witness for the prosecution, testifying primarily about how the fossil record refutes "flood geology" and supports evolution.

On January 5, Judge Overton delivered his eloquent opinion, declaring the Arkansas act unconstitutional because so-called "creation science" is only a version of Genesis read literally—a partisan (and narrowly sectarian) religious view, barred from public-school classrooms by the First Amendment. Legal language is often incomprehensible, but sometimes it is charming, and I enjoyed the wording of Overton's decision: ". . . judgment is hereby entered in favor of the plaintiffs and against the defendants. The relief prayed for is granted."

Support for Overton's equation of "creation science" with strident and sectarian fundamentalism comes from two sources. First, the leading creationists themselves released some frank private documents in response to plaintiffs' subpoenas. Overton's long list of citations seems to brand the claim for scientific creationism as simply hypocrisy. For example, Paul Ellwanger, the tireless advocate and drafter of the "model bill" that became Arkansas Act 590 of 1981, the law challenged by the ACLU, says in a letter to a state legislator that "I view this whole battle as one between God and anti-God forces, though I know there are a large number of evolutionists who believe in God. . . . it behooves Satan to do all he can to thwart our efforts. . . ." In another letter, he refers to "the idea of killing evolution instead of playing these debating games that we've been playing for nigh over a decade already"—a reasonably clear statement of the creationists' ultimate aims, and an identification of their appeals for "equal time," "the American way of fairness," and "presenting them both and letting the kids decide" as just so much rhetoric.

The second source of evidence of the bill's unconstitutionality lies in the logic and character of creationist arguments themselves. The flood story is central to all creationist systems. It also has elicited the only specific and testable theory the creationists have

offered; for the rest, they have only railed against evolutionary claims. The flood story was explicitly cited as one of the six defining characteristics of "creation science" in Arkansas Act 590: "explanation of the earth's geology by catastrophism, including the occurrence of a worldwide flood."

Creationism reveals its nonscientific character in two ways: its central tenets cannot be tested and its peripheral claims, which can be tested, have been proven false. At its core, the creationist account rests on "singularities"—that is to say, on miracles. The creationist God is not the noble clockwinder of Newton and Boyle, who set the laws of nature properly at the beginning of time and then released direct control in full confidence that his initial decisions would require no revision. He is, instead, a constant presence, who suspends his own laws when necessary to make the new or destroy the old. Since science can treat only natural phenomena occurring in a context of invariant natural law, the constant invocation of miracles places creationism in another realm.

We have already seen how Whitcomb and Morris remove a divine finger from the dike of heaven to flood the earth from their vapor canopy. But the miracles surrounding Noah's flood do not stop there; two other supernatural assists are required. First, God acted "to gather the animals into the Ark." (The Bible tells us [Genesis 6:20] that they found their own way.) Second, God intervened to keep the animals "under control during the year of the Flood." Whitcomb and Morris provide a long disquisition on hibernation and suspect that some divinely ordained state of suspended animation relieved Noah's small and aged crew of most responsibility for feeding and cleaning (poor Noah himself was 600 years old at the time).

In candid moments, leading creationists will admit that the miraculous character of origin and destruction precludes a scientific understanding. Morris writes (and Judge Overton quotes): "God was there when it happened. We were not there. . . . Therefore, we are completely limited to what God has seen fit to tell us, and this information is in His written Word." Duane Gish, the leading creationist author, says: "We do not know how the Creator created, what processes He used, for He used processes which are not now operating anywhere in the natural universe. . . . We cannot discover by scientific investigation anything about the creative processes used by God." When pressed about these quotes, creationists tend to admit that they are purveying religion after all, but then claim that evolution is equally religious. Gish also says: "Creationists have repeatedly stated that neither creation nor evolution is a scientific theory (and each is equally religious)." But as Judge Overton reasoned, if creationists are merely complaining that evolution is religion, then they should be trying to eliminate it from the schools, not struggling to get their own brand of religion into science classrooms as well. And if, instead, they are asserting the validity of their own version of natural history, they must be able to prove, according to the demands of science, that creationism is scientific.

Scientific claims must be testable; we must, in principle, be able to envision a set of observations that would render them false. Miracles cannot be judged by this criterion, as Whitcomb and Morris have admitted. But is all creationist writing merely about untestable singularities? Are arguments never made in proper scientific form? Creationists do offer some testable statements, and these are amenable to scientific analysis. Why, then, do I continue to claim that creationism isn't science? Simply because these relatively few statements have been tested and conclusively refuted. Dogmatic assent to disproved claims is not scientific behavior. Scientists are as stubborn as the rest of us, but they must be able to change their minds.

In "flood geology," we find our richest source of testable creationist claims. Creationists have been forced into this uncharacteristically vulnerable stance by a troubling fact too well known to be denied: namely, that the geological record of fossils follows a single, invariant order throughout the world. The oldest rocks contain only single-celled creatures; invertebrates dominate later strata, followed by the first fishes, then dinosaurs, and finally large mammals. One might be tempted to take a "liberal," or allegorical, view of Scripture and identify this sequence with the order of creation in Genesis 1, allowing millions or billions of years for the "days" of Moses. But creationists will admit no such reconciliation. Their fundamentalism is absolute and uncompromising. If Moses said "days," he meant periods of twenty-four hours, to the second. (Creationist literature is often less charitable to liberal theology than to evolution. As a subject for wrath, nothing matches the enemy within.)

Since God created with such alacrity, all creatures once must have lived simultaneously on the earth. How, then, did their fossil remains get sorted into an invariable order in the earth's strata? To resolve this particular knotty dilemma, creationists invoke Noah's flood: all creatures were churned together in the great flood and their fossilized succession reflects the order of their settling as the waters receded. But what natural processes would produce such a predictable order from a singular chaos? The testable proposals of "flood geology" have been advanced to explain the causes of this sorting.

Whitcomb and Morris offer three suggestions. The first—hydrological—holds that denser and more streamlined objects would have descended more rapidly and should populate the bottom strata (in conventional geology, the oldest strata). The second—ecological—envisions a sorting responsive to environment. Denizens of the ocean bottom were overcome by the flood waters first, and should lie in the lower strata; inhabitants of mountaintops postponed their inevitable demise, and now adorn our upper strata. The third—anatomical or functional—argues that certain animals, by their high intelligence or superior mobility, might have struggled successfully for a time, and ended up at the top.

All three proposals have been proven false. The lower strata abound in delicate, floating creatures, as well as spherical globs. Many oceanic creatures—whales and teleost fishes in particular—appear only in upper strata, well above hordes of terrestrial forms. Clumsy sloths (not to mention hundreds of species of marine invertebrates) are restricted to strata lying well above others that serve as exclusive homes for scores of lithe and nimble small dinosaurs and pterosaurs.

The very invariance of the universal fossil sequence is the strongest argument against its production in a single gulp. Could exceptionless order possibly arise from a contemporaneous mixture by such dubious processes of sorting? Surely, somewhere, at least one courageous trilobite would have paddled on valiantly (as its colleagues succumbed) and won a place in the upper strata. Surely, on some primordial beach, a man would have suffered a heart attack and been washed into the lower strata before intelligence had a chance to plot temporary escape. But if the strata represent vast stretches of sequential time, then invariant order is an expectation, not a problem. No trilobite lies in the upper strata because they all perished 225 million years ago. No man keeps lithified company with a dinosaur, because we were still 60 million years in the future when the last dinosaur perished.

True science and religion are not in conflict. The history of approaches to Noah's flood by scientists who were also professional theologians provides an excellent example of this important truth—and also illustrates just how long ago "flood geology" was conclusively laid to rest by religious scientists. I have argued that direct invocation of miracles and unwillingness to abandon a false doctrine deprive modern creationists of their self-proclaimed status as scientists. When we examine how the great scientist-theologians of past centuries treated the flood, we note that their work is distinguished by both a conscious refusal to admit miraculous events into their explanatory schemes and a willingness to abandon preferred hypotheses in the face of geological evidence. They were scientists *and* religious leaders—and they show us why modern creationists are not scientists.

On the subject of miracles, the Reverend Thomas Burnet published his century's most famous geological treatise in the 1680s, *Telluris theoria sacra* (*The Sacred Theory of the Earth*). Burnet accepted the Bible's truth, and set out to construct a geological history that would be in accord with the events of Genesis. But he believed something else even more strongly: that, as a scientist, he must follow natural law and scrupulously avoid miracles. His story is fanciful by modern standards: the earth originally was devoid of topography, but was drying and cracking: the cracks served as escape vents for internal fluids, but rain sealed the cracks, and the earth, transformed into a gigantic pressure cooker, ruptured its surface skin; surging internal waters inundated the earth, producing Noah's flood. Bizarre, to be sure, but bizarre precisely because Burnet would not abandon natural law. It is not easy to force a preconceived story into the strictures of physical causality. Over and over again, Burnet acknowledges that his task would be much simpler if only he could invoke a miracle. Why weave such a complex tale to find water for the flood in a physically acceptable manner, when God might simply have made new water for his cataclysmic purification? Many of Burnet's colleagues urged such a course, but he rejected it as inconsistent with the methods of "natural philosophy" (the word "science" had not yet entered English usage):

They say in short that God Almighty created waters on purpose to make the Deluge . . . And this, in a few words, is the whole account of the business. This is to cut the knot when we cannot loose it.

Burnet's God, like the deity of Newton and Boyle, was a clock-winder, not a bungler who continually perturbed his own system with later corrections.

We think him a better Artist that makes a Clock that strikes regularly at every hour from the Springs and Wheels which he puts in the work, than he that hath so made his Clock that he must put his finger to it every hour to make it strike: And if one should contrive a piece of Clockwork so that it should beat all the hours, and make all its motions regularly for such a time, and that time being come, upon a signal given, or a Spring toucht, it should of its own accord fall all to pieces;

would not this be look'd upon as a piece of greater Art, than if the Workman came at that time prefixt, and with a great Hammer beat it into pieces?

Flood geology was considered and tested by early-nineteenth-century geologists. They never believed that a single flood had produced all fossil-bearing strata, but they did accept and then disprove a claim that the uppermost strata contained evidence for a single, catastrophic, worldwide inundation. The science of geology arose in nations that were glaciated during the great ice ages, and glacial deposits are similar to the products of floods. During the 1820s, British geologists carried out an extensive empirical program to test whether these deposits represented the action of a single flood. The work was led by two ministers, the Reverend Adam Sedgwick (who taught Darwin his geology) and the Reverend William Buckland. Buckland initially decided that all the "superficial gravels" (as these deposits were called) represented a single event, and he published his *Reliquiae diluvianae (Relics of the Flood)* in 1824. However, Buckland's subsequent field work proved that the superficial gravels were not contemporaneous but represented several different events (multiple ice ages, as we now know). Geology proclaimed no worldwide flood but rather a long sequence of local events. In one of the great statements in the history of science, Sedgwick, who was Buckland's close colleague in both science and theology, publicly abandoned flood geology—and upheld empirical science—in his presidential address to the Geological Society of London in 1831.

Having been myself a believer, and, to the best of my power, a propagator of what I now regard as philosophic heresy, and having more than once been quoted for opinions I do not now maintain, I think it right, as one of my last acts before I quit this Chair, thus publicly to read my recantation . . . .

There is, I think, one great negative conclusion now incontestably established—that the vast masses of diluvial gravel, scattered almost over the surface of the earth, do not belong to one violent and transitory period. . . .

We ought, indeed, to have paused before we first adopted the diluvian theory, and referred all our old superficial gravel to the action of the Mosaic flood. . . . In classing together distant unknown formations under one name; in giving them a simultaneous origin, and in the determining their date, not by the organic remains we had discovered, but by those we expected hypothetically hereafter to discover, in them; we have given one more example of the passion with which the mind fastens upon general conclusions, and of the readiness with which it leaves the consideration of unconnected truths.

As I prepared to leave Little Rock last December, I went to my hotel room to gather my belongings and found a man sitting backward on my commode, pulling it apart with a plumber's wrench. He explained to me that a leak in the room below had caused part of the ceiling to collapse and he was seeking the source of the water. My commode, located just above, was the obvious candidate, but his hypothesis had failed, for my equipment was working perfectly. The plumber then proceeded to give me a fascinating disquisition on how a professional traces the pathways of water through hotel pipes and walls. The account was perfectly logical and mechanistic: it can come only from here, here, or there, flow this way or that way, and end up there, there, or here. I then asked him what he thought of the trial across the street, and he confessed his staunch creationism, including his firm belief in the miracle of Noah's flood.

As a professional, this man never doubted that water has a physical source and a mechanically constrained path of motion—and that he could use the principles of his trade to identify causes. It would be a poor (and unemployed) plumber indeed who suspected that the laws of engineering had been suspended whenever a puddle and cracked plaster bewildered him. Why should we approach the physical history of our earth any differently?

Theodore K. Rabb, professor of history at Princeton University, has written on the history of science. Here he satirizes the current creationism-evolution controversy.

Theodore K. Rabb

GALILEO'S LATEST MEMO

TO: Charles Darwin
FROM: Galileo Galilei
SUBJECT: Your current troubles

Since I once had to deal with the science vs. Bible problem, maybe I can cheer you up by reminding you of what I had to go through to establish the sun as the center of the solar system.

Actually, the trouble started with Copernicus. He was a perfectly respectable churchman, but the theologian who published his book, one Osiander, thought it safest to add a preface saying that the heliocentric theory was only a hypothesis. The sun was put at the center, and the earth made to move around it, just for the sake of some calculations; the theory was not necessarily a true description of the heavens.

Osiander wanted to be extra careful not to offend those who believed the older, geocentric theory, based on the Bible.

These traditionalists, however, did not want anyone teaching Copernicus's ideas. Martin Luther himself rebutted Copernicus by citing the biblical passage in which Joshua makes the sun stand still. Others quoted Ecclesiastes: "The earth abideth for ever. The sun also ariseth, and the sun goeth down, and hasteth to his place where he arose." Another favorite was the 93rd Psalm, which can be translated as "The earth also is stable, that it cannot be moved."

Some critics preferred arguments from common sense. (I can't bore you with everything they said, so I'll cut out their excess verbiage, and mine, too.) One famous scholar, Jean Bodin, said that "no one in his senses will ever think that the earth, heavy and unwieldly from its own weight and mass, staggers up and down around its own center and that of the sun."

But the main objections related to the Bible, and these finally led the Roman Church to declare the Copernican view contrary to Holy Scripture. It would be arrogant, Pope Urban VIII said, to teach Copernican notions: "To speak about the subject as if it were anything but a hypothesis would be tantamount to constraining God within the limits of your ideas."

The critics of Copernicus took heart because scientists could not agree among themselves. Some thought Copernicus right; others thought him wrong; and yet others tried to find a compromise in between. But their disputes did not make the biblical argument any more relevant, as I pointed out: "These men have resolved to fabricate a shield for their fallacies out of the mantle of pretended religion and the authority of the Bible. These they apply, with little judgment, to the refutation of arguments that they do not understand and have not even listened to. Contrary to the sense of the Bible, they would extend its authority until even in purely physical matters they would have us altogether abandon reason and the evidence of our senses in favor of some biblical passage.

"I think that in discussions of physical problems we ought to begin not from the authority of scriptural passages, but from sense-experiences and necessary demonstrations. Nothing physical which sense-experiences sets before our eyes, or which necessary demonstrations prove to us, ought to be called in question upon the testimony of biblical passages. I do not believe that the same God who has endowed us with senses, reason, and intellect has intended us to forgo their use. He would not require us to deny sense and reason in physical matters which are set before our eyes.

"It would perhaps fit in better with the decorum and majesty of the sacred writings to prevent every shallow and vulgar writer from giving to his compositions an air of authority by inserting in them passages from the Bible. Such authors would impose upon others an obligation to subscribe to conclusions that are repugnant to manifest reason. God forbid that this sort of abuse should gain countenance and authority, for then in a short time it would be necessary to proscribe all the contemplative sciences. Truly demonstrated physical conclusions need not be subordinated to biblical passages, but the latter must rather be shown not to interfere with the former.

"If in order to banish the opinion in question if it were sufficient to stop the mouth of a single man then that would be very easily done. But it would be necessary to forbid men to look at the heavens."

As you know, they did stop my mouth. When I proved Copernicanism beyond a doubt, I was condemned by the Inquisition. My punishment was to repeat the seven penitential psalms once a week for three years, under house arrest. The decision frightened many scientists, including Descartes and crippled Catholics' work in astronomy. And yet, in the long run we astronomers won out, because, to quote my friend Kepler, "so great is the power of truth." Eventually the church actually apologized to me—ironically, though, it did so at this very time, the late 20th century, when anti-Copernicanism has appeared in a new guise: anti-Darwinianism.

The point of view of the academic world toward the creationist controversy is represented by Robert M. O'Neil, president of the University of Wisconsin System, in an article, "Creationism, Curriculum, and the Constitution."

Robert M. O'Neil

CREATIONISM, CURRICULUM, AND THE CONSTITUTION

In 1927, the *Scopes* case could be dismissed as an episode, either comic or tragic, with little legal significance. One cannot so lightly view the current legal controversies over the teaching of the origins of human life. At last count, the legislatures of twenty-two states had before them bills which would mandate the teaching of creationism along with evolu-

Reprinted by permission from the March-April 1982 issue of *Academe* pp. 21–26.

tion. Two states, Arkansas and Louisiana, have in fact adopted such laws. Earlier, the school boards of Dallas, Texas, Columbus, Ohio, and Charleston, West Virginia, had enacted similar policies. Meanwhile there is mounting evidence that creationist pressures have distorted both the content and the choice of public school textbooks.

Many educators have responded with unusual alarm; for example, the strong statement issued early this year by the board of the American Association for the Advancement of Science indicts creationist mandates as "a real and present threat to the integrity of education and the teaching of science." To the AAAS Board, creationism must be rejected as having "no scientific validity." Yet an Associate Press poll only a few weeks earlier recorded three-quarters of the American people as favoring the teaching of biblical theory of the origins of life in the public schools. Such tension between the academic community and the popular will is likely, as indeed has happened here, to bring the issue before the courts.

Creationism has been before the courts several times and in different forms since the *Scopes* trial. The past year has seen two celebrated cases, one in the California state courts, the other in the federal courts in Arkansas. The Arkansas case, in which a federal district judge in January struck down that state's equal-time law on constitutional grounds, will be discussed more fully below. The earlier California case, though legally inconclusive, deserves at least brief mention. It was the first legal challenge mounted by the Creation Science Research Center against curricula which stress the Darwinian view of life's beginnings. A family named Seagraves brought suit against California education officials, protesting state department policies which they felt emphasized evolution to the detriment of creationism. Following several days of testimony—none of it on the underlying educational or religious questions—the trial court dismissed the complaint. But in the process it ordered the state board to reaffirm its 1972 position that evolution should be taught as "theory," rather than as "dogmatism." The California

State Board had also shifted the debate from the science-curriculum framework into the social science context. That portion of the state policy was unaffected by the *Seagraves* decision.

Superficially at least, the California result pleased both parties. The creationists succeeded in obtaining judicial imprimatur for the State Board's "anti-dogmatism" on evolution teaching. Evolutionists, on the other hand, avoided a court judgment which would require the teaching of Genesis, either in science or the social science course. On balance, the creationists may actually have carried the day. Beyond the national publicity which drew attention to the creationist position, Professor Harvey Siegel of Sonoma State University perceived further gain:

The court, by directing that evolution be taught as theory, not fact, left a clear impression that alternative theoretical accounts of the origins of life (notably the creationist account) are acceptable alternatives to evolutionist theory. . . . The effect of the decision is to suggest that creationism *does* deserve to be recognized as scientifically legitimate.

Thus, while inconclusive in a technical legal sense, the *Seagraves* case may have ominous portent.

The more significant suit, of course, is the one brought in the federal courts testing the constitutionality of the Arkansas "equal time" law. That statute, like one passed a few months later in Lousiana, reflected ingenuity and sophistication in seeking to avoid possible constitutional traps. Where earlier laws invoked or implied religious grounds for teaching creationism, the Arkansas statute not only makes no explicit mention of religion, but, in fact, vigorously disclaims a sectarian foundation. The law says that what must be taught along with Darwinian evolution is "creation science," a doctrine defined as "the scientific evidences for creation and inferences from those scientific evidences." While the phenomena described in the law conform precisely to the account set forth in the Book of Genesis, the statute disclaimed any nexus; e.g., "this act does not require or permit instruction in any

religious doctrine or materials. . . . Treatment of either evolution science or creation science shall be limited to scientific evidences for each model and inferences from those scientific evidences and must not include any religious instruction or references to religious writings." Whether such disclaimers would preclude an inference of Biblical inspiration is but one of several intriguing legal issues which now deserve analysis.

At the outset, something should be said of two claims which appear among the "legislative findings of fact." Noting that "only evolution science is presented to students in virtually all of those courses that discuss the subject of origins," the Arkansas and Louisiana legislatures went on to "find" that such curricula both abridge the free exercise of religion and breach the wall of separation between church and state. Thus, the new laws are offered as protective, rather than subversive, of constitutional rights—allegedly designed to give the creationist family a wider choice and freer inquiry through the public schools while taking nothing away from the family committed to a Darwinian view of history.

These claims have at least a superficial appeal. They have been considered several times, however, and rejected by state and lower federal courts. In Houston and in Charleston, West Virginia, parents brought suit in the early 1970s seeking to enjoin on religious freedom grounds the continued offering of evolution-only science and social-science courses. In both cases, the federal courts made short shrift of the plaintiffs' claims. In the Houston case, parents argued that the public schools gave forbidden support to a "religion of secularism" and thus violated the First Amendment prohibition of the establishment of religion. The court found the connection, if any, between the secular curriculum and "religion" so tenuous as to fall far beyond the constitutional ban. School officials had in no way inhibited free discussion of the origins of human life, and such discussion might well include exploration of Genesis.

The rejection of a comparable claim in the

West Virginia case was even sharper: "A complete loosening of imagination is necessary to find that placing the books and materials in the schools constitutes an establishment of religion contrary to the rights contained in the Constitution." On the "free exercise of religion" claim, this court observed dispositively that the First Amendment "does not guarantee that nothing about religion will be taught in the schools nor that nothing offensive to any religion will be taught in the schools" and concluded that none of the school board's policies "constitutes an inhibition on or prohibition of the free exercise of religion." In both cases, the courts of appeals affirmed with brief opinions and thus put an end to such litigation.

More recently, however, "counter-religious" claims have emerged in a different setting. Several challenges to compulsory-attendance laws and to state regulation of church-affiliated schools have attacked the allegedly restrictive character of the public school curriculum. Here, too, the courts have been consistently unsympathetic. Despite the Supreme Court's holding in 1976 that Amish children could not be compelled to attend school beyond the eighth grade, lower courts have sustained mandatory attendance laws over creationist objections to the public school curriculum.

These arguments deserve a better answer than the courts have yet given them. In fact, the creationist position was forcefully developed in a student Note several years ago in the *Yale Law Journal*. The author concluded that, given the strength and nature of religious opposition to noncreationist curricula, "exclusive instruction in the general theory of evolution in public school classrooms abridges the free exercise of religion." The proposed solution was precisely the one which Arkansas and Louisiana were soon to adopt: a provision for "equal time," at least in communities with substantial creationist sentiment. Such a policy would "neutralize" a curriculum which might otherwise offend religiously conservative families by omitting the Genesis theory. While a sufficient answer to these claims has not yet been offered by the courts, and can-

not be developed here, more remains to be said in future litigation.

The equal-time laws are constitutionally vulnerable on two broader grounds: the possible breach of separation of church and state, and the possible stifling of free expression in the classroom. The former is the more familiar and accessible claim, the latter a more novel but intriguing one.

The constitutional background for the establishment claim is relatively well developed. Fourteen years ago, the Supreme Court settled the issue first raised in the *Scopes* case by holding, in *Epperson* v. *Arkansas*, that a state could not forbid, for religious reasons, all teaching of evolution. The earlier Arkansas law (adopted in 1928) made it a crime for any teacher in a public school, or state college or university, to teach or use a textbook which teaches "that mankind ascended or descended from a lower order of animals." The Court found such a law violative of the First Amendment's establishment clause, because its origin and inspiration were plainly religious. There was, moreover, no possible secular rationale for banning the teaching of Darwinian theory. The sole aim of the law, said the Court, was "to blot out a particular theory because of its supposed conflict with the biblical account, literally read."

This decision put to rest all laws which flatly forbade the teaching of evolution. State legislators did not abandon the quest, however. Soon after *Epperson*, Tennessee amended its old "Scopes" law to require that any biology book treating evolution must state "that it is a theory as to the origin and creation of man and his world and is not represented to be a scientific fact." Text books also were required to give "commensurate attention" and "equal emphasis" to "the origins and creation of man and his world as the same as recorded in other theories including, but not limited to, the Genesis account in the Bible." This law did not forbid the teaching of evolution. But it did demand a disclaimer of evolution's scientific validity, and it did ensure equal stature for the Genesis theory. (Tennessee also declared that the Bible should not be considered a "textbook" and, thus, did not need to balance both theories or include the evolutionary disclaimer.)

Both state and federal courts rejected the new Tennessee law, finding it well within the ban of *Epperson*. Lawmakers had expressed a clear preference for a Judeo-Christian view, which was sectarian as well as religious. The fact that evolution was not banned, but simply disparaged, did not help. Also, the Tennessee law created a serious risk which the courts had anticipated in other religious cases: involving school authorities in making inevitably theological choices among curricular options.

Two other cases enlarge the context. A decade ago, a student teacher in North Carolina was summoned by the principal because she gave an evolutionary answer to a student's question about the origins of life. When the teacher admitted that she had impugned the accuracy of Genesis, she was discharged. Her suit for reinstatement was successful; the federal district court found the principal's order constitutionally unacceptable under *Epperson*.

The last case, in some ways the most intriguing, involves a textbook rather than a law or administrative order. The Indiana State Textbook Commission approved several biology books for local district adoption. One of the texts, *Biology: A Search for Order in Complexity*, was challenged by a group of parents because it included some creationist material in its treatment of the origins of human life. A state trial judge carefully examined both the text and the teacher's manual and upheld the parents' challenge: "The prospect of biology teachers and students alike, forced to answer and respond to continued demand for correct fundamentalist Christian doctrine, has no place in public schools." This decision shows an intriguing application of *Epperson* to teaching materials, though a worrisome one because of the precedent it creates for judicial involvement in review of textbook selection.

None of the foregoing cases gives an adequate answer to the constitutional issue recently raised in Arkansas. The legislature obviously had acquired some sophistication between 1928 and 1980; statements of religious purpose, support, and rationale were totally absent from the new equal-time law, and the summary action of the lawmakers left no legislative history. Thus, if the establishment-clause claim were to succeed, a more elaborate approach would be required. Several possibilities exist.

First, this case may fall within *Epperson* on the basis of extensive testimony revealing an essentially religious rationale for so-called "creation science." Essentially, the argument contains two prongs: that "creation science" is meaningful only in concordance with the Genesis view of the origins of human life; and that, despite its terminology, "creation science" bears no resemblance to scientific theory or principle in any other context. Such evidence is at least persuasive to an establishment-clause claim resembling the successful challenge in *Epperson*.

A second and more elaborate approach invokes the tripartite test developed in cases striking down public aid to parochial schools. There, the Supreme Court has asked (a) whether the law has a "secular legislative purpose"; (b) whether "its principal or primary effect" either "advances or inhibits religion"; and (c) whether it fosters "an excessive entanglement with religion." The "equal-time" laws, it has been argued, fail at least the first two of these tests. If, in fact, "creation science" has no established scientific basis, then it is without the requisite secular legislative purpose. If, moreover, its content parallels precisely that of Genesis, then the effect of its inclusion in the curriculum seemingly "advances . . . religion." The possible relevance of the third test is less clear. The enforcement of equal-time laws might or might not entail the sort of "governmental entanglement" which is more obvious in the context of state aid to church-related schools.

The three parts of the test are, however, cumulative rather than alternative; governmental action will survive judicial review under the establishment clause only if it meets all three criteria and not simply one or two. Thus, even the absence of a "secular legislative purpose" behind the equal-time law may seal its fate. To that end, the kind of testimony summarized above would surely be persuasive. Both the evidence of a religious rationale and the absence of any respectable scientific basis would taint the effort to include "creation science" in the school curriculum.

The federal district judge in the Arkansas case found such a challenge to the equal-time law constitutionally compelling. His long and thoughtful opinion saw no escape from the conclusion that Arkansas had done more subtly what the Supreme Court had said a decade earlier it could not do without breaching the wall between church and state: "Since creation science is not science . . . the only real effect of [the equal-time law] is the advancement of religion. It was simply and purely an effort to introduce the biblical version of creation into the public school curricula." In the absence of any convincing proof that "creation science" was in fact a recognized branch of scientific thought, Judge Overton concluded confidently "that the purpose and the effect of [the statute] is the advancement of religion in the public schools." That was something the Supreme Court had said repeatedly that states could not do—both in *Epperson* and later in the parochial-school aid cases. Moreover, there was substantial risk of that very "governmental entanglement" which the high Court had warned against: "Involvement of the state in screening texts for impermissible religious references will require state officials to make delicate religious judgments. The need to monitor classroom discussion in order to uphold the Act's prohibition against religious instruction will necessarily involve instructors in questions concerning religion." Thus, for several closely related reasons, the ingenuity of the drafters of the legislation and of the Arkansas legislature had failed to avoid the constitutional perils against which the Supreme Court has so often cautioned.

However persuasive the establishment-clause claim, there remains a wholly different constitutional issue. To inhibit the freedom of teachers in so sensitive an area is always ominous. The Arkansas trial court in the *Epperson* case initially struck down the 1928 anti-evolution law on grounds of free speech rather than religion, finding that the statute "tends to hinder the quest for knowledge, restrict the freedom to learn, and restrain the freedom to teach." This issue accompanied the establishment clause claim to the Supreme Court, but it became superfluous to a judgment resting on other constitutional grounds.

At least one other suit challenging evolution-teaching bans did raise an academic-freedom claim. A Mississippi parent argued in federal court that the anti-Darwinian law disadvantaged her daughter in the competition for college admission. Since the student did not do well on standardized tests, an imcomplete science education would, the mother argued, impede her academic progress and impair prospects for her success in later life. The claim was ingenious, but it became moot when the court followed *Epperson* and struck down the Mississippi law on familiar establishment-clause grounds. This issue remains in the background awaiting the time when the religious-freedom argument may fail and a court would thus be required to deal with this constitutionally novel contention.

In order to remove the religious question altogether, let us hypothesize a different and perhaps implausible case, a state law requiring all geography teachers to balance regular instruction in "round science" with teaching of "flat science" in describing the earth's surface. The analogy to creationism is, of course, imperfect. Whatever uncertainty there may be about the Darwinian explanation of the origins of life, there is no doubt whatever about the curvature of the earth. Nonetheless, a state law demanding equal time for "flat science" would pose the question even more starkly, although without any possible establishment clause. The pure question of academic or intellectual freedom for the teacher would thus become the sole constitutional issue, and, for that reason, this bizarre hypothesis may be helpful.

States have long been held to have broad latitude in prescribing curricula for the public schools. Many state laws already impose mandates that may be educationally troublesome but are not necessarily unconstitutional. At least seven states, for example, require teaching about the "evils of communism" and others require that the benefits of "capitalism" or "free enterprise" be balanced against any discussion of socialist or communist economic systems. Such laws undoubtedly restrict the teacher's freedom to shape a curriculum or to choose course materials. Quite clearly, a university professor's liberties could not be impaired in such ways. Yet, at the elementary or secondary level, such laws do not in and of themselves seem constitutionally defective. Only some additional consideration would transform a law which may seem absurd or intrusive into one that would be unconstitutional.

A first possible challenge would be an essentially procedural one, a claim that the operative terms were excessively vague and thus left the teacher without adequate guidance. Courts have recognized the vice of vagueness or overbreadth in some analogous areas, for example, several loyalty oath cases of the 1960s in which state laws were struck down in large part because they left conscientious teachers and other public employees without adequate guidance as to the conduct which was either required or forbidden. Particularly germane is the decision invalidating Washington State loyalty oath which made all teachers pledge that they would "by precept and example promote respect for the flag and [federal and state] institutions [and] undivided allegiance to the [federal] government." The Court believed that a responsible teacher was entitled to a clearer definition of his or her responsibilities, and it warned that a conscientious person might well foreswear advocacy or opinion which was, in fact, constitutionally protected—simply because the boundaries of the mandate were so imprecise. A challenge

to a loosely worded curricular mandate, for example, one which failed adequately to define "flat science," might be successful by analogy to the Washington state loyalty oath decision.

A second challenge might rest upon the negative implication of such a mandate. Some of the language from concurring opinions in the *Epperson* case might be helpful. Justice Potter Stewart, in a brief concurrence, offered his rather narrow view of the decision:

A state is entirely free, for example, to decide that the only foreign language to be taught in its public school system shall be Spanish, but would a state be constitutionally free to punish a teacher for letting his students know that other languages are also spoken in the world? I think not.

It is one thing for a state to determine that the subject of higher mathematics, or astronomy, or biology, shall or shall not be included in its public shcool curriculum. It is quite another thing for a state to make it a criminal offense for a public school teacher so much as to mention the existence of an entire system of respected human thought. That kind of criminal law, I think, would clearly impinge upon the guarantees of free communication contained in the First Amendment. . . .

Whether Justice Stewart would perceive the "flat science" mandate as so hostile to the accepted status of "round science" as to fall under his ban is problematic. A teacher might, however, be able to show how dramatically the traditional and accepted view of the curvature of the earth was disrupted and disparaged by the requirement that absurd notions of "flat science" receive equal time.

This latter analysis suggests a third possible approach. Conceivably, a geography teacher in our hypothetical state could adduce evidence of an impermissible chilling effect upon the learning environment. It is one thing for a legislature or school board to remove or require a particular text or unit when that requirement does not totally undermine a major premise of the course. If, however, the requirement has the effect of precluding any meaningful discussion of fully accepted scientific truth, perhaps a sufficient "chilling" of the classroom discussion and the whole learning process could be shown. One might draw upon several federal appellate decisions in the early 1970s which upheld teachers' rights to use certain words in classroom discussion without risking dismissal or suspension. In one such case, involving a senior English teacher who emphasized a taboo word in a respected magazine article, the federal court of appeals ordered the teacher reinstated, finding that "the general chilling effect of permitting such rigorous censorship" could not be condoned. There are, of course, obvious differences. For one, the administration had reached in to punish the use of a particular word. The proscribed word, moreover, appeared in a respectable literary context and (the court observed in passing) could be found in many works available in the school's own library. Had the teacher instead been required, while discussing the essay, to tell his class that the taboo word offended many persons, the analogy to the equal-time situation would be closer, and the outcome of the "dirty word" case might well have been different. But, despite the differences, the development of an academic-freedom claim may still be worth pursuing in this context. (There is, of course, much uncertainty about the extent to which teachers below the collegiate level can claim an academic freedom comparable to the liberty of inquiry which college and university professors possess. That issue has been much discussed elsewhere, and mere mention of it must suffice here.)

A final argument may have the greatest appeal. Clearly the "flat science" mandate would force most geography teachers to profess in class an abhorrent belief. On several occasions, courts have found that state laws which so constrain a citizen's speech raise serious constitutional questions. When New Hampshire put the motto "Live Free Or Die" on its license plates, some citizens objected and one sought legal relief. The Supreme Court upheld on First Amendment grounds the individual motorist's wish to avoid displaying the motto: "The First Amendment protects the right of individuals to hold a point of view different from the majority and to foster . . . an idea they find morally objectionable." (The court then considered several alleged governmental interests but found them insufficient to outweight the individual's right not to be made a purveyor of the abhorrent motto.)

There is at least one school case which applies this principle. An upstate New York teacher refused, as a matter of conscience, to lead the morning flag salute and the Pledge of Allegiance. Many years earlier the Supreme Court had held that states could not require *students* to salute the flag or say the pledge. That judgment did not, however, necessarily protect teachers from having to set a patriotic example for their pupils. The federal appellate court now applied the "abhorrent-belief" concept to the teacher as well, holding that the school district could not constitutionally compel a teacher to lead the pledge or to salute the flag against his or her beliefs.

A teacher required to tell his or her students that the earth may be flat would face a comparable crisis of conscience. Particularly where the mandated view is scientific nonsense (much more clearly than creationism), the individual teacher's constitutional plea has a special poignance. While there is no precedent precisely in point, the "abhorrent-belief" cases would surely have bearing. While academic freedom does not protect the high school teacher as it does the university professor, the teacher is not entirely without constitutional protection.

This brief analysis reveals the far greater difficulty of resolving "equal-time" issues in a nonreligious context. Where the establishment-clause attack could not be mounted, the prospects for constitutional relief are far less clear. Yet there is no doubt—in the words of the resolution recently passed by the AAAS Board—that such curricular mandates pose "a real and present threat to the integrity of education and the teaching of science."

CHAPTER SIX

A NEW BOGYMAN: SECULAR HUMANISM

A most improbable new devil, "secular humanism," has been suddenly invented by fundamentalist religious leaders, and the campaign attacking this ancient philosophy has equaled in virulence the witch hunts of the 1950s.

Like many eccentric religious movements, the current uproar over secular humanism appears to have started in California. In the 1960s, Max Rafferty, then California's Superintendent of Public Instruction, was criticized for the schools' failure to educate. Rafferty, who later moved on to Alabama, disclaimed responsibility. In a report sponsored by him, published in 1969, humanists were blamed for progressive education, promoting birth control, materialism, abandoning absolute ethical and moral standards, infiltrating the U.S. Supreme Court, replacing religion with science, and sexual promiscuity.

The hue and cry by evangelical extremists continued. Under pressure by them, in 1976 the Conlan Amendment was introduced seeking to deny federal funds to any educational program teaching or supporting secular humanism. The amendment was defeated in the U.S. Senate but passed in the House of Representatives. By 1980 opposition to secular humanism had become a key plank in the platform of the Moral Majority, along with anti-detente, anti-welfare, anti-abortion, anti-ERA, anti-gay rights, anti-sex education in public schools, and anti-gun control. Radio and television programs nationwide have been used in the crusade against humanism.

Humanism in its classical sense places emphasis on the present life rather than the hereafter. An important phase of the Renaissance in Europe, beginning in the fourteenth century, was special attention to Greek and Latin works, often referred to as the humanities. The movement was a reaction against the narrow scholasticism characteristic of the medieval system of learning and theology. Simultaneously, there was a revival of interest in literature and art. Such early humanists as Petrarch, Boccaccio, Lorenzo de Medici, Erasmus, and Sir Thomas More were primarily concerned with humanity, beauty, and the natural world.

Modern humanism has three principal aspects: *religious* humanism, putting faith in man rather than God, rejecting all supernaturalism; *social* humanism, which stresses such ideals as love, loyalty, kindness, service, and honesty; and *literary* humanism, which aims to re-emphasize the study of literature and culture as a balance to the technical studies in the educational system.

A background survey of the current controversy is provided by Kenneth L. Woodward and Eloise Salholz, writing for *Newsweek*. They conclude that "In rejecting humanism the fundamentalists are, in a sense, rejecting the entire Western tradition."

Kenneth L. Woodward and Eloise Salholz

THE RIGHT'S NEW BOGYMAN

During last year's political wars, the preacher-politicians of the Moral Majority transformed the terms "liberal" and "liberalism" into synonyms for godlessness and immorality. Now, in the wake of last November's conservative landslide, the fundamentalist New Right has shifted its terminology and tactics to confront a new bogyman. The target is what Christian fundamentalists label "humanism"—and their campaign against anyone they regard as a humanist threatens to become as virulent as the anti-communist crusade of the 1950s.

In the Western tradition, humanism is not really a philosophy. Rather, it is an attitude that recognizes the dignity of man and the importance of culture to his full development; it therefore emphasizes, as the poet T. S. Eliot put it, the superiority of "breadth, tolerance . . . and sanity" over "narrowness, bigotry and fanaticism." In the fundamentalist view, however, humanism becomes very nearly its own opposite: a narrowly anti-Christian creed that denies God, glorifies self-indulgence and preaches everything from Darwin's theory of evolution to socialism and pornography. With the influence of humanists in government, the media and public education, says the Moral Majority's Rev. Jerry Falwell, "secular

humanism has become the religion of America." It has, he declares, "taken the place of the Bible."

That apocalyptic message has become the rallying cry of a diverse field of right-wing political and religious groups, and it is being repeated with increasing frequency throughout the nation. The Christian Broadcasting Network, for example, has sold 1,813 prints of "Let Their Eyes Be Opened," a half-hour film that warns about the pervasive influence of humanism in the public schools while regaling audiences—most of them Bible-study and prayer groups—with peephole views of scantily clad teen-age prostitutes.

The crusade's most vigorous apostle is San Diego preacher Tim LaHaye, a self-styled Biblical family counselor who has used his anti-humanist zeal to achieve considerable political clout. Earlier this year LaHaye organized the Council for National Policy, an informal coalition of New Right activists that for the first time puts well-heeled conservatives like oil billionaire Bunker Hunt and fundamentalist preachers in regular touch with right-wing political tacticians, U.S. senators—and the White House. As council president, LaHaye figured prominently at a lavish dinner party recently given in Washington, D.C., by conservative fundraiser Richard Viguerie and attended by a number of Cabinet and White House officials. "We share a basic commitment to moral values," LaHaye says of his new political-religious coalition. As he noted in "The Battle for the Mind," a book he wrote about the humanist threat, "We must remove all humanists from public office and replace them with pro-moral political leaders."

So far, the anti-humanist campaign's main battleground has been in the public schools. Armed with fundamentalist tracts with titles like "Secular Humanism: The Most Dangerous Religion in America," activists criticize textbooks, intimidate teachers and block sex-education programs. In Alabama, businessman Leo Yambrek enlisted the support of Gov. Forrest (Fob) James's wife in an anti-humanist crusade that succeeded in eliminating five history and social-studies textbooks from the state's education curriculum. In New Hampshire, former Congressional candidate Bob Sweet has taken to the lecture circuit warning parents and teachers against the dangers of godless humanism in the classroom. And in the wealthy Dallas suburb of Plano, Texas, a group called Concerned Parents for Quality Education has written congressmen—and the White House—demanding that all traces of humanism be removed from the Plano schools. "It's a pervasive campaign, an epidemic and a real attack on public education," says Dorothy Massie of the National Education Association's teacher rights department. "It's really a witch hunt, only now the witches are humanists."

"Paranoid." Who are the humanists whom the fundamentalists are hunting? There is no clear answer. In the classic mode of what American historian Richard Hofstadter has called "the paranoid style in American politics," the fundamentalists seem to have created a conspiracy where none actually exists. LaHaye, for instance, warns darkly that America is being victimized by "275,000 humanists" who control everything from the Supreme Court and the Federal government to the nation's universities, labor unions and media. But in "The Battle for the Mind" (350,000 copies of which are currently in print), he manages to identify only a handful of card-carrying secular humanists—chiefly the hundred-odd signers of a windy 1973 tract called the "Humanist Manifesto II." This group of prominent, self-described nontheists—among them, science-fiction writer Isaac Asimov, behavioral psychologist B. F. Skinner and philosopher Sidney Hook—denounced religion in the name of the "scientific method." In doing so, they set themselves off from the mainstream of humanist tradition—a tradition in which man's rela-

tionship to God is as important a subject as any other human activity.

Despite its obscurity, the "Humanist Manifesto" has been used by fundamentalists to back up their charge that secular humanism is a religion—and as such should not be taught in public schools. The basis of that argument was set out in a 1978 article in the Texas Tech Law Review by attorneys John W. Whitehead and John Conlan. According to Whitehead and Conlan, secular humanism received what amounted to official recognition as a religion when the Supreme Court decided to allow principled nontheists to register as conscientious objectors to military service. As a result, they wrote, "Traditional theism, particularly Christianity, [was] disestablished as the State's presuppositional base in exchange for the religion of Secular Humanism." What were the humanist religion's tenets? To define them, Whitehead and Conlan turned to the "Humanist Manifesto"—which asserts the supremacy of human reason and science over religious faith and the authority of the Bible.

Narrow Test. Like many conspiracy theories, the anti-humanist argument contains elements of truth. Until the establishment of universal public education in the late nineteenth century, most American higher education—and much secondary schooling as well—took place in Christian schools. Not all of them, however, would have passed the modern fundamentalist's narrow test for Biblical inerrancy. In any case, the appearance of totally secular universities did have a profound influence on the thinkers and activists who eventually shaped public education in America. "John Dewey and most of the other progressive architects of the public-education system grew up in small-town, Protestant America," says church historian Martin Marty. "But after they went to university, they dismissed all religion as the dull, small-town Protestantism they had known." Today, however, apart from an occasional celebrity skeptic like Skinner, there are few dyed-in-the-wool secular humanists left on campus who do much more than serenely ignore religion.

The fundamentalist attack on humanism is aimed at far more than just contemporary secularism. It represents a challenge to the root values of Western culture and the tradition of Christian humanism that lies at its core. As evangelical educator David Hicks notes, "The dialectic between pagan humanism and Christianity . . . undergirds all Western thought, culture and education." Just as Saint Augustine used the scaffolding of Platonism to create the first system of Christian theology, so did Saint Thomas Aquinas draw on Aristotle to fashion his magnificent medieval synthesis of reason and revelation. Even the great Protestant reformers, Calvin and Luther, were trained as humanists; indeed, it was their humanistic studies that led them to their rediscovery of the Bible. And in Erasmus and Saint Thomas More, Renaissance humanism merged with Christian learning and sanctity.

"The Christian humanist does not feel skittish about using the word *humanism*," evangelical scholar Mark Noll has written, "since at the heart of his faith stands the confession that God—the originator of everything right and good—himself became man." The fundamentalists seem oblivious to this notion. "They know a lot about Jesus," Noll says, "but they would know a lot more about him if they also knew Aquinas and Pascal."

But the fundamentalist mind is essentially bellicose; it demands an enemy to fight, not books to read. Modern fundamentalism, after all, got off the ground in the 1920s when Biblical literalists abandoned the secular university and all it represented in favor of their own Bible colleges—sanctuaries that scorned humanistic learning as satanic. In their view, seminal thinkers like Plato and Aristotle were worth discussing only as examples of pagan error. Both Falwell and LaHaye were educated at such schools, and today both head fundamentalist colleges that continue this essentially anti-intellectual tradition.

The fundamentalist critique of humanism is breath-takingly simple. "All books are based either on man's thoughts or God's thoughts," LaHaye argues in "The Battle for the Mind." The notion that Christianity could be enriched or informed by outside sources is thus considered completely invalid. Indeed, LaHaye criticizes Aquinas for reintroducing Aristotelian thought in the Christian West, remarking: "It is an irony of history that a man who was sainted by his church as a scholar was responsible for reviving an almost dead philosophy, which has become the most dangerous religion in the world today—humanism." This notion that anything not inspired directly by Biblical truth is inevitably anti-Christian applies to more than just philosophy. Among others, LaHaye excoriates Michelangelo for sculpting a nude David—when the Bible makes it clear in Genesis that, having fallen from grace, man should cover his nakedness. "The Renaissance obsession with nude 'art forms'," LaHaye declares, "was the forerunner of the modern humanist's demand for pornography in the name of freedom."

Alienation. Such bizarre indictments may say less about humanism than about the fundamentalists' profound alienation from the life of the mind. As the Roman Catholic philosopher Jacques Maritain observed, "Humanism is inseparable from civilization or culture." In rejecting it, the fundamentalists are, in a sense, rejecting the entire Western tradition.

They may also be rejecting some potential allies—chiefly those orthodox Christians, both Catholic and Protestant, who are equally upset by sexual promiscuity, drugs and moral indifference. The fact is, fundamentalists share a common enemy with orthodox Christians and devout Jews: secularists in every walk of life who deny that man has a transcendent dignity and destiny. Together, they might well find a way to bring teaching *about* religion back into the nation's schools and check the zealotry of those social planners who would manipulate the young at the expense of parental authority.

Fundamentalists have only recently awakened to these problems, and to the fact that the United States is no longer—if it ever was—the Christian nation they yearn for. America is a complex, pluralistic nation whose problems demand of its citizens all the breadth, tolerance and sanity that Eliot said humanism has to offer. And if that takes the form of a religious faith, it must feed on more than resentment and fear.

A detailed account in the *New York Times* describes the effect of the war on humanism on libraries and education.

Dena Kleiman

PARENTS' GROUPS PURGING SCHOOLS OF "HUMANIST" BOOKS AND CLASSES

In Onida, S.D., birth control information has been removed from the high school guidance office, and the word "evolution" is no longer uttered in advanced biology. "Brave New World" and "Catcher in the Rye" have been dropped from classes in literature. The award-winning children's book "Run Shelley, Run" has been banned from the library.

In Plano, Tex., teachers no longer ask students their opinions because to do so, they have been told, is to deny absolute right and wrong. In Des Moines, Iowa, a high school student production of "Grease," the hit Broadway musical, was banned. In Mount Diablo, Calif., Ms. Magazine is off the school library shelves; it is available only with permission from both a parent and a teacher.

LOBBYING METHODS SOPHISTICATED
Emboldened by what they see as a conservative mood in the country, parents' groups across the nation are demanding that teachers and administrators cleanse their

local schools of materials and teaching methods they consider antifamily, anti-American and anti-God.

Armed with sophisticated lobbying techniques and backed by such national organizations as Moral Majority, the Eagle Forum and the Christian Broadcasting Network, these parents are banding together to remove books from libraries, replace textbooks, eliminate sex education courses and balance lessons of evolution with those of Biblical creation, at least. They also seek to revise such things as the open classroom, new math and creative writing, asserting that these relatively unstructured academic approaches break down standards of right and wrong and thus promote rebellion, sexual promiscuity and crime.

"SECULAR HUMANISM" OPPOSED
There have always been disgruntled parents of one political persuasion or another. But visits to several cities and interviews with educators and leaders of the movement in cities around the nation show that today's groups are far more numerous, well organized and vocal. Their focus is no longer a specific book or course of study but rather the very nature of public education itself. The philosophy of "secular humanism," they say, permeates every facet of school life, from learning the alphabet to high school lessons in American history.

"Secular humanism is the underlying philosophy of all schools," said Terry Todd, national chairman of Stop Textbook Censorship, a group based in South St. Paul, Minn., which argues that "decent" books such as "The House of Seven Gables," "A Midsummer Night's Dream," "Huckleberry Finn" and "Robinson Crusoe" have been censored in favor of "humanist" literature. "Those of us who understand know how it is infiltrated, know how it is inculcated in the children."

Lottie Beth Hobbs, president of the Pro-Family Forum in Fort Worth, Tex., which distributes a leaflet entitled "Is Humanism Molesting Your Child?" said, "Humanism is everywhere. It is destructive to our nation, destructive to the family, destructive to the individual."

According to these groups, "humanism" has become the unofficial state religion. Its omnipresence, they contend, particularly within the nation's schools, is responsible for crime, drug abuse, sexual promiscuity and the decline of American power.

THE PHILOSOPHY CALLED HUMANISM

There is a philosophy called humanism, which places man at the center of the universe, encourages free thought and scientific inquiry without deference to a supreme being and offers no absolute standard of ethics.

But critics of the antihumanist movement, including teachers, parents and administrators, charge that the campaign is based more on hysteria than fact. They see "secular humanism" as a meaningless catch-all term used by these groups to describe all the nation's ills. While they acknowledge that humanism is the underlying philosophy of modern society, they dispute the belief that its acceptance is a result of conspiracy. Nor do they believe that it has been destructive to mankind.

"I think secular humanism is a straw man," said Paul Kurtz, a professor of philosophy at the State University at Buffalo, a leading humanist. "They are looking for someone to blame."

"Substitute the word humanist for Communist of the fifties or Bolshevik of the twenties," said Dorothy Massie of the National Education Association. "This time the target is public school education."

Based primarily in predominantly white suburbs and small towns, the protesting parent's groups, which number in the hundreds, have names such as Young Parents Alert, People Concerned With Education, Parents of Minnesota and Guardians of Education. They include many parents who have never been involved in organized activity before but have decided to join with others now because they fear that the problems of urban school systems are slowly encroaching on those of their own home towns. Direct mail, toll-free telephone numbers and cable television provide easy access to others who share their concerns.

BRAINWASHING IS ALLEGED

Through brochures, films and pamphlets distributed at parents meetings, these parents are being told that humanism "brainwashes" students to accept suicide, abortion and euthanasia and that it encourages them to lie, alienates them from their parents, fosters such "socialistic" anticompetitive practices as the open classroom and conditions them to think that there is no such thing as right or wrong.

"Some of you may have elementary or secondary children who experience stomach aches, headaches, nightmares or other similar complaints and/or disorders that cannot be accounted for," warns a pamphlet entitled "Parental Guide to Combat the Religion of Humanism in Schools," distributed by Parents of Minnesota. "Look in your schools! Modern educational materials and the techniques used may be what is causing those problems."

"I worry about my sons," said Lore Finley, whose two sons attend grade school in Blunt, S.D., and who only recently has become aware of the movement against secular humanism. "We do not have any rules in school; no right, no wrong. I don't like secular humanism. It teaches anything goes: if you feel it's O.K., do it."

What these parent groups are asking for, they say, is a return to many of the teaching practices and textbooks of 30 years ago, as well as the Christian values and principles upon which, they argue, the country was founded. They are asking specifically for history texts that emphasize the positive side of America's past, economics courses that stress the strengths of capitalism and literature that avoids divorce, suicide, drug addiction and other harsh realities of life.

RATING TEXTBOOKS FOR PARENTS

On another level, they advocate a return to academic "basics," contending that the abandonment of such disciplines as penmanship has led to slackening of standards and declining achievement. They want reading programs that focus on phonics rather than whole word recognition, writing programs that stress good spelling over creativity. They also want, they say, a curriculum and an approach to teaching that clearly delineates between right and wrong.

"There is just too much negativism," said Mel Gabler, who with his wife, Norma, operates the largest "textbook clearinghouse" in the country, advising parents' groups on the moral acceptability of textbooks from their home in Longview, Tex. The Gablers say inquiries have increased 50 percent since President Reagan was elected in November.

"There is an uneasy feeling that maybe we've bent over backwards with being broadminded," said Dr. Scott Thompson, president of the National Association of Secondary School Principals.

According to Judith Krug of the American Library Association, since last November there have been attempts to remove, restrict or deny access to 148 different books in 34 states.

In Buhler, Kan., for example, "The Kinsman," a science fiction novel by Ben Bova, was removed from the library of the Prairie Hills Middle School because parents complained that it was sexually suggestive. In Gretna, Va., a parent-teacher committee at the high school voted to cut out or ink over "Howl" by Allen Ginsberg and "Getting Down to Get Over" by June Gordon, which involves the trauma of a woman who was raped, both of which are in "The Treasury of American Poetry."

In Muskego, Wis., students must now have written permission to check out the feminist health manual "Our Bodies, Ourselves." In Branson, Mo., an issue of Sports Illustrated was returned to the publisher in a brown paper bag because it emphasized bikini swim suits. In French Lick, Ind., "Death of a Salesman" has been banned from a high school English class because it contains obscenities.

CURBING VARIOUS TEXTBOOKS

Because of successful challenges by such groups as the Gablers, numerous health, social studies, English and science textbooks have already been removed or revised to comply with parental complaints. Most recently, the Alabama Board of Education voted to remove "Justice in America" and "Unfinished Journey," both published by Houghton Mifflin and widely used in social studies classes across the country, from the state's approved textbook list in response to parental complaints that they were filled with secular humanism.

"We feel we brought the best of scholarship and accumulated as accurate and objective a book as we can possibly publish," Gary Smith, corporate counsel for Houghton Mifflin, said of "Unfinished Journey." "We found it difficult to find substance to support the charges made."

Many attempts to ban books have met failure. Others are still tied up in litigation, such as Pico v. Island Trees, a case involving a ban on Long Island in 1976 of nine books, including "Slaughterhouse Five" by Kurt Vonnegut Jr., "The Fixer" by Bernard Malamud, and "Down These Mean Streets" by Piri Thomas. The Long Island case is currently on appeal to the Supreme Court and could become an important test case of a school board's right to decide the contents of a school library [*Island Trees* decision, pp. 74ff].

Even in areas where censorship efforts have failed, teachers and others say that the battles themselves have had a chilling impact in certain cases on what goes on in the classroom.

AVOIDING CONTROVERSIAL SUBJECTS

"I think about what I'm doing twice," said Betty Duke, who teaches ninth grade history at Vines High School in Plano, a suburb of Dallas, where no specific book has been eliminated. "Is there anything controversial in this lesson plan? If there is, I won't use it. I won't use things where a kid has to make a judgment."

In South St. Paul, a suburb of St. Paul, Minn., all books that could possibly be considered controversial must be so labeled. They must then be reviewed by committee and either rejected or accepted by the school board. Rather than be subjected to that procedure, teachers in the school system simply have not changed the curriculum in more than six years and continue to use books that may in fact no longer be relevant.

"We want and need to update contemporary literature," said Joyce Johnson, who teaches language arts at South St. Paul Senior High School. "But we won't make suggestions because they would only be labeled out of context."

LEARNING ABOUT HUMANISM

Peter Carparelli, the principal of Helena Senior High School in Montana, said that many of his teachers had become anxious since a meeting last month when a discussion of the sex education curriculum turned into a forum on the ills of secular humanism. "There is this feeling that you're being questioned," he said.

"Anything that I think possibly controversial I tape," said George H. Tanner, one of several teachers at Montello High School in Wisconsin who began taking cassette tape recorders to class after parents accused them of "anti-God" statements they deny making.

Parents become aware of "secular humanism" and the campaign to cleanse the schools in different ways. Some first heard about it by means of religious television, newspapers or at religious services. Many others have been invited to community meetings and have been shown films and given pamphlets from such national organizations as the Gablers, the Pro-Family Forum, the Eagle Forum, Moral Majority, the Heritage Foundation and America's Future.

Some of the pamphlets currently in circulation include "Weep for Your Children," "The Hate Factory" and "Anti-God Humanists Are 'Conditioning' Our Children."

QUICK NETWORK REACTION

A 29-minute film produced by the Christian Broadcasting Network and entitled "Let Their Eyes Be Opened" has already sold over 1,800 copies at $125 each to individuals and groups across the nation. The film shows, among other things, aborted fetuses and teen-agers who have taken an overdose of drugs. It attempts to show that teen-age prostitution, pornography and murder are all a result of secular humanism in the schools.

"Two years ago I didn't even know what secular humanism was," said Joy Cook of Blunt, S.D., president of the local parents group attempting to purge it from the schools. "Now I realize you can be a humanist without knowing it and that there are humanists doing everything."

Mrs. Cook, who has a son at Sully Buttes high school in Onida and another child in grade school in Blunt, first heard about secular humanism when she was working to oppose the proposed equal rights amendment. She was told to call a lobbyist in North Dakota, who in turn said that she would put Mrs. Cook in touch with someone who could tell her more about humanism. Fifteen minutes later, Mrs. Cook said, she received a phone call from Mel Gabler of Texas, who sent her a package of materials.

Mrs. Cook now subscribes to at least a dozen national organizations sympathetic to her cause and keeps their literature in cardboard boxes and files in her living room. She plays host to sessions around her kitchen table to inform her neighbors of humanism's dangers and is always an outspoken participant at school board meetings. She, among others in the community, was in favor of banning "Run Shelley Run" by Gertrude Samuels, which was chosen by the American Library Association as Best Book for Young Adults in 1974 and which deals, in sometimes stark language, with the problems of a teen-age runaway.

"We have to get rid of secular humanism," said Donald J. Rykhus, superintendent of schools in Onida and Blunt, S.D. The only way that can be done, he said, was by getting rid of "liberal, real liberal, personnel."

"I worry for my son," said Vicky Brooks,

who teaches English at Sully Buttes high school and opposed the ban. "I don't want him to be in a community where if you disagree you are wrong. I want him to be able to evaluate opinions and be able to think. People who can't think are ripe for dictatorship."

Paul Kurtz and Edwin H. Wilson

HUMANIST MANIFESTO II

Recently over a hundred and twenty religious leaders, philosophers, scientists, writers and social scientists throughout the world have signed a new Humanist Manifesto, updating a 1933 document, Humanist Manifesto I, whose signers at that time included John Dewey, the philosopher.

PREFACE

It is forty years since *Humanist Manifesto I* (1933) appeared. Events since then make that earlier statement seem far too optimistic. Nazism has shown the depths of brutality of which humanity is capable. Other totalitarian regimes have suppressed human rights without ending poverty. Science has sometimes brought evil as well as good. Recent decades have shown that inhuman wars can be made in the name of peace. The beginnings of police states, even in democratic societies, widespread government espionage, and other abuses of power by military, political, and industrial elites, and the continuance of unyielding racism, all present a different and difficult social outlook. In various societies, the demands of women and minority groups for equal rights effectively challenge our generation.

As we approach the twenty-first century, however, an affirmative and hopeful vision is needed. Faith, commensurate with advancing knowledge, is also necessary. In the choice between despair and hope, humanists respond in this *Humanist Manifesto II* with a positive declaration for times of uncertainty.

As in 1933, humanists still believe that

This article first appeared in *The Humanist* September/October 1973 and is reprinted by permission.

traditional theism, especially faith in the prayer-hearing God, assumed to love and care for persons, to hear and understand their prayers, and to be able to do something about them, is an unproved and outmoded faith. Salvationism, based on mere affirmation, still appears as harmful, diverting people with false hopes of heaven hereafter. Reasonable minds look to other means for survival.

Those who sign *Humanist Manifesto II* disclaim that they are setting forth a binding credo; their individual views would be stated in widely varying ways. This statement is, however, reaching for vision in a time that needs direction. It is social analysis in an effort at consensus. New statements should be developed to supersede this, but for today it is our conviction that humanism offers an alternative that can serve present-day needs and guide humankind toward the future.

TEXT OF THE MANIFESTO

The next century can be and should be the humanistic century. Dramatic scientific, technological, and ever-accelerating social and political changes crowd our awareness. We have virtually conquered the planet, explored the moon, overcome the natural limits of travel and communication; we stand at the dawn of a new age, ready to move farther into space and perhaps inhabit other planets. Using technology wisely, we can control our environment, conquer poverty, markedly reduce disease, extend our lifespan, significantly modify our behavior, alter the course of human evolution and cultural development, unlock vast new powers, and provide humankind with unparalleled opportunity for achieving an abundant and meaningful life.

The future is, however, filled with dangers. In learning to apply the scientific method to nature and human life, we have opened the door to ecological damage, overpopulation, dehumanizing institutions, totalitarian repression, and nuclear and biochemical disaster. Faced with apocalyptic prophesies and doomsday scenarios, many flee in despair from reason and embrace irrational cults and theologies of withdrawal and retreat.

Traditional moral codes and newer irrational cults both fail to meet the pressing needs of today and tomorrow. False "theologies of hope" and messianic ideologies, substituting new dogmas for old, cannot cope with existing world realities. They separate rather than unite peoples.

Humanity, to survive, requires bold and daring measures. We need to extend the uses of scientific method, not renounce them, to fuse reason with compassion in order to build constructive social and moral values. Confronted by many possible futures, we must decide which to pursue. The ultimate goal should be the fulfillment of the potential for growth in each human personality—not for the favored few, but for all of humankind. Only a shared world and global measures will suffice.

A humanist outlook will tap the creativity of each human being and provide the vision and courage for us to work together. This outlook emphasizes the role human beings can play in their own spheres of action. The decades ahead call for dedicated, clearminded men and women able to marshal the will, intelligence, and cooperative skills for shaping a desirable future. Humanism can provide the purpose and inspiration that so many seek; it can give personal meaning and significance to human life.

Many kinds of humanism exist in the contemporary world. The varieties and emphases of naturalistic humanism include "scientific," "ethical," "democratic," "religious," and "Marxist" humanism. Free thought, atheism, agnosticism, skepticism, deism, rationalism, ethical culture, and liberal religion, all claim to be heir to the humanist tradition. Humanism traces its roots from ancient China, classical Greece and Rome, through the Renaissance and the Enlightenment, to the scientific revolution of the modern world. But views that merely reject theism are not equivalent to humanism. They lack commitment to the positive belief in the possibilities of human progress and to the values central to it. Many within

religious groups, believing in the future of humanism, now claim humanist credentials. Humanism is an ethical process through which we all can move, above and beyond the divisive particulars, heroic personalities, dogmatic creeds, and ritual customs of past religions or their mere negation.

We affirm a set of common principles that can serve as a basis for united action—positive principles relevant to the present human condition. They are a design for a secular society on a planetary scale.

For these reasons, we submit this new *Humanist Manifesto* for the future of humankind; for us, it is a vision of hope, a direction for satisfying survival.

RELIGION

First: In the best sense, religion may inspire dedication to the highest ethical ideals. The cultivation of moral devotion and creative imagination is an expression of genuine "spiritual" experience and aspiration.

We believe, however, that traditional dogmatic or authoritarian religions that place revelation, God, ritual, or creed above human needs and experience do a disservice to the human species. Any account of nature should pass the tests of scientific evidence; in our judgment, the dogmas and myths of traditional religions do not do so. Even at this late date in human history, certain elementary facts based upon the critical use of scientific reason have to be restated. We find insufficient evidence for belief in the existence of a supernatural; it is either meaningless or irrelevant to the question of the survival and fulfillment of the human race. As nontheists, we begin with humans not God, nature not deity. Nature may indeed be broader and deeper than we now know; any new discoveries, however, will but enlarge our knowledge of the natural.

Some humanists believe we should reinterpret traditional religions and reinvest them with meanings appropriate to the current situation. Such redefinitions, however, often perpetuate old dependencies and escapisms; they easily become obscurantist, impeding the free use of the intellect. We need, instead, radically new human purposes and goals.

We appreciate the need to preserve the best ethical teachings in the religious traditions of humankind, many of which we share in common. But we reject those features of traditional religious morality that deny humans a full appreciation of their own potentialities and responsibilities. Traditional religions often offer solace to humans, but, as often, they inhibit humans from helping themselves or experiencing their full potentialities. Such institutions, creeds, and rituals often impede the will to serve others. Too often traditional faiths encourage dependence rather than independence, obedience rather than affirmation, fear rather than courage. More recently they have generated concerned social action, with many signs of relevance appearing in the wake of the "God Is Dead" theologies. But we can discover no divine purpose or providence for the human species. While there is much that we do not know, humans are responsible for what we are or will become. No deity will save us; we must save ourselves.

Second: Promises of immortal salvation or fear of eternal damnation are both illusory and harmful. They distract humans from present concerns, from self-actualization, and from rectifying social injustices. Modern science discredits such historic concepts as the "ghost in the machine" and the "separable soul." Rather, science affirms that the human species is an emergence from natural evolutionary forces. As far as we know, the total personality is a function of the biological organism transacting in a social and cultural context. There is no credible evidence that life survives the death of the body. We continue to exist in our progeny and in the way that our lives have influenced others in our culture.

Traditional religions are surely not the only obstacles to human progress. Other ideologies also impede human advance. Some forms of political doctrine, for instance, function religiously, reflecting the worst features of orthodoxy and authoritarianism, especially when they sacrifice individuals on the altar of Utopian promises. Purely economic and political viewpoints, whether capitalist or communist, often function as religious and ideological dogma. Although humans undoubtedly need economic and political goals, they also need creative values by which to live.

ETHICS

Third: We affirm that moral values derive their source from human experience. Ethics is *autonomous* and *situational*, needing no theological or ideological sanction. Ethics stem from human need and interest. To deny this distorts the whole basis of life. Human life has meaning because we create and develop our futures. Happiness and the creative realization of human needs and desires, individually and in shared enjoyment, are continuous themes of humanism. We strive for the good life, here and now. The goal is to pursue life's enrichment despite debasing forces of vulgarization, commercialization, bureaucratization, and dehumanization.

Fourth: Reason and intelligence are the most effective instruments that humankind possesses. There is no substitute: neither faith nor passion suffices in itself. The controlled use of scientific methods, which have transformed the natural and social sciences since the Renaissance, must be extended further in the solution of human problems. But reason must be tempered by humility, since no group has a monopoly of wisdom or virtue. Nor is there any guarantee that all problems can be solved or all questions answered. Yet critical intelligence, infused by a sense of human caring, is the best method that humanity has for resolving problems. Reason should be balanced with compassion and empathy and the whole person fulfilled. Thus, we are not advocating the use of scientific intelligence independent of or in opposition to emotion, for we believe in the cultivation of feeling and love. As science pushes back the boundary of the known, man's sense of wonder is continually renewed, and art, poetry, and music find their places, along with religion and ethics.

THE INDIVIDUAL

Fifth: The preciousness and dignity of the individual person is a central humanist value. Individuals should be encouraged to realize their own creative talents and desires. We reject all religious, ideological, or moral codes that denigrate the individual, suppress freedom, dull intellect, dehumanize personality. We believe in maximum individual autonomy consonant with social responsibility. Although science can account for the causes of behavior, the possibilities of individual *freedom of choice* exist in human life and should be increased.

Sixth: In the area of sexuality, we believe that intolerant attitudes, often cultivated by orthodox religions and puritanical cultures, unduly repress sexual conduct. The right to birth control, abortion, and divorce should be recognized. While we do not approve of exploitive, denigrating forms of sexual expression, neither do we wish to prohibit, by law or social sanction, sexual behavior between consenting adults. The many varieties of sexual exploration should not in themselves be considered "evil." Without countenancing mindless permissiveness or unbridled promiscuity, a civilized society should be a *tolerant* one. Short of harming others or compelling them to do likewise, individuals should be permitted to express their sexual proclivities and pursue their life-styles as they desire. We wish to cultivate the development of a responsible attitude toward sexuality, in which humans are not exploited as sexual objects, and in which intimacy, sensitivity, respect, and honesty in interpersonal relations are encouraged. Moral education for children and adults is an important way of developing awareness and sexual maturity.

DEMOCRATIC SOCIETY

Seventh: To enhance freedom and dignity the individual must experience a full range of *civil liberties* in all societies. This includes freedom of speech and the press, political democracy, the legal right of opposition to governmental policies, fair judicial process, religious liberty, freedom of association, and artistic, scientific, and cultural freedom. It also includes a recognition of an individual's right to die with dignity, euthanasia, and the right to suicide. We oppose the increasing invasion of privacy, by whatever means, in both totalitarian and democratic societies. We would safeguard, extend, and implement the principles of human freedom evolved from the *Magna Carta* to the *Bill of Rights*, the *Rights of Man*, and the *Universal Declaration of Human Rights*.

Eighth: We are committed to an open and democratic society. We must extend *participatory democracy* in its true sense to the economy, the school, the family, the workplace, and voluntary associations. Decision-making must be decentralized to include widespread involvement of people at all levels—social, political, and economic. All persons should have a voice in developing the values and goals that determine their lives. Institutions should be responsive to expressed desires and needs. The conditions of work, education, devotion, and play should be humanized. Alienating forces should be modified or eradicated and bureaucratic structures should be held to a minimum. People are more important than decalogues, rules, proscriptions, or regulations.

Ninth: The separation of church and state and the separation of ideology and state are imperatives. The state should encourage maximum freedom for different moral, political, religious, and social values in society. It should not favor any particular religious bodies through the use of public monies, nor espouse a single ideology and function thereby as an instrument of propaganda or oppression, particularly against dissenters.

Tenth: Humane societies should evaluate economic systems not by rhetoric or ideology, but by whether or not they *increase economic well-being* for all individuals and groups, minimize poverty and hardship, increase the sum of human satisfaction, and enhance the quality of life. Hence the door is open to alternative economic systems. We need to democratize the economy and judge it by its responsiveness to human needs, testing results in terms of the common good.

Eleventh: The principle of moral equality must be furthered through elimination of all discrimination based upon race, religion, sex, age, or national origin. This means equality of opportunity and recognition of talent and merit. Individuals should be encouraged to contribute to their own betterment. If unable, then society should provide means to satisfy their basic economic, health, and cultural needs, including, wherever resources make possible, a minimum guaranteed annual income. We are concerned for the welfare of the aged, the infirm, the disadvantaged, and also for the outcasts—the mentally retarded, abandoned or abused children, the handicapped, prisoners, and addicts—for *all* who are neglected or ignored by society. Practicing humanists should make it their vocation to humanize personal relations.

We believe in the *right to universal education.* Everyone has a right to the cultural opportunity to fulfill his or her unique capacities and talents. The schools should foster satisfying and productive living. They should be open at all levels to any and all; the achievement of excellence should be encouraged. Innovative and experimental forms of education are to be welcomed. The energy and idealism of the young deserve to be appreciated and channeled to constructive purposes.

We deplore racial, religious, ethnic, or class antagonisms. Although we believe in cultural diversity and encourage racial and ethnic pride, we reject separations which promote alienation and set people and groups against each other, we envision an *integrated* community where people have a maximum opportunity for free and voluntary association.

We are *critical of sexism or sexual chauvinism*—male or female. We believe in equal rights for both women and men to fulfill their unique careers and potentialities as they see fit, free of invidious discrimination.

WORLD COMMUNITY

Twelfth: We deplore the division of humankind on nationalistic grounds. We have reached a turning point in human history where the best option is to *transcend the limits of national sovereignty* and to move toward the building of a world community in which all sectors of the human family can participate. Thus we look to the development of a system of world law and a world order based upon transnational federal government. This would appreciate cultural pluralism and diversity. It would not exclude pride in national origins and accomplishments nor the handling of regional problems on a regional basis. Human progress, however, can no longer be achieved by focusing on one section of the world, Western or Eastern, developed or underdeveloped. For the first time in human history, no part of humankind can be isolated from any other. Each person's future is in some way linked to all. We thus reaffirm a commitment to the building of world community, at the same time recognizing that this commits us to some hard choices.

Thirteenth: This world community must *renounce the resort to violence and force* as a method of solving international disputes. We believe in the peaceful adjudication of differences by international courts and by the development of the arts of negotiation and compromise. War is obsolete. So is the use of nuclear, biological, and chemical weapons. It is a planetary imperative to reduce the level of military expenditures and turn these savings to peaceful and people-oriented uses.

Fourteenth: The world community must engage in *cooperative planning* concerning the use of rapidly depleting resources. The planet earth must be considered a single *ecosystem.* Ecological damage, resource depletion, and excessive population growth must be checked by international concord.

The cultivation and conservation of nature is a moral value; we should perceive ourselves as integral to the sources of our being in nature. We must free our world from needless pollution and waste, responsibility guarding and creating wealth, both natural and human. Exploitation of natural resources, uncurbed by social conscience, must end.

Fifteenth: The problems of *economic growth and development* can no longer be resolved by one nation alone; they are worldwide in scope. It is the moral obligation of the developed nations to provide—through an international authority that safeguards human rights—massive technical, agricultural, medical, and economic assistance, including birth control techniques, to the developing portions of the globe. World poverty must cease. Hence extreme disproportions in wealth, income, and economic growth should be reduced on a worldwide basis.

Sixteenth: Technology is a vital key to human progress and development. We deplore any neo-romantic efforts to condemn indiscriminately all technology and science or to counsel retreat from its further extension and use for the good of humankind. We would resist any moves to censor basic scientific research on moral, political, or social grounds. Technology must, however, be carefully judged by the consequences of its use; harmful and destructive changes should be avoided. We are particularly disturbed when technology and bureaucracy control, manipulate, or modify human beings without their consent. Technological feasibility does not imply social or cultural desirability.

Seventeenth: We must expand communication and transportation across frontiers. Travel restrictions must cease. The world must be open to diverse political, ideological, and moral viewpoints and evolve a worldwide system of television and radio for information and education. We thus call for full international cooperation in culture, science, the arts, and technology *across ideological borders*. We must learn to live openly together or we shall perish together.

HUMANITY AS A WHOLE

In closing: The world cannot wait for a reconciliation of competing political or economic systems to solve its problems. These are the times for men and women of good will to further the building of a peaceful and prosperous world. We urge that parochial loyalties and inflexible moral and religious ideologies be transcended. We urge recognition of the common humanity of all people. We further urge the use of reason and compassion to produce the kind of world we want—a world in which peace, prosperity, freedom, and happiness are widely shared. Let us not abandon that vision in despair or cowardice. We are responsible for what we are or will be. Let us work together for a humane world by means commensurate with humane ends. Destructive ideological differences among communism, capitalism, socialism, conservatism, liberalism, and radicalism should be overcome. Let us call for an end to terror and hatred. We will survive and prosper only in a world of shared humane values. We can initiate new directions for humankind; ancient rivalries can be superseded by broad-based cooperative efforts. The commitment to tolerance, understanding, and peaceful negotiation does not necessitate acquiescence to the status quo nor the damming up of dynamic and revolutionary forces. The true revolution is occurring and can continue in countless nonviolent adjustments. But this entails the willingness to step forward onto new and expanding plateaus. At the present juncture of history, commitment to all humankind is the highest commitment of which we are capable; it transcends the narrow allegiances of church, state, party, class, or race in moving toward a wider vision of human potentiality. What more daring a goal for humankind than for each person to become, in ideal as well as practice, a citizen of a world community. It is a classical vision; we can now give it new vitality. Humanism thus interpreted is a moral force that has time on its side. We believe that humankind has the potential intelligence, good will, and cooperative skill to implement this commitment in the decades ahead.

Two thoughtful studies of the "humanist phantom," by Charles Krauthammer and James David Besser, appeared in the July 25, 1981, issue of *The New Republic.*

Charles Krauthammer

THE HUMANIST PHANTOM

I should not have any inclination to call myself a humanist, as I think, on the whole, that the non-human part of the cosmos is much more interesting and satisfactory than the human part.
—Bertrand Russell

Most of us have only a vague idea what humanism is. We tend to think of a humanist as someone who is concerned with other humans, a humanitarian, an all-around nice guy. For example, that's how Deborah Weisner of Auburn, Maine, sees it. For five days last March she was held hostage on a Pakistani jetliner by armed hijackers. UPI reported that after her release "[she] said that she had sympathized with the terrorists and believed their leader was a 'humanist' until he shot a passenger before her eyes." Now, any definition of humanist that includes a pistol-packing Albert Schweitzer up until the moment he shoots someone dead before your eyes is a broad definition indeed. There used to be a narrower definition. Beginning with the Renaissance and for about 400 years thereafter, the title "humanist" was generally reserved for Greek and Latin scholars and for students of classical forms in art and literature. "In my old-fashioned terminology," wrote George Santayana, "a humanist means a person saturated by the humanities. Humanism is something cultural; an accomplishment, not a doctrine."

Not anymore. If you hold to the Santayana (or the Weisner) view of humanism, you will have difficulty understanding the current hysteria on the religious right over humanism. That is because for the right it has a different meaning. Jesse Helms summarized it neatly: "Basically, we are talking about faith in God versus secular humanism." Note the prefix "secular," the characteristic identifier of this type of humanism and the key to what Reverend Jerry Falwell calls "its satanic influence"—to wit, its atheism. Among evangelicals, secular humanism has become the talk of the tube. Falwell warns that it "challenges every principle on which America was founded. It advocates abortion-on-demand, recognition of homosexuals, free use of pornography, legalizing of prostitution and gambling, and free use of drugs, among other things." Worst among these "other things" is that it "promotes the socialization of all humanity into a world commune." Reverend Tim LaHaye, another founder of the Moral Majority and author of its antihumanist bible, *The Battle for the Mind*, is the movement's historian. He explains that humanism "snuck into" America via European rationalists such as Voltaire and now it has become "the most dangerous religion in the world." But Phyllis Schlafly says not to worry. The tide is turning. "The humanists should be worried—because the public has begun to see through their hypocrisy in fastening their atheist ideology on the public schools. . . ."

This is moderate, mainstream antihumanism. For the truly bloodcurdling stuff one has to travel to the deep end of the anti-humanist spectrum. Here one finds, among others, pastor Leo Wine of Ashland, Oregon. He did a series of radio programs on humanism. One began with a look at current humanist activities:

Why are the humanists promoting sexual perversion? Because they want to create such an obsession with sex among our young people that they will have no time or interest for spiritual pursuits. . . . So what do we have? Humanist obsessions: sex, pornography, marijuana, drugs, self-indulgence, rights without responsibility.

Then he panned upward for the larger over-view:

Humanists control America. America is supposed to be a free country, but are we really free? . . . Now the humanist organizations—ACLU, AHA [American Humanist Association]—control the television, the radio, the newspapers, the Holly-wood movies, magazines, porno magazines, and the unions, the Ford Foundation, Rockefeller Foundation. . . . They, 275,000 humanists, have infiltrated until every department of our country is controlled by the humanists.

And they have plans for the future:

Humanists will continue leading us toward the chaos of the French Revolution. After all, it is the same philosophy that destroyed France and paved the way for the dictator Napoleon Bonaparte. This time the humanists hope to name their own dictator who will create out of the ashes of our pro-moral republic a humanist utopia, an atheis-tic, socialistic, amoral humanist society for Amer-ica and the rest of the world. In fact, their goal is to accomplish that takeover by or before the year 2000.

Nor is the fear of secular humanism re-stricted to paranoid pastors, television huck-sters, or Moral Majoritarians trying to drum up converts and donations. When the South-ern Baptist Convention met in Los Angeles last June, the *New York Times* reported blandly that it "approved resolutions con-demning pornography, anti-Semitism and secular humanism. . . ." Interesting com-pany. The resolution "encourage[s] Baptists to become informed about and voice opposi-tion to the tenets of secular humanism" and calls for an educational effort to "explain the nature and inherent danger of secular humanism."

The antihumanist campaign also has found its way into the classroom. School-boards throughout the country evaluate textbooks based on the critique of Educa-tional Research Analysts, a textbook re-viewing outfit that is a Geiger counter for humanist contamination. It is run by a re-tired Texas couple, Mel and Norma Gabler. In 1979 the *American School Board Journal* cited them as perhaps the two most powerful individuals in American education. The cur-rent issue of *Moral Majority Report* hails

them as an inspiration to those "who think there is little they can do to fight the human-ism that increasingly dominates public education." In that same issue, Mel (who refers to the public schools as "government seminaries" of secular humanism) candidly lists the kinds of humanist influence he fer-rets for in textbooks: situation ethics, self-centeredness, evolution, negations of Christianity, death education, international-ism, and sexual freedom.

The antihumanists have even made sev-eral forays, with mixed results, into the political arena. In 1976 Representative John Conlan of Arizona introduced an amend-ment to withhold federal funds for any edu-cational activity involving "the religion of humanism." Conlan lost on the House floor, but he did get the House to cut off funding for an entire public school curriculum enti-tled "Man: A Course of Study" (man, for reasons unrelated to feminism, being the offending concept). This year a suit was filed in California to force the public schools to teach the "creationist" rebuttal to evolution. The plaintiffs lost, but shortly thereafter Arkansas passed a law mandating equal time for creationism in the public schools. Jesse Helm's human life amendment and Roger Jepsen's omnibus Family Protection Act are guaranteed to carry on the antihumanist cru-sade in Congress.

What is behind all the rending of garments over secular humanism? Clearly, for Falwell and Company, humanism does not mean humanitarianism or a love of Greek poetry (though he might have some reservations about that, too). It is a handy catchall to evoke all the changes of the postwar Amer-ican cultural revolution: challenges to tradi-tional sexual morality, civil and parental au-thority, and religious orthodoxy; to work, family, neighborhood, and church, as Ronald Reagan puts it. Ultimately, it is a reaction to a decline in religious values. Now, there is nothing particularly new or necessarily dangerous about conservatives opposing secularization and calling for a reli-gious renewal. What *is* new, and potentially dangerous, is that the current reaction has identified a single cause for the secular trend and dubbed it humanism. This poses a logical problem. If humanism simply means irreligion, then to blame the decline of religion on the rise of humanism is a tautology. On the other hand, if humanism is the evangelical creed of a small band of proselytizing zealots, then to blame the decline of religion on humanism is paranoia. The religious right, apparently, has chosen paranoia. It is a clever tactic. What otherwise would have been a shadowy struggle against a 500-year-old historical trend—secularization—is transformed into a crusade against a militant ideology controlled by a vanguard of party activists—the humanists. A generation ago the pernicious sappers of our vital spiritual juices were called "godless Communists." Now they are "secular humanists."

Who are these people hiding under (in?) the beds of God-fearing Christians? There is in fact an organization of humanists, but they are hardly a group on whom to pin the decline of Western civilization. Forty years ago they banded together into the American Humanist Association. They then proceeded to wander in the same political wilderness as the militant vegetarians and agrarian anarchists. It took the far right to put them on the map.

A glance at the current issue of the *Humanist*, the American Humanist Association's magazine, gives a good idea of what they are up to. The cover story is "Humanistic Revolution in Health Care," a paean to the Pritikin diet. It is followed by articles on sexual equality, genetic altruism, the makings of a good person, and the like. The *Humanist* would be indistinguishable from other publications promoting good causes except for several unnerving characteristics. First, it has a consistent strain of gratuitous antitheism which endows each piece with a triumphant "God-is-really-dead" tone. In this issue, for example, an article describing a politician's fight with the local Catholic hierarchy over birth control is entitled "The Man Who Defeated God." Second, a slightly crackpot secular millenarianism prevails. There is the promise of salvation in

every new discovery, scientific or social: if only the Pritikin diet were accepted, 150,000 lives a year would be saved; or, if only we had sexual equality, we would have the "key to solving such globe-threatening problems as nuclear war, totalitarianism, and social injustice all across the board." That same spirit compels the almost obsessive habit of ending each article with an uplifting reference to all humankind, a kind of humanist hallelujah.

It is difficult, however, to make such benign eccentricities the object of a holy war. For the religious right to sustain its malevolent fantasies about humanism, it turns not to today's *Humanist* but instead to a more venerable source, the *Humanist Manifesto*, I and II. The first of these was issued in 1933 and signed by 34 intellectuals (John Dewey was one). Its object was not to reject religion but to replace the traditional creeds with a new one: "religious humanism." It was to be the "vital, fearless and frank religion" that new realities demanded. By today's standards the manifesto is a mild, naive affirmation of faith in science, reason, and "manly attitudes." It rejects the traditional belief in God and calls for man to create his own ethics; it rejects "acquisitive and profit-motivated society" and calls for a "socialized and cooperative economic order" with "the equitable distribution of the means of life." The content is vaguely Marxist, humane and minus the class antagonism. But the pretentions of the 15 numbered principles are decidedly biblical. Take humanist principle number one: "religious humanists regard the universe as self-existing and not created." This statement tells us nothing about the universe, since "self-existing," though the kind of word that might inspire an Escher painting, is philosophically empty. It is a thinly disguised declaration about (the nonexistence of) He-who-is-supposed-to-have-created-the-universe, a politely humanist way of saying that in the beginning God did *not* create the heavens and the earth.

Forty years later the *Humanist Manifesto* began to look a bit dated. So a sequel—*Humanist Manifesto* II—was produced. By now there were many more signers. They included biomedical types like Francis Crick and B. F. Skinner; philosophers like Sidney Hook; civil liberty lobbyists like the heads of Planned Parenthood and the Association for the Repeal of Abortion Laws; and liberal—very liberal—churchmen, mostly Unitarians with a rabbi thrown in here and there. By now, the pretense that humanism was a new religion or in any way "religious" was dropped. The new manifesto was frankly antireligious, although it did, with Christian charity, concede that "traditional religions are surely not the only obstacles to human progress." All the hallmarks of the old humanism are there: a naive faith in science ("We need to extend the uses of scientific method . . . to build constructive social and moral values"); a rejection of God ("We find insufficient evidence for belief in the existence of a supernatural," $p > 0.05$, no doubt, or, for you lawyers, case dismissed); the enshrinement of "self-actualization" as the goal of life; the assertion that ethics is "autonomous and situational needing no theological sanction"; an attack on orthodox religion for "unduly repress[ing] sexual conduct"; an affirmation of the right to birth control, abortion, and permission to express "sexual proclivities" and pursue "lifestyles" and a definition of civil liberties that includes "the right to die with dignity, euthanasia and the right to suicide." In keeping with the fashion of the times, a few new clichés are appended: a commitment to decentralized decision-making, a salute to "the energy and idealism of the young," an appeal for "a world order based upon transnational federal government," and bows to ecology and a new world economic order for the third world. All in all, a mixture of old-fashioned earnest atheism and late-1960s radical libertarianism, floating in a gelatinous universalism worthy of a UN preamble. It is the creed one might expect of a socially conscious, passionately naive microbiology major.

Neither *Humanist Manifesto* made a great impact. The 1933 version might have served the already religiously defrocked as a benign, mildly socialist alternative to Stalinism; the 1973 version, as a highly scientistic corrective to some of the neo-romantic irrationalism of the late-1960s. Today's tepid *Humanist* magazine reflects the same sensibilities. And it shares the same intellectual marginality. It remains an enthusiastic, slightly utopian, and doggedly atheistic forum for a small group of believers. But that's not how its opponents see it. They see these humanists and their manifestos marching across the centuries leaving devastation in their wake. Recently, Alabama removed from its approved list of school texts a history book which parental groups claimed promoted secular humanist values. One complaint was about a reference to Erasmus as a "Christian humanist." One critic asked: "How can a Christian be a humanist? . . . It is impossible to be a Christian humanist. . . . If you embrace the humanist manifesto, you embrace that there is no God."

The entire evangelical attack on the humanist nemesis is at roughly the same level of sophistication. And the saddest consequence of this crazy crusade is that it has corrupted an important social issue: what happens to a free society when a major source of its values—religion—declines? Conservatives are not the only ones who are troubled by this question. Arthur Schlesinger once wrote that "the most important thing for the preservation of civilization is a belief in moral standards. That belief is really most solid when it is founded upon a fervent belief in a supernatural order." Years later he added,

I am impressed, for example, by the way the declining faith in the supernatural has been accompanied by the rise of the monstrous totalitarian creeds of the 20th century. As Chesterton once said, "The trouble when people stop believing in God is not that they thereafter believe in nothing; it is that they thereafter believe in anything."

Schlesinger is not the first to appreciate the political and social functions of religious belief. As Terry Eastland points out (*Commentary*, June 1981), the founding fathers held a similar view. They recognized that individual liberty alone was insufficient for sustaining a republican order. For society to remain intact, the centrifugal forces of simple libertarianism had to be balanced by countervailing forces promoting civic and moral virtue. Respect for the gods and the *polis* provided that for the Greeks. The founding fathers believed that the prevailing Protestant culture, with its belief in Divine Providence, would do the same for America.

But that religious order has declined. In intellectual circles today, a belief in the supernatural is treated with condescension if not contempt. Several years ago the great Australian neurobiologist, Sir John Eccles, ended a Harvard lecture on brain organization by admitting that although evolution could account for the brain, it could not, in his view, account for the mind, with its mysterious capacity for consciousness and thought: only something transcendent could account for that. The audience began hissing.

In the scientific world, to insist on the need for a religious sensibility is considered a lapse of judgment; in the political world, it is considered a retreat to sentimentality if not reaction. But in my view it is a mistake to assume that rejecting the lunacy of the far right means we must deny the value to society of a religious sensibility. The connection between decline in spirituality and social pathology has been noted by Schlesinger. And it has been argued most forcefully not by Jerry Falwell but by Alexander Solzhenitsyn. In his fire and brimstone Harvard address of 1978 Solzhenitsyn ascribed the present "state of weakness of the West" to:

. . . the prevailing view of the world which was first born during the Renaissance and found its political expression from the period of the Enlightenment . . . rationalistic humanism or humanistic autonomy: the proclaimed and enforced autonomy of man from any higher force above him . . . [This] anthropocentricity, with man seen as the center of everything that exists . . . did not admit the existence of intrinsic evil in man nor did it see any higher task than the attainment of happiness on earth. . . . That provided access for evil of which in our days there is a free and constant flow.

Solzhenitsyn does not engage in the easy demagoguery of the American right in blaming our current condition on a small band of satanic conspirators. When Solzhenitsyn speaks of humanism, his definition is the only honest and useful one: the doctrine of man-centeredness which has characterized half a millenium of Western thought. And when Solzhenitsyn denounces this doctrine and calls for a return to the spiritual fold, he knows he is ordering the tides to turn back. But that is not his only message. We don't have to will ourselves into his idealized theistic past to appreciate his warnings against anthropocentric arrogance—against an insufficient appreciation of man's capacity for evil and, therefore, of the dangers of absolute freedom. Most of us are not prepared to learn our theology from Solzhenitsyn. But that is not a reason to reject his message about the limits of liberty and the need to reestablish—in our law and politics and culture—communal values. Restoring these values is a task secularists and skeptics should address without fear that it will put them on the road to Lourdes, or to Lynchburg, Virginia. Ignoring these values simply guarantees that they will remain the exclusive domain of comically dogmatic manifesto signers and dangerously intolerant twice-born preachers.

James David Besser

ANTIHUMANISM ON THE AIR

The radio preachers start talking at dawn and continue with numbing intensity far into the night. More than a million Americans faithfully tune in to their 15-minute concoctions of fire and brimstone, dulcet-toned pleading, right-wing ideology, and born-again religion. And with the advent of the "new right" and the growing sophistication of groups like the Moral Majority, radio evangelists can no longer be dismissed as representing a politically and culturally meaningless fringe. Currently there are

Reprinted from the July 25, 1981, issue by permission of *The New Republic.* © 1981 The New Republic Inc.

more than 1,300 radio stations nationwide with extensive religious programming that reaches as many as 115 million listeners a week. The number of religious stations is increasing at a rate of two per week.

Most religious stations are profit-making ventures. Air time is sold to the independent ministries that produce and distribute programs. Preachers make frequent pitches for contributions. For nationally syndicated programs, the goal is to generate enough revenue through local contributions to be self-sustaining in each market.

In the Washington, D.C. area, two stations broadcast more than 70 programs every day. WFAX went into the religious radio business in 1948. WABS ("We Always Broadcast Salvation") changed from an all-news format four years ago. To get an idea of the flavor of what the religious stations broadcast, I recently spent several days listening to the two Washington outlets. What I heard says a great deal about the kinds of issues that are galvanizing the religious right.

"Ask the Pastor" presents modern marriage as a grim struggle resulting from the unwillingness of many women to accept God's laws. "Part of the judicial decree of God in response to the sin that Eve committed was to place her in subordination to her husband," Pastor Andy Christianson says, citing appropriate Scripture. "Sometimes women rebel, and this is called womens' liberation." Brother Roloff covers child rearing. His theme is corporal punishment. (His enthusiasm for physical punishment as the best disciplinary method also guides his Lighthouse home for errant children and has embroiled him in a legal battle with the Texas attorney general.) "No Christian," he reassures listeners, "will beat a child until he maims him or cripples him or kills him. Love will always stop him at the proper time. A child needs enough punishment to break his stubborn will and let him throw up the white flag and say 'Daddy, you win, I surrender.' "

After a chorus of "My Country, 'Tis of Thee," Dr. Vernon Schroeder articulates a theme that is no longer rare on born-again radio, though it runs counter to the traditional fundamentalist respect for civil law. Shroeder advocates a kind of civil disobedience based on a view of the Bible as inerrant and absolute. He tells his audience that God's law always takes precedence over civil law, especially in this age of abortion, birth control, homosexuality, and the assorted ungodly laws of unrighteous men. "The time is coming, my friends, when we will be forced to make a decision whether we will deny God and obey civil government, or deny civil government and obey God. . . . In a few short hours, we will be thrust under the hand of godless government regulations, and then we must make our decision."

Old-time radio preachers such as Dale Crowley, who has been broadcasting the Gospel and chasing evolutionists for half a century, still condemn the social gospel, the liberal notion that churches should work to redeem society through the broad ethical principles of Christianity. But the new radio evangelists have been forced to rename the enemy, since they have come to assume the role of social redeemers themselves. "They're using 'secular humanism' as a kind of updated term for the social gospel," says William Fore, director of communications for the National Council of Churches, another favorite target of fundamentalist broadcasters. "Humanism is second only to communism as a scare word." On his program, Vernon Shroeder calls humanism "anti-God and anti-Christ." On the "Family Freedom Hour," Pastor Brothers portrays it as a sinister, well-organized conspiracy especially designed to influence young people. The *Humanist Manifesto*, he says, lists its goals: atheism, birth control, abortion, free sexual choice, and world government.

Several other groups are favorite targets. Planned Parenthood is excoriated almost hourly for advocating the same sins as the humanists, in addition to more traditional sins such as bestiality and incest. Homosexuals fare no better. One caller on the daily talk show on WABS reads selections from the Bible that seem to advocate the execution of homosexuals. And the radio ministries are doing what they can to boost the anti-evolution revival. Theories of evolution, according to Pastor Carver on the "Christian-Jew Hour," are part of the "doctrine of Demons." Several ministers ridicule the idea that their listeners' ancestors might have been apes or "blobs." Jerry Falwell calls evolution the "cornerstone of secular humanism."

Jews are treated with ambivalence on evangelical radio, but programs are aimed more at reinforcing the commitments of converted Jews than at making new converts. Often they are described as members of an obdurate, misguided race. "To my Jewish friends, I say this: you blew it 2,000 years ago," thunders Brother Shambock. On the "Christian-Jew Hour," the tone is patient and condescending. Sermons are loaded with biblical quotes showing Jews—and Catholics, Mormons, and vegetarians—the error of their ways. But to the millenialists who dominate the religious airwaves (the James Watt view of an abbreviated earthly future is taken as given), the repopulation of modern Israel with unconverted Jews is the key event in their prophesies of the rapture that will precede the imminent return of Christ. The messianic Jews focus on the ways in which Jews can accept Christ as the Messiah prophesied in the Old Testament and still retain their cultural identity. The messianic programs are sprinkled with Yiddish words, Hasidic-sounding music with Christian lyrics, and personal testimonies in which earnest young converts document the spiritual poverty of growing up Jewish.

Born-again radio emphasizes that Christians should strive to divorce themselves from a sinful society. The leader of a Washington-area Baptist youth group tells the audience the qualities he tries to instill in children: being saved, surrendering to God, being soul winners, studying the Bible, and separation. "We want our young people to be separated from the world," he says firmly. Genuine Christians are portrayed as a long-suffering minority who pay at every turn for their convictions. As radio preachers shed the fundamentalist distrust

of politics, they increasingly come to portray themselves as moral crusaders who are bound together, at least in part, by the perceived hostility of the outside world.

No broadcaster uses this concept more effectively than Jerry Falwell, guiding light of the Moral Majority, whose "Old Time Gospel Hour" is broadcast on 389 TV and 450 radio stations nationwide. Real Christians, Falwell says, inevitably will be controversial and unpopular figures in this troubled time. He invokes a long list of evils: abortion, George McGovern, the ACLU, political and religious liberalism, homosexuality, divorce, and sex education— "academic pornography," he calls it. Christians who take the correct positions on these moral dilemmas, he suggests, must be willing to suffer. "The right stands," he says, "are the difficult ones." The theme of persecution by the forces of unrighteousness—liberal clergymen, politicians, and bureaucrats—works its way into his plea for funds. "Satan," he intones, "would love to silence the voice of the 'Old Time Gospel Hour.' "

The daily talk shows on WABS provide an opportunity for listeners to express their own righteous anger. One caller describes the 29 things the Communists are doing to overthrow our "Christian" nation. "Sex education," she says, "is done deliberately to destroy the minds of American youth and destroy their ruggedness." Other callers describe Ernest Lefever, Jesse Helms, and South Africa as staunch defenders of the Christian faith and accuse unnamed public officials of being homosexuals. Surprisingly few callers fit stereotypes of the backwoods fundamentalist. They are generally articulate and well read in current politics. But facts are reshaped to fit into rigid politico-religious schemes. When a caller suggests that most of the Soviet Union's space satellites are really orbiting warheads, and another argues that the Ku Klux Klan is merely a victim of the liberal press, no one disagrees. "You're not giving me the facts as I like to hear them," a caller tells a guest on one edition of the program.

The programs are a smashing success with their audiences. Chaplain Ray "wins criminals from crime to Christ" through his prison radio ministry. Marilyn Hickey, in a kind of hyperkinetic baby talk, says that "Jesus can be your pain deadener and disinfectant." Pastor Epley's services reverberate with the wails of the afflicted and the shouted praise of those who witness his diagnoses and cures. David Weber warns that zip codes, Social Security numbers, and government computers are among the tools the Antichrist will soon use to identify his followers, who have been marked with the number 666. Already, he says, uniform product codes on food packages contain the dangerous digits.

The high-pitched vehemence of many radio preachers contrasts sharply with the new wave of slick, toned-down television ministries. The nationally telecast "700 Club" is more reminiscent of the "Tonight Show" than of steamy rural Pentecostal churches. The television ministers, because they emphasize the proselytizing function, have repackaged fundamentalism to sell to a broader market. The radio preachers focus instead on the already-saved. And because they are not concerned about impressing the non-fundamentalist world, they probably reflect more accurately the feelings of the foot soldiers in this growing army of the righteous.

The religious right is fragmented into many factions, each claiming moral purity, each interpreting the absolute world of God in a different way. On the surface, nothing seems more unlikely than a stable coalition of such diverse groups. But a coalition *has* developed which tolerates major doctrinal differences as long as there is agreement about certain highly charged symbolic issues. Radio preachers may quibble about the chronology of Armageddon, but increasingly they agree about the political advantages of focusing on issues such as sex education, homosexuality, humanism, and evolution. They often express their satisfaction with the rising conservative tide, and their determination to help direct the current. Jerry Falwell sums up the basic tenet that has, for the moment, unified the electronic evangelists: "One man and his God," he says, "constitute a majority."

CHAPTER SEVEN

WHO OR WHAT IS OBSCENE?

It has been suggested that ever since Adam made nudity seem indecent by wearing a fig leaf, a continuous debate has gone on to determine what is or is not obscene. There seems slight prospect that the dispute will ever be resolved to the satisfaction of opposing forces.

Among the issues that may never find acceptable answers to all factions are these: (1) Does obscenity or pornography do anyone any harm? (2) Does pornography have a deleterious effect on social morality? (3) Does the First Amendment, which guarantees free speech, protect obscenity? (4) Can obscenity laws be enforced, using community standards (as proposed by the Supreme Court) or any other criteria?

A major attempt to bring an end to the long-drawn-out controversy and to find some solutions occurred, beginning in 1967, with passage by the U.S. Congress of Public Law 90–100. The act was a response to a belief that the business of obscenity and pornography had increased to such an extent it had become "a matter of national concern." A federal commission was authorized to investigate the spread of pornography and its effects on American society and to produce recommendations for its control.

The Commission on Obscenity and Pornography began its work in January 1968, with the appointment of members by President Lyndon Johnson. The chairman was William B. Lockhart, University of Minnesota law school dean. Subsequently, the great moral leader Richard Nixon appointed an ultra-conservative member to offset what he considered a liberal bias in the Johnson appointees. The total membership was thus brought to eighteen.

The commission's principal recommendations, supported by twelve of its eighteen members, proposed, among other things, the repeal of all laws against pornography for "consenting adults," the adoption of state laws prohibiting the distribution of pictorial, but not written, pornography to "young people," and the launching of "a massive sex education effort" to "contribute to healthy attitudes" and to "reduce interest in and dependence upon clandestine sources of information."

Noteworthy among the commission's findings were the following: (1) The sexual behavior of most people is not changed substantially by exposure to erotica, nor are attitudes toward sexual morality altered significantly. (2) Adult sex offenders have been less exposed to erotica as teenagers than have other adults and there is no evidence that exposure to pornography leads significantly to sex crimes. (3) Patrons of "adults only" bookstores and movies are generally not lonely social misfits, but "predominantly white, middle-class, middle-aged, married males in business suits or neat casual attire." (4) The majority of Americans believe that adults should be allowed to read or see pornography if they so wish.

A coalition statement on the COP report was issued by the American Civil Liberties Union and other sponsoring organizations. There it was pointed out that the report represented two years of intensive efforts by dedicated commission members, working under a congressional mandate. The report did not recommend abolition of all laws regulating censorship. It did, however, recommend abolition of obscenity laws prohibiting distribution of materials to adults who chose to receive them. Doubt is expressed in the report that so-called obscene books and films affect the morals or social behavior of individual readers. A wide program of sex education and further scientific investigation are urged. The commission was united in its concern about censorship and the need for freedom of thought, freedom of expression, and freedom of choice.

The committee's report, a lengthy document of 1,053 pages, came off the press in 1970. Key sections are the Preface, the nonlegislative recommendations, and legislative recommendations, reproduced here.

U.S. Commission on Obscenity and Pornography

REPORT

PREFACE

Congress, in Public Law 90–100, found the traffic in obscenity and pornography to be "a matter of national concern." The Federal Government was deemed to have a "responsibility to investigate the gravity of this situation and to determine whether such materials are harmful to the public, and particularly to minors, and whether more effective methods should be devised to control the transmission of such materials." To this end, the Congress established an advisory

Reprinted from *Report of the U.S. Commission on Obscenity and Pornography* (Washington: U.S. Government Printing Office, 1970), pp. 1–4, 47–64. Footnotes have been omitted from the portion of the text reproduced here. In addition to the official report, the full text appears in a Bantam Books edition (1970).

commission whose purpose was "after a thorough study which shall include a study of the causal relationship of such materials to antisocial behavior, to recommend advisable, appropriate, effective, and constitutional means to deal effectively with such traffic in obscenity and pornography."

Congress assigned four specific tasks:

(1) with the aid of leading constitutional law authorities, to analyze the laws pertaining to the control of obscenity and pornography; and to evaluate and recommend definitions of obscenity and pornography;

(2) to ascertain the methods employed in the distribution of obscene and pornographic materials and to explore the nature and volume of traffic in such materials;

(3) to study the effect of obscenity and pornography upon the public, and particularly minors, and its relationship to crime and other antisocial behavior; and

(4) to recommend such legislative, administra-

tive, or other advisable and appropriate action as the Commission deems necessary to regulate effectively the flow of such traffic, without in any way interfering with constitutional rights. . . .

Material may be deemed "obscene" because of a variety of contents: religious, political, sexual, scatological, violent, etc. The Commission has limited its concern to sexual obscenity, including sadomasochistic material, because the legislative history indicated this as the focus of congressional concern as reflected by the linking of obscenity with pornography in the Act creating the Commission. The application of obscenity laws has been directed in recent times almost exclusively to sexual obscenity; indeed, court decisions regarding permissible legal definitions of the term "obscene" have appeared in recent years to delimit its application to such sexual obscenity. Thus, the Commission's inquiry was directed toward a wide range of explicit sexual depictions in pictorial and textual media.

Just as obscenity may involve a variety of contents and judgments, so also may "antisocial" behavior and moral character. A declining concern with established religions, new questions as to the wisdom and morality of war, changes in attitudes toward races and minorities, and conflicts regarding the responsibility of the state to the individual and the individual to the state may all be considered to represent changes in the moral fiber of the nation. To some, these phenomena are considered to be signs of corroding moral decay; to others, signs of change and progress. It was impossible during the brief life of the Commission to obtain significant data on the effects of the exposure to pornography on nonsexual moral attitudes. Consequently, the Commission has focused on that type of antisocial behavior which tends to be more directly related to sex. This includes premarital intercourse, sex crimes, illegitimacy, and similar items.

Discussions of obscenity and pornography in the past have often been devoid of fact. Popular rhetoric has often contained a variety of estimates of the size of the "smut"

industry and assertions regarding the consequences of the existence of these materials and exposure to them. Many of these statements, however, have had little anchoring in objective evidence. Within the limits of its time and resources, the Commission has sought, through staff and contract research, to broaden the factual basis for future continued discussion. The Commission is aware that not all issues of concern have been completely researched nor all questions answered. It also recognizes that the interpretations of a set of "facts" in arriving at policy implications may differ even among men of good will, Nevertheless, the Commission is convinced that on most issues regarding obscenity and pornography the discussion can be informed by important and often new facts. It presents its Report, hopeful that it will contribute to this discussion at a new level. Since it may be anticipated that in any controversial area some of the research will be questioned as to method and the validity and reliability of the results, the Commission hopes that responsible scientific organizations will carefully scrutinize these studies and that new and continuing research will result.

I. NON-LEGISLATIVE RECOMMENDATIONS

The Commission believes that much of the "problem" regarding materials which depict explicit sexual activity stems from the inability or reluctance of people in our society to be open and direct in dealing with sexual matters. This most often manifests itself in the inhibition of talking openly and directly about sex. Professionals use highly technical language when they discuss sex; others of us escape by using euphemisms—or by not talking about sex at all. Direct and open conversation about sex between parent and child is too rare in our society.

Failure to talk openly and directly about sex has several consequences. It overemphasizes sex, gives it a magical, non-natural quality, making it more attractive and fascinating. It diverts the expression of sexual interest out of more legitimate channels, into less legitimate channels. Such failure makes teaching children and adolescents to become fully and adequately functioning sexual adults a more difficult task. And it clogs legitimate channels for transmitting sexual information and forces people to use clandestine and unreliable sources.

The Commission believes that interest in sex is normal, healthy, good. Interest in sex begins very early in life and continues throughout the life cycle although the strength of this interest varies from stage to stage. With the onset of puberty, physiological and hormonal changes occur which both quicken interest and make the individual more responsive to sexual interest. The individual needs information about sex in order to understand himself, place his new experiences in a proper context, and cope with his new feelings.

The basic institutions of marriage and the family are built in our society primarily on sexual attraction, love, and sexual expression. These institutions can function successfully only to the extent that they have a healthy base. Thus the very foundation of our society rests upon healthy sexual attitudes grounded in appropriate and accurate sexual information.

Sexual information is so important and so necessary that if people cannot obtain it openly and directly from legitimate sources and through accurate and legitimate channels, they will seek it through whatever channels and sources are available. Clandestine sources may not only be inaccurate but may also be distorted and provide a warped context.

The Commission believes that accurate, appropriate sex information provided openly and directly through legitimate channels and from reliable sources in healthy contexts can compete successfully with potentially distorted, warped, inaccurate, and unreliable information from clandestine, illegitimate sources; and it believes that the attitudes and orientations toward sex produced by the open communication of appropriate sex information from reliable sources through legitimate channels will be normal and healthy, providing a solid foundation for the basic institutions of our society.

The Commission, therefore, presents the following positive approaches to deal with the problem of obscenity and pornography.

1. The Commission recommends that a massive sex education effort be launched. This sex education effort should be characterized by the following:

a) its purpose should be to contribute to healthy attitudes and orientations to sexual relationships so as to provide a sound foundation for our society's basic institutions of marriage and family;

b) it should be aimed at achieving an acceptance of sex as a normal and natural part of life and of oneself as a sexual being;

c) it should not aim for orthodoxy; rather it should be designed to allow for a pluralism of values;

d) it should be based on facts and encompass not only biological and physiological information but also social, psychological, and religious information;

e) it should be differentiated so that content can be shaped appropriately for the individual's age, sex, and circumstances;

f) it should be aimed, as appropriate, to all segments of our society, adults as well as children and adolescents;

g) it should be a joint function of several institutions of our society: family, school, church, etc.;

h) special attention should be given to the training of those who will have central places in the legitimate communication channels—parents, teachers, physicians, clergy, social service workers, etc;

i) it will require cooperation of private and public organizations at local, regional, and national levels with appropriate funding;

j) it will be aided by the imaginative utilization of new educational technologies for example, educational television could be used to reach several members of a family in a family context.

The Commission feels that such a sex education program would provide a powerful positive approach to the problems of obscenity and pornography. By providing accurate and reliable sex information through legitimate sources, it would reduce interest in and dependence upon clandestine and less legitimate sources. By providing healthy attitudes and orientations toward sexual relationships, it would provide better protection for the individual against distorted or warped ideas he may encounter regarding sex. By providing greater ease in talking about sexual matters in appropriate contexts, the shock and offensiveness of encounters with sex would be reduced.

2. The Commission recommends continued open discussion, based on factual information, on the issues regarding obscenity and pornography.

Discussion has in the past been carried on with few facts available and the debate has necessarily reflected, to a large extent, prejudices and fears. Congress asked the Commission to secure more factual information before making recommendations. Some of the facts developed by the Commission are contrary to widely held assumptions. These findings provide new perspectives on the issues.

The information developed by the Commission should be given wide distribution, so that it may sharpen the issues and focus the discussion.

3. The Commission recommends that additional factual information be developed.

The Commission's effort to develop information has been limited by time, financial resources, and the paucity of previously existing research. Many of its findings are tentative and many questions remain to be answered. We trust that our modest pioneering work in empirical research into several problem areas will help to open the way for more extensive and long-term research based on more refined methods directed to answering more refined questions. We urge both private and public sources to provide the financial resources necessary for the continued development of factual information so that the continuing discussion may be further enriched.

The Federal Government has special responsibilities for continuing research in these areas and has existing structures which can facilitate further inquiry. Many of the questions raised about obscenity and pornography have direct relevance to already existing programs in the National Institute of Mental Health, the National Institute of Child Health and Human Development, and the United States Office of Education. The Commission urges these agencies to broaden their concerns to include a wider range of topics relating to human sexuality, specifically including encounters with explicit sexual materials.

4. The Commission recommends that citizens organize themselves at local, regional, and national levels to aid in the implementation of the foregoing recommendations.

The sex education effort recommended by the Commission can be achieved only with broad and active citizen participation. Widespread discussion of the issues regarding the availability of explicit sexual materials implies broad and active citizen participation. A continuing research program aimed at clarifying factual issues regarding the impact of explicit sexual materials on those who encounter them will occur only with the support and cooperation of citizens.

Organized citizen groups can be more constructive and effective if they truly represent a broad spectrum of the public's thinking and feeling. People tend to assume, in the absence of other information, that most people's opinions are similar to their own. However, we know that opinions in the sexual realm vary greatly—that there is no unanimity of values in this area. Therefore, every group should attempt to include as wide a variety of opinion as is possible.

The aim of citizen groups should be to provide a forum whereby all views may be presented for thoughtful consideration. We live in a free, pluralistic society which places its trust in the competition of ideas in a free market place. Persuasion is a preferred technique. Coercion, repression and censorship in order to promote a given set of views are not tolerable in our society.

II. LEGISLATIVE RECOMMENDATIONS

In general outline, the Commission recommends that federal, state, and local legislation should not seek to interfere with the rights of adults who wish to do so to read, obtain, or view explicit sexual materials. On the other hand, we recommend legislative regulations upon the sale of sexual materials to young persons who do not have the consent of their parents, and we also recommend legislation to protect persons from having sexual materials thrust upon them without their consent through the mails or through open public display.

The Commission's specific legislative recommendations and the reasons underlying these recommendations are as follows:

A. Statutes Relating to Adults

The Commission recommends that federal, state, and local legislation prohibiting the sale, exhibition, or distribution of sexual materials to consenting adults should be repealed. Twelve of the 17 participating members of the Commission join in this recommendation. Two additional Commissioners subscribe to the bulk of the Commission's Report, but do not believe that the evidence presented at this time is sufficient to warrant the repeal of all prohibitions upon what adults may obtain. Three Commissioners dissent from the recommendation to repeal adult legislation and would retain existing laws prohibiting the dissemination of obscene materials to adults.

The Commission believes that there is no warrant for continued governmental interference with the full freedom of adults to read, obtain or view whatever such material they wish. Our conclusion is based upon the following considerations:

1. Extensive empirical investigation, both by the Commission and by others, provides no evidence that exposure to or use of explicit sexual materials play a significant role in the causation of social or individual harms such as crime, delinquency, sexual or nonsexual deviancy or severe emotional disturbances. This research and its results are described in detail in the Report of the Effects Panel of the Commission and are summarized above in the Overview of Commission findings. Empirical investigation thus supports the opinion of a substantial majority of persons professionally engaged in the treatment of deviancy, delinquency and antisocial behavior, that exposure to sexually explicit materials has no harmful causal role in these areas.

Studies show that a number of factors, such as disorganized family relationships and unfavorable peer influences, are intimately related to harmful sexual behavior or adverse character development. Exposure to sexually explicit materials, however, cannot be counted as among these determinative factors. Despite the existence of widespread legal prohibitions upon the dissemination of such materials, exposure to them appears to be a usual and harmless part of the process of growing up in our society and a frequent and nondamaging occurrence among adults. Indeed, a few Commission studies indicate that a possible distinction between sexual offenders and other people, with regard to experience with explicit sexual materials, is that sex offenders have seen markedly *less* of such materials while maturing.

This is not to say that exposure to explicit sexual materials has no effect upon human behavior. A prominent effect of exposure to sexual materials is that persons tend to talk more about sex as a result of seeing such materials. In addition, many persons become temporarily sexually aroused upon viewing explicit sexual materials and the frequency of their sexual activity may, in consequence, increase for short periods. Such behavior, however, is the type of sexual activity already established as usual activity for the particular individual.

In sum, empirical research designed to

clarify the question has found no evidence to date that exposure to explicit sexual materials plays a significant role in the causation of delinquent or criminal behavior among youth or adults.

2. On the positive side, explicit sexual materials are sought as a source of entertainment and information by substantial numbers of American adults. At times, these materials also appear to serve to increase and facilitate constructive communication about sexual matters within marriage. The most frequent purchaser of explicit sexual materials is a college-educated, married male, in his thirties or forties, who is of above average socio-economic status. Even where materials are legally available to them, young adults and older adolescents do not constitute an important portion of the purchases of such materials.

3. Society's attempts to legislate for adults in the area of obscenity have not been successful. Present laws prohibiting the consensual sale or distribution of explicit sexual materials to adults are extremely unsatisfactory in their practical application. The Constitution permits material to be deemed "obscene" for adults only if, as a whole, it appeals to the "prurient" interest of the average person, is "patently offensive" in light of "community standards," and lacks "redeeming social value." These vague and highly subjective aesthetic, psychological and moral tests do not provide meaningful guidance for law enforcement officials, juries or courts. As a result, law is inconsistently and sometimes erroneously applied and the distinctions made by courts between prohibited and permissible materials often appear indefensible. Errors in the application of the law and uncertainty about its scope also cause interference with the communication of constitutionally protected materials.

4. Public opinion in America does not support the imposition of legal prohibitions upon the right of adults to read or see explicit sexual materials. While a minority of Americans favors such prohibitions, a majority of the American people presently are of the view that adults should be legally able to read or see explicit sexual materials if they wish to do so.

5. The lack of consensus among Americans concerning whether explicit sexual materials should be available to adults in our society, and the significant number of adults who wish to have access to such materials, pose serious problems regarding the enforcement of legal prohibitions upon adults, even aside from the vagueness and subjectivity of present law. Consistent enforcement of even the clearest prohibitions upon consensual adult exposure to explicit sexual materials would require the expenditure of considerable law enforcement resources. In the absence of a persuasive demonstration of damage flowing from consensual exposure to such materials, there seems no justification for thus adding to the overwhelming tasks already placed upon the law enforcement system. Inconsistent enforcement of prohibitions, on the other hand, invites discriminatory action based upon considerations not directly relevant to the policy of the law. The latter alternative also breeds public disrespect for the legal process.

6. The foregoing considerations take on added significance because of the fact that adult obscenity laws deal in the realm of speech and communication. Americans deeply value the right of each individual to determine for himself what books he wishes to read and what pictures or films he wishes to see. Our traditions of free speech and press also value and protect the right of writers, publishers, and booksellers to serve the diverse interests of the public. The spirit and letter of our Constitution tell us that government should not seek to interfere with these rights unless a clear threat of harm makes that course imperative. Moreover, the possibility of the misuse of general obscenity statutes prohibiting distributions of books and films to adults constitutes a continuing threat to the free communication of ideas among Americans—one of the most important foundations of our liberties.

7. In reaching its recommendation that government should not seek to prohibit con-

sensual distributions of sexual materials to adults, the Commission discussed several arguments which are often advanced in support of such legislation. The Commission carefully considered the view that adult legislation should be retained in order to aid in the protection of young persons from exposure to explicit sexual materials. We do not believe that the objective of protecting youth may justifiably be achieved at the expense of denying adults materials of their choice. It seems to us wholly inappropriate to adjust the level of adult communication to that considered suitable for children. Indeed, the Supreme Court has unanimously held that adult legislation premised on this basis is a clearly unconstitutional interference with liberty.

8. There is no reason to suppose that elimination of governmental prohibitions upon the sexual materials which may be made available to adults would adversely affect the availability to the public of other books, magazines, and films. At the present time, a large range of very explicit textual and pictorial materials are available to adults without legal restrictions in many areas of the country. The size of this industry is small when compared with the overall industry in books, magazines, and motion pictures, and the business in explicit sexual materials is insignificant in comparison with other national economic enterprises. Nor is the business an especially profitable one; profit levels are, on the average, either normal as compared with other businesses or distinctly below average. The typical business entity is a relatively small entrepreneurial enterprise. The long-term consumer interest in such materials has remained relatively stable in the context of the economic growth of the nation generally, and of the media industries in particular.

9. The Commission has also taken cognizance of the concern of many people that the lawful distribution of explicit sexual materials to adults may have a deleterious effect upon the individual morality of American citizens and upon the moral climate in America as a whole. This concern appears to

flow from a belief that exposure to explicit materials may cause moral confusion which, in turn, may induce antisocial or criminal behavior. As noted above, the Commission has found no evidence to support such a contention. Nor is there evidence that exposure to explicit sexual materials adversely affects character or moral attitudes regarding sex and sexual conduct.

The concern about the effect of obscenity upon morality is also expressed as a concern about the impact of sexual materials upon American values and standards. Such values and standards are currently in a process of complex change, in both sexual and nonsexual areas. The open availability of increasingly explicit sexual materials is only one of these changes. The current flux in sexual values is related to a number of powerful influences, among which are the ready availability of effective methods of contraception, changes of the role of women in our society, and the increased education and mobility of our citizens. The availability of explicit sexual materials is, the Commission believes, not one of the important influences on sexual morality.

The Commission is of the view that it is exceedingly unwise for government to attempt to legislate individual moral values and standards independent of behavior, especially by restrictions upon consensual communication. This is certainly true in the absence of a clear public mandate to do so, and our studies have revealed no such mandate in the area of obscenity.

The Commission recognizes and believes that the existence of sound moral standards is of vital importance to individuals and to society. To be effective and meaningful, however, these standards must be based upon deep personal commitment flowing from values instilled in the home, in educational and religious training, and through individual resolutions of personal confrontations with human experience. Governmental regulation of moral choice can deprive the individual of the responsibility for personal decision which is essential to the formation of genuine moral standards. Such regulation would also tend to establish an official moral orthodoxy, contrary to our most fundamental constitutional traditions.

Therefore, the Commission recommends the repeal of existing federal legislation which prohibits or interferes with consensual distribution of "obscene" materials to adults. These statutes are: 18 U.S.C. Section 1461, 1462, 1464, and 1465; 19 U.S.C. Section 1305; and 39 U.S.C. Section 3006. The Commission also recommends the repeal of existing state and local legislation which may similarly prohibit the consensual sale, exhibition, or the distribution of sexual materials to adults.

B. Statutes Relating to Young Persons

The Commission recommends the adoption by the States of legislation set forth in the Drafts of Proposed Statutes in Section III of this Part of the Commission's Report prohibiting the commercial distribution or display for sale of certain sexual materials to young persons. Similar legislation might also be adopted, where appropriate, by local governments and by the federal government for application in areas, such as the District of Columbia, where it has primary jurisdiction over distributional conduct.

The Commission's recommendation of juvenile legislation is joined in by 14 members of the Commission. Two of these, feel the legislation should be drawn so as to include appropriate descriptions identifying the material as being unlawful for sale to children. Three members disagree. Other members of the Commission, who generally join in its recommendation for juvenile legislation, disagree with various detailed aspects of the Commission's legislative proposal. These disagreements are noted in the following discussion.

The Commission's recommendation of juvenile legislation flows from these findings and considerations:

A primary basis for the Commission's recommendation for repeal of adult legislation is the fact that extensive empirical investigations do not indicate any causal relationship between exposure to or use of explicit sexual materials and such social or individual harms such as crime, delinquency, sexual or nonsexual deviancy, or severe emotional disturbances. The absence of empirical evidence supporting such a causal relationship also applies to the exposure of children to erotic materials. However, insufficient research is presently available on the effect of the exposure of children to sexually explicit materials to enable us to reach conclusions with the same degree of confidence as for adult exposure. Strong ethical feelings against experimentally exposing children to sexually explicit materials considerably reduced the possibility of gathering the necessary data and information regarding young persons.

In view of the limited amount of information concerning the effects of sexually explicit materials on children, other considerations have assumed primary importance in the Commission's deliberations. The Commission has been influenced, to a considerable degree, by its finding that a large majority of Americans believe that children should not be exposed to certain sexual materials. In addition, the Commission takes the view that parents should be free to make their own conclusions regarding the suitability of explicit sexual materials for their children and that it is appropriate for legislation to aid parents in controlling the access of their children to such materials during their formative years. The Commission recognizes that legislation cannot possibly isolate children from such materials entirely; it also recognizes that exposure of children to sexual materials may not only do no harm but may, in certain instances, actually facilitate much needed communication between parent and child over sexual matters. The Commission is aware, as well, of the considerable danger of creating an unnatural attraction or an enhanced interest in certain materials by making them "forbidden fruit" for young persons. The Commission believes, however, that these considerations can and should be weighed by individual parents in determining their attitudes toward the exposure of their children to sexual materials, and that legislation should aid, rather than undermine, such parental choice.

Taking account of the above considerations, the model juvenile legislation recommended by the Commission applies only to distributions to children made without parental consent. The recommended legislation applies only to commercial distributions and exhibitions; in the very few instances where noncommercial conduct in this area creates a problem, it can be dealt with under existing legal principles for the protection of young persons, such as prohibitions upon contributing to the delinquency of minors. The model legislation also prohibits displaying certain sexual materials for sale in a manner which permits children to view materials which cannot be sold to them. Two members of the Commission, who recommend legislation prohibiting sales to juveniles, do not join in recommending this regulation upon display; one member of the Commission recommends only this display provision, and does not recommend a special statute prohibiting sales to young persons.

The Commission, pursuant to Congressional direction, has given close attention to the definitions of prohibited material included in its recommended model legislation for young persons. A paramount consideration in the Commission's deliberations has been that definitions of prohibited materials be as specific and explicit as possible. Such specificity aids law enforcement and facilitates and encourages voluntary adherence to law on the part of retail dealers and exhibitors, while causing as little interference as possible with the proper distribution of materials to children and adults. The Commission's recommended legislation seeks to eliminate subjective definitional criteria insofar as that is possible and goes further in that regard than existing state legislation.

The Commission believes that only pictorial material should fall within prohibitions upon sale or commercial display to young persons. An attempt to define prohibited textual materials for young persons with the same degree of specificity as pictorial materials would, the Commission believes, not be advisable. Many worthwhile textual works, containing considerable value for young persons, treat sex in an explicit manner and are presently available to young persons. There

appears to be no satisfactory way to distinguish, through a workable legal definition, between these works and those which may be deemed inappropriate by some persons for commercial distribution to young persons. As a result, the inclusion of textual material within juvenile legislative prohibitions would pose considerable risks for dealers and distributors in determining what books might legally be sold or displayed to young persons and would thus inhibit the entire distribution of verbal materials by those dealers who do not wish to expose themselves to such risks. The speculative risk of harm to juveniles from some textual material does not justify these dangers. The Commission believes, in addition, that parental concern over the material commercially available to children most often applies to pictorial matter.

The definition recommended by the Commission for inclusion in juvenile legislation covers a range of explicit pictorial and three-dimensional depictions of sexual activity. It does not, however, apply to depictions of nudity alone, unless genital areas are exposed and emphasized. The definition is applicable only if the explicit pictorial material constitutes a dominant part of a work. An exception is provided for works of artistic or anthropological significance.

Seven Commissioners would include verbal materials within the definition of materials prohibited for sale to young persons. They would, however, also include a broad exception for such textual materials when they bear literary, historical, scientific, educational, or other similar social value for young persons.

Because of changing standards as to what material, if any, is inappropriate for sale or display to children, the Commission's model statute contains a provision requiring legislative reconsideration of the need for, and scope of, such legislation at six-year intervals.

The model statute also exempts broadcast or telecast activity from its scope. Industry self-regulation in the past has resulted in little need for governmental intervention. If a need for governmental regulation should arise, the Commission believes that such regulations would be most appropriately prepared in this specialized area through the regulating power of the Federal Communications Commission, rather than through diverse state laws.

The Commission has not fixed upon a precise age limit for inclusion in its recommended juvenile legislation, believing that such a determination is most appropriately made by the States and localities which enact such provisions in light of local standards. All States now fix the age in juvenile obscenity statutes at under 17 or under 18 years. The recommended model statute also excludes married persons, whatever their age, from the category of juveniles protected by the legislation.

The Commission considered the possibility of recommending the enactment of uniform federal legislation requiring a notice or label to be affixed to materials by their publishers, importers or manufacturers, when such materials fall within a definitional provision identical to that included within the recommended state or local model juvenile statute. Under such legislation, the required notice might be used by retail dealers and exhibitors, in jurisdictions which adopt the recommended juvenile legislation, as a guide to what material could not be sold or displayed to young persons. The Commission concluded, however, that such a federal notice or labelling provision would be unwise. So long as definitional provisions are drafted to be as specific as possible, and especially if they include only pictorial material, the Commission believes that the establishment of a federal regulatory notice system is probably unnecessary; specific definitions of pictorial material, such as the Commission recommends, should themselves enable retail dealers and exhibitors to make accurate judgments regarding the status of particular magazines and films. The Commission is also extremely reluctant to recommend imposing any federal system for labelling reading or viewing matter on the basis of its quality or content. The precedent of such required labelling would pose a se-

rious potential threat to First Amendment liberties in other areas of communication. Labels indicating sexual content might also be used artificially to enhance the appeal of certain materials. Two Commissioners favor federally imposed labelling in order to advise dealers as clearly and accurately as possible about what material is forbidden for sale to young persons, placing the responsibility for judging whether material falls within the statute on the publisher or producer who is completely aware of its contents and who is in a position to examine each item individually.

Finally, the Commission considered, but does not affirmatively recommend, the enactment by the federal government of juvenile legislation which would prohibit the sale of certain explicit materials to juveniles through the mails. Such federal legislation would, the Commission believes, be virtually unenforceable since the constitutional requirement of proving the defendant's guilty knowledge means that a prosecution could be successful only if proof were available that the vendor knew that the purchaser was a minor. Except in circumstances which have not been found to be prevalent, as where a sale might be solicited through a mailing list composed of young persons, mail order purchases are made without any knowledge by the vendor of the purchaser's age. Certificates of age by the purchaser would be futile as an enforcement device and to require notarized affidavits to make a purchase through the mails would unduly interfere with purchase by adults. The Commission has found, moreover, that at present juveniles rarely purchase sexually explicit materials through the mail, making federal legislative machinery in this area apparently unnecessary.

C. Public Display and Unsolicited
   Mailing

The Commission recommends enactment of state and local legislation prohibiting public displays of sexually explicit pictorial materials, and approves in principle of the federal legislation, enacted as part of the

1970 Postal Reorganization Act, regarding the mailing of unsolicited advertisements of a sexually explicit nature. The Commission's recommendations in this area are based upon its finding, through its research, that certain explicit sexual materials are capable of causing considerable offense to numerous Americans when thrust upon them without their consent. The Commission believes that these unwanted intrusions upon individual sensibilities warrant legislative regulation and it further believes that such intrusions can be regulated effectively without any significant interference with consensual communication of sexual material among adults.

PUBLIC DISPLAY

The Commission's recommendations in the public display area have been formulated into a model state public display statute which is reproduced in the Drafts of Proposed Statutes in Section III of this Part of the Commission Report. Three Commissioners dissent from this recommendation.

The model statute recommended by the Commission (which would also be suitable for enactment in appropriate instances by local government units and by the federal government for areas where it has general legislative jurisdiction) prohibits the display of certain potentially offensive sexually explicit pictorial materials in places easily visible from public thoroughfares or the property of others. Verbal materials are not included within the recommended prohibition. There appears to be no satisfactory way to define "offensive" words in legislation in order to make the parameters of prohibition upon their display both clear and sufficiently limited so as not to endanger the communication of messages of serious social concern. In addition, the fact that there are few, if any, "dirty" words which do not already appear fairly often in conversation among many Americans and in some very widely distributed books and films indicates that such words are no longer capable of causing the very high degree of offense to a large number of persons which would justify legislative interference. Five Commissioners

disagree and would include verbal materials in the display prohibition because they believe certain words cause sufficient offense to warrant their inclusion in display prohibitions.

Telecasts are exempted from the coverage of the statute for the same reasons set forth above in connection with discussion of the Commission's recommendation of juvenile legislation.

The recommended model legislation defines in specific terms the explicit sexual pictorial materials which the Commission believes are capable of causing offense to a substantial number of persons. The definition covers a range of explicit pictorial and three-dimensional depictions of sexual activity. It does not apply to depictions of nudity alone, unless genital areas are exposed and emphasized. An exception is provided for works of artistic or anthropological significance. The Commission emphasizes that this legislation does not prohibit the sale or advertisement of any materials, but does prohibit the public display of potentially offensive pictorial matter. While such displays have not been found by the Commission to be a serious problem at the present time, increasing commercial distribution of explicit materials to adults may cause considerable offense to others in the future unless specific regulations governing public displays are adopted.

UNSOLICITED MAILING

The Commission, with three dissents, also approves of federal legislation to prevent unsolicited advertisements containing potentially offensive sexual material from being communicated through the mails to persons who do not wish to receive such advertisements. The Federal Anti-Pandering Act, which went into effect in 1968, imposes some regulation in this area, but it permits a mail recipient to protect himself against such mail only after he has received at least one such advertisement and it protects him only against mail emanating from that particular source. The Commission believes it more appropriate to permit mail recipients to protect themselves against all such unwanted mail advertisements from any source. Federal legislation in this area was enacted just prior to the date of this report as part of the 1970 Postal Reorganization Act. Public Law 91-375, 91st Cong., 2nd Sess., 39 U.S.C. Sections 3010-3011; 18 U.S.C. Sections 1735-1737.

The Commission considered two possible methods by which persons might be broadly insulated from unsolicited sexual advertisements which they do not wish to receive. One approach, contained in the 1970 Postal Reorganization Act, authorizes the Post Office to compile and maintain current lists of persons who have stated that they do not wish to receive certain defined materials, makes these lists available at cost to mailers of unsolicited advertisements, and prohibits sending the defined material to persons whose names appear on the Post Office lists. A second approach, described in detail in the Commission's Progress Report of July, 1969, would require all mailers of unsolicited advertisements falling within the statutory definition to place a label or code on the envelope. Mail patrons would then be authorized to direct local postal authorities not to deliver coded mail to their homes or offices.

In principle, the Commission favors the first of these approaches employed by Congress in the 1970 Postal Reorganization Act. The Commission takes this view because it believes that the primary burden of regulating the flow of potentially offensive unsolicited mail should appropriately fall upon the mailers of such materials and because of its reluctance to initiate required federal labelling of reading or viewing matter because of its sexual content. The Commission believes, however, that under current mail-order practices it may prove financially unfeasible for many smaller mailers to conform their mailing lists to those compiled by the Post Office. Use of computers to organize and search mailing lists will apparently be required by the new law; few, if any, small mailers utilize computers in this way today. If the current lists maintained by the Post Office came to contain a very large number of names—perhaps one million or more—even a computer search of these names, to discover any that were also present on a mailing list sought to be used by a mailer, might be prohibitively expensive. If such were the case, the Commission would believe the second possible approach to regulation to be more consistent with constitutional rights. This approach, however, might place serious burdens upon Post Office personnel. The Commission was not able to evaluate the practical significance of these burdens.

In considering the definition appropriate to legislation regulating unsolicited sexual advertisements, the Commission examined a large range of unsolicited material which has given rise to complaints to the Post Office Department in recent years. A definition was then formulated which quite specifically describes material which has been deemed offensive by substantial numbers of postal patrons. This definition is set forth in the footnote. The Commission prefers this definitional provision to the less precise definitional provision in the 1970 Postal Reorganization Act.

D. Declaratory Judgment Legislation

The Commission recommends the enactment, in all jurisdictions which enact or retain provisions prohibiting the dissemination of sexual materials to adults or young persons, of legislation authorizing prosecutors to obtain declaratory judgments as to whether particular materials fall within existing legal prohibitions and appropriate injunctive relief. A model statute embodying this recommendation is presented in the Drafts of Proposed Statutes in Section III of this Part of the Commission Report. All but two of the Commissioners concur in the substance of this recommendation. The Commission recognizes that the particular details governing the institution and appeal of declaratory judgment actions will necessarily vary from State to State depending upon local jurisdictional and procedural provisions. The Commission is about evenly divided with regard to whether local prosecutors should have authority to institute such actions directly, or whether the approval of an official with state-wide jurisdiction, such as the State Attorney General, should be required before an action for declaratory judgment is instituted.

A declaratory judgment procedure such as the Commission recommends would permit prosecutors to proceed civilly, rather than through the criminal process, against suspected violations of obscenity prohibition. If such civil procedures are utilized, penalties would be imposed for violation of the law only with respect to conduct occurring after a civil declaration is obtained. The Commission believes this course of action to be appropriate whenever there is any existing doubt regarding the legal status of materials; where other alternatives are available, the criminal process should not ordinarily be invoked against persons who might have reasonably believed, in good faith, that the books or films they distributed were entitled to constitutional protection, for the threat of criminal sanctions might otherwise deter the free distribution of constitutionally protected material. The Commission's recommended legislation would not only make a declaratory judgment procedure available, but would require prosecutors to utilize this process instead of immediate criminal prosecution in all cases except those where the materials in issue are unquestionably within the applicable statutory definitional provisions.

WITHDRAWAL OF APPELLATE JURISDICTION

The Commission recommends against the adoption of any legislation which would limit or abolish the jurisdiction of the Supreme Court of the United States or of other federal judges and courts in obscenity cases. Two Commissioners favor such legislation; one deems it inappropriate for the Commission to take a position on this issue.

Proposals to limit federal judicial jurisdiction over obscenity cases arise from disagreement over resolution by federal judges of the question of obscenity in litigation. The

Commission believes that these disagreements flow in largest measure from the vague and subjective character of the legal tests for obscenity utilized in the past; under existing legal definitions, courts are required to engage in subjective decision making and their results may well be contrary to the subjective analyses of many citizens. Adoption of specific and explicit definitional provisions in prohibitory and regulatory legislation, as the Commission recommends, should eliminate most or all serious disagreements over the application of these definitions and thus eliminate the major source of concern which has motivated proposals to limit federal judicial jurisdiction.

More fundamentally, the Commission believes that it would be exceedingly unwise to adopt the suggested proposal from the point of view of protection of constitutional rights. The Commission believes that disagreements with court results in particular obscenity cases, even if these disagreements are soundly based in some instances, are not sufficiently important to justify tampering with existing judicial institutions, which are often required to protect constitutional rights. Experience shows that while courts may sometimes reverse convictions on a questionable basis, juries and lower courts also on occasion find guilt in cases involving books and films which are entitled to constitutional protection, and state appeals courts often uphold such findings. These violations of First Amendment rights would go uncorrected if such decisions could not be reversed at a higher court level.

The Commission also recommends against the creation of a precedent in the obscenity area for the elimination by Congress of federal judicial jurisdiction in other areas whenever a vocal majority or minority of citizens disagrees strongly with the results of the exercise of that jurisdiction. Freedom in many vital areas frequently depends upon the ability of the judiciary to follow the Constitution rather than strong popular sentiment. The problem of obscenity, in the absence of any indication that sexual materials cause societal harm, is not an appropriate social phenomenon upon which to base a precedent for removing federal judicial jurisdiction to protect fundamental rights guaranteed by the Bill of Rights.

The commission's report was condemned and rejected by President Nixon and found little support in Congress, which had instructed the commission to bring in recommendations for "advisable, appropriate, effective, and constitutional means to deal effectively with traffic in obscenity and pornography."

A statement prepared for the commission while it was still in session presented the point of view of the American Library Association.

Judith F. Krug

STATEMENT OF THE AMERICAN LIBRARY ASSOCIATION

Library service in the United States is built on the concept of intellectual freedom. The term is defined in the *Library Bill of Rights*, the Association's basic policy statement concerning the concept. This document states that it is the responsibility of library service to provide books and other materials representing all points of view concerning the problems and issues of our times. It further states that no library materials should be proscribed or removed from libraries because of partisan or doctrinal disapproval. In pursuance of the fulfillment of this philosophy, the document contends that the rights of an individual to the use of a library should not be denied or abridged because of his age, race, religion, national origins or social or political views.

Originally adopted in 1939, the *Library Bill of Rights* was extensively revised in 1948. Further revisions were approved by the Council, the governing body of the Asso-

Reprinted from *Newsletter on Intellectual Freedom* 19 (4): 59–62 (July 1970).

ciation, in 1961 and 1967. Each revision, while broadening the Association's interpretation of intellectual freedom, also reflected changes that had occurred in regard to the concept of the library. This institution is no longer the stronghold of the printed word, but now accommodates all materials that can help provide information and enlightenment. This means that not only books, magazines, and newspapers, but also tapes, pictures, films, recordings—indeed, all expressions regardless of form—have a valid, if not required, place in a library.

The same concern that led the Association to adopt the *Library Bill of Rights* led it, in 1940, to establish the Intellectual Freedom Committee. The Committee was charged with the responsibility "to recommend such steps as may be necessary to safeguard the rights of library users in accordance with the Bill of Rights of the United States and the *Library Bill of Rights* as adopted by the ALA Council." Among its many activities, the Intellectual Freedom Committee has developed supportive and interpretive documents relating to the Association's position on intellectual freedom. Prime among these is the *Freedom to Read Statement*, formulated in conjunction with the American Book Publishers Council. The *Statement* stresses the necessity for free access to all information and ideas, regardless of the form the expression takes.

ASSOCIATION POSITION REGARDING OBSCENITY AND PORNOGRPAHY

With particular reference to obscenity, the *Freedom to Read Statement* asserts the Association's belief that Americans can be trusted to recognize and reject obscenity. It further states that individuals in a free society do not need the help of organized censors to assist them in this task. One reason for this belief is that the Association cannot determine the individual or group in whom this power over all other individuals and groups can be vested.

As public servants, librarians are required to act in accordance with existing laws relating to obscenity. Such legislation, however, is directly in conflict with the goal of librarians to make available the widest diversity of views and expressions, including those which are unorthodox or unpopular with the majority. In this context, the *Freedom to Read Statement* implies that such legislation—insofar as it coerces the tastes of others, confines adults to materials deemed suitable for adolescents, or inhibits the efforts of creative people to achieve artistic expression—must be challenged by librarians through every legal means available.

In addition, it seems to the Association that laws dealing with so-called obscenity are contrary to the maintenance of a free society and, therefore, are contrary to the public interest. The Bill of Rights, particularly the First Amendment, has given to each citizen the right to think what he pleases on any subject and to express his point of view in whatever manner he deems appropriate, be it orally or graphically, publicly or privately. To utilize this "right" effectively, a man must have something to think about, something on which to base his own opinions and decisions. Generally, this is in terms of other men's thinking. Access to the ideas of other men, therefore, is a necessity.

This, then, is the philosophy guiding librarians in acquiring and making available information representing all points of view on all questions and issues. Freedom keeps open the path of novel and creative solutions and enables change to come by choice.

ALLEGED GRAVITY OF "SITUATION" CONSTITUTES SPECIOUS ARGUMENT

At the present time, the American Library Association does not view the alleged situation regarding obscenity and pornography as a grave one. It views it, rather, as one that is impossible to assess in objective terms. This view is predicated on three significant aspects of the situation.

First, to state that the situation is grave is to imply that an acceptable definition of obscenity and pronography is available. As the Commission, itself, stated in its *Progress*

Report of July, 1969, there is no generally accepted definition of either "obscenity" or "pornography." The Association believes, furthermore, that it is a practical impossibility to define these words. Each human being is an individual with his own wants, needs, and desires. These, in turn, have been determined by the various environments in which the individual has lived; by the values, principles, and goals instilled in him by his parents and others who were or are in positions to influence him; and finally, by the experiences that one has throughout his life.

To allow for human diversity, the Association, in the *Freedom to Read Statement*, assigned the responsibility of defining "obscene and pornographic materials" to the individual citizen, in accordance with his own judgment and tastes.

The Association reaffirms its belief in this *Statement* and suggests that if individuals can ever be considered identical to one another, perhaps it will be possible to determine a definition of "obscenity and pornography." Of course, if such a definition were to be imposed, that day when all individuals were alike would be much closer.

Secondly, to state that the situation is grave is to imply that there is a demonstrable relationship between allegedly obscene and pornographic materials and overt, antisocial acts. The Commission, however, has recognized in its *Progress Report* (July, 1969) that there is little, if any, reliable, empirical evidence to substantiate a belief in such a causal relationship. The Association contends that what an individual hears, sees, or reads serves to reinforce previously learned behavior. Seeing and hearing, and particularly reading, are acts of the mind. It does not follow that thought processes are invariably translated into overt action.

Furthermore, the Association adheres to the belief that it is the right and the responsibility of parents—not public officials—to guide their children, and only their children, to informational sources for any subject in which the children express a need or an interest. In line with this belief, the *Library Bill of Rights* specifically states that an individual shall not be restricted in his use of the library, whether materials or services, because of his age.

Thirdly, to state that the situation is grave is to imply that it somehow requires enforced legislative control. It implies further that there is a necessity for such suppression and that this necessity outweighs the benefit of continuing our national tradition of freedom of speech and freedom of the press. Implicit, furthermore, in this advocation of legal suppression is the belief that restrictions upon publication and dissemination of one kind of materials will not adversely affect the publication and dissemination of other kinds of materials. This, however, does not seem to be the case.

CENSORSHIP ATTEMPTS

A review of the history of censorship attempts and a survey of contemporary conditions indicate that suppression of one kind of materials *does* lead to the extension of the license to other kinds of materials. In effect, the acceptance of one kind of suppression fosters a climate for the acceptance and perpetuation of suppression in other areas.

To illustrate, the Association believes that our culture would have suffered if would-be censors in the past had succeeded in their attempts to eradicate or bowdlerize certain creative works which were repugnant to various segments of the society. Among these works are the comedies of Aristophanes, the plays of Shakespeare, the "Song of Songs" from the *Bible*, Chaucer's *Canterbury Tales*, Walt Whitman's *Leaves of Grass*, James Joyce's *Ulysses*, D. H. Lawrence's *Lady Chatterly's Lover*, J. D. Salinger's *Catcher in the Rye*, and more recently, Claude Brown's *Manchild in the Promised Land*. The writers of these works each expressed, with superlative skill, some aspects of our common humanity. Still, each of these works has been banned or mutilated at one time or another. Who is to say what pieces of outrageous literature will someday gain respectability and acceptance?

That suppression of allegedly obscene materials leads easily to suppression of other

kinds of ideas is illustrated by the popular view and treatment of the underground, "dissident," or "alternative" press. Many historians and educators have pointed out the social and historical value of the underground press as a recorder of a movement which escapes objective coverage in the conventional news media. It is estimated that, in an average underground newspaper, 30% may be morally objectionable to some. The remaining 70% deals with social and political issues. Yet, courts have found particular issues of the underground newspapers to be obscene. This leads the Association to believe that some individuals are utilizing the moral question which—granted—is able to arouse great emotions, as a screen from behind which social and political ideas, somewhat contrary to those currently in vogue, can be attacked.

SELF-CENSORSHIP

As a result of their controversial nature, underground newspapers have been banned from the library collections of some institutions. Printers, on occasion, have refused to handle the papers. Certain principals and college administrators have attempted to suppress the production of "underground" publications at their institutions. Police have arrested street vendors, sometimes confiscating their publications through extra-legal methods. College editors have resigned to protest administrational censorship. Well-known underground publications have ceased activity completely because of an inability to withstand legal and extra-legal intimidation and censorship. The long-range result may be the eventual curtailment or extinction of a valuable historical record and a truly "alternative" voice.

What effect has "creeping censorship" had on the library? During the summer of 1969, the mayor of Memphis, Tennessee, received national news coverage when he proclaimed *Portnoy's Complaint* to be a "dirty book." He did not believe that it should be in the library, and certainly was against using taxpayers' money for "this kind" of material. It did not matter that the book was No. 1 on the Bestseller List, nor did it matter that the Memphis Public Library had almost 100 requests for the book.

Just three months ago, the mayor of Madison, Wisconsin, launched a crusade against the public library to remove all allegedly obscene materials.

A librarian in a Chicago Public High School placed Claude Brown's *Manchild in the Promised Land* in her office and required any student wishing to read it to bring a note from his teacher. She believed the book to be detrimental to any individual in the school who would read it, since it clearly reflected the individual's current situation.

A librarian from a small Chicago suburb refused to have *"Portnoy's Complaint* or any book like that" in her collection. Books "like that" included medical texts and particularly, art books.

A librarian in the Missouri State Library was fired for writing a letter to the local newspaper protesting the suppression of an underground newspaper published and distributed by University of Missouri students.

In St. Louis County (Missouri), some book dealers and librarians are finding it politically expedient to remove "controversial books from their shelves at the suggestion of police."

In New Orleans, a new ordinance, which combines the provisions of *Ginzberg v. New York*, the "variable obscenity law," with certain provisions of the 1968 Postal Law, allows any individual to walk into a book store or a public library and demand that any piece of material be removed from the shelf. We understand that if the bookstore owner or the librarian should not carry out this directive, he is liable to criminal prosecution.

In the Los Angeles Public Library, the professional staff asked the city attorney for an opinion in regard to California's "variable obscenity law," which went into effect November 10, 1969. The Assistant City Attorney, in response, stated that if a librarian is in doubt, he must—for his own good—censor the materials.

CLOSING

All of these examples, occurring in rapid succession, lead the Association to believe that we are functioning in a "repressive" climate and that any further controls may prove completely stifling. Of particular concern to the Association is that individual or group of individuals who would be chosen to determine what the general public is permitted to read, see, and hear. Some of the finest minds in our society have wrestled with the problem of exactly what is to be deemed "obscene and pornographic." We are no closer to a generally acceptable definition today than we were when the Bill of Rights was adopted. Of course, this is undoubtedly one of the reasons for the First Amendment to the United States Constitution.

Since a definition of the term or terms seems impossible and since, as noted previously, there is little, if any, reliable empirical evidence to substantiate the belief of a causal relationship between certain materials and behavior, it would seem to the Association that any further concrete action *must* be based on a strictly personal point of view. We strongly advocate personal points of view—and, in fact, the entire profession is geared to helping people arrive at personal points of view. But we do not believe that we have yet reached the juncture where citizens in this country must be dictated to by individuals and/or groups of individuals in accordance with the beliefs that these persons hold.

The Association recognizes that many people find much of what is uttered or printed in the various communications media to be offensive or objectionable. That there is fear and concern is easily documented by reference to reactions in the press and other media. The success of nationally organized community efforts to rally large numbers of supporters of "decent literature" to their cause is further evidence of the widespread concern. The Commission, itself, is a visible manifestation of the fact that the tastes of many people have been offended. The fear is obvious. The justification for this fear is not obvious.

The American Library Association contends that the dangers of legislative control of any materials are far easier to prove and much more significant in their implications. We maintain that it is the responsibility of those who believe in repression to show, beyond a reasonable doubt, that their way is superior to free choice.

In accordance with these beliefs and its basic philosophy regarding intellectual freedom, the American Library Association urges the Commission on Obscenity and Pornography not to recommend any further controls on the population's access to materials of any kind.

A professor of law at Stanford University, Herbert L. Packer, writing in *Commentary* several months after publication of the commission's report, analyzed legal and other aspects of the matter.

Herbert L. Packer

THE PORNOGRAPHY CAPER

Presidential commissions, as Elizabeth B. Drew once put it in the *Atlantic*, are often "self-inflicted hotfoots." The tangled story of the Commission on Obscenity and Pornography serves as a paradigmatic example of the truth of this observation. After documenting that assertion, I shall try to come to grips with the substance of the Report and the data on which it rests. Finally, I want to explore a possible constitutional doctrine that could render moot legislative arguments about what kind of conduct to forbid.

My bias in this essay is that of a lawyer who believes pornography to be a nuisance rather than a menace. Effective legal controls for this nuisance I consider to be a worse nuisance than what they attempt to suppress, which a democratic, open society can ill afford.

Reprinted from *Commentary*, February 1971, by permission; all rights reserved. Footnotes have been omitted.

I

The Commission owes its existence to the initiative of Senator John McClellan (D., Ark.). He, joined by Senator Karl Mundt (D., S. Dak.) and others, introduced a resolution that found the traffic in obscenity and pornography to be "a matter of national concern." What John McClellan thinks is a matter of "national concern" clearly becomes just that. He steered his resolution through the Senate Judiciary Committee, through the House, and it became law as P.L. 90–100. This law directed the President to set up an advisory commission whose purpose was: "After a thorough study which shall include a study of the causal relationship of such materials to anti-social behavior, to recommend advisable, appropriate, effective, and constitutional means to deal effectively with such traffic in obscenity and pornography." The Commission was further directed:

1. with the aid of leading constititional law authorities, to analyze the laws pertaining to the control of obscenity and pornography; and to evaluate and recommend definitions of obscenity and pornography;

2. to ascertain the methods employed in the distribution of obscene and pornographic materials and to explore the nature and volume of traffic in such materials;

3. to study the effect of obscenity and pornography upon the public, and particularly minors, and its relationship to crime and other antisocial behavior; and

4. to recommend such legislative, administrative, or other advisable and appropriate action as the Commission deems necessary to regulate effectively the flow of such traffic, without in any way interfering with constitutional rights.

P.L. 90–100 became law in October 1967 and President Johnson appointed the Commission's members in January 1968. In July 1968 Congress funded the Commission and extended its tenure to provide two years for its studies.

I have no idea what backstairs maneuvers accompanied the selection of the members. The Commission at its first meeting in July 1968 elected William B. Lockhart as its chairman. Although it is most unusual for a Commission to elect its own chairman, Lockhart was a natural choice. He is dean of the University of Minnesota Law School, and a leading academic authority on obscenity laws. (It may or may not be a coincidence that the White House, on announcing the composition of the Committee in January, stated that Mr. Lockhart would be the chairman.)

The Commission set about its work quietly, eschewing public hearings and proceeding with the help of a carefully selected staff, to commission, carry out, and review the studies that Congress had expected. The first public hint of trouble came in the late fall of 1969 when two members of the Commission—Commissioners Hill and Link—conducted "runaway" public hearings in eight cities, contrary to the Commission's announced policy. These hearings, whose general tenor was strongly in favor of tightening legal controls, were extensively reported in the press.

As the time for publication of the Report drew close, a number of odd incidents occurred. The first was the publication of what purported to be the Commission's Report which sounded very much like a Birchite document. Many people thought this document a parody. Among lawyers, it was thought to be a hoax perpetrated by law students. Although its provenance is unknown to me, one ought to compare this spurious document with the dissenting views expressed in the genuine report by Commissioners Hill and Link, who had conducted the "runaway" hearings. There is a marked similarity.

Then the text of the Report was prematurely "leaked" to the House Subcommittee on Postal Operations. The leak was made by an unidentified Commission member to Representative Robert Nix (D., Pa.), who on August 11 and 12 conducted hearings before the Subcommittee on the leaked report. The hearings were pretty much given over on the first day to a refutation of the as-yet-unpublished findings of the Commission. The star witness, Professor Victor B.

Cline, of the University of Utah—who reappears as the dissenters' principal expert on the behavioral sciences—said:

This review is limited by the fact that I don't have most of the original studies which are cited and used as evidence in coming to many of [the Commission's] conclusions. . . . Despite this, enough details are given and I am acquainted with some of the studies sufficiently to comment on them.

Professor Cline's sense of grievance is a bit hard to understand, since he was trying to refute an unpublished purloined Report.

President Nixon's sole appointee to the Commission—Charles H. Keating, Jr., a Cincinnati lawyer and founder of Citizens for Decent Literature—had been warning the President for about eleven months "not only that the pornographers will have taken a giant step toward winning the war but that your administration will receive the blame." The warning was quickly heeded. Ronald Ziegler, the President's flack, declared to reporters without being asked: The President has views at variance with those of the Report. Thus, before the Report was even submitted to him, the President dissociated himself from it.

The Associated Press also obtained a "leaked" version of the final report, which then became extensively publicized. As the controversy grew hotter, Commissioner Keating, Nixon's man on the Commission, filed suit to enjoin publication of the Report on the ground that the Commission had denied him sufficient time to prepare a dissent. He obtained a preliminary injunction. But, finally, Keating and Lockhart agreed that Keating could have until September 29 to file his dissent. Since the Report was scheduled to go to the President and Congress on September 30, had it been delayed beyond that date, it might never have been released. Mr. Keating met his deadline and the Government Printing Office printed just enough copies of the whole Report and the various dissents for the officials immediately involved. I have never seen the GPO Report, nor do I have any expectation of seeing it. Private enterprise rapidly filled the breach.

Just seventeen days after the Commission's Report was made public, the Senate rejected it. On October 17, the Senate passed a condemnatory resolution introduced by Senator McClellan by a vote of 60 to 5; and President Nixon, in a statement released at the height of the 1970 campaign, denounced the document. There is no good reason to suppose that the President even glanced at the Report. Thus hundreds of thousands of dollars and thousands of man-hours later, the Commission's work had become a source of personal pain for many of its members and the occasion for national cries of shame.

II

What did the Report say to outrage the Senate and the President at a time when the political wars were at their hottest? Just this: (1) "Extensive empirical investigation . . . provides no evidence that exposure to or use of explicit sexual materials play a significant role in the causation of social or individual harms such as crime, delinquency, sexual or non-sexual deviancy or severe emotional disturbances." (2) "Public opinion in America does not support the imposition of legal prohibitions upon the right of adults to read or see explicit sexual materials." (3) "Therefore, the Commission recommends the repeal of [federal, state, and local] legislation" which prevents adults from getting access to what has previously been labeled "obscene."

The Commission also recommended that the states should enact legislation preventing the exposure of young persons to pictorial erotica—by which textual material is to be excluded—and prohibiting public displays of pictorial erotica. The Commission recommended that Congress legislate against unsolicited mail advertising. In fact, Congress has already done just that. But, of course, these modest legislative proposals have not saved the Commission from attack on the repeal proposals just cited.

The Commission's Report, whose legislative recommendations take up only twenty-eight pages, is based on four reports prepared by panels of the Commission. These include: (a) a report on traffic and distribution of sexually-oriented materials in the United States; (b) a report on the impact of erotica; (c) a report on positive approaches: the development of healthy attitudes toward sexuality; and (d) a report on legal considerations relating to erotica. I shall comment only on the second panel report. All four consume over 400 pages in the Bantam edition. Another 175 pages are taken up primarily by the dissents of three members of the Commission.

Perhaps the best way of discussing the Commission's findings is to put them in the context of the bitter and venomously personal attacks of the dissenters. They were Morton A. Hill, S.J., president of Morality in Media, New York; the Rev. Winfrey C. Link, administrator of the McKendree Manor Methodist Retirement Home, Hermitage, Tennessee; and the aforementioned Charles H. Keating, Jr., appointed by the President. These several gentlemen—the dissent of Messrs. Hill and Link is concurred in by Mr. Keating, who then voices a disagreement of his own—open their dissent with the statement that: "The Commission's majority report is a Magna Carta for the pornographer." They quickly dispose of the Commission's empirical evidence with the observation that inquiry into effects is beside the point because the central question is whether and to what extent society may establish and maintain moral standards. I should have thought that the question was not that, but rather *how* society may do that. Precisely, the question is not (as the dissenters seem to think) a moral question but a functional question asking what laws enforced by what sanctions and involving what costs will enable society (meaning *our* society) to establish and maintain morals. Unfortunately, neither the Report nor the dissent illuminates that question. As I shall presently show, the Report fails just because it does not illuminate that question. However, since it is hard for the dissenters to keep reiterating their central proposition for 175 pages, they first attack the chairman,

Dean Lockhart, and the Commission's General Counsel, Professor Paul Bender, both of whom they identify as members of the American Civil Liberties Union, whose subversive nature apparently (to the dissenters) requires no comment. They attack the Report of the Legal Panel which had summarized the state of the law with respect to obscenity. One would have to be a legal illiterate to accept the dissenters' attempt to frame a counter-Legal Report, consisting as it does of a mishmash of headnotes, quotations from legal encyclopedias, and excerpts from Supreme Court opinions (interspersed with ominous comments such as "Justice Fortas is no longer on the Court").

The Legal Panel Report is uninspired. It is a straight-faced but hopeless attempt to give some intellectual coherence to the Supreme Court's lucubrations on the subject. As I shall suggest below, this effort was misguided. Yet the Panel Report is as game an effort to summarize the bewildering state of constitutional law on obscenity as I have seen in print.

The most controversial portion of the Commission's Report is unquestionably the Panel Report on the "Impact of Erotica." Of the six members of this Panel only one (Dean Lockhart, sitting *ex officio*) was not a behavioral scientist. Although the dissenters had opened their attack by claiming that empirical studies were irrelevant, they here enlisted the support of Professor Cline to mount what is their most effective engagement against the Report. To me, it is odd that this Panel Report neglected to deal with the "aesthetic objections" to erotica (the Report's own term). Students of literature like George Steiner have dwelt on the pernicious effects of erotica not only on readers but also on the creators of what passes for "literature." The gist of the "aesthetic" objection is that pornography corrupts taste, primarily the taste of those who seek to supply what the consumer wants. While I believe that writers like Steiner are profoundly right, it is hard to see what remedy laws can provide for the evils they discern. The Panel Report would have been strengthened had this been pointed out.

The "behavioral scientists" reached two conclusions from their empirical evidence: (1) Public opinion does not support legal efforts to prevent adult Americans from reading or seeing whatever they like; (2) it cannot be demonstrated that pornography causes crime or delinquency. Their conclusions are based on a review of the empirical literature, on analysis of crime statistics, and on research commissioned by the Panel.

The Panel commissioned a very elaborate attitudinal study. This particular document comes down to the facts that (a) only 2 per cent of their interviewees spontaneously mentioned the prevalence of erotica as an important national problem, and that (b) most Americans think that erotica has undesirable effects on people's behavior, but that (c) when this attitude is more carefully examined it appears that with respect to the respondent's own experience, socially desirable or neutral effects of exposure to erotica predominate. To give two examples of the variation between people's perception of the effects of erotica and their own experience the study reports as follows:

Effect	% who say it has effect	Effect on respondent	Effect on someone known to respondent	Effect on no one known
Provide info re sex	61%	24%	15%	22%
Lead to a breakdown of morals	56%	1%	13%	38%

They further report that 51 percent of their sample would "be inclined to favor the availability" of erotica if it were "clearly demonstrated" that such material had no harmful effects while 79 per cent would oppose availability if it were shown that harmful effects occurred. Fifty-one per cent is a pretty slim majority, particulary considering the quoted qualifications.

Finally, the authors of the Panel Report state that people who identify harmful results are more likely to have seen less erotic material recently, to be less educated, older, and more conservative than . . . whom? Than their "counterparts," we are told, whoever that may be. The complete study, including the ten volumes of *Technical Reports*, may supplement these data. Yet it is, at best, very poor strategy for a report to be as dogmatic and unsupported as this one appears to be. The attitudinal study that the Panel commissioned is a pretty damp firecracker.

Obviously, the empirical studies of effects are far more important than the public-opinion studies, since the latter fall if the former are weak. Citing Masters's and Johnson's *Human Sexual Response* as demonstrating that it is possible to measure human sexual arousal, the Panel Report moves on to an examination of behavioral responses to erotica. The Panel Report relies exclusively (with one exception) on second-hand studies. By second-hand I mean both people's asserted recollections of their previous exposure to erotica and their own statements about their arousal when experimentally exposed to erotica. These second-hand studies, which owe nothing to Masters and Johnson, are simply hearsay which the Panel analyzes for many tedious pages. The Commission appears to have sponsored only one study that may justly be called "experimental." That study sparked a controversy that made headlines.

The experiment, conducted at the University of North Carolina so outraged Congressman Nix that he devoted the second day of his hearings to raking the principal investigator—James L. Howard, assistant professor of psychiatry at the University of North Carolina Medical School—over the coals (at one point he gratuitously observed that had Dr. Howard not volunteered to testify, he would have been subpoenaed.) Twenty-three male students had volunteered to participate in this experiment. While I cannot share Congressman Nix's sense of outrage, I tend to view the experiment as trivial and of doubtful relevance. By hooking up the subjects' penises to measuring devices (it is not reported whose ingenuity was responsible for devising the hardware, or perhaps, software) the principal investigator succeeded in demonstrating that over a three-week period the subjects became satiated with erotica. After a short layoff, their interest returned. Consequently, the study concluded triumphantly that the hypothesized satiation effect was confirmed, as anyone could have told the experimenters. This seems to me a good example of how rigor and triviality are related in empirical behavioral work. One may well conclude that, if the controversy had been foreseen, the Panel would probably not have commissioned this experiment. One may also wonder whether not commissioning it would have been a defeat for "behavioral science."

The culminating section of the Panel Report on Effects is entitled "Erotica and Antisocial and Criminal Behavior." This is where the behavioral approach stands or falls: as the Report plainly concedes, people's attitudes toward erotica depend on whether a harmful effect can be shown to exist. The Report claims that the existing research "provides no substantial basis for the belief that erotic materials constitute a primary or significant cause of the development of character defects or that they operate as a significant determinative factor in causing crime or delinquency."

As I have previously said, the Panel Report is based on a review of the empirical literature, on an analysis of crime statistics, and on studies that the Panel had commissioned. That remains true of this culminating section of the Panel Report. It is terribly difficult to prove a negative. Burying the reader in a cloud of studies and in statistical analysis only compounds the difficulty. The statistical analysis is flawed because the Panel forgot to define "delinquency." If delinquency includes conduct that would not be criminal in an adult—like being a wayward child, or a child in need of correction—which the concept usually does include, then I fail to see how any amount of statistical analysis can possibly demonstrate anything whatever about the connection between X (which is undefined) and Y (exposure to erotica).

The studies, of which one comparing a group of convicted rapists with a matched group of nonsex offenders is typical, tend to demonstrate almost nothing except that such studies prove nothing. We are told that this study shows:

All subjects were asked at what age they first saw each of fifteen erotic depictions, and mean ages of first exposure were computed for each of the two groups and each of the types of erotica. The data in Table 36 show that the mean age of first exposure of the rapists was one-half a year or more later than that of the matched nonsex offenders in reference to eight of the fifteen items and one-half a year or more earlier in reference to two. The biggest difference between the groups for which nonsex offenders had a mean age of first exposure of 14.95, and rapists a mean age of first exposure of 18.19. Rapists were also found to have a generally later mean age of first exposure to erotica than a nonmatched sample of college students and a lower age than a nonmatched sample of members of men's clubs.

Who needs it?

After 140 pages of examining "the data," the Panel Report on the Impact of Erotica finally sputters out with the observation that:

. . . [I]t is obviously not possible, and never would be possible, to state that never on any occasion, under any conditions, did any erotic material ever contribute in any way to the likelihood of any individual committing a sex crime. Indeed, no such statement could be made about any kind of nonerotic material.

Thanks a lot, fellows.

While the behavioral studies, which are the heart of the Effects Panel's case, prove almost nothing, the dissenters devote many pages to picking holes in the data which likewise prove almost nothing. They muster much material to support their assertion that erotica does cause criminal behavior. This material is worthless: it consists almost exclusively of anecdotal reports by police. While the proponents of the majority position have not succeeded in proving their case, the dissenters may have inadvertently strengthened the case by resorting to half-truths, distortions, and, to paraphrase the old story about statistics, "damned lies." The most clearly disgusting passage in the entire report comes when Mr. Keating in his separate dissent prints the names and addresses of the leading distributors of pornography. Mr. Keating is plainly guilty of aiding and abetting the distribution of pornography.

The predominantly behavioral tone of the Report strikes me as a disservice to the position that the majority espouses. Given the fact that the behavioral sciences have so little to say about the connection between erotica and people's behavior, a far better ploy, in my judgment, would have been to acknowledge this deficiency and simply to state the recommendations without attempting to justify them as resting on anything but the liberal, humane, and pluralistic values that presumably motivated the majority of the Commission. That course would have given the dissenters much less to snipe at and would have cost the Commission much less in money, time, and finally, credibility. By relying so heavily and so misguidedly on the behavioral sciences, the Commission's Report suffers terribly in readability. The effort may have been very costly in all the respects just stated.

III

The violence of the Presidential and Congressional reaction, provoked by the Report's behavioral tone, guarantees that it will be consigned to at least temporary oblivion. At this stage in the nation's history there is no chance whatever that the recommendations of the Commission will be enacted into law. The contrary may very well happen. I would bet that we are quite likely to see a spate of even tougher laws passed against pornography than we now have, fueled at least in part by the controversy over the Report.

That prospect does not dismay me, since there is no reason to suppose that we are willing to support a vigorous campaign of law-enforcement against pornography. Such a campaign would involve costs in money, manpower, and invasions of privacy that we as a society are unwilling to pay. Passing laws costs a great deal. Given the dimensions of our present crime problem, rhetoric (passing tough laws) is the administration's only weapon.

I think that our present use of the First Amendment as a constitutional means of limiting the effect of anti-pornography laws is misguided. The Supreme Court has got itself into a box; it must either function as a Supreme Board of Censors and read every allegedly dirty book and watch every allegedly dirty movie that is attacked before it or give up the unequal struggle. Potter Stewart's famous quip that he doesn't know the meaning of hard-core pornography but that he knows it when he sees it is a perfect illustration of the Court's dilemma. In the end, if we stick with the First Amendment I would guess that the pressure of their other business will compel the Supreme Court to get out of the obscenity business and leave it to the local boards of censorship. As for reinterpreting the First Amendment, that seems naive. First, the Supreme Court is so heavily mired in its old decisions. (In *Roth* v. *United States*, 354 U.S. 476 [1957], the Court held that "obscenity is not within the area of constitutionally protected speech or press." This decision and its numerous progeny placed the Court in the dilemma to which I have referred. While the Court can distinguish *Roth*, how can it overrule that decision and still rely on the First Amendment?) Second, the Black-Douglas absolutist position that freedom of speech means just that is indefensible: libel and incitement to commit a crime, to say nothing of conspiracy,

demonstrate that "speech is speech" can never mean that the First Amendment protects every form of speech.

In place of the First Amendment, I would suggest that the opponents of anti-pornography laws should rely instead on the doctrine of "substantive due process," which means simply that legislation which lacks a rational basis does not pass constitutional muster. "Substantive due process" is a doctrine that has been in bad odor for at least thirty-five years. It was used to strike down economic regulatory legislation. Holmes and Brandeis had labeled the doctrine as an effort to read the economic predilections of justices like the Four Horsemen (McReynolds, Van Devanter, Sutherland, and Butler) into the Constitution. And so it was. The effect of the great authority of Holmes and Brandeis, plus the effects of the changing views of constitutional law that their views induced the law schools to adopt, resulted in the present generation of judges and legal scholars becoming allergic to "substantive due process." The reluctance strikes me as being counter-productive for the liberal spirit in 1971. After all, it is the choice of minorities to be pluralistic rather than economic regulation which is at stake when the state uses the ultimate weapon of the criminal sanction to suppress such things as pornography. The "Brandeis brief" (which Brandeis developed before he took his seat on the Supreme Court) was originally a weapon against "substantive due process." The Brandeis brief was originally used to marshal economic facts to sustain economic regulatory legislation by demonstrating its rationality, thus undermining the old-fashioned substantive due process. The same technique, I believe, can be used to show that it is irrational to enforce morals legislation that attempts to suppress consensual transactions, like the sale of pornography. By mustering economic facts that demonstrate what a heavy price we pay in money and human resources, costs which could be allocated to more pressing social needs than the chimerical benefits of suppressing pornography, courts may eventually be brought to view morals legislation as irrational and, therefore, unconstitutional.

So far, the attack on morals legislation has had some limited successes without the benefit of a Brandeis brief. A variety of constitutional pegs exists: the Religion Clause of the First Amendment, the "cruel and unusual punishment" clause of the Eighth Amendment, the Ninth Amendment. But these *ad hoc* constitutional pegs are not good enough. The Supreme Court badly needs a unifying theory if the attack is to be truly successful. "Substantive due process" may well be that theory, if the Supreme Court can ever be led to overcome its "allergy" to it. Doctrinal purity—not producing *ad hoc*, result-oriented decisions—ought to be important to the Supreme Court. Doctrinal purity means essentially intellectual honesty. That seems to me to weigh the scales quite heavily in favor of "substantive due process."

However the Supreme Court may resolve the "substantive due process" problem, I suspect that it is to courts rather than to legislatures that we must look to begin the process of reforming our substantive criminal law to bring our commitments into balance with our capacities.

Stanley Kauffmann, writing in *The New Republic*, immediately after the commission's report appeared, offers some discerning comments.

Stanley Kauffmann

ON OBSCENITY

September 30, 1970, was a red-letter day in American social history. The majority report of the Federal Commission on Obscenity and Pornography, published that day, is a revolutionary document. I speak about it only on the basis of the extensive excerpts in *The New York Times*, but surely this is the central statement of the report:

The commission recommends that federal, state and local legislation prohibiting the sale, exhibition or distribution of sexual materials to consenting adults should be repealed.

That is not a new idea, but no one in his right mind would have predicted as recently as 1960 that a federal commission would make such a recommendation only ten years later.

A report, obviously, is an advice, not a law. (Far from a law, in this case; it was promptly denounced by Mr. Finch of the White House, the Postmaster General, leaders of both parties in the Senate, and the president of the National Conference of Catholic Bishops.) Obviously, too, the men and women of the commission are appointees, free of any need to please constituencies; and are specialists whose views are likely to be more sophisticated in this field than those of most elected legislators. (The chairman, William B. Lockhart, dean of the University of Minnesota Law School, has been called, by a pro-censorship lawyer, one of "the most careful American scholars in the obscenity field.") Nevertheless we have here the astonishing phenomenon of a commission appointed by a President of the United States voting twelve to five for a report whose gist, as little as ten years ago, could have been read only in the most liberal journals.

The dissenting minority reports are more predictable; the recurrent word there is "filth." Less predictable was the action of Charles H. Keating, Jr., President Nixon's one appointee to the commission (the others were appointed by President Johnson in 1968); Mr. Keating obtained a legal injunction, later lifted, to bar publication of the majority report. Even less predictable, in another vein, was the opinion filed by two sociologists on the commission, Professors Larsen and Wolfgang, recommending the abolition of *all* statutory restrictions in this field, for young persons as well as adults, on the ground that obscenity and pornography have long proved undefinable. The professors (who voted with the majority) would rather rely on "informal social controls," "improvements in sex education and better understanding of human sexual behavior" than on "ambiguous and arbitrarily administered laws."

The Lockhart report and the Larsen-Wolfgang supplement are strong stuff to come from a Washington podium. In a culture-tradition sense, they are anti-American. The Kerner report on civil disorders (1968) was an attempt to make American practice conform to expressed American principle. The recent Scranton report on campus unrest spoke to a nationally experienced horror. But the Lockhart report runs *counter* to a dominant strain in the American temperament. This country was founded by (literal) Puritans who came here for freedom of religion; but their religion was steeped in concepts of original sin, and their idea of freedom was a theocracy that brooked no opposition. (Remember Mary Dyer and Roger Williams.) The expansionist nineteenth century brought us evangelist fundamentalism, many of whose sermons, says Richard Hofstadter, "were composed for audiences terrified of their own sexuality." Immigration added large dollops of Irish Catholic and Italian Catholic and orthodox Jewish puritanism. (Small wonder that this is the country that invented burlesque.) So when this immense heterogeneous nation, a bit more two-faced than most nations in sexual morality, produces a quasi-official statement like the Lockhart report, it is a revolutionary act. Moral realities have at least dented desperately defended moral fictions. In the thick gloom that rolls in on us from all sides these days, this report is a flicker of light.

It comes at a time when libertarian views will be severely tested. I commented recently on some Danish porno films (July 11, 1970) and noted my shock at their availability in New York. (One of those films has since been seized, the distributor and three theater managers have been arrested. The case is pending.) All four films had a veneer of education and uplift. Last week I walked in off Seventh Avenue and saw a bill of films—American-made, I think—with no such veneer, which were even more explicit

in sexual detail and language; and in the intermission a stripteaser came out on the tiny stage, quickly disrobed, and did a blatantly suggestive naked dance. The porno book shops and peep shows of Times Square, and of many other cities, are by now commonplace. In some cities, it costs a dollar just to get into a shop and examine the books with the entrance fee deducted from the cost of purchases. Two days after the Lockhart report was published, *The New York Times* ran a story about live sex shows in Manhattan where you can go for five dollars and watch a couple copulate.

I'm glad that all these matters are in the news just as the report is published because it puts the central issue right on the line. The commission does not contend that pornography is desirable but that the law cannot deal with it satisfactorily. Some lawyers argue that the law cannot even deal with it legally in the light of the First Amendment. The commission relies on education and enlightenment to mitigate pornography. (I hope that educational methods are spelled out in the full report. It's easy to *say* education and enlightenment.) For myself, I wish any sane educational process the best of luck, but I would rely at least as much on some social turbulences and dissatisfactions that are already very evident. Before talking about them, I ought to say that I don't believe pornography will ever disappear completely or that no healthy man or woman should ever get any kind of kick from it.

A lot of radical nonsense has been published about the esthetics of pornography, particularly its literature. Discussion of style in porno books is affectation, I think. *Fanny Hill* is elegantly written, but the point of *Fanny Hill* is to make the reader masturbate if no partner is available, which is not the point of the last section of *Ulysses*. The elegance only makes the masturbation more snobbish. I'm not against masturbation; I'm not against publication of *Fanny Hill*; I'm making what I think is an important distinction, and differences of quality within the province of pornography do not affect that distinction. Still it's a pretty dull dog who has never got any kind of fun from a pornographic book, and *Fanny Hill* would still be amusing in Utopia.

But performed pornography, almost always lumped with fiction, is different. Pornographic action that is filmed or staged or posed for still photographs—pornography *done* by people, not invented by writers or draftsmen—runs right into the matters of social change mentioned above. Performed pornography is an exercise in the humiliation of women. (It can be argued that porno fiction humiliates them, too, in value, but at least they don't physically participate.) The men who are involved in porno performance, though not precisely ennobled, are not being so humiliated. They are treated as masters, usually, and the performances are done for their satisfaction. Those male performers are vicars for the almost entirely male audience. Performed porno is a species of male revenge on our social systems of courtship and monogamy, courtship in which a man has to woo a woman to get her to bed or wed him or both, monogamy in which he has nominally to forego the favors of other women all his life in order to get hers. Performed porno makes every man a sultan.

But it is time out from civilization. Vindictiveness is mean, essentially, and money-coercion is brutal—whether the coercion is on Madison Avenue, in Detroit, or in a sex-flick studio; and it's especially brutal when it produces, not just profit but pleasure.

The growing realizations about the historic mistreatment of women, some new aspects of community, the thorough reexamination of social values generally, some understanding of the interplay of money and sex, the growing hungers for moral honesty—all these forces which are now evident in our society, though hardly yet triumphant, are the real enemies of pornography. (The Lockhart report is one manifestation of the existence of those forces.) Censorship laws, besides being questionable in legality and enforcement, only make porno more desirable, particularly among those who don't like being bossed in their private lives,

and those laws do not alter basic causes. Once those obscurantist and provocative laws are out of the way, there will be more chance for the social changes already in motion to prosper.

A last point. The usual complaint against porno is that it distorts sex by depersonalizing it. I think this is inaccurate. Porno (performed) tells the truth about sex: that it *is* impersonal, that the complete identification of love with sex is a romantic fabrication. Many people, especially women, could not begin the sex act with partners to whom they feel no specific attraction, but the specifics fade as the act progresses, and it ends in the greatest commonalty of the human race. Porno is ruthless. It proves that love, or anything remotely like it, is not essential to sex, that love is an invention and has a limited congruence with sex.

But my own view is that love is a good invention, the best idea yet devised for getting through life with minimal loneliness. I suppose that plenty of loved and loving people go to porno shows occasionally, but still it can be said that porno is implicitly an attack on love by an audience of the insufficiently loved, who get their revenge by insisting that a screw is only a screw. And I don't like to see the love-invention attacked.

There is, as yet, no sure cure for lovelessness. Who can imagine a society entirely composed of happy mates? But maybe we can imagine a society whose concept of love discards the implications of restriction, a society where sexual health is as much a part of decent social obligation as physical health and cleanliness now are, where the "liberation" of women also means the liberation of men from the calculated and managerial subservience of women. Such a society would not need porno to "prove" that love is just sex after all. Such a society would have a better chance to arrive if our lungs were free of the sulphurous stench of porno laws.

Such a society is not flatly impossible, as things look. Officialdom has now made its first small recognition of that fact. The Lockhart report is just possibly epoch-making, and it's an epoch that needs to be made.

An exploration in depth of the obscenity issue in relation to the Constitution was made by Harriet F. Pilpel in the R. R. Bowker Memorial Lecture presented in 1973.

Harriet F. Pilpel

OBSCENITY AND THE CONSTITUTION

The First Amendment to the United States Constitution prohibits the local, state, and national governments from passing any laws abridging freedom of speech and the press— so as my two-year old grandson is fond of saying, "How come?" How come we are having problems on the obscenity front? The answer is deceptively simple: For many decades the United States Supreme Court had held that what is obscene is not entitled to the protection of the First Amendment, and the recent majority decisions of the Court on June 21 of 1973 reiterate this view.

What has been the result of those decisions and what can or should we do about them?

The portents are mixed: On Sunday, November 11, 1973, the *New York Times* carried the enlightening news that three dozen copies of Kurt Vonnegut's now-famous and well-regarded book *Slaughterhouse-Five* "were burned in Drake, North Dakota, this week on orders of the local school board." The rest of the story makes clear that the whole incident was set into motion by the complaint of a sophomore high school student that the book was "profane."

Some ministers at the meeting described the burned copies of the novel about the Allied bombing of Dresden, Germany, in World War II as "tools of the devil."

Student lockers were inspected on the chance that some might have defied the board's order to turn in all copies of the book. Other books scheduled to be destroyed because of allegedly profane

First of the new series of the R. R. Bowker Memorial Lectures. Reprinted with permission. Copyright © 1973 by the R. R. Bowker Co.

language are *Deliverance* by James Dickey, and an anthology of short stories by Ernest Hemingway, William Faulkner and John Steinbeck.

The school board also decided not to retain the English teacher who assigned the books to the students in Drake, a central North Dakota town of 700 persons.

Noting that none of the school board members had read the books they ordered destroyed, Mr. Severy (the teacher) said, "I say no one can make a judgment about a book without reading the entire book. Anything less is academically dishonest, anti-intellectual and irrational."

. . . the five-member board voted unanimously to burn the books and not to rehire Mr. Severy for next year.

The whole story evokes the indignant shade of Franklin Delano Roosevelt who signed the first proclamation reducing postage rates on books in the 1930s, indicating with a flourish, that this is the difference between Nazism and Democracy—they are burning books while we here are going to make them as available as possible.

Drake, North Dakota, please note. In Chile, of course, the art of book destruction is more advanced. There, according to the same *New York Times*, the citizens throw books out of the window to avoid being caught by the Junta with subversive material on their premises.

Earlier this fall, on September 4, 1973, the *New York Times* carried a story, "Crime In, Sex Out in New Film Season." Apropos of this: a great many years ago a sociologist wrote a book pointing out that increasingly we glorify violence, killing, and destruction, and condemn sex in all its manifestations. He forecast that the result would be a violent society—so far, he has turned out to be right and no doubt the recent United States Supreme Court obscenity rulings will make possible a further substantial lurch in that direction. The events in Drake, North Dakota, are a good example.

In the Sunday *New York Times*, preceding the one that carried the story about Drake, North Dakota, a headline read, "Film Pornography Flourishes Despite Court Ruling." According to the item, "It is still possible to see blue movies and purchase graphically explicit books in virtually all major cities." The paper then goes on to give details. It reminds me of the famous cartoon which showed a smiling and bowing Hitler who had just swallowed the Russian sickle. The caption read, "Wait until he tries to straighten up." I'm afraid this is the situation with the June 21 United States Supreme Court decisions on obscenity. We have not really felt the impact of these decisions because the state legislatures have not been in session, Congress had had more pressing matters to attend to, and state authorities may well feel constrained by the June 21 decisions to wait until the present generalized obscenity laws, many of which are probably unconstitutionally vague under those decisions, are replaced by the type of new statutes which the Court said were constitutionally permissible.

Of course, we can shrug and say, "this, too, will pass" as other repressive eras have slid into history. I am indebted to the Bowker Company's book called *Banned Books* for a list of some of the more distinguished precedents for the present "purity" decisions: There are the works of Homer which Plato thought should have been expurgated and of Confucius whose *Analects* were banned in 200 B.C. because the Emperor frowned on all literature except "practical" works on alchemy, husbandry, and medicine. Other authors whose books have been banned include: Francis Bacon, Baudelaire, Lewis Carroll, Darwin, Defoe, Freud (who was permitted to lecture in only one university in the United States), Goethe, Hemingway, Sinclair Lewis, Karl Marx, Montaigne, Ovid, Thomas Paine, Proust, Bertrand Russell, Sartre, Schiller, Shakespeare, Spinoza, Swift, Tolstoi, Trotsky, Mark Twain, Voltaire, H. G. Wells, and Zola, to mention only a few. (As with the case of President Nixon's "enemies list," an author not included on the list might well feel downgraded.)

The whole situation relating to obscenity today in this country brings to mind the airplane pilot who announced over the loudspeaker to the plane's passengers that he had "good news—and bad news. First the good news—we have a very strong tail wind and have an almost unprecedented ground speed of 700 miles an hour. Now for the bad news—our instrument panel isn't working so we don't know where we're going—but we're sure getting there fast."

That seems a pretty accurate description of today's obscenity volatility, and I thought what I would do today would be to sketch in briefly the good and the bad news on the obscenity front as of November 15, 1973. Before I do so, however, I would like to summarize briefly the situation as it existed before the United States Supreme Court redefined obscenity in its June 21 decisions and the essence of those decisions.

Obscenity did not really become an important issue in this country until the mid-nineteenth century. In the words of Supreme Court Justice William O. Douglas, "There was no recognized exception in the free press at the time the Bill of Rights was adopted which treated 'obscene' publications differently from other types of papers, magazines, and books." The anti-obscenity forces flowered in the Victorian era and were epitomized in the federal Comstock Act whose one hundredth birthday we celebrate—or more accurately should deplore—this year. It prohibited the importation, carriage by mail, or interstate commerce of "every obscene, lewd, lascivious, indecent, filthy or vile article, matter, thing, device, or substance." Many states adopted identical or similar "little Comstock Acts" of their own and a number of cities and towns followed suit. For example, "banned in Boston" became a commonplace and helped to promote nationwide sales of material so labeled. But despite the anti-obscenity laws, many courts handed down rational decisions. Under them the test of obscenity ceased to be the probable effect of material attacked as obscene on the most susceptible person in the community and instead became its probable effect on the average person. No longer could isolated passages be made the basis of an obscenity conviction—the test became the effect of the work as a whole, and defendants were held entitled to introduce expert testimony as to the merits and probable effects of a book. (My partner, Morris L. Ernst, was largely responsible for getting this established in the case of the *United States* v. *One Book Entitled "Ulysses" by James Joyce*, and in other cases.)

All this progress culminated in 1957 in the famous *Roth* v. *United States* decisions somewhat expanded subsequently by later decisions in the case of *A Book Named "John Cleland's Memoirs of a Woman of Pleasure"* v. *Attorney General of the Commonwealth of Massachusetts*, and in other cases.

In the *Roth* case, the United States Supreme Court pronounced unequivocally:

> . . . sex and obscenity are not synonymous. Obscene material is material which deals with sex in a manner appealing to prurient interest. The portrayal of sex, e.g., in art, literature and scientific works, is not itself sufficient reason to deny material the constitutional protection of freedom of speech and press. Sex, a great and mysterious motive force in human life, has indisputably been a subject of absorbing interest to mankind through the ages; it is one of the vital problems of human interest and public concern.

Basically, the Court had formulated a three-part test, and material had to fail all three parts of the test before it could be held obscene. The material in question had to: appeal to prurient interest, be patently offensive under current community standards, and be utterly without any redeeming social value.

It looked like "the end of obscenity," the title of my friend Charles Rembar's book on the subject. This possibility looked even more likely when in 1967 the Court decided the *Redrup* v. *New York* case and seemed to be saying that the test was no longer the character of the material itself but the manner in which it was promoted and to whom.

Thus, Ralph Ginzburg went to jail for, among other things, what the Court called "pandering." The Court really condemned him for distributing his publications "with the leer of the panderer," an offense incidentally with which he had not been charged. For example, it was said that efforts

had been made to mail his magazine *Eros* first from Blue Ball, Pennsylvania, then from Intercourse, Pennsylvania, and finally from Middlesex, Pennsylvania.

The Court also indicated its disapproval of the "thrusting" of obscenity on unwilling adults in public places, stating that such thrusting violated an aspect of the "right of privacy" in public of those who did not wish to see or hear it.

In addition the Court made clear that a different test would apply if the so-called obscene material were beamed directly to children—somewhat limiting its decision in the light of Justice Felix Frankfurter's warning in the earlier case of *Butler* v. *Michigan* that we must be careful not to tailor the reading, listening, or viewing of adults to what is fit for children, for to do so would be "to burn down the house to roast the pig."

It was not, of course, all good news after the *Roth* case and until the obscenity decisions this year. There was also some bad news. Two additional federal obscenity statutes were passed. One of these enables any person to prohibit a particular mailer from sending him *any* further mail because, in his opinion, mail previously received from that sender was obscene. The other requires any mailer of "sexually oriented material" to identify it as such, and not to send such mail to anyone who has indicated that such mail should not be sent to him by putting his name on a public list compiled for this purpose.

At the same time, there continued to be good developments. The Report of the Commission on Obscenity and Pornography concluded after extensive study that there was no causal connection between "obscenity" or "pornography" on the one hand and criminal behavior on the other—indeed that obscenity might well be a safety valve for those who might otherwise explode into unlawful conduct. President Nixon, of course, who is all in favor of sexual purity, rejected the report as he was later to reject two of the most important recommendations of the Report of the Commission on Population and the American Future. (He pretty much ignored the rest of that report.)

Then came the case of *Stanley* v. *Georgia* holding that a man had a constitutional right to enjoy obscenity—in this case a motion picture—in the privacy of his own home. Said the Court: "If the First Amendment means anything, it means that the State has no business telling a man, sitting alone in his own house, what books he may read or what films he may watch. Our whole constitutional heritage rebels at the thought of giving government the power to control men's minds."

The United States Supreme Court also held that a draft and war opponent had the constitutional right to wear in public a sweat shirt on the back of which was printed "Fuck the Draft" (which should be contrasted with a recent decision of the New Hampshire Supreme Court which held criminally liable the proprietor of a shop where a teen-age girl bought a button saying "Copulation—not Masturbation.")

The "Fuck the Draft" case involved facts which were summarized by the United States Supreme Court as follows—the Justice writing the opinion was John M. Harlan, not generally known as a liberal or free thinker.

On April 26, 1968, the defendant was observed in the Los Angeles County Courthouse in the corridor outside of division 20 of the municipal court wearing a jacket bearing the words "Fuck the Draft" which were plainly visible. There were women and children present in the corridor. The defendant was arrested. The defendant testified that he wore the jacket knowing that the words were on the jacket as a means of informing the public of the depth of his feelings against the Vietnam war and the draft.

The defendant did not engage in, nor threaten to engage in, nor did anyone as the result of his conduct in fact commit or threaten to commit any act of violence. The defendant did not make any loud or unusual noise, nor was there any evidence that he uttered any sound prior to his arrest.

. . . Against this background, the issue flushed by this case stands out in bold relief. It is whether California can excise, as "offensive conduct," one particular scurrilous epithet from the public discourse, either upon the theory of the court below that its use is inherently likely to cause violent

reaction or upon a more general assertion that the States, acting as guardians of public morality, may properly remove this offensive word from the public vocabulary.

The rationale of the California court (which upheld the defendant's conviction) is plainly untenable. At most it reflects an "undifferentiated fear or apprehension of disturbance [which] is not enough to overcome the right to freedom of expression."

. . . The constitutional right of free expression is powerful medicine in a society as diverse and populous as ours. It is designed and intended to remove governmental restraints from the arena of public discussion, putting the decision as to what views shall be voiced largely in the hands of each of us, in the hope that use of such freedom will ultimately produce a more capable citizenry and more perfect polity and in the belief that no other approach would comport with the premise of individual dignity and choice upon which our political system rests.

It should be noted, however, that during this interim period between the *Roth* case and the June 21 decisions, obscenity proceedings were brought against underground newspapers which were probably really under attack because of their dissident points of view. By and large, these efforts did not succeed. Indeed, the United States Supreme Court let pass language which it is likely none of them are apt to use.

It should never be forgotten that, in addition to the evil inherent in so-called obscenity censorship itself, the agenda of those who propound it almost always includes using obscenity charges as a means of suppressing views which are dissident, satirical, irreverent, or merely unpopular; in other words, that charges of obscenity are not infrequently the pretext for suppressing works because of the non-sex-related ideas which they contain. A recent example of this kind of effort can be seen in a United States Supreme Court *per curiam* opinion in 1972. The publisher of an underground newspaper called *Kaleidoscope* was convicted under a state obscenity statute and sentenced to two years in prison. His "crime" consisted of publishing two photographs of a nude couple embracing and the inclusion of a "sex poem." The Supreme Court decided that there was nothing obscene about the items in question and reversed the conviction of the underground publisher. The year before, in another case to reach the Court, police raids had been directed at the publisher of another underground newspaper, effectively putting it out of business. The foundation of the raids was a search warrant authorizing the seizure of "obscene articles and materials."

A most interesting example of an attempt to use the obscenity laws to suppress political comment can be seen in a case decided by the Supreme Court as late as March 19, 1973. It was brought by a student who had been expelled from a state university for distributing a newspaper containing "forms of indecent speech," particularly a cartoon depicting a rape of the Statue of Liberty by police, and a headline containing a well-known "twelve-letter word." A majority of the Court held that the cartoon and the headline could not be found obscene. (I am indebted to the American Civil Liberties Union, both the National and the ACLU of Southern California, for the discussion of these cases.)

Generally speaking, I have now summarized where we had arrived with respect to the laws on obscenity before the blow fell on June 21, 1973. But before I get to that, I'd like to say a few words on the *general* legal principles to be borne in mind when we come to our current good and bad news in the obscenity field. We should distinguish between local, state, and federal law; we should remember that the United States Supreme Court's reading of the Constitution takes precedence over all else. In the obscenity field above all, we should distinguish between civil and criminal law—between what lawyers call an *in personam* proceeding and a proceeding *in rem*. An *in personam* attack on obscenity grounds may result in a person being criminally punished; an *in rem* attack can result in a *work* but not a person being condemned. Many of us insist that there should be no obscenity prosecution, i.e., no criminal proceeding should be

legally permitted until a work has been declared obscene in a civil case. We should also bear in mind that the obscenity law embraces (that would seem to be the word) not only statutes but also court rulings and rulings of such administrative agencies as the Post Office (such as the ruling I once got permitting to remain in a novel such elegant expressions as "Go frig a rubber duck," and, "He left a train of busted cherries behind him"—the latter of which I thought at the time was simple allusion to fruit).

So now we come to the current bad news—the decisions of June 21. These decisions—all of them 5-to-4—made two changes in the basic test of obscenity formulated in the *Roth* case: Henceforth, the Court said, while the "appeal to prurient interest" and "patently offensive" tests are still in effect, they may be applied in the light of the *local* community where the questions are presented and not with reference to a national community as had been previously thought. The Court did not make at all clear what community it meant—the state, the city, the town, or the block. The Court referred to the differing standards between "Maine and Mississippi"—*states* on the one hand—and "New York City and Las Vegas, Nevada"—*cities* on the other—which is not helpful, although in general the opinions seem to look to the *state* being the relevant community. And the third of the *Roth* tests changed significantly. It is no longer true that a work can be suppressed only if it is "utterly without redeeming social value"; now a patently offensive work which appeals to prurient interest must have "serious literary, artistic, political, or scientific value" if it is to be saved from being banned as obscene.

Four judges disagreed entirely and agreed with each other that there should be no ban on obscenity addressed to adults in private. As they put it, "At least in the absence of distribution to juveniles or obtrusive exposure to unconsenting adults, the First and Fourteenth Amendments prohibit the state and federal governments from attempting wholly to suppress sexually oriented materials on the basis of their allegedly obscene contents."

The net result of the majority's holdings is an almost complete negation of the right established in the *Stanley* case to enjoy obscenity in private. As has been pointed out, the *Stanley* case now apparently means that you have the right to compose an obscenity in your attic, print or produce it in your basement, and look at it in your study or living room, but as soon as you try to take anything "obscene" into or out of your house you can be in serious trouble under the obscenity laws. Unfortunately, it is all too clear that this applies to books as well as other forms of expression. The Court essentially applied the same test to books as to anything else, but only after saying piously that "a book seems to have a different and preferred place in our hierarchy of values, and so it must be."

However, there is also some good news in these cases if you look at it from the vantage point of Morris Ernst's favorite distinction between the optimist and the pessimist—a glass of water half empty (the pessimist) or half full (the optimist).

Presumably we keep the gains we won before the *Roth* case—the test is the average adult, the work must be judged as a whole, and the defense in an obscenity case can introduce expert testimony on the worth of a work.

Moreover, all the cases were decided 5-to-4. Thus we're only one judge away from the four who would not hold anything obscene for consenting adults, and who would at the most permit to be banned as obscene only the thrusting of obscenity in public on unwilling adults and the distribution of obscene material to children. What the minority was really doing was to apply to obscenity the rule which is increasingly being applied to sex acts—the apparently emerging rule that no sex acts should be made criminal if engaged in by consenting adults in private. The majority in the June 21 obscenity cases rejected these limits, although it did seem particularly concerned at the prospect of the depiction of a nude couple copulating being shown to the public in Times Square (which is one of the few problems New York City has not yet had to face).

Also, it seems still to be true that a book must fail all three tests to be held obscene: It must appeal to prurient interest, it must be patently offensive under current community standards, and it must lack any serious literary, artistic, political, or scientific importance.

So far, the June 21 decisions have had very little effect. This is discussed in the *New York Times* November 4 story already referred to which is headlined "Film Pornography Flourishes Despite Court Ruling."

Moreover, the Court said that any prohibition of obscenity "must be carefully limited to areas of sexual conduct" and must be in very specific terms. In the words of the Court:

. . . we now confine the permissible scope of such regulation to works which depict or describe sexual conduct. That conduct must be specifically defined by the applicable state law, as written or authoritatively construed.

Then the Court added, to make its decision "clearer," as examples of the type of patent offensiveness which could constitutionally be held obscene, "descriptions of (a) ultimate sexual acts, normal or perverted, actual or simulated, or (b) masturbation, excretory functions and lewd exhibitions of the genitals."

Thus the Court also permits prohibition of specific descriptions of excretion. This is really a kind of schizophrenia—presumably specific sex acts are forbidden because they might be too titillating and lead to overt and "immoral" behavior; the only comparable fear I can imagine on which to base the forbidding of specific descriptions of excretion is that they might lead to too much, or maybe too little, excretory activity.

Perhaps the lack of clarity as to what community and national standards are applicable can be turned to advantage. Maybe it can be argued that when a book or a movie is selling well in an area, it is clearly not "patently offensive" under the standards of that community. If *Tropic of Cancer* or *Fanny Hill* or their present-day counterparts are on the best seller list of a place, surely that is proof positive that they are not patently offensive under the standards of that community. Moreover, the requirement that obscenity laws specifically describe what they proscribe may well render many of the present state obscenity laws unconstitutional, excepting the very specific statute now in effect in the State of Oregon. Here are some of the "specifics" set forth by that statute:

"Nudity" means uncovered, or less than covered, post-pubertal human genitals, pubic areas, the post-pubertal human female breast below a point immediately above the top of the areola, or the covered human male genitals in a discernibly turgid state. For purposes of this definition, a female breast is considered uncovered if the nipple only or the nipple and the areola only are covered.

"Obscene performance" means a play, motion picture, dance, show or other presentation, whether pictured, animated, or live, performed before an audience and which in whole or in part depicts or reveals nudity, sexual conduct, sexual excitement or sado-masochistic abuse, or which includes obscenities or explicit verbal descriptions or narrative accounts of sexual conduct.

"Obscenities" means those slang words currently generally rejected for regular use in mixed society, that are used to refer to genitals, female breasts, sexual conduct or excretory functions or products, either that have no other meaning or that in context are clearly used for their bodily, sexual or excretory meaning.

"Sado-masochistic abuse" means flagellation or torture by or upon a peson who is nude or clad in undergarments or in revealing or bizarre costume, or the condition of being fettered, bound or otherwise physically restrained on the part of one so clothed.

"Sexual conduct" means human masturbation, sexual intercourse, or any touching of the genitals, pubic areas or buttocks of the human male or female, or the breasts of the female, whether alone or between members of the same or opposite sex or between humans and animals in an act of apparent sexual stimulation or gratification.

"Sexual excitement" means the condition of human male or female genitals or the breasts of the female when in a state of sexual stimulation, or the sensual experiences of humans engaging in or witnessing sexual conduct or nudity.

It certainly seems to me that, by reason of the Court's requirement of sexual specificity, the basic federal obscenity law is also unconstitutional in its prohibition of every lewd, lascivious, obscene, filthy, disgusting article. Thus, at the moment—and perhaps accounting for the lack of the hundreds or thousands of new obscenity prosecutions following in the wake of the United States Supreme Court June 21 decisions which might have been expected—we may not have in effect many valid federal or state laws against obscenity. Of course, the other two federal statutes I have already mentioned— the laws governing sexually oriented mail and mail subjectively judged by the receiver to be obscene—may still be in effect, but standing by themselves they are a lesser threat than the major generally worded obscenity statute.

What do we do now, to cut down on the bad news and bring about the good?

ON THE LEGISLATIVE FRONT

1. Our first battle is to persuade the legislators not to pass any new general or "specific" prohibitions of obscenity, but to leave the subject alone since the Supreme Court decisions themselves show that the subject is really impossible to regulate. If an obscenity law must be passed, then try to get the legislation in the mold recommended by the dissenting judges, i.e., let it prohibit only the thrusting of obscenity in public and to children. Remember and stress at all times that the United States Supreme Court obscenity decisions leave it up to the legislatures. The Court doesn't say anyone *shall* or must pass *any* legislation, only that if they do, the legislation must conform with and cannot go further than its decisions allow.

2. Insist that, whatever the substantive law against obscenity is, there must always be an *in rem* proceeding against the work— a finding of obscenity in a civil suit before any criminal prosecution or conviction can

be based on the work. In no other way can the "chilling effect" of mammoth self-censorship be avoided. It should be some encouragement that on November 13, 1973 the United States Supreme Court, according to the *New York Times*, "declined to order a Federal District Court to set aside its order in which it said that the Ohio obscenity statute is unconstitutional to the extent that it permits authorities to forbid the showing of films deemed obscene, which have not been determined in a prior adversary hearing to be obscene." (No. 72-1613, *Huffman* v. *U.S.D.C. for Northern Dist. of Ohio.*)

3. Make the applicable standard a statewide standard, if you can't persuade a state to adopt a national standard. But bear in mind that there may be special situations where some areas in a state may do better if the standard is not statewide, for example, New York City, as opposed to the rest of New York state; San Francisco, as opposed to Orange County, California.

ON THE COURT SIDE

4. Continue stressing, as have Justices Black and Douglas for so many years, that (a) the basic constitutional freedoms of speech and the press mean what they say: they protect the recipients—the listeners and viewers—as well as the publishers and transmitters; (b) all obscenity laws are a form of thought control—a virulent restraint and a government effort to regulate not what we do, not even what we say, but what may come into our minds.

5. Stress also our newly won constitutional right of privacy—first declared in the Connecticut birth control case and more recently reaffirmed and extended in the abortion cases. We can hope that the next development will be a guaranty of the privacy of the mind against obscenity prohibitions because no matter how specifically defined the prohibited obscenity is, obscenity, as the dissenting judges pointed out, is really impossible to define.

6. Develop briefs, legal papers, and defense pleadings banks as part of a coordinated national effort and make their availability known. The federal government has given a grant of federal moneys to a religious institution (not Catholic) to do this kind of thing for obscenity prosecutors. I submit it can do no less for defendants in obscenity cases. It is, after all, the defendants who are trying to preserve rather than whittle down the constitutional rights of free speech and press. Why not a comparable grant to the Media Coalition, for example?

7. Attack as unconstitutional those parts of the obscenity laws which make distributors of obscene material, who are the conduits of the material, criminally liable if the material they merely distribute is held to be obscene. In other words, insist that the laws provide that conduits like libraries and bookstores can in no circumstances be held criminally liable until after it has been held in a civil proceeding that the material on the basis of which they are attacked is legally obscene. This should apply to librarians, booksellers, printers, and others who can be and sometimes are made the totally innocent victims of obscenity proceedings. (In practice, the book publishers and the producers of movies and television programs almost always do step up and defend the innocent distributors, but they cannot in the final analysis remove from their shoulders the burden of a criminal conviction.)

Here we really still have a chance to persuade not only the legislature but also the courts, including the United States Supreme Court. While it appears that a majority of the United States Supreme Court has sustained, in connection with juveniles, a rebuttable presumption that a bookseller knows the contents of the book he sells, this has not yet been held generally applicable or necessarily applicable to librarians. Here is what Justice Douglas in his dissent from one of the June 21 obscenity decisions had to say about the impact on librarians.

What we do today is rather ominous as respects librarians. The net now designed by the Court is so finely meshed that taken literally it could result in raids on libraries. Libraries, I had always assumed, were sacrosanct, representing every part of the spectrum. If what is offensive to the most influential person or group in a community can be purged from a library, the library system would be destroyed.

A few States exempt librarians from laws curbing distribution of "obscene" literature. California's law, however, provides: "Every person, who with knowledge that a person is a minor, or who fails to exercise reasonable care in ascertaining the true age of a minor, knowingly distributes to or sends or causes to be sent to, or exhibits to, or offers to distribute or exhibit any harmful matter to a minor, is guilty of a misdemeanor." (9 Ann. Calif. Code 313.1.)

8. If obscenity laws there must be, and if the reasoning of the dissenting judges in the June 21 decisions is not adopted, then urge that no law be passed which would limit the press or speech on any obscenity grounds unless the prosecutor proves beyond a reasonable doubt that the material challenged would give rise to a clear and present danger of illegal conduct on the part of those exposed to it.

The "clear and present danger" test appears to be still the only sound constitutional basis (and to have been formerly held to be such by the Supreme Court) for making criminal any speech and press except obscenity. It is Justice Douglas' position (and was Justice Black's) with regard to obscenity as well. Why shouldn't this same test apply to obscenity? There should be as free a marketplace for sexual ideas and descriptions as we have now with reference to other kinds of ideas and descriptions.

If Justice Black had been alive and on the bench on June 21 of this year, there might have been a majority on the other side in some of the cases decided June 21 based on a combination of this ground and the ground Mr. Justice Brennan expounded for himself and Justices Stewart and Marshall, namely, that obscenity laws are constitutional only to the extent that they prohibit public thrusting and dissemination to children.

Those of us who are pushing for freedom of the mind against the June 21 obscenity decisions do not have to look to a constitutional amendment to restore freedom of speech and the press in the fundamental area of sex (and excretion, I suppose) for the Constitution already states that neither the federal, nor state, nor local government may abridge freedom of the speech or the press. What we have to do is persuade our legislators that, as Justice Holmes said, the test and only test is the power of the thought to get itself accepted in the marketplace.

. . . When men have realized that time has upset many fighting faiths, they may come to believe even more than they believe the very foundations of their own conduct that the ultimate good desired is better reached by free trade in ideas—that the best test of truth is the power of thought to get itself accepted in the competition of the market, and that truth is the only ground upon which their wishes safely can be carried out. That, at any rate, is the theory of our Constitution. It is an experiment as all life is an experiment. . . . While that experiment is part of our system I think we should be eternally vigilant against attempts to check the expression of opinions that we loathe and believe to be fraught with death.

9. And we must keep litigating. When the Supreme Court majority sees that these June 21 decisions created more problems than they solved, perhaps the Court will again drift toward the position of the dissenting Justices. Moreover, experience suggests that *in fact* the United States Supreme Court majority view does not reflect the viewpoint of the country because, by and large, juries have been and continue to be unwilling to convict in recent obscenity cases.

It seems odd to me that the United States Supreme Court majority turned out to be so uptight on obscenity that they handed down what seems to me a series of un-lawyer-like decisions inconsistent with the Court's own recent thinking on the subject of freedom of choice as to human reproduction and freedom of the press. My guess is that this is so because for the most part the Court majority consists of middle-aged or elderly gentlemen of the upper middle class, basically afraid of two things:

(a) Themselves. In a sense they exemplify Walt Kelly's "We have met the enemy and it is us." Even at the risk of sounding Freudian, I would venture to surmise that many of the Justices are not completely comfortable about sex and therefore objectify their subjective concerns by saying in effect "this obscene material which we must look at in the course of our judging process can't and doesn't hurt us, but we're afraid it might hurt the rest of you."

(b) Bad taste. And, I suspect that is why so-called obscene material is offensive to the majority Justices. I honestly believe with Justice Douglas that the United States Supreme Court is worried about taste. As he put it, "The Court is at large because we deal with tastes and standards of literature. What shocks me may be sustenance for my neighbors. What causes one person to boil up in rage over one pamphlet or movie may reflect only his neurosis, not shared by others. We deal here with problems of censorship which, if adopted, should be done by constitutional amendment after full debate by the people."

The majority of the Court masks this conventional middle class distaste for the vulgar and profane with words like "protecting the public community," "the state's right to maintain a decent society," and "protecting the public environment" against such things "as a man and woman locked in a sexual embrace at high noon in Times Square," which the Chief Justice says would not be saved from being obscene "because they [the couple] simultaneously engage in a valid political dialogue." I'm all in favor of good taste, but I don't think it should be enshrined as a matter of constitutional law, and that, I think, is what the June 21 decisions have done.

In summary, all is not lost and needn't be. There are many specific things we can do, some of which I have mentioned, to blunt the edges of the June 21 obscenity decisions and bring them more rationally into the framework of our Constitution.

We have a very popular environmentalist slogan today, "Keep America Green." I have a further and equally or more important slogan to suggest, "Keep the minds of America free—defend the Constitution—get rid of anti-American obscenity laws." Remember, as Dean Roscoe Pound of the Harvard Law School pointed out, "The law of each age is ultimately what that age thinks should be the law." It would be a good thing if we were able to celebrate our two hundredth birthday as a nation, in 1976, free from the kind of censorship which is reflected in the June 21 United States Supreme Court decisions—decisions which stand as a threat to our "first" freedom—freedom of speech and the press—which, as Justice Benjamin Cardozo pointed out many years ago, are "the matrix—the indispensable condition" of our other freedoms.

The historic controversy over obscenity has taken on new dimensions with the advent of the "sexual revolution" of the 1970s and a greater tolerance of the courts toward expression in the realm of sex. In this more permissive climate, books, magazines, television, and especially the motion pictures have pressed to the outer limits in portraying explicit sex, including perversions, sexual abuse of children, and acts of sado-masochistic violence. Such excesses have led to widespread demands for controls over hard-core pornography. Demands have come not only from traditional moral arbiters but also from a number of intellectuals concerned with the dehumanizing and brutalizing effect of pornography on American society. In the following article lawyer Richard H. Kuh, an advocate of legislation that he believes would protect the moral fiber of society without threatening intellectual freedom, calls for a "thinking man's censorship." Written two years before the issuance of the report of the Presidential Commission on Obscenity and Pornography, the article favors two of the anti-obscenity restrictions recommended by the commission: laws to protect children and laws against invasion of privacy. Kuh adds a third restriction: unambiguous laws prohibiting display or sale of live or photographed sex in action, coupled with laws against the exploitation of sex through pandering.

Richard H. Kuh

OBSCENITY, CENSORSHIP, AND THE NONDOCTRINAIRE LIBERAL

Just three years ago, in New York City, the late Lenny Bruce was arrested and charged with putting on a series of indecent shows. His had been an undoubted satiric skill. One of his warmest partisans, however—one who had not in his enthusiasm, abandoned his critical faculties—had noted that Bruce's satiric talents had degenerated. "His use of obscenity," said Professor Albert Goldman of Columbia University's English Department, "has begun to resemble the twitching of a damaged muscle."

Yet, significantly, the day before Bruce's New York trial was to start, one read in the papers of a manifesto, signed by more than one hundred American leading intellectuals. The signatories included Lillian Hellman, Norman Mailer, Robert Lowell, Lionel Trilling—persons of undisputed credentials (whether or not with first-hand familiarity with Bruce's performances)—and Rudy Vallee and Elizabeth Taylor. Their manifesto declared that Bruce's arrest was: ". . . a violation of civil liberties. . . . It is up to the audience to determine what is offensive to them; it is not a function of the police department of New York or any other city to decide what adult private citizens may or may not hear."

Similarly, at the time the conviction of Ralph Ginzburg (publisher of *Eros*) was on review before the United States Supreme Court, another group—then well in excess of one hundred—submitted a brief indicating the impropriety of that conviction. Both the

Ginzburg friend-of-the-court brief and the Bruce manifesto underscored the premise that it was inconsistent with "liberalism," inconsistent with "intellectualism," to permit any censorship whatsoever.

Is censorship—any anti-obscenity legislation—inconsistent with the liberal mind? If not, what legislation may be appropriate? With apologies to the Viceroy people, is there such a thing as "the thinking man's censorship"?

To consider the first question, whether all censorship is inherently inconsistent with the liberal mind, one must start with some measure of agreement as to a meaning of the word *liberal*. And here I think it vital that we distinguish between the doctrinaire "liberal"—in my mind, no liberal at all—and the thinking man who holds certain rights holy, but who is willing to inspect fully other factors that may call for some impingement upon even these holy rights.

To the doctrinaire, the imprimatur of the truly "liberal" judge, the "liberal" advocate, the "liberal" intellectual, is his uncompromising adherence to the broadest possible interpretation of the Bill of Rights. To him, the individual is *always* to be preferred when his interests, and those of society, appear to collide. This all-out "liberalism"—specious, I believe—reached its apogee a few years ago when the Americans for Democratic Action issued a sort of Nielsen rating on the performance of United States Supreme Court Justices, and noted that the then Mr. Justice Arthur Goldberg had barely outpointed Mr. Justice William O. Douglas. The Goldberg opinions, and the Justice's adherence to the opinions of others, had more closely reflected the ADA views for the year than had the reported views of Justice Douglas. To me, this "liberal" rating of Supreme Court Justices according to the measure of their agreement with one's own ideas, was a dramatic abnegation of true liberalism. If we are to probe the question as to whether a true liberal can agree to some state-imposed limitations on obscenity, this doctrinaire approach must be rejected.

To me, a balance, a sense of weighing all relevant factors and not stubbornly deciding in advance that a single aspect must outbalance all else, is far closer to the heart of true liberalism. Applying this less fundamentalist liberal approach to the area of censorship, I find solid authorities for the proposition that a good liberal does not have to be blind to all else when freedom of speech and press are involved. My authorities include the voices of two undisputed intellectual leaders who, when considering the impact on the young of written materials that presently surround us, have advocated some degree of censorship.

Walter Lippmann commented in 1954 on the vogue of sadism in media of mass entertainment:

Censorship is no doubt a clumsy and usually a stupid and self-defeating remedy for such evils, but a continual exposure of a generation to the commercial exploitation of the enjoyment of violence and cruelty is one way to corrode the foundations of a civilized society. For my own part, believing as I do in freedom of speech and thought, I see no objection in principle to censorship of the mass entertainment of the young. Until some more refined way is worked out of controlling this evil thing, the risks to our liberties are, I believe, decidedly less than the risks of unmanageable violence.

And one whose credentials as a liberal and as an independent may even surpass those of Walter Lippmann, Norman Thomas, testifying before a Senate Committee, said:

I do not think the First Amendment gives any guarantee to men to seduce the innocent and to exploit the kind of unformed mind and unformed emotions of children and adolescents. I think there is a great deal of dangerous nonsense in this appeal to the First Amendment and to the freedom of the press when one is dealing with this kind of thing. . . . I think it is nonsense to say that we are so bound by a very extreme interpretation of the freedom of the press that we cannot act.

The "thinking man's censorship" then would seem to embrace pornography and the young. Are there other areas as well?

I believe that there are three areas in which the liberal can not only countenance censorship, but in which he may call for it: 1) this area of the sale to children of matter deemed offensive in light of their tender years; 2) the area of public display—billboards and shop windows—of materials likely to be deemed offensive to passersby, using public streets; and 3) a very narrow area having to do with adult viewing of the most extreme hard-core pornography, coupled with restrictions on the tasteless public huckstering of borderline items—a "pandering" standard.

First, as to pornography and children. Liberals in our community have always been deeply concerned with the welfare of our young. We see this in the emphasis liberals have long placed upon integration in the education of the young; we see it in the area of liberal lobbying for increased budgets for education; and we see it in the liberal's interest in such projects as Operation Headstart. The attitude of the liberal in terms of raising the young has been the antithesis of laissez-faire. It has been one of advocating maximum government intervention: government protection for, and aid to, the young.

More than two thousand years ago, a courageous intellectual—one who was to forfeit his life in the cause of independence of thought and expression—deeply interested in the education of the young, advocated censorship of the fiction to which they might be exposed. Plato's *Republic* tells us of Socrates urging: "The first thing will be to establish a censorship of the writers of fiction, and let the censors receive any tale of fiction which is good and reject the bad; and we will desire mothers and nurses to tell their children the authorized ones only."

Today's liberal, profoundly interested in the sound development of the young, may—proudly—share similar views. Living in our psychiatrically oriented culture, the liberal sees man as a person of multiple capacities, multiple dimensions. Life involves many things: work, love, home, travel, hi-fi, art, the theater and cinema, physical fitness, self-expression. Yet pornography is one-dimensional. In the hands of the young whose attitudes toward life are being molded, pornography presents shadows, not people. Women become playtoys, sexual objects, dimensions; they are not sensitive, feeling, thinking humans. Hugh Hefner of *Playboy* preaches to males that "Sex is fun," and Helen Gurley Brown of *Cosmopolitan* responds for females that "Fun is sex." There is more to sex, and more to fun, than this however; and over-exposure to this narrowly hedonistic approach cannot foster the development of healthy children. Margaret Mead has noted:

. . . every society has the task of bringing up children who will focus their capacities for sexual feeling on particular persons, with or without overt bodily expression, and who will not only refrain from large amounts of undirected, objectless sexual behavior, but will be able to produce the proper intensity of feeling, expressed or unexpressed, for the proper object.

And a committee of psychiatrists of the New York Academy of Medicine, reporting in 1963 on the impact of pornography on the young, commented: "Such reading encourages a morbid preoccupation with sex and interferes with the development of a healthy attitude and a respect for the opposite sex."

The liberal, with this knowledge of the way today's pornography tends to draw the individual away from the full life, the way it derogates from a healthy attitude towards the opposite sex, should not shy at favoring censorship that would bar merchants from selling pornography to the young. Proper legislation would not, inexorably, keep all possibly obscene materials out of the hands of minors. But, by forbidding *sales* to the young of such items, it would—to a large extent—let parents (and schools and libraries), those charged with raising youth, make the decisions as to what materials children might see.

The liberal in our society, ordinarily, is a strong believer in parental responsibility. As a parent he endeavors to surround his youngsters with love and security, with appreciation of aesthetic values; he tries to screen out crass, perverted, violent items, at least until his children have reached sufficient maturity to enable them to wrestle intelligently with these items, to recognize their abnormality, and to appreciate that they are not acceptable parts of everyday life. Such a liberal should find his ideals served by legislation that would backstop individual parents in their efforts to keep merchants from selling pornography to their children.

The *second* area in which censorship of pornography may be agreeable to the liberal mind is that involving public displays. Every city has its honky-tonk newsstands, festooned with crass magazine covers—girlie magazines as well as those catering to the homosexual trade. New York City's Times Square, several years ago (in connection with a movie premiere), was decked with a forty-foot poster of a nude Jane Fonda.

THE RIGHT TO BE ALONE

The liberal bridles at the concept of captive audiences. In 1952, Mr. Justice William O. Douglas, dissenting in *Public Utilities Commission of the District of Columbia v. Pollak*, 343 U.S. 451, in expressing his objections to licensed radio transmission, including commercial messages, in street cars, urged that people had the right to be left alone. That right, I believe, is not strained unduly by the suggestion that it includes the right to walk through New York City's Times Square without seeing a forty-foot nude Jane Fonda, "sexploitation" movie marquees with blown-up stills of nudism or of sadistic encounters in a Paris bordello, or burlesque billboards featuring the exaggerated physiques of the current strippers. All these portrayals may have some appeal, it is conceded, to some of the people all of the time, and possibly even to all of the people some of the time, but the existence of such moments of private titillation does not commend the propriety of these items being foisted upon us, willy-nilly, whenever we choose to walk our cities' streets.

The liberal, today, is worried about civic beauty. He supported the 1963 Federal Highway Beautification Bill concerning junkyards and billboards on highways. He takes at least mild pleasure in the vigor of Ladybird Johnson and Mrs. Mary Lasker in encouraging the planting of azaleas and dogwoods and cherry trees in our communities. He fights Consolidated Edison in New York when there is a threat to chop at the scenic Hudson. By the same token, he should not cow at fighting for something that may render some of our cities a little bit less honky-tonk.

At least tacit support for the constitutionality of legislation that would ban offensive public displays is found in the statement of Supreme Court Justice Potter Stewart dissenting in the *Eros* case (*Ginzburg* v. *United States*, 383 U.S. 463). Mr. Justice Stewart there said:

Different constitutional questions would arise in a case involving an assault upon individual privacy by publication in a manner so blatant or obtrusive as to make it difficult or impossible for an unwilling individual to avoid exposure to it.

And Mr. Justice William J. Brennan, Justice Stewart's colleague, writing in the *Harvard Law Review*, in 1965, remarked that:

. . . government is not powerless to say that you cannot blare by loudspeaker the words of the first amendment in a residential neighborhood in the dead of night, or litter the streets with copies of the text. In other words, though the speech itself be under the first amendment, the manner of its exercise or its collateral aspects may fall beyond the scope of the amendment.

Without deprecating from the articulateness of our high court Justices, the argument was best expressed in the remark of a beautiful, sharp-witted, talented, turn-of-the-century actress. "I don't mind at all what people do," said Miss Patrick Campbell, "as long as they don't do it in the streets and frighten the horses."

PORNOGRAPHY AND THE ADULT'S PRIVATE LIFE

The *third*—and most difficult and least consequential—area in which some extremely limited censorship of pornography may be agreeable to the liberal involves the private (off-the-street) conduct of adults.

The American Civil Liberties Union protests that, in the absence of ability to prove that pornography works *tangible* harm upon adults—that it leads to crime—there should be no limitations upon it whatsoever. (It is obvious that, despite demonstrable relationships between pornography and crime *in extremely rare cases*, no connection *ordinarily* exists.) The ACLU's insistence, and that of other liberals, upon a showing of *concrete* damage before they will tolerate censorship is wholly inconsistent with liberal demands when the goring is of other oxen. Thus, liberals, generally, are deeply concerned with *morality*, not simply results. Law enforcement wiretapping, with properly supervised court orders, can be an undisputably helpful tool in society's protection; but it is—to most liberals—anathema, "dirty business." Its asset value in law enforcement's arsenal must yield, the liberal proclaims, to the immorality of its use. Confessions, vital in many criminal cases, should not be used, the liberal is apt to insist, even though voluntarily elicited, as morality requires that ours be an accusatory—not an inquisitorial—system.

Liberals, being adept at outlawing conduct that they find repugnant, and doing so wholly, on grounds of *morality*, why must they bridle at outlawing pornography as immoral? Why isn't sexual immorality, and the banning of items that abrade and shock our sexual morality, a cause that liberals can embrace?

Anthropologist Margaret Mead has noted: "Every known human society exercises some explicit censorship over behavior relating to the human body, especially as that behavior involves or may involve sex." Retired federal judge, and long-time law partner of the Supreme Court's Justice Abe Fortas, Thurman Arnold, noted in discussing pornography:

Society requires a public denunciation of this almost universal sin whether or not it leads to positive harmful conduct. . . . The fact that laws against obscenity do not have a rational or scientific basis, but rather symbolize a moral taboo, does not make them any the less necessary. They are important because men feel that without them the state would be lacking in moral standards.

Even D. H. Lawrence, whose *Lady Chatterly's Lover* led to litigation that, in large measure, began to shape today's attitude of permissiveness, conceded:

But even I would censor pornography, rigorously. . . .[Y]ou can recognize it by the insult it offers, invariably to sex, and to the human spirit. . . . Pornography is the attempt to insult sex, to do dirt upon it. . . . Ugly and cheap they make the human nudity, ugly and degraded they make the sexual act, trivial and cheap and nasty. . . .

If obscenity legislation may be appropriate in these three areas, what form should it take?

On March 21, 1966, when the United States Supreme Court handed down its opinion affirming Ralph Ginzburg's obscenity conviction, Ginzburg commented that pornography was "not definable, not measurable, a bag of smoke." And Ginzburg was an authority; pornography was something he knew well. The statutes talk in terms of banning items that are "obscene, lewd, lascivious, indecent, filthy or disgusting." The courts, intending to lend interpretative aid, invoke phrases such as "appeals to prurient interest," is "patently offensive," or is "hard core." But, as is obvious, neither the adjectives nor the Court phrases tell us just what it is that is to be banned.

The uncertainty is highlighted by a remark of one of the Justices of the Supreme Court, a tribunal relied upon in affording guidance to 200,000,000 Americans—and particularly to judges, lawyers, and police. Mr. Justice Potter Stewart, writing in 1964 in a case involving movie censorship, expressed his disinclination to define that which, in his judgment, might be censored. "*Perhaps,*" said Justice Stewart, "*I never could succeed in intelligibly doing so. But I know it when I see it*, and the motion picture involved in this case is not that." What guidance is there in that opinion?

The need, of course, is for precision if we are to have censorship. The lack of precision in existing laws is responsible for the prime evil of censors' blue-pencillings: *subjectivity*. Censorship, under laws that mean a thousand different things to a thousand different judges, prosecutors, and jurors, becomes almost wholly a matter of personal taste. And no liberal can countenance having either his, or his childrens', reading or viewing bobtailed according to the taste of another individual, be he a Comstock, a Bowdler, or a particular prosecutor, or judge. On the other hand, we are all used to heeding many clear laws—such as those banning the use of drugs, those barring public intoxication, those penalizing bigamy—whether or not we believe that they make sense, or that the areas on which they impinge should be the province of our legislators. And so if precise censorship laws can be drafted, focusing logically on the three areas herein suggested, and stating with great specificity what may and may not be shown, such laws may afford a program for fighting the ills of obscenity, without making inroads on meaningful freedom of expression.

GUIDELINES FOR LEGISLATION

A proper statute could articulate that parents, schools, churches, museums, and public libraries would be free to give (or through institutional bookstores to sell) youngsters whatever they thought appropriate for the child's education. Having clearly so said, our solons might then declare that it would be a crime for others to sell a youngster (an appropriate cut-off age would have to be set) any book, magazine, picture or other object that contained a description of human sexual activity or that portrayed nudity. The legislation would define, with great specificity, what constituted "sexual activity" or "nudity." And such definitions could readily be framed free of the elusive adjectives, "obscene," "lewd," or "lascivious," and free of the equally elusive phrases, "pruriently appealing," "hard core," or "patently offensive." (Specific drafts are suggested in my book, *Foolish Figleaves? Pornography in—and Out of—Court.*)

Similarly, legislation could provide that public commercial displays showing nudity or sexual activity were taboo.

Such statutes would apply equally to bar the sale to a youngster, or the public display *commercially*, of a Botticelli or a Playboy nude, or of one produced by the crassest pornographer. But with a built-in statutory safety-valve that created complete leeway for parents, schools, churches, libraries, and museums in terms of the young, and similar leeway for noncommercial public displays of art, the subjective judgments that have been the bane of obscenity enforcement could be removed.

There is authority to suggest that the United States Supreme Court would sustain such legislation even though, concededly, it would—to some extent—inhibit freedom of expression. In *Prince* v. *Massachusetts*, 321 U.S. 158, in 1944, that Court held that limitations on a youngster's religious freedom, that barred her from tendering religious tracts in bars and certain other places, could be enforced, although the same limitations, were they applied to adults, would have violated the freedom of religion clause of the First Amendment. Youngsters, then, can be deprived of the constitutional rights of an adult. And in *Berman* v. *Parker*, 348 U.S. 26, in 1954, the high Court held that legislation might be directed at protecting community aesthetic considerations.

In the third area, that of obscenity and adults, legislation might specify that any display or sale of live or photographed sex in action would be criminal. Such "exhibitions," undeniably "hard core" photographs, or stag movies appeal to voyeuristic tastes. They make of sex a spectator sport, derogating from that essential privacy with which it has been traditionally cloaked in our western culture. Even though the free choice of adults is involved, could liberals not agree that such a limited restraint constitutes no meaningful interference with freedom of speech, press—or assemblage? Without such restraint, consideration of contemporary "happenings" and commercial films suggests that such showing will be upon us in the immediate future. The late Father John Courtney Murray, Jesuit scholar-priest, whose independence of thought and speech, and whose intolerance of church censorship pressures, had seen him, over the years, in trouble with his own church, said: "The genuine artist knows instinctively that, although art may 'say all,' there are certain things that it is never allowed to say explicitly."

Lastly, in this area of obscenity and adults, a statute that explicitly barred the commercial exploitation of morbid interests in sex or sadomasochistic conduct should not shock a liberal. Such a statute would, essentially, be one requiring honest marketing. Since 1957, the law has spoken of "redeeming social interest" as removing items from the pale of censorship. Yet it is dishonest to examine a book like *Fanny Hill*, and to justify its sale because of its purported "redeeming social importance," when we know that such social values as it may have have never been used in its marketing or advertising, and no one—out of court—ever seriously considered those values. John K. Hutchens, reviewing *Fanny Hill* in *The Herald Tribune* when it was reissued in 1963, commented on Peter Quennell's introduction to the memoirs:

Mr. Quennell makes a game try as he goes about attributing to Cleland's erotic classic a degree of "elegance and energy," "undoubted historical value," and even "a definite literary appeal".... There is a little something in this, though if you could get a subsidy from one of those rich foundations you might enjoy a long, profitable career before you found anyone who ever read Fanny Hill's memoirs for any of the above-noted reasons.

A pandering statute would be, essentially, a marketing statute. It would safeguard items that were marketed on the basis of such "redeeming social importance" as might be claimed for them. But recognizing, as the Supreme Court has repeatedly declared, that pornography is not protected free speech, a pandering statute would penalize the publisher, distributor, or vendor of seemingly obscene items who intruded upon the public with his lip-licking claims of promised prurience.

In presenting this outline of "the thinking man's censorship," I am aware that there are self-styled liberals who, without pausing to analyze, will hoot at efforts to reconcile censorship and freedom of speech. Such persons may be those who were described by Pulitzer Prize winning poet Phyllis McGinley when, in her poem *In Praise of Diversity*, she wrote:

> His good has no nuances. He
>   Doubts or believes with total passion.
> Heretics choose for heresy
>   Whatever's the prevailing fashion.
> Those wearing Tolerance for a label
> Call other's views intolerable.

Wendy Kaminer, an attorney and activist in the feminist movement agaist pornography and violence against women, explains in the following article why legislative or judicial control of pornography is not the answer.

Wendy Kaminer

A WOMAN'S GUIDE TO PORNOGRAPHY AND THE LAW

Feminist protests against pornography often seem to posit a choice between the First Amendment rights of a few pornographers and the safety, dignity and independence of all women. Pornography is speech that legitimizes and fosters the physical abuse and sexual repression of women, and censorship appeals to some as a simple matter of self-preservation. A battle line has been drawn between "Feminists" and "First Amendment Absolutists"; the women's movement, which has been a struggle for civil rights and freedom of choice, has suddenly become tainted, in the popular view, with a streak of antilibertarianism.

None of this has been necessary. The bit-

ter debate over pornography and free speech derives from misconceptions on both sides about the methods and goals of the antipornography movement and the practical meaning of First Amendment guarantees of free speech. Feminists need not and should not advocate censorship, but we have every right to organize politically and to protest material that is degrading and dangerous to women.

Women can protest pornography with impunity under the First Amendment as long as they do not invoke or advocate the exercise of government authority. Only the government, by definition, can violate a First Amendment right. A woman who goes as far as "trashing" a porn shop could be convicted of a variety of offenses under the state criminal law and would probably be liable to a civil damage action by the damaged business, but she would not have violated any rights to free speech.

The First Amendment applies to government action at both the state and Federal levels. In practice, the control of obscenity or pornography is usually a matter of state law, although there are Federal statutes prohibiting interstate, international or postal traffic in obscene materials. But official regulation of speech, at any level, is governed by constitutionally mandated rules of legal procedure designed to protect the basic right *to* speak.

The heart of the First Amendment is its procedural safeguards against the imposition of prior restraints on any form of speech. It protects the act of expression, although it may not always protect the substance of what is said. Obscenity may, in principle, be prohibited under state law and is generally treated as a criminal offense. But the government may not restrain or prohibit any material before a judicial determination that it is, in fact, obscene. The government may not, in practice, take any general action, either civil or criminal, against a class of speech; it may only act against an individual utterance *after* it has been proved to fall within an unprotected class or to present an immediate threat to the national security.

The First Amendment works by narrowly proscribing the power of the government to enforce speech-related prohibitions. Its enforcement process is borrowed from the criminal law. All speech is presumed protected until proved otherwise, just as all defendants in criminal cases are presumed innocent until proved guilty. In each case, the government bears a heavy burden of proof, and a conviction of guilt or a finding of obscenity depends on the weight of the evidence. Every instance of speech must be judged individually, on its own merits, before it may be prohibited, just as every criminal defendant must be tried before she may be sentenced.

Obscenity is not, in theory, protected by the First Amendment. In 1957, in *Roth* v. *United States*, the Supreme Court held that obscenity was simply not speech and could be prohibited. But, the practical problems of defining obscenity and separating it from protected speech are overwhelming. The current definition of obscenity was enunciated by the Supreme Court in 1973 in *Miller* v. *California*. It is material "that the average person, applying community standards, would find . . . as a whole, appeals to the prurient interest," material that "depicts or describes, in a patently offensive way, sexual conduct specifically defined by the applicable state law" and material that "taken as a whole, lacks serious artistic, political, or scientific value."

Most hard-core pornography would probably be found legally obscene under *Miller* and could therefore be prohibited. But effective, generalized enforcement of obscenity laws is not possible without violating the very basic prohibition of prior restraints. As the law stands now, every single book, magazine, or film must be proved to be obscene, in a separate judicial proceeding, before it may be enjoined. This makes it almost impossible for the government to take any generalized action against businesses that regularly deal in pornography. A bookstore selling allegedly obscene material cannot be closed by the state until every book in it has been found obscene, in court.

A store with an inventory of 1,000 books cannot be closed because of 50 or 100 or even 500 obscenity convictions. The state could not restrain the sale of remaining or future stock; until it has been proved obscene, it must all be presumed to be protected speech. Broad civil injunctive relief against pornography-related businesses is barred by the prohibition of prior restraints, regardless of the number of underlying obscenity convictions.

Even individual convictions for obscenity are difficult to obtain, and the process in each case is complicated by First Amendment procedures. The seizure of any allegedly obscene material for use in a pending trial must be based on a narrowly drawn judicial warrant and cannot completely cut off access to the material. Thus, a District Attorney may seize one copy of a book as evidence in a given case, but he cannot prohibit its sale or distribution before a hearing or judicial determination of obscenity. Seizures of material for evidence in obscenity cases must comport with due process requirements under the First Amendment as well as with Fourth Amendment standards for search and seizure. Obscenity prosecutions are long, costly and unpredictable, and are, necessarily, a piecemeal approach to the "problem" of pornography.

The attempt to define and control obscenity simply hasn't worked for feminists or First Amendment lawyers alike. The Court has been struggling with a legal definition for the past twenty years, ever since the current obscenity doctrine was formulated in *Roth*. The definition has undergone relatively minor changes since then, the most important being the shift to local standards of "prurience." In addition, the Court changed the requirement that the work in question be "entirely without redeeming value" to an evaluation of the work "as a whole." These changes have apparently not increased the general number of obscenity prosecutions or the rate of convictions.

Moreover, the current definition of obscenity is conceptually unsound, for it does not set forth a predictable, objective test even for hard-core, sexually explicit material. Instead, it involves a balancing of the social and cultural utility of the material at issue with community standards of prurience. This belies the principle on which it is based: that obscenity can be identified and prohibited.

There is, of course, a good deal of frustration among feminists about ineffective obscenity laws and a natural concern for developing feasible legal alternatives. It has been suggested that pornography could be readily prohibited because it is dangerous and incites violence against women, based on the "clear and present danger" standard traditionally invoked by the Court in free-speech cases. The perception that pornography is dangerous is basic and one that must be impressed upon the public consciousness, but it does not translate so simply into First Amendment law.

The clear and present danger standard would actually afford greater legal protection to pornography than current obscenity laws. It is a strict standard of review, governing the regulation or prohibition of *protected* speech. It is, arguably, sounder constitutional law than the formulation of obscenity as "nonspeech," and it more accurately reflects a feminist view of pornography as dangerous propaganda, but it would substantially restrict government control over obscene material. The clear and present danger standard is more logically invoked in *defense* of pornography. It was, in fact, unsuccessfully raised by the defendant in the *Roth* case. Feminists who urge the adoption of this standard should understand its legal and political implications, otherwise they may find themselves unwittingly on the side of pornographers and First Amendment absolutists.

The clear and present danger standard describes a very narrow exception to the general restriction of government power over protected First Amendment activity. It was formulated to review instances of official repression of political speech: clear and present danger essentially means an immediate threat to the national security. The standard was first enunciated by the Supreme Court in 1919, after World War I, to allow for prosecutions for antidraft pamphleteering under the Espionage Act; it was used in the early 1950s to uphold convictions for allegedly "subversive" speech under the Smith Act; it has recently been invoked unsuccessfully by the Justice Department in an attempt to restrain the publication of the Pentagon Papers. It is applied in cases in which the government appears as the "aggrieved party," i.e., in its role as guardian of national security. Its use in a pornography case would raise an initial problem of identifying a plaintiff; pornography may be a crime against women, but it is not necessarily a crime against the state.

Adoption of a clear and present danger standard to prohibit pornography would be an implicit admission that it is protected political speech, which would considerably heighten practical problems of proof and enforcement. It is probably easier to prove that a given instance of speech is "obscene" than to prove that it presents "an immediate danger," and the clear and present danger standard imposes a particularly heavy burden of proof on the government. It must demonstrate, in every case, with direct factual evidence, a compelling, even overwhelming, imminent threat to the national security. It is not enough that the speech at issue might be or could be dangerous. In addition, "clear and present danger" does not recognize the cumulative harmful effect of a certain kind of speech. It means a tangible, immediate and specific danger that can be avoided only by suppressing publication.

Sociological studies and expert testimony pointing to a connection between pornography generally and violence against women would not establish a clear and present danger in an individual case, as a matter of law. It might not even be properly admissible as evidence. Use of this sort of generalized evidence to demonstrate that a given instance of speech is dangerous would be like trying a defendant in a criminal case with evidence of "similar" crimes committed by "similar" people. Every instance of speech must always be tried on its own merits; restraints could still be imposed only on specific utterances actually found to present an immediate danger. Moreover, a retreat to a clear and present danger standard and the acceptance of pornography as protected speech would actually strengthen these prohibitions against prior restraints.

The final irony is that in politicizing pornography, feminists are unintentionally signaling a need for a return to a more "permissive" clear and present danger standard in obscenity cases. Pornography is being redefined by women in terms of power, instead of sex and "prurience"; it is being characterized as dangerous political speech. The courts are being asked to weigh the alleged connection of pornography with violence against the underlying right of speech. This is the kind of balancing involved in a clear and present danger case, but, again, it applies to protected speech and presumes the strongest restriction of government authority in accordance with the First Amendment. By framing pornography as political speech, feminists are, in some senses, legitimizing it in ways that First Amendment absolutists never could.

This does not mean that pornography protests are necessarily counterproductive, but it underscores the need to understand fully the legal process in shaping an effective anti-pornography movement. It makes little sense for feminists to focus on a legal war against pornography or to direct much energy to reformulating obscenity prohibitions.

The primary obstacles to effective legal control of pornography are procedural, not definitional; it's not so much a matter of the standard used to identify unprotected speech in each case, which may change, but the procedures by which they are applied, which must remain constant. We cannot blame the failure of the system to enforce obscenity laws on a dearth of women judges, prosecutors, or jurors, because the problem is not in the way in which pornography is perceived but with the ways in which laws must be enforced. We must understand that procedural safeguards cannot be suspended simply to deal with pornography or any other single class of speech. These procedures are meaningless if not applied in every instance because they are specifically designed to insure a consistent legal process. In First Amendment cases, they also insure the narrow enforcement of laws affecting speech, so as not to infringe upon or deter protected activities. The underlying principle of the First Amendment is that the danger of government having the power to regulate speech and political dissent by a system of prior restraints far outweighs any possible harm that free speech might cause.

We simply cannot look to the government to rid us of pornography; legally, there are no "final solutions." The feminist movement against pornography must remain an antidefamation movement, involved in education, consciousness-raising and the development of private strategies against the industry. We have a crucial role of our own to play in a marketplace in which pornography is flourishing. But it is essential for us to maintain a larger political perspective and a sense of ourselves as one of many competing private interest groups. We can and should speak out and take action against pornographers, because they constitute a hostile group with interests antithetical to our own that threaten our independence and our psychic and physical well-being, but, we cannot ask the Government to speak for us.

Legislative or judicial control of pornography is simply not possible without breaking down the legal principles and procedures that are essential to our own right to speak and, ultimately, our freedom to control our own lives. We must continue to organize against pornography and the degradation and abuse of women, but we cannot ask the government to take up our struggle for us. The power it would assume in order to do so would be far more dangerous to us all than the "power" of pornography.

A lighter touch comes from Malcolm Cowley, well-known literary critic and editor, speaking about "dirty books" to the Virginia Library Association.

Malcolm Cowley

DIRTY BOOKS

Thank you Mr. Chairman. I might add that this is the first time in my life that I have addressed a meeting of librarians. I regard it as a privilege.

The subject is "Dirty Books." I shall start by reminding you of the situation that prevailed in the literary world of the 1920's, when there were continual battles over censorship and when many books were suppressed either because of the stories they told or because of their using bad words.

In regard to stories, the general rule was that guilt must lead to punishment and that illicit sexual relations, if presented at all, must end unhappily. Ernest Hemingway's first novel, *The Sun Also Rises*, published in 1926, does portray such relations. But it was not suppressed and the publisher, Charles Scribner's Sons was not even hailed into court. The principal reason why the book escaped prosecution was that the heroine, although clearly a nymphomaniac, was also clearly unhappy. Hemingway's second novel, *A Farewell to Arms* describes another illicit union, but this leads to the death of the heroine, and so the book could be placed on sale in every city but Boston, which was then more straitlaced than the rest of the country.

Before the novel appeared in 1929, there had been arguments in the publisher's office about some of the words that Hemingway used. Old Charles Scribner, then the head of the house (the present Charles Scribner is his grandson) was extremely conservative, but not unworldly. He asked Maxwell Perkins, Hemingway's editor, what the words were that bothered him. Perkins hesitated,

Reprinted by permission of the author from *Virginia Librarian* 14: 8–17 (Winter 1967).

blushed and then wrote the words on a pad. Old Mr. Scribner glanced at them and said, "Why, Max, you can't even *speak* those words." Many of them disappeared from the printed text.

There is also a story which Perkins denied to me, that he left the pad lying on his desk when he went out to lunch. According to the story, his secretary looked at the bad words and found they were written under a rubric printed at the top of the pad: THINGS TO DO TODAY.

In those days there were separate battles over each of the forbidden words, first in publishers' offices and later, often, in court. When *The Great Gatsby* appeared in 1925, one of Scribner's venerable strockroom clerks looked reproachfully at a pile of copies. He opened one of them to a page he remembered, put his finger on the page, and said, "To think that Scribner's would publish a book with that word in it!" The word was really a phrase, "The poor son-of-a-bitch," spoken as an epitaph at Gatsby's funeral. Son-of-a-bitch soon passed into current fictional usage and began to appear in the newspapers, but even as late as 1944, Lillian Smith's generally high-minded novel, *Strange Fruit*, was surpressed in Boston because of another word which I am sure Miss Smith, a Southern lady, had written with a sense of performing a necessary but utterly distasteful duty. No, I do not propose to repeat the word in mixed company, although you can find it in scores and hundreds of recent novels, where it has become as trite and meaningless as "geewhillikens."

For my part, I lament the deline in prestige and power of what used to be the bad words in the language, the obscene or blasphemous words that could not be printed. One might read the polite fiction and drama of two centuries, say from 1725 to 1925, without finding the words themselves, though sometimes they appeared in softened forms like "heck" or "darn" or even "d--m." Sometimes there were shocked or sly illusions to their survival in spoken English. In spite of the horror they aroused, or partly because of it, they had a recognized place and function, but now they have lost them both.

Their place until World War I was in the language of mule skinners, caterwaulers, gandy dancers, bindle stiffs, pine butchers, gobs, leathernecks, and others whose hardy lives were seldom shared by women. Their primary function was to express a variety of strong emotions, including pain, amazement, outrage, admiration, loathing, and exuberance, but seldom romantic yearning. On occasion they might serve as admonishments or even prayers. "Giddap!" the teamster shouted when the wheels were deep in mud. "Giddap, you——" whereupon he uttered what novelists liked to call "a picturesque flood" or "a crimson stream" of profanity. The novelists in using such phrases betrayed an ambiguous attitude toward the words in question. They seemed to imply that the words were "low" socially, but also that they expressed the strength of the lumberjack, the freedom of the wanderer, the daring of the soldier, and the hairy maleness of anyone who spoke them.

Anyone who used bad words where ladies might overhear them was not worth a tinker's curse, people said of him undamningly. That suggests another function of the words. They were an exclusively male idiom that helped to keep women in a protected but subordinate position. Though many of them referred to sexual acts, they did not kindle the fires of passion; instead they tried to quench the fires by making passion ugly and ridiculous. Anthropologists report that in many of the South Sea cultures the men of the tribe build a clubhouse where they gather to converse in a special male language that women are forbidden to speak under pain of ostracism or even death. In much the same fashion, those bad Anglo-Saxon words were the language of what amounted to a vast clubhouse where men could live untamed by female gossip and unsubdued by yearning.

How did the bad words lose their quality of being a secret language for men? The process may have started in France during the First World War when American boys of sheltered families discovered that there was an extensive oral literature, mostly British or Negro, in which bad words were used to comic and sometimes hilarious effect. The boys in uniform committed some of that literature to heart, including songs like "Frankie and Johnny" and "The Bastard King of England," which they later sang at parties in the States. Often the listeners included girls, also from sheltered families, who heard the words without visible blushes, and in fact were proud to be learning the passwords into the forbidden world of men.

"Frankie and Johnny" was sung in public, though in a somewhat expurgated version, at the first performance of a play by E. E. Cummings, *Him*, produced at the Provincetown Playhouse in 1927. Soon afterward the song was included in the printed version of the play that was issued by a New York publisher. Without the expurgation, Cummings' play would have had to be published in Paris, if it was published at all.

Paris was the port of refuge for authors who insisted on using bad words or presenting situations that offended American censors. Everybody knew that Joyce's *Ulysses* had been published there in 1922, after an American magazine, *The Little Review*, had been suppressed for printing extracts from it. D. H. Lawrence followed Joyce's example. When he finished *Lady Chatterley's Lover* in 1928, he sent the manuscript to Paris without even looking for an English or American publisher. There were, however, serious disadvantages in foreign publication, as Joyce and Lawrence both discovered. Not only did the author forego his English and American sales, except to tourists, but he could not even apply for an American copyright on his work. The result was that unscrupulous dealers in the printed word could profit from the notoriety of *Ulysses* and *Lady Chatterley* by bringing out expurgated editions of the two books in New York without asking the authors' permission or paying them royalties.

In spite of those disadvantages, there was a succession of small publishing houses in Paris—including Pyramid Press, Obelisk

Press, and Olympia Press—that made a business of publishing dirty books in English. At least there was a succession of names, though I think most of them concealed the single personality of Maurice Girodias, who was later to have his troubles with the French authorities. Girodias used to hire authors for a small sum—Paris being full of impecunious Americans—to write books for his special market. Some of these authors later became famous, as notably, Nathanael West (who wrote *The Dream Life of Balso Snell* for Paris publication), Henry Miller (who wrote *The Tropic of Cancer*, in 1931, and its many successors), and Terry Southern (who wrote most of *Candy*, but was given a collaborator because the publisher complained that his story was somewhat lacking in appeal to the prurient-minded). It is to be noted, however, that the dirty-book business was not confined to Paris and Brussels and Tokyo. In those Prohibition days, New York was full of bookleggers who printed small editions of the pornographic classics with illustrations and sold them for what they would bring— often as much as $100 a copy. Anyone could buy whatever book he pleased, as he could buy any sort of liquor, if he was able to pay the price and had the right connections.

The immense change since the 1920's has been the series of upheavals by which the underground or under-the-counter book trade has become an overground that grows in dimensions year by year until it now has the look of an uncovered city dump grandly infested with rats. I don't want to be vehement about the present situation. It has some obvious advantages for writers and for readers, too—since they have gained the right to buy at a reasonable price some distinguished works of fiction that used to be outside the law. But it has also led to the publication of a great many dull, emotionally deadening, badly written, and unnecessary books.

As for the written language, that vast storehouse from which all books are requisitioned, I doubt whether it has been improved by the upheavals of the last three or four decades. What it has gained amounts to no more than a few exact but ugly synonyms. Today a novelist would not dare say that one of his characters uttered "a crimson stream of profanity." Instead he would set everything down phonographically, and the crimson stream would be found to consist of a few stereotyped phrases repeated in a disordered sequence. The bad words have lost their mystery and magic. They are like the venerated idols of a tribe, kept in a secret sanctuary, but finally captured by invaders. When brought to light they are revealed to be nothing but coarse-grained and shapeless blocks of wood.

Passing from once forbidden words to once reprobated situations, we find that the change in literary standards has also proved a handicap to the novelist in his search for truly dramatic effects. Once, if he had nothing else to write about, he could always deal with the seduction of a virtuous woman. It was a subject that enthralled both the novelist and his readers. Samuel Richardson, for example, described the seduction of Clarissa Harlowe in six volumes, which were followed by a seventh volume devoted to Clarissa's death and the just punishment of her seducer. There is not a single contemporary novelist who could deal with a seduction at such length; they all seem to lack the necessary belief in its importance. In contemporary novels we find seductions described in a hasty chapter or even dismissed in a paragraph, with the result in the latter case that the author has to find a new subject, perhaps another seduction, to fill out the rest of the page.

I have mentioned the series of upheavals by which the underground book trade of the 1920's has emerged to the light and become almost respectable. Of course the first upheaval was Judge John M. Wollsey's decision in 1933 that the United States Customs Bureau exceeded its powers when it confiscated and destroyed copies of Joyce's *Ulysses*. The book was soon published in an American edition without noticeably corrupting the morals of the country, though it had already begun to exert a deep influence on the writing of American fiction. There were other upheavals in the years that immediately followed the Second World War, but these depended less on judicial decisions than on the liberties taken by some of our most successful novelists. Norman Mailer, James Jones, and John O'Hara all made extensive use of the once forbidden words and situations. They all had trouble with the censors, although their books were not suppressed except locally and then only in the paperback editions. Generally speaking the censors were in retreat, and the novelists marched forward uttering what used to be called a picturesque torrent of obscenity.

The next decisive battle in the courts was over the American publication of *Lady Chatterley's Lover*. D. H. Lawrence had written the novel out of a deep conviction that our ideals regarding marriage were false to human nature and should be condemned. His condemnation took the form of presenting an adulterous love affair as though it were a high moral achievement. He also used most of the forbidden words, or had the hero use them, but for the paradoxical purpose (in which he did not succeed) of evoking passion and tenderness, whereas the words had been used in the past to ridicule both emotions. When Lawrence wrote the book in 1928, he was deliberately trying to affront respectable people, and he knew that it could not be published in England or the United States—although he hoped that it might appear at some later time when his doctrines had done their work.

In 1959 Grove Press decided that the time had come, and it published *Lady Chatterley* in a hard-cover edition. A small book club, Reader's Subscription, distributed a circular in which it offered the novel to its subscribers. At this moment the Postmaster General, Arthur E. Summerfield, ruled that the book was unmailable and confiscated the circulars. There was a Post Office hearing at which I was one of two expert witnesses, or so they called us, summoned by Grove Press; the other was Alfred Kazin. I testified that after thirty years the doctrines preached in *Lady Chatterley* had been accepted by a rather wide segment of the population; one

could hear them from marriage counselors and even read them in articles published by *The Ladies Home Journal*. As for the bad words in the book, I testified that every one of them had been printed during the past ten years in some widely read American novel.

At this, counsel for the Post Office Department, Sol. J. Mindel, said to me slyly, "I haven't heard you repeating any of those words, Mr. Cowley."

The laugh was on me, but it wasn't ill-humored, and in fact Mr. Mindel couldn't put any passion into his condemnation of *Lady Chatterley*. Later I heard that the Post Office referee wanted to give a verdict in favor of the publisher, but that he had been overruled by Mr. Summerfield, who was an automobile dealer by profession and an ardent defender of the existing order. Still later the case was tried in the United States District Court for New York, where the presiding Judge was my friend and neighbor Frederick van Pelt Bryan. Partly on the basis of the book's literary merits, Judge Bryan ruled that it could be distributed without interference from the Post Office Department. It soon appeared on the newsstands for ninety-five cents, in what was announced as the first printing of two million copies.

Two years later there was another case involving Grove Press, which had taken advantage of the Chatterley decision to publish an American edition of Henry Miller's *Tropic of Cancer*. I was again invited to serve as an expert witness, but this time I had an instinct that I had better keep quiet. What I had discovered in myself was an unexpected residue of conservatism. Although I admired the book for its literary virtues of naturalness, vigor, and perfect honesty, and although I was glad to see it sold in bookstores, where presumably it would be purchased by adults who thought twice about spending $7.50, I didn't know that I was eager to have it displayed on newsstands for ninety-five cents, since it wasn't, so it seemed to me, the best sort of work for high-school boys and girls.

This brings up a general problem about censorship: if used at all, should it be the same at all levels? At present, many situations can be presented on the stage that cannot be presented in motion pictures. Many others are permissible in motion pictures but not on television, which goes into the home and is devotedly watched by children. On television there is a difference between the pictures or the situations that can be shown at 6 o'clock and those that can be shown at midnight after the children have gone to bed. Now, should the same sort of distinction be made between hardcover books and those distributed at low prices to a mass audience? Judges don't think so, and it may be that the judges are right. But then again it may be that the judges have been wrong in some of their recent decisions.

Almost all the decisions, going back to those on *Lady Chatterley* and *Tropic of Cancer*, have favored the publishers of dirty books. The only man whose conviction was allowed to stand (it is still under appeal) was Ralph Ginsburg, publisher of *Eros* (and more recently of *Avant Garde*), and his crime was not that of bringing out prurient magazines, but the secondary crime of appealing to prurient tastes in his advertising. The clinching point was that he tried to set up his headquarters in Intercourse, Pennsylvania. The advertising men for other publishers have been warned to be more discreet, but, after reading some recent issues of *The New York Times Book Review*, one can hardly say that they have taken the warning.

Grove Press is still the most enterprising of the half-dozen publishers in the field. In addition to maintaining an extensive list of books, including some of considerable merit, it also publishes *Evergreen Review*, which is served by an imaginative advertising director. Thus, in presenting his current bi-monthly issue, he asks:

Do hippies have a more swinging sex life than squares? What does the hippie mean when she talks about love? And sex? What is sex like when you're high on LSD? What's all this talk about her new pan-sexuality? Just how communal is her sex? What happens to her kids if the family goes out the window? Is acid turning out a new mutant genera-

tion? And what would happen if all America turned on? You'll find frank replies to these and many other bold questions in the current issue of *Evergreen Review*. Hippie Louis Rappaport, in an exclusive interview, tells it like it is—exactly like it is—on the hippie scene . . .

Hippie sex is just one of the many exciting, sometimes outrageous features in our current issue. Here's a rundown of some of the others . . .

The full-page advertisement continues with a list of articles that I feel no uncontrollable impulse to read:

Is the Square Left Doomed? Not only doomed, but dead, says Ralph J. Gleason in a passionate piece that puts down politics and puts the hippies at the very center of the radical movement to save America before it's too late.

What happens at Lance (A Mag for Men) when its fiction editor, stoned on schizojuice (blood tapped from the veins of an insane Commie-fag-spade-Chinese drug fiend) concocts a story of NECK-ROPHILIA a la Krassner—a brandnew story by Terry Southern, famous author of *Candy*, plus exciting new fiction by Boris Vian and James Brunot . . . and many other features.

For those who are enthralled by the advertisement and reply in these words: "Gentlemen: I want to be tuned into *Evergreen Review* for 12 issues (bi-monthly). . . . Enclosed is my check for $9"—for such as find themselves on the *Evergreen* wave length, there is promised a choice among seven premiums, all books published by Grove Press. They include, among others:

My Secret Life. Anonymous Victorian gentleman's sexual memoirs. Deluxe giant paperbound ed. (10″ × 13″) complete and uncut, boxed. Retail $9.50. FREE.

120 Days of Sodom and other Writings. The Marquis de Sade. A shocking work Sade considered his masterpiece. Retail $15. FREE.

The Olympia Reader. Maurice Girodias, Ed. Some of the finest writing and illustrations ever censored! Retail $12.50. FREE.

All seven books offered as premiums—from which offer I should judge that their sale in bookstores has been lagging—are what used to be called hard-core pornography. They are books of the type that used to be published in Paris or Brussels and smuggled past the customs, or else furtively printed in New York by bookleggers whose principal stock in trade was a mailing list of rich men who collected such items. Grove Press has driven those underground publishers out of business. It has even started a new series of Black Circle Books in which all the titles are defiantly pornographic. A recent advertisement in *The Times Book Review* includes these two choice items:

Harriet Marwood, Governess. Anonymous. A modern underground classic with overtones of Sacher-Masoch. [In other words, a book that would presumably appeal to masochist.]

Sadopaideia. Anonymous. Rediscovery of an Edwardian work first privately printed in 1907, and "Being the experiences of Cecil Prendergast, Undergraduate of the University of Oxford, showing how he was led through the pleasant paths of masochism to the supreme joys of sadism."

There is absolutely no reason I can discover why books like these should be publicly distributed. They are not books, properly speaking, but hasty concoctions designed to gratify the tastes of people addicted to what used to be called perversions of various types. Except for such people, they are of interest only to sociologists, who could always obtain them through specialized dealers. Why should they be placed on public sale and advertised in *The New York Times*?

Grove Press is by no means the only publishing house that has been active in the dirty-book business. Among others, G. P. Putnam's Sons, one of the oldest names in American publishing, caused a sensation some years ago when it reissued *Fanny Hill*, after the book had survived two centuries of surreptitious life. Having lost the charms of the forbidden, it turned out to be well written, but dull and repetitious after the first few chapters. Putnam's also published *Candy*, which, as I said, had first been issued in Paris by the Olympia Press. Meanwhile Olympia had been driven out of business by the French government, which has become more puritanical than the government in Washington. Maurice Girodias, the proprietor of Olympia, has transferred his activi-

ties to New York, as one learns from a recent advertisement in *The Times Book Review*:

The Olympia Press man opens shop in New York. Send your Mss to Maurice Girodias, 440 Park Ave., South, New York City.

Lyle Stuart, Inc. is a smaller firm that specializes in sensational items overlooked by Grove Press. In the September 17 issue of *The Times Book Review* it advertises a series of illustrated books, "Historical Eroticism." Among them, to quote from the advertisement, "*Checan* boldly presents the erotic elements in Peruvian art. $50. . . . *Shunga* reveals the turbulent life of passion that lies behind the screens erected by modern Japan in deference to the prudery of visiting foreigners. . . . $50. . . . *Roma Amor*. . . . The 'scandalous' collection of the famous Museum of Naples reproduced for the first time with color photographs . . . not only do they attain a rare degree of technical perfection: they are also unprecedently frank. . . . $35." Obviously the series is designed to appeal to those with visual, not audial, imaginations and well-stocked bank accounts.

There is also the firm of Bernard Geis Associates (most of the Associates have withdrawn from the partnership), which makes a specialty of collecting scandals from the motion-picture world and using them as the subject of novels which are written to order. *The Valley of the Dolls* was its great success, though a more recent work, *The Exhibitionist*, is also appearing on best-seller lists. *The New York Times* daily reviewer said of it, in part:

What is offensive about "The Exhibitionist" is not that it's a stupid book aimed at a presumable stupid market, but that it makes so little pretense to be anything else. It does pretend to be pornography. Not quite hard-core, of course, for the intended market is presumed to disapprove of the real thing while slobbering after substitutes.

A Putnam advertisement for Norman Mailer's latest book, *Why Are We in Vietnam?* says in a so-called balloon: "Frankly, we didn't know whether the American public could take it. Obviously they could." After Mailer's book, of which reviewers complained that they could not quote so much as a paragraph in their reports because of its omnipresent obscenity, it would appear that the American public, or part of the public, can take absolutely anything. And it is being given anything: sadism, masochism, voyeurism, fetishism, pederasty, lesbianism, bestialism, necrophilia. The list of clinical perversions is rather limited, and they are all being presented in book after book with what has become an appalling monotony.

There are more and more complaints from book reviewers. Many of you have read, but I do not apologize for repeating here, the *New York Times* Sunday review of Mailer's book. It was written by Anatole Broyard, not regarded as a prude, and it says in part:

Every page is studded—the word is used advisedly—with sexual references, generally boasts or threats, Kilroy was here, there and everywhere. In an aggressively modern book like this, it goes without saying that the acts are always gratuitous. There is no question of love, affection, or even desire: sex is simply a form of protest. . . .

Nostalgic readers might see here one of the indirect results of the lifting of censorship. In the goody-good old days, novelists were forced to treat sex as a meaningful act. To be publishable, it had to be part of the development of character, to occur in a context of inevitability. Now sex occurs in no context whatever—not even a bed—and it is about as meaningful as Berkeley students shouting four-letter words over a loudspeaker.

. . . the literature of sexual heroism doesn't make for good writing or reading.

There is also resistance on the part of librarians. Once again I quote from *The Times*, which says in a recent Sunday issue.

Just before its sales conference the other day, Scribner's editors held a meeting that was somewhat more genteel. The guests were reviewers, a few bookstore owners, a good many neighborhood librarians, and the purpose was to go over the books scheduled for January through April. At the center of a long table in a ballroom of the Pierre, there was Charles Scribner, head of the house, who presided. Flanking him were Harry Brague and Burroughs Mitchell, big-wheel editors. Flanking them were other editors, and as each book came up the editor in charge was allowed four minutes to describe it.

It took about eight minutes to prove once again how library oriented—or indeed how young-adult-reader library oriented—book publishing is these days. Editors with books suitable for the young—in libraries—had a note of triumph, those without seem faintly apologetic. A book entitled "The Red Pavilion" came up. This is a mystery by Robert van Gulik, the Netherlands Ambassador to Japan, and in describing it, Mr. Brague said sadly, "It's not recommended for children in libraries." Someone wanted to know why. "It's o.k. if you want a handbook on prostitution, gambling, debauchery and murder," said Mr. Brague.

It would seem that reviewers to some extent, and librarians in a more practical fashion, are almost the only forces that limit the publication of handbooks on prostitution, gambling, debauchery, and murder.

One question is whether this state of affairs is likely to continue. I would not set myself forward as a prophet, but still I might offer the reflection that social issues in this country seldom continue a movement in one direction. Instead they veer crazily from one extreme to another, from conservatism to radicalism, from right to left, then back again to the right, but not all the way back; certain changes will prove to be permanent. Thus, I should guess that the change in the language itself will be permanent and that the bad words will never regain the power they had for our parents and grandparents. The new attitudes toward sex are likely to represent another permanent change for better or worse—not in the sense that the present attitudes will persist, but in the broader sense that we are not likely to return to the older attitudes either in life or in fiction. It is safe to predict, however, that there will be a reaction against the tasteless permissiveness that now prevails in writing and publishing. Yes, the censors will come back in some fashion, as they came back in France, and the Supreme Court of some future day will write new decisions to authorize their return.

As for librarians, whom I have the honor to address, they do not determine the taste of the community; they record that taste, and they have as their privilege the right of preserving the written word in its integrity. But this does not mean that they have to accept every written word, including those that belong on the walls of water closets, as if it were handed down from Mount Sinai. Fortunately they are privileged to exercise a certain wise discrimination.

Art Buchwald has the last word on the theme "dirty books."

Art Buchwald

DIRTY BOOKS

Linda Peeples was giving the dinner. When dessert was finished she said, "I have some exciting news for all of you."

"So tell us already," someone said.

"My son George just read his first book."

We all raised our wine glasses to toast the occasion.

"How old is George?" Reilly asked.

"He'll be 18 next month," Linda said.

"That's fantastic," Rowan said. "My son is 21 and he hasn't read a book yet."

"George has always been a bright student," Linda bragged.

"What book did he read?" Frannie Huff wanted to know.

"J. D. Salinger's *Catcher in the Rye.*"

There was an embarrassed silence at the table.

"What's wrong?" Linda wanted to know.

"*Catcher in the Rye* is a dirty book," I said. "Where did he get his hands on such filthy literature?"

"He found it in the school library," Linda said.

Exstrom was outraged. "You ought to report the librarian to the school board. They probably don't even know it's there."

"But George seemed to enjoy it," Linda said defensively.

"Sure he enjoyed it," Reilly said. "It's full of sex and bad words. But it doesn't belong

Reprinted with permission of the author, L.A. Times Syndicate, 1982.

in a high school library. The next thing you know, George will be reading *Huckleberry Finn* and Kurt Vonnegut's *Slaughterhouse Five.*"

"Or Studs Terkel's *Working,*" I said.

"Not to mention Somerset Maugham's *Of Human Bondage.*"

"Are they all bad books?" Linda asked.

"The worst. They've ruined kids for life," I said.

"But we've been trying to get George to read a book since he was 12 years old. *Catcher in the Rye* was a breakthrough, and it would break his heart if we told him he couldn't read any more like it."

"There are books and there are books," Exstrom said. "My daughter came home from her English class with William Faulkner's *Sanctuary*, and I told her if she ever brought anything like that in the house again I'd throw it in the furnace. I also reported her teacher to the principal."

I said, "If more parents took an interest in what their kids were reading we wouldn't have such a rotten society."

"Well, it's too late now," Linda said. "George has already read *Catcher in the Rye*. What do I do?"

"Watch him closely," Frannie Huff said. "Search his room. If you find a book by John Steinbeck or James Baldwin under his bed, then you know he's in real trouble and I would take his library card away from him."

"I wish I had kept a closer eye on my son. I let him read Hemingway's *The Sun Also Rises* when he was 15 years old, and the next thing I knew he checked out Malamud's *The Fixer,*" Exstrom said.

"Where do you find out what books are bad for children's minds?" Linda wanted to know.

"There are organizations all over the country that will supply you with lists," I said. "We get our guidance from a couple who censors books in Texas."

"What's George reading now?" Reilly asked.

Linda said "Voltaire's *Candide.*"

"I hate to tell you this," said Frannie Huff, "But you have a sick kid on your hands."

CHAPTER EIGHT

THE PRESS UNDER PRESSURE

The framers of the First Amendment to the Constitution of the United States recognized both the natural right of the citizen to self-expression without fear of government repression and also the need in a democracy for an informed electorate. In exercising this constitutional guarantee, the nation's press, printed and electronic, has often come into conflict not only with various elements in society but also with the government itself. These conflicts have sometimes arisen over differing interpretations of the meaning of the First Amendment. An examination of certain specific issues threatening freedom of the press reveals serious problems in four areas: (1) government secrecy versus the people's right to know, (2) libel and the invasion of privacy, (3) free press versus fair trial (conflict between the First and Sixth Amendments), and (4) the application of the First Amendment to radio and television.

GOVERNMENT SECRECY VERSUS THE PEOPLE'S RIGHT TO KNOW

It is argued that if a democracy is to survive and flourish, the people, who make the ultimate decisions by electing officials and legislators to reflect their views, must know what is happening in their government and what actions their representatives are taking. At the same time, it has long been recognized that there are certain areas, national defense being the most obvious, where some secrecy is essential. And so there is an ever present debate between the two forces: secrecy and openness in government.

Thomas I. Emerson

THE DANGER OF
STATE SECRECY

Secrecy has always been a crucial feature of the governmental process, but the expansion of government functions and the development of mass communications have given it new dimensions and made it a challenging issue of our day. Thus the American people and the whole world were taken to the brink of atomic war in the Cuban missile crisis, without knowing what was going on. In the U-2 affair, not only was the country unaware of the flights over Soviet territory but one of our most revered Presidents was caught in a flagrant lie. Cambodia was subject to intensive bombing for more than a year while the American people were told it was not happening and elaborate machinery was set up by the military bureaucracy to conceal the facts. Most recently, a massive network of deceit has been uncovered in the White House itself.

These are just a few of the shocking peaks of government secrecy; the day-to-day ramifications of secrecy permeate every level of government and create more pervasive and equally difficult problems. The effect of secrecy upon the operation of modern government is baleful and the task of controlling it is enormous. All that can be done here is, very briefly, to examine some of the basic philosophic and political considerations that underlie the use of secrecy in government, make note of some constitutional and statutory tools for dealing with the problem, and suggest some working rules for achieving a more just and effective mode of operation.

It long has been recognized that information is a source of power. The President controls foreign relations in large part because he alone has access to critical information about events in foreign countries and our responses to them. Similarly, the power

Thomas I. Emerson, "The Danger of State Secrecy," *The Nation*, March 30, 1974. Copyright 1974 *Nation* magazine, The Nation Associates, Inc.

of the executive branch to formulate an economic program, such as one to deal with the energy crisis, flows out of the massive volume of facts and figures stored in the files of the bureaucracy. And the withholding of information from other participants in the governmental process is well understood to be a method of aggrandizing and in fact monopolizing power. Control of access to the factual material closes off public debate, eases the task of responding to criticism, and ultimately confines the whole decision-making process to those who possess the crucial information.

As a general proposition, secrecy in a democratic society is a source of *illegitimate* power. This is so for a number of reasons.

In the first place, withholding of information by any part of the government is in direct conflict with democratic principles of decision making. Under our constitutional theory, the people are the masters and government is the servant, and it is incongruous that the master should be denied the information upon which to direct the activities of his servants. This is not just abstract theory. Regardless of how well the democratic process may work, regardless of the extent to which our mechanisms of government actually allow the ordinary citizen to participate in making choices, *no* rational choice can be made in the absence of adequate information.

Furthermore, under our constitutional system each branch of government has a part to play. For one branch to keep secret from another branch information it needs to perform its function, is to undermine the whole principle of the separation but coordination of powers. In the case of the legislative branch, the need for access to information possessed by the executive is virtually coextensive with that of the executive branch. In the case of the judicial branch, the need is less extensive but fully necessary in those areas where it exists.

Second, withholding information from citizens of a democratic society is unjust, morally wrong. We fully accept that when the government makes a decision about the fate of an individual, such as to confine him to prison or deprive him of his property, justice requires that he be afforded due process of law. And due process involves, as its most basic element, that the citizen be furnished all the information upon which the decision in his case is founded. What difference does it make whether the governmental decision at issue affects only a single citizen or many citizens collectively? There may be practical difficulties in establishing appropriate procedures in the latter case, but the issue of affording justice is the same. In other words, in our society the individual has a moral right to exercise control over his own destiny. It is the minimum price demanded by him, and owed to him, for bowing to collective authority.

Third, to the extent that information is withheld from a citizen the basis for government control over him becomes coercion, not persuasion. The citizen is given no rational ground for accepting a decision; he must submit to it as a matter of force. It is the obligation of democratic government to suppress the use of coercion and encourage the factor of acquiescence, but no such policy is possible when the operation of government is secret. Indeed, secrecy is the very mark of totalitarian government.

Fourth, secrecy is politically unwise. In the long run it leads not to support of government but to disaffection. One reason for this is that the concealment of information tends to engender anxiety, fear, panic and extremism. It eliminates the possibility that the citizenry can face its problems on a rational basis and leaves room only for irrational response. Moreover, the disaffection thus aroused leads to suppression, and that in turn demands more secrecy. The process, as we are beginning to be aware, can accelerate.

Fifth, secrecy is totally inconsistent with the ultimate need for confidence in government that is essential to successful administration of public affairs and peaceful social change. Concealment of information by its nature leads to affirmative deception. In the end, however, much of the information will come out, partly by the passage of time, partly by leaks, partly by the efforts of a free press. The result is a credibility gap, one of the most ominous developments in modern government.

Broadly speaking, then, secrecy in government accompanies evil in government. There is, indeed, a symbiotic relationship—government wrongs are kept secret because they are evil; and evil is done because it can be kept secret.

Historically, no clear mandate for banning secrecy in government resulted from the work of the Constitutional Convention (indeed its own sessions were secret). The Constitution expressly provides that some operations of Congress might be kept from public view in that, while each house is obliged to keep and publish a journal of its proceedings, it is not required to publish "such parts as might in [its] judgment require secrecy." And President Washington refused on several occasions to provide Congress with documents which he determined should be withheld in the public interest. On the other hand, some provisions of the original Constitution were designed to eliminate secrecy in the workings of government. In voting on bills in each house, the "yeas and nays of the members . . . on any question shall, at the desire of one-fifth of those present, be entered on the journal." Similar provision for public accountability was made with respect to voting on the overriding of a Presidential veto.

Not until recent times, however, did a constitutional basis for open government begin to emerge. The applicable doctrines are derived mainly from modern ideas concerning the separation of powers, the First Amendment and due process of law. Limitations are to be found primarily in the constitutional right of privacy. But despite some advance in these concepts, as yet only the bare outlines of effective constitutional doctrine can be discerned.

Separation of powers is normally conceived as prohibiting each branch of government from interfering with the work of another, but it can also be viewed affirmatively in more modern terms, as including the right of each branch to receive from another such assistance as it needs to carry out its functions. As already noted, this would give the legislative branch virtually unlimited access to any information possessed by the executive branch, because the power of Congress to appropriate funds, to oversee the work of the executive branch, and to enact laws generally would give it a right of access to almost the entire spectrum of information held by the executive.

The principal constitutional limitation upon these powers, advanced by the executive branch historically and currently, has been the doctrine of executive privilege. More detailed treatment of the legitimate scope of executive privilege is reserved for later consideration. Here it suffices to say that, while the doctrine has been relied on from time to time over the years (though the term "executive privilege" is a more recent coinage), the issues have ordinarily been settled in the political rather than the judicial arena, and usually by compromise. As a result, there is little constitutional law on the subject. The only court decisions which deal squarely with it are the rulings of the District and Circuit courts for the District of Columbia in the recent Watergate tapes case. Both those courts forcefully rejected the extravagant contention of Mr. Nixon and his lawyers that executive privilege allowed the President to withhold any information that he deemed required secrecy in the "public interest." The exact scope of executive privilege, however, remains undefined.

The main constitutional basis for the proposition that the operations of government should be open to the ordinary citizen lies in the First Amendment. Here again, the constitutional provision has been traditionally conceived as enforcing a negative—that the government shall not in any manner interfere with the right of individuals or groups to freedom of expression. Two additional features of First Amendment law, however, have recently begun to take shape, and both are directly related to the maintenance of open government.

The first deals with the right of reporters, scholars and other gatherers of facts to have access to sources of information. Obviously any system of freedom of expression must recognize the establishment and maintenance of such a right. An untrammeled privilege to speak on a subject, but with no opportunity to obtain the relevant facts about that subject, guarantees but an empty freedom. The Supreme Court has dealt with this problem in only one case, involving the power of grand juries to compel newspaper reporters to reveal information obtained by them under a pledge of confidentiality. The Supreme Court recognized the basic constitutional right, agreeing that "news gathering" does "qualify for First Amendment protection," and adding, "without some protection for seeking out the news, freedom of the press could be eviscerated." But it refused to accept the specific First Amendment claim made in the case. Thus the general principle has been established but its application so far is limited.

The other development concerns what has come to be called the public's "right to know." The obverse of the right to speak, it embraces the right of persons to listen, to read, to observe; in short, to receive communications from others. The right to know implies, further, a right of access to the information necessary to enrich and make meaningful the basic guarantee. This right to know is a much more amorphous constitutional concept than the right to speak, and hence far more difficult to reduce to workable operating rules. Nevertheless it is fundamental to any system of freedom of expression that would meet the needs of a democratic society.

The Supreme Court first clearly acknowledged a constitutional right to know in a 1965 decision invalidating a federal statute that sought to impose restrictions upon receiving mail from abroad which had been designated by the government as "Communist political propaganda." In 1969 the Supreme Court, upholding the right of persons to read pornography in the privacy of their own homes, reaffirmed that "[i]t is now well established that the Constitution protects the right to receive information and ideas.'' And in the same year, in a case upholding the fairness doctrine for broadcasting, the Supreme Court declared that "[i]t is the right of the viewers and listeners not the right of the broadcasters, which is paramount." Yet the Supreme Court, once again, has been loath to accord real substance to the right it has recognized in theory. In its most recent decision it declined to give any weight to the contention by a group of scholars that the government's refusal of a visa to a Belgian Marxist economist, who had been invited to lecture in the United States, violated their constitutional right to know.

The third possibility for invoking constitutional doctrine to bar secrecy in government grows out of an expansion of current concepts of due process of law. This ancient legal precept, first formulated in the Magna Carta, affirms that government decision making must follow procedures which the community recognizes to be just.

Due process has been applied most extensively to decision making by the judicial branch. And it is fair to say that, as a general proposition, it forbids the use of secret information in the judicial process. The basic rule in criminal cases is that, if the government refuses to reveal evidence upon which it relies, or withholds evidence known to be relevant to guilt or innocence, the court will dismiss the prosecution. No exceptions are permitted, even when national security is invoked as grounds for refusing to disclose. In civil cases the general rule is open to some exception. Thus, where a citizen sued the government for damages and sought information in the possession of the government, the Supreme Court held that the government might refuse to supply the information when national security would be jeopardized. On the other hand, where the government brings the civil action, the same rule as in criminal cases would seem to apply.

The requirements of due process also apply to decisions of the executive branch. In fact it is in the field of administrative law that the greatest expansion of due process has occurred. Here again, as in the judicial process, reliance upon evidence not disclosed to the parties was a general proposition prohibited by due process concepts. Only in loyalty cases, where the government appeals to national security, have the courts wavered at all. Further, the right to compel disclosure of evidence in the possession of the government has steadily expanded.

Due process has had least application in the legislative sphere. Yet even here its concepts have been applied to the operation of legislative investigating committees.

The basic notions of due process, as already suggested, can clearly be extended to the use of secrecy in government operations. Decision making on a collective scale, it can be asserted, ought to follow the rules of fairness to the same degree as decision making that is directed against specific individuals or organizations. Access to all the facts, by all interested parties, is as essential to a just result in the one situation as in the other. The only difference is that in the individual case the facts are usually specific, whereas in the collective case they are general. This may make some difference in the form of rules necessary to implement the constitutional right, but it does not change the nature of the right asserted. One must concede, however, that the problem of government secrecy has thus far not been approached in these terms.

To complete the constitutional picture, it is necessary to consider the limitations imposed upon the obligation of the government to make information available to all citizens. As noted previously, these flow primarily out of the constitutional right of privacy. The right of privacy was first formulated by the Supreme Court in the Connecticut birth control case of 1965. Its parameters remain largely undefined, but the main concept is that the constitution recognizes with respect to each person a zone of privacy from which the government, its agents and its laws are excluded. The zone of privacy derives from the right of a person to live as an individual, in respects to which he or she is not responsible to the collective, and intrusions by the collective are constitutionally forbidden.

It follows that some information in the possession of the government may not be publicly disclosed without violating the constitutional right of privacy. The information thus protected would involve mainly personal matters found in personnel files, loyalty dossiers, or investigative reports not matured into litigation. The drawing of a specific line between public and private matter might not be easy in individual cases, but it would occasion no more difficulty than many other lines drawn in the course of constitutional adjudication. The goal is simply to eliminate from the public forum material that is of legitimate concern only to the individual involved.

This sketch of a constitutional framework for open government suggests the possibility of developing fundamental constitutional principles into a mandatory protective structure. But that point has not yet been reached, nor does it seem imminent. Meanwhile, reliance must be placed upon the possibility of solving the problem through legislation.

The basic power of the legislature to eliminate or curtail secrecy in government through statutory enactment is not open to question. The legislative branch is authorized to make laws dealing broadly with the organization and operation of the executive and judicial branches. The only limits upon this power would arise from a constitutional claim asserted on the basis of executive privilege, a possibly similar claim urged by the judiciary, and claims of privacy advanced by individual citizens. The scope of executive privilege, as noted above, is uncertain, but it is unlikely that the courts would employ that doctrine to nullify in any substantial degree statutory directions that the executive furnish the legislature with specified materials. The other limitations would present minimal problems to an open system.

Unfortunately, the existing statutory structure is primitive and ineffective. The Freedom of Information Act, passed in 1966, starts out bravely by asserting that "[e]ach agency, on request for identifiable records . . . shall make the records promptly available to any person." Thereafter, however, the statute provides for nine exceptions which take away most of what was previously granted. One of these exceptions, for example, provides that the statute does not apply to matters that are "specifically required by Executive order to be kept secret in the interest of national defense or foreign policy." This removes all classified material from the operation of the Act. Furthermore, the Supreme Court has held that the courts have no power under the Act to review the executive decision as to whether material was properly classified or to force the executive to separate out classified from unclassified material embodied in a single document. In addition, the executive agencies have interposed serious administrative obstacles to the obtaining of information, even when it is rightfully available under the statute. State statutes, mostly providing for open meetings of legislative bodies, have made even fewer inroads on government secrecy.

The statutory scheme for eliminating government secrecy needs a substantial overhauling. That revision is not likely to come, however, until there is more general agreement on basic principles and more careful study of specific working rules. To that problem we now turn.

Remarkably little attention has been paid to the details of a system of nonsecret government. Discussion has centered around broad questions of whether executive privilege should exist, or has focused on the validity of executive privilege in a particular situation. Thus the development of a comprehensive set of basic principles and working rules has been slow to mature.

The underlying principle must be that decisions which the government makes without disclosing to all parties concerned the full information on which they are based cannot be considered a legitimate exercise of governmental power. This principle derives from the philosophical and political considerations set forth earlier. It means that any withholding of information in the governmental process must be an exception, expressly justified as such. The basis for making an exception must be that nondisclosure is unarguably essential to the performance of a proper government function. It is not sufficient that disclosure would simply make the function more difficult to perform or would change it in some way. Quite the contrary, it is to be expected that open operation of government, such as the deliberation of a legislative committee, might result in substantial change both in form and substance. Only where secrecy is inherent in a specific operation can it be justified.

Starting from these premises, one must define specific areas of exceptions. The first involves the advice privilege. It authorizes withholding information relevant to that part of the decision-making process which relies upon free and frank discussion with subordinate, coordinate or superior officials. The justification is a sad but true reflection on modern bureaucracy—unless such an exchange of ideas, trying out of proposals, and general brainstorming is kept confidential, the whole process of reaching a reasoned decision is acutely impeded. This exception is most applicable to decision making in the executive branch, where the bureaucratic process is especially inhibited unless protection is afforded for new, experimental or offbeat ideas. It is also applicable to some parts of the judicial process, particularly in connection with court conferences for decision making or in relations between a judge and his law clerk. The exception is least applicable to the legislative process, being limited, perhaps, to personal interchange between members of the legislature and to the relation of a member to his staff. Furthermore, in its application to all branches of government, the advice exception applies only to statements of opinion or ideas, not to matters of fact; it is not legitimately invoked with respect to discussions involving commission of a crime; and it requires the separation of privileged material from unprivileged, with only the format subject to nondisclosure.

A second exception relates to national security. The largest amount of government secrecy, administered mainly through the classification system, is based on that claim and most of it is unjustified. There are few issues of national security which do not demand public discussion on the basis of all available information. It is inconceivable for example, that in a democratic society such major decisions as the military buildup in Vietnam should be made by a few top government officials, to the total exclusion of the rest of the country. It should be noted that the Supreme Court, in holding that warrantless wiretapping was not justified as a matter of national security, has rejected the basic contention that reasons of national security authorize government operations in violation of constitutional principles.

The national security exception, therefore, should be limited to those situations where nondisclosure is clearly justified as a matter of immediate military necessity. This would confine the exception largely to information concerning the development of new weapons and actual tactical military operations. Acceptance of such limited exceptions would, of course, bring about a drastic change in methods of making decisions concerning national security matters. The burden of showing the need for broader exceptions, however, is difficult to meet.

A third exception must be devised for some aspects of foreign relations. This is probably the most troublesome area to define or keep within bounds. The complexities are many. Thus other countries may not adhere to our views or practices with regard to disclosure of matters of mutual concern; negotiations with foreign nations involve a bargaining process, a situation which raises special problems discussed hereinafter; and relations with other countries sometimes involve the use of procedures, such as espionage and counter-espionage, which cannot be brought within the democratic principles upon which the theory of disclosure is premised. On the other hand, most of the information that has to do with foreign relations is of vital concern to the legislative branch and to the citizen. It is a safe assumption that much more information can be made public, without jeopardizing our foreign relations, than is now provided. The answer would seem to lie in framing exceptions in terms of those features which have just been noted as causing the major problems. Nondisclosure would not be justified merely because requested by another country: it would have to live with our policy. But secrecy would be permissible to the extent necessary to prevent revelation of bargaining positions, and protect espionage or counter-espionage activities.

A fourth exception is justified where decision making is the result of a bargaining process and the disclosure of information at a premature stage would jeopardize the negotiations. Such a situation arises in collective bargaining with a union of government employees, in advance disclosure of a position of litigation, or in other procedures which involve development of fall-back positions. Under such circumstances the government should be entitled to the same advantages as its opponent, or a nongovernment bargainer. The withholding of such information, which in any case would be temporary, would seem permissible.

The fifth exception, already mentioned, concerns protection of the right of privacy and would extend to certain personnel, loyalty and investigative files. Here the emphasis is upon the personal nature of the information. The material is normally not a matter of public concern and nondisclosure would not seriously affect the conduct of public business.

A final word needs to be said about the administration of such a system of open government. Experience to date with the Freedom of Information Act has shown that two administrative matters are of prime importance. One involves the problem of separating secret from nonsecret material when both kinds are embodied in the same document or occur in the same conversation. This separation may pose some difficulties, including some cost, but it is essential that the effort to separate be pursued to the maximum degree possible. The other essential administrative requirement is that the deci-

sion of whether to disclose or keep secret must not be entrusted exclusively to the branch of government which possesses the information. A neutral arbitrator is imperative. In practical terms this means that the courts should have power to review all actions of the executive and legislative branches on these issues and to make final determinations on the basis of the applicable principles of law.

The above formulations, though only rough approximations, may point the way to the kind of legal structure that is necessary to maintain an effective system of open government. If we can succeed in this, we shall go far to make the exercise of government power legitimate and to encourage its use only in the degree necessary to solve our pressing problems. And we shall almost certainly make future Watergate disasters impossible.

Attempts by the federal government and its agencies to suppress information by the device of prior restraint have multiplied in recent years. The Central Intelligence Agency has generally persuaded the courts that adverse revelations by former employees are impermissible for publication.

Most widely publicized was the Pentagon Papers case, eventually won by the press. Citing the doctrine of "executive privilege," which has no constitutional basis, the President may withhold information from Congress and the press, usually on the basis of "national security." About 95 percent of the contents of the Pentagon Papers, relating to the War in Vietnam, had been released or declassified when the *New York Times* decided to publish the complete record. Legal steps were taken by the Justice Department to ban publication. The U.S. Supreme Court rejected the government's application for prior restraint and upheld the press' freedom to publish. Following the Court's decision (*New York Times v. United States*), the *Times* said in an editorial:

The New York Times

"THE PENTAGON PAPERS"
CASE

The historic decision of the Supreme Court in the case of the United States Government vs. The New York Times and The Washington Post is a ringing victory for freedom under law. By lifting the restraining order that had prevented this and other newspapers from publishing the hitherto secret Pentagon Papers, the nation's highest tribunal strongly reaffirmed the guarantee of the people's right to know, implicit in the First Amendment to the Constitution of the United States.

This was the essence of what The New York Times and other newspapers were fighting for and this is the essence of the Court's majority opinions. The basic question, which goes to the very core of the American political system, involved the weighing by the Court of the First Amendment's guarantee of freedom against the Government's power to restrict that freedom in the name of national security. The Supreme Court did not hold that the First Amendment gave an absolute right to publish anything under all circumstances. Nor did The Times seek that right. What The Times sought and what the Court upheld, was the right to publish these particular documents at this particular time without prior Governmental restraint.

The crux of the problem lay indeed in this question of prior restraint. For the first time in the history of the United States, the Federal Government had sought through the courts to prevent publication of material that it maintained would do "irreparable injury" to the national security if spread before the public. The Times, supported in this instance by the overwhelming majority of the American press, held on the contrary that it was in the national interest to publish this information, which was historic rather than current operational nature.

If the documents had involved troop movements, ship sailings, imminent military plans, the case might have been quite different; and in fact The Times would not have endeavored to publish such material. But this was not the case; the documents and accompanying analysis are historic, in no instance going beyond 1968, and incapable in 1971 of harming the life of a single human being or interfering with any current military operation. The majority of the Court clearly recognized that embarrassment of public officials in the past—or even in the present—is insufficient reason to overturn what Justice White described as "the concededly extraordinary protection against prior restraint under our constitutional system."

So far as the Government's classification of the material is concerned, it is quite true, as some of our critics have observed, that "no one elected The Times" to declassify it. But it is also true, as the Court implicitly recognizes, that the public interest is not served by classification and retention in secret form of vast amounts of information, 99.5 per cent of which a retired senior civil servant recently testified "could not be prejudicial to the defense interests of the nation."

Out of this case should surely come a total revision of governmental procedures and practice in the entire area of classification of documents. Everyone who has ever had anything to do with such documents knows that for many years the classification procedures have been hopelessly muddled by inertia, timidity and sometimes even stupidity and venality.

Beyond all this, one may hope that the entire exercise will induce the present Administration to re-examine its own attitudes toward secrecy, suppression and restriction of the liberties of free man in a free society. The issue the Supreme Court decided yesterday touched the heart of this republic; and we fully realize that this is not so much a victory for any particular newspaper as it is for the basic principles of freedom on which the American form of government rests. This is really the profound message of yesterday's decision, in which this newspaper rejoices with humility and with the consciousness that the freedom thus reaffirmed carries with it, as always, the reciprocal obligation to present the truth to the American public so far as it can be determined. That is, in fact, why the Pentagon material had to be published. It is only with the fullest possible understanding of the facts and of the background of any policy decision that the American people can be expected to play the role required of them in this democracy.

It would be well for the present Administration, in the light of yesterday's decision, to reconsider with far more care and understanding than it has in the past, the fundamental importance of individual freedoms—including especially freedom of speech, of the press, of assembly—to the life of the American democracy. "Without an informed and free press," as Justice Stewart said, "there cannot be an enlightened people."

A former member of the staff of the *Washington Post* examines the decision of the U.S. Supreme Court in the case of the Pentagon Papers and assesses its significance for a free press.

Ben H. Bagdikian

WHAT DID WE LEARN?

To the casual eye, the newsroom of the Washington *Post* at mid-afternoon of June 30 must have looked normal—normal, that is, for the *Post*: cramped, noisy, anarchic-democratic, the most interesting journalistic slum in America. There were no obvious signs of stress created by nearly three weeks of the most extraordinary events in the history of American journalism.

At one end of the newsroom the *Post's* owner and publisher, Katharine Graham, and its executive editor, Benjamin Bradlee,

and a small band of associated sufferers were awaiting word from company lawyers at the Supreme Court building, two miles away. In the middle of the newsroom, Mary Lou Beatty, deputy national editor, held an open telephone line to the Supreme Court pressroom, waiting for the paper's court reporters to be handed the printed decision. In a communications room, Eugene Patterson, then managing editor, monitored the wire machines in case the word came first from them. Suddenly Miss Beatty held up her hands as she listened to a court reporter at the other end of the line riffle through the fifty-six-page decision. She yelled toward the executives, "It looks as though we've won." Then Gene Patterson rushed out of the wire room, leaped onto a desk, and with his hands cupped around his mouth shouted, "We win, 6-to-3!"

In the euphoria of the newsroom that afternoon and throughout the country's journalistic establishment in the weeks since, something ominous seems to have escaped notice. It is not the fact that the newspapers and journalists might be criminally prosecuted or cited for contempt when asked to testify about their sources—though at this writing there is a grand jury sitting and the Government is emanating strong signals. The journalists are affluent and well known and will march to court with much public notice and skilled lawyers, and at worst will probably avoid the psychopathic horrors of contemporary prisons; it is the uncelebrated little people who get quietly locked up on dubious grounds without glory.

The euphoria is unjustified because the Supreme Court decision probably signalizes not the triumphant end, but the start of a struggle. The astonishing cluster of major issues involved in the court case moves onward with an uncertain future; legitimacy of the war in Vietnam; deception by the Government; secrecy in government; and freedom of the press.

This is not to slight the accomplishments so far. The New York *Times* acquired the Pentagon Papers first and took the icy plunge without benefit of precedent. Once the *Times* was silenced, the *Post* went ahead knowing that it would be hauled into court and knowing that the Nixon Administration hates the *Post* and the *Times* with a passion deeper than Spiro Agnew's thesaurus. Other metropolitan papers followed the silencing of the *Post* and *Times* with their own slices of the secret papers. Like relics of St. George, whose spine is in Portofino, skull in Rome, a hand in Genoa, a finger in London, the bits and pieces of the Pentagon Papers had escaped their secret reliquary in the crypts of the Government and reappeared throughout the country in a finally credible sense of reality about the Government and the war and a metastasized affront to the Espionage Act. The major papers did not shirk their duty and the Supreme Court upheld them.

But the Supreme Court victory should not obscure some troublesome facts. Courts officially ordered American newspapers not to publish certain materials because these materials offended the Government (like all censoring governments, Mr. Nixon's claimed that the offensive material would do grave and irreparable harm to the nation). From June 15 to June 30 there was official, effective, court-enforced suppression of information in the hands of American newspapers. Nothing prevents the Government from bringing similar suits in the future, and win or not in the Supreme Court it can suppress information for a period of time and intimidate a paper.

Government antagonism to the press is not new or bad. The press shouldn't expect to be loved. Franklin Roosevelt had a running battle with publishers, Harry Truman ridiculed "newspaper talk," Dwight Eisenhower viewed the press with cool contempt, John Kennedy enjoyed periodic outbursts of venom on the subject, and Lyndon Johnson's sentiments about newspapers would cause Bella Abzug to blush. But this Administration has a special attitude toward the working press that is ideological and cultural, it has a political stake in spreading hatred of the metropolitan press, and unlike other administrations that fought with the press this one has an itch for the jugular.

A major reason given by some judges for refusing the Government request was that Congress had not yet passed a law giving the President the power to censor the press. If such a law existed, these judges said, the decision might have been different. In 1917, in a time of war and hysteria about spying, Congress specifically voted down an amendment to the Espionage Act that would have made the President a censor. In 1950 during the height of McCarthyism, the Espionage Act was amended to say—with puzzling implications—that nothing in the Act shall infringe on freedom of the press. Secrecy in government is by Executive Order, not law.

Given the Nixon Administration approach to the free press and broadcasting, the tendency of this court is not encouraging. Only three justices—Black, Douglas, and Brennan—explicitly turned their backs on the idea of both presidential and Congressional power to censor. Justice Black said that when he reads that the First Amendment says Congress shall make no law abridging freedom of the press, he interprets "no law to mean no law." To which Erwin Griswold, Solicitor General, representing the Government, replied, "I can only say, Mr. Justice, that to me it is equally obvious that 'no law' does not mean 'no law'. . . . The First Amendment was not intended to make it impossible for the Executive to function or to protect the security of the United States." Each of the nine justices felt impelled to write a separate opinion, and if one reads these for attitudes on the legitimacy of Congress' taking up a measure to give the President censorship powers, the apparent willingness to accept this is 6-to-3.

The reversed 6-to-3 is ironic, but so was much more in the case. The New York *Times'* regular law firm, Lord, Day & Lord, did not take up the case. Its head is former Attorney General Herbert Brownell. The Washington *Post's* law firm, Royall, Koegel & Wells, did take up the case. Its former head is the present Secretary of State and presumably one of the aggrieved parties in the printing of the Pentagon Papers, William P. Rogers. The case also saw those "strict constructionists," John Mitchell and Richard Nixon, asking the Supreme Court to "make law"—that is, give the president powers that Congress had refused.

Some judges asked in all earnestness why a responsible newspaper would not ask the Government what part of official papers it could publish. It is a discouraging question, asking that papers accept informally what the First Amendment forbids officially, putting a construction on "responsible" that makes the press an instrument of official policy on the most vital issues. This was not the kind of issue the framers of the Constitution had in mind. King George III didn't mind if the colonial press reported on the weather; it was all that disrespectful information about royal governors and tax collectors that it printed without the advice and consent of the local Governor. The First Amendment was not written with the idea that the press would be free to print the names of donors to the Santa Claus Fund but have to ask the Government for permission to write about war and peace.

In addition there seemed in some justices to be a personal hostility to the press. Chief Justice Burger wrote, "To me it is hardly believable that a newspaper long regarded as a great institution in American life would fail to perform one of the basic and simple duties of every citizen with respect to the discovery or possession of stolen property or secret government documents. That duty, I had thought—perhaps naïvely—was to report forthwith, to responsible public officers. This duty rests on taxi drivers, Justices, and the New York *Times*." He added in a footnote, "Interestingly, the *Times* explained its refusal to allow the Government to examine its own purloined documents by saying in substance this might compromise their sources and informants! The *Times* thus asserts a right to guard the secrecy of its sources while denying that the Government of the United States has that power."

Judge Blackmun exhibited the same feelings. He wrote, ". . . the Washington *Post*, on the excuse that it was trying to protect its source of information, initially refused to reveal what material it actually possessed. . . ." He concluded, "I strongly urge, and sincerely hope, that these two newspapers will be fully aware of their ultimate responsibility to the United States of America. . . ."

What emerged throughout the case was a dangerous naïveté among judges, lawyers, and others about government propaganda, the frequency with which government agencies break the law or improperly invade privacy, and the true relationship between the federal government and the press in Washington. The grim and terrible condemnations about "secrets" look different when you know that highly placed government officials, beginning with the President of the United States and his Cabinet, the Joint Chiefs of Staff and their staffs, regularly and systematically violate the Espionage Act— or at least the Attorney General's interpretation of it—by knowingly and deliberately disclosing secret information to the press. . . .

The quantity of military secrets that appear in the press is directly related to appropriation hearings for the military services. If the Air Force wants a few billion dollars for a new weapons system, it leaks a few secrets that put the system in a good light. Two days later the Navy leaks other secrets about the same weapons system showing that it fails much of the time. Or the State Department, wanting to bluff another nation, lets out a secret that is a half-truth, then denies it the next day as "newspaper talk." And perhaps the Pentagon, which disapproved anyway, leaks the whole story of how the State Department leaked a half-truth. The net result is probably good because it is the only present remedy to secret government, but the point is that the U.S. Government is the biggest player in town of the Leaking Secrets Game. Only when the secrets are embarrassing do the words "national security" come into play.

The idea that in matters of secrecy and responsibility the press is beholden to "the United States of America" sees the Government as a policy monolith. There is no such entity, either in the Constitution or in practice. It is a pluralistic organism whose parts work on each other with various mechanisms, one of the more important being information. If the press did not obtain secrets or was not handed secrets on a silver platter, the Government would have to invent some other way of getting out sequestered information.

The harm done by disclosure of secrets is minimal; the harm done by concealing information inside the secrecy system is enormous. President Kennedy ultimately told the New York *Times* that it should have printed more about the Bay of Pigs invasion of Cuba rather than less. Both the *Times* and the *Post* knew about the U-2 airplane flights over Russia months before the story broke. Both suppressed it in what they thought was the national interest. Soviet Russia knew about the plane all the time—its radar picked it up—but for a while it lacked planes and missiles with the range to shoot down the plane. Nonpublication merely kept the information from the Russian and American publics, a convenience to each government whose implications are interesting indeed. Ultimately the U-2 was shot down, with the result that lives were endangered, a summit conference was wrecked, and a presidential visit to Moscow cancelled—the usual scenario of what it is said will happen if secrets are published.

It seems safe to predict catastrophe if information is disclosed. If the information is protected by secrecy the prediction can never be tested, and keeping the secret seems the more prudent course. But intelligent, diligent men differ on the consequences of printing sensitive information. Justice White examined the Government lists of "worst cases" it wanted suppressed in the Pentagon Papers and said he was confident that publication by the *Post* and *Times* "will do substantial damage to public interests." Justice Stewart looked at the same lists and said, "I cannot say that disclosure of any of them will surely result in direct, immediate, and irreparable damage to our nation or its people."

The judges were not the only ones who differed on the wisdom of publishing. There were arguments within the papers themselves. The *Post* reached its initial decision after about twelve continuous hours of intense debate. The argument, involving lawyers, editors, reporters, and management, was fierce and prolonged. It ran through one deadline and was finally resolved five minutes before the deadline for the main edition. In the end, Katharine Graham took the full weight of argument and said yes.

As the lawyers and later the judges began looking beneath the awesome claim of TOP SECRET they began to see that it was seldom justified. List after list submitted by the Government to the Court in secret was shown to be filled with items already in the public domain or already known to adversary nations. The Government official brought in to testify in secret court session on how bad it would be to publish the documents later told Congress that at least 6,000 pages of the 7,000 should not be classified.

Newspapermen in Washington already knew things like that. Last year during the heat of an armaments debate, the *Post* received in a plain envelope without return address a Xerox of a document marked, SECRET—SENSITIVE. We called the Pentagon to confirm the document's authenticity and then printed it in full. It was a memorandum from Secretary of Defense Melvin Laird to his service secretaries and other military officials telling them they should say nothing in public that might imply that it would be good to have a moratorium on deploying MIRV missiles or ABMs. It was a directive to subordinates on what to say in public on an important public issue—a natural enough impulse from an official trying to win an argument among his rival officials in government. But *secret?* The *Post* received a letter from the Department of Defense telling it to turn over the memo under pain of prosecution under the Espionage Act.

When Mr. Laird was a member of the opposition in Congress, he wrote a stiff letter, in October of 1966, demanding to know the Government's negotiating position in the Vietnam war, including how many

American troops we were offering to pull back in return for how many enemy troops. He demanded publicly that the Government "should spell out clearly and unequivocally what our short-term aims and long-term objectives are with regard to South Vietnam and Southeast Asia."

The issues involved are too profound to argue about whose ox is being gored, though that impels much of the secrecy machinery. What is more basic is that even when there is a discernible reason for keeping information secret, every piece of information marked SECRET erodes the basis for a free society. It excludes the citizen from the process of his own government, and that is a cost that has to be put into the "national security" equation.

This country was started on the assumption that legitimate government derives its powers from the consent of the governed, and if that means anything those who are governed have to know what their government is doing. Yet we have lived under the spreading mystique of the official secret for so long that there is an assumption that information about public affairs is the private property of the Government. Somewhere, somehow, the burden has shifted from the Government having to prove why it should conceal information, to the citizen, who now has to prove why he should be told. The Solicitor General even argued the analogy of the copyright law to the Supreme Court.

The country seems to have lost sight of the fact that true security lies in knowledge, not secrecy. During the Supreme Court hearing Justice Stewart asked the *Times*' lawyer, Alexander Bickel, whether he would change his insistence on the Constitutional right to publish if doing so would result in the death of "100 young men whose only offense had been that they were nineteen years old and had low draft numbers."

The information in the Pentagon Papers covers the years 1945-1968. The documents were not published during that period. More than 1 million Indochinese have been killed, more than 50,000 young Americans were killed, we have spent $120 billion dollars, and have descended into one of the most poisonous eras in our time. The calculation of the costs of secrecy is not small.

The need for press freedom is not simply an intellectually elegant idea. The perfect secret is useless because information is powerful only if it causes men to understand their environment better. If information is secret, not enough people know enough to put the information to use, nor to correct errors. The open society avoids catastrophic accumulations of maladjustment because everyone in the system is free to express himself and be heard by those who can make adjustments. "Responsibility" is not a safe standard. What is irresponsible to one man is responsible to another, or at another time. When Richard Nixon was a member of Congress he and his friends were prepared to send men to jail for suggesting normalizing relations with the Communist government of mainland China. It was a "bad," "treasonable," "subversive" idea. President Richard Nixon is now planning to go to China in order to start normalizing relations with the Communist government of mainland China.

The free marketplace of ideas, and the press's role in it, is not a luxury, nor is it a sometime thing to be tolerated only when it pleases the authorities. The press itself needs to remember its obligations. When the press insists on making its own decisions on publishing official information independent of government it is sometimes painted as arrogant. But the reverse is true. For a newspaper to know something to be accurate and important and not to trust the public with it is arrogant. To withhold the truth from the public is to hold the public in contempt.

Justice Burger was amazed that the press would not give up its documents while criticizing government secrecy. Justice Blackmun thought that the *Post* was using protection of its sources as an "excuse." The fact is that government has the full force of its police powers to shut off the porosity of information that saves the United Government from the sickness of secrecy.

The anger of government at press intrusion is an ancient emotion. Roger L'Estrange was Licenser of the Press in London in 1680. He said: "A newspaper makes the multitude too familiar with the actions and councils of their superiors and gives them not only an itch but a kind of colorable right and license to be meddling with the Government."

Governments never like to be meddled with. But it happens to be the whole idea of the American political system.

Having won in the Supreme Court, the press now must fight the more insidious self-censorship that comes when it tries to avoid future confrontations, when it concedes in the newsroom what it won in the courts. Better than Roger L'Estrange is the more contemporary wisdom of Elmer Davis, who said in the height of the Joe McCarthy era:

"Don't let them scare you. For the men who are trying to do that to us are scared themselves. They are afraid that what they think will not stand critical examination; they are afraid that the principles on which this Republic was founded and has been conducted are wrong. They will tell you that there is a hazard in the freedom of the mind and of course there is, as in any freedom. In trying to think right you run the risk of thinking wrong. But there is no hazard at all, no uncertainty, in letting somebody else tell you what to think; that is sheer damnation."

A continual conflict goes on between the press and other media whose job it is to seek out information and to inform the public and governmental agencies apparently intent on suppressing unfavorable facts. Using as disguises national security and budget reductions, fearful bureaucrats resist complying with the provisions of the Freedom of Information Act. The Freedom of Information Act was originally enacted by Congress in 1966 and was substantially strengthened in 1974. Under the law citizens may demand information on government activities in any except top-secret matters.

Under a presidential order issued in October 1981, government officials may classify information even if they are uncertain whether secrecy is needed to protect national security. The order reversed long-standing government policy that mandates a firm determination of national security danger before a secrecy stamp can be applied—a policy that had been endorsed by President Nixon in 1972 and President Carter in 1978.

The new order, which the President can implement on his own authority, includes other changes that increase governmental power to deny public access to documents related to national security. The order states, "If there is reasonable doubt about the need to classify information, the information shall be considered classified." In contrast, a directive issued earlier by Henry Kissinger as national security adviser stated, "If the classifier has any substantial doubt as to which security classification is appropriate, or as to whether the material should be classified at all, he should designate the less restrictive treatment."

The Carter order in 1978 contained similar language, declaring that in cases of "reasonable doubt the less restrictive (security) designation should be used, or the information should not be classified." The order stated further, that government officials must "determine whether the public interest in disclosure outweighs the damage to national security that might reasonably be expected from disclosure."

The 1981 order loosens the guidelines for what government information can be withheld as "confidential." The classification previously applied was reported to have kept 75 percent of the 300,000 government documents from public view each year. Under the revised rules the "confidential" stamp could be applied to documents for which unauthorized disclosure "reasonably could be expected to cause damage to the national security." A former member of the National Security Council staff described the changes as "an enormous step backward."

The new presidential order eliminates a rule under the Carter administration that classified documents should be reviewed within six years to decide whether national security requires that they continue to be kept secret or they should be released to the public, and further that all documents should be released except in extraordinary circumstances. The revised rule simply declares that "information should be classified for as long as required by national security considerations." Also, information previously released to the public may be reclassified.

Jack C. Landau

PRESIDENT REAGAN AND THE PRESS

The free flow of information and news is headed for a most difficult period due to pressure from two sources: unrelenting and continuous pressure from the state and federal courts and dangerous new threats launched by the Reagan Administration.

President Reagan and his top advisors have initiated a coordinated campaign to impose massive content censorship and information restrictions on government news reporting to the public.

In addition, the Congress, either on its own or in consort with the Administration, has joined in a number of these censorship efforts.

Meanwhile, litigation against the press continues to increase all over the nation and judges continue to pressure the press on many constitutional fronts, especially closed courtrooms, libel, and confidential sources.

Therefore, taken together, there is now an unprecedented combination of legal and political forces moving to strangle critical channels of information traditionally relied on by the press to inform the public.

The Administration effort covers a whole range of news including reporting on foreign affairs, national defense policy, law enforcement, intelligence practices, consumer affairs, environmental and pollution threats

Reprinted with permission from the February-March 1982 issue of The News Media & the Law.

and government legal settlements—to mention some of the most troublesome.

The government also has resorted to the full range of information restriction weapons: the criminal law of prosecutions and contempt; the civil law of injunctions, fines and impoundments; executive regulations; published policy statements and the office of the Presidency itself.

FOREIGN AFFAIRS AND DEFENSE POLICY

Starting in the spring of 1981, the Administration began its campaign to limit news reporting on foreign affairs and defense policy which it decided to label as "national security"—a disinformation effort designed to appeal to patriotism.

These included supporting the "Agent Identities Bill" which would make it a crime to name an intelligence agent even if he is breaking federal law and regulations; seeking a total exemption for the CIA from the FOI [Freedom of Information] Act; and proposing regulations to keep secret massive collections of historical documents now available to scholars and journalists.

Other news restriction efforts in the foreign affairs area were: a CIA ruling that it would only brief reporters if they would brief the Agency on what they knew; telling the Supreme Court that the identities of foreign government officials, who were naturalized American citizens, should be kept secret, and finally requiring that all interviews with the press on foreign affairs and defense must be pre-cleared by White House officials.

The White House pre-clearance memo was subsequently revoked after a stormy confrontation between White House officials and reporters.

CONFIDENTIAL SOURCES

While the Reagan Administration efforts to violate editorial privacy have not yet reached the level of the Nixon efforts, there are a number of disturbing developments to be noted including:

Allowing intelligence agents to once again infiltrate and spy on the press with the approval of the attorney general; giving lie detector tests to government employees suspected of leaking information, and undermining the Justice Department guidelines for subpoenas to the press by refusing to defend the guidelines in court.

Also, Attorney General William French Smith has said he would support surprise raids on newsrooms to discover the source of national security leaks.

FEDERAL FOI ACT

The Administration is supporting a bill, introduced by Sen. Orrin Hatch (R-Utah) which would mutilate existing public accountability available under the Federal FOI Act.

The bill would establish new and wholesale secrecy for many types of government documents now available including those showing: that the FBI, IRS and other law enforcement agents are violating the law or the constitution; that dangerous consumer products and fraudulent services are being offered to the public; that communities are endangered by pollution or other environmental threats, and that intelligence agents are violating Presidential policy statements.

In addition, the bill would keep secret details of government legal settlements, even those done by conflict of interest or bribery offers and would establish massive new red tape obstacles for reporters and scholars wanting to use the FOI Act.

PRIOR RESTRAINT ON PUBLICATION

Even in this area—considered the classic area of First Amendment protection—the Administration has forged ahead somewhat successfully mainly by resorting to its claims of protecting the national security.

It has announced it will seek court injunctions against all former agents who want to publish books and articles even if they disclose no classified information and will enforce no-notice passport cancellations against citizens who publish articles officials believe harm national security.

It has continued to threaten a CBS freelancer with an espionage prosecution for importing books containing American embassy cables which are freely sold in Teheran bookstalls; has continued to hold up the importation of books and newspapers from Cuba and, through the Deputy Director of the CIA, has suggested that all university research—which could be helpful to the Soviet Union—should be pre-cleared by the government.

It has also supported the Federal Criminal Code Reform bill which contains a number of troublesome provisions including one which would permit a news organization to be held in contempt for defying an unconstitutional order prohibiting a newspaper from publishing the news.

COPYRIGHT OF GOVERNMENT INFORMATION

Perhaps all of these efforts are best symbolized by the Administration's support of a bill which would, for the first time in history, charge citizens "royalties" and "fees" for the commercial value of government information.

The theory seems to be that the "government" is something separate and apart from the "people"—some type of private corporation—and therefore its information is not the "people's" information. This would reverse 200 years of law and tradition that government information belongs to the people and may be used by them for free.

In a sense, that is what the Reagan Administration campaign to restrict news reporting is all about. They are saying to the public: this is "our government," not "your government;" this is "our information" not "your information"—and if you publish "our information" without our approval, we will jail you, or fine you, or restrain you or impound you or wiretap you or intimidate your sources or close down the records of whole agencies.

In short, the Administration is saying: "We are not accountable to 'you' (the public), we are only accountable to 'us' (the government)."

Is that the kind of country we all want?

A *New York Times* columnist believes that true freedom of the press is to decide for itself what to publish and when to publish it; true responsibility of the press must be to assert that freedom.

Tom Wicker

OUR ALL-TOO-TIMID PRESS

The First Amendment does not say anything about "responsibility." This observation, which I have offered to hundreds of disbelieving and usually disapproving audiences, invariably brings some challenger to his or her feet with something like the following inquiry (usually varied more in its degree of choler than in wording): "Do you mean to say that the press has a right to be irresponsible?"

I mean to say nothing of the sort, although it's true—just to be argumentative—that irresponsibility does not appear to the layman's eye to be a constitutional violation. But it's just as well for journalists in particular to recall the skeptical judgment in *The Federalist* of Alexander Hamilton—who opposed as unnecessary a Bill of Rights for the Constitution:

What is the liberty of the press? Who can give it any definition which would not leave the utmost latitude for evasion? I hold it to be impracticable; and from this I infer that its security, whatever fine declarations may be inserted in any constitution respecting it, must altogether depend on public opinion, and on the general spirit of the people and of the government.

Just so. And with that in mind, no journalist should advocate to the public the idea that the press has "a right to be irresponsible"; no one could agree to that. Nor should any journalist wish the press or broadcast news to *be* irresponsible. Aside from their pride in their craft and its institutions, their desire to do their personal work well, and their concern that the public should be informed, all

journalists know that popular contempt for and fear of press irresponsibility are as grave threats—and more justified ones—to a free press as are government attempts to silence it. And, as Hamilton foresaw, that part of the First Amendment might not long survive a hostile, determined public opinion.

Granting all that, a certain case for tolerance of irresponsibility still has to be made. That is to say, if the American press is to remain free—even in the somewhat limited sense that necessarily results from the conflict of this freedom with the other equally guaranteed freedoms in the Constitution and the Bill of Rights—it cannot have responsibility imposed on it by legislation, judicial interpretation, or any other process.

Freedom contains within itself the possibility of irresponsibility. No man is truly free who is not permitted occasionally to be irresponsible; nor is any institution. Responsibility, it goes without saying, is profoundly important; and the highest freedom of all may well be the freedom to conduct one's life and affairs responsibly—but by one's own standards of responsibility. It's a mean freedom in which a mere failure of responsibility brings a jail term or a fine or some other societally imposed penalty—and no freedom at all if standards of responsibility are uniform, designed to prevent rather than to punish failures, and set by higher authority.

Yet some of the most sweeping restrictions on the freedom of the press have been proposed in the name of preventing press irresponsibility. What is lost sight of is that if responsibility can be imposed, freedom must be lost; and of those who advocate various means of ensuring the responsibility of a supposedly free press, two questions should be asked:

Who defines responsibility? In numerous instances, the difficulty editors and reporters have in determining a responsible course in disputed circumstances has, I believe, been demonstrated—notably in the case of *The New York Times*'s treatment of the Bay of Pigs story. In literally thousands of other instances—most of them less important but many on the same level of seriousness—editors have no hard-and-fast rules to follow, save those of experience, ethics, and common sense—all of which vary from person to person. Editors may, and often do, differ on what is responsible—even as *Times* editors differed among themselves on handling the Bay of Pigs story. There simply is no certainty, in most instances, as to what constitutes a responsible course in an enormous number of cases that editors and reporters have to face.

Most journalists believe that the multiplicity of editorial decisions likely to result in any given case is a major safeguard against irresponsibility and misinformation. All editors won't make the same decision based on the same set of facts—a story played on page one by the *Times* may be printed inside *The Washington Post*; a quotation in the one story may not appear in the other; different lines of interpretation may well be taken by the two papers and by any number of others, with the result that the same story appears in many versions and with a greater or lesser degree of prominence. This rich diversity not only works against the possibility that any story can be covered up or manufactured but it also offers a reasonable guarantee that differing viewpoints on the same events will reach the public.

Not only, therefore, would the imposition of standards of responsibility on the press move it away from diversity and toward uniformity of presentation but it would require an instrument big enough and comprehensive enough to define responsibility in an immense number of instances, for a huge number of publications and broadcasters. No such instrument exists, save the government.

Who enforces responsibility? This is a simpler problem. Once responsibility is defined, obviously nothing of sufficient power and scope exists to force the defined responsibility on the entire press—again save the government.

Thus, if we are to be *sure* of a responsible press, the only way is through a government that both defines and enforces responsibility. Not just Richard Nixon would have leaped at *that* opportunity. It need scarcely even be pointed out that in such circumstances, the condition of the American press would be a far cry from freedom.

Would that matter?

Obviously, a totally government-controlled press would make much difference to liberty in America; but that is not what most of those who demand greater press responsibility have in mind. They more often set forth a supposedly middle course—yielding a little freedom in a beneficial trade-off to gain some responsibility.

The middle-course argument is respectable. It cannot be maintained by the most ardent First Amendment advocate that democracy is not reasonably healthy in Britain, where the press is under much greater restraint than it is in the United States. Libel laws that sharply restrict publication and broadcasting; a heavy bias toward privacy rather than publication in laws governing press reports on criminal justice proceedings and other actions of the courts; the Official Secrets Act that governments of both parties frequently invoke, apparently not always in matters of indisputable national security; and the quasi-governmental Press Council to monitor and criticize press activities—have these stifled the larger British democracy? From my side of the Atlantic, I cannot say that they have.

For whatever reasons, the history of British politics is by no means as marked by venality and corruption as is that of the United States, and governing ethics and traditions there appear so settled that serious violations of them—for example, a power grab such as that represented by the Watergate complex of offenses—are far less likely. Secrecy by the British government has been widely accepted for centuries. Profound policy miscalculations—the Suez War, for example—bring quick political retribution, Official Secrets Act or no, while more egregious American blunders in Vietnam and Cambodia for years produced in the United States mostly a "rally-round-the-President" effect, until the press—primarily television—finally turned the public against the war (by printing and broadcasting *news*, not editorials).

Therefore, press restraints perhaps amenable to British democracy—although not many British journalists really consider them so—would not necessarily be fitting in the United States. Should a Watergate occur in the United Kingdom, colleagues in the British press say, the governing party plausibly accused of conniving in the burglary of opposition party headquarters and then of obstructing justice to conceal the crime would soon be turned out of office, despite restrictions on reporting such a story. But it was a challenging American press that kept Watergate in the public eye and ultimately forced the various actions that led to Richard Nixon's resignation—at that, two years after the offense.

But the existence of restrictions on the British press, together with the evident survival of the essential British democracy, leads many serious and reasonable persons to suggest not government control of the American press but similar instruments of responsibility in this country's journalistic practice.

When the Senate in 1977 established an oversight committee for the so-called intelligence community, for example, one of the committee's first studies was of the need, if any, for a limited form of Official Secrets Act in the United States—an effort to protect the CIA from the public rather than the public from the CIA that stood the committee's supposed responsibility on its head.

The discussed act's reach would ostensibly have been limited to barring disclosures of "sources and methods" of gathering intelligence—"ostensibly" because although "sources and methods" describes an arcane art and is a term therefore supposedly capable of being strictly defined and narrowly applied, both the FBI and the CIA have in the past shown themselves capable of slipping large abuses through tiny loopholes. It

was, for example, supposedly to protect sources and methods that some of the CIA's mail-opening and surveillance operations were illegally pursued.

Whatever the situation in Britain, in this country—as I hope I have demonstrated—secrecy has too often been used to shield blunders, crimes, and ineptitude. Alert citizens should not accept without sharp questioning a secrecy law designed to give a secret agency even greater powers of covering up its operations than it already has. And unless Congress were to show an uncharacteristic willingness to include a "shield" provision for reporters—which it has never done in other legislation of less importance and which would be of dubious constitutionality—a likely consequence would be about as follows:

The leak of a secret protected by the act would appear as a news story in a newspaper or on a broadcast. An inquiry would be launched; but as usual, the identity of the leaker (who could be prosecuted under the new law) would not be learned. The reporter-recipient of the leak would be subpoenaed to appear before a grand jury and would be asked the identity of his source, with a view to prosecuting the leaker. It would be made clear that no other means existed of obtaining this information vital to enforcement of the Official Secrets Act and the orderly administration of government.

The reporter would abide by his professional code of ethics and would refuse to answer. He would then be held in contempt and ordered to jail—although there might be no evidence of any damage to national security as a consequence of his or her story. A lot of reporters would have a lot of second thoughts—chilling indeed—about accepting leaks of so-called security secrets under such a threat.

Would that serve the cause of responsibility? Once again, the answer depends upon who defines responsibility in any given case; but those who place a high value upon a "robust and uninhibited press" and who have learned to be skeptical of the government's assertions of "national security" are not likely to think so.

But even if no such drastic step as instituting an Official Secrets Act was taken, why not more restrictive libel and privacy laws? Would they limit press freedom so severely as to threaten the public's right and need to know? And what about a non-governmental press council, at least to criticize—constructively, as well as punitively—press performance, even if the council had no real power to punish or penalize?

The question of more severe libel and privacy laws requires, essentially, a value judgment. There isn't much doubt that greater protection from press charges than is now provided for public officials would limit the ability of the press to act as a check on the power of government; but some reasonable persons believe the press has too much latitude to criticize government, expose its workings, penetrate needed confidentiality, and hinder its effectiveness. Similarly, no one should be in doubt that stricter protection of individual privacy from searching press inquiry would frequently prevent needed public exposure and discussion of personalities, institutions, and processes; but few in the press would deny that the power of the press has too often been the instrument by which have come unwarranted personal humiliations, embarrassments, misfortunes, and losses of reputation and livelihood.

As for a U.S. press council, the National News Council has been financed and supported by the Twentieth Century Fund, which is neither conservative nor antipress. Neither have been the first workings of the council, which is supported by many in the press and broadcasting and which has no connection with the government. Its purpose is to conduct quiet private investigations of controversial press or broadcasting decisions and to report publicly on whether or not those decisions were taken responsibly and on reasonable grounds. The council has no power, other than the force of its disapproval, to penalize news organizations.

Concerned journalists have argued that the press and broadcasting ought to cooperate wholeheartedly with the News Council. Most news organizations, they say, would have nothing to fear; and it would be better for those who might be culpable to be censured by a private group with press interests at heart than by unsympathetic courts or legislatures. Besides, say the advocates, by certifying in most disputed cases that editorial decisons have been responsibly and reasonably taken, the council would more often reassure the public than threaten the press.

In short, these journalists view the News Council as a good public relations instrument for the press. Not only would news organizations appear to be trying to police their own work and that of colleagues but most would periodically be given a good bill of health by a respected panel of citizens, while irresponsible publications and broadcasts would be sternly reprimanded by a council backed by the press itself.

But there is another underlying reason why there has been considerable press support for the News Council. Seldom stated outside newsrooms, journalism classes, or press club bars, it is that the News Council idea offers a safe way to "clean up the press before the government comes in and does it for us." This suggests that even many who are themselves deeply involved in American journalism believe that there are so many excesses and malpractices that need to be cleaned up that the press really does face possible governmental control. And that points straight to the fundamental reason why I personally am opposed to the News Council, to more restrictive privacy and libel laws, and to all other schemes for enforcing the responsibility of a supposedly free press—reasonable as some of these schemes undoubtedly appear in their proposals for only limited sacrifices of freedom.

The overwhelming conclusion I have drawn from my life in journalism—nearly 30 years so far, from the *Sandhill Citizen* to *The New York Times*—is that the American press, powerful as it unquestionably is and protected though it may be by the Constitution and the laws, is not often "robust and uninhibited" but is usually timid and anxious—for respectability at least as much as for profitability. Those whose ideas of the press is bounded by the exploits of Woodward and Bernstein on the one hand and by the Pentagon Papers on the other do not usually understand that such remarkable efforts as these—whether or not they are viewed as necessary or excessive—are limited exceptions to long-established practice.

Undoubtedly, in the more than a decade since Dwight Eisenhower roused the Goldwaterites with his attack on "sensation-seeking columnists," the press has become more activist and challenging, particularly in covering politics and government—though *not* business and financial institutions. On the evidence of press performance in that decade—the disclosure of duplicity and ineptitude in Vietnam; the exposure of political corruption in the Nixon administration; the demonstration of grave threats to American liberty by the "Imperial Presidency," the FBI, the CIA, and other security agencies—I assert the necessity to encourage the developing tendency of the press to shake off the encumbrance of a falsely objective journalism and to take an adversary position toward the most powerful institutions of American life.

By "adversary position," I don't mean a necessarily hostile position; I use the word in the lawyer's sense of cross-examining, testing, challenging, the merits of a case in the course of a trial. Such an adversary is opposed only in the sense that he or she demands that a case be made: the law stated, the facts proven, the assumptions and conclusions justified, the procedure squared with common sense and good practice. An adversary press would hold truth—unattainable and frequently plural as it is—as its highest value and knowledge as its first responsibility.

Such a press should be encouraged in its independence, not investigated—even by its friends—when it asserts that independence. A relatively toothless News Council that nevertheless could summon editors and reporters, notes and documents, film and outtakes, in order to determine publicly whether editorial decisions had been properly made *by the News Council's standards* would be bound to have an ultimately inhibiting effect on editors, publishers, and broadcasters—not all of whom would therefore be dismayed. Most, it's safe to say, would rather be praised for someone else's idea of responsibility than risk being questioned or criticized for their own independence.

Somewhat similarly, tighter libel and privacy laws would surely narrow the area open to editorial judgment—and some editors and publishers might welcome such laws just for that reason. Some might even yearn privately for an Official Secrets Act because its proscriptions would relieve them of having to decide such difficult questions as whether or not to publish so-called national security stories and of the loud accusations of irresponsibility that inevitably follow such decisions, no matter how they are made.

My belief is that the gravest threat to freedom of the press is not necessarily from public animosity or mistrust, legislative action or court decision. Certainly even though absolute press freedom may sometimes have to accommodate itself to other high constitutional values, the repeal or modification of the First Amendment seems unlikely. At least as great a threat, I believe, comes from the press itself—in its longing for a respectable place in the established political and economic order, in its fear of the reaction that boldness and independence will always evoke. Self-censorship silences as effectively as a government decree, and we have seen it far more often.

In the harsh sunlight of a robust freedom, after all, nothing stands more starkly exposed than the necessity to decide and to accept the responsibility for decision. If the true freedom of the press is to decide for itself what to publish and when to publish it, the true responsibility of the press must be to assert that freedom.

But my life in journalism has persuaded me that the press too often tries to guard its freedom by shirking its responsibility and that this leads to default on both. What the press in America needs is less inhibition, not more restraint.

LIBEL AND THE INVASION OF PRIVACY

One of the earliest exceptions made to First Amendment guarantees was to protect the individual citizen from false and abusive treatment and invasion of privacy by the press. The courts over the years developed the doctrine that would except, however, political (and later public) figures from protection against critical comment in the press. Today a delicate interplay is taking place between publishing and individual rights under the First Amendment, witness the current case of General Westmoreland against CBS News over treatment of the general in a documentary on Vietnam.

Various commentators, viewing the increasing number of libel suits and enormous damages awarded when such suits are won by the plaintiffs, are alarmed at their impact on a free press, suggesting that the courts are being used to muzzle the press. This is the concern of Alan U. Schwartz, a California lawyer specializing in the field of communications, who fears that recent Supreme Court decisions may result in excessive self-censorship by reporters.

Alan U. Schwartz

USING THE COURTS TO MUZZLE THE PRESS

Censorship, in some form or other, exists in every country in the world. While the brutal repressions of the Soviet Union are very different from the inhibitions imposed by the Official Secrets Act in Great Britain, for example, the reason for governmental restrictions on speech and press are essentially the same in both cases: the need for balance—sometimes horribly distorted, sometimes restrained and well-meaning—between the right of individuals to information and the right of a state to self-protection. Despite certain periods of almost hysterical

repressive measures (the Alien and Sedition Acts, the Comstock era, the McCarthy witch-hunt, to mention a few), the United States has been perhaps the least restrictive of countries in imposing burdens upon free communication.

Nevertheless, throughout our history such creative legal minds as Madison and Jefferson and, more recently, Justices Black and Douglas have felt that *any* restriction on free communication, regardless of the apparent worthlessness of the "speech," presents an inherent danger to a free society and is an invitation to the imposition of further and perhaps more important limitations on the public's "right to know." They point out that the First Amendment to our Constitution states categorically that "Congress shall make no law . . . abridging the freedom of speech, or of the press." And they argue that when our Founding Fathers enacted this fundamental right they did so with the intention of excluding government entirely from the role of censor. After all, they were still licking their wounds from the spiritual, economic, and political manhandling they had received from the government of King George III.

Inevitably, though, the practical experience of government in an increasingly complex society has resulted in the overlap of many "interpretations" of seemingly explicit constitutional provisions, and it is perhaps naive to maintain that speech and press can, or should, operate independent of inhibition in modern society. The power of the media—the press, radio and television, books, magazines, and motion pictures—has grown almost geometrically in recent decades. Unchecked, it could control the minds, actions, and destiny of our people. Yet the apparatus of government has become so large and so complicated that piercing scrutiny by the media is necessary. So it is monolith against monolith, preferably with one checking and balancing the other, while our society grows more hydra-like and more unmanageable. This is a dangerous and explosive situation, but one with which we must cope if we are to make it through these increasingly difficult times.

The Supreme Court of the United States, a group of nine men, usually middle-aged or older, appointed for life by the president with the "advice and consent of the Senate," is the body empowered to oversee this battle of titans for the good of the public and in conformity with the principles of the Constitution. The degree of freedom of communication we are allowed is often determined not by any specific law but rather by the way the Court interprets the First Amendment. Our history has shown that repressive judicial decisions are often more damaging to free speech than the strictest governmental edict. Therefore, if we are to judge how well our system of government has managed the "balancing act" between free speech and self-preservation, we must look carefully at the thinking of the present nine justices, and at the direction they are taking. In the areas of libel and privacy law, the portents are grim.

On March 2, 1976, the U.S. Supreme Court decided the libel case of *Time, Inc.* v. *Mary Alice Firestone*. The shock waves from this decision are now being felt by journalists, publishers, and broadcasters everywhere. Mrs. Firestone sued *Time* magazine for libel, claiming injury to her character and reputation because it reported in its "Milestones" section that she had been divorced by her wealthy husband "on grounds of extreme cruelty and adultery." She had, in

fact, been found guilty only of extreme cruelty. A Palm Beach jury awarded Mrs. Firestone $100,000 in damages despite the acknowledged facts that Mrs. Firestone was a well-known society woman who had given press conferences during the trial, that the case had attracted widespread publicity in Florida, and that *Time's* reporters had tried conscientiously to get their information straight from an admittedly ambiguous opinion of the Florida judge who made the award.

The *Firestone* decision is really a continuation of a series of recent decisions by the Supreme Court in the fields of libel and privacy which have created new dangers for journalists trying to report on matters of public interest.

The Supreme Court's attempt to fashion a modern law of libel and privacy began in 1964 with the now famous case of *The New York Times* v. *Sullivan*. The Court there held that in order for a public official to win a libel action he must prove "actual malice." This the Court defined as a showing "with convincing clarity" that the statement complained of was made "with knowledge that it was false or with reckless disregard of whether it was false or not." The theory of the case, of course, was that it is in the interest of our society that a robust and free press criticize public officials without fear of liability for mere error or even negligence. In a number of subsequent cases the Court extended this doctrine to require that "public figures" (as well as public officials) prove actual malice, and in the 1967 privacy case of *Time* v. *Hill*, this malice requirement was also applied to actions brought by individuals who were neither "public officials" nor "public figures" for invasion of their right of privacy when those actions are based on "false reports of matters of public interest." Finally, in 1971, with a short-lived burst of enthusiasm for the First Amendment, a majority of the Court extended the "public interest" doctrine of *Time* v. *Hill* to libel as well as privacy cases (*Rosenbloom v. Metromedia, Inc.*).

However, after *Rosenbloom*, death and

retirement began to alter the Court's character, and the press began to encounter stormy weather. In 1974, a changed Court decided in *Gertz* v. *Robert Welch, Inc.* that the Supreme Count had gone too far three years earlier. It replaced the reasoning in *Rosenbloom* with the position that proof of actual malice would no longer be required in libel cases brought by private individuals involving matters of public interest. All such a person need prove was some degree of "fault," (presumably negligence) on the part of the reporter, publisher, or broadcaster. Ironically, the vote of Justice Blackmun was pivotal in this decision. Although he had decided in favor of the public interest exception in the Rosenbloom case, he changed his vote in the Gertz case. Blackmun explained, "If my vote were not needed to create a majority I would adhere to my prior view"— a strange reason on which to base a substantial change in the policy of the United States toward the First Amendment.

Then, after more changes in the personnel of the Court, came *Firestone.* Justices Black and Douglas, who for many years supported the position that the First Amendment placed an absolute ban on government interference with freedom of speech and press, were gone. Justice John Paul Stevens, only recently appointed to replace Justice Douglas, did not take part in the case. In this splintered decision, the so-called "majority" opinion is written by Justice Rehnquist, joined by Justices Burger and Blackmun. Justices Powell and Stewart support the judgment of the majority but for different reasons. In a sentence reminiscent of Blackmun's disclaimer in the Gertz case, Justice Powell (with Stewart agreeing) states: "In order to avoid the appearance of fragmentation of the Court on the basic principles involved, I join the opinion of the Court." Again bedrock principles of protection for the First Amendment seemingly are governed by brotherly behavior among justices. No wonder journalists and others concerned with the free expression of ideas felt a chill in the air.

The issues in the Firestone case are crucial to the survival of a free press in this country. First, five justices decided that despite her social position and despite the notoriety of the case and its extensive coverage by the press, Mary Alice Firestone was not a "public figure" as previously defined in the decisions of the Supreme Court. Both Justice Brennan and Justice Marshall in their dissents find this hard to understand, especially when one remembers that Mrs. Firestone herself called several press conferences during the litigation and subscribed to various clipping services. The majority of the Court seems to be saying that although Mrs. Firestone was obviously involved in public controversy, that controversy was not deemed significant enough for judicial recognition. Clearly, that decision severely limits the scope of the term "public figure," and since mere negligence is all that is required to be proved in a libel case involving someone who is not a public figure, once again the sphere of protection for the press has been reduced. If the Supreme Court cannot agree in any consistent fashion as to who is a public figure, journalists who attempt to make use of this "qualified privilege" to comment (short of actual malice) on behavior, do so at their peril.

The Firestone case has an aspect considerably more frightening for the media than the narrowed definition of a public figure. In defending against his wife's suit for divorce, Russell Firestone counter-claimed on the grounds of her "extreme cruelty and adultery." The judge was clearly aware of evidence relating to the adultery of both parties:

. . . [the] extramarital escapades of the plaintiff [Mrs. Firestone] were bizarre and of a amatory nature which would have made Dr. Freud's hair curl. Other testimony . . . would indicate that defendant was guilty of bounding from one bed-partner to another with the erotic zest of a satyr . . . much of this testimony [is] unreliable. Nevertheless, it is the conclusion and finding of the court that neither party is domesticated . . ."

Having first made such explicit reference to the Firestones' sexual activities, the judge, in granting Mr. Firestone's claim, ordered that "the equities in this case are with the defendant; that defendant's counter-claim for divorce be and the same is hereby granted, and the bonds of matrimony which have heretofore existed between the parties are hereby forever dissolved." This order, as well as an examination of the judicial proceedings, led to the *Time* magazine characterization that the divorce was granted "on grounds of extreme cruelty and adultery."

Since Mrs. Firestone was held not to be a public figure, she did not have to prove that *Time* magazine was guilty of malice in making the statements it did; rather, according to the Supreme Court of Florida, she merely had to prove "negligence." One of her lawyers was smart enough to point out that although Mr. Firestone's claim was on the grounds of both extreme cruelty and adultery and the judge's order did not refer to any specific grounds for divorce, the fact that the judge awarded Mrs. Firestone alimony was proof that he had granted Firestone a divorce merely on the grounds of extreme cruelty. The reason: under Florida law one cannot get alimony if divorced on grounds of adultery. Despite the incredible complexity of this matter, even for a lawyer, and the vagueness and lack of clarity of the judge's decision in the case, the Supreme Court of Florida decided that *Time* magazine was negligent in including adultery as a ground for the divorce and therefore was liable to Mrs. Firestone for defamation to the tune of $100,000.

A majority of the Supreme Court agreed that Mrs. Firestone was not a public figure and that all she was required to prove was that *Time* was guilty of "fault" in inaccurately reporting the judge's verdict. But a majority couldn't agree on whether *Time* had been negligent enough to be held liable. As Justice Powell said: "The decision of the Circuit Court [the court awarding the divorce] may have been sufficiently ambiguous to have caused reasonably prudent newsmen to read it as granting divorce on the ground of adultery." Despite this, Powell, joined by

Justice Stewart, agreed with the majority to send the case back to the local court to make a decision there as to whether *Time* magazine was at "fault" for being negligent.

To a journalist reporting a judicial decision, the peril of this opinion is obvious. As the Supreme Court has said in another case, "Where the document reported on is so ambiguous as this one was, it is hard to imagine a test of 'truth' that would not put the publisher virtually at the mercy of the unguided discretion of a jury." If those reporting on judicial proceedings are held to a standard which requires a knowledge of legal niceties and judicial obscurantism which even most lawyers don't have, such proceedings will be reported only reluctantly—and sketchily—by newsmen, and in many cases articles of great importance will have to be read by batteries of lawyers before they are allowed to reach the public eye.

The cases reported in various parts of the country since the Gertz decision tend to require "negligence" rather than "malice" in holding publications responsible for defamatory remarks made about people who are involved in matters of public interest but who are not public officials or public figures. The few exceptions have not been numerous enough to warm the chill the Supreme Court is sending our way.

A recent privacy case is even more ominous. In *Virgil* v. *Time, Inc.*, the top federal appeals court in California held that a well-known body surfer was entitled to a jury trial for invasion of privacy because of an article about him in *Sports Illustrated* for which he agreed to be interviewed and *the truth of which he never challenged.* Even though the appeals court admitted that Virgil was a public figure for most purposes, it held, "We conclude that unless it be privileged as newsworthy, the publicizing of private fact is not protected by the First Amendment." The appeals court then ordered that a jury should decide whether the information about Mr. Virgil was "newsworthy." "In determining what is a matter of legitimate public interest, account must be taken of the customs and conventions of the community; and in the last analysis what is proper becomes a matter of the community mores.''

In an action that shocked many constitutional lawyers the Supreme Court declined to review the appeals court decision, thereby letting the California decision stand as law. As a result, a jury in California will now be asked to decide whether the article published by *Sports Illustrated* dealt only with the "newsworthy" aspects of Mr. Virgil's life or whether it crossed the forbidden boundary into the private, "non-newsworthy" part of his life. Under this formula truth becomes immaterial. The test is whether community mores (and *what* community? one may ask) have been offended. The peril to the journalist is extreme. He interviews a public figure with that person's consent. He publishes or broadcasts an accurate account of the interview using his best judgment as to what is newsworthy about the person, only to find, to his overwhelming cost and expense (and that of his editor and publisher) that a jury in the town where his subject resides has decided that he stepped over the line and behaved "improperly."

The effect of this decision on the public is even more serious. Is Representative Hays's relationship with his administrative assistant a "newsworthy" event or one that really deals with his private life? How would a jury in his hometown feel about it? And what reporter (and what newspaper, magazine, or television station) would or should take the chance that led to the defeat of *Sports Illustrated* in the Virgil case? Taken in the context of its new libel decisions, the Supreme Court's refusal to hear the Virgil case cannot but give rise (at least until the Court changes its collective mind or its constituency) to yet another ice age in the history of the First Amendment.

These recent decisions, while seemingly unfair and even dangerous, should not obscure the very real complexity of the issues with which the Supreme Court has been wrestling in the fields of libel and privacy. While freedom of speech and press may be protected under our Constitution, it

is, as Justice Brandeis once commented, the public's "right to know" rather than the journalist's "right to publish" which is the heart of the matter protected. And this "right to know" does not, and should not, be extended to matters of intimacy having no conceivable relationship to information which will enable the public to make informed judgments about matters in which they have a legitimate interest. In other words, the First Amendment should protect the communication of newsworthy information, as the Virgil case says, but not the dissemination of intimate details of one's private life completely unconnected with one's public position or activities.

The justices who decided *Firestone* and *Virgil* are not bad men attempting to prevent the rest of us from getting needed information. Rather they are trying to balance interests in the public and private spheres which are at best very difficult to define and evaluate. However, what these men seem to have forgotten or ignored is the nature of censorship itself. Wherever it exists, its effects are more extensive than its immediate application. Therefore, these Court decisions, unfortunate enough in themselves, extend judicial obscurantism in areas where clarity is needed, and thereby make future self-censorship by journalists even more likely. As the history of censorship in the Soviet Union and elsewhere has shown, the most far-reaching and insidious result of state censorship is self-censorship. Faced with unclear laws (or laws unevenly applied) and severe penalties for their violation, one tends to hold back, to overedit, to censor one's own material before allowing it to slip into the public stream.

Publishers and broadcasters of all kinds are now coming to realize that the cost of defending libel and privacy suits—and the uncertainty of result because of unclear guidelines—adds another link of self-censorship to the chain which can eventually strangle free expression through governmental intimidation rather than action. As the New York *Times* discovered when it defended its publication of the Pentagon Papers, and as Alfred A. Knopf, Inc. discovered when it fought for publication of the Marchetti book on the CIA, tens, even hundreds of thousands of dollars may be needed to protect the publication of challenged material. No wonder publishers are becoming more cautious about what they publish and are thereby making writers more cautious about what they write. Unfortunately, no appeal is available from this kind of censorship, because the hand of government remains invisible to the naked eye.

The great mistake being made by the Supreme Court lies in its failure to recognize that despite the undeniable value our society places on the protection of the individual for invasion of privacy and defamation, the First Amendment demands higher priority on unfettered communication. Where the two are in conflict, the latter must prevail. While many will feel it vulgar to disclose, for example, that Representative Howe was arrested for soliciting prostitutes, or that Harrold Carswell (a former Nixon candidate for the Supreme Court) has been accused of homosexual solicitation, these stories should not be judged by their tastelessness but rather by their relevance to information which the public needs. A press denied the opportunity to commit occasional errors in judgment and taste, will inevitably contribute to its own emasculation.

Ironically, in the recent case of *Nebraska Press Association* v. *Stuart* (the "Nebraska Gag Decision"), the Supreme Court unanimously struck down a judge's order which would have prohibited newsmen from publishing confessions or admissions made by an accused murderer to law-enforcement officials or other third parties. While recognizing that overzealous newsmen can often publicize material that reduces the chances for a fair trial, the Court held that the need for public information about judicial proceedings outweighs the dangers inherent in pretrial publicity. The burden of protecting confidentiality, the Supreme Court said, rested on the lower courts, rather than on

the press. In reaching this result, Chief Justice Burger pointed out the extreme danger of prior restraint upon the dissemination of information:

> a prior restraint . . . has an immediate and irreversible sanction. If it can be said that a threat of criminal or civil sanctions after publication "chills" speech, prior restraint "freezes" it at least for the time.

But "gag" orders still occur, and the Supreme Court has recently declined to review two convictions of reporters for refusing to disclose their sources. One wonders how Chief Justice Burger and his colleagues can fail to recognize that self-censorship—by newsmen, editors, and publishers—caused by unclear and inconsistent guidelines, creates the most effective (and most rigid) prior restraint of all.

From *Times* v. *Sullivan* to *Rosenbloom* v. *Metromedia*, a period of seven years, a Supreme Court influenced by Justices Warren, Black, Douglas, and Brennan expanded First Amendment protection for news reporters in a fashion consistent with the public's ever-growing need to know, and consistent also with the basic tenets of the First Amendment. The result was a climate of journalistic criticism and investigation which produced the revelations of the Pentagon Papers and Watergate. It was a time in which the press—and other media—finally came into its own, stubbing toes, barging in where it wasn't wanted, sometimes being vulgar, sometimes being wrong, but uncovering the essential insight, the unmentionable question, the buried fact, which allowed American society to see what its government was actually doing.

Now, the pendulum is swinging the other way. In five short years, from *Rosenbloom* to *Firestone*, the Supreme Court has taken a number of confused steps backward, leaving journalists, broadcasters, and publishers at the mercy of unclear laws, inconsistent judges, and subjective juries. As a result of *Gertz* and *Firestone*, no one can say for sure what the law for libel is in this country, who constitutes a public figure, when malice must be proved, what standards of negligence will be applied to reporters making valiant efforts to untangle judicial cats' cradles, what incredibly expensive and time-consuming legal proceedings might threaten.

How will a conscientious but financially limited reporter know the extent to which he may report judicial proceedings (confusing as some of they are) without liability for defamation or invasion of privacy? How many newspapers, magazines, and local television stations will be able to risk the expense of a full-scale libel action in order to report the kind of governmental low-jinks which led to the "Plumbers Case" or Watergate? The result of this "chilling effect" may well be the destruction of the press's necessary role as critic of the judiciary. While cases like *Firestone* may eventually be overturned, the time in which they remain in force (or in limbo) is a time of dark caution for the press, and therefore for the country. (As this article went to press, the California judge who originally decided the Virgil case reversed his decision and held that the *Sports Illustrated* piece was indeed "newsworthy." Absent clear Supreme Court guidelines, who can say which way the pendulum will swing?)

A Harvard law professor and author of *The Assault on Privacy* believes that the public's right to privacy needs increased protection against the press.

Arthur R. Miller

OVERZEALOUS REPORTERS VS. THE RIGHT TO PRIVACY

During the past few years, Americans have become increasingly sensitive to the right of individual privacy. Popular concern over the computerization of personal information,

This article first appeared in the *Los Angeles Times* April 16, 1978. Used by permission of the author.

governmental surveillance of citizens, the excessive zeal of the FBI and CIA and the abuses of Watergate has led to a remarkable series of statutes, administrative regulations and judicial decisions designed to limit data collection, to extend the rights of those on whom files are kept and prevent access to dossiers by those with no legitimate need to know their contents.

The nation's press has begun to argue that it needs immunity from these new rules. But I believe the media have it backward; it is the public's right to privacy that needs increased protection against the press.

Although I appreciate that the nation's journalists have served as a bastion against abuse of governmental power, as in the case of Watergate, I reject the suggestion that the media have such a paramount status that the judgment of editors as to what is newsworthy need not be balanced against other social considerations.

After all, as Justice William O. Douglas once observed, "The right to be let alone is indeed the beginning of all freedom." The U.S. Supreme Court has protected the privacy of personal association, ideology, the home, the marital relationship and the body. Similarly, an individual's desire to control the dissemination of information about himself is a natural part of personal autonomy and should not be dismissed as some kind of eccentric Greta Garbo-Howard Hughes syndrome.

Many people feel embarrassed or demeaned when information about them is disclosed or exchanged, even though it may be accurate and not professionally or socially damaging. To some, loss of privacy equals loss of dignity. Lewis Carroll put it well in "Alice's Adventures in Wonderland": "Oh, 'tis love, 'tis love, that makes the world go round!" the Duchess remarks, prompting Alice to whisper, "It's done by everybody minding their own business!"

We live in a crowded, complex world, one in which a host of decisions affecting our daily lives—whether we are insurable, credit-worthy, employable or eligible for government benefits—are made by people we never see, using information over which we have no control. The individual is increasingly at the mercy of information brokers who covet, collect and abuse personal information on other people.

Ironically, while the media decry these developments, they assert their right to investigate our private lives—an act which surely contributes to the erosion of privacy and emphasizes the need for protection. An excessively zealous newspaper, television network or radio station poses a significant threat to our right to be let alone. Indeed, disclosures in the public press about one's private life can be more devastating than dissemination of the same information by a credit bureau.

With the help of the courts, we must protect our right of privacy by balancing it against the legitimate needs and First Amendment rights of America's media. The courts, after all, have accorded extraordinary protection to journalists in recent years, thereby creating the contemporary imbalance between individual rights and press prerogatives. The media's liability for defamation has been limited, the scope of executive privilege has been contained and publication restrictions based on national security have been overcome. The courts have done these things by expansively interpreting the First Amendment and striking down countless attempts to intimidate journalists by repressive agency regulations or governmental practices.

Despite these court victories, the press now claims that it is threatened by America's growing social sensitivity to privacy. Journalists apparently think they are engaged in a never-ending series of life-and-death cliffhangers. Challenged by one Goliath after another, media Davids must repeatedly sally forth to slay the enemy. This strikes me as a highly distorted and egocentric view of the universe. Spiro Agnew notwithstanding, not everyone is out to get the media.

I am not persuaded that press freedom will come tumbling down like a house of cards unless every competing social interest is subordinated to this one right. However fragile

the condition of newspapers at the time of the American Revolution, the present economic power of the broadcast networks and publishing giants casts serious doubt on any suggestion of media vulnerability.

WHY DOES THE PRESS WORRY?
Why do journalists insist on pressing their prerogatives to the limits? Why is it that the press reacts like a terrified hemophiliac to the slightest pinprick of criticism? Apparently, it fears that recognizing the importance of any other public interest may inhibit news gathering and is the first step toward erosion of the media's special status. But the nation's press can remain vibrant without a license to intrude on our privacy. The law already affords the media so much protection that tempering journalistic zeal by requiring a modicum of respect for people's privacy poses no real risk that anything of news value will be lost.

Moreover, other, profound human values are at stake. People involuntarily thrust into the glare of publicity pay a terrible price when they lose their right to be let alone. Oliver Sipple, who lunged at Sara Jane Moore and deflected her revolver as she fired at President Ford, paid that price in 1975, when the media revealed his membership in San Francisco's gay community.

Unless reporters are deterred from excessive and unwarranted curiosity, many of us may be inhibited from participating in society's affairs. Any risk of dampening press enthusiasm for newsgathering must be measured against creating a public fear, what George Orwell called "the assumption that every sound you made was overheard, and, except in darkness, every move was scrutinized."

Despite this specter, the press begrudges us some of the measures recently taken to protect our privacy. For example, it demands immunity from laws that deny unfettered access to certain criminal records—typically those of juveniles and of people who have been rehabilitated.

Vigorous and diligent reporters can effectively monitor the criminal-justice system without examining the records of individuals who have paid their debt to society, who have met the stringent prerequisites for having their record sealed and who deserve a second chance. Why should society not draw a protective curtain over the record of a youthful peccadillo that has never been repeated? It is inexcusably self-serving for the press to say that those who are protected by such curtains must be sacrificed on the altar of the First Amendment's absolute primacy.

The media ask for prerogatives unavailable to anyone else. For example, some journalists argue that a reporter who trespasses or uses false pretenses to enter someone's home should not be accountable if the resulting story "benefited the public." In short, when the press is concerned, the end justifies the means. Yet if a police officer entered a private home without a lawful warrant, we would be outraged by his violations of the rules against intruding on a citizen's private domain—even if the officer believed his entry would "benefit the public."

To permit the press to justify intrusive conduct because it "benefited the public" is an open-ended invitation to arbitrary and capricious actions. It could encourage certain elements of the press to invade the privacy of people and institutions with whom it disagrees. The media understand this risk, having reacted with shock to the revelation that various governmental intelligence organizations have spied on political dissidents and infiltrated various liberal organizations.

Should we not react with comparable shock if ultraconservative and right-wing journalists engage in similar conduct? And how could we condone violation of the privacy and associational freedoms of the members of the American Independent Party, the John Birch Society or even the American Nazi Party, by liberal elements of America's press?

Accepting the notion that the end justifies the means compromises the rule of law. Higher "justification" was precisely the defense employed by the Nixon administration. The press argues that there is a difference between surveillance by a governmental agent and by a reporter. True, but it happens to be one of degree, not principle. Our fear of official surveillance reflects a healthy apprehension about the oppressive use of governmental power. But in mid-20th century America, the power of media institutions has become such that, as a practical matter, the ramifications of intrusive behavior by the government, the media—or any other powerful social institution—are much the same.

Insisting on increased media sensitivity to privacy may be a modest incursion on editors. But the First Amendment does not give the press unfettered discretion. In various contexts, courts have decided that certain other values are worth protecting, even if it means second-guessing the journalist. The Supreme Court's recent conclusion that the Constitution does not give a television station immunity to broadcast the Human Cannonball's entire theatrical performance shows that our respect for property rights allows people to exploit their talents without fear of appropriation by the media. In the libel field, the courts have tried to achieve a principled accommodation between free speech and the integrity of an individual's reputation. And under certain circumstances, the law gives a rape victim's name a privacy-type protection.

To be sure, the courts are extremely reluctant to substitute their judgment for that of the media in determining what is "newsworthy." But, by exercising this restraint, judges have made journalists unaccountable and, in some cases, have abandoned the lambs to the wolves. In some contexts, particularly in gossip and "where are they now" columns, the media rationale underlying a decision of newsworthiness is circular: "When we publish it, people read and find it interesting; that makes it newsworthy and gives us the right to acquire and print it."

WHAT IS NEWSWORTHY?

"Interesting" is not synonymous with "newsworthy." What is "newsworthy" about the activities of someone unconnected with the events of the day, especially a person who has been seeking anonymity for years? Even our "interest" in Jacqueline Kennedy Onassis doesn't make her every movement "newsworthy" and justify photographers following her day in and day out. Nor does our "interest" in the drug difficulties of a teen-age child of a senator or governor make it "newsworthy." The drug problem can be reported upon without identifying individuals; their relation to prominent citizens is irrelevant.

The apparently unauthorized entry into the locked apartment of David R. Berkowitz, accused of the "Son of Sam" murders, shows how far some journalists may go in quest of "a story," a real problem during this post-Watergate period of media euphoria and muscle-flexing.

The press claims that it is accountable to its readership. I doubt that. Americans are captivated by gossip. We revel in the latest pratfalls of celebrities of every description and derive vicarious pleasure from the intimate discussions of Dear Abby and the like.

No one disputes the public's "right to know." But like any platitude, it is only a generalization. The deeper questions are: "Know what?" and "What practices may the press employ to gather information?" As things now stand:

The press may publish demonstrable falsehoods, subject only to remote threat of liability.

The media claim the right to publish *any* "truth," no matter how private it may be or how prurient the interest to which it caters.

Some journalists justify using improper and intrusive techniques in terms of the "benefit" produced by their stories.

In our complex society, rights frequently collide. Thus, it is imperative that no institution press its special prerogatives to the utmost. I believe that the press would further its own long-term interests if it more equitably balanced individual privacy against the public's right to know, and if it developed principles that would stay the typesetter's hands when the former seem paramount.

William J. Brennan, Jr., U.S. Supreme Court Associate Justice, delivered the decision in 1964 in a major libel suit against the *New York Times*. The key question dealt with public officials and the law of libel.

William J. Brennan, Jr.

"UNINHIBITED, ROBUST, AND WIDE-OPEN"

We are required for the first time in this case to determine the extent to which the constitutional protections for speech and press limit a State's power to award damages in a libel action brought by a public official against critics of his official conduct.

Respondent L. B. Sullivan is one of the three elected Commissioners of the City of Montgomery, Alabama. He testified that he was "Commissioner of Public Affairs and the duties are supervision of the Police Department, Fire Department, Department of Cemetery and Department of Scales." He brought this civil libel action against the four individual petitioners, who are Negroes and Alabama clergymen, and against petitioner the New York Times Company, a New York corporation which publishes the New York Times, a daily newspaper. A jury in the Circuit Court of Montgomery County awarded him damages of $500,000, the full amount claimed, against all the petitioners, and the Supreme Court of Alabama affirmed.

Respondent's complaint alleged that he had been libeled by statements in a full-page advertisement that was carried in the New York Times on March 29, 1960. Entitled "Heed Their Rising Voices," the advertisement began by stating that "As the whole

Justice William J. Brennan, Jr., speaking for the majority in *New York Times v. Sullivan.* 376 U.S. 254 (1964). Case citations omitted.

world knows by now, thousands of Southern Negro students are engaged in widespread non-violent demonstrations in positive affirmation of the right to live in human dignity as guaranteed by the U. S. Constitution and the Bill of Rights." It went on to charge that "in their efforts to uphold these guarantees, they are being met by an unprecedented wave of terror by those who would deny and negate that document which the whole world looks upon as setting the pattern for modern freedom. . . ." Succeeding paragraphs purported to illustrate the "wave of terror" by describing certain alleged events. The text concluded with an appeal for funds for three purposes: support of the student movement, "the struggle for the right-to-vote," and the legal defense of Dr. Martin Luther King, Jr., leader of the movement, against a perjury indictment then pending in Montgomery. . . .

It is uncontroverted that some of the statements contained in the two paragraphs were not accurate descriptions of events which occurred in Montgomery. Although Negro students staged a demonstration on the State Capitol steps, they sang the National Anthem and not "My Country, 'Tis of Thee." Although nine students were expelled by the State Board of Education, this was not for leading the demonstration at the Capitol, but for demanding service at a lunch counter in the Montgomery County Courthouse on another day. Not the entire student body, but most of it, had protested the expulsion, not by refusing to register, but by boycotting classes on a single day; virtually all the students did register for the ensuing semester. The campus dining hall was not padlocked on any occasion, and the only students who may have been barred from eating there were the few who had neither signed a preregistration application nor requested temporary meal tickets. Although the police were deployed near the campus in large numbers on three occasions, they did not at any time "ring" the campus, and they were not called to the campus in connection with the demonstration on the State Capitol steps, as the third paragraph implied. Dr.

King had not been arrested seven times, but only four; and although he claimed to have been assaulted some years earlier in connection with his arrest for loitering outside a courtroom, one of the officers who made the arrest denied that there was such an assault. . . .

Because of the importance of the constitutional issues involved, we granted the separate petitions for certiorari of the individual petitioners and of the Times. . . . We reverse the judgment. We hold that the rule of law applied by the Alabama courts is constitutionally deficient for failure to provide the safeguards for freedom of speech and of the press that are required by the First and Fourteenth Amendments in a libel action brought by a public official against critics of his official conduct. We further hold that under the proper safeguards the evidence presented in this case is constitutionally insufficient to support the judgment for respondent. . . .

Thus we consider this case against the background of a profound national commitment to the principle that debate on public issues should be uninhibited, robust, and wide-open, and that it may well include vehement, caustic, and sometimes unpleasantly sharp attacks on government and public officials. . . . The present advertisement, as an expression of grievance and protest on one of the major public issues of our time, would seem clearly to qualify for the constitutional protection. The question is whether it forfeits that protection by the falsity of some of its factual statements and by its alleged defamation of respondent.

Authoritative interpretations of the First Amendment guarantees have consistently refused to recognize an exception for any test of truth, whether administered by judges, juries, or administrative officials— and especially not one that puts the burden of proving truth on the speaker. . . . The constitutional protection does not turn upon "the truth, popularity, or social utility of the ideas and beliefs which are offered. . . ."

That erroneous statement is inevitable in free debate, and that it must be protected if the freedoms of expression are to have the "breathing space" that they "need . . . to survive, . . ." was also recognized by the Court of Appeals for the District of Columbia Circuit in Sweeney v. Patterson. . . . Judge Edgerton spoke for a unanimous court which affirmed the dismissal of a Congressman's libel suit based upon a newspaper article charging him with anti-Semitism in opposing a judicial appointment. . . .

Just as factual error affords no warrant for repressing speech that would otherwise be free, the same is true of injury to official reputation. Where judicial officers are involved, this Court has held that concern for the dignity and reputation of the courts does not justify the punishment as criminal contempt of criticism of the judge or his decision. . . . This is true even though the utterance contains "half-truths" and "misinformation. . . ." If judges are to be treated as "men of fortitude, able to thrive in a hardy climate, . . ." surely the same must be true of other government officials, such as elected city commissioners. Criticism of their official conduct does not lose its constitutional protection merely because it is effective criticism and hence diminishes their official reputations.

If neither factual error nor defamatory content suffices to remove the constitutional shield from criticism of official conduct, the combination of the two elements is no less inadequate. This is the lesson to be drawn from the great controversy over the Sedition Act of 1798 . . . which first crystallized a national awareness of the central meaning of the First Amendment. . . . That statute made it a crime, punishable by a $5,000 fine and five years in prison, "if any person shall write, print, utter or publish . . . any false, scandalous and malicious writing or writings against the government of the United States, or either house of the Congress . . . or the President . . . with the intent to defame . . . or to bring them or either of them, into contempt or disrepute; or to excite against them, or either or any of them, the hatred of the good people of the United States." The Act allowed the defendant the defense of

truth, and provided that the jury were to be judges both of the law and the facts. Despite these qualifications, the Act was vigorously condemned as unconstitutional in an attack joined in by Jefferson and Madison. In the famous Virginia Resolutions of 1798, the General Assembly of Virginia resolved that it "doth particularly protest against the palpable and alarming infractions of the Constitution, in the two late cases of the 'Alien and Sedition Acts,' passed at the last session of Congress. . . . Congress [The Sedition Act] exercises . . . a power not delegated by the Constitution, but, on the contrary, expressly and positively forbidden by one of the amendments thereto—a power which, more than any other, ought to produce universal alarm, because it is levelled against the right of freely examining public characters and measures, and of free communication among the people thereon, which has ever been justly deemed the only effectual guardian of every other right. . . ."

Madison prepared the Report in support of the protest. His premise was that the Constitution created a form of government under which "The people, not the government, possess the absolute sovereignty." The structure of the government dispersed power in reflection of the people's distrust of concentrated power, and of power itself at all levels. This form of government was "altogether different" from the British form, under which the Crown was sovereign and the people were subjects. "Is it not natural and necessary, under such different circumstances," he asked, "that a different degree of freedom in the use of the press should be contemplated? . . ." Earlier, in a debate in the House of Representatives, Madison had said: "If we advert to the nature of Republican Government, we shall find that the censorial power is in the people over the Government, and not in the Government over the people. . . ." Of the exercise of that power by the press, his Report said: "In every state, probably, in the Union, the press has exerted a freedom of canvassing the merits and measures of public men, of every description, which has not been confined to the strict limits of the common law. On this footing the freedom of the press has stood; on this foundation it yet stands. . . ." The right of free public discussion of the stewardship of public officials was thus, in Madison's view, a fundamental principle of the American form of government.

Although the Sedition Act was never tested in this Court, the attack upon its validity has carried the day in the court of history. Fines levied in its prosecution were repaid by Act of Congress on the ground that it was unconstitutional. . . . Calhoun, reporting to the Senate on February 4, 1836, assumed that its invalidity was a matter "which no one now doubts. . . ." Jefferson, as President, pardoned those who had been convicted and sentenced under the Act and remitted their fines, stating: "I discharged every person under punishment or prosecution under the Sedition Law because I considered, and now consider, that law to be a nullity as absolute and palpable as if Congress had ordered us to fall down and worship a golden image. . . ." The invalidity of the Act has also been assumed by Justices of this Court. . . . These views reflect a broad consensus that the Act, because of the restraint it imposed upon criticism of government and public officials, was inconsistent with the First Amendment.

There is no force in respondent's argument that the constitutional limitations implicit in the history of the Sedition Act apply only to Congress and not to the States. It is true that the First Amendment was originally addressed only to action by the Federal Government, and that Jefferson, for one, while denying the power of Congress "to control the freedom of the press," recognized such a power in the States. . . . But this distinction was eliminated with the adoption of the Fourteenth Amendment and the application to the States of the First Amendment's restrictions. . . .

What a State may not constitutionally bring about by means of a criminal statute is likewise beyond the reach of its civil law of libel. The fear of damage awards under a rule such as that invoked by the Alabama courts here may be markedly more inhibiting than the fear of prosecution under a criminal statute. . . . Alabama, for example, has a criminal libel law which subjects to prosecution "any person who speaks, writes, or prints of and concerning another any accusation falsely and maliciously importing the commission by such person of a felony, or any other indictable offense involving moral turpitude," and which allows as punishment upon conviction a fine not exceeding $500 and a prison sentence of six months. . . . Presumably a person charged with violation of this statute enjoys ordinary criminal-law safeguards such as the requirements of an indictment and of proof beyond a reasonable doubt. These safeguards are not available to the defendant in a civil action. The judgment awarded in this case—without the need for any proof of actual pecuniary loss—was one thousand times greater than the maximum fine provided by the Alabama criminal statute, and one hundred times greater than that provided by the Sedition Act. And since there is no double-jeopardy limitation applicable to civil lawsuits, this is not the only judgment that may be awarded against petitioners for the same publication. Whether or not a newspaper can survive a succession of such judgments, the pall of fear and timidity imposed upon those who would give voice to public criticism is an atmosphere in which the First Amendment freedoms cannot survive. Plainly the Alabama law of civil libel is "a form of regulation that creates hazards to protected freedoms markedly greater than those that attend reliance upon the criminal law. . . ."

The state rule of law is not saved by its allowance of the defense of truth. A defense for erroneous statements honestly made is no less essential here than was the requirement of proof of guilty knowledge which, in Smith v. California . . . , we held indispensable to a valid conviction of a bookseller for possessing obscene writings for sale. We said:

For if the bookseller is criminally liable without knowledge of the contents, . . . he will tend to restrict the books he sells to those he has inspected; and thus the State will have imposed a restriction upon the distribution of constitutionally protected as well as obscene literature. . . . And the book-seller's burden would become the public's burden, for by restricting him the public's access to reading matter would be restricted. . . . [H]is timidity in the face of his absolute criminal liability, thus would tend to restrict the public's access to forms of the printed word which the State could not constitutionally suppress directly. The bookseller's self censorship, compelled by the State, would be a censorship affecting the whole public, hardly less virulent for being privately administered. Through it, the distribution of all books, both obscene and not obscene, would be impeded.

A rule compelling the critic of official conduct to guarantee the truth of all his factual assertions—and to do so on pain of libel judgments virtually unlimited in amount—leads to a comparable "self-censorship." Allowance of the defense of truth, with the burden of proving it on the defendant, does not mean that only false speech will be deterred. Even courts accepting this defense as an adequate safeguard have recognized the difficulties of adducing legal proofs that the alleged libel was true in all its factual particulars. . . . Under such a rule, would-be critics of official conduct may be deterred from voicing their criticism, even though it is believed to be true and even though it is in fact true, because of doubt whether it can be proved in court or fear of the expense of having to do so. They tend to make only statements which "steer far wider of the unlawful zone. . . ." The rule thus dampens the vigor and limits the variety of public debate. It is inconsistent with the First and Fourteenth Amendments.

The constitutional guarantees require, we think, a federal rule that prohibits a public official from recovering damages for a defamatory falsehood relating to his official conduct unless he proves that the statement was made with "actual malice"—that is, with knowledge that it was false or with reckless disregard of whether it was false or not. . . .

Reversed and remanded.

Writing in the international journal *Index on Censorship*, Robert G. Picard, editor of the Freedom of Information Center Reports, School of Journalism, University of Missouri, shows how the fear of costly legal actions is inhibiting journalists and may lead to self-censorship.

Robert G. Picard

SELF-CENSORSHIP THREATENS U.S. PRESS FREEDOM

American publishers and broadcasters are increasingly exercising self-censorship to avoid costly litigation; the result is a decline in press freedom, say journalists and legal experts in the United States.

The self-censorship is denying the public a wide range of information because journalists fear libel and privacy suits, and confrontations with government attorneys which can result in legal fees of up to $200 an hour.

The cost of lawyers for the number of suits filed against the media has increased. The media have also increased their legal costs because a large number of papers and broadcasting enterprises have chosen to hire permanent legal staffs.

The attorneys on media staffs are not only handling legal defences for their employers—they have also moved into the editorial decision-making process, encouraging self-censorship and making decisions on whether articles will be printed or broadcast.

"There's a lot of self-censorship by editors unwilling to rock the boat. They fear the heavy court costs that could come from a

Reprinted by permission of the Fund for Free Expression from *Index on Censorship* 2 (3): 15–17 (June 1982).

tough investigative article," says Bruce Sanford, a former *Wall Street Journal* reporter who is now an attorney for United Press International and the Society of Professional Journalists.

His analysis is echoed by Dan Paul, Attorney for the *Miami Herald*. "Costs of trying libel suits . . . quashing subpoenas, fending off privacy actions and obtaining news under freedom of informaion laws are already substantial, and the burden is growing," he says. "Because of this burden the hometown newspaper or small radio station may decide to steer clear of news prone to generate litigation costs or search warrants. That is chilling."

Floyd Abrams, an attorney who has represented *The New York Times* and other major media clients, believes such censorship may increase. "If things develop to the point where large jury verdicts [large awards made by juries] or large counsel fees on a yearly basis are the norm and not the exception, then I don't have any doubt that publications will be obliged to trim their sails. . . . The real danger is that the public would never know," he warns.

Many journalists and attorneys believe that libel victories by plaintiffs may be increasing the number of suits in recent years because high damages awarded by juries could be an incentive for many individuals to pursue a case even if it is unwarranted.

"The country is in a litigious mood—everybody sues these days, and even if there are no real grounds, suits are expensive to defend," says Art Spikol, a columnist for *Writer's Digest*.

The cost of defending any suit, with attorney fees averaging $1,000 a day, is enough to scare most media managers, and many news organizations have begun settling even unwarranted suits with out-of-court payments in order to avoid more costly defence costs and the possibility of large jury verdicts.

CUTTING COSTS

In a celebrated case the *San Francisco Examiner* sought to reduce its liability in a libel suit brought against it by two policemen and a prosecuting attorney. The case involved stories in the paper that alleged a police frame-up against a member of a youth gang.

The story was written by a freelance reporter and a member of the *Examiner* staff. When the suit was filed, the paper chose to cut its litigation costs and attempted to reduce its liability by refusing to defend the freelance writer and blaming the alleged libel on him. As a result, both reporters sought separate counsel because they felt the paper did not have their interests at heart.

A defence committee, composed of horrified colleagues, raised $20,000 to pay the reporters' legal bills for the trial. Because the finding against the reporters in the trial has been appealed, defence costs have gone up, perhaps as much as double, as have costs for the *Examiner*, which also lost its initial case.

Defence costs in libel suits involving other parties have resulted in high expenditures. Litigation costs of nearly $100,000 were recently encountered by newspapers in Palm Beach, Florida, and Baton Rouge, Louisiana, when they lost and appealed sizable libel cases. Although both won their cases on appeal, they still had to bear defence costs.

John Zollinger, publisher of the *New Mexico Independent*, laments, "It's no joke anymore. . . . You win and you still pay."

The *Grass Valley* (California) *Union* is preparing to fight a $5.4 million slander suit, which will go to trial early in 1982. A religious school for troubled teenagers is seeking damages from this small daily newspaper for questions asked by a reporter who was investigating rumours of impropriety in financial and other activities at the school. Since the suit was filed executives of the paper and its parent corporation, Pioneer Newspapers, have killed stories about the school and its directors out of fear of further difficulties. "We're so gun-shy at this point that if anybody were to say 'sue', we'd just shake," says one reporter.

The National News Council recently considered a complaint against the controversial drug rehabilitation organization, Synanon.

The case brought by United Press International involved a "retraction project" in which Synanon sent nearly 1,000 letters to news services, publishers and broadcasters demanding corrections and retractions of nearly every story carried about the group in 1978 and 1979. During that period members of Synanon and the group's founder were charged and tried for attempted murder after a rattlesnake had been placed in the mailbox of an attorney involved in a suit against Synanon.

Although the letters threatened possible legal action against the media. Synanon denied using the letters as threats or harassment. Most editors saw them as threats, however, and some claimed the letters were in retaliation for the negative coverage Synanon had received because of the snake incident or because of the publicity generated when the *Point Reyes* (California) *Light* received the Pulitzer Prize for its investigations of the group.

The National News Council heard testimony indicating that some journalists, particularly those in medium and small news organisations, had chosen to cease coverage of Synanon to avoid possible legal confrontations with the group.

J. Hart Clinton, publisher of the *San Mateo* (California) *Times* and *News-Leader*, told the council that he had twice run retractions about Synanon stories and was trying to avoid further involvement with the group. "I have instructed my newsroom not to publish any more material on Synanon unless it is extremely important and we know it is accurate. I don't want to be harassed," he said.

A California-based news service, which was a target of the retraction project, reported that a quarter of its subscribers refused to publish any stories about Synanon after being threatened with suits over a column distributed by the service. "They can't afford lawsuits. Their liability insurance for the most part calls for them to pay the first $7,500, and that's a lot of money for a small paper," said Fred Kline, owner and editor of Capitol News Service.

Although the exact amount of money spent by news organisations consulting with attorneys about the Synanon demands is unknown, a conservative estimate of one hour of consultation for each of the 1,000 letters sent would result in $100,000 of legal expenses.

Costs of this kind are making many organisations more careful in choosing the type of information they will publish, broadcast or distribute, and many are reportedly increasing the amount of stories they choose to censor.

DEFENDING RIGHTS

In addition to litigation costs posed by libel and other suits, the media in America are confronted with significant costs when they attempt to defend press rights and privileges. The high cost of First Amendment defences is reportedly keeping many publishers and broadcasters from pursuing such cases and leading some to censor material which might bring them into conflict with the government.

When *The Progressive* magazine decided to challenge the government's attempt to restrain publication of an article about the H-bomb, the litigation costs nearly forced the journal out of business, [see *Index on Censorship* 1-1980, pp. 51–54]. The magazine, which had already been losing about $100,000 a year, spent nearly $250,000 pressing its case before the government dropped its efforts.

"Our lawyers said at the outset this was likely to be a protracted and horrendously expensive case that could jeopardise the survival of the magazine," says Editor Erwin Knoll. But he reports that supporters have raised much of the money needed for defence costs and that only $60,000 remains unpaid.

"As legal costs go up and legal complications grow ever more ramiferous and Byzantine, publishers may increasingly try to avoid these types of difficulties," warns Knoll. "If we were still bearing the $60,000 debt from the last go around . . . and knowing fully the burdens of pursuing such a case, we would do it again. But we would do it with the knowledge that the magazine would not be likely to survive."

Knoll believes few publications with circulations the size of his (40,000) would elect to pursue such an expensive and potentially harmful course.

The 1980 U.S. Supreme Court ruling limiting the closure of trial to the press and public was also an expensive victory for the press. The costs were borne solely by Richmond Newspapers Inc. which pursued the case after a Virginia judge closed a murder trial in which the defendant was acquitted.

According to Publisher J. Steward Bryan III, the final costs of the case are not tallied yet, but he expects them to be between $75,000 and $100,000. "I don't think there are many newspaper companies who could afford this kind of case. Even daily newspapers with between 20,000 and 25,000 circulation couldn't possibly afford it," he says.

AVOIDING CONTROVERSY

Challenges to broadcast licences are also proving expensive, and pressure groups are more and more challenging the licences in order to force changes by broadcasters. It is estimated that even the simplest challenge requiring legal representation before the Federal Communication Commission can cost a broadcaster between $50,000 and $100,000.

Few broadcast licence challenges have proved successful, but many are being made only to force changes in station policy or programming content rather than to take the licence away from the broadcaster. Owners who must pay large fees for defence costs are often saddled with the challengers' legal costs as well when they come to an agreement that halts the proceedings.

Such costs have the apparent result of encouraging many broadcasters to avoid controversial subjects which may bring about the need for legal representation.

In the mid-1970s, Richard Schmidt, general legal counsel for the American Society of Newspaper Editors, noted "a subtle but pervasive attitude of self-censorship

motivated by fear of libel suits." Today, he still believes the litigious climate is making publishers exercise self-censorship.

"Self-censorship is rather prevalent," he says, "but it can't be proved with empirical evidence. It's something publishers don't like to talk about, but I hear about it in conversations at conferences all the time."

Avoiding litigation by self-censorship adds a raw economic factor to an industry that has claimed to be guided by the interests of society and ethical principles. It is an unfortunate reality that there can be no appeal of this kind of censorship because it is instituted by the media themselves and is usually unseen and undetected by their audiences.

"Self-censorship has always been the most pervasive form of censorship," notes Erwin Knoll, editor of *The Progressive*. "Keeping out of trouble has always been publishers' main interest."

LIBEL INSURANCE

The development of cable, satellite and other new information delivery systems is expected to multiply demands for legal representation and increase the probability of self-censorship. The new media are expected to face libel, privacy and other suits, as well as challenges citing FCC and antitrust regulations as their audiences and programming increase.

The popularity of libel and First Amendment insurance policies may help some media, however.

About half of the 1,750 daily newspapers and 425 weeklies now carry libel insurance, but deductibles of up to $25,000 can pose problems because some cases are settled or ended at costs below that level. Premiums for weekly newspapers begin at about $150 per year and small dailies can get coverage for $240 per year. Larger papers, and those located in California, Oklahoma, South Carolina, Hawaii and Alaska, pay premiums because they are more likely to do the type of reporting that brings on lawsuits and because those states have laws or juries that tend to place the media at a disadvantage in litigation. Most libel insurance policies cover only the cost of damages awarded, not the costs of legal representation.

The increasing interest in libel insurance has led to the establishment of First Amendment insurance, which aids the media in pursuing or defending themselves in cases involving the First Amendment. About 300 companies, mostly daily newspapers, have purchased policies ranging from $100,000 to $1 million in coverage. The premiums for these policies are about the same as those for libel insurance, but they are designed to cover the costs of legal representation only.

Critics of such policies argue that the insurance will not be effective against self-censorship because they actually encourage more litigation, which will only increase the cost of insurance. They also point out that the smaller news organisations, which are most prone to self-censorship, often cannot afford the policies.

Not all newspapers that can afford coverage purchase it. The prestigious *New York Times*, for instance, does not carry libel insurance and has a policy of never settling a libel suit with an out-of-court payment. The paper's executives believe that such actions only encourage unwarranted litigation.

Concern about litigation has prompted several developments, including industry-wide and in-house seminars on libel and other litigation to better acquaint reporters, editors, and media executives with the issues and to develop ways to avoid litigation. A Libel Defense Resource Centre has been established by industry organisations to gather information on libel litigation and study developments. . . . In the future, the centre hopes to be able to coordinate defence efforts in suits brought against different media by individuals or groups.

The litigious spirit of the nation has been heightened by some journalists becoming "First Amendment junkies" who seek legal relief whenever they feel any privileges have been infringed, according to Don Reuben, an attorney who has represented *The Chicago Tribune, The New York Daily News* and *Time,* Inc. Reuben recently warned journalists attending an Illinois newspaper association meeting that such a "knee-jerk reaction" allows bad cases to be brought to court which can bring unfavourable rulings that cost fellow journalists existing freedoms. It is ridiculous to seek confrontation and to test cases that have no real importance or that could be counter-productive, he said.

Whether the media in the United States will be able to break loose of the bonds of litigation costs, self-imposed censorship and the continued growth of the litigious spirit remains to be seen. But many observers in America believe few efforts by the media are directed toward those goals.

FREE PRESS VERSUS FAIR TRIAL

On the surface, it appears that there is a fundamental conflict between the First Amendment, with its uncompromising declaration against any law abridging freedom of speech and press, and the Sixth Amendment, which provides various safeguards for persons accused of crimes. Under the American system of checks and balances, both the press and the courts have essential roles to play. The issues are well defined by Richard M. Schmidt, Jr., General Counsel for the American Society of Newspaper Editors, writing for *The Quill* magazine.

Richard M. Schmidt, Jr.

FIRST AND SIXTH:
SIBLING RIVALRY

The First Amendment written to the Constitution provided in part: "Congress shall make no law . . . abridging the freedom of speech or of the press."

The Sixth provided in part: "In all criminal prosecutions, the accused shall enjoy the right to a speedy and public trial, by an impartial jury of the State and district wherein the crime shall have been committed. . . ."

For the 185 years since their adoption, the two amendments have found themselves in an uncomfortable relationship, if not one that in recent years has become outright combative.

As the U.S. Supreme Court noted in its most recent and most significant press case involving the conflict: "The problems presented by this case [*Nebraska Press Association* v. *Hugh Stuart*] are almost as old as the Republic. Neither in the Constitution nor in contemporaneous writings do we find that the conflict between these two important rights was anticipated, yet it is inconceivable that the authors of the Constitution were unaware of the potential conflicts between the right to an unbiased jury and the guarantee of freedom of the press."

One of the earliest cases to reach the Supreme Court involving the problem of free press and fair trial was *United States* v. *Reid* (1851). The defendant, accused of murder, demanded a new trial because two jury members allegedly had read a newspaper account of the proceedings while the trial was in progress. However, the Supreme Court stated, "There was nothing in the newspapers calculated to influence their decision, and both of them swear that these papers had not the slightest influence on their verdict."

As early as 1878, the Supreme Court (*Reynolds* v. *United States*) stated, "The theory of the law is a juror who has formed

Reprinted by permission of the author from *The Quill* September 1976, pp. 25–27.

an opinion cannot be impartial. Every opinion which he may entertain need not necessarily have that effect. In these days of newspaper enterprise and universal education, every case of public interest is, almost as a matter of necessity, brought to the attention of all the intelligent people in the vicinity, and scarcely anyone can be found among those best fitted to be jurors who has not read or heard of it, and who has not some impression or some opinion in respect to its merits. It is clear, therefore, that upon the trial of the issue of fact raised by a challenge for such cause, the court will practically be called upon to determine whether the nature and strength of the opinion formed are such as in law necessarily to raise the presumption of partiality."

In the Reynolds case, the Court quoted from Chief Justice John Marshall's opinion in the trial of Aaron Burr in 1807, stating, "Light impressions which may fairly be presumed to yield to the testimony that may be offered, which may leave the mind open to a fair consideration of the testimony, constitute no sufficient objection to a juror; but that those strong and deep impressions which close the mind against the testimony that may be offered in opposition to them, which will combat that testimony and resist its force, will constitute a sufficient objection to him."

In 1976, the Court again turned to the Burr trial. Chief Justice Warren Burger said, "The trial . . . presented Chief Justice Marshall, presiding as a trial judge, with acute problems in selecting an unbiased jury. Few people in the area of Virginia from which jurors were drawn had not formed some opinions concerning Mr. Burr or the case, from newspaper accounts and heightened discussion both private and public. The Chief Justice conducted a searching voir dire [interrogation] of the two panels eventually called and rendered a substantial opinion on the purposes of voir dire and the standards to be applied. . . . Burr was acquitted, so there was no reason for appellate review to examine the problem of prejudicial pretrial publicity."

For the first half of the 20th century the battle of free press-fair trial was relatively quiescent with one notable exception, that being Bruno Hauptmann's internationally publicized trial for the abduction and murder of the Lindbergh child. The carnival atmosphere of that trial was widely criticized in retrospect by not only the bench and bar but the press.

In 1961, the case of *Irvin* v. *Dowd* reached the United States Supreme Court. For the first time in history the Court reversed a state court conviction on the sole ground of prejudicial pretrial publicity. The defendant had been indicted for murder, was granted a change of venue to an adjoining county, denied a second change of venue and a continuance. Ten murders within a four-month period had been committed in the county in which he was indicted, and, shortly after the arrest of the defendant, the police issued a press release stating he had confessed to six of the murders. Radio stations in the community broadcast citizens' opinions as to the defendant's guilt and their suggestions as to what punishment he should receive. The press stories in both print and the electronic outlets referred to the defendant's past convictions for other crimes, his juvenile record, a military court-martial and accusations that he was a parole violator.

The jury of twelve ultimately selected contained eight jurors who in voir dire examination had expressed the opinion that the defendant was guilty as charged.

AN IMPOSSIBLE STANDARD
The Supreme Court reversed the conviction but stated:

> To hold that the mere existence of any preconceived notion as to the guilt or innocence of an accused, without more, is sufficient to rebut the presumption of a prospective juror's impartiality, would be to establish an impossible standard. It is sufficient if the juror can lay aside his impression or opinion and render a verdict based on the evidence presented in court.

In the early 1960s, a person was charged with kidnaping, murder and bank robbery in Louisiana. In a 20-minute film interview with the local sheriff the defendant's confession was broadcast over television on three consecutive days to an audience of more than 100,000 people out of a total population in the area where he was to be tried of approximately 150,000.

The defendant was convicted by a jury, two of the members of which were deputy sheriffs of the parish where the trial was held, and three members who stated on voir dire they had seen the televised interview. The Supreme Court, in the majority opinion (*Rideau* v. *Louisiana*) reversing the conviction, referred to the lower court proceedings as a "kangaroo court" and pointed out that the defendant had no lawyer to advise him of his right to stand mute on camera.

In 1965, the Supreme Court dealt with the question of whether the televising of a criminal trial, over the objections of the defendant, interfered with the due process guarantee in the Fourteenth Amendment. In a 5–4 decision, the Court held on the facts of the case as presented that the defendant was prevented from obtaining a fair trial (*Estes* v. *Texas*).

Next came the watershed decision of *Sheppard* v. *Maxwell*.

Dr. Sam Sheppard was convicted in 1954 in Ohio for the murder of his wife. The various appeals in this case had gone all the way to the U.S. Supreme Court, which denied review in 1956. Later, he filed an application for a writ of habeas corpus alleging that he had been deprived of a fair trial because of the court's failure to protect him from prejudicial publicity. In 1966 the U.S. Supreme Court, in a majority opinion written by Justice Tom C. Clark, held that the "carnival atmosphere" at the trial, coupled with the pervasive pretrial publicity containing what the Court considered to be prejudicial material, made a fair trial impossible.

In recent years, the Sheppard case has been misinterpreted by many as making permissible gag orders on the press and denying the press access to information concerning criminal trials. The Supreme Court had outlined methods of protecting the right to fair trial, such as change of trial venue, postponement of the trial until public attention subsides, intensive voir dire (interrogation of prospective jurors), and emphatic and clear instructions to the jury to decide the issues only on evidence presented in open court. However, Justice Clark made clear that the Court was not suggesting, or even intimating, "gagging" the press. In his opinion he stated, "A responsible press has always been regarded as the handmaiden of effective judicial administration, especially in the criminal field. Its function in this regard is documented by an impressive record of service over several centuries. The press does not simply publish information about trials but guards against the miscarriage of justice by subjecting the police, prosecutors, and judicial processes to extensive public scrutiny and criticism. This Court has, therefore, been unwilling to place any direct limitations on the freedom traditionally exercised by the news media, for 'what transpires in the courtroom is public property.'"

Prior to *Sheppard* v. *Maxwell*, various press organizations throughout the country began to work with the organized bar and in some instances with representatives of the bench to open up a dialogue and develop statements of "principles," "codes," or "guidelines" relating to pretrial publicity and the coverage of trials by the press. Among the states pioneering in this effort were Washington, Oregon and Colorado.

While differing in many details, all acknowledged presumption of a defendant's innocence and his right to a fair trial. And all of the statements recognized the right and responsibility of the press to inform the public of the conduct of its criminal justice system. Most of the statements also urged that the press not publish—particularly just before the start of a trial—any information concerning a confession or a prior criminal record.

At the national level, the American Bar Association's Advisory Committee on Fair Trial and Free Press, chaired by Justice Paul C. Reardon of the Massachusetts Supreme Judicial Court, issued a report which became extremely controversial with the media, par-

ticularly as to the use of contempt power in certain circumstances against the press. But even this 1968 report clearly disavowed any "direct restrictions on the media."

RECOMMENDED PROCEDURES

In 1975, the committee issued a "Recommended Court Procedure to Accommodate Rights of Fair Trial and Free Press." But, again, this report, while not universally acclaimed by the press, unequivocally rejected the imposition of any direct restraints upon the media. The report states, "It is clear that the free flow of information concerning court business is important and necessary not only to the requirements of a free press and a fair public trial, but the greater public understanding of the judicial function and the rule of law. . . ."

Until the 1970s, the courts appeared to be content with reversing convictions of those whose trials they thought had been prejudiced by pretrial publicity. Then, despite the repeated statements of the highest court in the land concerning prior restraints on the press and the various press guidelines and studies which cautioned against any direct restraints on the press, a wave of gag orders began to be entered by lower courts.

In 1971, a U.S. District Court in Louisiana ordered that ". . . no report of the testimony taken in this case today shall be made in any newspaper or by radio or television, or by any other news media. . . ." The Baton Rouge *State Times* defied the order, as did its sister paper, the *Morning Advocate*. The reporters who wrote the stories were found in criminal contempt. On appeal, the Fifth Circuit Court of Appeals found the order of the lower court to be an unconstitutional prior restraint on freedom of the press. But it also held that the reporters were obligated to obey the order until it was reversed and that the court *could* hold the reporters in contempt even though the order was unconstitutional. The U.S. Supreme Court denied review.

The Baton Rouge case appeared to encourage trial courts throughout the country to enter gag orders upon the motion of the defense, the prosecution, or upon their own initiative, and the First and Sixth amendments appeared to be engaged in mortal combat.

Then, in October 1975, six members of one family were murdered in a small Nebraska town. A suspect was arrested and the event was given widespread news coverage locally and nationally. The prosecuting and defense attorneys joined in asking the court with initial jurisdiction to enter a restricting order because of the "reasonable likelihood of prejudicial news which would make difficult, if not impossible, impaneling of an impartial jury and tend to prevent a fair trial." Local and national news organizations jumped into the battle. Action was taken to overturn the lower courts' rulings in the Nebraska Supreme Court and the U.S. Supreme Court. While denying a motion to expedite review or to stay the order of the State District Court pending the defendant's trial, the U.S. Supreme Court, for the first time, agreed to review whether the press could be enjoined from publishing news on pending criminal trial proceedings.

The Court stated, after reviewing previous cases of prior restraint, but not specifically concerning the defendant's right to fair trial, "The thread running through all these cases is that prior restraints on speech and publication are the most serious and the least tolerable infringement on First Amendment rights." Further, "A prior restraint, by contrast and by definition, has an immediate and irreversible sanction. If it can be said that a threat of criminal or civil sanctions after publication 'chills' speech, prior restraint 'freezes' it at least for the time."

THE MAJOR RESPONSIBILITY

The Court also said, ". . . [P]retrial publicity—even pervasive, adverse publicity—does not inevitably lead to an unfair trial. The capacity of the jury eventually impaneled to decide the case fairly is influenced by the tone and extent of the publicity, which is in part, and often in large part, shaped by what attorneys, police and other officials do

to precipitate news coverage. The trial judge has a major responsibility. What the judge says about a case, in or out of the courtroom, is likely to appear in newspapers and broadcasts. More important, the measures a judge takes or fails to take to mitigate the effects of pretrial publicity—the measures described in *Sheppard* [v *Maxwell*]—may well determine whether the defendant received a trial consistent with the requirements of due process. . . ."

Justice William J. Brennan Jr., joined by Justices Potter Stewart and Thurgood Marshall, went further than the majority opinion: ". . . Damage to that Sixth Amendment right could never be considered so direct, immediate and irreparable, and based on such proof rather than speculation, that prior restraints on the press could be justified on this basis." And, they continued, ". . . [T]he press may be arrogant, tyrannical, abusive, and sensationalist, just as it may be incisive, probing, and informative. But at least in the context of prior restraints on publication, the decision of what, when, and how to publish is for editors, not judges."

However, the Court's *majority* opinion emphasized that its ruling was confined to the record before it. It refused to rule out the possibility that in some future case a showing of an adequate threat to a fair trial would possess ". . . the requisite degree of certainty to justify restraint. This Court has frequently denied that First Amendment rights are absolute and has consistently rejected the proposition that a prior restraint can never be employed."

Recognizing the extraordinary protections afforded by the First Amendment, the Court discussed what it described as obligations of the press under the First Amendment ". . . something in the nature of a fiduciary duty to exercise the protected rights responsibly—a duty widely acknowledged but not always observed by editors and publishers. It is not asking too much to suggest that those who exercise First Amendment rights in newspapers or broadcasting enterprises direct some effort to protect the rights of an accused to a fair trial by unbiased jurors.

"The authors of the Bill of Rights did not undertake to assign priorities between First Amendment and Sixth Amendment rights ranking one as superior to the other. In this case, the petitioners would have us declare the right of an accused subordinate to their right to publish in all circumstances. But if the authors of these guarantees, fully aware of the potential conflicts between them, were unwilling or unable to resolve the issue by assigning to one priority over the other, it is not for us to rewrite the Constitution by undertaking what they declined."

While refusing to elevate First Amendment rights above the Sixth Amendment, the Court did say, ". . . [T]he barriers to prior restraint remain high and the presumption against its use continues intact." This in itself should serve to cool the conflict.

A policy of the Board of Directors of American Civil Liberties Union reflects the organization's dilemma over two conflicting civil rights values: First Amendment freedom and the need to maintain rigorous standards of due process in criminal proceedings. Favoring sanctions against law enforcement officers and officers of the court rather than against the press directly, the policy aims at greater cooperation between press, bar, and bench.

American Civil Liberties Union

PREJUDICIAL PRE-TRIAL PUBLICITY

One of the most difficult problems the Union has been called upon to resolve is that raised by the publicizing of pending criminal trials. On the one hand, the Union has steadfastly

Minutes of the Board of Directors, American Civil Liberties Union, February 6–7, 1971; March 28, October 18, 1966. Reprinted by permission of the American Civil Liberties Union.

held as its core principle the inviolability of First Amendment freedoms, including freedom of the newspapers and electronic media to report all matters that they hold to be newsworthy. On the other hand, it has consistently urged even more rigorous standards of due process in criminal proceedings, including methods of ensuring impartial judges and juries.

Any attempt to suggest proper guidelines in this area doubtlessly will offend what many regard as a virtually absolute right to report events that qualify as news. Yet it is equally certain that the release or reporting of information relating to a criminal prosecution can, in a significant number of instances, effectively destroy the right of an individual to a fair trial. For, in a widely publicized case, that defendant often must either take his or her chances with a jury whose members have been exposed on numerous occasions to the press' version of the crime, or forego the constitutional right and protection of a jury trial, trusting to the supposedly greater objectivity of a judge.

The general recognition of the need to assure a fair trial has resulted in the adoption, by the American Bar Association and other professional, legal and journalistic organizations, of new standards for this area.

The ACLU concurs in many of these new standards aimed at preserving the historic right to a fair trial without unduly limiting public discussion and public understanding of the machinery of justice.

Regarding specific standards, the ACLU recommends that all officials involved in the enforcement of law and prosecution of criminal defendants under the local, state, and federal laws abide by the following guidelines which apply to the release of information to news media from the time of a prosecutor's focus on the particular defendant until the proceeding has been terminated by trial or otherwise:

1. No statement of information should be released for the purpose of influencing the outcome of a trial.

2. Subject to specific limitations imposed by law or court order, officials may make public the following:
   a) Defendant's name, age, residence and similar background other than race, religion, employment, and marital status;
   b) Substance or text of charge;
   c) Identity of investigating and arresting agency and length of investigation;
   d) Time and place of arrest;
   e) But none of the above information should be disclosed where such disclosure would be prejudicial comment on the case or circumstances of arrest.

3. No information should be released concerning the criminal or arrest record or confession of a person accused of crime.

4. No information should be released by officials concerning:
   a) Observations about a defendant's character.
   b) Statements, admissions, confessions, or alibis attributable to a defendant.
   c) References to investigative procedures (fingerprints, polygraph tests, etc.).
   d) Statements concerning identity, credibility, or testimony of prospective witnesses.
   e) Statements concerning evidence or argument in the case.
   f) Circumstances surrounding arrest (residence, use of weapons, etc.).

5. Officials in charge of custody of a defendant must protect the defendant from being photographed or televised while in custody. No photograph of defendant should be released unless they serve a proper investigative function.

6. None of these restrictions are intended to apply to release of information concerning a person accused of crime when such release is deemed necessary to apprehend him or her.

The most troublesome issue has been the question of how best to enforce these informational standards in order to ensure the defendant's right to a fair trial. The Union has taken note of the cooperation between the bar and the press which has resulted in the formulation of voluntary press guidelines. Such voluntary press codes have apparently been adopted in almost half of the states. They are premised on the theory of self-regulation by the press and ultimately rely on the discretion of news editors.

The main difficulty is whether the voluntary compliance approach is effective in preserving the defendant's right to a fair trial. Until it is shown that the voluntary approach is effective in safeguarding the defendant's right to a fair trial, we favor the direct application of sanctions against the public officials who release prejudicial information. If, in addition to these restrictions, news media want to refrain voluntarily from publishing any prejudicial information they do obtain, the ACLU would, of course, support such self-restraint. But we cannot support voluntary codes in lieu of sanctions against law enforcement officials.

Regarding the use of sanctions, the ACLU favors directing sanctions against law enforcement officers and prosecuting attorneys responsible for presenting a case to the press instead of to the court. One simple method of control is the adoption of specific administrative measures and policy statements by police departments and prosecuting attorneys' offices to guide the conduct of employees. Improper release of information would thereby be grounds for disciplinary action.

In addition, a procedure should be adopted by rule or statute in all courts, allowing judges to admonish publicly law enforcement officers and prosecution attorneys responsible for aiding or creating prejudicial publicity. The court could also refer the matter to the appropriate bar association committee on ethics. Aside from the advantages of its deterrent effect, the proposal would enable a judge to act immediately after the release of prejudicial publicity, rather than wait, as is now done, until the trial to exercise his or her limited power of instructing a jury to disregard newspaper comment—when it is generally too late to dissipate the effects of a prejudicial reporting.

The ACLU believes that a defense attorney in criminal proceedings should not be subject to judicial sanctions for pretrial statements to the press concerning his or her client or the circumstances to which the pending litigation relates. There are several reasons for treating defense counsel in criminal prosecutions differently from prosecution attorneys:

1. Public prosecutors are apt not to prosecute cases that are against the general public sentiment, while defense counsel often have the burden of representing an interest or person that is disfavored by the majority of the community;

2. There is a generally held presumption that the prosecutor has acted in the public interest in proceeding against the defendant, and therefore statements by the prosecutor are more readily believed. On the other hand, there is no such presumption that the defense counsel is acting in the public interest; his or her remarks will be received by the public with the thought that they are made on behalf of the client whom "the people," through the prosecutor, have charged with a crime;

3. Defense counsel often faces a community sentiment already well-marshalled against the defense;

4. The concept of "fair trial" in the present context is essentially to guarantee the accused individual a trial by a jury that is free of prejudice. Absent this premise there would be little reason for adding judicial sanctions to enforce the nearly universally accepted professional self-restraint counsel have traditionally imposed on themselves to assure that the judicial process is a fair one.

The present narrow scope of the traditional challenge for cause should be expanded to permit challenge of any juror who has gained a substantial degree of knowledge about a case from pre-trial publicity, whether or not the juror thinks he or she is impartial. This method would also be a further discouragement to police and prosecuting attorneys who might instigate prejudicial publicity in the hope of making convictions easier to obtain, because it would disqualify many prospective jurors and thus delay trial. When pre-trial publicity, despite all precautions, reaches virtually all members of a community, a change of venue is usually possible. In appropriate cases where extensive pretrial publicity, prejudicial to the defendant, has emanated from the government, the defendant shall be entitled to a dismissal of the charges. In any event, difficulty in securing an impartial jury is a reasonable price to pay for ensuring that the right to a fair trial will not be destroyed by intentional efforts to sway the community through publicity.

The Union feels that at the present time it would be a mistake to enact sanctions directly against the press. Unless experience under the new rules regulating conduct of officials who are more intimately a part of the judicial process shows them to be inadequate, the press should not be subjected to controls that may well violate fundamental constitutional rights.

The ACLU suggests that the Judicial Conference of the United States explore the problem of the potential bias that inflammatory publicity may create in judges, with a view to adopting standards governing the conduct of judges in sensational, well-publicized cases.

The conflict over free press and fair trial came to a head in 1966 with publication of the Reardon Report by the American Bar Association, which recommended restrictions against release of information by law enforcement officers, attorneys, and officers of the court, sources from which the press gets its information. Disagreement with this approach encouraged members of the bar, the press, and the bench in a number of states and cities to draft mutually acceptable and voluntary guidelines that would recognize the two basic constitutional rights. One such statement of principles was adopted in California.

State Bar of California

JOINT DECLARATION REGARDING NEWS COVERAGE OF CRIMINAL PROCEEDINGS IN CALIFORNIA

I. STATEMENT OF PRINCIPLES

The bench, bar, and news media of California recognize that freedom of the press and the right to fair trial, as guaranteed by the First and Sixth Amendments to the Constitution of the United States, sometimes appear to be in conflict. They believe, however, that if the principles of fair trial and free press are applied responsibly in accord with high professional ethics, our society can have fair trials without limiting freedom of the press.

Accordingly, the following principles are recommended to all members of the bar and the press in California.

1. The news media have the right and responsibility to gather and disseminate the news, so that the public will be informed. Free and responsible newsmedia enhance the administration of justice. Members of the bench, the bar, and the news media should cooperate, consistent with their respective ethical principles, in accomplishing the foregoing.

2. All parties to litigation, including the state, have the right to have their causes tried fairly by impartial tribunals. Defendants in criminal cases are guaranteed this right by the Constitutions of the United States and the State of California.

3. Lawyers and journalists share with the court responsibility for maintaining an atmosphere conducive to fair trial.

4. The news media and the bar recognize

the responsibility of the judge to preserve order in court and to conduct proceedings in such a manner as will serve the ends of justice.

5. Editors in deciding what news to publish should remember that:

   a) *An accused person is presumed innocent until proven guilty.*

   b) *Readers, listeners, and viewers are potential jurors or witnesses.*

   c) *No person's reputation should be injured needlessly.*

6. No lawyer should use publicity to promote his version of a pending case. The public prosecutor should not take unfair advantage of his position as an important source of news. These cautions shall not be construed to limit a lawyer's making available information to which the public is entitled. Editors should be cautious about publishing information received from lawyers who seek to try their cases in the press.

7. The public is entitled to know how justice is being administered, and it is the responsibility of the press to give the public the necessary information. A properly conducted trial maintains the confidence of the community as to the honesty of its institutions, the competence of its public officers, the impartiality of its judges, and the capacity of its criminal law to do justice.

8. Journalistic and legal training should include instruction in the meaning of constitutional rights to a fair trial, freedom of the press, and the role of both journalist and lawyer in guarding these rights.

9. A committee of representatives of the bar, the bench, and the news media, aided when appropriate by representatives of law enforcement agencies and other interested parties, should meet from time to time to review problems and to promote understanding of the principles of fair trial and free press. Its purpose may include giving advisory opinions concerning the interpretations and application of these principles.

These principles have been endorsed, as of February 15, 1970, by the following. The State Bar of California, California Freedom of Information Committee, California

Newspaper Publishers Association, California Broadcasters Association, Radio and TV News Directors, and the Executive Board of the Conference of California Judges.

II. STATEMENT OF POLICY
To give concrete expression to these principles in newsmen's language the following statement of policy is recommended for voluntary adoption by California newspapers and news broadcasters.

Our objective is to report the news and at the same time cooperate with the courts to assure the accused a fair trial.

Protection of the rights of an accused person or a suspect does not require restraint in publication or broadcast of the following information:

His or her name, address, age, residence, employment, marital status, and similar background information.

The substance or text of the charge, such as complaint, indictment, information and, where appropriate, the identity of the complaint.

The identity of the investigating and arresting agency, and the length of investigation where appropriate.

The circumstances surrounding an arrest, including the time and place, resistance, pursuit, possession and use of weapons, and a description of items seized.

Accuracy, good conscience, and an informed approach can provide non-prejudicial reporting of crime news. We commend to our fellow newsmen the following:

Avoid deliberate editorialization, even when a crime seems solved beyond reasonable doubt. Save the characterizations of the accused until the trial ends and guilt or innocence is determined.

Avoid editorialization by observing these rules:

Don't call a person brought in for questioning a suspect.

Don't call a slaying a murder until there's a formal charge.

Don't say solution when it's just a police accusation or theory.

Don't let prosecutors, police or defense attorneys use us as a sounding board for public opinion or personal publicity.

Exercise care in regard to publication or broadcast of purported confessions. An accused person may repudiate and thereby invalidate a confession, claiming undue pressure, lack of counsel, or some other interference with his rights. The confession then may not be presented as evidence and yet have been read by the jurors, raising the question whether they can separate the confession from evidence presented in court. If you do use a "confession" call it a statement and let the jury decide whether the accused really confessed.

In some circumstances, as when a previous offense is not linked in a pattern with the case in question, the press should not publish or broadcast the previous criminal record of a person accused of a felony. Terms like "a long record" should generally be avoided. There are, however, other circumstances—as when parole is violated—in which reference to a previous conviction is in the public interest.

Records of convictions and prior criminal charges which are matters of public record are available to the news media through police agencies or court clerks. Law enforcement agencies should make such information available to the news media upon appropriate inquiry. The public disclosure of this information by the news media could be prejudicial without any significant contribution toward meeting the public need to be informed. The publication or broadcast of such information should be carefully considered.

IN SUMMARY
This Statement of Policy is not all-inclusive; it does not purport to cover every subject on which a question may arise with respect to whether particular information should be published or broadcast. Our objective is to

report the news and at the same time cooperate with the courts to help assure the accused a fair trial. Caution should therefore be exercised in publishing or broadcasting information which might result in denial of a fair trial.

"Freedom of the press must not prevent a man on trial for his life from receiving a fair trial." In the following article noted trial lawyer Louis Nizer presents a strong case for restricting the press coverage of criminal trials, recommending the adoption of the English doctrine of constructive contempt of court.

Louis Nizer

TRIAL BY HEADLINE

When the Profumo scandal exploded in England, the public there took to importing American newspapers to satisfy its curiosity. Under English law and tradition, British newspapers would not prejudice the fair trial of those involved by publishing in advance the lurid details of a government minister who was accused of endangering government secrets by his sexual adventures. Contrast this with the conduct of our press, prosecutors and police in the Richard F. Speck case. There, eight nurses in Chicago were tied by a man who calmly assured them he intended no harm, then took them one by one into another room and killed them.

Such a horrible multiple crime, of course, produced an inflamed atmosphere. yet before trial, newspapers screamed the statements of prosecution authorities that "Speck is guilty. We have an open-and-shut case against him"; that thirty-two fingerprints left on the scene of this horrendous crime were identified as his (no cross-examiner had yet been afforded an opportunity to examine the prints before trial and question the expert

Reprinted with permission of the author and the McCall Publishing Company from the February 1967 issue of *McCall's*.

who would testify for the prosecution, if by chance there was a discrepancy); that he had a prior record of sex offenses, such as a "tendency" to self-exposure; that he once had been convicted of burglary.

A jury would later be chosen from a public drenched with details of Speck's "guilt," established by assertions outside the courtroom. He might very well be the murderer; but then why not offer the overwhelming proof for the first time in a courtroom, where the jurors would be unprejudiced by prior reports and the evidence would be sifted for admissibility by rules based on centuries of experience? Why endanger any conviction by publicity that preconditions a jury and therefore makes possible a reversal and escape for an inhuman killer?

The Supreme Court reversed the conviction of Dr. Samuel Sheppard for murdering his wife after he had served nine years, on the ground that the trial judge had permitted "massive, pervasive and prejudicial publicity." The court held that charges and rumors (such as that Sheppard had an illegitimate child and that he balked at taking a lie-detector test), never introduced as evidence, were aired in the press and on television. Later, Dr. Sheppard was judged an innocent man, who spent nine years in jail because the press made it impossible for him to get a fair trial. Can the retrial ever take the place of a fair first trial?

The Supreme Court set aside the conviction of Billie Sol Estes on similar, though less aggravated, grounds. Before Jack Ruby's serious illness, scene of the new trial was shifted to Wichita Falls, Texas, to provide a more impartial forum. The Illinois Supreme Court ordered that Speck be tried in Peoria, not Chicago.

There was a time when local prejudice could be overcome by a change of venue—that is, a shift of the trial to another locale. The theory was that the intense passions at the scene of the crime had made unlikely an impartial hearing. However, today, when radio and television carry the neighbors' and the sheriff's comments to every town and hamlet, a change of venue is probably useless.

The Warren Commission Report referred to the orgy of statements on television, by police and witnesses, that condemned Oswald as President Kennedy's assassin. It concluded that had Oswald lived, "opportunity for a trial by twelve jurors free of preconception as to his guilt or innocence would have been seriously jeopardized by the premature disclosure and weighing of evidence against him."

Police officers, nightclub entertainers, acquaintances, janitors and other "witnesses" who had touched the periphery of Oswald's life spoke freely before the television cameras. They were so intoxicated by world attention they forgot to say, "I don't know." They were full of knowledge, often completely false. The errors they made, such as the police officer's wrong identification of the make of Oswald's rifle, have fed the contentions of a spate of books, now being published, that seek to impugn the authoritative Warren Commission Report.

Jurors are instructed not to read newspapers or listen to radio or watch television. They are also forbidden to discuss the case with anyone during the trial. Sometimes they are sent to a hotel during the trial, with no access to newspapers or electronic devices. It has been said humorously that ours is the only country in which the jurors are locked up while the defendant goes home. Human nature being what it is, these admirable precautions against outside influence cannot be trusted too far. What juror will refrain from talking to his wife about the exciting day's events? In a famous case, how often does a juror shut his eyes to newsprint or his ears and eyes to radio and television reports?

In the Candy Mossler trial, in which she and her nephew, Mel Powers, were accused of killing her husband, a Miami newspaper chided the jurors for their lack of comely appearance. Immediately thereafter, there was a general sprucing up of the jurors' attire, proving that they were reading the newspapers.

Let us examine specific illustrations of prejudice from out-of-court publicity about a defendant's guilt.

Suppose the prosecutor announces triumphantly that he has obtained a complete confession from the accused. At the trial, that confession may never be admitted into evidence, because of the claim that it was obtained by duress or that the prisoner was not advised of his constitutional right not to incriminate himself or to obtain counsel. If so, it would be barred. The prosecutor would then be obliged to prove his case by external evidence, without using the defendant's own statement against him. There is a considerable school of thought that before anyone's liberty or life is sacrificed, the burden should rest on the state, with its enormous investigative and other resources, to prove its case without depending on the word of the defendant himself to impale him.

Therefore, the prosecutor should await a trial before announcing a confession, which must still pass legal muster. Otherwise, the jury is prejudiced by knowledge of a confession or other evidence a court may rule it should never hear.

And another illustration: Suppose the prosecutor announces that the accused has a long list of prior arrests and convictions. Under our law, arrests can never be offered in evidence at the trial. A man may be innocent, although arrested.

For the same reason, even if a defendant has been *convicted* of a prior crime, this fact may not be offered affirmatively as evidence of guilt of the charge for which he is being tried. Only if the defendant chooses to take the stand and testify on his own behalf may he be cross-examined about his prior convictions. However, the jury is carefully instructed by the judge that such evidence may be considered only in evaluating the defendant's *credibility*, not as evidence of guilt for the crime with which he is charged.

In any event, if the defendant does not take the stand at all, as he has a right not to do, his prior convictions may never be alluded to at all. Since he doesn't testify, his credibility is not involved, and that would be the only reason to offer his prior record into evidence. So we see again that announcement before trial, by district attorneys, police officers or witnesses, that the defendant has a record of arrests or convictions is evil, because it fills a prospective juror's mind with matter that would or might be excluded at the trial.

The same is, of course, true about pronouncements before trial by defense counsel that his client is innocent, or that he has been maltreated by the police, or that certain witnesses will give exculpatory testimony. Such assurances also upset the exquisite balance of judicial scales, where only weights tested by the judge's rulings on admissibility may be used.

When the jury system was first developed in the thirteenth century, jurors were chosen from the neighborhood where events occurred, so that they might know more about the case in question. Through evolution, rules of evidence separated the chaff from the fact, and hearsay was excluded. Then a juror who knew anything about the case in advance of the trial was excluded, because the "facts" he brought with him into the jury had not passed through the process of truth-finding. Thus there was a complete reversal of juror qualification. Now, if a juror has even read about a case or has been influenced by external impressions, he is disqualified to sit.

The subject of "trial by newspapers" has become a broadly debated national issue. In October, 1966, a 226-page report of the American Bar Association proposed restrictions on pretrial publicity. If adopted, they will prevent officials from providing the press with any prejudicial information that might lead to wrongful conviction or acquittal. The suggested code was met with a storm of protest. "Would inhibit the news media in the coverage of law enforcement," said the Des Moines *Register and Tribune*. "The cure is far more dangerous than the suspected ailment," cried the Miami *Herald*. "The more the press blasts the serious criminal, the better we like it," stated a Boston police commissioner.

But the fact remains that today's communications do hinder the judicial process.

The press is relentless in feeding public curiosity. In the Sam Sheppard case, the Cleveland *Press* unabashedly ran these headlines: "Why Isn't Sam Sheppard in Jail?," "Quit Stalling—Bring Him In." In other cities, stories on other crimes include: "So-and-So, who was arrested about 6:30 P.M. Wednesday, is reported to have told enforcement officers he did not know why he had killed the woman." "Death Quiz Yields Beating Confession. Admits Attack on Coed. Link Parolee to 2nd Crime." "Ex-con Admits Shooting Salesman. Aide in Theft Also Slain, Body Hidden." It is hard to determine the precise number of cases in which possible prejudice is created by news coverage and public statements. But according to the American Bar Association survey, there were between January, 1963, and March, 1965, approximately one hundred reported decisions in which the question is raised. And this is only the top of the iceberg.

Some news media do attempt to practice voluntary restraint. The Straus Broadcasting Group recently instituted a code by which reporters eliminate mention of confessions and prior criminal records of suspects except under circumstances of "overriding need." Media groups, sometimes in conjunction with the bar, have set up codes in various states, including Massachusetts, Oregon, Louisiana and Kentucky. But the codes vary in their specific guidelines, and the individual media do not always follow them. The Massachusetts guide, for example, is not followed by the daily papers in three large cities, including Boston.

How can an editor live up to a gentlemanly code of forebearance when, as in the Speck case, his competitor prints reams of material about how "Speck was jailed in Dallas in January, 1965, for holding a butcher's knife to a woman's throat"?

We are dealing here with nothing less than constitutional rights. The Sixth Amendment of our Constitution provides: "In all criminal prosecutions, the accused shall enjoy the right to a speedy and public trial, by an impartial jury." The First Amendment guarantees the right of freedom of speech and of the press, which rightly encompasses newspapers, radio and television. Both the First and Sixth Amendments protect precious rights. Neither must be sacrificed in favor of the other. Indeed, one cannot be violated without both being injured. The real question is not which is to be preferred, but rather how to accommodate them to achieve a just balance. Otherwise, there is the paradox that occurred in the case of Maryland vs. Baltimore Radio Show, where the American Civil Liberties Union filed a brief in support of free press, while the Maryland Civil Liberties Union opposed its parent organization and filed a brief in defense of fair trial.

Freedom of the press must not prevent a man on trial for his life from receiving a fair trial. The alternative is to slip into lynch law. In the famous case of Bridges vs. California, the Supreme Court said, "Free speech is not so absolute or irrational a conception as to imply paralysis of the means for effective protection of all the freedoms secured by the Bill of Rights. The claims on behalf of freedom of the press encounter claims on behalf of liberties no less precious."

The Bill of Rights is not self-destructive. Freedom of expression need not nullify the guarantees of impartial trials. Frequently, those who defend the present practice of the press speak of its "right to know." There is no such right. The press has "the right to publish." No citizen owes the duty to the press to inform it about his or her personal life. No district attorney need report the progress of an investigation. No lawyer must confide his trial plans.

However, when the trial finally does take place, then the public and the press may attend, and the right to publish becomes sacrosanct. In the famed Jelke trial, the judge barred the public and press during the prosecution's presentation of lurid evidence about the charge of operation of a prostitution ring. (In New York, the judiciary state law permits a judge, at his discretion, to close the courtroom to all but the participants when the issue involves rape, abortion, sodomy, bastardy or divorce.) A newspaper claimed that it had been deprived of its constitutional right to know and brought a proceeding to test its right. Jelke also appealed, on the ground that he was entitled to the Sixth Amendment's guarantee of a public trial. Jelke's appeal was granted; the newspaper's was not. Public trials are for the benefit of defendants, not newspapers. Attendance of the public prevents the courts from becoming instruments of persecution, such as existed during the Spanish Inquisition and the English Court of the Star Chamber. However, as one court reminded the press, "People are not arrested to provide news stories or telecasts. They are arrested to be brought to justice."

Indeed, many of the lurid stories in the press are motivated not by a desire to protect the public interest, but rather to feed the morbid curiosity of readers and increase circulation. The great majority of newspapers are responsible institutions impelled by high ideals of public service. But there appears to be a Gresham's Law of the press, by which the tawdry and sensational newspapers drive the more responsible ones down to their own standards.

There are honest arguments made by newspapers that their coverage helps public officials stay alert and keeps the public alert about public officials. For example, an editorial in a Chicago newspaper pointed out with pride that its revelation that Richard Speck has a tattoo on his arm inscribed "Born To Raise Hell" had helped his identification by a doctor in the hospital where he was taken after a suicide attempt. It did not add that Speck had escaped earlier arrest by half an hour because he was warned by screaming headlines that he was "the most wanted man in America."

It is argued that the very enormity of the crime would seem to justify public information even if it encroached on a defendant's right to a fair trial. But when we yield to this ancient "the end justifies the means" argument, we ultimately weaken the law. The corollary is always to strengthen lawlessness.

Freedom of the press is not an end in itself; it is the means to an end—*proper* public information. Every right is subject to abuse, and our society is founded on the principle of preventing our privileges from trespassing too far on other privileges. From red traffic lights to the prohibition against possession of dangerous weapons, from the laws of libel to the draft for service in the armed forces, we limit our freedom of speech and action for the common good. Restraint, whether voluntary or imposed, is an essential condition for the fullest enjoyment of freedom in a complex society. The press has enjoyed such extreme license, and the consequences to the administration of criminal justice have been dire. Supreme Court Justice Robert H. Jackson once wrote in a decision that "trial by newspaper is one of the worst menaces to American justice."

When a jury is selected, the lawyers inquire of each one whether he or she has read or heard about the case in the newspapers, on radio or television. In a well-publicized case, the answer is inevitably yes. The key question is then put: "Would you be influenced thereby, or do you think you can remove all that from your mind and decide this case solely on the evidence presented in this courtroom?" Some will admit they can't or that they are not sure they can. They will be excused "for cause." However, there are jurors who honestly feel uninfluenced or who are anxious to sit on an exciting case. They will say that pretrial publicity has not influenced them one whit. Such a juror cannot be challenged "for cause" and, since a lawyer has only a limited number of arbitrary challenges, may be allowed to remain. Chief Judge Desmond of the New York Court of Appeals has bluntly referred to the "incredible statements of jurors that they can read such stuff and wipe it off their minds."

Nor is the press solely responsible for this sullying of the judicial process. Prosecutors, police and defense counsel who feed the press must bear the onus, too. As the Warren Commission Report found, it was the desire of the police authorities to accommodate television cameras that exposed Oswald to his fatal shooting. The Warren Report commented on "a regrettable lack of self-discipline by the newsmen" and held that "primary responsibility for having failed to control the press and check the flow of undigested evidence to the public must be borne by the [Dallas] Police Department."

Some "exterior" force, some sanction is obviously necessary to protect the right to a fair trial. Anyone who thinks this is an abstruse question need only pray that he or she does not fall into the toils of the law. Then only will there be an appreciation for the magnificent safeguards that preserve the presumption of innocence. The torment of standing accused by one's government is indescribable. In such a predicament, one is grateful for every constitutional right that gives the individual a chance to be acquitted, despite the great resources of the state.

What, then, is the remedy to overcome the present frequent corruption of the atmosphere surrounding a trial, of eliminating implanted prejudice in jurors, which defeats their "impartiality," guaranteed by the Sixth Amendment?

For remedy, we need not grope in the darkness. We need only look at the historic example provided in England under the same Anglo-Saxon philosophy of law that guides us. Because England has succeeded in curbing its press, so as to create a proper balance between its right to publish and an individual's right to a fair trial. How? By a device called "constructive contempt of court," which holds newspaper publishers who interfere with judicial process liable to fines and imprisonment.

In the famous Crippen case, an enterprising editor published a cable saying that a man named Crippen had been arrested in Canada and had confessed to killing his wife. Judge Darling fined the editor two hundred pounds and costs. In the Crumbles murder case in 1924, the *Evening Standard* sent special "criminal investigators" to the scene and published reports of their efforts. The editor was fined a thousand pounds and costs, with a warning that such conduct in the future would be punished by imprisonment. The most severe penalty was meted out in 1948 to the editor of the *Daily Mirror*, who was sent to jail for three months, and his company was fined ten thousand pounds and the cost of the proceedings. This resulted from editorials commenting on the case of John George Haigh, who had been accused of murdering a woman and then disposing of the body in an acid bath. The newspaper called him a vampire, said he was charged with other murders and gave the names of his other alleged victims.

Reform in our country should take two directions. First, law-enforcement officials—prosecutors, police and the bar—must not, prior to trial, issue statements or disclose:

1. Confessions.
2. Criminal records of the accused.
3. Opinions as to his guilt.
4. What witnesses will testify to.

Goaded by the threat of legislation, such as a bill introduced by Senator Wayne Morse and ten other Senators, which would punish violations in federal criminal cases, a voluntary code may be adopted by enforcement agencies. This may be further stimulated by the recent issuance of the American Bar Association report, which suggests similar revisions in the bar's canon of ethics and enforces them by threat of judicial and Bar-Association reprimand and, in severe cases, disbarment and punishment for contempt of court.

The second phase of reform involves the press itself. Newspapers, radio and TV should, in my opinion, pledge that before a trial begins, they would publish only the following data:

1. The name, age and address of the accused.
2. How, when and where the arrest was made.
3. The charge and the identity of the complainant.
4. The fact that a grand jury has returned an indictment and that a trial date has been set.

During the progress of the trial, they would adhere to the rules mentioned above for prosecutors, police officials and lawyers: not to refer to a confession, or to a prior criminal record of the accused, or to testimony that has been stricken out by the court, or to opinions about guilt or innocence or the credibility of witnesses, unless admitted into evidence.

After all, what the newspapers are being asked to do is simply to delay the publication of details until a trial takes place.

The need for reform is heightened by the fact that when the higher courts reverse a conviction because of pretrial publicity, a vicious criminal may be freed. It is more important to protect the constitutional rights for all citizens than to incarcerate one offender; but this sacrifice can be avoided. If we adopt a sensible procedure to eliminate trial by newspapers, we will protect society by incarcerating a guilty felon, who will not escape because his trial was prejudiced by prosecutor and the press.

Some newspapers, out of a sincere conviction that they perform a public service by rejecting all restraints on a free press, or because they are more eager to mind the till than till the mind, will ignore these rules. Then the courts should adopt the English doctrine of constructive contempt of court and punish them. Thus the tiny minority of rebellious newspapers will not be able to prevent the responsible mass of the press from putting into balance the freedom of the press and the accused's right to an impartial jury.

We ought to delay no longer. "Let us not be guilty," as Voltaire said, "of the good things we did not do."

The associate editor of the *New York Times*, while recognizing the abuses of the press in covering trials and applauding the efforts of the legal profession to discipline its members to ensure a fair trial, itemizes the things the press will *not* do to endanger its freedom to publish.

Clifton Daniel

FAIR TRIAL AND
FREEDOM OF THE PRESS

My position on the Free Press—Fair Trial issue begins with some stipulations.

First of all, we of the press can readily admit that, in our zeal to publish, we sometimes do violence to the rights of defendants—unintentionally, inadvertently, without malice, but, nevertheless, deplorably.

In the second place, we can concede that the *manners* of newspapermen are not always impeccable. We are highly competitive. We work against the clock. We push. We shove. We probe. We ask embarrassing questions. Sometimes we do a little browbeating.

In the third place, we can acknowledge also that the press sometimes swarms over a news story in such a way that the story becomes warped and distorted. Instead of merely covering the news, the press by its very numbers, its energy and its activity, becomes a participant in the news, and transforms it into something it would otherwise never have been. Incidentally, when I speak of the press in this context, I include television and radio.

In the fourth place, we newsmen are ready to agree that there is need for reform and that we must be more conscientious in our concern for the rights of individuals.

The press in general will interpose no objection to anything the bar, the bench and the police may do in the way of disciplining their own people, although we may feel constrained to point out the risks and evils inherent in restricting the free flow of information to the public, which we all serve.

I am certain that some further restrictions on the legal profession, the judiciary and the law enforcement agencies are on the way. They will be imposed by professional associations or ordered by the appellate courts. I think you will find that most newspapers will not seriously resist them, and that conscien-

Reprinted by permission of the publisher from *Case and Comment* September-October 1966.

tious and responsible newspapers will tend to applaud them.

Those are my stipulations.

WHAT THE PRESS WILL NOT DO

Now, let me tell you a few things I am quite sure the press will *not* do.

1. We will not submit to censorship.

We will not be told by policemen, lawyers or judges what we may or may not print. We are not inclined, speaking plainly, to hand over control of the press to political-minded prosecutors and judges who may be running for election and seeking the support of the very newspapers they are empowered to censure and control.

We do not believe that a law degree necessarily makes a man more civic-minded than a degree in journalism, or that elevation to the bench is equivalent to canonization.

2. We will not surrender our freedom to publish anything that is said or done in public, provided we do not transgress the laws of libel and the generally accepted standards of decency and good taste. In particular, as long as policemen and lawyers feel free to make outrageously prejudicial statements, we will feel free to print them—if only to show how outrageous they are.

Freedom of the press is really a very small part of the issue we are considering here.

A much broader question is the freedom that law enforcement officers, lawyers and judges allow to themselves.

Judges fret about the publication of the prior criminal records of defendants.

How much does it matter as long as the law allows the defendant to be questioned about his record once he takes the stand?

Newspapers are berated for printing so-called confessions.

Lawyers might better use their time in investigating how such confessions are obtained and how they find their way into the hands of newspapermen.

Sometimes lawyers seem to us to be too much concerned with the *appearance* of justice, and not enough concerned with the *reality* of it.

Lawyers seem to be too preoccupied with

individual cases, and not worried enough about the thing that worries serious newspapermen most—the general climate surrounding law enforcement and the administration of justice.

You will perhaps recall an arrest that was made in New York in April of 1965.

The New York Times version of the story began:

A slender, nearsighted 19-year-old drifter in the Brownsville section of Brooklyn was charged yesterday with stabbing Janice Wylie and Emily Hoffert to death in their East Side Apartment last year.

The police said the suspect, George Whitmore Jr., had admitted killing the two career girls. They said he also had confessed to the slaying of a Brooklyn woman on April 14.

No public official, no bar association president, no judge in the whole city of New York, so far as I am aware, objected to our using the terms "admitted killing" and "confessed to the slaying."

The only protest we received, and it was a vigorous one, came nine months later when the indictment against George Whitmore was abandoned, and we published an allegation that the police had concocted his confession for him.

Would the confession, 61 pages long and detailed in the extreme, have ever been discredited if the newspapers hadn't challenged it?

3. Newspapers will not yield up the privilege of publishing anything said in open court. If judges feel that such things may be prejudicial, they must use the remedies already available to them. They can clear the courtroom; they can call counsel to the bench or to their chambers; they can excuse the jury; they can enjoin the jurors not to read newspapers or listen to radio and television; they can lock up the jury; they can expunge anything they like from the record. But they cannot edit our newspapers.

The same sort of thing might be said of the judge in the Ruby trial.

What matters most is not what newspapers say but what lawyers and judges do. The press, for the most part, merely holds up a mirror to these actions.

4. We will not surrender the power of the press to expose and criticize the acts of public officials, including prosecutors and judges.

There is undoubtedly something to be said for the British rule which bars pre-trial publication of confessions and the previous records of defendants. But there is also a danger in the British rule. It could impair our long-established and very serviceable American concept of freedom of the press, and seriously inhibit the press in the performance of one of its most vital functions. That function is to keep public servants honest.

For all practical purposes the British rule would bar investigations by newspapers or, to be more precise, the publication of the results of investigations by newspapers. Newspapermen, of course, are not judges, but they are investigators, and to prevent the publication of their investigations would cost us a great deal in terms of the integrity of our public life.

5. We newspapermen will not do some of the ridiculous things that lawyers now seem to be suggesting we should do.

If a notorious hoodlum is hailed into court, we will not describe him simply as a loving husband, a kind father, a devoted son, a good provider and a churchgoer, while, at the same time, suppressing all mention of his criminal record and questionable activities. We will call a crook a crook—if it is perfectly clear that he *is* a crook.

6. We will not submit to legislation that clearly abridges the constitutional guarantee of a free press. We will fight any such legislation to the highest court.

I have read, as I am sure you have, several of the statutes proposed for the purpose of limiting pre-trial publicity and assuring a fair hearing for defendants. It looks to me as if some people are using sledgehammers to kill gnats.

The problem to which this legislation is addressed is not of enormous dimensions. Only a tiny fraction of criminal cases is ever reported in the press, and in only a fraction of this fraction is there any question of doing violence to the rights of defendants.

In New York City, 11,724 felonies were committed in January of 1965. Only 41 of those cases were mentioned in the Daily News, and the News gives more attention to crime than any other paper in town. If there were violations of defendants' rights in any of the other 11,683 cases—and who can doubt that some violations did occur?—they cannot in any way be charged to the newspapers.

7. We will not accept any compulsory code of conduct for the press. We doubt that such a code would be constitutional. We see no practical means of enforcing it without licensing the press, and licensing would destroy the freedom of the press.

I don't think anyone who has not lived under a dictatorship can appreciate the atmosphere of a country where the press is *not* free, where the newspapers never speak until spoken to.

I spent a part of my career in the Soviet Union. When I was there some ten years ago, it was possible for a man to be arrested without even his family knowing about it, much less his friends and his professional associates. He was simply missing. His family inquired, but his friends dared not do so, and his neighbors kept their doors locked, and listened at the keyhole.

The newspapers never reported his arrest. No hint of the charges against an ordinary citizen was ever given to the general public, even if he were brought to trial. The highest dignitaries of the state could disappear overnight, and nothing was heard of them until arrest, trial and execution were simultaneously announced in one terse communique.

Now, I know we are not taking about instituting the Soviet system of justice. But we *should* be talking about the abuses that can take place and *do* take place when the work of the police and the courts and the prisons is hidden from public view.

One wonders what would have happened in Philadelphia, Miss. if there had been no newspapermen—Northern and Southern newspapermen—prying into the disappearance of the three civil rights workers there in the summer of 1964. Would the bodies *ever* have been found? Would anybody *ever* have been indicted for the murders?

THE ENGLISH APPROACH

Before I worked in Russia, I spent ten years of my life in London, and people sometimes ask me why we simply don't adopt the British rule on pre-trial publicity in this country.

As you know, through the stringent exercise of the contempt power of the courts, newspapers in Britain are effectively restrained from publishing prejudicial material about a defendant after he has been charged and before he is brought to trial. In essence, the newspapers can say only that a crime has been committed and someone has been arrested. Further details come out only when they are heard in court.

As long as I lived in England, I was never conscious of any oppressive abridgement of the British public's right to share vicariously in the delights and pleasures of the criminal classes. The British popular press is more scurrilous and scandalous and more prurient than anything published in this country. The British newspaper reader has to wait, but in the end he gets his four-pence worth of thrills.

Still, I don't think the system is appropriate for the United States. In Britain, judges are appointed, not elected. Lawyers serve the prosecution today, the defense tomorrow, depending on who hires them. The rights of accused persons are more consciously protected. Justice is swifter.

In the United States it might be three months, six months, a year or two years before a criminal is brought to trial on a major charge. There is plenty of time in between for tampering with justice.

In this country, the preliminary hearing is usually a pro forma matter. In Britain, the preliminary hearing is held quickly, and the principal issues in the case are immediately and fully disclosed.

I recall covering the trial of Klaus Fuchs,

the atom spy. He was in police court within 10 days after his arrest, and the principal evidence against him was presented and available for publication. Within 26 days, he was standing in the dock at the Old Bailey. The trial was concluded in an hour and a half, and he was on his way to prison.

When cases are so promptly disposed of, there is less need for pre-trial disclosure of the facts in the newspapers.

Up to this point I have been largely negative in my reaction to suggestions for limiting pre-trial publicity and ensuring the rights of defendants.

WHAT THE PRESS WILL DO

Now, let me be more positive and tell you some of the things I think the press will do.

In the first place, we newspapermen are more than ready to engage in discussions between the press and the bar, the bench and law enforcement authorities.

We hope these discussions can be predicated on the assumption that all of us believe in the principle of a fair trial for every defendant. We are, after all, citizens before we are lawyers and newspapermen. We have a common interest in preserving the rights of our fellow-citizens, not to mention our own rights.

Second, the press is prepared to draw up a code of etiquette for newsmen and seek approval of it from professional journalistic and broadcasting organizations.

Third, we are prepared to offer advice to public authorities on procedures for pool coverage of news events, whenever pooling seems desirable or necessary to prevent the kind of gross interference with the news that occurred in Dallas three years ago.

Fourth, we are more than willing to see that young journalists, those just entering the profession, are alerted to the damage that can be done to the rights of individuals by carelessness, sensationalism and over-zealousness.

It is simple enough to alert students to these dangers. Journalism schools regularly offer lectures on the laws of libel. There is no reason why they should not have lectures on the rights of defendants. Some schools already do. And it would be a fine thing if these lectures could be delivered by lawyers and judges.

Fifth, the American press will be responsive to more frequent admonitions from the bench and representations from the bar, provided such admonitions are clearly designed to insure a fair trial and are not self-serving efforts to suppress news.

Finally, we are more than willing, in cooperation with the bar and the bench and independent scholarly institutions, to seek a consensus on the limitations that we should place upon ourselves to protect the rights of individuals. This might lead to the drafting of guidelines or a statement of principles.

JOURNALISTIC AND LEGAL ETHICS

One might imagine from some of the things said lately that journalism knows no law but the law of the jungle. As a matter of fact, in this country we have already set certain standards of journalistic performance that are generally accepted. From the beginning of my career, I was indoctrinated in American journalism's code of accuracy, fairness, objectivity and good taste. There is no law to enforce this code, but it is widely and scrupulously honored.

On The New York Times, it is expressed in the credo that was given to us by Adolph Ochs when he bought the paper in 1896. That credo was: "To give the news impartially, without fear or favor, regardless of any party, sect or interest involved."

We would be quite willing to add, "And without prejudice to the rights of any individual."

As Alfred Friendly of the Washington Post has said, "The press is in a mood to move." It might move more quickly if it could see more signs of movement in the legal profession.

Canon XX [of the Canons of Professional Ethics, captioned "Newspaper Discussion of Pending Litigation"], as Mr. Friendly points out, has been on the books for a long time.

Lawyers can be disbarred for violating it, but no disbarments have yet occurred, in spite of all the abuses you complain about.

Should newspaper reporters be given the same right to protect their news sources, even from court orders, as the immunity granted to lawyers, doctors, and clergy? Failing to be given such immunity by the courts, the press has looked to legislative relief. Columnist Anthony Lewis opposes a special journalist's privilege.

Anthony Lewis

PRESS POWER AND THE FIRST AMENDMENT

It is the particular function of the press to raise skeptical questions, to doubt infallibility. I find it incongruous, therefore, and unbecoming, to have the press claim a broad immunity from being questioned itself. That is the common theme of two positions taken recently by many leading figures in the media: in favor of Congress legislating a reporter's privilege not to testify in legal proceedings; against proposals for a press council.

I am dubious about the privilege bills because I do not think that any legislation can foresee all the difficult problems involved and balance the social interests wisely. I believe a press council would be a good thing for the public and more especially for the press. On these issues I differ with most of my colleagues on *The New York Times* and elsewhere. So be it.

There is common ground between us on the threat to freedom today. We have a government in Washington that has arrogated power to itself, even the power to take this country into war. Some of its officials have shown that they will not hesitate to lie and cheat in order to keep that power. Against

Reprinted by permission of the author and the Educational Fund for Individual Rights from *Civil Liberties Review* 1: 183–85 (Fall 1973).

that threatening concentration a free press is an essential social weapon. It has performed with great courage and independence recently, notably in the *Times's* decision to publish the Pentagon Papers and the *Washington Post's* tenacity on Watergate. The administration sees the news media as its enemy and has used all the pressures available to stop exposure and criticism, including the device of subpoenaing journalists. Local governments concerned to prevent disclosure of corruption have done the same.

It is against this background that the demand for a special journalist's privilege has arisen. The immediate reason is a pressing one: reporters must rely on sources who will not identify themselves; unless the sources can be confident that they will not be disclosed, they will not talk; and in case after case authorities are trying to make reporters disclose them.

All this was argued as ground for journalists to have a *constitutional* privilege under the First Amendment, at least unless the authorities could convincingly show an essential need for their testimony. But in June 1972, the Supreme Court rejected that argument by a vote of five to four. The contest then shifted to Congress, with a campaign by the media for legislation granting an absolute privilege. As the managing editor of the *Times*, A. M. Rosenthal, put it: "I am urging passage of legislation prohibiting the use of subpoena powers in all matters relating to the free press provisions of the First Amendment."

Whatever individual states or the federal government may do, I do not believe legislative shield laws are the proper approach. To testify when called is in general not only a legal obligation but a civic duty. The exemptions are narrow, and the thrust of the law has been to remove what have been called "barriers to the truth" in the law of evidence except as to protection from compelled self-incrimination. Why, then, should such a sweeping new exemption be created for the press?

The argument is that the vital function of

the press justifies special treatment. I agree that the function is vital, but it is impossible for me to say that it qualifies for treatment different from many other interests. The Constitution protects the freedom of not only the press but books and films and scholarship, and every citizen's freedom of speech, thought, and association.

When the commission investigating the tragedy at Attica interviewed prisoners involved in the rebellion, it promised not to identify who said what. After publication of the report, authorities tried to find out; but the commission's counsel, Arthur Lyman, said he would go to jail himself before disclosing the names. Was there less public interest in confidentiality there than in the case of a reporter's sources?

Samuel Popkin, an associate professor at Harvard, actually did go to jail in November, 1972, rather than answer questions before a grand jury about the names of officials who might have known about the Pentagon Papers. How would one distinguish his claim of scholarly integrity from a journalist's?

Ralph Nader is not a journalist, but no newspaper or magazine or radio station has done what he has in exposing the malfunctioning of government agencies. Should he have less legal protection in keeping the names of his sources confidential?

It is of course possible for Congress to draw a line and say that only regular reporters for established media should have a new privilege. But I think such a distinction would be logically and morally insupportable. I do not have it in me to believe that I should have a privilege denied, under similar circumstances, to Arthur Lyman or Samuel Popkin or Ralph Nader.

Apart from the difficulty—for me the impossibility—of defining in a statute *who* should be privileged, there is the question of *what* testimony should be covered. Should a reporter be able to avoid testifying if he was involved in criminal activity himself? If he was the only person to see a crime committed? If the defendant calls him as the only alibi witness in a criminal trial? These questions are hardly exhaustive; they merely in-

dicate that there are other interests in a civilized society than those of the press.

All the difficulties in defining the scope of any new privilege suggest to me that there can be no absolute rules. Rather, the public interest in privacy should be weighed in every relevant case against the general duty to testify—whether a journalist or scholar or whoever is involved. It should be crucial to see whether the authorities showed a real need for the demanded testimony or were just fishing, endangering "confidential source relationships without a legitimate need of law enforcement."

The quoted words are from Justice Powell's concurring opinion in the privilege cases. To me they show how the problem should be handled: by courts, weighing competing interests case-by-case as only courts can. If the Supreme Court and other courts had followed Justice Powell's wise formulation, instead of dealing with the claim of privilege as a matter of power, of yes-or-no, we should not be in the fix we are now. Men who abuse power would not have been encouraged to harass the press.

It may be that without a legislated absolute privilege some reporters will have to go to prison to protect their sources. That is a price that sometimes has to be paid in protests against tyranny. The social advantage of that kind of resistance, of fighting through the courts instead of getting a blanket exemption in advance, is that it focuses public attention on the real evils: the abuse of investigative power, the perversion of the grand jury, the vindictive character of some who govern us.

A final reason for skepticism about a testimonial privilege for the press alone is that it looks like special pleading. And a good many people already have a suspicion that the media tend to apply gentler standards to themselves than they do to others.

That brings us to the press council. A study for the Twentieth Century Fund, drawing on the successful experience in Britain and elsewhere, suggested the creation of a National News Council with six members from the media and nine representing the public and as chairman the esteemed former chief justice of the California Supreme Court, Roger Traynor. The *Times* responded by saying it would not take part, arguing that the council would weaken defenses against the real threats to freedom, and others were negative also.

There is space to make only a point or two. One is that the public has an intense interest in the press today—and rightly so, considering its influence. There is widespread hostility, and doubt about media accuracy and fairness. A press council is a modest step, a most cautious one, to meet these public concerns. It would regulate nothing and order nobody; its only power would be to ask questions and publish its views.

Is the press so perfect that it does not need that kind of scrutiny? I think the growth of serious press criticism in such journals as the *Columbia Journalism Review* and [MORE] has been highly beneficial to newspapers, magazines, and broadcasters. We think criticism strengthens governments and other institutions; why will it weaken ours? By opposing the idea of a press council the media appear to seek what Stanley Baldwin attributed to the press lords of his day: "power without responsibility, the prerogative of the harlot throughout the ages."

RADIO AND TELEVISION UNDER THE FIRST AMENDMENT

Should radio and television, forms of communication not anticipated by the framers of the Bill of Rights, be given the same protection under the First Amendment as the printed press? Leaders in the broadcast industry have long sought equal treatment, but the Federal Communications Commission, backed by the courts, has insisted on controls over both content and distribution of programs. On the other hand, there is a growing movement to extend broadcasting's so-called fairness doctrine to the newspaper press, in order to guarantee the airing of opposing points of view on controversial issues. The president of United Press International makes a case for equal treatment for radio and television.

William Small

RADIO AND TELEVISION TREATED LIKE DISTANT COUSINS

It was almost as if those fine fellows, our Founding Fathers, had sat down with quill pen in hand and Walter Cronkite in mind to frame the First Amendment thusly: "Congress shall make no law . . . abridging the freedom of speech, or of the press except, of course, on radio and television. There, Congress shall feel free to set government stan-

Reprinted by permission of the author from *The Quill* September 1976, pp. 30–32.

dards on fairness in news, bureaucratic definitions on what constitutes a need to reply, and slide-rule obligations on the care and treatment of political candidates."

If they didn't indicate such foresight, the Founding Fathers should be here today to see their political descendants do it for them. Jefferson and Madison and all those other fellows might find it hard to hide a smile as they see political figures and federal appointees and even Supreme Court justices rationalize why certain parts of the press can be fully free but some others free some of the time, partly so, in most cases.

The late Justice Hugo Black felt the First Amendment was absolute, it meant just what it said. The prevailing belief in most quarters is that this isn't quite so in the case of broadcasting.

Had broadcast journalism not emerged in recent times as the source for most of the people to get most of their news, this might be wryly amusing. It is not.

There are cliches to defend the bend-the-amendment position. One is that "the airwaves belong to the people." Former Secretary of State Dean Rusk, who has little patience with that one, has noted that the North Star and gravity also "belong to the people."

It has been noted that the government's right to regulate content because it is delivered over publicly owned airwaves means, with equal logic, that the government can regulate newspapers and magazines which are delivered over publicly owned streets or through the publicly owned post office.

Regardless of who owns the airwaves, the more important question is how they are used and, in terms of a free press, is the government's hand going to have a grip on that usage.

There is the scarcity argument. It states that government must license radio and television because the broadcast spectrum is limited. This is true; however, "limited" and "scarce" are not the same thing. As many have pointed out, there are several times as many radio and TV stations broadcasting daily as there are daily newspapers in America. Not everyone can own a television station, but very few of us can start a daily newspaper either.

Scarcity was the core of the so-called Red Lion decision by the Supreme Court in 1969. This was a definitive high-court ruling on the question of how far the Federal Communications Commission can go in imposing a "fairness doctrine." The Court, in fact, ruled that the FCC can go all the way, that the First Amendment was *not* fully applicable to the broadcaster.

The Court said in Red Lion, "Just as the Government may limit the use of sound-amplifying equipment potentially so noisy that it drowns out civilized private speech, so

may the Government limit the use of broadcast equipment." Agreed. That is exactly what the original legislation of radio was meant to do, to control the broadcast spectrum so that—as happened in the 1920s—one broadcaster does not infringe on the broadcast channel of the next. It is quite a different thing to extend that concept to the insertion of government into what is being said.

The Red Lion ruling also said, "It is the right of the viewers and listeners, not the right of the broadcasters, which is paramount." That, too, is a common argument in favor of a controlled broadcast press. It assumes, somehow, that broadcasters are oblivious or callous towards their viewers. A strong argument can be made that that is not the case.

Take the Fairness Doctrine. William S. Paley, the chairman of CBS, noted that "we in broadcasting have no quarrel with fair coverage of news and public issues. We insisted on it, and lived by it, as the record shows, before the Fairness Doctrine came into being. What we object to is setting up the government as the arbiter of the fairness of our coverage—usurping the function of those directly responsible for news and public affairs broadcasts."

"Fairness" has such a marvelous ring. How can one oppose it? Paley noted, "Whenever I hear the misnomer, 'Fairness Doctrine,' I am reminded of Voltaire's remark about the Holy Roman Empire—that it was neither holy, nor Roman, nor an empire."

Paley called the Fairness Doctrine

an open defiance of the First Amendment. We all would be outraged if the government were allowed to impose standards of fairness on the contents of newspapers or magazines. . . . Yet, under the Fairness Doctrine, we are enduring a situation where government—through an administrative agency—can impose such standards on the contents of broadcast journalism. Thus, we find full First Amendment protection denied to the very media—radio and television—that have become the primary source of news and information for the American public.

The irony of the Fairness Doctrine is that broadcasters can fulfill it by tucking away an interview or a contrary viewpoint somewhere in the schedule. NBC found the FCC insisting that it do so after it produced a first-rate documentary called "Pensions: The Broken Promise" in September 1972. On the same day that "Pensions" won a Peabody Award as "a shining example of constructive and superlative investigative reporting," the FCC ruled that it should have presented more material on those pension plans that were sound and reliable. NBC could have had someone on the "Today" show or elsewhere to placate the Washington bureaucrats. Instead, it went to court to fight the ruling.

Up through the courts it went and the FCC was reversed. Finally the Court of Appeals ruled for "Pensions" and the Supreme Court rejected a request to review. Julian Goodman, chairman of NBC, two and a half tedious years later, noted

Over those months, as NBC's legal expenses mounted and lawyers' time burned away, there were those who said, "Why don't you give them five minutes and talk about good pension plans and get rid of it? What can it cost?" I suspect that Samuel Adams in 1773 heard someone say, "Come on, Sam. Pay the tax on the tea. What difference does a few dollars make?" The cost, quite simply, is our freedom.

Goodman concluded, "It is easier for broadcasters to steer clear of controversial issues because of the high price tag that can be placed on freedom of expression. It *is* easier to give in. But it is not in the public interest."

It means lawyers and money to fight and only five minutes of air time to give in. Give in enough, however, and you have the most damaging impact of government in the newsroom, the so-called chilling effect of the "Fairness Doctrine." Richard Salant, president of CBS News, once noted that FCC inquiries result in reporters, producers, executives stopping and spending days "to dig out stuff and try to reconstruct why they did what they did." You don't have to do that often before your enthusiasm for taking on controversy slows down.

The Supreme Court, in Red Lion, did not find this persuasive. In a critical review of that decision in the *Texas Law Review* (April, 1974), P. M. Schenkkan wrote, "The Court approved an entire system of direct government intervention in broadcasting upon a mere hypothesis of public injury and dismissed the possible chilling effect as mere speculation."

There are those who argue that the government imposition of "fairness" means many voices will be heard. There are others who contend that not more voices but fewer will be heard and those opinions will be bland and safe.

Americans don't lack exposure to ideas if they seek them out. One estimate is that the average American probably has access to at least eight radio stations, two newspapers, all the magazines he can afford, and six or seven television channels. The danger in the information flow is not the scarcity of voices but hearing some who have nothing to say.

FED UP

If all of this has the ring of a broadcast journalist who is sick and tired of intrusions into the daily work of editorial judgments by the need to worry about and respond to the specter of the bureaucrat in the newsroom, it is just that. Let editors edit, reporters report. The public will, as it should, be the proper judge.

In the political arena, the equal time provisions of Section 315 create similar problems. You can't set up debates between candidates. You can't do documentaries involving candidates except when they are incidental to the main subject which therefore, can't be "them." One presidential election ago, before candidate George Wallace was shot, CBS had to kill an hour-long documentary about the Wallace movement. It was an important political phenomenon and deserved better than death in the cutting room.

Under the political equal-time provisions, a violation of Section 315 means equal time for lots of candidates (maybe as many as 100 declared or would-be candidates in 1976), ranging from Lar (America First) Daly, who has run for president seven times going back to 1948 and for the Senate seven and the House thrice and three times for governor of Illinois, to Merril Riddick, an 80-year-old Montana prospector who believes in the Puritan ethic and turning garbage into electricity. Giving time, and lots of it, to these minor figures, no matter how pure their motives, is what keeps us from a repetition of broadcasts like the Kennedy-Nixon debates of 1960.*

Broadcasters have found few sympathizers to their problems. One came, unsolicited, last October when the chairman of the Federal Trade Commission, Lewis A. Engman, gave an eloquent speech to the UCLA law school on the Fairness Doctrine. He spoke to the traditional arguments from scarcity of channels to multiplicity of voices and finally addressed the question of the intent of the framers of the First Amendment, saying, of the contention that they would have excluded broadcasting from its protection, "That is literalism requiring suspension of reason to accept."

Chairman Engman asks us to
recall [that] the 18th Century philosophical underpinning for the First Amendment was that no one had the right to control the speech of anyone else. Freedom to express one's opinion was deemed an inalienable right which could not be abrogated by government.

The fashionable mid-20th-Century explanation that the First Amendment is a legal expression of our conviction that if everyone were allowed to speak his mind, the truth would somehow emerge, may be correct. But it was not the reason the First Amendment was adopted.

It is crucial that this be understood. For, to suggest that freedom of speech is merely a privilege granted by the government in the belief that it will lead to truth—which some have done in embracing the Fairness Doctrine—is to suggest that freedom of speech is no more than a political expedient. Government might as easily decide the opposite—that uninhibited speech was a nui-

*Since this article appeared, there were, of course, presidential campaign debates in 1976 and 1980.—Ed.

sance, that it resulted in rumor, gossip, lies and self-serving half-truths; that it was not, therefore, in the public interest. More than a few governments around the world have reached precisely that conclusion.

THE PRINCIPLE STANDS
Broadcasters have tried again and again to show that they belong under the full protection of the First Amendment. Few in government, hardly any in the courts, and not many in the general public hear them. In the case of *CBS* v. *the Democratic National Committee*, Justice William O. Douglas, was one of the few.

He wrote,

My conclusion is that the TV and radio stand in the same protected position under the First Amendment as do newspapers and magazines. The philosophy of the First Amendment requires that result, for the fear that Madison and Jefferson had of government intrusion is perhaps even more relevant to TV and radio than it is to newspapers and other like publications.

Said Douglas, "One hard and fast principle which it announces is that government should keep its hands off the press. That principle has served us through days of calm and eras of strife and I would abide by it. . . ."

In the 1969 case *Red Lion Broadcasting Co. v. Federal Communications Commission*, the U.S. Supreme Court upheld the "fairness doctrine" which required radio and television stations that aired controversial issues to present opposing views or give the opposition opportunity to reply. Five years later, in the case *Miami Herald Publishing Co. v. Tornillo*, the court ruled that the same principle could not be applied to the newspaper press to give balance to public issues. Jerome A. Barron, law professor at George Washington University, disagrees with the *Tornillo* decision, arguing that the First Amendment gives constitutional protection not to the "press" but to "freedom of the press," and that this protection encompasses the right of the people to have access to the newspaper press as they now have to the electronic press under the "fairness doctrine."

Jerome A. Barron

ACCESS TO THE PRESS: A NEW FIRST AMENDMENT RIGHT

In American law the classic question of free expression has always been whether something already said or published can be the subject of legal sanction. It has been the stated purpose, not always accomplished, of our constitutional law to try to keep as much as possible of what is said and published out of the reach of legal sanction. Therefore, for those who are able to obtain access to the media our law is a source of considerable strength. But what about those whose ideas are too unacceptable to gain entrance to the media? Is it time to focus our attention not only on the protection of ideas already published but on making sure that divergent opinions are actually able to secure expression in the first place?

The failure of existing media in this regard is revealed paradoxically by the advent of the sit-in and now the riot. These are really an inadequate underground press which bear tragic witness to the unwillingness of existing mass communications to present unpopular and controversial ideas. If southern newspapers had given voice to the Negro community's real feelings about segregation during the past 50 years a whole society would not have been so startled by the sit-in. If the northern press had given some space to the feelings of the Negro community about discrimination in housing and slum living in general, they would not have been so startled by the riots in Detroit, Newark and New Haven. Recently stories appeared in the press about a newspaper in Lynchburg, Virginia, which would only publish obituaries of Negroes if they were purchased as commercial advertisements. But this was just a particularly unattractive symptom of a basic problem—the horror of upsetting the community applecart—which dominates the press in this country. The dissenter is thus driven to look for novel, even violent, techniques to capture the attention of the public. Paradoxically, when he does this he reaches instantly the network coverage, the front-page story, which otherwise he could never have obtained. For now the trappings of violence and shock have a claim both to "news" and, less avowedly, to entertainment which the commercial bias of the media instantly picks up for immediate coverage.

The grand language of the First Amendment has been used by the media to say that government may impose no responsibilities on them. But constitutional protection is given not to the "press" but to "freedom of the press." What was desired was assurance for the interchange of ideas. But the present structure of the mass media is away from rather than toward ideas. Ideas suggest disagreement and disagreement is not good for business. As V. O. Key wrote in his "Public Opinion and American Democracy": "Newspaper publishers are essentially people who sell white space on newsprint to advertisers." In the light of this, the present constitutional status of the American press is a romantic one. The theory is that the "marketplace of ideas" is self-executing and that according to some Darwinian principle the best ideas will secure primacy over all competing ones.

A more mundane but more candid approach to the First Amendment ought to lead to the realization that a right of expression which is dependent on the sufferance of the managers of the mass media is pitifully anemic.

The difficulty with doing anything about this situation is that the First Amendment has conventionally been thought of as prohibiting *governmental* restraints on expression. But what of private restraints on expression?

Suppose a monopoly newspaper publisher decides that a certain cause or person shall simply receive no space in its pages? What remedy does such a person have? Presently the answer to this question is simple: none. What would seem necessary would be an approach to free speech and free press—the area which constitutional lawyers describe as First Amendment problems—which would recognize that forbidding governmental restrictions on expression is quite useless if the power to prevent access to the channels of communication may be exercised at the pleasure of those who control them. The mandate for a free press is not a constitutional gift to publishers alone. The reader, the public, and in a larger intellectual sense, the world of ideas, all have a stake in the press. That indeed is the reason for the special status of the press in the United States.

The lack of any obligation on newspapers to publish minority viewpoints is particularly aggravated by the rise of the one-newspaper city. Little attention has been given to the problems raised by the vanishing numbers and the general blandness of the American press. In New York City where 14 English language newspapers were published in 1900, only two morning papers and one afternoon paper survive. Nor is this a big-city phenomenon. In a book significantly entitled "Freedom or Secrecy," J. Russell Wiggins of the *Washington Post* offered these statistics on the lack of competition in the American press:

The number of newspapers in the United States declined from 2202 in 1909–10 to 1760 in 1953–4. The number of cities with competing daily newspapers declined from 689 to only 87. The number of cities with non-competing dailies increased from 518 to 1301. Eighteen states are now without any locally competing daily newspapers.

The goal of informing the public is the reason that the American Constitution has a First Amendment which says that "Congress shall make no law . . . abridging the freedom of speech, or of the press," in the first place. As Mr. Justice Brandeis put it 40 years ago, the First Amendment rests on the premise that free expression is indispensable to the "discovery and spread of political truth" and

that "the greatest menace to freedom is an inert people." It might be said that the decline in the number of newspapers and the rise of monopoly situations is offset by the fact that newspapers not only compete with each other but with radio and television as well. But what is the effectiveness of radio and television competition in terms of informing the public?

Marshall McLuhan's singular insight into the electronic media is that the attraction they have for us is in their form, rather than in what they have to say. What intrigues us is the television screen itself. The implication from this would appear to be that the electronic media are not very well suited to making public issues meaningful. The question then arises: perhaps on balance the existing press *is* doing this informing job well enough. The fact that the press is in fewer hands than ever has not resulted in a desire on the part of its controllers to bend us, Orwellian fashion, to their political will. The problem is that the media, print and electronic, share a common blandness, a pervasive aversion for the novel and the heretical. The reason for this is that the controllers of the media have no political wish to dominate. They are business men and their stance is essentially one of political neutrality. It is simply not good business to espouse or even give space to heresy and controversy.

Despite the foregoing, there appears to be no change in the approach to the First Amendment and to the press from the romantic view which has thus far prevailed. Judicial indifference to the problem of access to the press was vividly underscored by a case decided by the Supreme Court in 1964. There the Supreme Court reversed a $500,000 libel suit which Commissioner Sullivan of Montgomery, Alabama, had won against *The New York Times* in the state courts of Alabama. Among other things, Commissioner Sullivan charged that he was libelled by a political advertisement appearing in the *Times* on March 29, 1960, entitled "Heed Their Rising Voices," which protested the handling of a civil rights demonstration by Birmingham, Alabama, police.

Mr. Sullivan was the Birmingham City Commissioner in charge of the Police Department. The Supreme Court of the United States created a new privilege for newspapers sued by public officials for libel: no damages would be allowed unless the official suing could show that the newspaper acted in "actual malice." As a legal matter, "actual malice" is most difficult to prove. Therefore the decision in *New York Times* v. *Sullivan* amounted to a grant to the press of a new and relatively complete freedom, where articles about public officials are concerned, from the libel laws. The rationale of the decision, as Mr. Justice Brennan put it, rested on the "principle that debate on public issues should be uninhibited, robust, and wide-open, and that it may well include vehement, caustic and sometimes unpleasantly sharp attacks on government and public officials."

But the disturbing aspect of the *New York Times* decision is its romantic and unexamined assumption that limiting newspaper exposure to libel suits will automatically result in removing restraints on expression and thus lead to the "informed society." Although the Supreme Court changed the law of libel for the benefit of newspapers, the court did nothing in the way of demanding something in exchange from the press such as a requirement to provide space for reply by the public officials which newspapers choose to attack.

What is particularly disturbing is that the newspaper freedom from libel litigation begun in the Supreme Court is being extended by the lower courts to attacks in the press on non-elected persons, so-called "public figures," as well as public officials. Thus when Linus Pauling was attacked by the *National Review* he sued for libel; the New York Court took the position that Pauling was equivalent to a public official in that like such an official he had voluntarily entered public life and debate and therefore that newspapers and magazines should have the same freedom to attack him, without fear of libel suit, in the interest of "uninhibited and robust" public discussion.

One would not quarrel with this approach

if some awareness were also displayed that as the law presently stands if someone in the public eye becomes a source of irritation to a publisher, he may attack such a person both without too much concern for the libel laws and with no duty to provide such a person an outlet for his views. How much does this contribute to "wide-open" public discussion? Probably very little. One can rationalize and say that the *New York Times* case is a victory for the left and the Pauling case a victory for the right. But both represent a defeat for the goal of providing the public with a balanced presentation of controversial public issues.

Nevertheless the legal horizon is not entirely bleak. A case offering very encouraging possibilities for the future was decided by the United States Court of Appeals for the District of Columbia in 1966. In that case, various Negro churches and organizations brought suit against the Federal Communications Commission for renewing the license of the owner of a Broadcast station in Jackson, Mississippi. The Negro organizations, claiming to speak for the 45% of Jackson which is Negro, claimed that the station had failed to provide effective opportunity for the expression of views in favor of integration although the station gave very effective opportunity for expression of segregationist views. The Federal Communications Commission took a narrowly technical position and said that the Negro organizations were not the appropriate persons to challenge renewal. Only those could challenge renewal who were in the broadcast business: in other words in direct competition with the station.

The Court held that the interests of community groups in broadcast programming was sufficient to entitle the Negro organizations to demand a full hearing on whether the Jackson station ought to have its license renewed. The Jackson, Mississippi, broadcast case marks the beginning hopefully of a new judicial awareness that our legal system must protect not only the broadcaster's right to speak but also public rights in broadcasting. It amounts to recognition that there is a community or public interest involved in the media as well as the interest represented by management. The Court put the matter with stark simplicity: "(T)he freedom of speech protected against government licensees of means of public communication to exclude the expression of opinions and ideas with which they are in disagreement." *(sic)* Furthermore, the Court said that requiring broadcast licensees to use their license so that the listening public may be assured of "hearing varying opinions on the paramount issues facing the American people is within both the spirit and letter of the first amendment."

That such a decision comes out of a broadcasting context is not too surprising for the FCC has long had a rule, the so-called fairness doctrine, that broadcasters have an obligation to provide balanced presentation of a constitutional issue of public importance. It is a kind of "equal time" for ideas requirement. The rule has not been a great success. The path of evasion is too obvious: avoid controversy and you won't have to give time to viewpoints you don't like. On the other hand, failure to provide balanced presentation of controversial issues might result in a refusal to grant a broadcast licensee, who only has his license for three years, renewal. Such decisions are now more likely since it has been held as a result of the Jackson, Mississippi, case that groups in the community as well as other broadcast stations and applicants have a right to call the station to account.

The new development in broadcasting is in sad contrast to the situation of the press. In this area, not only has there been no new ground broken but, indeed, as we have seen, developments are if anything retrogressive. Thus the Court in passing in the Jackson, Missippippi, case remarked: "A newspaper can be operated at the whim or caprice of its owners; a broadcast station cannot." Is it not time to rethink whether mass circulation newspapers, many of which are monopoly situations, ought to continue to be operated entirely "at the whim or caprice" of the owner?

I would hope that the new awareness of the listener's stake in broadcasting would lead to a similar concern for the reader's stake in the press. Obviously the daily press cannot be at the disposal of the vanity of the public. Everyone cannot be written about and every idea cannot be given space. In the *United Church of Christ* case, the Jackson, Mississippi, Negro organizations were allowed to contest the station's license although this certainly did not mean that in the future just any listener could contest a licensee's renewal application. The basic test is whether the material for which access is desired is in fact suppressed or undercovered. If it is, it is still not necessary to give space to every group associated with the suppressed viewpoint as long as one such group is allowed to present its case. The machinery for implementing some guarantee of confrontation of ideas could be achieved independently of legislation through the courts themselves by decision. In the *New York Times* case the Supreme Court created a new relative freedom from libel for newspapers by the method of "interpreting" the First Amendment. Similarly, techniques could be used to fashion a right of access to the press for the public. If this approach does not work, then a carefully worded right of access statute which would aim at achieving a meaningful expression of divergent opinions should be attempted. The point is that we must realize that private restraints on free expression have become so powerful that the belief that there is a free marketplace where ideas will naturally compete is as hopelessly outmoded as the theory of perfect competition has generally become in most other spheres of modern life.

Clifton Daniel of the *New York Times* objects to the proposal of Professor Barron to mandate the right of access and right of reply to the nation's newspaper press. Such requirement by law would be both impractical and unconstitutional. He suggests alternate ways of achieving fairness.

Clifton Daniel

RIGHTS OF ACCESS
AND REPLY

So far as I am concerned, we can begin with a stipulation. I am perfectly prepared to concede that there is a problem of access to the press in this country. However, the dimensions of the problem have been greatly exaggerated, and the proposed legal remedies are either improper or impractical.

My contention is that the remedies should be left largely to the press itself and to the reading public, and that adequate remedies are available.

About the dimensions of the problem: I suppose there *are* some publishers and editors who capriciously and arbitrarily refuse to print material with which they disagree. But I don't know them.

In an adjudication made two years ago, the British Press Council, which is the official British forum for complaints against the press, had this to say: "We are finding more and more that even quite large localities cannot support more than one newspaper. We are satisfied, however, that most editors of such newspapers are now accepting it as a duty to see, as far as possible, that events and views of interest to all shades of opinion are impartially reported while reserving the editorial right to come down on one side or the other."

Exactly the same thing could be said—and truthfully said—about the press in this country. More than thirty years ago, Eugene Meyer, who had quarreled with the New Deal, resigned from the Federal Reserve Board, and bought *The Washington Post*, set out deliberately to find a New Deal columnist for his newspaper. He thought his readers were entitled to get the New Deal point of view as well as his own.

Hundreds of American publishers and editors take the same attitude today. They go out of their way to find columnists and

commentators who are opposed to their own editorial policies.

New ideas are not being suppressed. On the contrary, a hurricane of dissent is blowing through the world. It is shaking the foundations of all our institutions. Can anyone here doubt the truth of that statement?

When and where has it ever before been possible for a man like the Rev. Ralph D. Abernathy to reach an audience of millions by simply painting a few signs, assembling 150 poor people, and appearing before the television cameras at the gates of Cape Kennedy?

The great guru of the right of access, Prof. Jerome Barron of the George Washington Law School . . . speaks of insuring "access to the mass media for unorthodox ideas."

I thought until I got into this argument that the main complaint against the press was that we were giving too much access to the unorthodox—hippies, draft-card burners, student rioters, black militants, and the people who make dirty movies and write dirty books. At least, that's the message I get from the mail that comes across my desk.

In spite of the mail, I still concede that there is a problem of access to the press. But its dimensions are not great and the solutions proposed are not practical.

Advocates of the right of access blandly ignore the problems and techniques of editing a newspaper. Prof. Barron speaks of the press as having "an obligation to provide space on a non-discriminatory basis for representative groups in the community."

Note the key words: Space. Non-discriminatory. Representative groups.

First: Space! How much space?

The *New York Times* received 37,719 letters to the editor in 1968. At least 85 to 90 percent of these letters, in the words of our slogan, were "fit to print." However, we were able to accommodate only six per cent. If we had printed them all—all 18 million words of them—they would have filled up at least 135 complete weekday issues of *The New York Times*. Yet, every letter-writer probably felt that he had some right of access to our columns.

Some letter-writers and readers have been aggressively trying to enforce that presumed right. For many months the adherents of an artistic movement called Aesthetic Realism have been petitioning and picketing *The New York Times*, demanding reviews for books and paintings produced by members of the movement. Criticism, incidentally, would be meaningless if critics were required to give space to artistic endeavors they consider unworthy of it.

Art galleries in New York plead for reviews. They contend that it is impossible to succeed in business without a critical notice in *The Times*. That is probably true. But no one, surely, is entitled to a free ad in the newspapers. No artist has a *right* to a clientele. He has to earn his audience by the forcefulness of his art, the persuasiveness of his talent. How much more cogently does this apply to political ideas!

Non-discriminatory! Discrimination is the very essence of the editing process. You must discriminate or drown.

Every day of the year *The New York Times* receives an average of a million and a quarter to a million and a half words of news material. At best, we can print only a tenth of it. A highly skilled, high-speed process of selection is involved—a massive act of discrimination, if you like—discrimination between the relevant and the irrelevant, the important and the unimportant.

When I was preparing these remarks, I suggested to my secretary that she buy a bushel basket, and fill it with press releases, petitions, pamphlets, telegrams, letters and manuscripts. I wanted to empty the basket here on this platform just to show you how many scoundrels, scroungers and screwballs, in addition to respectable citizens and worthy causes, are seeking access to the columns of our newspaper.

Actually, 168 bushels of wastepaper, most of it rejected news, are collected and thrown away every day in the editorial departments of *The New York Times*. Do you imagine that the courts have the time to sort it all out? Do they have the time and, indeed, do they have the wisdom? Even if judges do have the time to do my job as well as their own, I think Ben Bagdikian, the leading critic of the American press, is right when he says that "judges make bad newspaper editors."

Representative groups! What constitutes a representative group? Who is to decide? I would say that representative groups already have access to the press. It's the unrepresentative ones we have to worry about.

I am not prepared to argue that it's easy for anybody with a cause or a grievance to get space in the newspaper. Indeed, it isn't easy. In my opinion, it shouldn't be. When you begin editing by statute or court order, your newspaper will no longer be a newspaper. It will be "little more than a bulletin board," as Mr. Jencks [Richard W. Jencks, President, Columbia Broadcasting System Broadcast Group] has said, "—a bulletin board for the expression of hateful or immature views."

Nowhere in the literature on access to the press do I find any conspicuous mention of the hate groups. Does this newfangled interpretation of freedom of the press mean that an editor would be obliged to give space to ideas that are hateful to him? Must he give space to advertisements that are offensive to his particular readers? Must a Jewish editor be forced to publish anti-Semitism? Must a Negro editor give space to the Ku Klux Klan?

Prof. Barron, it seems to me, looks at these problems in a very simplistic way, and defines them in parochial terms. All but the most localized media have national connections of some sort: They broadcast network television programs. They buy syndicated columnists. They subscribe to the services of the great national news agencies. An idea that originates in New York is, within a matter of minutes, reverberating in California.

In determining who is to have access to the press, who would decide how widely an idea should be disseminated? Must it be broadcast in prime time on the national networks? Must it be distributed by the Associated Press and United Press to all their clients? And must all the clients be required to publish or broadcast it? Just asking these questions shows how impractical it is to enforce access to the press by law or judicial fiat.

It is impractical in another sense. In contested cases, it might take a year or more to gain access to the press for a given idea or item of news. And if there is anything deader than yesterday's news, it's news a year old.

Not only is it impractical to edit newspapers by statute and judicial interpretation, but it would, in my view, be improper—that is to say, unconstitutional.

My position on that point is a very simple one: Freedom of the press, as defined by the First Amendment, means freedom of the press. It doesn't mean freedom *if,* or freedom *but.* It means freedom *period.* Prof. Barron's proposition, however exhaustively elaborated, cannot disguise the fact that it involves regulation of the press—freedom *but.*

I cannot guess what the makers of our Constitution would have said about television, but I have a pretty good idea of what they meant by freedom of the printed word, and they certainly did not mean that it should be controlled, regulated, restricted or dictated by government officials, legislators or judges. Indeed, the makers of the Constitution meant exactly the opposite— that officialdom, constituted authority, should keep its hands off the press, that it should not tell newspapers what to print or what not to print.

To repeat: My proposition does not mean that there is no need for greater access to the press. It simply means that legislators and judges should not be—indeed cannot be— the ones to decide how much access there should be. Editors should decide, under the pressure of public and official opinion, constantly and conscientiously exercised.

There are effective devices that the newspapers and their readers could employ. Mr. Bagdikian mentions some of them in the *Columbia Journal Review:*

1. Start a new journalistic form: an occasional full page of ideas from the most thoughtful experts on specific public problems.
2. Devote a full page a day to letter-to-the-editor.
3. Appoint a fulltime ombudsman on the paper or broadcasting station to track down complaints about the organization's judgment and performance.
4. Organize a local press council of community representatives to sit down every month with the publisher.

Press councils have already been tried in several small cities. They work well. A press council for New York City—or perhaps a media council, taking in broadcasters as well as newspapers and magazines—is under consideration by the Twentieth Century Fund. In September, 1969 the Board of Directors of the American Society of Newspaper Editors went to London to make a study of the British Press Council.

There are also other ways, as Mr. Bagdikian says, "of keeping the press a relevant institution close to the lives of its constituents."

One way is hiring reporters from minority groups, as the newspapers are now doing. Not only is opportunity given to the minorities, but also they bring into the city room the special attitudes of their communities.

In New York the communities themselves, with outside help, are bringing their problems to the attention of the press. Community representatives have been meeting with newspaper editors and broadcasting executives under the auspices of the Urban Reporting Project. A news service is being organized by the project to provide continuous reporting from the neglected neighborhoods to the communications media.

In one of the neighborhoods—Harlem—a new community newspaper, the *Manhattan Tribune,* has been established to train Negro and Puerto Rican journalists.

I am aware that not everybody with a cause can afford a newspaper to promote it. It is not as difficult, however, to launch a new newspaper as some people would have you believe.

In 1896 a small-town publisher, Adolph S. Ochs, came to New York from Chattanooga, Tenn., borrowed $75,000, bought the moribund *New York Times,* and converted it into an enterprise that is now worth

$400 million on the American Stock Exchange.

They say nobody will ever be able to do that again. But I wonder.

Fourteen years ago, Norman Mailer, the novelist, and Edwin Fancher put up $5,000 apiece to start an offbeat, neighborhood weekly in Greenwich Village. Altogether, only $70,000—less than Adolph Ochs needed to gain control of *The New York Times*—had to be invested in the *Village Voice* before it turned a profit. Its circulation is now more than 127,000—greater than the circulation of 95 per cent of United States dailies. Its annual profit is considerably more than the capital that was required to launch it.

From the beginning, the *Village Voice* has been a forum for those unorthodox opinions that are said to be seeking access to the press.

It was the *Village Voice* that blazed the trail for the underground press. While you may think that the underground press is scatological and scurrilous, its existence is nevertheless welcome proof that our press is indeed free, and that the First Amendment does not have to be reinterpreted, rewritten or wrenched out of context to give expression to unorthodox ideas.

I had not intended in these remarks to discuss the right of reply. But I think I should respond to Commissioner Cox [FCC Commissioner Kenneth A. Cox], who says that Congress could constitutionally apply equal time and right-of-reply obligations to newspapers.

I don't agree with him. The First Amendment very plainly says—it couldn't be plainer—that Congress shall make *no law—no law*—abridging freedom of the press.

However, the right of reply does not provide as much of a problem for newspapers as enforced access to the press. Indeed, the right of reply is widely recognized and accepted. In practice, most newspapers recognize a prior-to-publication right of reply when dealing with controversial matters.

On *The New York Times*, we have a standing rule that anyone who is accused or critized in a controversial or adversary situation should be given an opportunity to comment before publication. The rule is sometimes overlooked in the haste of going to press. It is often not possible to obtain comment from all interested parties, but the principle is there and the effort is required. More importantly, the same is true of the news agencies which serve practically every daily paper and broadcasting station in the United States.

The right of reply after publication is also widely accepted. However, I would caution against creating an absolute right of reply or trying to enshrine such a right in law. Newspapers, it seems to me, *must* have the right to refuse to publish a reply, provided they are willing to accept the consequences of doing so—a suit for damages for example. [In 1974 in the case of *Miami Herald Publishing Co. v. Tornillo*, the U.S. Supreme Court ruled that Florida's right to reply statute was unconstitutional, a violation of the First Amendment's guarantee of a free press. This seemed to close the door to a government-mandated right of access to the newspaper press as advocated by Professor Barron.]

CONTRIBUTORS

BEN H. BAGDIKIAN
is a journalist, editor, and author who was awarded the Most Perceptive Critic Citation, American Society of Journalism Administrators in 1978. His list of published works includes *The Information Machines: Their Impact on Men and the Media* (1971).

JEROME A. BARRON
is dean of the National Law Center, George Washington University, author of *Freedom of the Press for Whom? The Right of Access to Mass Media* (1973), and coauthor of *Handbook of Free Speech and Free Press* (1979) and *Constitutional Law: Principles and Policy, Cases and Materials* (1980).

JAMES DAVID BESSER
is a Washington, D.C., writer.

WILLIAM JOSEPH BRENNAN, JR.
has served as a justice of the United States Supreme Court since 1956.

ART BUCHWALD'*s*
syndicated column appears in 550 newspapers worldwide. He has also published many books, including *While Reagan Slept* (1983), *Laid Back in Washington* (1981), *I Never Danced at the White House* (1979), and *The Buchwald Stops Here* (1978).

SCOTT CAMPBELL
is a Boston-based freelance writer.

MALCOLM COWLEY,
a literary critic and social historian, is best known for his work on the American writers of the "Lost Generation" of the 1920s. Cowley was the literary editor for *The New Republic*, 1929–44, and is author of collections of criticism and studies of writers' roles in society.

CLIFTON DANIEL
is an associate editor of the *New York Times*.

RICHARD LEWIS DARLING,
dean of the School of Library Service, Columbia University, was president of the
Freedom to Read Foundation from 1974 to 1977.

THOMAS I. EMERSON,
professor of law at Yale University, is author of *Toward a General Theory of the First
Amendment* (1966) and *The System of Freedom of Expression* (1970).

STEPHEN JAY GOULD
writes a monthly column for *Natural History* and books that make science accessible
to a broad spectrum of readers. His most recent books are *Hen's Teeth and Horse's
Toes: Further Reflections in Natural History* (1983), *The Mismeasure of Man* (1981),
and *The Panda's Thumb* (1980).

NAT HENTOFF
is a staff writer for the *Village Voice*. He frequently writes and speaks on First
Amendment issues. *The Day They Came to Arrest the Book* (Delacorte, 1982), a
book for young readers, is among his recent publications.

WENDY KAMINER
is an attorney active in the feminist movement against pornography and violence
against women.

STANLEY KAUFFMANN's
film reviews have appeared regularly in *The New Republic* since 1958. He is also the
drama critic for *Saturday Review* as well as author and editor of books about film and
of criticism.

DENA KLEIMAN
is a writer on the staff of the *New York Times*.

CHARLES KRAUTHAMMER
is senior editor of *The New Republic*.

JUDITH F. KRUG
has been the executive director of the Freedom to Read Foundation since 1969 and
the director of the Office for Intellectual Freedom of the American Library Association since 1967.

RICHARD H. KUH
is an assistant district attorney in the New York County District Attorney's Office as
well as author of *Foolish Figleaves? Pornography in and out of the Court* (1967) and
numerous articles in popular and professional publications.

PAUL KURTZ
is a professor of philosophy at the State University of New York–Buffalo and editor of a long list of books that includes *The Philosophy of the Curriculum* (1975), *The Ethics of Teaching and Scientific Research* (1977), and *University and State* (1978). He is editor of *The Humanist*.

JACK C. LANDAU
is the editor of *The News Media and the Press*.

ANTHONY LEWIS,
recipient of the Pulitzer Prize for national reporting in 1955 and 1963 was chief of the London bureau of the *New York Times* from 1965 to 1972 and is now a *New York Times* editorial columnist. Lewis is also author of *Gideon's Trumpet* and *Clarence Earl Gideon and the Supreme Court*.

GENE LYONS,
an educator and political scientist, is a resident of Little Rock and a frequent contributor to various magazines.

The late LEROY C. MERRITT
was editor of the ALA *Newsletter on Intellectual Freedom*, Dean of the University of Oregon's School of Librarianship, and author of *Book Selection and Intellectual Freedom* (1970).

ARTHUR R. MILLER,
in addition to being the host of the syndicated TV show, Miller's Court, is a Harvard law professor, chairman of the Massachusetts Security and Privacy Council, and author of *The Assault on Privacy: Computers, Data Banks, and Dossiers* (1971).

DOROTHY NELKIN
holds a joint appointment in the program on science, technology, and society and the Department of City and Regional Planning at Cornell University.

LOUIS NIZER,
lawyer and author, is famous for his courtroom dramatizations such as *My Life in Court* (1962), *The Jury Returns* (1966), and *Reflections without Mirrors* (1978).

ROBERT M. O'NEIL,
president of the University of Wisconsin, is author of *Free Speech: Responsible Communication under Law*, second edition (1972), *The Courts, Government and Higher Education* (1972), and *Classroom in the Crossfire* (1981).

WILLIAM R. OVERTON
is a U.S. District Judge in the Eastern District of Arkansas in Little Rock.

HERBERT L. PACKER
is a law professor at Stanford University and author of *The Limits of the Criminal Sanction* (1968).

ROBERT G. PICARD
edits the *Freedom of Information Center Reports* and the *Freedom of Information Digest.*

HARRIET F. PILPEL
is a lawyer who has lectured, written, made TV and radio appearances, and served on numerous committees and advisory boards to share her views and knowledge of a wide spectrum of social concerns ranging from marriage, family law, birth control, and the status of women and senior citizens to civil liberties, copyright, and communications media.

THEODORE K. RABB
is a professor of history at Princeton University and the author of books about European history and the history of the family. He has been a board member of the American Association for the Advancement of the Humanities, to name just one of the scholarly organizations with which he is involved.

R. BRUCE RICH
is a partner in a New York law firm and counsel to the Association of American Publishers Freedom to Read Committee.

ELOISE SALHOLZ
is a staff writer for *Newsweek.*

RICHARD M. SCHMIDT, JR.,
a Washington-based lawyer, chaired the Washington Journalism Center from 1979 to 1981 and is general counsel for the American Society of Newspaper Editors.

ALAN U. SCHWARTZ
is a California lawyer specializing in the field of communications and counsel to both the American Association of Publishers' International Freedom to Publish Committee and P.E.N.

WILLIAM SMALL
is the president of United Press International and has written *To Kill a Messenger: Television and the Real World* (1970) and *Political Power and the Press* (1972).

CAL THOMAS
is vice president of the Moral Majority and a former reporter for NBC News.

STANLEY WELLBORN
is on the staff of the *U.S. News and World Report.*

TOM WICKER
is a regularly featured columnist in the *New York Times* and author of seven novels and four nonfiction works.

EDWIN WILSON
is executive director emeritus, American Humanist Association.

KENNETH L. WOODWARD
is a staff writer for *Newsweek*.

MARK G. YUDOF
is a law professor at the University of Texas at Austin.

EDITORS

Robert B. Downs has had a distinguished career in librarianship. He is emeritus dean of library administration at the University of Illinois, Urbana. In addition to serving as dean of library administration there (1958–71), he was director of the library and library school (1943–58). He has been president of the American Library Association, Association of College and Research Libraries, and the Illinois Library Association. Among his many publications are *Books That Changed the World, Books That Changed America, Famous American Books, In Search of New Horizons*, and the predecessor to this volume, published in 1960. He is the recipient of the Lippincott Award, the Clarence Day Award, the Melvil Dewey Medal, and the Syracuse Centennial Medal and is a Guggenheim Fellow.

Ralph E. McCoy also has had a notable career in librarianship. He is emeritus dean of library affairs at Southern Illinois University, Carbondale, having served as dean from 1955 to 1976. Subsequently he was interim director of libraries at the University of Georgia and interim director of the Association of Research Libraries. He has been president of the Association of College and Research Libraries and the Illinois Library Association, chairman of the Library Advisory Committee to the U.S. Public Printer, and has held committee appointments in ALA, the Bibliographic Society of America, and the American Council of Learned Societies. He is the author of *Freedom of the Press: An Annotated Bibliography, Freedom of the Press: A Bibliocyclopedia*, and *Personnel Administration for Libraries*.

INDEX